GATS 2000

New Directions in Services Trade Liberalization

Pierre Sauvé
Robert M. Stern
Editors

CENTER FOR BUSINESS AND GOVERNMENT
Harvard University

BROOKINGS INSTITUTION PRESS
Washington, D.C.

Copyright © 2000
THE BROOKINGS INSTITUTION
1775 Massachusetts Avenue, N.W., Washington, D.C. 20036
www.brookings.edu

Library of Congress Cataloging-in-Publication data

GATS 2000 : new directions in services trade liberalization / Pierre
Sauvé and Robert M. Stern, editors.
   p. cm.
Includes bibliographical references.
  ISBN 0–8157–7717–5
  1. International trade. 2. General Agreement on Trade in Services
(1994) 3. Service industries—Government policy. 4. International
business enterprises. 5. Free trade. I. Sauvé, Pierre, 1959–. II. Stern,
Robert Mitchell, 1927–. III. Title.
  HD9980.6 .G37 1999   99–050583
  382′.92—dc21   CIP

9 8 7 6 5 4 3 2 1

The paper used in this publication meets minimum requirements of the
American National Standard for Information Sciences—Permanence of Paper
for Printed Library Materials: ANSI Z39.48-1984.

Typeset in Adobe Garamond

Composition by Northeastern Graphic Services
Hackensack, New Jersey

Printed by Automated Graphic Systems
White Plains, Maryland

To Harry Freeman,
friend, supporter, and services pioneer

Foreword

Since the end of World War II remarkable progress has been achieved in lowering barriers to trade among countries under the auspices of the General Agreement on Tariffs and Trade (GATT) and most recently the World Trade Organization (WTO). Tariffs have been substantially eliminated, and many other nontariff barriers have been reduced.

It is striking, however, that while the attention of the world's shapers of trade policy has been focused principally on removing barriers to trade in goods, most of the world's economic activity, especially in the developed countries, is concentrated in services. Indeed, trade in services remains an area in which policymakers around the world find themselves grappling for answers posed by the remarkable diversity, complex regulatory geometry, and fast-changing nature of modern service economies.

This volume brings together contributions from many of the world's leading specialists in services trade to help develop a comprehensive yet workable agenda for that part of the next WTO round that will concentrate on services, specifically the "built-in" services left from the agenda of the Uruguay Round, and is called GATS 2000.

The individual chapters were originally presented at a conference in Washington, D.C., in June 1999 and since have been revised for publication under the editorial guidance of Pierre Sauvé of Harvard University and the Organization for Economic Cooperation and Development and Robert Stern of the University of Michigan. The conference was jointly sponsored by the American Enterprise Institute, the Brookings Institution, the Center for Business and Government at Harvard University's John F.

Kennedy School of Government, and the Education and Research Foundation of the Coalition of Service Industries (CSI).

Financial support for this project was provided by the CSI Education and Research Foundation, the European Commission, the Mark Twain Institute, the Sanwa Research Institute, Teleglobe Inc., the government of Canada, the French government's Direction des Relations Economiques Exterieures (DREE), and the Ministry for International Trade and Industry (MITI) of Japan. The editors are especially grateful to Harry Freeman, president of the Mark Twain Institute, for helping to inspire the project and providing much guidance and support.

Special thanks also go to Kimberly Bliss and Linda Gianessi of the Brookings Institution for the diligence and professionalism with which they coordinated this publication and managed the research project's finances; to Bonnie Jessup, whose tireless efforts were key to organizing, running, and making a success of the conference from which this book originated; and to Vicky Macintyre, James Schneider, and Theresa Walker of the Brookings Institution Press for expeditiously copyediting the work and Carlotta Ribar for proofreading the pages in record time. Gratitude is also extended to Janet Walker, who provided overall editorial management; Susan Woollen, who coordinated development of the cover; and Rebecca Clark, who, as marketing director for the press, takes over from here.

The views expressed in this book are exclusively those of the authors and should not be ascribed to those institutions with which they are affiliated, to the people whose assistance is acknowledged, to the organizations that supported the project, or to the trustees, officers, or staff members of the Brookings Institution.

ROGER B. PORTER   MICHAEL H. ARMACOST
Director   *President*
Center for Business and Government   *The Brookings Institution*
Harvard University

Contents

ix

GATS 2000

1 | *New Directions in Services Trade Liberalization: An Overview*

PIERRE SAUVÉ *and*
ROBERT M. STERN

T HE URUGUAY ROUND OF TRADE TALKS broke new ground by broadening the scope of world trade rules to cover trade areas never before subject to multilateral disciplines. Services, which encompass activities from banking, transportation, travel, telecommunications, and audio-visual services to professional services such as engineering and the law as well as the dizzying array of Internet-based service offerings, have been with little doubt where such broadening was most significant in economic terms.

Services account for more than 70 percent of production and employment in advanced industrial societies, levels that many of the developing world's emerging economies are today fast approaching. With the negotiation of the General Agreement on Trade in Services (GATS) the policies affecting access to and conditions of competition in service markets are today firmly rooted in the multilateral trading system. The pathbreaking rules established by GATS govern one of the world economy's most dynamic sectors, bringing much needed transparency and fairness to the $2.2 trillion worth of services traded globally on an annual basis.

Despite the growing domestic and international importance of services and the increased worldwide recognition of that importance, efforts to reap the benefits of more open services markets had until recently lagged far behind efforts devoted to opening markets for manufactured goods. The entry into force of GATS in 1995 marked a watershed by providing the first multilateral set of binding rules and disciplines with which to launch orderly trade and investment liberalization for services.

Although the Uruguay Round negotiations were generally more successful in developing trading rules than in increasing market access opportunities (whether for services or agriculture), they nonetheless laid a firm foundation for future negotiations. That future is already upon the international community as it intensifies preparations for a new round of GATS talks, which the Uruguay Round's built-in agenda has set for January 1, 2000 in Geneva.

The essays that make up this volume address the most pressing questions now arising in services trade. Some of these were in fact not addressed by the first generation of GATS negotiators. This volume is intended to help shape the policy choices that members of the World Trade Organization (WTO), whether from developed or developing countries, will need to make as they resume negotiations under GATS. It should also prove of interest to those involved in regional attempts at liberalizing trade and investment in services. The essays have been written with policymakers and practitioners in mind. They speak first to those in government, business, and nongovernmental circles who will deal directly with difficult policy challenges—old and new—in the next set of GATS talks.

The GATS 2000 negotiations will confront two central challenges: completing the incipient framework of GATS rules and disciplines so as to ensure the agreement's (and the WTO's) continued relevance in a globalizing environment, and achieving greater overall trade and investment liberalization than was possible during the Uruguay Round and in subsequent sectoral negotiations.[1]

What are the stakes of the next GATS round in terms of trade and investment liberalization? And what are the benefits associated with multilateral attempts to achieve such liberalization? Much of the analysis in this volume focuses on these two challenges. They are important, not least because, unlike in the Uruguay Round, negotiators will enter the GATS 2000 Round against the backdrop of a tested, if far from complete or fully satisfactory, framework of rules and disciplines and a machinery for negotiating liberalization commitments. The task of setting priorities on where scarce negotiating resources should best be spent in the GATS

---

1. The subsequent sectoral negotiations have covered basic telecommunications, financial services, maritime transport, and labor mobility issues (so-called temporary movement of service suppliers).

2000 talks should accordingly prove easier. In turn, this should help make a success of a negotiating cycle that many WTO members intend to keep relatively short.

Two reasons can be adduced to explain the greater ease that GATS members may experience in setting priorities for the next round. First, there has never been a lull in GATS negotiations, which have been going on since the inception of the Uruguay Round and the entry into force of the WTO in 1995. Second, and closely related, WTO members have been able to internalize a great deal of the learning by doing that has characterized the agreement's development. However, a critical ingredient to the success of the next round is that members heed some of the lessons they have learned, especially when it comes to proposals to amend the architecture of GATS rules or seek alternative routes to trade and investment liberalization under existing rules. WTO members must similarly keep an eye to the future by ensuring that GATS rules properly anticipate the development of new technologies and the greatly expanded scope they offer for new forms of service delivery within and across borders.

In keeping with the conference format in which the following essays were originally presented, the volume is organized into five parts. Parts I to IV address the challenge of how best to complete and refine the incipient framework of rules negotiated during the Uruguay Round, while part V is chiefly devoted to a discussion of various negotiating modalities for the new round.

Part I. The Benefits of Services Trade and Investment Liberalization

The four chapters that make up the book's opening part provide a clearer sense of the economic and commercial significance of what is at stake in the GATS 2000 Round. Such stakes are considerable.

The opening chapter by Guy Karsenty attempts to measure the value of commercial transactions carried out globally under GATS's four modes of supply: (1) cross-border trade, (2) commercial presence (or investment), (3) consumption abroad, and (4) the movement of natural persons (service suppliers). Karsenty notes that although knowledge of the size and nature of internationally traded services remains sketchy, efforts undertaken during the last decade to improve trade statistics, including data on sales of services by local affiliates of multinational firms (so-called establishment-related trade), have greatly improved our knowledge of the flows involved.

Karsenty estimates that total measurable trade in services as defined by GATS is $2.2 trillion. This represents 7.6 percent of world GDP and close to a third of total trade. These are significant amounts, especially for a sector that was long regarded as nontradable. Although cross-border trade and commercial presence, GATS's two major modes of delivery, account for four-fifths of total trade in services, Karsenty shows that, on the basis of available statistics, "traditional" trade in services—defined to measure cross-border transactions—is today larger in absolute size than establishment-related trade in services. Such a finding interestingly contrasts with GATS's negotiating reality, which has seen most commercially meaningful liberalization commitments focused on establishment-related trade. Karsenty's findings draw attention to the untapped potential for cross-border liberalization that GATS members will undoubtedly pay closer attention to in the next negotiations, particularly in light of the explosive growth of electronic commerce.

Karsenty also documents the relative insignificance of trade involving the movement of service providers. Although data on this subject are notoriously poor, such a finding is broadly in line with the political sensitivities typically associated with this highly restricted mode of supply, one in which a number of developing-country GATS members enjoy a strong comparative advantage.

The lack of a clear statistical description of services did not prove a decisive issue in the Uruguay Round, given the attention that negotiators devoted to the development of rules and disciplines. However, to the extent that matters of trade and investment liberalization will loom more importantly in the GATS 2000 Round, Karsenty argues that the need for improved services statistics could become more pronounced, whether in setting quantitative negotiating objectives or in measuring the balance of concessions resulting from negotiations. Efforts to deepen the nascent dialogue between statisticians and GATS negotiators and greater research efforts in this often neglected area will be needed to ensure that statistical reporting systems take better account of negotiating needs. Improvements in services data may similarly allow political proponents of trade and investment liberalization to more credibly measure the resulting gains and to better document how economic adjustment operates in the sector.

Although there is little doubt that improved data on trade flows are needed to support services negotiations, it is arguably more important from an economic perspective to gather data that shed light on barriers restricting competition in services markets. The chapters by Karsenty and by Tony Warren and Christopher Findlay illustrate how data on barriers affecting trade in services remain noticeably weaker and less comprehensive than those available for trade in goods. This is a matter of concern on several levels, not least of which is that a paucity of information on the extent and impact of impediments to services trade plays into the hands of those interested in limiting liberalization reform efforts. Warren and Findlay stress that transparency of policy affecting services trade and investment is critical for successful reform, whether it is enacted unilaterally or pursued through trade negotiations. Making the costs of protection as transparent as possible can go a long way toward building coalitions that support liberalization, particularly among user industries. It will also allow policymakers to have greater confidence in their chosen path of reform.

Like Karsenty, Warren and Findlay note that the need for a more complete inventory of barriers to trade and investment in services will likely be greater in the GATS 2000 Round given its heavier emphasis on liberalization-related matters. Gaining a clearer sense of existing barriers and establishing a more explicit hierarchy of their nature, importance, and sectoral incidence are critical to assessing the potential for trade expansion and the magnitude of the welfare gains that may be obtained by pursuing liberalization.

Warren and Findlay outline a methodology aimed at securing greater information about impediments to services trade that they developed as part of a research project funded by the Australian Research Council. This methodology involves three stages. First, available qualitative evidence that compares the way nations discriminate against potential entrants in various service industries is collected. This evidence is then transformed into a frequency index, coupled with an attempt to weigh discriminatory policies by their economic significance. Second, the impact of the policies as measured by the frequency indexes is assessed against national differences in domestic prices or domestic quantities, with the effect of other factors explaining national differences taken into account. And third, the measured impact of the frequency indexes (the coefficient) on prices or quantities is incorporated into a general equilibrium model to assess the economywide impacts of the policies at issue. Where possible, partial equilibrium modeling can also be undertaken to allow the specific impacts of liberalization to be more clearly understood.

Warren and Findlay show that despite the overall dearth of information it is still possible to develop weighting schemes by which policy measures affecting international services transactions can be compared. Measures of impediments to trade in services are becoming available that can legitimately be used as tools for the documentation and comparative assessment of reform efforts and liberalization commitments. The increased sophistication of their measurement techniques has several implications for the negotiating process: information may be more readily available to help set priorities at the national and international levels; liberalization commitments can be codified more easily, which should in turn facilitate cross-sectoral negotiations; and, perhaps more controversially, the adoption of a negative list approach (whereby all nonconforming measures are generated by the negotiations) to scheduling GATS commitments may be facilitated by the greater information disclosures that such techniques afford.

Warren and Findlay make a persuasive argument for giving priority attention to improving data and qualitative information on barriers to entry, trade, and investment that affect services. International organizations such as the World Bank, the UN Conference on Trade and Development (UNCTAD), and the Organization for Economic Cooperation and Development (OECD), all of which have recently begun work in this area, should cooperate more closely. Multinational businesses should also devote resources required to launch what the chapter by Pierre Sauvé and Christopher Wilkie calls an "operation transparency," which would entail drawing up non–legally binding lists of nonconforming measures affecting trade and investment in services. At the WTO level, some progress was made in the Uruguay Round with the creation of the Trade Policy Review Mechanism. However, TPRM resources, and the wealth of information contained in country reports, have yet to be marshaled with a view to generating the type of comparative analytical work that could help underpin future negotiations.

The chapters by Geza Feketekuty and Rudolf Adlung move away from quantitative matters to focus on normative issues. Perhaps the greatest *acquis* of GATS is how it has allowed a fuller appreciation of the dual nature of services. That is, services are burgeoning economic activities but also, and most important from a political economy perspective, they provide the infrastructure that allows modern economies to function. This dual nature and how such duality has shaped the evolution of GATS rules and disciplines are much in evidence in both papers.

Feketekuty offers a comprehensive survey of some of the architectural shortcomings of GATS while advancing practical means to strengthen the agreement both as a system of rules and an instrument of liberalization. He contends that the five years that have elapsed since the adoption of GATS is too short a period to form any conclusive judgments. Empirical evidence from GATT and other agreements, and experience gained in the context of European integration, suggests that more than a decade may elapse before new institutional arrangements are actively used by governments and businesses in managing their affairs. Still, Feketekuty observes that beyond the results of negotiations carried out to date (which show significant variance across countries and sectors), GATS itself has had a major impact by triggering national debates on the optimality of national regulatory systems in important service sectors. This debate has led in many countries to significant liberalization of domestic and foreign trade through domestic regulatory reforms. Although such reforms may not always be bound in schedules of commitments, they offer a clear objective that negotiators should aim to lock in during the GATS 2000 Round.

Feketekuty argues that while the conceptual foundations of GATS are solid, negotiators could usefully revisit some of its structural deficiencies, many of which resulted from a hasty transfer of concepts borrowed from the GATT system. Efforts to overcome the lack of precision (and of user friendliness) of GATS's current approach to scheduling liberalization commitments need to rank high on the next round's agenda of structural reform. There is also a need to remedy the confusing overlap that characterizes the relationship between market access (Article XVI) and national treatment (Article XVII). He also sees merit in spelling out more clearly the hierarchy of precedence that flows from GATS's three-tiered architecture (framework, sectoral annexes, and schedules of commitments).

Like other contributors, Feketekuty does not advocate reopening the debate over the merits of positive and negative list approaches to liberalization. GATS members should concentrate instead on drafting clear guidelines for scheduling commitments, something that was not done in the Uruguay Round, and stand prepared for a detailed and labor-intensive peer review of national schedules. As is suggested by William Drake and Kalypso Nicolaïdis elsewhere in this volume, Feketekuty foresees the need to revisit the increasingly blurred lines of demarcation among modes of supply and regulatory jurisdictions arising from the advent of electronic commerce. Looking to the future, he encourages trade negotiators to think about ways to gradually integrate GATT and GATS disciplines under one body of common rules. This challenge already arises in government procurement and is likely to surface as attention turns to the more inherently generic domains of investment and competition policy.

Rudolf Adlung's chapter focuses on the political economy of adjusting to services trade and investment liberalization, a subject that often receives insufficient attention in negotiating circles. The costs and benefits—economic, social, and political—of adjusting to the heightened competition that open markets bring will be important in determining WTO members' participation in and contribution to the GATS 2000 Round. Although the greater immediacy and concentrated costs of policy reform and trade liberalization tend to outweigh the longer-term and more widely diffused benefits associated with greater market openness, Adlung shows how forces have in recent years combined to facilitate reform efforts in services and encourage nonreciprocal forms of autonomous liberalization.

He notes that users of services have become increasingly vocal in opposing supplier inefficiencies, technological change poses an ever increasing challenge to maintaining traditional rents, and the adjustment costs associated with greater competition are more manageable in political and social terms to the extent that labor experiences less disruption from services trade liberalization. On the last point Adlung notes how barriers to intersectoral mobility are noticeably lower for services employees than for people involved in farming, mining, or steel production. What is more, unlike manufacturing or the production of primary commodities where adjustment often tends to proceed in a depressed sectoral environment, structural change in services frequently coincides with periods of economic expansion fueled by the pursuit of regulatory reform, privatization, and external trade and investment liberalization. An environment of liberalized trade and investment can more easily absorb the resources that adjustment releases, all the more so as additional sources of supply enter newly contestable markets.

Adlung notes that trade policy considerations have on the whole been of secondary importance as a source of services liberalization. To be sure, GATS did provide an opportunity to give greater permanency (so-called lock-in) and legitimacy to unilateral domestic policy undertakings, with positive implications for production and trade. But it has yet to prove a central reform stimulus per se. An important question, then, concerns the incentives that may have to be built into the GATS 2000 Round to encourage countries to more readily pursue reform efforts via GATS. According to Adlung, an important challenge will be to come up with negotiating concepts ranging from formula-based approaches to liberalization to the development of an opt-out clause in the form of emergency safeguard provisions that could help translate reform efforts into bound commitments.

Adlung sees indications that the hitherto free-riding developing countries of GATS are increasingly aware that binding commitments signal that reforms are permanent and irreversible. The next round, he believes, particularly if it involves more comprehensive (rather than unduly sector-specific) negotiations, may generate some rebalancing of commitments across countries and sectors, particularly in user industries (finance, travel, IT-intensive manufacturing) that may be loath in a more competitive environment to carry the burden of services protection.

Part II. Completing the GATS Framework: The Built-in Agenda

Negotiators will enter the GATS 2000 Round with much unfinished business from the Uruguay Round. More than a dozen years after the Uruguay Round's inception, the framework of GATS rules and disciplines is still very much under construction, with work outstanding on the five fronts that this and the following part of the volume focus on. These are emergency safeguards, subsidies, government procurement, movement of natural persons, and domestic regulation.

That GATS should be seen as a work in progress is hardly surprising considering the diversity of activities it encompasses and the rapid pace at which developments in technology and regulatory approaches affect policymaking and rulemaking. As the essays featured in part IV show, GATS negotiators are already confronted with policy choices on many fronts, ranging from more comprehensive rules on investment to the integration of generic competition policy that targets private anticompetitive conduct or the development of rules aimed at facilitating services trade through electronic means.

Before turning their attention to these challenges, GATS members must finish what the Uruguay Round left unfinished. Since 1994 little progress has been made on these leftover issues, some of which (for example, emergency safeguards against injurious and unanticipated import surges) had been earmarked for completion by mid-1997. In part, this reflects the fact that much attention was devoted during this period to completing outstanding sectoral negotiations, particularly in telecommunications and financial services. But it also reflects other forces. In the case of emergency safeguards and subsidies, and quite apart from the fact that such issues divide the WTO membership along developmental (North-South) lines, problems have arisen from the sheer technical complexity inherent in developing disciplines in hitherto uncharted areas. In the case of government procurement, progress has doubtless been hampered by the manner in which WTO members have approached the subject, with calls for the development of multilateral disciplines for services procurement sitting alongside existing multilateral disciplines applying to services under the Government Procurement Agreement (GPA) as well as calls for non-binding rules to improve transparency and due process in public purchasing. Progress has also been slowed because each component, and none more so than rules governing the mobility of people, involves some North-South tension.

The chapter by Gilles Gauthier examines emergency safeguards and subsidies. It asks whether it is feasible and indeed desirable to extend such disciplines to services. Two core issues are addressed: whether the GATT model for goods would work for services and whether new rules would contribute to deepening and broadening the liberalization objectives of GATS.

Gauthier offers two conclusions on safeguards. First, the economic rationale for them is ambiguous: they are costly to consumers and producers and to economic efficiency in general. Second, for various practical and conceptual reasons flowing from the particularities of services trade and the architecture of GATS (multiple modes of supply, difficulty in determining product "likeness"), as well as the paucity of data required for credible injury determinations, a generic GATT-like safeguard clause is largely unworkable for services. Gauthier comments that the case for safeguards is further reduced by the fact that GATS already features many safeguard-like provisions, not least of which is the ability it affords countries to pursue a sequenced à la carte approach to trade and investment liberalization. Still, recognizing that "the art of trade policy strikes a balance between what policymakers practice and what economists preach," he notes that one cannot easily dismiss the political economy imperative for developing safeguard disciplines. This is the insurance policy function they may perform by encouraging GATS members to undertake more liberal commitments. Should a consensus favoring the adoption of a GATS safeguard clause arise, Gauthier suggests that GATS members inscribe emergency safeguards in their schedules for individual sectors, with general disciplines or criteria conditioning their use. He argues that sector-specific measures should be of limited duration so as to delay liberalization commitments only temporarily and should be triggered by transparent domestic procedures, applied on a most favored nation basis, and subject to appropriate notification, reporting, and surveillance requirements.

Gauthier notes that the subject of subsidy disciplines has not given rise to the same intensity of debate and discussion as that of safeguards. For this reason, deciding on the desirability or feasibility of introducing disciplines will require a more thorough identification phase to determine the extent to which subsidies exist in services industries and the circumstances in which they may result in adverse trade or investment effects. This process has only just begun among GATS members. There may well be valid reasons to temper expectations, as witnessed by the generally disappointing experience of attempts by the Industry Committee of the Organization for Economic Cooperation and Development to monitor industrial subsidies or the swiftness with which subsidy-related issues fell off the negotiating table in recently abandoned negotiations on the Multilateral Agreement on Investment.

As for safeguards, determining the feasibility of subsidy disciplines will need to factor in the specificities of services trade. Although Gauthier suggests that some guidance could come from the WTO's Agreement on Subsidies and Countervailing Measures, it is not a panacea. In particular, consideration of a countervailing mechanism would appear undesirable from the standpoint of both policy and concept. Export subsidies, which are prevalent in large infrastructure projects, and investment incentives, which have recently proliferated beyond the OECD area to a number of emerging economies, may deserve further consideration, particularly in the context of discussions on how best to improve GATS provisions relating to commercial presence.

The chapter by Simon Evenett and Bernard Hoekman examines the case for embedding disciplines on government procurement in GATS. It concludes forcefully that they may not be necessary and that the domestic and foreign welfare effects of discriminatory procurement regimes will likely be negligible and transient to the extent that domestic markets remain contestable. The authors draw attention to an important characteristic of procurement markets: the fact that many procured services may not be viably supplied across borders, commercial presence typically representing the preferred route in light of the natural advantages that flow from local establishments. For this reason a country's foreign investment regime assumes crucial importance in maximizing the economic efficiency and domestic welfare gains from an open procurement regime. Market presence is indeed a precondition for foreign firms to contest procurement markets. If they are not permitted access to the market, which in practice means establishing a commercial presence, procurement regimes and possible multilateral disciplines are largely irrelevant.

Clear and practical policy implications flow from Evenett and Hoekman's analysis. Because the economic damage inflicted by discriminatory procurement policies depends on the contestability of markets, the optimal policy response should be to encourage open and competitive markets and vigorously enforce competition policy. This policy is one that many countries can easily pursue on their own. The authors emphasize the removal of barriers to entry and presence in markets, especially on commercial presence. Priority in the GATS 2000 Round should be devoted to easing market access and national treatment commitments under GATS and not on developing GATS-specific disciplines on government procurement.

While Evenett and Hoekman suggest that trade and investment liberalization may ultimately obviate the need for multilateral procurement disciplines applicable to both goods and services, they recognize the value of promoting transparency in procurement as a means of reducing corruption and rent seeking. They argue that although the case for the multilateral agreement on transparency and due process in public procurement currently being considered by WTO members is much stronger than the economic case for seeking to ban discrimination, any procurement disciplines in the WTO should apply to both goods and services.

The chapter by Allison Young focuses on the movement of service providers, a topic not commonly viewed as forming part of GATS's built-in agenda of unfinished business. Yet, built-in and unfinished are apposite terms to affix to the first attempt ever to contend with labor mobility within the multilateral trading system. Negotiated at the behest of developing countries with large pools of highly skilled (and competitively priced) labor and multinational companies, and drawing on the pioneering provisions developed in the 1987 Canada–United States Free Trade Agreement, the so-called mode 4 of GATS governing the movement of persons to provide services broke important new ground, affirming the conceptual equivalence between capital and labor under GATS.

Young's examination of the schedules of GATS commitments shows that a significant liberalization of mode 4 was not achieved in the Uruguay Round nor in the follow-up sectoral negotiations. The reasons are not hard to come by. Attempting to liberalize the movement of natural persons as service suppliers raises complex and highly sensitive domestic regulatory issues concerning immigration and labor market policy. Faced with demands from developing countries and businesses for liberalizing such movement, immigration and labor ministries are being forced, somewhat reluctantly, to undertake the difficult technical and political task of figuring out how to respond to such demands as the trade policy community gives the subject renewed attention in the run-up to the GATS 2000 Round. The challenge of overcoming such reluctance and securing greater regulatory lock-in—indeed of getting the two policy communities to view the world similarly enough so that tensions can be mediated and progress made—remains formidable. How then can this be achieved?

As a first step, Young says that GATS members need to be clearer on what constitutes mode 4 trade. Greater clarity is all the more important in light of the general opaqueness of GATS's rules and scheduling guidelines. The absence of agreed definitions of employment categories or functions means that inconsistency and vagueness plague interpretation of GATS schedules. Such vagueness also means that immigration and labor ministries tend to retain excessive regulatory discretion. Such transparency problems need to be remedied to lend more certainty to scheduling and open new negotiating possibilities in future rounds. Young suggests that GATS members should be encouraged to submit to comprehensive peer reviews of their schedules where mode 4 commitments are concerned.

Also requiring attention are job and skill-level classifications, the absence of which has typically prompted regulatory authorities to maintain restrictive policies. Young's proposed solution is to underpin mode 4 commitments with nomenclature developed by the International Labor Organization in its International Standard Classification of Occupations (ISCO). There remains also the challenge of overcoming the restrictive effects that nondiscriminatory regulations in licensing, technical standards, or qualification procedures may pose to the cross-border deployment of service providers. Young recalls that Article VI:4 of GATS makes some effort to remedy this problem, adding that it could be useful to subject relevant aspects of immigration and labor market development policies to the article's tests of necessity or of least-trade-restrictiveness.

Addressing the interests of developing countries with respect to the movement of service providers represents another important challenge of the coming round. Young suggests that efforts be directed toward listing sectors and activities that could be excluded from an economic needs test, particularly in areas where skill shortages are predicted to occur in the labor markets of developed countries. She cautions, however, that this might prove difficult in certain occupations, such as computer programming or software development, where professional regulation is largely absent, and comments on the crucial importance of encouraging feedback from business in negotiating and implementing mode 4 commitments. Finally, her analysis of restrictions maintained by the quadrilateral countries (Canada, the European Union, Japan, and the United States) suggests that scope does exist for making all of their mode 4 commitments more transparent and commercially meaningful.

Part III. Domestic Regulation and GATS

There is general agreement that the subject of domestic regulation will lie at the heart of the GATS 2000 Round. Indeed, the three essays in this part of the volume tackle what will undoubtedly be one of the most difficult and challenging aspects of the coming talks: ensuring that worldwide regulatory reform remains a powerful means of securing effective market access conditions for services. That challenge is formidable not only because regulation is pervasive in virtually every service sector but also because of the weakness of current GATS disciplines governing domestic regulations.

Article VI (Domestic Regulation) of GATS is provisional and badly in need of clarification and strengthening. But how best to perform such strengthening without unduly curtailing national regulatory freedom? Of related interest are determining the extent to which government regulations can be based on principles of economic efficiency and good governance and the more narrowly GATS-specific extent to which such principles can, amidst considerable sectoral diversity, be pursued through the creation of meaningful horizontal (non-sector-specific) disciplines.

A critical additional challenge of the GATS 2000 Round will be to achieve greater lock-in vis-à-vis the broad and diverse community of domestic regulators. The sheer novelty, universality, and technical complexity of GATS, coupled with the lack of a proper culture of dialogue and consensus building between trade negotiators and domestic regulators, contributed to an outcome that saw most GATS members err on the side of regulatory caution. This was generally true for both agreed rules and liberalization undertakings. The fundamental changes in technology and in recent approaches to regulation afford a more congenial setting for constructive and forward-looking dialogue between these two policy communities. More often than not, such a dialogue will need to involve competition policy officials.

GATS members have been grappling with domestic regulation and its qualitative bearing on market access ever since the conclusion of the Uruguay Round. Recognition of the weaknesses of framework provisions on this crucial issue has led to sectoral experimentation, most notably in accountancy and basic telecommunications where complementary disciplines were developed to ensure that trade and investment liberalization is properly underpinned by regulatory environments that are friendly to competition and market access.

Both experiments raise the still unresolved problem of the desirability and feasibility of horizontal versus sectoral approaches to the interface of domestic regulation and market access. The diversity of services sectors and the difficulty negotiators have experienced in making certain policy-relevant generalizations have imparted a strongly sector-specific approach to domestic regulation under GATS. Yet even though services sectors vary greatly, the underlying economic and social reasons for regulatory interventions—market failures arising from natural monopolies or oligopoly, asymmetric information about the quality of services or service providers, and externalities, as well as distributional considerations—typically do not differ. GATS negotiators will need to focus more resolutely on these reasons in the coming round to determine the scope that may or may not exist to create meaningful horizontal disciplines on domestic regulation.

Both the basic telecommunications and accountancy negotiations showed that Article VI is concerned only with nondiscriminatory regulatory measures. What this means in practice is that if a GATS member has not scheduled a national treatment commitment in a sector, there is little that Article VI can do to discipline regulatory behavior in that sector. The lesson for negotiators is important as they enter the GATS 2000 Round. That is, under the current GATS architecture, which is unlikely to undergo major surgery in the talks, improvements in market access and national treatment need to go hand in hand with efforts to strengthen GATS rules on domestic regulation.

The chapter by Geza Feketekuty provides an overview of the various regulatory principles that governments should follow to achieve greater economic efficiency and improve governance. It also outlines the practical ways GATS could be modified to better reflect such principles. These principles, which involve transparency of laws, regulations, and regulatory objectives; due process in the administration of laws and regulations; predictability; nondiscrimination; performance-based criteria; and the use of market mechanisms, aim not at imposing social objectives on governments but rather at ensuring that such objectives are achieved most efficiently.

In implementing such regulatory principles, Feketekuty advocates a three-pronged approach:

—strengthening the generic disciplines of Article VI of GATS, which he sees as particularly well suited to overcoming problems of burdensome nondiscriminatory regulations affecting more lightly regulated professions and services related to the information economy;

—negotiation of sectoral agreements in heavily regulated sectors along the lines of the pathbreaking Reference Paper on Basic Telecommunications or as was done in the Agreement on Accounting Services; and

—improvement of commitments incorporated in national schedules so as to better deal with differences in national legal systems, cultural practices, or institutions.

Feketekuty calls attention to the need for negotiators to apply the principle of subsidiarity to WTO negotiations on regulatory issues so as to ensure that efficient regulation is carried out at the lowest level of governance consistent with the achievement of various policy objectives. Noting that future negotiations on trade in services will inevitably become more intrusive of domestic regulatory sovereignty, he argues that the work of the WTO on regulatory issues will need to become increasingly transparent to allay public concerns about the multilateral trade body's perceived democratic deficit.

The chapter by Kalypso Nicolaïdis and Joel Trachtman explores the nature of domestic regulation and the factors that influence the negotiation of appropriate regulatory principles. It provides a vivid reminder of the extent to which nascent GATS provisions are still untested, weaker on balance than those pertaining to trade in goods, and subject to interpretation. The authors describe a range of options for policing domestic regulation under GATS, including an assessment of the kind of criteria that should guide the fundamental trade-off between trade and investment liberalization objectives and legitimate domestic constraints. The chapter usefully bridges the analysis contained in the Feketekuty and Beviglia Zampetti chapters by asking specifically how the objective of market access friendlier domestic regulation can be achieved by developing more precise commitments under Article VI:4 of GATS as well as by implementing mutual recognition agreements under GATS Article VII. Nicolaïdis and Trachtman consider that gaining a clearer sense of the boundary between these two modes of liberalization represents an important challenge to the negotiating community.

They begin by describing existing constraints on domestic rule-making, including those imposed by national treatment obligations in scheduled sectors and the nullification and impairment standard of Article VI:5. They recall how the issue of regulatory jurisdiction—who regulates what?—is far more complex for trade in services than for trade in goods. Like Feketekuty, Nicolaïdis and Trachtman explore the potential for greater discipline under Article VI:4, including the possibility of increased general (horizontal) discipline through the establishment of more rigorous or intrusive standards such as proportionality or necessity. Such an adjudicated approach is then contrasted with a more political approach emphasizing the development of requirements of recognition or harmonization, either multilaterally under Article VI:4 or among a subset of members under Article VII.

Nicolaïdis and Trachtman take no general stand on generic versus sector-specific approaches to the domestic regulation–market access interface. They note that there is a choice between more general principles, such as national treatment, proportionality, or necessity, to be interpreted and applied as disciplines over time by panel rulings and more specifically sectoral rules requiring recognition or harmonization achieved through political agreement. As they comment, the choice "depends on particular factors capable of evaluation by negotiators." In more sensitive sectors they believe that it may be premature to develop detailed rules of recognition and harmonization. Rather, depending on particular sectoral circumstances and state preferences, they think it may be preferable to allow experience to develop with the application of general standards by dispute resolution panels, while concurrently allowing the development of more spontaneous, politically driven recognition and harmonization agreements.

Nicolaïdis and Trachtman usefully remind would-be practitioners of what mutual recognition agreements (MRAs) entail in operational terms. As does Beviglia Zampetti, they note how effective MRAs require some prior harmonization, partial and reversible transfers of recognition powers, and credible verification procedures. They provide practical recommendations aimed at ensuring that MRAs better meet their stated liberalizing objectives, starting with the negotiation of a framework agreement setting out requirements for MRAs. Such an agreement could usefully contain

provisions encouraging parties to continue progress—indeed to keep negotiating—as well as transitivity clauses requiring recognition between all
members of interlocking MRAs. It could also aim to set up a multilateral
system of accreditors on the enforcement side; as well as guidelines on how
and when to achieve some minimal degree of regulatory harmonization.

Americo Beviglia Zampetti focuses on recognition, governed by Article
VII of GATS. He discusses the experience of MRAs as well as the challenges
that need to be met in designing successful arrangements of this type. He recalls the difficulties of designing MRAs in the context of multilevel regulation, noting the generally sobering experience of attempts by federal states or
economic unions to craft MRAs when the prime locus of regulatory jurisdiction stands removed from those entities undertaking contractual treaty obligations. Uncertainty over the feasibility of overcoming such a political
constraint casts a potentially ominous shadow over the ultimate benefits
flowing from MRAs. Such problems are compounded by the tendency, even
in unitary states, toward regulatory regimes that contain a mix of legislation
and self-regulation by independent (and typically private) bodies. Indeed,
the increasing presence of nongovernmental voluntary bodies in rule-making and standard-setting poses special challenges of accountability when an
MRA is being negotiated. This is so even while information and opinions
from such expert bodies may serve an essential legitimizing function in the
design, negotiation, and implementation of such arrangements. Beviglia
Zampetti believes that MRAs concluded between professional bodies
should be looked at as private contracts, implying that only agreements concluded between states can be legally enforced under world trade rules.

He also draws attention to the topic, also raised by Nicolaïdis and
Trachtman, of the relationship between MRAs and MFN treatment. Noting that an important function of Article VII is to provide MFN cover to
MRAs (to legitimize MRAs as agreed partial departures from MFN treatment), Beviglia Zampetti cautions that recognition agreements could increase discrimination in international trade. Although Article VII attempts
to strike a delicate balance by allowing MRAs to proceed as long as third
countries have the opportunity to accede or demonstrate equivalence, his
worries may well be valid to the extent that many GATS members have
chosen to notify MRAs under Article V of GATS, which deals with
integration agreements, rather than Article VII.

The deficiencies in Article VII lead him to argue, like Nicolaïdis and
Trachtman, in favor of a framework agreement on MRAs to clarify the
meaning of "recognition," defining it as a form of "equivalency"; spell out

the roles of subnational and voluntary bodies; and incorporate features for settling multilateral disputes. Such an agreement would also specify minimum requirements MRAs would need to meet so as to hem in the effects of the MFN exception and work to ensure that managed recognition does not in fact become a covert means for discriminatory managed trade. In so doing, a framework agreement would more firmly anchor the practice of MRAs within the multilateral trading system while encouraging their use by an increasing number of WTO members.

Part IV: Investment, Competition, and the Electronic Commerce Revolution

As if the task of prioritizing the long list of issues left over from the Uruguay Round were not daunting enough, GATS negotiators head into the next round of negotiations with a heavy menu of policy choices on several new rule-making fronts, all of which are germane to adapting GATS to the demands of a globalizing world economy. The three chapters contained in this part address those new policy areas that beckon with greatest force: investment, competition policy, and the electronic commerce revolution.

The chapters by Pierre Sauvé and Christopher Wilkie on investment and by Mark Warner on competition policy investigate closely related matters. The analysis and policy recommendations in both display considerable symmetry of tone and scope. They acknowledge the desirability of equipping the multilateral trading system with more comprehensive disciplines with which to govern conditions of entry and presence in markets and curtail private anticompetitive conduct. Both, however, believe that such an objective will continue to elude the WTO in the coming round. Accordingly, they suggest that the attention of trade negotiators be directed toward incremental steps anchored in existing WTO disciplines. Such an objective, as it happens, can be usefully pursued through GATS. Indeed, both suggest that GATS offers by far the most potent means by which to further what Sauvé and Wilkie call the "creeping multilateralization" of disciplines in both policy areas.

Sauvé and Wilkie recall how various forces—economic, political, and juridical—have recently dampened interest in an ambitious investment agenda at the WTO. They draw attention to the sobering, if ultimately useful, lessons emerging from the recent failure to conclude negotiations on an OECD-based Multilateral Agreement on Investment (MAI), all of which are relevant to better understanding where the global investment agenda may be headed in the coming round.

Beyond adverse developments in international sentiment toward investment agreements, Sauvé and Wilkie suggest that there may well be more fundamental reasons to scale back rule-making ambitions on trade and investment in the WTO. Recalling the remarkable growth in foreign direct investment flows registered during the last two decades in the absence of multilateral rules, they draw attention to the political economy of liberalizing the investment regime, which has seen a strongly liberalizing dynamic of policy change take root around the world with little or no evidence of significant or durable policy reversal. Such a trend begs the larger question of the particular type of market or policy failure that multilateral investment rules could redress.

Sauvé and Wilkie's advocacy of a GATS-based focus on investment rule-making and liberalization stems from their belief that by far the greatest and most economically significant number of discriminatory and presence-impairing measures are maintained in services. To be sure, national investment policies continue to influence (and potentially distort) corporate decisions and investment flows in manufacturing and primary industries, most notably as a result of onerous performance requirements and wasteful spending on investment incentives. Yet just as the MAI negotiations revealed a limited appetite in OECD countries for potentially intrusive investment protection rules, the scope for curtailing spreading recourse to investment incentives or significantly broadening the list of measures prohibited under the Agreement on Trade-Related Investment Measures (TRIMs) shows little promise in their view. They advocate a "pragmatic way forward"—steps to improve the investment friendliness of GATS. These include

—clarifying the definition of commercial presence;

—strengthening the investment protection features of GATS;

—improving the clarity of GATS's scheduling technology;

—promoting greater transparency on investment incentives;

—ensuring that GATS commitments reflect the regulatory status quo;

—progressively reflecting unilateral liberalization measures in country schedules;

—devising formula-based approaches to liberalization; and

—increasing regulatory transparency by preparing nonbinding lists of nonconforming measures.

The chapter by Mark Warner begins with a discussion of the numerous

GATT provisions that deal with matters related to competition policy: Articles III (National Treatment), XI (Quantitative Restrictions), XVII (State Trading Enterprises), and XX(d) (Exceptions) as well as the safeguards code; the mandate to review the relationship between investment and competition policy in Article 9 of the TRIMs Agreement; GATS Articles VIII (Monopolies and Exclusive Service Providers) and IX (Business Practices); and the "Reference Paper on Regulatory Principles" appended to the Agreement on Basic Telecommunications (which a third of WTO members have accepted in whole or in part). He draws attention to the ways competition rules can be instrumental in promoting market access for services. This is particularly the case where public sector enterprises, state-owned enterprises, and companies with exclusive or special rights operate (sometimes in competition with privately owned firms, as is the case in energy, postal, and telecommunications services).

Warner suggests that incremental competition rule-making offers the best way forward for WTO members. This is particularly true for services, where negotiations on basic telecommunications have shown the way. He believes that the GATS 2000 Round offers a ready theater for further sectoral experimentation. Accordingly, an important challenge for negotiators is to ensure that, wherever feasible, trade and investment liberalization commitments be properly complemented (either in country schedules or through guidelines such as those developed in the "Reference Paper" for basic telecommunications). Warner suggests that only when a sufficient number of sectoral experiments have been satisfactorily conducted should GATS members try to derive lessons and develop generic disciplines, the breadth of which could subsequently extend to trade in goods. To the extent that GATS members hold true on their stated intention of keeping the GATS 2000 Round to three years, the task of developing and agreeing to WTO-bound competition disciplines may yet have to wait until another round.

In their chapter William Drake and Kalypso Nicolaïdis explore a topic that did not confront the first generation of GATS negotiators but is sure to figure prominently in the coming talks: the information revolution's implications for global services trade rules. When GATS was designed during the Uruguay Round, cross-border trade in services generally involved transactions between organizations over private networks. But the rapid growth, globalization, and mass popularization of the Internet since GATS's inception has dramatically broadened the potential scope of internationally traded services. Drake and Nicolaïdis note that new end-use services such as health care, education, and customized finance, or e-shopping deliverable directly to consumers have now been added to the existing infrastructural services.

They examine some of the issues that global electronic commerce (GEC), especially Internet commerce, can be expected to raise for GATS in the coming round and beyond. They begin by recalling that GEC is not a sector. Nor is it confined to services. Agricultural, manufactured, and intangible goods are also traded electronically, so there are implications for the GATT as well. Further, the growth of GEC raises important questions with respect to the Agreement on Trade-Related Aspects of Intellectual Property Rights as well as for other WTO instruments and issues.

They believe that the Internet poses fundamental challenges that trade policy in general and GATS negotiations in particular cannot ignore. This is so not only because electronic commerce blurs the functional boundaries that used to exist between suppliers and customers, ways of delivering services across barriers, and goods and services, but also because it leads to a blurring of national borders and regulatory jurisdictions.

They caution, however, against conferring too large a role to trade policy in answering such challenges. Instead, their analysis suggests the need for WTO members to focus more modestly and pragmatically on how best to strengthen the open environment in which Internet commerce has so far flourished. Drake and Nicolaïdis discuss alternatives for addressing this objective in a WTO setting. These options include a horizontal approach straddling both goods and services and predicated on the idea of technological neutrality; common law reliance on jurisprudence arising from the results of WTO dispute settlements; revision of relevant GATS provisions, particularly those pertaining to the scheduling of liberalization commitments; and agreement on more specific rules set out in a basic telecommunications-like reference paper or an annex to GATS. Declaring themselves generally neutral about the optimal institutional path to pursue, they nonetheless believe that some rules specific to e-commerce are called for in light of the current architecture of GATS.

In arguing for reforming GATS the authors caution that from a technical standpoint it may be that not all gaps or ambiguities in coverage need to or can be resolved in the next trade round. Its explosive growth notwithstanding, Internet-based GEC is still a relatively new phenomenon. The technology is changing rapidly, and transactional dynamics, business models, and national policies are still in flux. Under these circumstances it will be difficult for WTO negotiators to devise rules that promote trade and will remain appropriate.

The authors remain unconvinced that a quick fix consisting of only the most minimal additions to or clarifications of GATS would be the best result of the coming round. Even if the round actually concludes in 2003, global economic commerce will have expanded dramatically, which will probably lead governments to adopt a variety of national policies to deal with emerging problems. Without a multilateral consensus on at least core principles during the 2000 Round, there may be a risk that such policies will impede global economic commerce or lead to conflicts that the WTO's dispute settlement system is not yet equipped to handle.

Thus although adopting detailed rules on some points may have to wait, the authors believe flexible guidelines that take into account the specificities of GEC should be established. Among the most pressing concerns are solving definitional and classification problems, strengthening the Telecommunications Annex, establishing permissible domestic regulatory objectives, including consumer protection (while also attempting to specify some criteria of permissibility), and banning customs duties on transmissions if developing countries can be convinced that it is in their interest. Drake and Nicolaïdis also suggest the usefulness of developing language clarifying the workings of GATS transparency, national treatment, and competition policy—related provisions in the GEC environment, or at least reaching an informal agreement on their interpretation. In addition, they argue that liberalization commitments need to be strengthened, including commitments on electronic transmission services (telecommunications and Internet access) and on sectors and modes of supply of particular interest to developing countries. Even if formal agreement cannot be reached on all these issues in the 2000 Round, working through them could yield greater consensus in some respects.

Part V. GATS 2000: Challenges Ahead

The four chapters in the last section of this book offer perspectives on the GATS 2000 Round. The first three explore how best to increase liberalization of services. As it happens, there are many routes available to countries seeking expanded liberalization of services trade and investment. One route—that afforded by unilateral regulatory reform—is explored by Bernard Hoekman and Patrick Messerlin. Countries may seek to promote greater market contestability at the regional level, an option exercised frequently in recent years. The question arises then of how the WTO can best discipline egregious regional discrimination and marshal regional interest in services trade liberalization into a force for subsequent multilateral lock-in, an issue taken up in the concluding chapter by Sherry Stephenson.

At the multilateral level, which saw the first round of liberalization negotiations conducted primarily on the exacting grounds of bilateral requests and offers, interest is high among GATS members in developing complementary negotiating modalities aimed at generating more bound commitments while economizing on time and negotiating effort. Considerable attention has been focused on so-called formula-based approaches to liberalization, a topic that figures prominently in the chapters by Patrick Low and Aaditya Mattoo and by Rachel Thompson. Low and Mattoo point to the importance of looking at liberalization through the perspective of improvements in the GATS rule-making apparatus. They emphasize that the next round's twin objectives of stricter disciplines and greater liberalization commitments cannot (and should not) be divorced from one another, as some business groups are prone to do. Rather, determined efforts need to ensure that GATS rules evolve in ways that lead to deeper, more transparent and commercially meaningful GATS bindings.

Low and Mattoo start from a simple yet powerful premise: if GATS rules do not impose unambiguous disciplines on the design and conduct of policy at the national level, they will not be enforceable internationally. Nor will they foster a strong commitment to continuing trade and investment liberalization. Their conclusion that "it is possible to make significant improvements to GATS and to make it a much more effective instrument of liberalization without fundamental structural changes that are, in any case, of doubtful political feasibility," is clear and compelling and will doubtless resonate loudly at the negotiating table.

Low and Mattoo's quest to improve GATS leads them to identify four means: improving the clarity of the agreement, using the existing structure to generate more effective liberalization, deepening the disciplines on domestic regulations, and improving the negotiating dynamic. Although their proposals build on an existing commitment to successive rounds of negotiations aimed at achieving progressively greater liberalization (Article XIX(1) of GATS) and on existing negotiating mandates to develop new rules, they believe that an explicit mandate is needed for work on improving the clarity of the agreement. They contend that some of the ambiguities in GATS are indeed fundamental, turning on questions of interpretation that make a significant difference to the nature of members' obligations and the extent of market access and rule-based certainty delivered by the agreement.

Areas for clarification include the relationship between market access and national treatment to specify precisely the scope of existing and future national treatment commitments. At present, credible alternative interpretations carry starkly different implications. Low and Mattoo also call for clarification of the relationship among modes of supply concerning commitments on given services, an issue of growing prominence with respect to mode 1 (cross-border trade) and mode 2 (consumption abroad) when it comes to electronic commerce. They also call on negotiators to confirm that the principle of technological neutrality applies within modes. In other words, within a mode of supply, a service is to be regarded as a "like" product independently of the means by which it is delivered. Once again, this subject is of potentially greatest importance in the electronic delivery of services.

Low and Mattoo recall that strengthening the domestic regulation provisions of GATS Article VI only makes sense where specific market-access commitments have been made. Otherwise the value of good regulation can simply be nullified by restrictions on access to the market. For this reason, they urge that work on domestic regulation and improving the quality of liberalization commitments proceed in tandem. Meaningful liberalization requires that the provisions on domestic regulations be strengthened. They suggest that the basic approach should be horizontal so as to take advantage of economies of scale in rule-making and lessen the risk of regulatory capture. Sector-specific regulatory provisions may sometimes be necessary to supplement the horizontal approach. They note that horizontally based regulation implies generalization of existing initiatives, depending on the source of market failure that the regulatory intervention is designed to address. Where a problem arises from monopolistic or oligopolistic control over essential facilities, the approach should be to develop regulatory principles along the lines of those negotiated in the basic telecommunications sector. Where other market failures are present, a "necessity test" should be applied, on the basis of economic efficiency criteria.

In considering the best means of promoting further liberalization, Low and Mattoo argue that GATS members should develop clearer negotiating guidelines in the 2000 Round. The absence of adequate nomenclature for scheduling purposes has made it difficult to interpret the true nature of commitments, and there is a critical need to gain a more precise understanding of discriminatory and access-impairing measures listed in country schedules.

They also urge GATS members to make greater use of phased-in commitments to liberalization, as a number of countries did in the telecommunications negotiations. They note how precommitment can be a valuable instrument for planning the opening of a market and guaranteeing adequate time to ensure that necessary conditions are in place when additional competition is introduced into the market.

Like Thompson, Low and Mattoo explore making greater use of various formulas that have been used in sectoral liberalization negotiations. They note that a model schedule can be helpful where ambiguity over sectoral definitions coexists with potential consensus on how much liberalization is achievable. Understandings such as those developed in financial services also make sense where some members are willing to undertake deeper commitments or accept stricter rules but need to develop a common understanding as to the content of such liberalization or rules. Similarly, the idea of developing standardized sets of additional commitments, such as the procompetitive regulations in the basic telecommunications reference paper, has significant appeal and may find a place in negotiations in other network-based industries.

The chapter by Bernard Hoekman and Patrick Messerlin develops rules of thumb aimed specifically at policymakers from developing countries to harness the negotiations on services to their domestic regulatory reform agendas. A corollary of their approach is that governments should seek to lock in regulatory reform policies at the national level. This prompts the authors to call for greater unilateralism in liberalization matters. Accordingly, they look at scheduled commitments under GATS as a useful complement to domestic regulatory reform efforts.

They recommend that policymakers attempt to reduce dispersion in the support given to service activities. Uniformity of protection across sectors should be primary. This in turn requires that information be compiled to allow decisionmakers to identify priorities and assess the effects of existing regulatory interventions across sectors.

Hoekman and Messerlin's emphasis on unilateral liberalization stems from their view that governments cannot easily rely on reciprocal exchange of concessions in services. First, protection in services takes the form of nontariff, behind-the-border measures, which are much more difficult to translate into tariff equivalents and thus do not offer ready-made ways to gauge the welfare-improving effects of bound concessions. The lesser scope for reciprocity-based negotiations also reflects the fact that services exporters typically play a smaller countervailing role than goods exporters do.

Indeed, in many developing countries, opposition to reform and liberalization cannot be counterbalanced by export interests seeking better access to foreign markets. Under such circumstances the authors believe it fair to assume that much of what is required to ensure that the WTO process is a facilitator of the adoption of policies supportive of economic development—promoting cheaper imports of intermediate inputs and maintaining an open policy toward foreign direct investment—will have to be undertaken unilaterally.

Reliance on the unilateral steps required to pursue a growth-enhancing domestic regulatory reform agenda and promote the greater contestability of services markets does not eliminate the benefits from multilateral cooperation. The authors note that a GATS-centered liberalization can be beneficial in moving the world closer to the ideal of free trade by helping remove regulatory barriers to entry in service industries and break the political deadlock that may occur when domestic vested interests are powerful enough to block welfare-enhancing reform. Hoekman and Messerlin also note that GATS negotiations are an important means of expanding the global information base regarding the height and impact of barriers to trade and investment that affect services. Future efforts to expand GATS disciplines should, they contend, center on expanding the sectoral coverage of the agreement and strengthening the transparency and information collection and dissemination functions of the WTO Secretariat.

The chapter by Rachel Thompson sets out some practical options for what can be described as cross-cutting or formula-based approaches to liberalizing services trade and investment. She discusses what a large number of WTO members already see as one of the most promising ways of ensuring that the GATS 2000 Round is conducted efficiently and produces meaningful outcomes.

Echoing Low and Mattoo, she notes that although formula-based approaches have featured more prominently in tariff negotiations on trade in goods, they are hardly newcomers to trade in services. Indeed, ingenious use was made of liberalization formulas in GATS negotiations on financial services and basic telecommunications. The challenge for the coming round is to devise a menu of options that could be pursued horizontally or could apply to clusters of sectors, individual modes of supply, or across particular types of measures (for example, foreign ownership restrictions or residency requirements as conditions of professional licensing).

She recalls the significant negotiating benefits that formula-based approaches may produce: greater economies of scale and effort in negotiating, easier setting of liberalization targets against which progress and results can be measured, improved public understanding of negotiating objectives and outcomes, and improved consistency, clarity, and user friendliness of resulting schedules of commitments. Formulas may also facilitate precommitting to future liberalization, called for by Low and Mattoo, and contribute to achieving the uniform pattern of protection across countries and sectors that Hoekman and Messerlin advocate. Moreover, rather than a GATT-like focus on the reciprocal exchange of concessions, the "concerted unilateralism" inherent in the pursuit of formula-based liberalization promotes greater awareness of the economic benefits of open services markets and of bound commitments while affording GATS members the opportunity to determine for themselves how best to achieve a stated negotiating target.

Thompson usefully notes the particular benefits that developing countries may derive from formula-based approaches to liberalization. Indeed, formulas provide resource-poor countries an opportunity to shape a packaged approach to market access commitments into which their particular interests and negotiating priorities are integrated from the outset. In the case of services, where stand-alone negotiations on movement of natural persons and maritime transport have not succeeded and where developing countries' other commercial interests are likely to be very specific, a formula package that includes specific liberalization in particular sectors could prove highly valuable.

Like Low and Mattoo, Thompson cautions against expecting too much from negotiating formulas. They are not a cure-all, but a means toward a larger end: that of using the WTO to promote economic efficiency and impart greater credibility and permanency to domestic reform efforts. What is more, and as several essays in this volume emphasize, the feasibility and ultimate effectiveness of formula approaches for services must go hand in hand with needed improvements in a number of framework provisions. These provisions pertain particularly to scheduling and the overlap between national treatment and market access, and the possible adoption of such new disciplines as emergency safeguards.

Thompson recalls that formulas provide a complementary route to liberalization. They are not about to replace bilateral request-offer procedures. Indeed, formulas offer a way of making request-offer procedures multilateral. They can reduce but not remove the need for requests and require that offers be more thoroughly scrutinized against a commonly agreed benchmark. Her concluding section provides a comprehensive list of liberalization formulas and informational requirements needed to test their feasibility. Both are matters to which GATS negotiators are certain to pay close attention.

Article V of GATS allows WTO members to participate in regional trade agreements that discriminate against third-country services and service suppliers. It is the services equivalent of GATT's controversial Article 24 on free trade areas and customs unions. Sherry Stephenson's chapter addresses questions that have received scant attention in policy circles: the extent to which the pursuit of regional (preferential) liberalization of trade and investment in services contributes to liberalization at the multilateral level and is properly circumscribed and contained by multilateral rules. The recent proliferation of regional integration agreements (RIAs) containing provisions on trade and investment in services (many of which have yet to be notified to the WTO) and the inconclusive nature of RIA examinations conducted by the WTO's Committee on Regional Trading Arrangements give added urgency to these matters.

Stephenson recounts the tortured negotiating history that led to the adoption of Article V. Recalling Feketekuty's analysis, she points out how the decision to transpose to services the disciplines developed five decades ago for trade in goods resulted in rules that are weak and lack clarity. To some extent such deficiencies may be deliberate, reflecting the unwillingness of key GATS members, many of whom were involved in regional rule-making efforts when Article V discussions were proceeding, to be seriously constrained by multilateral disciplines.

To ensure that regional trading arrangements remain useful engines for multilateral trade liberalization, Stephenson contends that the nexus between regional and multilateral approaches to liberalization must be clarified. As things stand, Article V disciplines generate considerable uncertainty over the type of barriers to trade and investment in services that RIAs should be expected to eliminate. This is also true with regard to the meaning and measurement of the tests that RIAs should be required to meet to gain WTO approval (for instance, "substantial" sectoral coverage, removal of "substantially" all discriminatory measures, and no net rise in the overall protection affecting third-country services or service providers). She proposes that multilateral guidelines be developed that would clarify the application and interpretation of conditions under which RIAs can be deemed WTO-compatible in services.

Stephenson also draws attention to the multiplicity of RIAs to which some GATS members have recently adhered and the proliferation of stand-alone sectoral agreements, trends that are most acute in the Western

Hemisphere. Apart from the fact that such stand-alone agreements (none of which has been listed as an exception to the MFN provision of GATS) appear to exist in a legal gray area, Stephenson asks whether the treaty congestion resulting from overlapping disciplines and differing liberalization timetables may not defeat the purpose of closer regional ties by adding to transaction costs and fuelling juridical uncertainty. If the answer is affirmative, there may be grounds to argue that RIAs are not as a class conducive to multilateral liberalization.

Conclusion

We have tried here to capture the essence of the analysis of each of the essays. No such attempt can ever do full justice to the richness of their content. Nor has an attempt been made to highlight the insights provided in the commentaries appended to the essays. Using the overview as a guide, readers are urged to read the chapters and comments that will be of greatest interest to them in identifying the most salient issues that will make up the agenda for the GATS 2000 negotiations.

PART ONE

Why Are We Doing This? Recalling the Benefits of Services Trade and Investment Liberalization

2 | *Assessing Trade in Services by Mode of Supply*

GUY KARSENTY

THE GENERAL AGREEMENT ON TRADE IN SERVICES (GATS) was concluded during the Uruguay Round of trade negotiations without the support of relevant statistical information. Quantitative information on the amount of trade covered by the agreement was not available, nor was it roughly estimated. In addition, although GATS defined trade in services by modes of supply, their relative importance was simply unknown. Sectoral commitments scheduled according to these modes could not be matched with quantitative information and thus be assessed or compared.

The lack of a clear statistical picture did not prove a decisive issue since the two major achievements of these first multilateral service trade negotiations were expected to develop a framework of enforceable rules and to bind current regimes, rather than to achieve significant trade liberalization or rollback per se.[1] However, the forthcoming service negotiations will aim at extending trade liberalization starting from the situation resulting from the implementation of GATS and subsequent sectoral negotiations, for

The views expressed in this paper are those of the author and should not be attributed to the World Trade Organization.

1. According to Hoekman (1994), "Commitments made in the Uruguay Round are best described as bound standstill agreements for policies pertaining to service sectors. Abstracting from ongoing talks on financial services, liberalization awaits future rounds of negotiations."

example, in telecommunications and financial services. Statistics ought to play a more prominent role in this new context, whether to set negotiating priorities or to exchange concessions. It is thus becoming crucial to fully understand how, and to what extent, available statistical information could support these negotiations. If the statistical systems are to be improved from a negotiating perspective and a fruitful dialogue engaged between negotiators and statisticians, the statistical community must become fully acquainted with negotiating concepts and data needs.[2]

A major obstacle to the availability of GATS-relevant statistics is the divergence between the GATS legal framework and the traditional statistical framework used for statistics on trade in services, namely, balance of payments statistics. As defined by the International Monetary Fund (IMF) in its current *Balance of Payments Manual* (BPM5), the balance of payments statistical framework is based on the concept of *residency* and aims at recording *transactions* between resident and nonresident *transactors*.[3] The GATS modes of supply do not ignore residency but go beyond this concept by using an amalgam of additional notions such as *nationality, territorial location,* and *ownership* or *control.*

A more striking example of divergence between traditional statistics and the GATS framework concerns the supply of services through *commercial presence*, which is simply not recorded in the balance of payments accounts. A commercial presence company is normally resident in the economic territory where it is established, and its supplies in this territory escape recording in the balance of payments as they relate to transactions between residents. However, the inclusion of commercial presence as a way to supply international services is a major innovation of GATS, as well as an important mode of supply that needs to be measured and compared with the other modes of supply.[4] The foreign affiliates trade in services (FATS) statistical framework was created as a response to this challenge. More generally, statisticians and compilers have undertaken the difficult task of improving statistics on trade in services by taking explicit account

---

2. Henderson (1997) established a classification that differed little from the one used by service negotiators during the Uruguay Round but that was more appropriate for compilation in the balance of payments context, at least in Canada. In many other countries, however, the dialogue between negotiators and statisticians has not been as successful.

3. See IMF (1993). The conceptual criterion for the determination of residency is the center of economic interest, but the criterion of more than one year of intentional residence is used in practice.

4. A comparison between cross-border supply and commercial presence using the U.S. data published in the Survey of Current Business was also carried out by Chang and others (1999).

of negotiating needs. These efforts will be embodied in the *Manual on Statistics of International Trade in Services* (MSITS) soon to be finalized.[5] The aim of the manual is to provide compilers of statistics on trade in services with an internationally agreed conceptual framework that will meet users' needs, including those of services trade negotiators. However, considering that the manual's first priority is to ensure consistency with existing international statistical standards, its recommendations will not generate statistics that would exactly match modes of supply.

Hence the overall purpose of this discussion is to assess trade in services by modes of supply. Its specific objectives are to clarify the relationships between GATS and currently available statistics; identify goals for improvement of statistical systems by analyzing the current statistical deficiencies, from the GATS viewpoint; show how current statistics could be used to better support the negotiating process, that is, to identify major markets, major exporters, or to measure relative degrees of specialization; and assess the size of international trade in services in the GATS sense, as well as the relative importance of modes of supply. The chapter also provides some discussion of the prospects for improving the availability of relevant statistics on trade in services in the short and medium term. This discussion will, I hope, give an impetus to new research in these rather neglected areas in the economic literature, as well as in related issues such as the quantitative assessment of potential trade liberalization gains.

Mode 1: Cross-Border Supply

Article I ("Definitions") of GATS describes four possible means by which trade in services may arise. The first of these modes is defined as "the supply of a service from the territory of one Member into the territory of any other Member." This is commonly referred to as *cross-border supply*, or mode 1. It is similar to the traditional notion of trade in goods, wherein both the consumer and the supplier remain in their respective territories when the product is delivered. For a service product, this situation may arise when the service can be embodied in a transportable medium, such

---

5. The manual is currently being drafted under the auspices of the Inter-Agency Task Force of Statistics on International Trade in Services, which comprises representatives from International Organizations such as the EUROSTAT, International Monetary Fund, Organization for Economic Cooperation and Development (OECD), United Nations, United Nations Conference on Trade and Development (UNCTAD), and World Trade Organization (WTO).

Table 2-1. *Balance of Payments Current Account*

Major structure	Major structure
Goods and services	Income
Goods	Compensation of employees
Services	Investment income
Transportation	Current transfers
Travel	
Communication services	
Construction services	
Insurance services	
Financial services	
Computer and information services	
Royalties and license fees	
Other business services	
Personal, cultural, and recreational services	
Government services, not included elsewhere	

as a paper document or on computer diskette, or can be digitized and transmitted through telecommunication links.

In some respects, mode 1 supply is also similar to current services transactions between residents and nonresidents, as recorded in balance of payments statistics. Table 2-1 shows the structure of the balance of payments current account as defined in BPM5, with particular emphasis on the categories having a relationship with trade in services.[6] However, mode 1 differs from the transactions recorded in the category of balance of payments *services* in that GATS coverage excludes government services.[7] These services are included in the BPM5 category *government services, n.i.e.* It also excludes situations in which the consumer moves to the territory of the supplier to consume the service, in which case the transaction is recorded under *travel* in the balance of payments account. These transactions correspond to the second GATS mode of supply, that relating to the movement of consumers.

It follows that the statistical indicator based on the BPM5 components and defined as services minus travel and government services, n.i.e may be used as a proxy measure of cross-border supply. However, transactions occurring when the supplier moves to the territory of the consumer to

6. For more information on these components, see IMF (1993, pp. 61–69).

7. GATS, Article I, describes services as including services in any sector except services supplied in the exercise of governmental authority.

Table 2-2. *World Exports of Cross-Border Services, Value, and Share in GDP and Exports of Goods and Services, 1985 and 1997*

Value and share	1985	1997
Value (billions of dollars)	270	890
Share in GDP (percent)	2.2	3.1
Share in exports of goods and services (percent)	11.9	13.0

supply its services are also included in this statistical indicator, though they are excluded from the definition of mode 1. As a result, this indicator will tend to overestimate transactions under mode 1. This overestimation is presumed to be minimal at the level considered in this discussion, namely, total cross-border services.[8] It would not be the same if this indicator were used as a proxy of cross-border services in certain detailed services, such as professional services. In addition, this overestimation does not, a priori, introduce any specific bias for the identification of major markets, major exporters, or countries with high relative degrees of specialization.

Between 1985 and 1997 exports of cross-border services rose more than threefold, from US$270 billion to US$890 billion (table 2-2).[9] Exports of cross-border services grew significantly faster than GDP, and more rapidly than exports of goods and services.[10] As a result, in 1997 their share in GDP amounted to 3.1 percent, while their share in exports of goods and services reached 13 percent. Cross-border trade in services is obviously a significant component of international trade and has contributed to economic growth during the past decade.

As table 2-3 shows, the relative share of country groups in world exports and imports of cross-border services was fairly stable in 1985 and 1997, with two notable exceptions. Africa's share, on one hand, declined by half, to 3 percent; Asia's share, on the other hand, increased from 20 percent in 1985 to 29 percent in 1997. This gain was made at the expense

8. Major subcategories of cross-border services pertain almost entirely to mode 1. This is the case for transportation, communication, financial services, and royalties and license fees, which account for an estimated 56 percent of cross-border services. This estimate is based on the share of commercial services components shown in WTO (1997).

9. In 1998, commercial services, that is, *cross-border services* and *travel*, decreased by 2 percent. Statistical developments in 1998 are discussed in the WTO press release, March 1999 (see http:\\www.wto.org).

10. In "exports of goods and services," goods are measured on a balance of payments basis rather than on a customs basis, so as to ensure consistency between goods and services. Also, services refer to the BPM5 *services* component, excluding *government services, n.i.e.*

of Africa and economies of the Middle East and those in transition, which are not shown in table 2-3.

The export side is marked by a general decrease in the importance of developed countries, which, while still accounting for nearly three-quarters of world exports, saw a drop of five percentage points during the period. This decline affected mainly Western Europe, while North America benefited from a slight increase. Such a loss was counterbalanced by the performance of Asian countries, which pushed up the Asian group as a whole to a gain in world share of six percentage points during that period.

Table 2-4 identifies the major exporters and importers in cross-border services trade in 1997. While the sixteen major exporters account for three-quarters of world trade in cross-border services, the corresponding share for major import markets is only 67 percent. The higher concentration on the export side may reflect the fact that many service sectors, such as telecommunication services, have a limited number of dominant suppliers, whereas any person or firm is potentially a consumer of these services. The first seven importers—the United States, Japan, and five countries of the European Union—account for about half of world trade in cross-border services. This shows the importance of the commitments inscribed under mode 1 in the schedules of these three major markets.

As might be expected, major exporters in cross-border services consists mainly of major economies. Other countries, though possibly of more modest economic size, may rely heavily on mode 1 exports for their foreign ex-

Table 2-3. *Shares in World Exports and Imports of Cross-Border Services, Selected Country Groups, 1985 and 1997*
Percent

Country group	Exports		Imports	
	1985	1997	1985	1997
World	100	100	100	100
Developed countries	78	73	67	68
Other countries	22	27	33	32
North America	18	19	14	14
Latin America	3	3	6	5
Western Europe	51	47	42	42
European Union (15)	45	41	38	39
Africa	3	2	6	3
Asia	18	24	20	29

Table 2-4. *Top Sixteen Exporters, Importers, and Countries with Highest Specialization in Cross-Border Services, 1997*
Percent

Importer	Share	Cumulative share	Exporter	Share	Cumulative share	Country	Specialization ratio
United States	11.1	11	United States	16.7	17	Kiribati	71
Japan	9.9	21	United Kingdom	7.8	25	Nepal	54
Germany	8.0	29	Japan	7.2	32	Mozambique	53
Italy	5.9	35	Germany	6.6	38	Netherlands Antilles	52
France	5.1	40	France	5.9	44	Cape Verde	52
United Kingdom	4.8	45	Netherlands	4.8	49	Greece	37
Netherlands	3.7	49	Italy	4.7	54	Egypt	37
Canada	2.7	51	Belgium-Luxembourg	3.2	57	Djibouti	36
Belgium-Luxembourg	2.6	54	Hong Kong, China	3.0	60	Ethiopia	34
Republic of Korea	2.4	56	Singapore	2.7	63	Philippines	32
China	2.2	58	Republic of Korea	2.3	65	Vanuatu	30
Spain	2.2	61	Canada	2.3	67	Latvia	29
Taipei, China	1.8	62	Switzerland	2.0	69	Samoa	28
Malaysia	1.7	64	Spain	1.9	71	Jordan	27
Austria	1.6	66	Austria	1.7	73	Antigua and Barbuda	26
Indonesia	1.5	67	Sweden	1.6	74	Seychelles	25

change earnings. Those countries can be identified through an indicator of relative specialization. A first approach might be to scale exports of cross-border services in relation to some indicator of the size of the country, such as its gross domestic product (GDP), which already includes exports of cross-border services. A second approach would be to use exports by all modes of supply as the scaling factor, thus giving an indication of specialization in relation to the other modes of supply. Unfortunately, the lack of data on all modes of supply for all countries prevents the use of such a specialization indicator. A third approach, which is adopted here, is simply to use the ratio of cross-border services to exports of goods and services.[11] It reveals specialization in relation to the other modes of supply, and also to exports of goods, which is probably more relevant in the context of comprehensive trade negotiations. This methodology is used to identify countries with higher specialization ratios (table 2-4). The picture that emerges is radically different from that depicting major exporters, which are not present here. North America is not represented, and there is only one country from Western Europe, Greece. Asia is only represented by small countries, with the exception of the Philippines.

The cross-border services indicator is thus a useful means of identifying major exporters and importers, as well as countries having a high export specialization in this mode. The extent of mode 4 trade that this indicator reflects is presumed to be marginal, but further research is obviously needed to verify this assumption. The MSITS will recommend that compilers provide a breakdown of balance of payments service transactions between modes 1 and 4. However, given the current lack of information on relevant statistical procedures and the need for unambiguous and precise definitions of these modes, these recommendations will likely be assigned low priority. Unless one or more countries undertake specific research or conduct surveys in this area, the statistical perception of the mode 4 component of cross-border services transactions will remain limited for the foreseeable future.

Mode 2: Consumption Abroad

GATS defines the second mode of supply as "the supply of a service in the territory of a Member to the service consumer of any other Member."

11. In line with specialization indices often used in the economic literature, this ratio could also be further divided by the same ratio calculated for all countries. However, inasmuch as the latter is a constant, the new ratio would not change the rankings shown in table 2-4.

This situation arises when the consumer moves to the territory of the supplier, as in the case of tourism services. This mode is often referred to as *consumption abroad*, or *movement of consumers*, or *mode 2*. The consumer, although being abroad, remains a resident of its home country, thus giving rise to transactions between residents and nonresidents. The result is an import of services for the country of the consumer and an export for the supplying country. These transactions correspond to those recorded in the balance of payments travel category of the service account, as shown in table 2-1. Travel is thus a candidate for statistical indicator for mode 2.[12]

Activities such as ship repair abroad, where only the property of the consumer moves, or is situated abroad, are also covered under GATS.[13] The result is a downward bias of travel as a proxy of mode 2. This underestimation is presumably more than compensated by the inclusion of goods bought by travelers not covered by GATS.[14]

The line between mode 2 and mode 1 is often unclear for the electronic supply of services, as well as for some types of financial service transactions such as bank deposits or property insurance.[15] In principle, these transactions should be recorded in the relevant balance of payments service categories and thus be included in the mode 1 estimate.[16]

Unlike the other categories that define service products, travel refers to a demand-oriented activity and relates to specific transactors—travel-

12. In addition, intermediate service inputs of a commercial presence should normally also be accounted for in mode 2, since the consumer, in the GATS sense, may be a *natural person* as well as a *juridical person*. However, for purposes of simplification, this dimension of mode 2 is ignored in this discussion.

13. GATT (1993).

14. Data collected by the World Tourism Organization on international tourism receipts broken down by major expenditures categories for fifteen countries reveal that "shopping" accounts for less than 12 percent of total expenditures in five cases, more than 12 percent and less than 22 percent in four cases, and more than 22 percent and less than 50 percent in six cases.

15. Some members indicated in their schedules under some financial services that if the supply of services involved "solicitation" or active marketing, mode 1 would apply, while mode 2 would cover other cases. In the case of electronic supply, it has been proposed that mode 1 and mode 2 be distinguished according to whether the measure restricted the ability of foreign suppliers to supply services, or that of domestic consumers to buy the services. This rule might help in classifying the measures, but not in clarifying the statistical treatment of modes of supply.

16. For purposes of simplification, however, some countries may allocate all payments in foreign currencies by credit cards to "travel," so the ambiguity between mode 1 and mode 2 is also reflected in the balance of payments statistical treatment.

17. All balance of payments services categories are linked to the UN central product classification (CPC, 1998), except the ones defined by transactors' characteristics, that is, travel and government services n.i.e. According to BPM5, §241, "unlike other services, travel is not a specific type of service but an assortment of services consumed by travelers."

Table 2-5. *World Exports of Travel, Share in GDP, and Share in Exports of Goods and Services, 1985 and 1997*

Value and share	1985	1997
Value (billions of dollars)	120	430
Share in GDP (percent)	1.0	1.5
Share in exports of goods and services (percent)	5.2	6.3

ers—rather than to transactions on specific products.[17] As a result, although travel corresponds to one mode of supply, it is not generally further subdivided by service products to allow an analysis of mode 2 in individual service sectors. However, the classification of tourism expenditures in the *Recommendations on Tourism Statistics* includes the major travel categories: accommodation; food and drinks; local transport; recreational, cultural, and sporting activities; and shopping.[18]

As table 2-5 shows, exports of travel services rose from US$120 billion in 1985 to US$430 billion in 1997 and thus outpaced cross-border services. Travel's share of GDP reached 1.5 percent in 1997, a 50 percent increase over the 1985 level. Its share in exports of goods and services increased from 5.2 percent in 1985 to 6.3 percent in 1997. The performance of travel was thus even more striking than that of cross-border services, which was considered remarkable during the 1985–97 period.

Table 2-6 shows some of the similarities between regional developments in travel exports and those in cross-border services discussed in the preceding section: a decrease in the share of developed countries, principally in Western Europe (particularly in the European Union), and a marked increase in the share of the Asian group. Note, too, that the relative importance of developed countries is not as pronounced in the travel category, compared with that in cross-border services. Travel is an important source of revenue for many developing countries. The import side is also characterized by a substantial decline in the share of developed countries. However, this overall decrease is the result of opposite regional trends. While North America lost one-third of its share, dropping from 26 percent in 1985 to 16 percent in 1997, the European Union experienced a notable increase, from 35 percent in 1985 to 40 percent in 1997. The general tendency of Asia to expand also applies to its travel market, which repre-

18. Recommendations on Tourism Statistics, World Tourism Organization, Madrid, 1993.

Table 2-6. *Shares in World Exports and Imports of Travel Services, Selected Country Groups, 1985 and 1997*

Country group	Exports		Imports	
	1985	1997	1985	1997
World	100	100	100	100
Developed countries	74	68	76	71
Other countries	26	32	24	29
North America	22	22	26	16
Latin America	7	6	5	5
Western Europe	50	44	40	44
European Union (15)	44	39	35	40
Africa	3	3	3	3
Asia	13	19	18	25

sented a quarter of world imports in 1997, compared with an 18 percent share in 1985.

The top sixteen importers of travel account for 73 percent of the world total, while the corresponding share for exporters is 69 percent (table 2-7). Travel does not follow the export concentration pattern of cross-border services. This is not too surprising, since travel exports (inbound tourism) are a demand-oriented activity that reflects the importance of tourism destinations. They are selected on the basis of various criteria (history, culture, specific geographical conditions) or the quality of certain services (education, health-related services). By contrast, travel import levels (outbound tourism) are mainly determined by income distribution.

Nor is it surprising to see which countries have higher specialization ratios in travel (table 2-7). These are small countries that have exceptional geographical conditions and that rely heavily on travel services for their economic development, or countries specializing in certain types of travel services, such as gambling in the case of Macao.

Mode 3: Commercial Presence

Recognizing that the supply of services often requires proximity between the supplier and the consumer, GATS defines the third mode of supply as "the supply of a service by a service supplier of one Member, through commercial presence in the territory of any other Member."

Table 2-7. *Top Sixteen Exporters, Importers, and Countries with Highest Specialization in Travel Services, 1997*
Percent

Importer	Share	Cumulative share	Exporter	Share	Cumulative share	Country	Specialization ratio
United States	13.4	13	United States	19.7	20	Anguilla	89
Germany	11.7	25	Italy	6.9	27	Bahamas	76
Japan	8.4	34	France	6.5	33	Maldives	69
United Kingdom	7.2	41	Spain	6.2	39	St. Lucia	66
Italy	4.2	45	United Kingdom	5.3	45	Montserrat	66
France	4.2	49	Germany	3.8	48	Antigua and Barbuda	61
Hong Kong, China	3.1	52	China	2.8	51	St. Kitts and Nevis	61
Canada	2.9	55	Austria	2.6	54	Grenada	60
Netherlands	2.6	58	Hong Kong	2.6	56	Macau	58
China	2.6	60	Australia	2.1	59	Barbados	57
Austria	2.6	63	Canada	2	61	Comoros	55
Russian Federation	2.6	66	Switzerland	1.9	62	Samoa	52
Belgium-Luxembourg	2.1	68	Thailand	1.8	64	Sierra Leone	52
Taipei, China	2.1	70	Mexico	1.8	66	Haiti	51
Republic of Korea	1.8	72	Russian Federation	1.7	68	St. Vincent and the Grenadines	44
Switzerland	1.7	73	Turkey	1.6	69	Cyprus	44

Commercial presence covers not only juridical persons in the strict legal sense, but also legal entities that share some of the same characteristics, such as corporations, joint ventures, partnerships, representative offices and branches.[19]

The supplier may be viewed from two perspectives: that of the legal entity in the home country ("a service supplier in one Member") and that of the "commercial presence" in the country where the service is to be supplied, the host country. Article XXVIII further specifies the type of relationship that must link the two entities for mode 3 to be effective: the "commercial presence entity" must be owned or controlled by the entity located in the home country.[20] The host country entity is generally referred to as a foreign affiliate and the home country entity as the parent company.

A foreign affiliate is usually established as a result of capital flows taking the form of foreign direct investment (FDI). Balance of payments statistics record international FDI flows, income and stocks in the financial accounts, current account, and international investment position (IIP) balance sheets.[21] However, since the foreign affiliate is normally a resident of the host country, its supplies in this territory are not recorded but are regarded as transactions between residents in the balance of payments sense.[22] In the absence of statistical information on such transactions, a new statistical framework, FATS, is being designed to provide information on *commercial presence*. Some preliminary steps have already been taken to collect the necessary data.[23] FATS statistics are designed to measure the operations—such as sales, employment, or value added—of enterprises that are majority-owned by entities located in foreign economies. Inward FATS statistics relate to foreign affiliates established in the compiling economy, while outward FATS statistics refer to foreign affiliates abroad owned by residents in the compiling economy.

19. GATT (1993).

20. In the GATS sense, "own" refers to ownership of more than 50 percent of the equity interest of a company, and "control" means the power to name a majority of its directors or otherwise to legally direct its actions.

21. For balance of payments statistics, direct investment, as opposed to portfolio investment, implies the objective of obtaining a *lasting interest* by the investor in the direct investment enterprise, and the ownership of 10 percent of the ordinary share or the voting power is considered to be sufficient to reflect *lasting interest*. See IMF (1993, para. 362). This is somewhat different from the 50 percent FATS counterpart, or from the GATS definition of commercial presence.

22. However, these transactions may give rise to international income that is recorded.

23. It should be recognized that the United States has been collecting FATS statistics for some time, although not under this appellation.

FATS statistical concepts and the GATS notion of commercial presence are very much alike, although some differences need to be mentioned. First, while GATS refers to majority ownership or control, FATS data are based on *majority ownership* alone. Statisticians have selected this criterion because it is statistically well defined and operational. This means that FATS does not address all companies covered by GATS; that is, FATS does not include the minority-owned companies that are controlled.[24] However, the difference between these categories is not generally deemed to be significant.[25]

Another difference is that GATS covers services whether produced by a service company or a company classified in the manufacturing sector, whereas FATS statistics aim at measuring the output of companies classified according to their primary activity. The methodology used in this discussion uses the total products of companies classified in service sectors as a proxy for service products.[26] However, companies classified in the other sectors, such as agriculture or manufacturing, often have secondary (and sometimes important) service-producing activities. Similarly, companies classified in service sectors may also produce goods. The effect of this approximation of service product by service activity is unclear. Finally, mode 3 covers only the supply of foreign affiliates in their host countries, whereas FATS variables such as gross output also include sales to foreign markets (exports).[27]

The FATS statistical estimates presented in this chapter were based on two sources. Data for the United States are from the U.S. Survey of Current Business (U.S. Department of Commerce, October 1998), and those for the other countries are from an OECD/EUROSTAT survey of the activities of domestic firms and foreign affiliates.[28] The methodological appendix to this chapter provides information on the way in which such estimates were derived.

These estimates are shown in table 2-8. Global value added by foreign

24. The term "minority-owned" refers to a level of ownership between 10 and 50 percent.

25. U.S. Department of Commerce (1998a, p. 48) indicates that the gross product of majority owned affiliates of foreign companies (50 percent ownership) in the United States accounts for 80 percent of that of all affiliates (10 percent ownership). Thus the mode 3 related gross output nonmeasured by FATS ranges from zero to 20 percent and represents those affiliates that are controlled but not majority owned.

26. Another approach was used for the United States. U.S. Department of Commerce (1998b) shows "sales of services" for all the economic sectors. It was thus possible to sum it up for all these sectors.

27. Exception made of U.S. Department of Commerce (1998b), which shows "sales of services to U.S. persons" for inward FATS, and "sales of services to foreign persons" for outward FATS.

28. OECD (1998). These results are also presented in WTO (1999)

Table 2-8. *World Services Value Added and Gross Output from Foreign Affiliates, 1997*

Value and ratio	Value added	Gross output
Value (billions of dollars)	550	820
Ratio to GDP (percent)	1.9	2.9
Ratio to exports of goods and services (percent)	8.0	12.1

affiliates in services sectors is estimated to be US$550 billion in 1997, or 1.9 percent of world GDP. However, value added cannot be compared with exports, since it does not include intermediate consumption. Gross output, a better indicator of commercial presence, was estimated at US$820 billion the same year.[29] These estimates should be interpreted with caution, however. Most countries have just started to work in this new statistical area, and the data are still not reliable. In addition, gross output and, in some cases, value added, were estimated using other FATS variables, as explained in the appendix.

Since FATS data are only available for a few countries and in most cases data collection is of recent vintage, they cannot be used to analyze general trends and regional shares. An alternative is to use FDI stocks for such analyses, on the ground that the output of a foreign affiliate is a function of the size of related foreign investments.[30] Using the outward FDI stock as a proxy for mode 3, table 2-9 reveals the dominance of developed countries, which accounted for some 90 percent of world FDI stocks in 1997. These countries have nonetheless lost six percentage points since 1985, despite a 6 percent gain for Western Europe. North America's share dropped from 43 percent to 30 percent during the period. Asia increased its share to 8 percent in 1997, up noticeably from 2 percent in 1985. The distribution of inward FDI stocks is more regular, the non–developing countries being recipients of 30 percent of world FDI stocks in 1997. During this same period, country groups experienced a similar general trend in the change of their inward and outward shares, with the

29. As explained in the appendix to this chapter, data from countries reporting FATS statistics (developed countries) were extrapolated using the share of these countries in world FDI stock. However, given that the share of these countries in FDI stock is much higher than their share in FDI flows, if FDI flows were used rather than stocks, the estimates of world gross output and value added would have been much higher.

30. The lack of data prevented the use of a more relevant indicator such as FDI stocks in service sectors. Many countries do not report FDI stocks broken down by activity. Some regional aggregates and world totals for FDI stock in services could not be computed.

Table 2-9. *Shares in Inward and Outward FDI Stocks, Selected Country Groups, 1985 and 1997*

Percent

Country group	Outward		Inward	
	1985	1997	1985	1997
World	100	100	100	100
Developed countries	96	90	72	68
Other countries	4	10	28	30
North America	43	30	33	25
Latin America	1	1	7	11
Western Europe	44	50	34	37
European Union (15)	41	45	31	35
Africa	1	1	3	2
Asia	2	8	14	17

Source: UNCTAD (1998, table I.3 and annex tables B3 and B4).

exception of Latin America, whose outward share stagnated while its inward share shot up from 7 percent in 1985 to 11 percent in 1997.

FDI stock data may also be used to proxy major exporters and importers through the commercial presence mode of supply. Table 2-10 lists the major countries with their outward and inward share in FDI stocks in 1997. The concentration of outward FDI stocks is striking. The top four countries account for more than half of world FDI stocks, the top eight for three-quarters, and the top sixteen for 93 percent. By contrast, inward FDI stocks are more evenly distributed. It may be noted that one developing country, China, is the third largest host country with FDI stocks. However, the fact that the figures used represent total FDI, rather than FDI in services, may limit the accuracy of the results for mode 3.

Mode 4: Presence of Natural Persons

Direct contact between the consumer and the supplier is often necessary not only for supplies channeled through a commercial presence, but also for those coming through an individual. Accordingly, the fourth mode of supply is defined as "the supply of a service by a service supplier of a Member, through presence of natural persons of a Member in the territory of any other Member." An "Annex on the Movement of Natural Persons Supplying Services under the Agreement" states (paragraph 1): "This An-

Table 2-10. *Countries with Higher Shares in World Inward and Outward FDI Stock, 1997*

Percent

Inward country	Share	Cumulative share	Outward county	Share	Cumulative share
United States	20.9	21	United States	25.6	26
United Kingdom	7.9	29	United Kingdom	11.7	37
China	6.3	35	Germany	9.2	47
France	5.0	40	Japan	8.0	55
Belgium-Luxembourg	4.1	44	France	6.4	61
			Netherlands	6.0	67
Germany	4.0	48	Switzerland	4.4	71
Canada	4.0	52	Canada	3.9	75
Netherlands	3.7	56	Hong Kong, China	3.9	79
Brazil	3.7	60			
Australia	3.7	63	Italy	3.5	83
Spain	3.2	66	Belgium-Luxembourg	2.7	85
Mexico	2.5	69			
Italy	2.3	71	Sweden	2.1	88
Singapore	2.3	73	Australia	1.5	89
Indonesia	1.8	75	Spain	1.4	90
Switzerland	1.6	77	Singapore	1.2	92
			Taipei, China	1.0	93

nex applies to measures affecting natural persons who are service suppliers of a Member, and natural persons of a Member who are employed by a service supplier of a Member, in respect of the supply of a service." The annex further indicates that GATS does not apply to measures affecting individuals seeking access to the employment market, or to measures regarding citizenship, residence, or employment on a permanent basis.

The GATS definition and the annex provisions appear to cover two distinct categories of natural persons: self-employed individuals and employees. "Self-employed" refers to individual foreign service suppliers who move to the territory of the consumer for the supply of their services. "Employees" relate to foreign natural persons who are employed by a service supplier in respect of the supply of a service. In this case, the employer may be located abroad, or in the country of the consumer in the case of a commercial presence.

The earnings of foreign employees in foreign-owned or controlled companies are recorded under the balance of payments income category, *compensation of employees*, provided they are established abroad for less than one year. In this regard, GATS excludes permanent employment but does not provide any guidelines on how to distinguish it from employment of a temporary nature. When country commitments give specific time limits, they are generally greater than one year. "Compensation of employees" also contains income received by foreign individuals in domestic companies, normally not covered by GATS.[31]

In all other cases of individuals moving abroad to supply a service, whether on their own behalf or on behalf of their employer, related statistical information is recorded in the balance of payments accounts. However, the balance of payments treatment of such transactions is not straightforward. It depends first on whether the individual is, or is perceived to be, supplying work or supplying a service. If the supplier is contracted and paid for its service, the transaction is normally recorded in the balance of payments current account in the service entry corresponding to the type of service. If the supplier is contracted and paid for its work, the resulting income is normally recorded under compensation of employees.[32]

Thus both the balance of payments service categories and compensation of employees contain information on mode 4. However, the bulk of service categories pertain only to mode 1. Furthermore, the compensation of employees category also contains transactions that are not related to a service supply in the GATS sense, such as income of foreign workers employed in national firms.

One methodology that can be used to derive a mode 4 estimate from balance of payments components would be to first downscale compensation of employees to discount income not related to a service supply, and then to rescale the result to take into account the mode 4 transactions included in the balance of payments service components. Unfortunately, not enough quantitative information is available to use this methodology. Alternatively, one may simply use compensation of employees as a statistical indicator for mode 4, assuming that the upward bias resulting from the

31. Strictly speaking, income received in domestic companies is excluded from GATS. However, some commitments under mode 4 refer to mode 4 as covering short-term employment. Thus there is a certain degree of legal uncertainty (commitments are part of GATS) with respect to the coverage of mode 4.

32. Before BPM5, the category *compensation of employees* was referred to as *labor income*. This category comprises wages, salaries, and other benefits earned by individuals such as seasonal, short-term, and border workers in economies where they are not resident.

Table 2-11. *World Income in Compensation of Employees, Share in GDP,*
and in Exports of Goods and Services, 1985 and 1997

Value, share, ratio	1985	1997
Value (billions of dollars)	10	30
Share in GDP (percent)	0.09	0.11
Ratio to exports of goods and services (percent)	0.5	0.5

inclusion of noncovered income is roughly compensated by the downward bias resulting from the omission of the components that are not related to mode 4.[33] However, no quantitative evidence is available to test the validity of this assumption.

Table 2-11 shows figures on world income in compensation of employees—the mode 4 proxy—as well as its relative importance in GDP and in exports of goods and services. World income in compensation of employees, estimated at US$30 billion in 1997, is quite small in comparison with the other modes of supply. It represents less than 4 percent of cross-border trade in services. Even if mode 4 were indeed underestimated, it would not dramatically change this conclusion. Note, however, that its share in GDP rose slightly, from 0.09 percent in 1985 to 0.11 in 1997, while its share in exports of goods and services has stagnated.

The relatively small size of mode 4 trade does not come as a complete surprise. Compare, as a typical example of a mode 4 service, an on-site software service produced by *one* individual, over a period of a couple of months, with a software ordered to a foreign company (mode 1) that may allocate a full team of experts and mobilize significant resources to deliver the required product. Incidentally, the small value of the mode 4 estimate also suggests that the impact of the mode 4 ingredient on the mode 1 indicator is marginal, thereby reinforcing confidence in the mode 1 indicator.

Table 2-12 reveals that although most income payments (imports) in compensation of employees originate in developed countries, other countries receive (exports) a substantial part of world income, as much as 36 percent in 1997. The major importing country groups are in Western Europe. The European Union alone accounts for some 44 percent of the

33. Following some studies by UNCTAD and the World Bank, WTO (1998) used a statistical indicator defined as the sum of "compensation of employees," "worker's remittances," and "migrant transfers," However, "migrant transfers" does not seem to be related to mode 4, and "worker's remittances" referring to long-term migrants is only very loosely related to mode 4. In addition, there is no evidence that compensation of employees alone does not already overestimate mode 4.

Table 2-12. *Shares in Exports and Imports of Compensation of Employees, Selected Country Groups, 1985 and 1997*
Percent

Country group	Exports		Imports	
	1985	1997	1985	1997
World	100	100	100	100
Developed countries	64	64	82	88
Other countries	36	36	18	12
North America	0	0	9	12
Latin America	9	3	0	3
Western Europe	55	55	64	65
European Union (15)	55	52	45	44
Africa	0	3	9	3
Asia	18	30	9	9

total, and the other European countries in the group for 21 percent, while North America accounts for 12 percent and Asia 9 percent. The major exporting groups are the European Union and Asia.

As may be seen from table 2-13, there is a high degree of concentration in both exports and imports in compensation of employees. The top four importers account for more than half of world imports, and the top sixteen for 87 percent. On the export side, the four major counties benefit from 48 percent of world revenue in compensation of employees, while the corresponding figure for the major sixteen countries is 85 percent. No specific pattern seems to emerge with regard to the level of development or geographical conditions.

Table 2-13 also identifies countries with higher specialization ratios, that is, countries for which compensation of employees is a major source of revenue. These comprise developing countries, including least-developed ones, as well as countries in transition. For the first one, Lesotho, such revenue represents 1.6 times the value of total exports of goods and services combined.

Total Trade in Services and Relative Importance of Modes of Supply

When trade in services is summarized by modes of supply, all modes reached an estimated US$2,170 billion in 1997, or 7.6 percent of world

Table 2-13. *Top Sixteen Exporters, Importers, and Countries with Highest Specialization in Compensation of Employees, 1997*
Percent

Debtor	Share	Cumulative share	Creditor	Share	Cumulative share	Country	Specialization ratio
Switzerland	19.3	19	Philippines	17.5	18	Lesotho	160
Germany	14.1	33	Belgium-Luxembourg	12	30	Armenia	39
United States	12.8	46	Germany	11.5	41	Albania	16
Belgium-Luxembourg	7.2	53	France	7.2	48	Djibouti	16
Japan	5.4	59	Italy	5.6	54	Rwanda	15
Italy	5	64	Thailand	5.1	59	Philippines	14
United Kingdom	4.8	69	United Kingdom	5	64	Kiribati	14
Israel	3.9	73	Switzerland	3.5	67	Mozambique	12
France	3.4	76	Japan	3.4	71	Moldova	8
Netherlands	2.8	79	Austria	2.8	74	Swaziland	8
Bahrain	1.8	81	Republic of Korea	2.2	76	Syrian Arab Republic	4
Russian Federation	1.7	82	Mexico	2.1	78	Côte d'Ivoire	3
Norway	1.6	84	Netherlands	2	80	Fiji	3
Australia	1.2	85	South Africa	1.6	82	Thailand	2
South Africa	1.1	86	Australia	1.6	83	Iceland	2
Sweden	1.0	87	Denmark	1.6	85	Slovenia	2

Table 2-14. *Trade in Services by Modes of Supply, Share in GDP, and in Exports of Goods and Services, 1997*

Mode	Proxy used	Value (billions of dollars)	Total share in all	Share in GDP (percent)
Mode 1	Balance of payments commercial services minus travel	890	41.0	3.1
Mode 2	Balance of payments travel	430	19.8	1.5
Mode 3	FATS gross output in services	820	37.8	2.9
Mode 4	Balance of payments compensation of employees	30	1.4	0.1
Total		2,170	100.0	7.6

GDP (table 2-14). Cross-border supply is estimated to be the major component, accounting for 41 percent of the total, closely followed by commercial presence with 38 percent. Stated differently, both modes account for some 80 percent of the total trade in services. The share of consumption abroad, some 20 percent, is about half of each of the first two modes, while the presence of natural persons is not estimated to be statistically significant (1.4 percent).

These figures should be interpreted as very rough estimates. The definitions of these estimates carry intrinsic limitations, and many of the underlying figures are unreliable. Despite their limitations, however, these indicators may still prove quite relevant for analyzing trade in services and supporting service negotiations. At the same time, the need for empirical research on the refinement of these indicators and on the improvement of statistical information is great. It is hoped that the forthcoming issue of a *Manual on Statistics of International Trade in Services* will trigger national initiatives to improve statistical systems on trade in services. The generalization of FATS statistics as a new statistical domain might also be a major statistical development in the short to medium term that may encourage the international statistical community to collect and disseminate GATS-relevant data. Although the Secretariat of the Organization for Economic Cooperation and Development (OECD) might include this topic in its regular statistical program, no agency is yet ready for such an undertaking for the non-OECD countries. The key element to such statistical improvements will be political support to statisticians who are currently facing a surge in new demands in a general context of budget constraints.

Appendix: Data Sources and Methodology

The balance of payments service statistics used to estimate mode 1 and 2 were extracted from the World Trade Organization's Statistical Data Base (SDB), which contains IMF and national sources. Data on compensation of employees used to estimate mode 3 were extracted from the monthly IMF balance of payments statistics on CD-ROMs. World growth rates were calculated on the basis of available data and applied to missing periods.

For commercial presence, foreign affiliates value added by industry was available for the United States, Japan, France, Finland, and the Czech Republic in the following sectors (industries): "wholesale and retail trade," "hotels and restaurants," "transport, storage, and communications," "financial intermediation," "real estate, renting and business services," and "other community and personal services."[34] Then, gross output was derived in each industry using the gross output/value added ratio.[35] For the United States, an alternative method was also applied. "Sales of services to U.S. persons by non-banks majority-owned U.S. affiliates of foreign companies" was used in place of gross output in services, and an average between the estimates was obtained by these two methods.[36] For all countries in the sample, value added and gross output in services were obtained by summation across service industries. Finally, their shares in world FDI stocks were used to extrapolate world value added and gross output from foreign affiliates.[37] If FDI flows had been used rather than stocks, the estimates of world gross output and value added would have been much higher.

References

Central Product Classification (CPC). 1998. *Statistical Papers,* version 1.0, series M, no. 77. New York: United Nations.

Chang, Phillip, Guy Karsenty, Aaditya Mattoo, and Jürgen Richtering. 1999. "GATS, The

34. See OECD (1998).
35. Computed from United Nations (1997).
36. Sales of services are from U.S. Department of Commerce (1998b).
37. Shares in world FDI stocks were drawn from UNCTAD (1998).

Modes of Supply and Statistics on Trade in Services." *Journal of World Trade* 33 (June): 93–115.

General Agreement on Tariffs and Trade (GATT). 1993. *Scheduling of Initial Commitments in Trade in Services: Explanatory Note*. TN/GAS/W/164. Geneva: World Trade Organization.

Henderson, Hugh. 1997. "Building Bridges: A Canadian Perspective on Linking Service Categories of the World Trade Organization and of Balance-of-Payments Compilers." Paper prepared for the Tenth Meeting of the IMF Committee on Balance of Payments Statistics, Washington, D.C. (October 22–24).

Hoekman, Bernard. 1994. *Tentative First Steps: An Assessment of the Uruguay Round Agreement on Services*. Washington, D.C.: World Bank.

International Monetary Fund (IMF). 1993. *Balance of Payments Manual*. 5th ed. Washington, D.C.

———. Yearly. *Balance of Payments Statistics Yearbook*. Washington, D.C.

Organization for Economic Cooperation and Development (OECD). 1998. *Joint OECD/EUROSTAT Survey on the Activity of Domestic Firms and of Foreign Affiliates in the Service Sector: First Results*. DSTI/EAS/IND/SWP(98)16. Paris (October).

United Nations Conference on Trade and Development (UNCTAD). 1998. *World Investment Report 1998*. Geneva.

United Nations. 1997. *National Accounts Statistics: Main Aggregates and Detailed Tables, 1994*. New York.

U.S. Department of Commerce. 1998a. "Foreign Direct Investment in the United States." *Survey of Current Business*, June, 39–67.

———. 1998b. "U.S. International Sales and Purchases of Private Services." *Survey of Current Business*, October, 71–116.

World Trade Organization (WTO). 1997. *A Review of Statistics on Trade Flows in Services*. Background Note by the Secretariat S/C/W/27. Geneva (November 10).

———. 1998. *Presence of Natural Persons (Mode 4)*. Background Note by the Secretariat S/C/W/75. Geneva (December 8).

———. 1999. *Recent Developments in Services Trade—Overview and Assessment*. Background Note by the Secretariat S/C/W/94. Geneva (February 9).

3 | *Measuring Impediments to Trade in Services*

TONY WARREN *and*
CHRISTOPHER FINDLAY

A N IMPORTANT QUESTION for economic research today is how to characterize, assess, and measure the economic impact of policy affecting services trade. Without such details, it is difficult to mobilize the key interests against protectionism in domestic economies, forge coalitions for reform, and improve the confidence of decisionmakers in the strategies, design, transparency, and implementation of national trade policies. Yet little attention has been given to the services sector, and barriers to trade in services remain opaque, given the nature of the transactions involved.

Moreover, where information on such barriers is available, it is often in qualitative form and needs to be culled from a wide range of sources. This chapter shows how this sort of information can be combined into robust assessments of policy that can help explain market outcomes. This in turn opens up new opportunities to use such measures in the design of reform programs and in the international negotiations associated with their implementation.

The next section reviews the nature of trade in services and the impediments involved. The following sections spell out a case for greater

The authors would like to thank Philippa Dee, Greg McGuire, Pierre Sauvé, and Robert Stern for their comments on this paper, and the Australian Research Council for its support.

transparency, a method for achieving that transparency in a variety of sectors, related modeling issues, and implications for the negotiating process. The methodologies described should make the scope of the General Agreement on Trade in Services (GATS) less of an impediment to its implementation.

What Are the Barriers to Trade in Services?

A service may be defined as an economic activity that adds value to another economic unit, either directly or indirectly, through a good belonging to another economic unit.[1] Consequently, a defining feature of services is that they require direct interaction between producers and consumers (or at least a consumer's assets) before the service can be rendered.[2]

Service Transactions

The fact that producers and consumers must interact before a service can be rendered influences the manner in which international transactions in services are conducted. If a service producer in one economy is capable of rendering the desired services, then a consumer residing in another country must somehow interact with the producer to acquire those services. GATS has developed a four-part typology of how such capabilities can be accessed internationally: through cross-border communications in which neither the producer nor the consumer moves physically, interacting instead through a postal or a telecommunications network; through the movement of a consumer to a supplier's country of residence; through the movement of a commercial organization to the consumer's country of residence; or through the movement of an individual service supplier to the consumer's country of residence.[3] Consequently, the concept of international services transactions encompasses foreign direct investment and the movement of labor, as well as traditional cross-border transactions. In this discussion, any policy that impedes service producers and consumers interacting through any of these channels (or modes of supply) is considered an impediment to international service transactions.

1. This definition is derived from the classic definition of services first proposed by Hill (1977, p. 317).
2. Hirsch (1989, pp. 45–60).
3. See GATS, Article I. See also Bhagwati (1984); Sampson and Snape (1985).

Categories of Impediments

Impediments to trade in services may be divided into two main categories: market access restrictions and derogations from national treatment.[4] Part III of GATS explicitly introduces the concepts of market access and national treatment into the architecture of international services trade. Surprisingly, GATS does not specifically define market access. Article XVI(1) simply obliges members to grant market access to scheduled industry subsectors, while Article XVI(2):(a)–(f) contains a list of measures considered to be limitations on market access. Article XVII(1) defines national treatment as treatment no less favorable than that accorded to like domestic services and service providers, subject to the limitations and conditions set out in the country's schedule of commitments.

Part III implies that market access and national treatment are broader in scope than the corresponding market access and national treatment provisions in GATT.[5] To begin with, the GATS provision on national treatment does not draw a distinction between frontier and internal constraints but embraces all policies that might discriminate between domestic and foreign suppliers. In contrast, national treatment in GATT extends to matters of internal taxation and regulation only. In effect, the GATS article on national treatment encompasses both national treatment and market access as normally defined.

More important, the GATS article on market access extends beyond traditional concerns of access for foreign service suppliers to all policies that restrict access to a market. This is a major extension of multilateral trade disciplines into the realm of domestic policy, particularly competition policy. It has therefore been suggested that "GATT is almost entirely concerned with relations between 'us' and 'them'; these provisions of GATS are not concerned with 'us' and 'them' but [with] 'some of us' on the one hand and 'the rest of us and them' on the other."[6]

Following this suggestion, we propose to operationalize the distinction between market access and national treatment by focusing on the concept of discrimination as follows:

—Market access means nondiscrimination between incumbents in a particular market and possible entrants (be they domestic or foreign). Hence, a legislated monopoly is considered a market access limitation.

---

4. For an early example of this kind of distinction in services, see UNCTAD (1994, chaps. 4–7).
5. See Hoekman (1995); Snape (1998).
6. Snape (1998, p. 284).

—National treatment means nondiscrimination between domestic and foreign service suppliers. Hence a policy limiting foreign investment is considered a breach of national treatment.

Why Measure Barriers to Trade in Services?

Owing to the nature of service trade, impediments to such trade tend to come in the form of nontariff barriers (NTBs), reflecting the difficulties inherent in imposing tariffs directly on either the service consumer or the service supplier as they interact across borders. NTBs are notoriously difficult to identify and measure. There have been few systematic attempts to collect information on barriers to entry beyond the periodic trade reviews conducted by national trade negotiators.[7] No equivalent of the United Nations Conference on Trade and Development (UNCTAD) database on NTBs yet exists for the services sector.[8] As a consequence, few studies have attempted to identify the barriers that do exist or to assess the impact of these barriers on economic outcomes. This is a matter of concern on several different levels.

At a policy development level, the lack of information on the extent and impact of impediments to trade in services undermines the liberalization process. Evidence is available to suggest that services industries remain protected for many of the standard political economy reasons: protection is primarily afforded to uncompetitive service industries with significant political muscle.[9] For those involved in multilateral and regional negotiations, this evidence tends to confirm what many already suspect. Negotiations on services encounter the same barriers to progress that are so familiar in negotiations on merchandise and agriculture. Powerful domestic interests limit the extent to which commitments to liberalization will be made. If anything, the barriers to progress in services are even greater because of the relatively widespread involvement of the public sector in service provision and of the private sector in service regulation.

---

7. The problem with these reports, or so-called black books, is that they are seldom comprehensive, simply reflect the interests of exporters, and are usually based on uncollaborated assertions from interested parties. Among the more widely distributed examples are the reports produced by the Office of the U.S. Trade Representative, the European Commission, the Japanese Ministry of International Trade and Industry, and the Canadian Department of Foreign Affairs and International Trade.

8. Although UNCTAD is currently developing its Measures Affecting Services Trade (MAST) database.

9. See Warren (1996, 1997, 1998).

Overcoming the forces of protection is no trivial task and the solution far from simple.[10] In the domestic political process, however, it is generally considered useful to make the costs of protection as transparent as possible. Not only does this help build coalitions of interest for liberalization, it allows policymakers to have greater confidence in the implications of any decisions they may make.[11] Without information on impediments to trade and investment in services and their consequent impact on the economy, policy reformers have fewer tools with which to push for liberalization.

At a negotiating level, the desire for reciprocity has played a major part in determining the pattern of specific commitments made under the auspices of GATS, as it has in other areas of multilateral trade negotiations.[12] Such a negotiating framework appears to lead multiproduct negotiations (whereby concessions in one industry are traded for concessions in another) to more liberal outcomes by extending the set of industries over which concessions can be traded:[13]

> The across-the-board approach has clearly enjoyed the most success. It establishes politically salient overall goals early in negotiation while permitting great flexibility in subsequent negotiations to deal with individual products, sectors, barriers, or framework and institutional issues. By contrast, the product and sector approaches are, taken alone, unlikely to generate enough political interest and momentum to move negotiations forward at an early stage.[14]

When dealing with NTBs, multiproduct negotiations become more difficult technically, because of the issues surrounding the comparability of concessions.[15] During the Uruguay Round, the problem of NTBs affecting agriculture was confronted directly with the development of the Aggregate Measure of Support (AMS) and attempts (subsequently watered down) to have this measure encompass all NTBs (and tariffs) affecting agriculture.[16] Service negotiators had no equivalent to the AMS, or even usable industry-level measures of impediments. During the Uruguay Round this may

10. See the various contributions on this point in Williamson (1994).

11. On the usefulness of such information in reform, see Corden (1994); Garnaut (1994); Destler (1995, pp. 304–05).

12. See Hoekman (1995); Warren (1996).

13. One of the major problems with the various post-round negotiations in services was that the sector-specific nature of the discussions limited the scope for successful bargaining.

14. Nau (1987, p. 76).

15. See Olechowski (1987, p. 126); Hoekman and Kostecki (1995, p. 68).

16. See Croome (1995, pp. 113–14).

not have been too significant a problem, as negotiations seemed to have focused on developing the necessary architecture, and the specific commitments made by members appear overwhelmingly to have been examples of binding the status quo. As the next round of services negotiations approaches, however, the lack of information on service impediments will undermine the potential for negotiated liberalization.

How to Measure Barriers to Trade in Services?

A research project initiated in 1997 under the auspices of the Australian Research Council has developed a method to help provide more information about services sectors impediments. This method consists of three steps:

—First, available qualitative evidence that compares the way nations discriminate against potential entrants in various service industries is collected. This evidence is then transformed into a frequency-type index, with every attempt made to weigh discriminatory policies by their economic significance.

—Second, the impact of the policies as measured by the frequency indices is assessed against cross-national differences in domestic prices or domestic quantities. The effect of other factors explaining cross-national differences is explicitly taken into account.

—Third, the measured impact of the frequency indices (the coefficient) on prices or quantities is incorporated into a general equilibrium model to assess the economy-wide impacts of the policies under consideration. Where possible, partial equilibrium modeling is also undertaken to provide insight into the specific impacts of liberalization.

The details of these steps are discussed next, with examples of some of the preliminary results, where appropriate.[17]

Step 1: Frequency Indices

As just mentioned, frequency-type measures of NTBs that affect services received little attention for many years because of the lack of suitable data on impediments. This problem was partly overcome thanks to the GATS requirement that countries agreeing to be bound by the multilateral

17. A full set of results from steps one and two can be found in Findlay and Warren (1999). The modeling results are to be published in early 2000.

trade disciplines would list in their individual GATS schedules those sectors in which they were prepared to make commitments and any specific barriers they wished to retain.

Quantification of the GATS schedules began with Bernard Hoekman's pioneering development of a three-category weighting method.[18] He examined all GATS schedules and for quantification purposes allocated a number to each possible schedule entry (that is, each possible market access or national treatment commitment in each mode in each industry subsector). Specifically, where a member has agreed to be bound without any caveats, a weight of 1 is allocated. A weight of 1 is also allocated in circumstances where a member declares that a particular mode of supply is "unbound due to lack of technical feasibility," if other modes of supply are unrestricted. A common example of this situation is the cross-border supply of construction and related engineering services. Where a member has agreed to be bound, but specific restrictions remain, a 0.5 weight is allocated. If a mode of supply is bound but specific reference is made to the horizontal commitments, a 0.5 weight is also allocated. This is commonly the case for commitments on the movement of natural persons, where immigration constraints continue to apply. Where a member has explicitly exempted that particular entry from the operation of GATS by recording an entry of "unbound" or by simply failing to make any commitments at all, a weight of 0 is allocated.

Hoekman used these measures to quantify the extent of commitments (the greater the number, the more commitments made). Other researchers have inverted the analysis and examined the number of commitments that have not been made (the greater the number the more illiberal the economy). We adopt the latter approach (and report results accordingly) because impediments to trade in services are the central concern here, rather than the extent of GATS coverage.

The Hoekman methodology has several drawbacks.[19] To begin with, it does not distinguish between barriers in terms of their impact on the economy, and minor impediments receive the same weighting as an almost complete refusal of access. Another is the coverage of the GATS schedules, many of which do not give an accurate picture of the actual barriers that are in place. This is particularly the case for developing economies, which have had difficulty providing the details required to meet the complexities of the agreement's scheduling process. There is also some suggestion that

18. Hoekman (1995).

19. Most of these problems are detailed by Hoekman (1995). But see also PECC (1995, chap. 5).

nations with liberal policies left some services unbound so as to maintain a retaliatory capability in future market access negotiations. Therefore some industries that are recorded in the Hoekman indices as impeded may be open, at least to suppliers from some economies.[20]

Various studies, including those produced as part of the Australian services project, have attempted to develop a more complex weighting system at a sectoral and mode of delivery level than that used by Hoekman, seeking to quantify differences in the effect of different partial commitments. More extensive databases have also been drawn upon to overcome some of the informational limitations with the GATS schedules. Brief summaries of these studies are provided next.

Cross-Sectoral Indices

At a cross-sectoral level, Alexis Hardin and Leanne Holmes made a comprehensive attempt to incorporate the relative economic impact of different policies into frequency data on the types of barriers affecting investment.[21] They identified five types of barriers to foreign investment, then developed weights within each of these categories on the basis of the perceived economic impact of each policy category. For example, they give a much greater weight to a policy that completely excludes foreign equity than to a policy that allows more than 50 percent but less than 100 percent foreign equity. Policies that limit investment in existing firms but allow greenfields investment are given a lower weight than those that limit all investment.

Moving beyond the GATS schedules, Hardin and Holmes included in their analysis the information contained in the individual action plans (IAPs) produced by members of the Asia-Pacific Economic Cooperation process.[22] These documents have the advantage of being closer to a negative rather than a positive list of barriers to services trade, although they are still far from an exhaustive description of impediments.

Applying their methodology to fifteen economies of the Asia-Pacific Economic Cooperation (APEC), Hardin and Holmes found that communications and financial services tended to be subject to the most stringent FDI controls (see table 3-1). Scores were particularly high for the communi-

---

20. However, a threat of future retaliation could itself be considered an impediment, in which case the data may not be too misleading.

21. Hardin and Holmes (1997).

22. See the APEC website at www.apecsec.org.sg.

Table 3-1. *FDI Restrictiveness Indices for Selected APEC Economies and Selected Sectors*

Percent

Economy	Business	Communications	Distribution	Education	Financial	Transport
Australia	18	44	18	18	45	20
Canada	23	51	20	20	38	24
China	36	82	28	53	45	46
Hong Kong, China	2	35	5	0	23	9
Indonesia	56	64	53	53	55	53
Japan	6	35	5	20	36	11
Korea, Republic of	57	69	63	55	88	57
Malaysia	32	42	8	8	61	12
Mexico	29	74	33	45	55	28
New Zealand	9	43	8	8	20	13
Papua New Guinea	30	48	30	30	30	30
Philippines	48	76	48	48	95	98
Singapore	26	52	25	25	38	25
Thailand	78	84	78	78	88	78
United States	1	35	0	0	20	3

Source: Hardin and Holmes (1997), App. A.2.
Note: The higher the score, the greater the degree to which an industry is restricted. The maximum score is 100 percent.

cations sector because many economies imposed ownership limits on telecommunications and broadcasting and completely closed postal services to
foreign entry. The least restricted sectors were found to include business and
distribution services.

Financial Services

Several frequency indices of impediments to trade and investment in
financial services reflect the preeminent position of this industry in the
world economy. Such indices can be found in the analysis of Aaditya
Mattoo, who has examined the market access commitments on financial
services made by developing and transition economies as part of the
post-round Agreement on Financial Services concluded in December
1997.[23] Mattoo attempts to unpack the partial commitments whereby
countries accept the GATS disciplines but to list policies that will continue
to limit market access. In particular, he distinguishes between limits on the
number of suppliers allowed in a market and limits on foreign equity in
existing suppliers. He concludes that there has been less emphasis on
introducing competition by allowing new entry than on allowing foreign
equity participation and protecting the position of incumbents.

Table 3-2 provides the GDP-weighted regional averages from the
Mattoo analysis, in a format that reflects the restrictiveness of each region.
Regions with higher scores have made fewer commitments. Of the regions
examined, Latin America appears to be the most restricted in direct insurance and Asia the most restricted in banking services.

The limitations of using information derived from international agreements such as GATS and the APEC individual action plans are graphically
demonstrated in Greg McGuire's detailed analysis of the Australian financial services policy regime (both state and federal).[24] Where applicable, he
includes prudential regulations in the definition of market access and
national treatment restrictions. A host of barriers are uncovered in this
manner, including government monopolies over the provision of certain
types of financial services, prudential regulation, restrictions on direct
foreign investment in banking and insurance, discriminatory government
licensing requirements, and government guarantees to selected financial

---

23. See Mattoo (1998). Mattoo focuses only on direct insurance, both life and non-life, and the acceptance of deposits and lending services. He also excludes the presence of natural persons from his analysis.
24. McGuire (1998).

Table 3-2. *GDP-Weighted Regional Restrictiveness Averages in Direct Insurance and Banking*[a]

Percent

	Direct insurance		Banking	
Region	Life insurance	Non–life insurance	Acceptance of deposits	Lending
Africa	44	48	32	43
Asia	59	58	72	67
Eastern Europe	47	49	40	39
Latin America	78	74	62	66

Source: Mattoo (1998, annex 1).

a. Figures are calculated as 1 – GDP-weighted average of the value of the most restrictive measure applied by a country to each mode in the sector. The higher the score, the greater the degree to which an industry is restricted. The maximum score is 100 percent.

service providers. Some 165 impediments are identified, compared with 38 financial service impediments listed in Australia's GATS schedule.

McGuire then applies the weighting methodology developed by Stijn Claessens and Tom Glaessner and finds that the Australian financial services market is fairly open compared with the eight Asian economies they analyzed (see table 3-3).[25] McGuire's results parallel Mattoo's findings in that banking services are more open than insurance services. Of the three financial service industries, the securities industry appears to be the most impeded. However, it is difficult to place too much weight on the scores for the Asian economies as they are based primarily on the GATS schedules and as such may understate the extent of the impediments in place. It would be informative to have McGuire's detailed data collection undertaken in other jurisdictions.

Building on this earlier research, McGuire and Michael Schuele constructed a set of indices of impediments to trade in banking services from a variety of sources, including the World Trade Organization (WTO) trade policy reviews, APEC IAPs, the International Monetary Fund, the office of the U.S. Trade Representative, and various commercial organizations.[26] McGuire and Schuele differentiated between impediments affecting commercial presence and those affecting operations (such as raising funds), and they differentiated between impediments affecting foreign banks and those

25. See Claessens and Glaessner (1998).
26. McGuire and Schuele (1999).

Table 3-3. *Restrictiveness Indices to Trade in Financial Services for Selected Economies*[a]

Economy	Banking	Securities	Insurance
Hong Kong, China	0.25	0.60	1.00
Australia	0.80	1.00	1.50
Indonesia	1.80	2.00	2.40
Korea, Republic of	3.30	2.90	2.40
Malaysia	2.60	2.50	2.90
Philippines	1.65	2.60	2.20
Singapore	2.50	2.30	.90
Thailand	2.15	3.00	2.20
India	2.75	2.90	4.00
Average	*1.98*	*2.20*	*2.17*

Source: McGuire (1998, table 4.2).

a. The higher the score, the more closed the financial services market. Scores range from 1 to 5.

affecting all banks. Each of the inputs into the indices were weighted to reflect the degree to which they are perceived to restrict access to the market. Figure 3-1 plots the index measuring impediments to foreign banks (the greater the score, the more restricted the market) against national income. The negative relationship between GNP per capita and financial market restrictions is immediately apparent.

Professional Services

Beyond financial services, the potential scope for frequency weighting systems is most clearly demonstrated by a pilot study of the Organization for Economic Cooperation and Development (OECD) on assessing barriers to trade in professional services.[27] Here a number of questions are asked within a flowchart format and scores allotted to the answers. The approach is designed to mimic the set of questions a service provider might ask when seeking access to a foreign market. For example: Can I gain physical access to the market (market access)? If I can gain access to the market, am I allowed to practice and to what extent (rights of practice)? Can I provide services as an independent firm (rights of establishment)? If I am required to practice in partnership with a local entity, what limitations does this place on me?

After scores are attributed to each answer, a detailed weighting system

27. OECD (1997).

Figure 3-1. *Foreign Restrictiveness Index in Banking and GNP per Capita at PPP Prices (1996)*

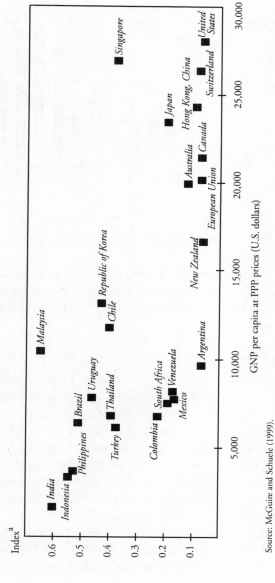

Source: McGuire and Schuele (1999).

a. The higher the score, the greater the level of impediment. Purchasing power parity (PPP) prices based on World Bank surveys undertaken since 1993. GNP per capita at PPP prices are used. GNP per capita using official exchange rates tends to undervalue low and middle income economies with relatively low prices.

Figure 3-2. *Restrictiveness Indices to Trade in Telecommunications Services for Top Twenty Service Trading Nations, 1997*

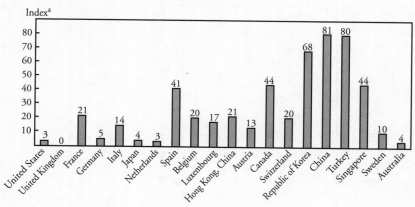

Index[a]

Source: Warren (1999a).
a. The higher the score, the greater the degree to which an industry is restricted. The maximum score is 100 percent.

is proposed. This method was used to examine accountancy services in Australia, Britain, France, and the United States. The United Kingdom was found to be the most liberal of the four countries, the United States to have the highest barriers.

Telecommunications

With the conclusion in February 1997 of the Agreement on Basic Telecommunications, the telecommunications component of the GATS schedule in many countries has changed drastically. Mary Marko has updated the Hoekman-type frequency indices on telecommunications to reflect the impact of the 1997 agreement for the sixty-nine member nations.[28] She finds that 58 percent of the basic telecommunications services market for all of these countries is now covered by either partial or full GATS commitments.

Moving beyond the GATS schedules, Tony Warren has used a 1997 survey by the International Telecommunications Union (ITU) to construct a set of policy indices for 136 countries.[29] These data have the distinct advantage of being drawn from a survey of actual policies, rather than inferring these policies from commitments made in trade negotiations.

28. Marko (1998).
29. Warren (1999a).

Five indices have been constructed, corresponding to the more important distinctions drawn in the GATS context, namely the differences between market access and national treatment and between trade and investment. Because data are limited, a distinction is made between access to mobile and fixed telecommunications markets only in relation to the market access restrictions on foreign investment.

In constructing these indices, Warren sought to incorporate economic and legal inputs by including a count of the number of firms actually competing in a market, as well as the formal policies. Figure 3-2 provides the unweighted average score across the five indices for the top twenty service trading nations. A high degree of variation is apparent, reflecting the continuing resistance among many countries to the liberalization of their telecommunications markets.

Transport

In the transport sector, McGuire, Schuele, and Tim Smith have developed a technique for assessing impediments to trade in maritime services.[30] The data on policy came from a variety of sources, including a questionnaire developed by the WTO's Negotiating Group on Maritime Services, GATS schedules, WTO Trade Policy Reviews, information from the office of the U.S. Trade Representative, OECD material, and APEC IAPs. In this case, separate indices were constructed to quantify restrictions on foreign maritime service suppliers and all maritime service suppliers.[31] The gap between the scores for these two types of entrants indicates the extent to which a country discriminates against foreign suppliers. The results for thirty-five economies in the Asia Pacific, America, and Europe reveal a large range in the degree of restrictiveness.[32] Chile, the Philippines, Thailand, Turkey, and the United States appear to treat foreign-service suppliers significantly less favorably than domestic firms.

A similar technique is currently being used to develop indices of restrictiveness in air transport services. We discuss that case in more detail in our review of the application of modeling methods.

30. McGuire, Schuele, and Smith (1999).

31. Restrictions are grouped into two broad categories of those imposed on commercial presence and "others." The former includes rules on forms of presence, investment in onshore service suppliers, and permanent movement of people. The latter includes cabotage, port services, the UN Liner Code, treatment of conferences, and temporary movement of people.

32. Brazil, Chile, India, Indonesia, the Republic of Korea, Malaysia, the Philippines, Thailand, and the United States are among the most restricted markets.

Step 2: Partial Impact Measures

Having identified and systematized the various cross-national differences in policy, one is able to estimate the impact of these differences on core economic outcomes (such as prices and consumption) in some industries. The available research on the measurement of NTBs affecting trade in goods provides a useful starting point. Two broad methods of quantifying the economic impact of NTBs have been identified: *price-impact measures,* which examine the impact of NTBs on domestic prices by comparing them with world prices; and *quantity-impact measures,* which compare an estimate of trade volumes in the absence of NTBs with actual trade volumes.[33]

These types of price and quantity-impact measures have been considered impossible to replicate in relation to service industries because of the lack of data. A world price for many service industries is indeterminate. Similarly, the lack of data on systematic bilateral services trade and the highly aggregated nature of the current account data limit the potential for traditional quantity-impact models.[34]

As a consequence of these data concerns, it is necessary to identify alternative benchmarks against which to compare actual prices and quantities. Here the market power analysis associated with competition or antitrust regulation is instructive. The aim of such analysis is to compare actual market outcomes with those that would be expected to prevail if the market were competitive.[35]

Price-Impact Measures

Work being undertaken as a part of the Australian services research project is seeking to assess price impacts for the banking, telecommunications, and transport industries.[36] The theory underlying the approach is that if the market had no impediments to entry, then it would be competitive and prices would be expected to approach a firm's long-run marginal cost, defined as the cost of keeping a particular facility alive and well in the long run.[37] If impediments are present, however, there will be a wedge between price and marginal cost, which might affect not only the margin over costs

33. See Deardorff and Stern (1985).
34. See Ascher and Whichard (1991).
35. Areeda, Hovenkamp, and Solow (1995).
36. See also Bosworth and others (1997).
37. The excess of price over marginal cost as a proportion of price is known as the Lerner index. See Lerner (1934).

but also costs themselves. Costs might be higher because low-cost suppliers are excluded from the market or because protected firms are not operating at their lowest possible cost levels. For all these reasons—the margin effect, the cost-difference effect, and the cost-reduction effect—prices observed in the presence of impediments may exceed those in their absence.

As a first step in estimating the impact that impediments to trade in services might have on prices, Kaleeswaran Kalirajan and others examined the price-cost margins (or the "net interest margins") of 694 national and state commercial banks in twenty-seven economies.[38] Using a two-stage econometric technique, they were able to isolate the specific impact that the trade restrictiveness indices developed by McGuire and Schuele had on this margin while correcting for the factors that influence the size of the buffer banks need to manage their cash flow. Table 3-4 provides preliminary estimates of the price effect nonprudential impediments to foreign banks have on the margins for all banks in each of the economies, ranked from the largest effect to smallest. The estimated impacts for Malaysia, Indonesia, and the Philippines are the highest among the twenty-seven economies. The net interest margins are estimated to be at least 45 percent higher than they would be in the absence of restrictions on trade in banking services. For the more developed countries, the restrictions result in smaller margin increases, owing to their greater liberality.

The impact of policy variables on prices in maritime services is also being assessed. An estimate of shipping expenses (derived from comparisons of values at the point of export and the values at the point of import) in bilateral trades in each direction is the proxy for price variables. Statistical methods are being used to test for the significance of the policy measures for variations in prices, after allowing for the impact of other variables that will affect those charges, including the distance between them, the scale of the trade, indicators of the composition of the bilateral trade, the extent of imbalances in the trade flows, and the degree to which the routes are isolated from substitutes. The data set includes 506 observations. Under the method used, policy must be included separately in both partner economies. The results will help researchers determine whether a high degree of restrictiveness is necessary in both economies in order to drive up shipping charges, or whether a high degree in one partner alone is sufficient.

One disadvantage of analyzing margins of prices over costs in order to draw implications for prices is that protected firms tend to extract monop-

38. Kalirajan and others (1999).

Table 3-4. *The Impact of Liberalization on Net Interest Margins (NIMs) for Selected Economies*

Percent

Economy	Effect of impediments to foreign banks on NIMs
Malaysia	60.61
Indonesia	49.32
Philippines	47.36
Korea, Republic of	36.72
Chile	34.00
Thailand	33.06
Singapore	31.45
Colombia	18.35
Japan	15.26
Australia	9.30
Hong Kong, China	6.91
Switzerland	5.95
Argentina	5.34
Canada	5.34
European Union[a]	5.32
United States	4.75

Source: Kalirajan and others (1999).

a. The European Union excludes Finland, Ireland, and Luxembourg.

oly rents in the form of inflated costs rather than excess margins. In some industries, international data are available to deflate costs by producing a world's best-practice (technically and allocatively efficient) cost function using various statistical techniques, notably in markets for air transport and for telecommunications, as discussed shortly. With these frontier cost functions, it is possible to estimate the costs that the world's most efficient firm would incur if allowed into a country (facing that country's factor costs and market characteristics). A comparison of this adjusted cost measure with actual prices has the potential to give a more precise measure of the rents being created by impediments to trade and investment in services.

Quantity-Impact Measures

An alternative approach is to examine output, since price and output are simultaneously determined in a market. In particular, the demand for various services is likely to be greater the more competitive its supply, because the lower relative prices and higher service quality arising from competition will increase demand, while rivalry in investment will push out supply.

Several recent studies have sought to examine the impact of barriers to entry by focusing on the quantity of mobile telecommunications services consumed within an economy—rather than the quantity traded—and by comparing this with international benchmarks.[39] Their aim is to quantify the comparative impact on telecommunications consumption of limits on competition, controlling for other explanatory variables. Restrictions on competition are modeled directly by a count of the number of mobile operators in each country at each period.[40]

Another analysis included fixed network services, measured in terms of the number of mainlines per hundred persons, and expanded the policy variable beyond a simple count of the number of operators (fixed and mobile) to the ITU-derived indices of telecommunications policies discussed earlier.[41] Two sets of simulations were run. The first investigated the impact of restrictive policies on the number of main telecommunications lines per hundred persons in a country, controlling for other key variables explaining cross-national differences: GDP per capita, housing density, quality, and unmet demand. The second set of simulations undertook the same type of analysis except that it focused on the number of mobile/cellular handsets per hundred persons. Across the 130 or more countries that were examined, policy was found to have a statistically significant impact on the extent of the network.[42]

As a consequence of these insights, it is possible to simulate the impact on network penetration of full liberalization. If these predicted increases are calculated as a percentage of actual network penetration, then in combination with an estimate of the elasticity of demand, one can derive a tariff equivalent estimate. Figure 3-3 details the percentage increase in mainlines per hundred persons that the available international data would indicate likely if the top twenty service trading economies completely

39. See Ralph and Ludwig (1997); Ergas, Ralph, and Small (1998).

40. Ralph and Ludwig (1997) found that the presence of three or more mobile operators substantially increased market penetration in the 150 countries they examined. Movement from one to two operators had minimal impact. Ergas, Ralph, and Small (1998) found that mobile penetration in Australia is high by international standards (about twice the expected level), even when all other variables that affect penetration, including the number of suppliers, are taken into account. Interestingly, Australia has been above the predicted level of penetration only since it liberalized in the early 1990s. From 1987 to 1991 it was consistently below the forecast level.

41. See Warren (1999b).

42. Warren (1999b).

Figure 3-3. *Predicted Quantity Impact and Tariff Equivalents of Restrictions on Entry into the Market for the Supply of Telecommunications Fixed Networks, 1997*[a]

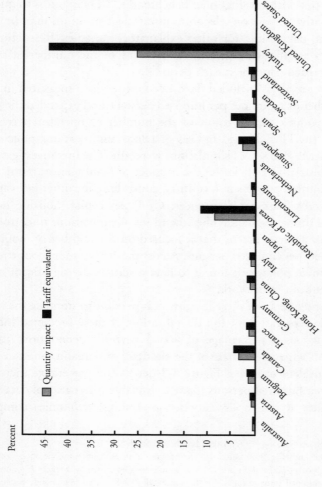

Percent

□ Quantity impact ■ Tariff equivalent

Source: Warren (1999)

a. The quantity impact is defined as the predicted quantity with free trade less the predicted quantity with current policies as a proportion of the latter. The tariff equivalent is defined as the predicted price with current policies less the predicted price with free trade as a proportion of the latter.

liberalized their telecommunications markets.[43] These percentage changes in quantities can be converted into tariff equivalents using estimates of elasticities of demand. For example, with an elasticity value of -1.2, the tariff equivalents also detailed in figure 3-3 can be generated.[44] For some countries, the tariff equivalents are quite small because of their highly liberal policy environment. For others, a significant increase in the actual number of mainlines and decrease in price could reasonably be expected if liberalization were to occur.

Step 3: Modeling

The price and quantity-impact estimates just outlined have three main drawbacks. First, the nature of the predicted reductions in price or increases in quantity remains a black box. Does liberalization affect economic outcomes through competition effects (reduced market power), cost reduction effects (increased efficiency), and cost differential effects (reduced input prices)? Second, such estimates fail to give a picture of the implications of reform for consumer and producer welfare. Third, even these techniques obviously fail to capture important intersectoral effects. What impact does liberalization of a particular service industry have on the economy as a whole? To overcome these limitations, it is necessary to undertake further economic modeling.

Partial Equilibrium Methods

Air transport markets illustrate the scope for using partial equilibrium modeling methods in the analysis of liberalization effects. Policymakers have various options at their disposal to reform international air transport where market access is often severely curtailed by a series of bilateral agreements.[45] Possible reform strategies include liberalization that permits the entry of further domestic suppliers without changing conditions of

43. China is excluded from figure 3-3 for reasons of scale, but the calculated quantity impact is 70.9 percent, which is consistent with the rates recorded by most developing economies.

44. The elasticity figure of -1.2 is the lower bound of various estimates on the price elasticity of international calls. See Warren, Hardin, and Bosworth (1997, p. 25). This figure is considered inappropriate for developing economies, where the price elasticity of demand is significantly lower.

45. For more details of the regulatory regime in international air transport markets, see Warren, Tamms, and Findlay (1999).

access for foreign suppliers, liberalization that permits commercial establishment by foreign carriers, and liberalization that permits the further entry by foreign carriers (for example, by allowing those currently excluded or restricted under the terms of the bilateral agreements to serve the route).

As noted earlier, liberalization can have an impact on prices and quantities as a consequence of three different effects:[46]

—*Competition effects.* These refer to the reduction in market power that occurs because of the removal of barriers to entry and the increase in the number of suppliers. Markups over costs are expected to be reduced because of this effect.

—*Cost-reducing effects.* These effects come from two sources in air transport markets. First, the greater intensity of competition in the markets affected leads suppliers to operate closer to the frontier levels of costs. Second, the relaxation of constraints otherwise imposed by the bilateral system facilitates the creation of networks, including new hubs. With greater freedom than before, and therefore more choice, airlines could be expected to achieve further cost reductions. This second set of effects therefore finds airlines moving closer to the minimum attainable levels of costs, given the input prices they pay.

—*Cost difference effects.* These arise because airlines based in different locations face different input prices. Airlines from different countries can deliver services to a particular market at varying costs. In other words, some countries are likely to have a comparative advantage in the provision of these services.

It is possible to identify these effects specifically by building on estimates of cost functions for air transport services. Using data from fifty airlines from twenty-seven countries over the period 1982–95, for example, Vanessa Tamms estimated a short-run variable cost equation. She also estimated a frontier function that can be used to assess the extent to which an airline lies off its frontier. These results can in turn be applied in partial equilibrium modeling to identify the effects of reform discussed earlier.[47] These models concentrate on supply and demand in air transport markets alone, but they include a series of markets over which airlines are likely to

---

46. See Elek and others (1999).

47. The cost estimates referred to in this paragraph are reported in Tamms (1999). Australia's Productivity Commission has undertaken modeling that captures these effects for air transport. The results will become available once the Australian government releases the commission's final report on international air services.

construct networks. In addition, they capture networking choices explicitly and incorporate forms of imperfect competition that make explicit the determination of markups over costs.[48]

The second major limitation of price or quantity impact measures is that they are unable to quantify the impact of liberalization on consumer and producer welfare. Airlines and consumers will be affected by reform, but in different ways. The impact of reform on consumers is relatively simple to describe: they gain from all three sorts of effects identified in this chapter. The impact on airlines is more complex. The competition effects reduce airline profits, but the degree of reduction is offset by cost reductions. The major airline beneficiaries of reform are likely to include those carriers with a comparative advantage in the provision of the service. In a market in which airlines provide differentiated services, however, even airlines that are relatively high-cost suppliers may see substantial gains from the scope to redesign their networks. Partial equilibrium modeling can be used to estimate the relative size of these effects on consumers and producers and also the scale of the net benefits, that is, the difference between consumer gains and airline gains or losses.

In summary, partial equilibrium modeling can be used to deal with the first two limitations of price and quantity-impact assessments of the impact of reform, namely the unpacking of the origins of the effects identified and their impacts on consumer and producer welfare in relevant markets. But by definition, the partial equilibrium methods fail to capture the intersectoral effects.

General Equilibrium Issues

The impact of liberalization on the wider economy can only be captured if the measures are incorporated into a general equilibrium model, such as a modified GTAP (global trade analysis project) model capturing the structure of service industries.[49] This will allow policymakers to quantify the costs of maintaining policies designed to exclude potential domestic and foreign entrants from their service markets.

Since services are an input into the production of most industries, an inefficient service sector can be very costly to the economy as a

48. For recent estimates of the frontier cost function for a set of telecommunications carriers, see Trewin (1999).

49. See Hertel (1997).

whole.[50] If a country reformed its tariff structure—even reducing rates to zero—but did not include the service sector in the liberalization process, then distortions would still remain and resource allocation would be affected. This point has usually been ignored in modeling work.

Modeling has been constrained, however, by the lack of data on the impact of policies that restrict services trade and investment. Some attempts have been made to convert frequency measures into tariff equivalents and then simulate the effects of reductions in barriers. According to one such study, the welfare gains from Uruguay Round cuts in industrial tariffs would have been three times higher if services barriers had also been cut by 25 percent.[51] Previous efforts at CGE (computable general equilibrium) modeling suggest that the various measures outlined here can be converted into tax equivalents for use in general equilibrium modeling.[52] They also indicate the importance of distinguishing between services supplied by substitute modes (that is, by local firms), by foreign-owned firms operating from a local base, and by foreign firms operating from home base (these are the same three modes of entry that we used as illustrations of reform in our discussion of the application of modeling methods to the air transport market).

It is equally important to determine how impediments affect restrictions on ongoing operations and those on establishment (both of which may apply to local and foreign-owned firms, and may apply differentially to foreign-owned firms, depending on how they want to access the market). Two other essential exercises are to determine the distribution of any rents created between local and foreign interests and to capture the possibility of perverse welfare effects from liberalization. The latter could occur when a form of service is subject to a tax in the initial equilibrium and its output falls as a result of liberalization, for example, as a consequence of the removal of tax on close substitute forms of delivery. The existence of these perverse effects supports the case for a broad program of reform in terms of sectoral coverage as well as modes of delivery.

Preliminary results showing how these features can be incorporated into a general equilibrium model are expected early in 2000. These will, for the first time, allow for a complete assessment of the economy-wide

50. See Hoekman and Primo Braga (1997). The intensity of production is an important factor to consider. The inefficiency of services supplied by arm's-length transactions could lead firms to provide a higher percentage of such services in-house.

51. Brown and others (1996).

52. For a review of these efforts, see Dee, Hardin, and Holmes (1999).

impacts of services liberalization and conversely will highlight the ongoing costs to economies of maintaining protection.

Conclusion

This chapter has demonstrated that weighting schemes can be developed for use in measuring policies affecting international services transactions. These schemes reflect some expectation of the economic significance of the restrictions involved. Over time, as the empirical work expands, the weights themselves may be determined endogenously.

Policy measures constructed in this way are also powerful explanators of market outcomes, although at this stage the assessments based on quantity impacts tend to work better than those based on price impacts (possibly because representative price data on services are difficult to obtain). This is especially the case where data on GATS policy can be supplemented by data from industry sources. If market data are available, the significance of the policy measures can be tested in terms of their impact on market outcomes. Where market data are not available, outcomes can be inferred from the policy measures, given the confidence in this methodology based on its applications in other markets.

More explicit modeling in either a partial or general equilibrium framework is always desirable, though sometimes costly. These modeling methods can be used to make explicit the mechanisms by which policy choices affect market outcomes. That information is hidden in the single-equation reduced-form calculations that are generally used in price or quantity-impact approaches. Modeling can also be used to derive other impact measures, including welfare effects and redistributive effects.

Because of their increased sophistication, the techniques discussed in this chapter are providing the first sound measures of impediments to trade in services that can be used in negotiations or in the documentation and comparative assessment of liberalization commitments. This has a number of major implications for international negotiations: information will be available to help set priorities at the national level; commitments in global (and regional) talks can be more easily codified, to the benefit of cross-sectoral negotiations; the constraint on the lack of incremental change—an inhibitor to reform because of the apparent all-or-nothing choices faced by negotiators—will be removed, since partial reform or sequencing will be more easily documented; and it will be easier to document commitments through a negative list approach because more information will be disclosed with these techniques. Negative lists in turn adduce greater pressure for liberalization as the schedules show what remains to be done in sectoral terms. By contrast, the current approach merely documents restrictive measures in sectors in which commitments to reform have been made. Above all, the information produced will enable economies to characterize their policy regimes and therefore participate meaningfully in the negotiations.

References

Areeda, Philip, Herbert Hovenkamp, and John Solow. 1995. *Antitrust Law: An Analysis of Antitrust Principles and Their Application.* Boston: Little, Brown.

Ascher, Bernard, and Obie Whichard. 1991. "Developing a Data System for International Sales of Services: Progress, Problems and Prospects." In *International Economic Transactions: Issues in Measurement and Empirical Research,* edited by P. Hooper and J. Richardson, 203–34. University of Chicago Press.

Bhagwati, Jagdish. 1984. "Splintering and Disembodiment of Services and Developing Countries." *World Economy* 7(2): 133–44.

Bosworth, Malcolm, Christopher Findlay, Ray Trewin, and Tony Warren. 1997. *Measuring Trade Impediments to Services within APEC: The Economic Implications of Liberalizing APEC Tariff and Nontariff Barriers to Trade.* USITC Publication 3101. Washington D.C.: U.S. International Trade Commission.

Brown, Drusilla, Alan Deardorff, Alan Fox, and Robert Stern. 1996. "Computational Analysis of Goods and Services Liberalization in the Uruguay Round." In *The Uruguay Round and Developing Economies,* edited by W. Martin and A. Winters. Cambridge University Press.

Claessens, Stijn, and Thomas Glaessner. 1998. "Internationalization of Financial Services in East Asia." Washington, D.C.: World Bank.

Corden, W. M. 1994. "Comment" in *The Political Economy of Policy Reform,* edited by J. Williamson, 111–13. Washington, D.C.: Institute for International Economics.

Croome, John. 1995. *Reshaping the World Trading System: A History of the Uruguay Round.* Geneva: World Trade Organization.

Deardorff, Alan, and Robert Stern. 1985. *Methods of Measurement of Non-Tariff Barriers.* Geneva: United Nations Conference on Trade and Development.

Dee, Philippa, Alexis Hardin, and Leanne Holmes. 1999. "Issues in the Application of CGE Models to Services Trade Liberalization." In *Identifying the Roadblocks to International Services Business,* edited by Christopher Findlay and Tony Warren. Sydney: Routledge (forthcoming).

Destler, I. M. 1995. *American Trade Politics.* 3d ed. Washington, D.C.: Institute for International Economics.

Elek, Andrew, Christopher Findlay, Paul Hooper, and Tony Warren. 1999. "Open Skies or Open Clubs? New Issues for Asia-Pacific Economic Cooperation." *Journal of Air Transport Management,* June.

Ergas, Henry, Eric Ralph, and John Small. 1998. "Declaration of GSM Roaming: An Economic Analysis." Mimeo submission to the Australian Competition and Consumer Commission.

Findlay, Christopher, and Tony Warren. 1999. *Identifying the Roadblocks to International Services Business.* Sydney: Routledge (forthcoming).

Garnaut, Ross. 1994. "Australia." In *The Political Economy of Policy Reform*, edited by J. Williamson, 51–72. Washington, D.C.: Institute for International Economics.

Hardin, Alexis, and Leanne Holmes. 1997. "Services Trade and Direct Foreign Investment." Staff Research Paper. Canberra: Industry Commission.

Hertel, T., ed. 1997. *Global Trade Analysis: Modeling and Applications.* Cambridge University Press.

Hill, T. P. 1977. "On Goods and Services." *Review of Income and Wealth* 24 (4): 315–38.

Hirsch, Seev. 1989. "Services and Service Intensity in International Trade." *Weltwirtschaftliches Archiv* 125: 45–60.

Hoekman, Bernard M. 1995. "Tentative First Steps: An Assessment of the Uruguay Round Agreement on Services." World Bank Policy Research Working Paper 1455. Washington, D.C. (May).

Hoekman, Bernard M., and Carlos Primo Braga. 1997. "Protection and Trade in Services: A Survey." CEPR Discussion Paper 1705. London: Centre for Economic Policy Research (September).

Hoekman, Bernard M., and Michel Kostecki. 1995. *The Political Economy of the World Trading System: From GATT to the WTO.* Oxford University Press.

Kalirajan, Kaleeswaran, Greg McGuire, Duc Nguyen-Hong, and Michael Schuele. 1999. "The Price Impact of Restrictions on Banking Services." In *Identifying the Roadblocks to International Services Business*, edited by Christopher Findlay and Tony Warren. Sydney: Routledge (forthcoming).

Lerner, A. 1934. "The Concept of Monopoly and the Measurement of Monopoly Power." *Review of Economic Studies* 1: 157.

Marko, Mary. 1998. "An Evaluation of the Basic Telecommunications Services Agreement." Centre for International Economic Studies Policy Discussion Paper 98/09. University of Adelaide.

Mattoo, Aaditya. 1998. "Financial Services and the WTO: Liberalization in the Developing and Transition Economies." Paper presented at the Measuring Impediments to Trade in Services Workshop, Productivity Commission, Canberra (April 30–May 1).

McGuire, Greg. 1998. "Australia's Restrictions on Trade in Financial Services." Staff Research Paper. Canberra: Productivity Commission.

McGuire, Greg, and Michael Schuele. 1999. "Restrictiveness of International Trade in Banking Services." In *Identifying the Roadblocks to International Services Business*, edited by Christopher Findlay and Tony Warren. Sydney: Routledge (forthcoming).

McGuire, Greg, Michael Schuele, and Tina Smith. 1999. "Restrictiveness of International Trade in Maritime Services." In *Identifying the Roadblocks to International Services Business*, edited by Christopher Findlay and Tony Warren. Sydney: Routledge (forthcoming).

Nau, H. 1987. "Bargaining in the Uruguay Round." In *The Uruguay Round: A Handbook for the Multilateral Trade Negotiations*, edited by J. Michael Finger and Andrzej Olechowski, 75–80. Washington, D.C.: World Bank.

Olechowski, Andrzej. 1987. "Nontariff Barriers to Trade." In *The Uruguay Round: A*

Handbook for the Multilateral Trade Negotiations, edited by J. Michael Finger and Andrzej Olechowski, 121–26. Washington, D.C.: World Bank.

Organization for Economic Cooperation and Development (OECD). 1997. "Assessing Barriers to Trade in Services: A Pilot Study on Accountancy Services." TD/TC/WP(97)26. Paris: Working Party of the Trade Committee.

Pacific Economic Cooperation Council (PEEC). 1995. *Survey of Impediments to Trade and Investment in the APEC Region.* Singapore: Asia-Pacific Economic Cooperation Secretariat.

Ralph, Eric, and J. Ludwig. 1997. "Competition and Telephone Penetration: An International Statistical Comparison." Paper presented to the Telecommunications Policy Research Center, Alexandria, Va., September 27–29.

Sampson, Gary, and Richard Snape. 1985. "Identifying Issues in Trade in Services." *World Economy* 8(2): 171–82.

Snape, Richard. 1998. "Reaching Effective Agreements Covering Services." In *The WTO as an International Organization,* edited by Anne O. Krueger, 279–85. University of Chicago Press.

Tamms, Vanessa. 1999. "Frontier Cost Estimates of the Impact of Restrictions on Trade in Air Transport Services." In *Identifying the Roadblocks to International Services Business,* edited by Christopher Findlay and Tony Warren. Sydney: Routledge (forthcoming).

Trewin, Ray. 1999. "Regulation and the Pricing of Telecommunications." In *Identifying the Roadblocks to International Services Business,* edited by Christopher Findlay and Tony Warren. Sydney: Routledge (forthcoming).

United Nations Conference on Trade and Development (UNCTAD). 1994. *Liberalizing International Transactions in Services: A Handbook.* New York: United Nations.

Warren, Tony. 1996. "The Political Economy of Services Trade and Investment Policy: Australia, Japan and the United States." Ph.D. diss., Research School of Pacific and Asian Studies, Australian National University.

———. 1997. "The Political Economy of Reform of Japanese Service Industries." *Pacific Economic Papers* 270. Canberra: Australian National University.

———. 1998. "The Political Economy of Telecommunications Trade and Investment Policy." In *Telecommunications and Socio-Economic Development,* edited by S. Macdonald and G. Madden. Amsterdam: Elsevier.

———. 1999a. "The Application of the Frequency Approach to Trade in Telecommunications Services." In *Identifying the Roadblocks to International Services Business,* edited by Christopher Findlay and Tony Warren. Sydney: Routledge (forthcoming).

———. 1999b. "Quantity Impacts of Trade and Investment Restrictions in Telecommunications." In *Identifying the Roadblocks to International Services Business,* edited by Christopher Findlay and Tony Warren. Sydney: Routledge (forthcoming).

Warren, Tony, Alexis Hardin, and Malcolm Bosworth. 1997. "International Telecommunications Reform in Australia." Staff Information Paper. Canberra: Industry Commission.

Warren, Tony, Vanessa Tamms, and Christopher Findlay. 1999. "Beyond the Bilateral System: Competition Policy and Trade in International Aviation Services." Paper presented at the American Economic Association Annual Meeting and meeting of the Transportation and Public Utilities Group, New York (January 3).

Williamson, John, ed. 1994. *The Political Economy of Policy Reform.* Washington, D.C.: Institute for International Economics.

4 | *Assessing and Improving the Architecture of GATS*

GEZA FEKETEKUTY

ONE OF THE MAJOR ACHIEVEMENTS of the Uruguay Round of Multilateral Trade Negotiations was the negotiation of the General Agreement on Trade in Services (GATS), the first comprehensive legal framework for the global liberalization of trade in services. In addition, countries negotiated national commitments on access to their markets in individual sectors and subsectors (agreeing to preserve the degree of access provided by current regulations), and on the treatment of foreign services and service suppliers within their national markets. The main thrust of this first round of negotiations on market access and national treatment was to persuade governments to preserve the degree of access provided by current regulations. The hard part of reducing the barriers built into existing government regulations was left largely to future rounds of negotiations.

Countries were aware of the need for further negotiations and agreed to resume them in the year 2000.[1] The agreement calls for successive rounds of negotiations for the liberalization of trade barriers, beginning with the round in 2000. It also calls for the resumption of negotiations on

---

1. See GATS, Article XIX:1: "In pursuance of the objectives of this Agreement, Members shall enter into successive rounds of negotiations, beginning not later than five years from the date of entry into force of the WTO agreement and periodically thereafter, with a view to achieving a progressively higher level of liberalization."

GATS rules, particularly with respect to issues such as subsidies, safeguards, government procurement, and regulations "relating to qualification requirements and procedures, technical standards and licensing requirements."[2] The Council for Trade in Services is charged with developing negotiating guidelines and procedures for each round of negotiations.[3] The existing provisions and their application, as input into the development of these negotiating guidelines and procedures, are the subject of this chapter.

In framing the negotiation guidelines and procedures, the Council should go beyond the built-in agenda and expand their terms of reference in several respects. First, the negotiators should be directed to develop procedures for the negotiation of national commitments that will ensure a substantial liberalization of barriers to trade in services. Second, the negotiators should be asked to fine-tune the legal framework and deepen the provisions of GATS, in order to enhance its clarity and effectiveness. Third, the World Trade Organization (WTO) Council should establish an institutional structure for the negotiation and administration of horizontal agreements that cover trade in both goods and services, since such agreements would not fall either under the Council for Trade in Goods or the Council for Trade in Services. In the future, it is likely to make more sense to negotiate agreements on issues of common concern to both trade in goods and trade in services on a unified basis, and to administer such agreements within a unified institutional structure.

An Initial Assessment of the Agreement

An international trade agreement such as GATS should be assessed on the basis of at least four criteria: whether the negotiating procedures achieve a reduction of trade barriers, whether the disciplines built into the agreement restrain the introduction of new trade barriers, whether the legal framework and the dispute settlement procedures facilitate the settlement of disputes arising over the interpretation of the commitments, and whether the agreement establishes a transparent and stable environment for enterprises engaged in international trade in services.

Five years have passed since the adoption of GATS. This is not a long enough period in which to form any conclusive judgments about the agree-

---

2. See Articles VX:1, X:1, XIII:2, and VI:4, respectively.
3. See Article XIX:3.

ment's effectiveness. The first round of negotiations on market access and national treatment commitments was designed not so much to achieve a substantial reduction in barriers to trade as it was to establish an initial set of national commitments that would preserve the existing degree of market access. Because the demand for services continues to grow rapidly, the provisions of the agreement have not been tested for their ability to withstand political and economic pressures for protection. Empirical evidence from other trade agreements such as the General Agreement on Tariffs and Trade (GATT) and the European Economic Community (EEC) suggests that such agreements often have to mature for a decade or two before enterprises or governments will actively use them in managing their affairs.

Although the data required to judge the operational effectiveness of GATS are in short supply, they do permit a preliminary assessment. Since the adoption of the agreement, there have been two multilateral negotiations under the GATS umbrella on market access and national treatment commitments: one on telecommunication services and the other on financial services.

The negotiations on basic telecommunication services led to the General Agreement on Basic Telecommunication Services (GBT), which will, over time, open the provision of basic telecommunication services to international competition. Another important result was the adoption of a reference paper that sets out a common framework for the regulation of competition in this area. In their submissions to the WTO on the preparation of the next round of multilateral trade negotiations, many governments have asked for a consideration of the wider application of the pro-competitive principles contained in the Reference Paper on Telecommunications.[4]

The negotiations on financial services were a more modest success. Few reductions were achieved in existing barriers to trade in financial services, and very few commitments of any kind were made with respect to cross-border sales of financial services. However, many governments did agree not to tighten existing barriers imposed on foreign financial institutions.

On the face of it, these sectoral negotiations contradict the conventional wisdom in the trade policy community that sectoral negotiations are unlikely to achieve much liberalization. Although it is premature to draw any conclusions about the comparative efficacy of horizontal negotiations across sectors, as opposed to sectoral negotiations, several observations can be made about the organization of these negotiations.

4. See, for example, WTO (1998, para. B.7; 1999, para. 5(b)).

In the negotiations on telecommunications, both business users and new telecommunications providers assisted in the development of national negotiating positions. Negotiations also benefited from substantial empirical evidence that deregulation and competition yielded economic benefits to both producers and consumers in the countries that had adopted such policies. In addition, they were reinforced and given a solid legal structure by the so-called Reference Paper, which sets out a framework for competition in this sector.

In financial services, little progress was achieved until an international effort was launched to persuade governments in developing countries of the domestic financial and economic benefits that would flow from an agreement. At the same time, one can only speculate if the development of a side agreement on prudential supervision would have established a basis for more progress.

A major issue in both the negotiations was the desire of many countries to persuade the United States to remove its reservation on most favored nation (MFN) treatment, that is, its right to negotiate preferential agreements with other countries. The United States had made it clear, however, that it would not remove its reservation on MFN treatment in these two sectors until enough countries had made substantial commitments in their national schedules in these sectors.

Beyond the concrete results of the negotiations carried out to date, GATS has had a major impact in many countries in triggering a national debate on the somewhat encrusted national regulatory systems in services. In many cases this debate has led to the substantial liberalization of both internal and external trade through autonomous domestic regulatory reforms. While national experiences with respect to the autonomous adoption of domestic reforms vary considerably, as seen in the various East Asian economies, they hold an important lesson for future liberalization efforts. An essential requirement for successful liberalization may well be the development of national consensus among consumers, providers, regulators, economic officials, and trade officials that regulatory reform and trade liberalization in a particular sector will spur economic growth and are therefore in the country's own interest, whatever happens in the broader global context.[5]

Turning from the impact of GATS on the liberalization of trade in

---

5. For an elegant and thorough discussion of the importance of approaching the liberalization of trade in services from the perspective of domestic regulatory reform, see chapter 17 in this volume.

services to the perceptions of potential stakeholders, anecdotal evidence suggests that the agreement and the associated appendixes and national schedules are not user-friendly and are somewhat opaque to the private sector. Comments by business managers and trade lawyers who have ventured to examine the national schedules of commitments have indicated that they are more confused than enlightened by the schedules and the provisions. Public perceptions have not been helped by what has been an often ill-informed debate among the experts. The confusion is to some extent due to the complexity of disentangling trade protection, overly restrictive approaches to national regulation, and the pursuit of legitimate public policy goals. Nevertheless, it can also be traced to a lack of clarity in the conceptual design of the agreement and the attendant schedules, a design flaw that could be addressed in the coming negotiations.

Assessing GATS Negotiating Procedures

To date, GATS negotiations aimed at liberalization have followed two approaches. The first is a bilateral exchange of requests and offers, followed by the bilateral negotiation of market access and national treatment commitments on an item-by-item basis, across all services sectors. The second consists of plurilateral or multilateral negotiations that have focused on individual sectors such as telecommunications and have covered not only market access and national treatment issues but also related regulatory issues.

As already noted, the relative success of these alternative approaches is difficult to evaluate. The initial round of across-the-board negotiations concentrated more on covering as many sectors as possible with an initial set of commitments that reflected the current level of market openness than on achieving a substantial liberalization of barriers. The two sectoral negotiations that were successfully concluded benefited from special factors such as the pressure of MFN exemptions and, in the case of telecommunications, the economic pressure generated by changes in technology.

The results require careful analysis because they go against the historical experience and the firm belief of the trade policy community that crosscutting negotiations are more successful in achieving liberalization than negotiations focused on individual sectors. Crosscutting negotiations are usually considered more successful because interests in other sectors that stand to gain from liberalization offset the opposition of vested interests in any one sector. The underlying assumption is that in any given sector some countries are competitive and other countries are uncompetitive, and current providers in uncompetitive protected markets stand to lose as a result of negotiations. They will therefore pressure the governments involved not to reduce the protective barriers. Broad negotiations allow sectoral trade-offs between those who lose and those who gain in every country. The resistance of providers in uncompetitive services is compounded in many services sectors by the potential resistance of sectoral regulators who have a vested interest in preserving their existing regulations and protecting their bureaucratic turf.

The accumulated wisdom of trade negotiators has to be tempered, however, by the recognition that liberalization in many services sectors cannot be achieved without substantial domestic regulatory reforms, and that such reforms cannot be achieved on a piecemeal basis and over the determined opposition of the regulators involved. As the less successful efforts in areas such as maritime and air transport show, without the cooperation of regulatory officials and the opportunity to make the case that regulatory reform in a particular sector is to everyone's advantage, little progress can be made. The more recent experience with negotiations in the accounting sector reinforces this point. Although negotiations were successfully concluded, they fell short of the desired results because of the determined opposition of some regulators.

Another lesson from past experience is that negotiations organized around targets such as tariff-cutting formulas are likely to be more successful than item-by-item negotiations having no overall target or goal. Targets provide benchmarks against which results based on highly detailed bilateral negotiations can be measured. They also help improve the efficiency of negotiation, public comprehension, and the consistency, clarity, and user friendliness of the final schedules.[6] Some practical steps for strengthening GATS along these lines are discussed in the remainder of the chapter.

The Conceptual Structure of GATS

The great difficulty in designing GATS was that barriers to trade in services are generally embedded in domestic regulations.[7] Unlike barriers

6. See chapter 16 in this volume.

7. For an extensive treatment of the challenges facing the negotiation of a comprehensive agreement on trade in services, see Feketekuty (1988).

to trade in goods, they do not take the form of transparent barriers imposed at the border against foreign services. Cross-border flows of services are largely invisible. Where governments have tried to protect their local service suppliers from foreign competition, they have embedded the protective measures in domestic regulations focused on the local consumption of services or the local provision of services. For example, regulations may stipulate that only car insurance provided by a local firm satisfies the compulsory insurance requirement for car registration, or that only locally owned and established firms may sell car insurance to consumers.

Another challenge was that domestic regulations frequently limit trade even if they do not explicitly discriminate against foreign providers. This was a crucial point because the regulatory involvement of governments in the provision of services has been much more intensive than their involvement in manufacturing. Regulations often limit the number of firms, the number of employees, the number of distribution outlets, the services that can be sold, prices, marketing practices, and distribution channels. These types of regulations protect existing firms from competition by new entrants, whether domestic or foreign. The rationale often provided for such intervention is that consumers need to be protected from the shady practices associated with excessive competition, or that consumers need to be assured of a stable supply of a reliable product at reasonable prices. Another rationale is that the market can support only a limited number of providers, both physically and economically, or that all economic activities related to the provision of services that contain a monopoly component have to be regulated to protect the consumer interest.

A third challenge for the designers of GATS was that trade, investment, labor mobility, and foreign consumption are far more interwoven in services than in goods. While the main argument for the negotiation of trade rules in services was that services were becoming tradable as a result of innovations in information technology, it did not seem to make much sense to limit a trade regime to cross-border trade. After all, the bulk of services sold by foreign service providers to consumers are still being sold through locally established firms. Interestingly, when confronted by a choice between cross-border sales and local establishment of foreign providers, many regulators decided they would prefer the latter.

GATS negotiators thus faced a threefold challenge: to remove discrimination in domestic regulations against services produced by foreign providers, to modify nondiscriminatory regulations that had the effect of restricting trade, and to deal with the four ways in which services could be traded (foreign consumption, cross-border trade, the sale of services through a foreign-owned local establishment, and the provision of a service by the resident of another country who has gained temporary entry). Although negotiators realized that the structure of the GATT rules would have to be changed to meet these challenges, they were nevertheless a product of the GATT system. They innovated where they had to, but otherwise they adapted legal concepts and terminology from the GATT system.

This grafting led to some of the major design flaws in the GATS regime. Therefore a review of the underlying structure of GATT is useful in order to understand the GATS framework.

The Basic Structure of GATT Rules for Trade in Goods

The GATT rules for trade in goods are woven around a few key notions: barriers should be imposed at the border; they should take the form of tariffs; the tariffs should be subject to negotiation; the resulting tariffs should be bound in national schedules; tariffs should be applied equally to goods imported from all member countries; and domestic regulations should not discriminate against foreign goods once they have crossed the border and paid the tariff. The GATT rules permit various exceptions to these basic rules, and they spell out how these rules are to be applied with respect to various types of government measures, but the core rules are those that implement the notions just mentioned.[8]

Under GATT, tariffs (and quotas where permitted) must be determined through the bilateral exchange of requests and offers. Successive rounds of negotiations proved that more liberalization could be achieved if such bilateral negotiations were based on multilaterally agreed targets or formulas.

The closest analog in goods to the central challenge in services—namely to curb the trade-restrictive impact of domestic regulations—was the need to curb the trade-distorting impact of domestic standards. The GATT rules on standards give governments the right to pursue domestic social objectives through the establishment of compulsory standards for the goods sold in domestic markets, but they require that the

8. For an elegant discussion of the underlying design of GATT, see Wilcox (1949).

resulting standards achieve the desired social objective in the least trade-distorting manner possible.

The Basic Structure of GATS Rules for Trade in Services

GATS addresses the trade-restrictive impact of regulations through three channels: general provisions on domestic regulation, sectoral annexes on the regulation of particular sectors, and the negotiation of national commitments on regulations that affect trade. The GATS rules are based on the following key principles: regulations that restrict trade should be subject to negotiation;[9] the results of such negotiations should be bound in national schedules;[10] the resulting commitments should apply equally to services and service providers from all other member countries;[11] and regulations should not restrict foreign services or service providers, or discriminate against them, in a manner that is inconsistent with the bound commitments.[12] Moreover, the rules define trade not only as the cross-border delivery of services, but also as the foreign consumption of services, the delivery of services by foreign-owned but locally established enterprises, and the temporary entry of natural persons for the explicit purpose of providing a service locally.[13] The binding of market access in services is less precise than in the case of goods because barriers in services take the form of discriminatory or burdensome regulatory requirements rather than tariffs.

This conceptual framework appears clear enough and thus cannot be the source of the major problems of GATS. Rather, the agreement's deficiencies are the result of the manner in which this underlying framework was implemented through the drafting of the legal provisions in GATS and the negotiation of the associated national schedules. After correctly analyzing the unique requirements of an effective GATS regime for services, the negotiators frequently fell back on GATT terminology and legal drafting, even where that did not provide the best fit. The ambitious nature of the undertaking and the continuing rapid pace of technological change in

---

9. Article XIX (Negotiation of Specific Commitments).
10. Article XX (Schedules of Specific Commitments).
11. Article II (Most Favored Nation Treatment).
12. Articles XVI (Market Access) and XVII (National Treatment), respectively.
13. Article I (Scope and Definition).

many services have also led to inevitable shortcomings that will need to be addressed in future negotiations.

The Hierarchy of Commitments in GATS

GATS provides for the negotiation of a hierarchy of commitments: general provisions, which apply to all services; annexes, which set out the rules for particular sectors (for example, telecommunications) or policy instruments (for example, visas for temporary service providers); and national schedules, which lay out an individual country's commitments on market access and national treatment. This architecture reflects the practical realities associated with the negotiation of increased discipline. National schedules reflect the reality that the liberalization of trade barriers cannot be achieved overnight and that not every country can move at the same pace. Sectoral agreements reflect the fact that in some sectors trade liberalization cannot be divorced from the establishment of compatible regulatory regimes, and in some cases from the modification of the current international regulatory regime. Sectoral agreements also may provide the best channel for achieving significant liberalization where the conditions are right, but the ability of any one country to liberalize its own regulations is facilitated either in economic or political terms by simultaneous reforms in other countries. The drafting of general provisions is, of course, the most efficient approach for advancing the liberalization of trade in services where such principles can be applied to all services.

The three-tier structure is analytically sound, though it does not make clear whether particular objectives are best achieved by concentrating negotiating resources at one level as opposed to another. The negotiation of the provisional agreement on accounting, for example, has raised the question of whether more progress could be made by focusing on another professional service, by developing a cross-cutting agreement for all professional services, or by improving the provisions of Article VI dealing with domestic regulation overall. No a priori answer presents itself, and in any case it probably depends on a political judgment of what can be achieved in different contexts, given the current political and economic realities.

The relationship among the commitments at the three levels is also somewhat unclear. For example, to what extent can reservations in national schedules override general provisions or those of sectoral annexes? Some general or sectoral provisions obviously refer to the right of members to enter reservations in the national schedules, but what about the other provisions? If member countries agree to adopt new definitions in the GATS agreement or in an annex, would that alter the definitions employed in the national schedules where the country did not specify that it was using a national terminology? It may well be desirable to spell out the hierarchy of commitments that would apply under different circumstances.

Market Access and National Treatment

GATS recognizes that trade in services can be hampered by either discriminatory regulatory requirements imposed only on foreign services or by restrictive regulations that are imposed on both domestic and foreign services. As mentioned earlier, however, the application of GATT concepts and terminology in GATS confuses the issue because they are used in ways that do not correspond closely with their application in GATT or clarify the intent of the commitments in the services context.

All quantitative limits on services or service providers are dealt with under the rubric of market access, whether such limits are being imposed on foreign services on a discriminatory basis or on both domestic and foreign services on a nondiscriminatory basis. National treatment is defined in the traditional GATT way as the nondiscriminatory application of domestic regulations to foreign services or service providers. This means that quantitative limits placed on foreign services or service providers fall under both the market access and national treatment provisions.[14]

The drafters of the agreement recognized that this overlap could create confusion in the scheduling of commitments because national commitments regarding the discriminatory application of quantitative regulatory controls could be entered in the schedules either as market access or as national treatment commitments. To avoid duplication and confusion,

---

14. For an in-depth discussion, see chapter 15 in this volume, by Low and Mattoo. Unlike them, I take the view that national treatment commitments should be independent of market access commitments, except insofar as a discriminatory restraint listed under the market access column ipso facto also constitutes a limitation on national treatment under the scheduling convention under Article XX. We may, in other words, hold different interpretations of the phrase "conditions and qualifications" in the following text from GATS Article XVII: "In the sectors inscribed in its Schedule, and subject to any conditions and qualifications set out therein, each Member shall accord services and service suppliers." I interpret this language as requiring the explicit enumeration of an exception to national treatment in either the market access or national treatment column. I do not believe that entering unbound in the market access column satisfies this requirement.

GATS Article XX:2 on the scheduling of commitments indicates that "measures inconsistent with both Articles XVI [on market access] and XVII [on national treatment] shall be inscribed in the column relating to Article XVI." Although this fix removes potential confusion with respect to the scheduling of discriminatory quantitative restrictions, it introduces a discrepancy between the text of the provisions on market access and national treatment on the one hand, and the content of the market access and national treatment columns in the national schedules on the other. This difference between the articles and the schedules has led some countries to wrongly assume that national treatment commitments become operative only after they have made a commitment on market access.

The intermingling of commitments on discriminatory and nondiscriminatory barriers has the further effect of mixing two laudatory, but separate goals: trade liberalization and domestic regulatory reform. Removing discriminatory regulation, whether in quantitative or qualitative form, is all about trade liberalization. Removing nondiscriminatory restraints on services is frequently an exercise in domestic regulatory reform. The use of nondiscriminatory quantitative restraints more often than not reflects a country's approach to the regulation of activity in a services sector, and telling a country to eliminate such restraints is tantamount to saying it must reform its approach to the regulation of that sector.

The intermingling of commitments on discriminatory and nondiscriminatory quantitative restraints raises a hurdle for countries that are willing to tackle the liberalization of trade barriers or the reform of domestic regulation in a services sector, but not both simultaneously. Yet the message being sent is that countries have to liberalize trade and reform their domestic regulations on services simultaneously. Although nothing in the agreement requires them to do both simultaneously, the organization of the schedule does not easily allow countries to highlight progress on either trade liberalization or domestic reform.

It is easy to see how the GATT mind-set about traditional notions of market access and national treatment influenced GATS structure and terminology. However, the net effect has been to create a great deal of confusion among businesses, trade officials, and other trade experts who are not thoroughly familiar with the details of the agreement. They naturally equate market access in services with the tariff bindings in GATT, and national treatment in services with its GATT counterpart. They fail to grasp that market access in services is potentially a more far-reaching commitment, since it covers both discriminatory and nondiscriminatory restraints on the production and sale of services; and that the deviations from national treatment in services are not as damning as they would be in a GATT context, since national treatment in many services equates to the complete absence of barriers to trade, and it grants nondiscriminatory treatment not only to services but also to service providers.

To cure the problems with market access and national treatment, the rule in Article XX should be reversed, and measures that impose quantitative limits on a discriminatory basis should be listed under national treatment rather than market access. This would allow countries to highlight progress on trade liberalization by scheduling commitments under the national treatment column, and to highlight progress on domestic regulatory reform by scheduling commitments under the market access column. Ideally, the market access column would be relabeled "nondiscriminatory quantitative restrictions on services," and the sequencing of the two columns would be reversed, with the national treatment column preceding the column on nondiscriminatory quantitative restraints. In an ideal world, the two relevant GATS provisions would also be retitled and reversed. Making all these changes may prove too difficult, but at a minimum the scheduling convention in Article XX needs to be reversed.

Top-Down (Negative List) versus Bottom-Up (Positive List) Approaches

One of the hotly debated issues in the course of the negotiations was whether the national schedules should list only deviations from an ideal state of national treatment and market access, or whether they should list only positive commitments to provide national treatment and market access for a particular service and mode of supply.[15] The first approach was referred to as the top-down or negative list approach, the second as the bottom-up or positive list approach. Those who favored a maximum degree of liberalization generally argued for the top-down approach, while those who were more reluctant to see much liberalization argued for the bottom-up approach.

A top-down approach is more liberalizing because it automatically accords new services or services that no one really cares about national

15. Commitments in the national schedules are broken down by sector and services products within each sector, by mode of supply (cross-border trade, foreign consumption, establishment of foreign services firms, and temporary entry of persons who are service providers), and by market access and national treatment commitments.

treatment and market access. Moreover, a top-down approach provides more information for potential exporters, since importing countries must indicate in their schedule any deviation from national treatment or the use of quantitative restraints on any tradable service. Under a bottom-up approach, new services, services no one cares about, or services on which the importing country does not wish to make a commitment are not covered in a country's national schedule. Foreign exporters therefore have no information on the treatment they might expect on such products.

Aside from differences over the desired degree of liberalization in services, the negotiators ran into a practical problem. Some countries were simply not equipped to identify all national and local laws that might conflict with the national treatment and market access provisions. In some cases they did not have the personnel to do it. In other cases their regulatory systems had not evolved to a state where they could identify potential inconsistencies, and they did not want to constrain their future ability to develop their own regulatory approach, or to put themselves in the uncomfortable position of having to renegotiate their commitments.

In the end, the negotiators chose to adopt a hybrid approach. In sectors where countries are prepared to make commitments, they must make a negative list, noting their reservations to market access and national treatment. However, they assume no commitments with respect to sectors not inscribed in their schedule. One might also call this a sector-by-sector top-down or negative-list approach.

In sectors inscribed in their schedules, countries can list limitations on market access and national treatment by spelling out in some detail the products on which they are not making a market access or national treatment commitment, and the precise manner in which market access or national treatment commitments are circumscribed with respect to such products. Alternatively, a country may list the specific provisions in its laws for which it is taking a reservation with respect to either market access or national treatment. In some cases a country may state that the commitment applies only to certain products or subsectors within a sector, and that it is making no commitments in other products or subsectors.

An examination of the schedules reveals that the issue is not primarily whether a top-down or bottom-up approach should be taken, but rather the degree of precision with which a country describes its limitations on market access and national treatment. There is a huge difference between whether a country declares a whole subsector unbound, takes a reservation for a broad law without listing the specific provisions that violate national treatment or impose quantitative restraints, or spells out in some detail the specific ways in which a particular law violates national treatment or imposes quantitative restraints.

Precision in the drafting of the reservations on national treatment and market access is desirable both because it guards against arbitrary protectionist measures and because it gives potential exporters more information on the provisions they must satisfy. In other words, precision helps achieve transparency, maximum liberalization, and greater certainty. The scheduling guidelines issued by the secretariat specifically indicate that countries should not merely list a law or measure that contains inconsistent provisions, but should spell out the specific provisions that are inconsistent.[16] Many of the existing schedules do not meet this standard. Hence one of the objectives of the coming negotiations should be to improve the quality of the schedules in this regard.

It is not worth revisiting the debate over top-down versus bottom-up approaches. Not only would the outcome likely be the same, but it would also miss the more important issue regarding the care and precision with which a country spells out the limitations it is putting on national treatment and market access, and the precise provisions of its laws that give rise to these limitations. This cannot be accomplished through broad conceptual arguments. It should be addressed through a detailed and labor-intensive peer review of national schedules, and the negotiation of a commitment by countries to bind a substantial portion of their schedules. Ironically, the schedules of new entrants have received a great deal more scrutiny than the schedules of existing members and therefore come closer to providing the kind of information that is desirable.

The Use of Negotiating Targets and the Negotiation of Rules

Each of the approaches to negotiation that have been used has its advantages and disadvantages. The bilateral approach, for instance, provides a broad basis for establishing a negotiating outcome that meets the interests of members, but it is also very labor intensive and all too easily loses sight of the forest as the negotiators argue over each tree. The sectoral approach provides a common target against which progress can be measured and it allows countries to address common regulatory issues that

16. See GATT Secretariat (1993).

might block progress in liberalizing restrictive regulatory measures, but it also limits the possibility of addressing the varied economic interests of members. The telecommunications sector may well be unique in that most countries found it in their economic interest to shift to more open competition domestically as well as internationally.

The question is whether the strength of the sectoral approach in setting a target could be applied on a more horizontal, cross-sectoral basis. In tariff negotiations under the GATT umbrella, tariff-cutting formulas, applied across the board, served this purpose. Since barriers in services do not take the form of tariffs but of a wide variety of regulatory measures, the use of targets is likely to involve the establishment of a more varied set of objective criteria against which progress in the negotiations can be measured. Some of these criteria could take the form of quantitative targets, whereas others may take the form of qualitative targets for the treatment of certain types of common regulatory issues.

One type of quantitative target could be based on the number of sectors in which countries have made binding commitments, and the degree to which such commitments cover both market access and national treatment and the four modes for the delivery of services. Negotiators might agree that developed countries cover, say, 95 percent of all sectors and subsectors, and that developing countries cover, say, 40 percent to 60 percent of their sectors and subsectors, based on their level of development. Similar percentages might be developed for the four modes.[17]

Quantitative targets might also be based on the types of quantitative restrictions included in Article XVI as the kind of measures that countries may not impose without listing such restrictions as exceptions in their national schedules in sectors where they have made any commitments. These limitations apply to the following categories: the number of service suppliers, whether in the form of numerical quotas, monopolies, exclusive service suppliers, or the requirement of an economic needs test; the total value of service transactions or assets in the form of numerical quotas or the requirement of an economic needs test; the total number of service operations or on the total quantity of service output expressed in terms of designated numerical units in the form of quotas or the requirement of an economic needs test; the total number of natural persons that may be employed in a particular service sector or that a service supplier may

17. For a thorough discussion of possible formulas, see chapter 16 in this volume. See also chapter 15.

employ and who are necessary for, and directly related to, the supply of a specific service in the form of numerical quotas or the requirement of an economic needs test; the specific types of legal entity or joint venture through which a service supplier may supply a service; and the participation of foreign capital in terms of maximum percentage limit on foreign share holding or the total value of individual or aggregate foreign investment.

Some targets or formulas may take the form of a suggested approach to a common regulatory issue or problem. Such qualitative targets would serve as negotiating guidelines, against which national measures could be compared. Negotiating guidelines do not become a binding part of the agreement.[18] If enough countries found a qualitative negotiating guideline useful, however, it could be given the status of a rule by being incorporated in a sectoral annex to the GATS agreement. The Reference Paper that forms a part of the General Agreement on Basic Telecommunications is an example of such a rule. The proposed rule could be open to any member for signature, and apply only to members that signed, or it could be made a universal obligation, which would bind all members who did not specifically enter a reservation in their national schedule.

Improving the Rules on Domestic Regulation

Given the importance of the regulatory dimension in the liberalization process, Article VI on domestic regulation plays a key role in the liberalization of trade in services. Article VI is the essential third leg of a three-legged stool, along with Article XVI on market access and Article XVII on national treatment. While Article XVI disciplines the use of quantitative restrictions, and Article XVII disciplines discriminatory treatment of foreign services and service providers, Article VI disciplines more hidden forms of protection buried in domestic regulations and their administration.[19] Article VI:1 requires that "in sectors where specific commitments are undertaken, each Member shall ensure that all measures of general application are administered in a reasonable, objective and impartial manner." Article VI calls for the negotiation of more detailed disciplines that

18. See chapter 16 in this volume.
19. For further discussion of the relationship between GATS Articles XVI and XVII, on the one hand, and GATS Article VI, on the other, see chapter 15 in this volume.

would help ensure that all measures are reasonable, objective, and impartial. It even spells out the objectives of such disciplines, by indicating that such disciplines shall aim to ensure that regulatory requirements are, among other things,

a) based on objective and transparent criteria, such as competence and the ability to supply a service;

b) not more burdensome than necessary to ensure the quality of the service;

c) in the case of licensing procedures, not in themselves a restriction on the supply of the service.

Pending the negotiation of the disciplines called for in VI:4, VI:5 applies the objectives listed in (a) to (c) to any new measures that may nullify or impair commitments made in the schedules.[20]

The negotiation of the disciplines called for in Article VI should clearly receive high priority in the new round of negotiations in services, and the negotiators would do well to start by converting the objectives listed under (a) to (c) into disciplines that would apply to all domestic regulatory measures with an impact on trade in services. Beyond these disciplines, they might consider adding some key principles to Article VI concerning the transparency of regulatory objectives, the appropriate use of market mechanisms, the scope of regulations, and the use of international regulatory standards.[21]

TRANSPARENCY OF REGULATORY OBJECTIVES.   The social objective served by a particular law or regulation should be transparent. That is, it should be clearly stated at the time the regulation is adopted. A clear statement of the desired social objective helps to remove possible confusion over the purpose of the regulation and makes it a great deal easier to judge whether a regulation is more burdensome than necessary to accomplish the desired

20. For a thorough treatment of the shortcomings of the GATS disciplines on domestic regulation, see chapter 10 in this volume.

21. Robert Howse, in his commentary on chapters 9–11 in this volume, articulates the strengths and weaknesses of what he terms the "neoliberal orthodoxy about regulation and its reform." His points about the difficult regulatory issues that are not resolved by the principles articulated here are well taken. The approach embodied here nevertheless rests on fifty years of experience under GATT in resolving day-to-day trade problems through bilateral consultations and multilateral dispute settlement based on generic principles. It seeks to draw a fine balance between international rule-making and the need for a degree of national regulatory sovereignty.

social objective. This principle is contained in the WTO agreement on accountancy services, which has been adopted on an ad ref basis.

APPROPRIATE USE OF MARKET MECHANISMS. Governments should use market mechanisms to promote desired social objectives, whenever that is feasible. The use of across-the-board economic incentives and disincentives is an economically efficient method of accomplishing desired social goals because it allows market forces to determine the most economically efficient manner of accomplishing the desired social goal. A corollary of this principle is that scarce resources should be auctioned whenever possible rather than allocated to incumbent firms on the basis of historic shares. An auction process is more likely to enable the most efficient firms to gain access to such resources and is more likely to ensure that the opportunity cost of using the scarce resource is properly reflected in the cost of supplying the service and the prices charged to consumers. Where regulations give existing producers or sellers preferential treatment in the allocation of scarce resources, they not only create domestic economic inefficiencies by discriminating against potentially more economically efficient new suppliers; they also distort international trade and competition. Moreover, there is a significant risk that the economic inefficiencies and trade distortions are magnified by political/interest group pressures and corruption.

MINIMIZING THE SCOPE OF REGULATIONS. Governments should seek to minimize the regulatory burden by limiting the scope of any regulation to what is necessary to accomplish the desired social objective. This principle could complement and reinforce the principle that government regulatory measures should not be more burdensome than necessary to ensure the quality of the service. This corollary principle would require governments to limit the scope of regulations to what is necessary for the achievement of the regulatory objective. This approach would in turn minimize the economic cost of such regulations. It is particularly relevant to the regulation of infrastructure services such as water, gas, electricity, telecommunications, and rail transportation. The tendency in the past has been for governments to regulate all aspects of economic activity in these sectors because the network for distributing these services often constitutes a natural monopoly. In more recent years many governments have recognized that they can more efficiently accomplish their objective of protecting consumers by separating the construction and operation of the distribution network from the provision of services over that network. In so doing, the government can regulate access to and use of the network monopoly, while leaving the supply of the services involved open to market competition. Efforts to minimize the scope of regulations to the minimum necessary to achieve the desired social objective help to minimize the economic cost of such regulations and the potential distortion of international trade and competition.

USE OF INTERNATIONAL REGULATORY STANDARDS.   Governments should use international standards where such standards would satisfy the desired social objectives. This principle is already included in Article VII:5, which deals with the negotiation of agreements recognizing the authorization, licensing, or certification of services suppliers by other governments. It requires that "wherever appropriate, recognition should be based on multilaterally agreed criteria." This principle is also a core principle embedded in the GATT Agreement on Technical Barriers to Trade, otherwise referred to as the Standards Code.

Domestic Regulation and Electronic Commerce

National schedules treat the four modes of trade in services as separate commitments. Countries thus have to specify the market access and national treatment commitments that apply to each mode of delivering services in a particular sector. (Where a country is prepared to commit itself to a particular mode across all sectors or where a reservation applies across all sectors, the schedule may contain a horizontal entry that applies to all sectors.) By addressing the four modes, the services framework covers much wider ground than GATT does, which only covers cross-border movement of goods.

The burgeoning of the Internet and electronic commerce has created the need for a more precise definition of the four modes. It used to be that foreign consumption of a service occurred when a traveler to another country purchased and consumed a service abroad. Cross-border trade occurred when the purchaser of a service was in one country and the seller in another country, and the service was transmitted from one country to the other country through a phone call or the mail. The sale of a service through a local establishment took place when a foreign-owned enterprise established a facility or a legal entity to produce or sell services in the local market. And the sale of services through the temporary entry of a natural person took place when a provider physically traveled to the importing country to produce the service.

Today these distinctions have become blurred, and it is not clear which set of market access and national treatment commitments apply under different circumstances, or whose regulatory jurisdiction applies under those circumstances. Take the issue of foreign consumption. If a consumer buys a service from a provider in another country over the Internet, under what circumstances should that transaction be treated as foreign consumption, or as cross-border trade, or as a purchase from a locally established enterprise?

Some have argued that direct marketing to consumers in a particular country should be considered local establishment, and the production of the service should be subjected to the local regulatory jurisdiction of the country of the consumer. Alternatively, if the purchaser acquires a service from a foreign producer who does not engage in targeted marketing, the sale might be considered cross-border trade, and the sale of the service subjected to the regulatory jurisdiction of the consuming country. But what if the consumer in question intends to consume the service abroad? Should the buyer's current physical location or the time of consumption be the key determinant?

To make things even more complicated, how does the physical location of the Internet service provider affect all of these distinctions? Suppose that a consumer in country *A* acquires access to the Internet from an Internet service provider in country *B*, using a local address in country *B*. For all practical purposes, it will appear to the service provider in country *B* that the purchaser is a local resident. To what extent can the government of country *A* hold the seller responsible for meeting its regulatory requirements?

One solution to such questions would be to follow strictly the treatment of analog transactions involving more traditional methods of acquiring services or goods abroad. The problem is that it is not always clear where a service was produced and where the service provider is located. This is particularly the case with the sale of information or some other form of intellectual property by multinational firms established in many countries.

An alternative approach would be to let the market sort out regulatory issues by allowing sellers and buyers to choose the regulatory jurisdiction that would apply to a particular transaction. Such an approach might be complemented by the development of private codes, which might receive some kind of recognition by individual governments and be enforced by all governments.

The Application of the MFN Principle

Another hotly debated issue in the negotiation of GATS was the application of the MFN principle. For many countries, the MFN principle is the cornerstone of the multilateral system. From an economic perspective, it avoids a distortion of the relative prices applicable to goods and services imported from or exported to different foreign countries. From a political economic perspective, it puts all members of a multilateral system on a more equal footing. Small countries in particular feel that the MFN principle gives them more equal standing with large countries and protects them from excessive bilateral pressure. The MFN principle also helps prevent the adverse political fallout of competitive bilateral negotiations, which historically contributed to a breakdown of global trade and exacerbated political tensions among countries between the two world wars.

On the other hand, some negotiators argued that differences in regulatory philosophy could lead to incompatible market structures. Also, differences in the quality of the regulations that are applied to service suppliers in different countries can affect the degree to which imported services meet the domestic regulatory objectives of the importing country in such areas as consumer protection and prudential supervision. Moreover, the opening of international competition in certain services such as international air passenger service, governed by bilateral agreements, would make sense only if the countries participating in the competition agreed to a new competition-based framework.

The debate concluded with another compromise. The MFN principle was incorporated as a generic principle of GATS. However, countries were permitted to enter reservations on the application of the MFN provision in particular sectors. A number of countries availed themselves of this opportunity in heavily regulated sectors. After the subsequent negotiation of sectoral agreements on telecommunication and financial services, however, most countries withdrew their MFN reservations in these sectors.

Another part of the compromise was the introduction of two provisions that allow for the negotiation of bilateral or plurilateral agreements on the mutual recognition of regulatory standards. Countries are allowed to negotiate such agreements without automatically extending the benefits to third countries, provided third countries are given the opportunity to negotiate accession to such agreements on equivalent terms. The first such provision is included in Article VII of GATS, which deals with the recognition of experience or education obtained, requirements met, or licenses or certifications granted in connection with the authorization, licensing, or certification of services suppliers. The second such provision is included in the Annex on Financial Services, which allows countries to recognize prudential measures of any other country for the purpose of determining whether a financial institution from that country meets requisite prudential standards.

Like GATT, GATS provides for an MFN exception for free-trade agreements, which it refers to as economic integration agreements. However, the conditions set out in Article V of GATS for economic integration agreements are poorly drafted. This is another case where one suspects that the drafters borrowed heavily from the equivalent GATT provision without considering how the provision would be applied in services. It is difficult to see how the conditions set out in the article can be effectively monitored with the kind of data that are normally available on trade in services. Moreover, the kind of barriers that an economic integration agreement should be expected to eliminate is unclear, as is the degree of integration that should be expected in areas such as labor mobility and the recognition of professional qualifications.

Here, too, there is little point in holding another conceptual debate. What negotiators should do about national MFN exceptions is establish the conditions under which countries are prepared to eliminate their MFN reservations in individual sectors, and organize negotiations designed to satisfy those conditions.

With respect to mutual recognition agreements, the negotiations should focus on the development of model instruments for accomplishing the regulatory objectives of member governments. To date, few bilateral mutual recognition agreements have been negotiated under the terms of either GATS Article VII or the Annex on Financial Services to date, and there is no precedent for the accession of third parties. The negotiation of mutual recognition agreements in services between the United States and the European Union under the umbrella of the Transatlantic Dialogue represents one such effort. The Basle Accord among the countries that participate in the Bank for International Settlements could be seen as a prototype agreement on prudential supervision. How to approach the accession of third parties under the terms of either Article VII or the Annex on Financial Services is not clear. It would be desirable to encourage a great deal of experimentation in this area. Countries should explore a range of alternative approaches, including the development of voluntary codes and regulatory models.

Finally, the drafting of Article V should be improved. Negotiators should clarify the conditions that economic integration agreements should be expected to meet. Negotiators should also examine the kind of data that have been submitted by countries participating in such agreements, as well as the kind of data that might be readily available. On the basis of such analysis, they should develop more meaningful guidelines for the examination of such agreements.

A Plan for the Progressive Future Integration of GATT and GATS

Because services are different from goods, GATS evolved as a separate instrument for liberalizing trade in services and disciplining government regulations affecting such trade. Earlier in this chapter it was suggested that the negotiators did not go far enough in recognizing the differences between goods and services, and this led to confusion in the drafting of some GATS provisions. Thus it may come as a surprise that the chapter concludes with a discussion of the progressive integration of GATT and GATS in future negotiations. Yet it makes sense to start thinking about a common framework for disciplines that may apply in the future to both trade in goods and trade in services. This is not to suggest that the development of common disciplines should take up significant negotiating resources in the next round of negotiations. However, the fact that the current negotiations on transparency in government procurement apply to both goods and services is an indication that it is not too early to think about the accommodation of cross-cutting agreements within the WTO structure.

There are a number of reasons for believing that the current distinction between goods and services will be less important in the future. Since much of GATT is built around the negotiation of tariffs and the maintenance of the benefits that accrue from tariff bindings, many of its provision that apply uniquely to goods will no longer matter as tariffs on goods are eliminated. Moreover, much of the substance of trade negotiations in goods will shift to regulatory matters and industrial structure policy, issues at the core of GATS.

Although foreign investment and labor mobility are particularly important issues for trade in services, they are also increasingly relevant for trade in manufactured goods. It is somewhat of an anomaly that a firm that produces services can secure WTO commitments on the right to invest and establish, or on the entry of foreign professional personnel, but it cannot do so if it produces goods. What about firms that produce both goods and services on an integrated basis? Can they really separate management staff that supervise or advise manufacturing units from those who supervise or advise units producing services?

Note, too, that many goods come with a package of services that for many purposes are treated as goods when they are bundled together with the goods, and they are treated as services when they become separated. Where the unbundled goods and services are subject to different regulatory requirements, the difference in treatment can distort the most efficient way of packaging the components.

For all these reasons, it does not make much sense to negotiate commitments on establishment and labor mobility for service providers but not for goods providers. It is not clear at this stage how ministers in Seattle will wish to address issues related to investment. At a minimum, they should decide to pursue investment commitments on a sector-by-sector basis, much along the lines currently possible under GATS.

Should WTO ministers agree to launch comprehensive negotiations on investment, they would need to decide whether such negotiations should cover both goods and services within a single framework, or whether such negotiations should be divided between goods and services. While any common agreement on investment would have to be reconciled with existing commitments in GATS under mode 3 dealing with establishment, it is difficult to imagine the negotiation of a comprehensive agreement on investment that did not apply to both goods and services.

Moreover, as the WTO regime for trade in goods is extended to investment, many of the GATS provisions will become highly relevant for trade in goods. For example, GATT deals with standards but not with regulations that affect the production process. Once investment in manufacturing is covered, the provisions of GATS Article VI on domestic regulation and the provisions of Article VII on recognition of certificates and licenses could apply equally to manufacturing enterprises. Conversely, many of the provisions of the GATT Standards Code could be applied to trade in services.

Similar considerations apply with respect to trade and competition policy. GATS has pioneered the integration of competition provisions into trade disciplines in the telecommunications area. If and when the WTO embarks on a broader consideration of competition issues, it will presumably want to do so on an integrated basis, and will ultimately incorporate the existing GATS provisions into the new joint framework.

The globalization of production, which results in the unbundling and distribution of various steps in the production process to different countries, gives manufacturing many of the same characteristics as the production of services. Unbundled manufacturing contains many steps that may have been classified as manufacturing activities in the past but now fall into the category of business services. It can also be argued that partial processing of manufactured goods is more effectively treated as the production of a value added service rather than as the manufacturing of a good. The traditional concepts behind trade in goods and the entire GATT structure rest on the proposition that goods have an identifiable country of origin. It might be better to view partly manufactured goods that are shuttled from country to country as goods involving trade in services, rather than as goods that originated in the last port of call.

Hence there are strong arguments for integrating GATT and GATS rules on a step-by-step basis. One could imagine the development, over time, of new instruments that would establish common provisions for trade in both goods and services. Specific provisions of GATT and GATS could be replaced by the new common provisions, as negotiators succeeded in reconciling differences between the two agreements that do not arise from fundamental differences between goods and services. Ultimately, provisions that are specific to either goods or services could be treated as special provisions contained in separate subsidiary chapters of the new common framework of disciplines.

These are long-term ideas that are unlikely to affect the near-term negotiations in either goods or services. However, the advent of negotiations on common issues such as transparency in government procurement argues for the establishment of an institutional structure to accommodate agreements that apply to both goods and services.

Conclusion

The negotiation of the General Agreement on Trade in Services during the Uruguay Round was a major achievement. The negotiators of the agreement made creative adjustments in the tool kit of GATT concepts and terms to fashion a set of disciplines suited for trade in services. In the end, they proved too conservative in applying the GATT tool kit by not realizing the full implication of the changes they were required to make to fit the needs of the services world. As a result, GATS suffers from ambiguities in key provisions, which undermine the value of negotiated commitments and the effectiveness of the agreement. This chapter has presented some modest fixes that would help strengthen the agreement and the associated schedules of national commitments.

References

Feketekuty, Geza. 1988. *International Trade in Services: An Overview and Blueprint for Negotiations.* Cambridge, Mass.: Ballinger.

General Agreement on Tariffs and Trade (GATT) Secretariat. 1993. "Scheduling of Initial Commitments in Trade in Services: Explanatory Note." MTN.GNS/W/164. Geneva (September 3).

Wilcox, Clair. 1949. *A Charter for World Trade.* New York: Macmillan.

World Trade Organization (WTO). 1995. *The Results of the Uruguay Round of Trade Negotiations: The Legal Texts.* Geneva.

———. 1998. "Preparation for the 1999 Ministerial Conference: Communication from Australia." WT/GC/W/116. Geneva (November 28).

———. 1999."Preparation for the 1999 Ministerial Conference: EC Approach to Services." WT/GC/W/189. Geneva (June 2).

5 | Services Trade Liberalization from Developed and Developing Country Perspectives

RUDOLF ADLUNG

T HE CREATION OF the General Agreement on Trade in Services (GATS), as part of the Uruguay Round, has been hailed as one of the landmark achievements in the history of the multilateral system. The reasons are well known and do not need to be repeated in detail. For the purposes of this discussion, however, one particular feature is worth mentioning: the forward-looking character of the agreement. Article XIX (Negotiation of Specific Commitments) commits World Trade Organization (WTO) members to entering into successive rounds of services negotiations "not later than five years from the date of entry into force of the Agreement" and periodically thereafter, with a view to achieving "a progressively higher level of liberalization." With the approach of the new negotiations, a range of questions arise: What have been the driving forces, generators, or facilitators behind the Uruguay Round results in services? What are the challenges ahead? How well are WTO members equipped for the new round, or where could momentum come from?

Behind these questions lurks the problem of economic adjustment, in various guises. First, adjustment-related issues were among the main motivators of services liberalization, which, to varying degrees, has been bound under GATS. The failure of traditional regulatory regimes in major sectors, not least telecommunications, to accommodate new economic, institutional, and technical developments paved the way for domestic reform and, by the same token, external commitments. Second, the costs and benefits of future adjustment—economic, social, and political—associated with liberalization will determine in large part the extent to which WTO members participate in, and contribute to, the new services round.

The Momentum for Liberalization under Multilateral Rules

GATS was the result of a lengthy and onerous process. In the early preparatory stages, the United States was the only vocal proponent of a new round of trade negotiations and, as one of the core elements, the inclusion of services. Hugo Paemen, one of the chief negotiators for the European Communities (EC) in the later stages, recalls that "had it not been for the tenacity of the United States, the negotiations would never have taken place."[1] The U.S. demands were strenuously resisted by a group of developing countries, including India and Brazil, while the European Communities—not least because of their internal diversity—were unable or unwilling to lend strong support in the preparatory process.[2]

U.S. negotiating interests in services might be attributed to traditional mercantilist motives, reflecting the competitive strength of major U.S. services industries. The resistance of "hardliners," by contrast, could be ascribed among other things to infant industry considerations, concerns about national (economic) sovereignty, and fears that the new issues would deflect attention from their own trade interests in areas such as textiles and clothing. However, the alternatives to a new round reaching beyond the scope of GATT were, in one way or another, rather bleak. The "old" GATT would have barely survived. New exclusive trading systems would have emerged and nonparticipants might have found themselves exposed to bilateral pressure without external surveillance and constraints.

This picture is too simple, however, to fully match reality. It fails to explain why the European Communities started playing an increasingly dynamic role in services negotiations, initiating, for example, an interim

1. Paemen and Bensch (1995, p. 91).
2. See Paemen and Bensch (1995, p. 51): "Caught between what were in many respects the extreme positions of the United States on the one hand and the developing countries on the other, especially with regard to the 'new subjects,' the European Community quite understandably elected to sit on the fence."

agreement on financial services in mid-1995 to prevent the extended negotiations from collapse. And it is irreconcilable with the fact that a growing group of developing countries actively pursued their own negotiating interests. In terms of sectoral coverage, for example, the commitments undertaken in the round by some developing or even least-developed countries (see table 5-1) were as extensive as those of some members of the Organization for Economic Cooperation and Development (OECD). Moreover, five developing countries (Barbados, Cyprus, Kenya, Suriname, and Uganda) used the ratification process following the extended negotiations on basic telecommunications, in 1997, to voluntarily submit schedules without external prodding. While it is true that the large majority of commitments remained limited to locking in the status quo, or even something less, the mere thought that developing countries could join the bandwagon—and that elements of a common vision might emerge—would have been flatly dismissed only a decade ago. What could explain this policy shift?

Technical Change and High Investment Needs

In modern services sectors, typically telecommunications and numerous downstream activities, liberalization benefited from the inability of traditional monopolies to control alternative technologies. Observers have noted, for example, that telecom liberalization owes far less to legislation than legislation owes to rapid technical change undermining the status of entrenched monopolies.[3] Although telecom might be considered a special case in this respect, it ranks among the largest and most dynamic services industries, contributing about as much to U.S. gross domestic product (GDP) as the whole of agriculture, and is very closely knitted into a system of supplier and user industries.

Many administrations, subject to public sector rules and disciplines, found it increasingly difficult to meet the capital and management needs of modern services sectors. Again, telecommunications is a case in point. The 1995 WTO Trade Policy Review of the European Communities observed, for example, that the technical and financial constraints arising in the wake of unification had boosted telecom deregulation in Ger-

---

3. Sapir (1999, p. 59). While a few WTO members have reserved the right, in their schedules, to restrict calling-card and call-back services, enforcement would be problematic for technical reasons, quite apart from the economic costs associated with inefficient and expensive communication links.

Table 5-1. *Structure of Commitments by WTO Members*

Sectors committed[a]	Members
20 or less (N = 44)	Angola, Bahrain, Barbados, Benin, Botswana, Burkina Faso, Cameroon, Central African Republic, Chad, Congo, Republic of Congo, Costa Rica, Cyprus, Fiji, Gabon, Guinea, Guinea-Bissau, Guyana, Haiti, Honduras, Madagascar, Malawi, Maldives, Mali, Malta, Mauritiania, Mauritius, Mozambique, Myanmar, Namibia, Niger, Paraguay, Rwanda, St. Kitts and Nevis, St. Lucia, St. Vincent and Grenadines, Solomon Islands, Sri Lanka, Suriname, Swaziland, Tanzania, Togo, Uganda, Zambia
21–40 (N = 23)	Bangladesh, Bolivia, Brunei Darussalam, Burundi, Côte d'Ivoire, Djibouti, Dominica, El Salvador, Ghana, Grenada, Guatemala, Kenya, Macau, Mongolia, Nigeria, Papua New Guinea, Peru, Qatar, Senegal, Sierra Leone, Tunisia, Uruguay, Zimbabwe
41–60 (N = 10)	Antigua and Barbuda, Belize, Cuba, India, Morocco, Netherlands Antilles, Nicaragua, Pakistan, Trinidad and Tobago, United Arab Emirates
61–80 (N = 20)	Brazil, Ecuador, Egypt, Hong Kong (China), Israel, Jamaica, Kuwait, Liechtenstein, Poland, Romania, Singapore, Venezuela
81–100 (N = 12)	Argentina, Chile, Czech Republic, Dominican Republic, Indonesia, Lesotho, New Zealand, Panama, Slovak Republic, Slovenia, South Africa, Turkey
101–20 (N = 8)	Australia, Bulgaria, Canada, The Gambia, Latvia, Philippines, Switzerland, Thailand
More than 121 (N = 25)	Colombia, European Communities (15), Hungary, Iceland, Japan, Republic of Korea, Kyrgyz Republic, Malaysia, Mexico, Norway, United States

Source: WTO (1999a, p. 11).
a. N = number of members.

many.[4] In turn, Germany's increasingly liberal stance was an important element in winning over the majority of EC members to full liberalization of basic telephony from January 1998.

Modern broadcasting and telecommunication services have extended the scope for cross-border supply in areas such as audiovisual services (for

4. WTO (1995a, p. 130). The German experience is not without irony, however, as the old monopoly proved particularly unsuited when, following unification, the perceived advantages of public sector involvement—reliability, security of supply, and the like—were in high demand.

example, video on demand), health services (telediagnosis and teleanalysis), and education services (distance learning), thus gradually eroding geographic and regulatory barriers to trade in these areas as well.[5] For instance, the proliferation of new transmission channels has undermined the use of licensing to regulate broadcast content. Again, governments may have little choice but to acknowledge that traditional regulatory approaches have reached their limits.[6]

Defenders of old monopoly regimes, not least in telecommunications, tend to stress the positive effects on government income. The share of telecom revenue in GDP, generally between 2 and 3 percent in OECD countries, may exceed 5 or even 10 percent in certain developing and transition economies. Nevertheless, any contribution to public coffers needs to be set against the investment required in the sector, and the possibility of subjecting private concessionaires to taxation and other charges. Liberalization of telecom, transport, financial, and similar services does not imply giving business rights away for free.[7] Recall that regulated utilities tend to be rather inefficient sources of government income, not only in direct monetary terms, but even more important, in terms of the efficiency losses and distortions incurred by other industries.[8] High telecom rates, bank charges, or transport tariffs are tantamount, from an economic perspective, to taxing international market integration and deterring innovation in user industries.

Internal Policy Balance and the Influence of Vocal User Interests

To the chagrin of its proponents, the economic benefits associated with liberalization do not necessarily translate into political advantage. Affected producers may be screaming while more often than not the beneficiaries are not even aware of the stakes involved. Since suppliers are normally better organized than consumers and their losses easier to anticipate than user benefits, it may be simpler—and more politically rewarding

5. WTO (1999a).

6. For more details, see OECD (1997b, p. 11).

7. Of course, revenue from privatization may differ enormously between countries: while Deutsche Telekom raised US$13,360 million in 1996, Mongolia's national operator fetched no more than US$11 million in 1995. See Besançon and Kelly (1996, pp. 6 and 8).

8. The 1995 WTO Trade Policy Review of Uganda noted that although the country's telephone tariffs were high and heavily biased against long-distance and international calls, no more than 50 percent of the telecom bill was actually collected, owing to fraud and other factors (WTO, 1995b, p. 77). Since then, however, Uganda has embarked on significant reforms.

in the short term—to mobilize resistance to, than support for, change. However, while such imbalances help to explain liberalization problems in agriculture, textiles, or clothing, they do not reflect so clearly the situation in services. In sectors such as communication or banking, industry interests tend to enter on both sides of the policy equation as suppliers and downstream users. In the absence of telecom reform, the threat of the industrial relocation, for example, of communication-intensive services sectors such as securities brokers and investment banks, may be an effective tool in overcoming the opposition to change of traditional suppliers, and their employees.

However, conditions tend to vary significantly across services industries. In particular, supplier-user links may not be as strong as just outlined, the relevant groups may not have the same degree of policy access within the same jurisdictions, and locational change is not always a threat. Thus complaints by the tourism industry about protectionist aviation policies have gone largely unheeded.[9]

Factor Mobility in a Dynamic Environment

Although user interests tend to be more powerful in modern services than in traditional goods industries, liberalization may meet less sector-internal resistance. This is likely to happen for two reasons. First, mobility barriers tend to be lower for services employees than, for example, for farmers, miners, or steelworkers, whose professional mobility is often associated with regional relocation or the depreciation of acquired skills and expertise. An accountant, broker, or telecom technician may have fewer problems finding reemployment or moving across sectoral lines than a coal miner, steelworker, or farmer. Second, whereas structural change in agriculture, mining, and industry often occurs within a depressed sectoral environment, deregulation and liberalization policies in telecom, financial, or certain professional services coincide with, and may benefit from, economic expansion. Redundancies of traditional producers are offset by the emergence of new or more commercially attractive suppliers in the same sector.

Thus although the breakup of the Bell system in 1984 was followed

---

9. A study by the World Tourism Organization found that some countries were pouring more money into their domestic carriers than their entire travel and tourism industry was able to generate. See WTO (1998b, p. 8).

by a decline in employment in the U.S. telecommunications sector from 956,000 to 881,400 in three years, employment rebounded and reached 929,500 by the end of 1995. Net losses were registered only by the regional Bell operating companies; other parts of the industry expanded rapidly. For instance, jobs in wireless communication grew at an annual rate of 22.6 percent from 1988 to 1996. Reports for Japan suggest that the heavy job losses suffered by the monopoly operator, NTT, after deregulation in 1985 have at least been compensated by new entrants.[10] A cross-country study for twenty-six Asian and Latin American economies showed that between 1990 and 1994 employment in monopoly markets grew by about 3 percent as compared with 20 percent in the more open markets.[11]

The Virtues of Self-Bindings

The interest of governments in external policy bindings, as achieved in successive GATT rounds, has been compared to Ulysses' decision to have himself tied to the mast in order to resist the sirens.[12] Rather than alluding to popular mercantilist motives, the metaphor stresses the domestic policy rationale arguing for multilaterally agreed liberalization. It does not, however, appropriately capture the ensuing benefits. The economic gains expected from liberal policy bindings—in particular their impact on a country's generation of, and attractiveness for, scarce resources (physical, financial, and human capital)—might be equated with Ulysses' action amplifying the wind currents driving him back home to Ithaca.

An additional consideration may come into play, given the increasing role in world trade of regional arrangements: external disciplines are likely to facilitate policy coordination and cooperation between participants. The EC scheduling of elements of its internal market in financial and in telecommunication services can be viewed, in traditional GATT terminology, as a "concession" extended to fellow WTO members. However, the commitments undertaken—including full liberalization, from January 1998, of voice telephony in eleven of the fifteen member states—could also be considered an instrument of central policy surveillance and enforcement over member states or regions. In the event of noncompliance, it would be more convenient for the Commission and adversely affected

---

10. OECD (1997a, pp. 95 and 107).
11. Petrazzini (1996).
12. See, for example, Roessler (1985, p. 287).

EC countries not to take action under EC law, but to rely on other WTO members raising the issue in Geneva. Such surveillance and enforcement functions appear particularly relevant in services areas, given the wide policy coverage of GATS, which extends, for example, to investment issues.

Some developing countries have also used their GATS commitments as a policy lever to renegotiate the status of contractual monopolies and, by implication, invite potential competitors to prepare for entry. Cases in point are two recent accession countries, Seychelles and Latvia. For example, Latvia's (pre-)commitment on basic telecommunications provides for earlier liberalization, by a full ten years, than foreseen under a previous exclusivity arrangement with a private concessionaire.[13]

Structure of GATS: Flexibility Ensured

The wide coverage of GATS, particularly its inclusion of four modes of supply, offers an opportunity for comprehensive policy binding.[14] The agreement does not entail, however, any legal obligation as to the breadth and depth of the commitments made by individual members. Nor does it constrain, in principle, the ability of governments to employ regulatory measures, including licensing or qualification requirements or internal standards, for quality and similar reasons. WTO members are not required to sacrifice the levels of prudential regulation and consumer protection. Thus, although "liberalization"—that is, the abolition of quotas and similar entry barriers—can be viewed as an essential objective of the agreement, it is less ambitious in the realm of "deregulation"; Article XVII (National Treatment) is intended to constrain regulatory discrimination in favor of national services and suppliers, while Article VI (Domestic Regulation) seeks to prevent internal regulation from creating "unnecessary" barriers to trade.

GATS obliges each WTO member to submit a schedule specifying market access and national treatment obligations, but it does not prescribe the sectoral scope or the depth of the commitments made. Any commitment may be made subject to limitations, even allowing for the complete

13. In some cases, however, the use of the "GATS lever" seems to have caused friction between the authorities and the previous incumbents. See, for example, "Sonera Wants Compensation for Losing Latvian Monopoly," *Total Telecom*, November 4, 1998.

14. The four modes are cross-border supply, consumption abroad, commercial presence, and presence of natural persons.

exclusion of individual modes, and its entry into force may be delayed.[15] The substance of Uruguay Round schedules may thus differ greatly from one member to another, reflecting (foreign) negotiating interests and (domestic) policy positions. Small participants with nonlucrative home markets have found it relatively easy, in the absence of contravening domestic considerations, to avoid economically meaningful bindings.[16] Flexibility has been further enhanced by the possibility to exempt measures, in principle for limited periods, from most favored nation (MFN) treatment. MFN exemptions have been sought by about seventy members for some 380 measures; coverage and content have not always been clearly defined.[17]

The flexibility of the agreement was an important factor, possibly a precondition, to ensure its acceptance by all WTO members. Individual governments were able, within a given negotiating context, to accommodate domestic economic, political, and institutional constraints. However, flexibility proved to be a double-edged sword. Though it helped to launch GATS, it did not facilitate broadly based liberalization across members, sectors, and modes.

Starting Point for a New Round

Observers tend to agree that in the services area the Uruguay Round was more important in terms of rule-making than actual liberalization. The impact of GATS on services trade, it has been claimed, is marred by insignificant access commitments.[18] Recent cases of liberalization, not least in financial services, have been associated predominantly with IMF-supported programs or with developments in other fora, such as the Republic of Korea's accession to OECD, rather than genuine commitments under GATS.[19]

It is worth bearing in mind, however, that even standstill bindings are economically beneficial—in enhancing transparency and predictability—

15. Such precommitments are particularly frequent in public voice telephony, where 40 percent, or twenty-six of the sixty-two countries concerned, opted for this possibility.

16. For example, some countries have bound access in no sector other than luxury hotels, and even these commitments have been made subject to an economic needs test.

17. MFN exemptions could be listed only before the entry into force of the agreement. Exemptions related to the presence of natural persons (mode 4) are discussed in WTO (1998c).

18. See, for example, Snape (1998, pp. 287–89); Hoekman (1996, p. 101); Sauvé (1995, pp. 140–44).

19. Dobson and Jacquet (1998, pp. 31–67).

and that the substance of current schedules may turn out to be greater than initially envisaged. Some WTO members seem to think that Article XVII, for instance, guarantees national treatment only with regard to measures operated under a relevant mode (for example, investment grants or production subsidies under mode 3, commercial presence); others suggest that the article also protects from discriminatory effects potentially impinging on trade under other modes (in the absence of limitations, a member would thus need to ensure as well that its domestic subsidies do not adversely affect the cross-border supply or consumption abroad of like services). The crucial question, still awaiting authoritative interpretation, is whether the concept of like services extends, and ensures nondiscrimination, across different modes of supply within a given sector.[20] Although the new round offers an opportunity to address such issues, its success will not be measured predominantly by legal clarifications or additional status quo bindings, but by effective improvements over current regimes. What are the main areas for action?

The Uruguay Round *acquis* in the services area may be looked at from three perspectives: the level of commitments by members, the inclusion of individual sectors, and the coverage of modes. An overview of current schedules reveals significant imbalances in all three respects.[21]

—One-third of WTO members have committed on 20 services sectors and less of the 160 specified for scheduling, one-third have committed on between 21 and 80 sectors, and the remainder on up to 145 sectors (table 5-1).

—Across all schedules, tourism has proved by far the most attractive area for inclusion. Commitments have been made, with varying coverage, by 125 members; this is about three times the frequency of scheduling of health or education services (see figure 5-1).

---

20. See chapter 15 in this volume. A similarly sensitive interpretation problem—the coverage of the MFN obligation under Article II—was at the center of the banana dispute. Both the panel and the appellate body endorsed a broader view of the MFN principle, covering cases of both de jure and de facto discrimination, than hitherto used by the defendant (European Communities) and, possibly, other WTO members as well. For a description of services-related disputes in the WTO, see Zdouc (1999, pp. 295–346).

21. The results of the extended negotiations on financial services (Fifth Protocol to GATS) are not included. The information in table 5-1 is at the level of the 160-odd sectors that have been specified for scheduling purposes under GATS. Figure 5-1 is based on their aggregation to eleven large areas. Figure 5-2 is based on samples of two to four subsectors from each of these eleven areas; for details, see WTO (1999b). Note that the coverage of sectors as well as the restrictiveness of the limitations made may differ widely between individual schedules.

Figure 5-1 *Structure of Commitments by Sector*
Number of members

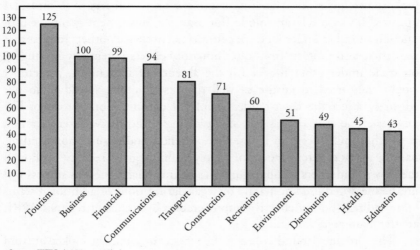

Source: WTO (1999a, p. 12).

—Among the individual modes of supply, consumption abroad (mode 2) has attracted the highest share of full commitments. About half of all entries examined in the context of this chapter were free of market access or national treatment limitations (see figure 5-2). The relevant shares for mode 1 (cross-border supply) are 30 and 35 percent for market access and national treatment, respectively, compared with 15 and 30 percent for mode 3 (commercial presence). Full bindings under mode 4 (presence of natural persons) are rare, reflecting the political and economic sensitivities associated with the physical presence of foreign service suppliers; they have been scheduled only by a few least-developed countries (e.g., Haiti in ten sectors and Angola in one sector).[22]

This picture, particularly its first two elements, is influenced in large part by variations in the participation of developing and transition econo-

22. Most members have turned the "negative approach" generally used for scheduling modal limitations—that is, the attachment of mode-specific market access or national treatment limitations to individual sectoral entries—into a "positive" or "bottom-up approach" for mode 4. The most frequent entries under that mode are in the form of a blanket "unbound" to which narrowly defined exceptions are added. In general, these exceptions focus on senior executives, experts, and other senior or skill-intensive staff transferred from abroad within the same company. Only a few commitments apply to untrained or self-employed persons as well. For more details, see WTO (1998c).

Figure 5-2. Structure of Commitments by Mode
Percent of full bindings[a]

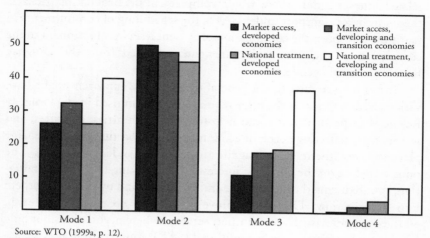

Source: WTO (1999a, p. 12).
a. Calculated on the basis of a sample of thirty-seven sectors deemed representative for various services areas.

mies. The situation is more uniform for developed economies; virtually all of them rank among the top third group of members in respect of sector coverage, with the individual commitments chosen from across all large services areas. The only major exceptions in terms of sectoral representation are education and health services, where four and eight developed countries, respectively, have not undertaken any commitments.[23]

Challenges Ahead

Given the current patterns of commitment, the impending services round might be viewed as a "rebalancing exercise." The overriding objective would be to promote the integration of Uruguay Round laggards—countries, sectors, and modes—into the system. In turn, this seems

23. In total, twenty-four developed countries, including the EC members, have been counted in this context. The nonparticipants in individual areas are Liechtenstein for construction services; New Zealand for environmental services; Canada and New Zealand for recreation services; Canada, Finland, Iceland, and Sweden for education services; and Canada, Finland, Iceland, Liechtenstein, New Zealand, Norway, Sweden, and Switzerland for health and social services. Given the high level of aggregation, these findings should be interpreted with care; any sort of commitment, regardless of the subsector(s) and the limitations, has been counted.

to require contributions from all sides, with varying intensity, depending on the area involved. Further issues earmarked for negotiation in GATS or related annexes and decisions would complement the negotiating package: the status of air transport under GATS, the scheduling of commitments in maritime transport, the continuation of current MFN exemptions, and the completion of the rule-making mandate inherited from the Uruguay Round's built-in agenda.[24]

It has been argued that a general or formulaic approach might have various advantages over the offer-request mechanism used in the Uruguay Round.[25] In particular, it could help to include countries, measures, and sectors that, reflecting a lack of economic interest on the part of the large players, have hitherto eluded significant reform or, at least, bindings. The onus would be on the domestic interest groups seeking to avoid liberalization, thus reducing the burden on administrations and users to cajole them into participation. This might prove difficult in areas such as health, education, audiovisual, and transport services, where negotiations not only involve trade officials—as in traditional GATT rounds—but also regulatory authorities with strong sectoral links.[26] Thus, as a starting point in the next round, all WTO members could undertake to commit on a minimum number of industries. Such an undertaking might call for the inclusion of at least X sectors from specified areas; this would permit members to prioritize basic services industries such as telecommunications that have strong cross-sectoral impacts on trade, investment, and innovation.[27] The relevant numbers might need to vary with the level of economic develop-

24. See chapters 6, 7, and 8 in this volume.

25. See chapters 12 and 16.

26. A general approach—based on "negative scheduling"—has been used in the modal context, starting from the assumption of full bindings in the absence of market access and national treatment limitations. Yet this has not prevented most members from scheduling a wide range of limitations and avoiding significant commitments, especially for mode 4 (natural persons). Richard Snape has raised the possibility of combining a comprehensive approach to sectoral coverage, through drastic structural changes in GATS. Commitments would apply to cross-border trade only; issues related to other modes would be treated under separate agreements. Barring some exemptions, all discriminatory measures would be converted into tariffs and subsequently made subject to negotiated reductions (Snape, 1998, pp. 289–92). However, there is no indication at present that WTO members would like to renegotiate the basic structure of the agreement. Difficult technical questions would need to be resolved if, for example, stricter licensing or deposit requirements for foreign suppliers were to be converted into tariffs. Where would the borderline be drawn between discriminatory measures deemed justified on prudential or other public policy grounds, on the one hand, and genuine departures from national treatment, on the other hand? And how would tariffs be assessed and collected in electronic trade?

27. See Feketekuty (1998, p. 92f.).

ment in order to make the approach, or the avoidance of discretionary provisions, acceptable to all WTO members.[28]

It would not come as a surprise, however, if a number of developing countries raised additional points, linking their position to an issue left open in the Uruguay Round—the creation of an emergency safeguard mechanism for services—or to compensatory "concessions" by developed members in particular for mode 4 (presence of natural persons).[29] The link with safeguards could amount to a trade-off between the level and range of commitments attainable in the next round and their stability over time. What would be gained in terms of liberalization, one might ask, if members could suspend obligations, possibly including "old" Uruguay Round commitments, at any time? Yet this might prove too skeptical a view as there is scope for counter requests. For example, if existing discretionary entries in schedules—unspecified economic needs tests and the like—were abandoned in return, a narrowly defined safeguards mechanism might not necessarily undermine stability. The existence of an "emergency exit" could also facilitate commitments on mode 4, although this might not be the outcome envisaged by most proponents of safeguards for services.

Given the uncertainties involved, it is reasonable to assume that the next round will continue to embrace strong sector-specific elements. The extended negotiations on basic telecommunications and financial services have revealed, despite the risks involved, the viability of this approach in specific circumstances.[30] But how well is the stage set for such an exercise? Can "GATS 2000" be viewed as a continuation (or repetition) of the Uruguay Round, with similar forces, interests, and coalitions at play? A closer look suggests that the scenario may have changed.

The United States and the European Communities—possibly the main instigators, facilitators, and mediators in the first round (at different stages, with differing emphasis)—may find it difficult to play the same role

28. Article XIX (Negotiation of Specific Commitments), para. 2, requires liberalization to "take place with due respect for national policy objectives and the level of development of individual Members, both overall and in individual sectors."

29. Article X (Emergency Safeguard Measures) provides for "multilateral negotiations on the question of emergency safeguard measures based on the principle of non-discrimination." The results should have entered into effect "not later than three years from the entry into force of the WTO Agreement," that is, January 1, 1998. The deadline has since been extended twice. In June 1999 the Council for Trade in Services decided that the negotiations should be concluded by December 15, 2000, and the results put into effect not later than the results of the next services round.

30. On the positive side, sectoral negotiations might help to prevent particularly difficult issues from derailing the whole process. See Snape (1998, p. 286f.).

again. In areas such as financial services and telecommunications, they have bound essential elements of their regimes on an MFN basis, without being obliged to make genuine changes at home. New commercially attractive offers may, however, require regulatory reforms and imply more significant commitments for mode 4 as well. In addition, the EC role might be complicated by the fact that, for all modes except cross-border trade (mode 1), negotiating competence is shared between the European Communities and the member states. Thus changes affecting the conditions of establishment or the issuance of work permits might need to be approved by each of the fifteen members. At the same time, the possibility of taking elements of established internal market legislation and offering them for external binding may be more limited in potentially relevant areas, not least air transport (traffic rights), than was the case in past negotiations on financial services and basic telecommunications.[31]

However, the focus of the negotiations will differ from the Uruguay Round. The creation of GATS marked a genuine breakthrough; it established the basic rules of the system and made all WTO members, to varying degrees, undertake specific commitments. Although the active participation of the United States and the European Communities will remain indispensable, given their economic weight, the need for (hegemonic) leadership might not be as strong as before.[32] The challenge is no longer to create an agreement and make it work, but—first and foremost—to attain higher levels of liberalization within an established framework and, second, to clarify existing rules and fill some perceived gaps.[33] Additional impetus might now come from other members, including some previous "free-riders" who had not undertaken significant obligations but benefited from MFN treatment.

31. It has been argued that whenever matters pertaining to GATS or to the Agreement on Trade-Related Aspects of Intellectual Property Rights are raised in the WTO, the EC negotiators have to "explain who is taking positions on what, negotiating about what and entering into further commitments on what. With a bit of negotiating skill, other WTO Members will have a field day in exploiting the situation." See Bourgeois (1995, p. 786). However, this is not the only possible scenario. Rather than promoting liberalization, internal frictions within negotiating entities, whether the EC or other participants, might well stifle the whole process.

32. This inference could also explain why virtually all members are hesitant to touch on the basic architecture of the agreement and thus restart the whole process.

33. For example, Wiener (1995, pp. 53–54) has noted that "if a leader initiates and guides a situation within the structure of a regime, and participants believe there to be sufficient benefits from participating, the leader can be regarded as acting legitimately. Most importantly, resources do not have to be invested into the normative framework. . . . Rather than resources, the leader requires *skills* to structure a multilateral context such that the concessions among participants themselves sustain interest in the particular round."

GATS 2000: Possible Sources of Momentum

There have been various indications, including the five "late submissions" in basic telecommunications, that developing and least-developed countries are increasingly aware of the economic advantages of policy bindings under GATS. Commitments for commercial presence may protect and thus attract foreign investment in a way similar to bilateral agreements, but can be attained without much negotiating effort. Governments might have been reticent to use the GATS option, however, for lack of information and experience. Some may be waiting for the new round as an opportunity to come forward, while others may first want to evaluate recent liberalization cases within the same region or income group and develop regulatory safeguards ensuring against liberalization-induced market upheavals and distortions.[34] In areas such as transport, banking, communication, or health, new rules may be required, for regional or social policy reasons, to guarantee the provision of universal services in a more open environment.

It appears safe to assume, however, that future liberalization will be by and large unaffected by regional or ideological divisions. Although the scope of current GATS commitments generally varies with the level of development, there are numerous country cases defying simple categorization, both among the Uruguay Round participants and the six recent accession countries (Bulgaria, Ecuador, Panama, Mongolia, Kyrgyz Republic, and Latvia; table 5-1). The schedules of Lesotho, the Gambia, or the Kyrgyz Republic, for example, are significantly wider in sectoral coverage than those of many more prosperous members.[35]

Once industries recognize that their foreign competitors benefit from a more liberal and predictable—that is, commercially attractive—domestic environment, governments will find it increasingly difficult to deny similar conditions at home. In addition, the liberalization of goods trade will amplify liberalization pressures in services. The closer their markets move toward uniform prices for identical products, the less scope will remain for

---

34. This "insurance factor" may play a particular role in services—despite the flexibility provided under GATS—as the legal implications of certain concepts are still being discussed. As mentioned earlier, this includes the question of whether the mode of supply affects the likeness of a service and thus whether the national treatment obligation is mode-specific or applies across modes within a given product category.

35. The two former cases, however, may be regarded by peers as more compelling examples than the schedules of accession countries, which were negotiated in other circumstances.

manufacturers (farmers, miners, and the like) to carry the burden of services protection or, in other words, suffer negative rates of assistance. In the same vein, the opening of some infrastructural services, such as banking and telecommunications, sets a precedent for liberalizing other sectors, such as air transport, which are governed by similar policy objectives and constraints.[36] Administrations will be facing increasing pressure from user industries such as the hotel and tourism sector, which are getting used to competitive conditions among certain suppliers, to create similar conditions elsewhere. And it would certainly not be convincing if such demands were rejected on regulatory or technical grounds, with reference, for example, to public service obligations or the complexity of existing government-to-government arrangements. Since regulatory solutions have been found to liberalization problems in telecommunications—a sector that has long operated within a dense network of bilateral price and access arrangements—it should be technically possible to solve similar problems in areas such as air transport.

The situation may be slightly different for "consumer services," that is, products essentially intended for final consumption (audiovisual services; residential construction; health, medical, and social services). In these sectors, the traditional policy equation—vocal and well-organized producer resistance versus more amorphous consumer interests—may continue to apply. However, new factors may emerge over time. Depending on the area, governments may find it increasingly difficult to ignore the proliferation of bypass technologies (video on demand, telemedicine, and the like), along with mounting cost pressures and fiscal constraints. For example, soaring health care budgets in a number of developed countries, partly attributable to demographic change, might prompt governments to reassess traditional notions of universal service.[37] In the longer run, they are facing the alternative of either assuaging incumbents and protecting their role in the system or defending basic

36. Even areas such as basic telecommunications or financial services continue to offer broad scope for widening and deepening current commitments. For example, while the signatories to the Fourth Protocol (basic telecommunications) account for more than 90 percent of world telecom revenue, they represent less than 60 percent of the WTO membership; the Fifth Protocol (financial services) has been signed by a comparable number of countries.

37. Observers have already pointed out a growing trend in Latin America (particularly in Chile and Brazil) and Central and Eastern Europe (Czech Republic, Hungary, and Poland) to decentralize or commercialize the health sector in a bid to contain cost pressures. Some countries have preferred to retain the public insurance monopoly but allow for competition between private and public health care providers. See WTO (1998a, p. 9f.).

objectives of the system and facilitating consumption abroad and access of natural persons under mode 4.

Concluding Remarks

In general, the stage seems well set for a new services round. For various reasons—technology, economics, and politics—services regimes throughout the world are gravitating in a more liberal direction. The forthcoming negotiations may be viewed by many participants, developed and developing countries alike, as an opportunity to mobilize support for policy reform and enhance credibility through external bindings. However, various problems remain to be solved in national capitals, in the WTO, and possibly other international organizations as well.

First, deregulation may need to be combined with re-regulation, that is, the introduction of new rules facilitating the transition to a more open system, ensuring competitive market conditions, and guaranteeing, where needed, the provision of universal services. Sector-specific guidelines, modeled on the Reference Paper for Telecommunications, could prove useful in other areas too.[38] To make them operational, however, regulatory content might still need to be developed by competent international organizations such as the World Bank, World Health Organization, or International Telecommunication Union.

Second, WTO members may have to improve—or clarify—individual areas of the agreement to facilitate its interpretation and application in practice. Among the critical issues are the distinction between modes 1 and 2, which has proved difficult to apply in electronic trade in particular, or a current overlap between market access and national treatment obligations, which leaves scope for confusion.

Third, from a more general perspective, the challenge remains to better integrate hesitant and more peripheral countries into the trading system. This leads back to the question of comprehensive versus sector-specific liberalization and, in this context, the possible role of negotiating arrangements that would encourage broader and deeper participation across members,

---

38. The paper was drafted in the context of the extended negotiations on basic telecommunications. It contains regulatory principles (competition safeguards, interconnection guarantees, neutrality of public service obligations, transparency of licensing criteria, independence of regulators, and so on) that were ultimately adopted, in full or with modifications, by fifty-nine of the seventy-two governments that undertook commitments in these negotiations.

sectors, and modes. Given current gaps, the "rebalancing" of commitments remains a challenging task economically, politically, and conceptually.

References

Besançon, Laurent, and Tim Kelly. 1996. "Telecom Privatisations: The New Realism." *ITU Speeches and Discussion Papers* (July): www.itu.int/ti/papers/privatisation.

Bourgeois, Jacques. 1995. "The EC in the WTO and Advisory Opinion 1/94: An Echternach Procession." *Common Market Law Review* 32: 763–87.

Dobson, Wendy, and Pierre Jacquet. 1998. *Financial Services Liberalization in the WTO.* Washington, D.C.: Institute for International Economics.

Feketekuty, Geza. 1998. "Setting the Agenda for the Next Round of Negotiations on Trade in Services." In *Launching New Global Trade Talks: An Action Agenda,* edited by Jeffrey J. Schott, 91–110. Washington, D.C.: Institute for International Economics.

Hoekman, Bernard M. 1996. "Assessing the General Agreement on Trade in Services." In *The Uruguay Round and the Developing Countries,* edited by Will Martin and L. Alan Winters, 88–124. Cambridge University Press.

Organization for Economic Cooperation and Development (OECD). 1997a. *The OECD Report on Regulatory Reform.* Vol. 2: *Thematic Studies.* Paris.

———. 1997b. *Policy and Regulatory Issues for Network-Based Content Services.* Document DSTI/ICCP/IE(96)9/REV1. Paris (August 4).

Paemen, Hugo, and Alexandra Bensch. 1995. *From the GATT to the WTO—The European Community in the Uruguay Round.* Leuven University Press.

Petrazzini, Ben A. 1996. "Competition in Telecoms—Implications for Universal Service and Employment." Industry and Energy Department Note 96. Washington, D.C.: World Bank (October).

Roessler, Frieder. 1985. "The Scope, Limits, and Function of the GATT Legal System." *World Economy* 8 (3): 287–98.

Sapir, André. 1999. "The General Agreement on Trade in Services: From 1994 to the Year 2000." *Journal of World Trade* 33 (1): 51–66.

Sauvé, Pierre. 1995. "Assessing the General Agreement on Trade in Services—Half-Full or Half-Empty?" *Journal of World Trade* 29 (4): 125–45.

Snape, Richard. 1998. "Reaching Effective Agreements Covering Services." In *The WTO as an International Organization,* edited by Anne O. Krueger, 279–293. University of Chicago Press.

Wiener, Jarrod. 1995. *Making Rules in the Uruguay Round of the WTO—A Study of International Leadership.* Dartmouth.

World Trade Organization (WTO). 1995a. *Trade Policy Review—European Union.* Geneva.

———. 1995b. *Trade Policy Review—Uganda.* Geneva.

———. 1998a. "Health and Social Services." Secretariat Background Note S/C/W/50. Geneva (September 18).

———. 1998b. "Tourism Services." Secretariat Background Note S/C/W/51. Geneva (September 23).

————. 1998c. "Presence of Natural Persons (Mode 4)." Secretariat Background Note S/C/W75. Geneva (December 8).

————. 1999a. "Recent Developments in Services Trade—Overview and Assessment." Secretariat Background Note S/C/W/94. Geneva (February 9).

————. 1999b. "Structure of Commitments for Modes 1, 2 and 3." Secretariat Background Note S/C/W/99. Geneva (March 3).

Zdouc, Werner. 1999. "WTO Dispute Settlement Practice Relating to the GATS." *Journal of International Economic Law* 2 (June): 295–346.

COMMENT BY
Bernard M. Hoekman

What is at stake in liberalizing services trade and investment? And what are the benefits and constraints associated with multilateral attempts to achieve such liberalization? These are the two major themes of part 1 of this volume. They are important questions. Clearly the greater the potential benefits of liberalization (the higher the costs of policies that restrict competition), the greater the priority that should be given to reform. There is therefore significant interest in seeking to quantify the potential benefits of liberalization. However, such reforms can in principle be undertaken unilaterally. This leads to the second question: why do it in a multilateral context?

The authors suggest a number of answers. One is the well-known political economy argument for multilateral trade negotiations: going to the World Trade Organization (WTO) may help overcome resistance to domestic reform if local forces with an interest in increasing exports can be mobilized to support liberalization. Another is that multilateral agreement can be a valuable mechanism for locking in or precommitting to reform, thereby reducing uncertainty and risk. Although reforms can and should be pursued autonomously, there is value in multilateral commitment, as it can help ensure that reforms are maintained over time through the threat of dispute settlement. The classic argument is that negotiation is required in order to get other countries to reduce their barriers on a reciprocal basis.

Rolf Adlung believes that governments generally have a conservative social welfare function and that the costs of reform weigh much more heavily than the benefits.[1] However, forces are emerging in the services context that facilitate (unilateral) reform: users of services have an incentive to oppose inefficiencies; technological change is making it difficult to maintain traditional rents; and the adjustment costs associated with greater competition are more manageable politically because labor tends to perceive fewer downsides from services liberalization. The implication is that much can be (and is being) achieved unilaterally. Why, then, pursue reform through the WTO? The main answer, Adlung suggests, is to achieve "lock-in" and commitment objectives. Hence a key policy issue is how to

---

1. See Corden (1974).

make the existing instrument (GATS/WTO) a more effective mechanism. Paradoxically, those who need it the most (presumably developing countries) use it the least, in that they have made the fewest commitments. Adlung does not fully address this issue. To do so, one would need to look at the gains from making binding commitments and identify what is "wrong" with GATS in this connection. Although some of the other contributions to this volume do mention this question, it still does not get the attention it merits.[2]

Tony Warren and Chris Findlay have a somewhat different and more negative outlook on the political economy of services reform. In their opinion, the standard political economy forces that impede reform may be worsened in the services context because the public sector is more of a player (both as a provider and as a regulator). The need for reciprocal exchange—negotiations—is therefore as great, if not greater, than in the case of merchandise trade. But then one must ask what can be traded? How to go about it? The traditional GATT approach is to trade market access "concessions"—lowering trade barriers on roughly equivalent trade flows. This requires information on the barriers to and volume of bilateral trade on a commodity-by-commodity basis. According to Guy Karsenty and Warren and Findlay, the available data on barriers and international services transactions remain a great deal weaker and less abundant than the information on merchandise trade.

The lack of data on the restrictiveness of current policies is particularly troublesome. As discussed by Karsenty, efforts undertaken during the last decade to improve trade statistics, including data on sales of services by local affiliates of foreign multinationals, have at least improved our knowledge of the flows involved. A noteworthy conclusion Karsenty draws from the available statistics is that trade in services (defined in the traditional, "cross-border" sense) is larger in absolute size than "foreign affiliate trade in services" (local sales achieved through establishment). Total measurable "trade" in services as defined by GATS is some $2.2 trillion, a significant amount, especially for a sector that was traditionally regarded as nontradable.

More data on trade flows are needed if decisionmakers desire to use traditional mercantilist negotiating techniques. They are also needed for analytical purposes. But much more important from an economic perspective are data on the barriers that restrict international competition. These

---

2. Although some innovative work on these questions has begun: see Francois (1977) and Francios and Martin (1999).

are major determinants of the potential for trade expansion and the magnitude of the welfare gains that may be obtained by pursuing liberalization. Little progress has been achieved in quantifying the impact of discriminatory restrictions on trade and investment flows. This makes it very difficult to provide quantitative estimates of what is at stake in the area of services policy reforms, although a rich literature is available on the sectoral or country-specific benefits of liberalizing trade in services.

Much better cross-country information is also needed on barriers to entry created or tolerated by governments. A revealing statistic quoted by Warren and Findlay illustrates the urgency of compiling such data: only 38 of 165 market access impediments that prevailed in the Australian financial services sector were scheduled under GATS. This not only illustrates the weakness of GATS as a transparency and a scheduling (commitment) device, but also confirms that the lack of comprehensive information on the effect of status quo policies impedes unilateral reform. Whatever one believes about the political economy rationale for having multilateral negotiations pursue service sector reform, the poor information on prevailing policies and consequent dearth of careful empirical analysis of the effects of these policies is a major constraint on reform efforts.

Great attention has been and will continue to be devoted to normative analyses of the GATS rules and disciplines. Making GATS a better instrument to promote the adoption of good policies for service sectors is clearly important, and such normative analyses are therefore valuable. Geza Feketekuty is particularly knowledgeable about GATS, having played a major role in its creation, and provides a good discussion of its weaknesses along with a number of innovative and practical suggestions to make it a more effective and useful instrument for international business and for consumers of services. But from a national perspective, especially for developing countries, the value of GATS will remain limited if it does not generate information on the level and effects of barriers to international competition and lead to a process in which the utility of existing policies is assessed by governments and civil society.

As is widely recognized, the scheduling technology that has been used in GATS does not greatly promote transparency. Thus it is essential to improve the available information on status quo policies. This will encourage countries to undertake national reform and help them determine where the multilateral process can support such efforts. Unfortunately, nothing in GATS or the WTO assists countries in generating comprehensive information on applied policies and evaluating the impact of these policies.

Some progress was made in the Uruguay Round in this regard with the creation of the Trade Policy Review Mechanism, but a great deal more can and should be done. Priority should be given to improving statistics and data on trade and entry restrictions in services. Using as a guide the role played by the OECD Secretariat in compiling information on agricultural policies in the 1980s, international organizations and multinational business should devote the resources required to document the status quo and put this information in the public domain. Without such an effort, multilateral discussions and negotiations on services may well be driven by special interests and put too much emphasis on "architectural improvements," as opposed to the achievement and support of the reforms needed to improve the economic development and growth prospects of WTO members. A great deal of information is already available to monitor the "state of competition" or the contestability of markets.[3] As Warren and Findlay demonstrate, substantial progress can be made with limited resources. What is required is a concerted effort.

References

Corden, Max. 1974. *Trade Policy and Economic Welfare.* Oxford: Clarendon Press.

Djankov, Simeon, and Bernard M. Hoekman. 1998. "Conditions of Competition and Multilateral Surveillance." *World Economy* 21: 1109–28.

Francois, Joseph F. 1997. "External Bindings and the Credibility of Reform." In *Regional Partners in Global Markets,* edited by Ahmed Galal and Bernard M. Hoekman, 35–48. London: Centre for Economic Policy Research.

Francois, Joseph F., and W. Martin. 1998. "Commercial Policy Uncertainty, the Expected Cost of Protection, and Market Access." Tinbergen Institute Working Paper (May).

---

3. See, for example, Djankov and Hoekman (1998).

COMMENT BY
Patrick Low

The General Agreement on Trade in Services (GATS) was a bold first attempt at rule-making in a previously uncharted area. But it was in many ways a preliminary effort, leaving much to be done. With all the expertise represented in this volume, I am sure that it will be possible to address some of the outstanding issues that need to be dealt with if GATS is to grow into a more useful commercial policy instrument.

To be effective, GATS needs to serve three primary functions. First, it must be an effective framework of clear, transparent rules. Second, it must serve as a vibrant instrument for continuing liberalization. Third, like the rest of the legal instruments that make up the World Trade Organization, GATS should be part of an effective system of dispute resolution. Clearly, GATS can only be enforceable if the rules are clear and if governments have assumed meaningful market access commitments. That is why these two aspects of GATS—as a system of rules and as an instrument of liberalization—should be given the utmost attention.

Some issues have already been identified as either requiring a complete overhaul, or at the very least significant clarification. First, the most favored nation (MFN) exemptions under GATS might have been defended as a necessary expedient at the time they were introduced, in order to prevent the wholesale removal of sectors from the purview of GATS. But surely this is a lacuna that must be addressed, not least to ensure that governments resist the temptation to invent new MFN exemptions in future negotiations.

A second issue is whether there is room to make national treatment commitments more pervasive and more biting. It is true that in a regime of rules that covers investment or commercial presence, national treatment becomes the cutting edge that defines market access, and for this reason governments were reluctant to grant national treatment too readily. If a structural change in the agreement that makes national treatment more automatic proves infeasible, then perhaps the emphasis should be on a bolder approach to granting national treatment within the existing schedules of specific commitments.

Third, as far as market access under Article XVI is concerned, a question that has been raised by some analysts is whether we could rely on price-based measures instead of quantity-based ones. This would certainly have something to recommend it in terms of economic efficiency, but it would require a redefinition of market access limitations under Article XVI. More generally, it is unclear that the permitted market access limitations under Article XVI of GATS can reasonably be regarded as exhaustive. And if they are not, it is difficult to expect certain kinds of limitations to be listed, or if they are listed, for them to fit adequately within the established framework. Another aspect of Article XVI in need of attention is the possibility of inscribing such vague and nonspecific notions as economic needs tests in the schedules. These remove a great deal of certainty as to what is being committed. We should also be certain that liberalization is being appropriately defined: it is unclear, for example, that increased foreign equity holdings in monopolistic enterprises represent genuine liberalization rather than a simple rent transfer from nationals to foreigners.

A fourth issue, and one of considerable complexity, is the precise nature of the relationship of market access under Article XVI and national treatment under Article XVII. Part of the problem is embodied in the GATS rules themselves, which contemplate a form of scheduling that makes the degree of intended discrimination in a market access commitment unclear. But even without this source of confusion, we still need to know whether a national treatment commitment is subsidiary to a market access commitment, or whether once granted, national treatment will apply to all future market access commitments as well. The answer to this question has far-reaching consequences for the value that one assigns to some nondiscrimination commitments in the schedules.

A fifth concern, related to the last one, is how we should interpret the relationship of commitments among different modes of supply. It is easy to see, for example, how full market access and national treatment commitments on cross-border supply (mode 1) could be severely undermined by subsidization of domestically established enterprises where commercial presence (mode 3) commitments do not prohibit such interventions. In general, to the extent that alternative means are available to supply a market, a lack of symmetry in commitments on the same sector in different modes can significantly undermine what is committed. One might argue that a nonviolation complaint would prosper in such circumstances, but greater clarity of this point would seem desirable.

A sixth area in need of attention is domestic regulation. This is essential in the field of services, where regulations are pervasive in virtually every sector. Article VI today is provisional in nature and badly needs clarification and strengthening. The recent work in the accountancy sector has raised some interesting issues. A horizontal approach would, in the first instance, seem preferable to a close focus on specific sectors when it comes to defining the rules to be applied to domestic regulation. The accountancy sector exercise also made clear the fact that Article VI is concerned only with nondiscriminatory measures of regulation. What this means in practice is that if a member has not scheduled a national treatment commitment in a sector, there is little that Article VI can do by way of imposing disciplines in that sector. Under the current GATS structure, therefore, improvements in market access and national treatment need to go hand in hand with efforts to strengthen the rules on domestic regulation.

Finally, many aspects of practices and procedures associated with scheduling need to be addressed. Some of these I have already mentioned, but the absence of an adequate nomenclature makes it very difficult to interpret the true nature of commitments. The tendency of many members to insert descriptive material of dubious legal status in the schedules serves to confuse matters further, as does inattention to the description of the precise nature of market access limitations under Article XVI.

Turning now to the question of GATS as an instrument for liberalization, the most obvious point to make is that very considerable scope remains for inscribing additional sectors in the schedules, as well as for removing market access and national treatment limitations on sectors already inscribed. It is also true that GATS would automatically become a more effective instrument of liberalization if issues such as those mentioned above were attended to adequately.

But what else could be done to promote further liberalization? An interesting question that is beginning to be discussed is whether scope exists for formula-like approaches to new negotiations, similar to those that have been applied from time to time in the area of goods. It may well be that a greater quantum of liberalization would be forthcoming if governments achieved prior agreement on the precise nature of liberalization commitments in individual sectors. We already have some experience with efforts like this in the use, for example, of model schedules in basic telecommunications and maritime transport services. We also have the precedent of the less than successful effort at standardization in the Understanding of Financial Services. Essentially, formula-like approaches offer greater clarity through precise definition of the activities to be covered and the exact nature of limitations to be imposed. By reducing uncertainty regarding these matters, and ensuring shared commitments among members, perhaps greater liberalization will take place.

Liberalization can also be promoted through a readier use of the schedules as instruments of precommitment. In basic telecommunications many governments did precisely this: they announced a liberalization timetable, which became legally binding by virtue of its inclusion in the schedule of commitments. In this way, governments not only defined their future intentions with clarity but also made it more difficult for these intentions to be challenged effectively by domestic interests opposed to liberalization.

Finally, the commitments of many members in a range of sectors represent markedly less than the actual regime in terms of the degree of openness that they express. While bindings at less than the policy status quo still have a certain value in setting a benchmark in terms of access, commitments would be even more valuable without the gap for discretion that "ceiling" bindings provide. Perhaps movement in this area could be linked to an agreement regarding a satisfactory safeguard mechanism under GATS.

PART TWO

Completing the GATS Framework: The Built-In Agenda

6 | Government Procurement of Services and Multilateral Disciplines

SIMON J. EVENETT *and* BERNARD M. HOEKMAN

Much of what is procured by governments comprises services. This is not surprising, since the production of services accounts for more than half of national income in many countries, and many governments outsource activities (including services) to the private sector. The absence of general rules on public purchasing practices is a major "hole" in the World Trade Organization's (WTO) edifice. A question confronting policymakers is whether this is in fact an important problem, and if so, what to do about it. In the context of the prospective "Services 2000" negotiations, the question is whether existing stand-alone disciplines should be incorporated into the General Agreement on Trade in Services (GATS), or whether a more general approach covering both goods and services is preferable.

This discussion focuses on the services dimension of the problem, to determine whether procurement favoritism is detrimental either to the welfare of the country pursuing it or to foreign countries. We conclude that

An earlier version of this essay was presented at the conference "Services 2000—New Directions in Services Trade Liberalization," University Club, Washington, D.C., June 1–2, 1999. We are grateful to Malcolm Bosworth, June Dong Kim, Juan Marchetti, Pierre Sauvé, Mark Warner, Tony Warren, and other conference participants for comments and discussion. The views expressed are those of the authors and should not be attributed to the World Bank.

procurement regimes for services, even those that explicitly discriminate against foreign suppliers, are unlikely to have major permanent repercussions on domestic or foreign welfare so long as the markets are contestable. For nations with strong competition policies, this undermines the case for stand-alone disciplines on the government procurement of services.

From a national policy perspective, the top priority is to remove market access barriers. Particularly important in this connection is the right of establishment (the ability to engage in foreign direct investment, FDI), for not only is proximity frequently required to supply services, but often purchasers of services need to source from local firms in order to ensure compliance and performance. Greatly expanding the market access and national treatment commitments under GATS will to a large extent obviate the need for multilateral rules on procurement. This is not to say there is no value in seeking multilateral disciplines that ensure procurement mechanisms are transparent; such mechanisms can help limit corruption and rent-seeking activities. Rather, in assessing the need for these rules it is important to distinguish between procurement policy (discrimination against foreign firms) and procurement practice (how products are actually purchased). The case for a multilateral agreement on transparency in public procurement is much stronger than the economic case for banning discrimination. But any such procurement disciplines should be horizontal and apply to both goods and services. In fact, this is the approach being pursued by WTO members, and our analysis bolsters the argument that separate disciplines on government procurement of services in GATS are unnecessary.

We begin the analysis by summarizing the major elements of the Government Procurement Agreement (GPA). To date this is the only multilateral agreement in this area, one that covers services as well as goods. Next, we look at the evidence on the size of procurement markets for services and examine the temporary and permanent economic effects of discrimination against foreign suppliers of services. We then turn to the policy implications of our findings, especially in relation to transparency and procedural safeguards.

Core Elements of the Government Procurement Agreement

Despite the importance of the national procurement markets, no general obligations are imposed on the procurement practices of members of the WTO. Government procurement practices were excluded from the reach of the General Agreement on Tariffs and Trade (GATT) in 1947, and it was only in 1979 that a number of countries negotiated a voluntary and stand-alone agreement on these practices. The resulting Government Procurement Agreement extends GATT's basic principles of nondiscrimination and transparency to the tendering procedures of specified government entities. At present the membership of the GPA remains limited: only Canada, the member states of the European Union (EU), Hong Kong, Israel, Japan, Korea, Norway, Singapore, Switzerland, and the United States signed the revised agreement after the conclusion of the Uruguay Round. Since then additional membership has come only from those countries that have acceded to the WTO and were confronted with significant pressure to join. The GATT precedent was followed in the WTO: the current GPA remains a voluntary instrument and procurement is not covered by GATS, although the GPA was extended to cover the procurement of services during the Uruguay Round.

The GPA's objectives are to contribute to the greater liberalization and expansion of world trade; to eliminate discrimination among foreign products, services, or suppliers; and to enhance the transparency of relevant laws and practices.[1] The agreement applies to any law, regulation, procedure, or practice regarding any procurement by entities listed in Appendix 1 of the agreement. Procurement covers all contractual options, including purchase, leasing, rental, and hire-purchase, with or without the option to buy (Article I). A so-called positive list determines the reach of the GPA: it applies only to entities that are listed in appendix 1 of the agreement. This appendix contains five annexes for each signatory. There are three entity annexes: Annex 1 lists covered central government entities; Annex 2 lists subcentral government entities; and Annex 3 lists all other entities that procure in accordance with the provisions of the agreement. Annex 3 is a catchall category that includes entities such as utilities. Annex 4 lists covered services, and Annex 5 relates to construction services. Only services expressly indicated by the signatory are covered by the GPA. The United States is the only party to the GPA to have included a negative list of services not covered by the agreement, rather than a positive list of services covered by the agreement.

The entities listed in the three annexes are subject to the rules and disciplines of the GPA with respect to their procurement of goods and

---

1. For a comprehensive discussion of the GPA, see Hoekman and Mavroidis (1997).

services if (1) the value of the procurement exceeds certain specified thresholds, and (2) the goods or services being purchased are not exempted from the coverage of the agreement. Table 6-1 sets out the various thresholds that apply to the procurement of goods and services for the three types of entities. For central government entities, there is a common minimum threshold of SDR 130,000 for purchases of goods and nonconstruction services. Thresholds can be as high as SDR 15 million for construction services procured by non–central government entities.

The range of products covered by the agreement is also indicated in the annexes. As far as goods are concerned, in principle all procurement is covered, unless specified otherwise in an annex. Thus a negative list approach is used to determine the coverage of the GPA for procurement of non-defense-related goods by scheduled entities. The procurement of goods by defense ministries or similar entities is often subject to a positive list: only items explicitly scheduled are covered. Procurement of services is also subject to a positive list: only the procurement by covered entities of services explicitly scheduled in Annexes 4 and 5 are subject to the GPA's rules, and then only insofar as no qualifications or limitations are maintained in the relevant annexes. In practice there is a close correspondence—often a one-to-one relationship—between sectors for which specific commitments on national treatment and market access were made in GATS and the services that are subject to the GPA disciplines.

Many parties made explicit derogations to the commitments that are contained in their annexes. These can be divided into two types. The first consists of a derogation from the nondiscrimination requirement (GPA, Article III). These generally specify that party X will not apply the nondiscrimination rule to the procurement by entities listed in Annex Y to firms originating in party R, S, or T "until such time as X has accepted that the parties concerned give comparable and effective access for X's undertakings to the relevant markets." This reflects a desire to attain reciprocity on either a product or an entity basis. The second type of derogation pertains to commitments on services (Annexes 4 and 5) and specifies that listed services are covered only to the extent that other parties to the GPA provide reciprocal access to that service. Canada, Finland, Korea, Switzerland, and the United States made such derogations. The mix of positive and negative list approaches for entities, products and services, varying thresholds, and the use of exceptions and derogations make it difficult to determine the effective scope of the GPA. Tables 6-2 and 6-3 summarize the various

Table 6-1. *Thresholds in Annexes 1, 2, and 3 of the GPA*
Thousands of special drawing rights

Category	Canada	EU-15	Israel	Japan[a]	Republic of Korea	Norway	Switzerland	United States
Annex 1[b]								
Goods	130	130	130	130	130	130	130	130
Services	130	130	130	130	130	130	130	130
Construction	5,000	5,000	8,500	4,500	5,000	5,000	5,000	5,000
Annex 2[b]								
Goods	355	200	250	200	200	200	200	355
Services	355	200	250	200	200	200	200	355
Construction	5,000	5,000	8,500	15,000	15,000	5,000	5,000	5,000
Annex 3[b]								
Goods	355	400	355	130	450	400	400	400
Services	355	400	355	130	450	400	400	400
Construction	5,000	5,000	8,500	15,000	15,000	5,000	5,000	5,000

a. For architecture services, Japan has thresholds of SDR 1.5 million for Annex 2 entities, and SDR 450,000 for Annex 1 and 3 entities.
b. Annex 1 consists of central government entities; Annex 2 consists of subcentral government entities; Annex 3 consists of all other entities scheduled by parties. In general, Annex 3 comprises public enterprises, public authorities, and public utilities.

Table 6-2. *Category Exemptions Invoked by GPA Signatories*

Country/entities	General notes
Canada	Small and minority businesses
Hong Kong	All consulting and franchise arrangements
Japan	Small and minority businesses
Annex 1: contracts to be awarded to a cooperative or association; Annexes 2 and 3: contracts that entities award for purposes of profit-making activities exposed to competitive market forces	
Korea	
All covered entities: single tendering and set-asides for small and medium-sized firms	
United States	Small and minority-owned firms

exceptions and nonapplication and reciprocity provisions that were imposed at the end of the Uruguay Round.

Nondiscrimination

The GPA has two key components: a nondiscrimination requirement, and a set of procedural disciplines relating to transparency. The two core nondiscrimination principles governing the GPA are most favored nation treatment (MFN) and national treatment (Article III). The former prohibits discrimination between foreign products; the latter prohibits discrimination between foreign and domestic suppliers. The nondiscrimination obligations apply irrespective of the customs treatment of the products or services that affect the procurement contract. That is, they "shall not apply to customs duties and charges of any kind imposed on or in connection with importation, the method of levying such duties and charges, other import regulations and formalities, and measures affecting trade in services other than laws, regulations, procedures and practices regarding government procurement covered by this Agreement" (Article III:3). Article III:2 requires parties to ensure that covered entities do not discriminate between locally established suppliers on the basis of degree of foreign affiliation or ownership or on the basis of the country of production of the good or

Table 6-3. *Product and Category Exemptions Invoked by GPA Signatories*

Country/entities	Services and construction	General notes
Canada		
Annex 2: steel	Coin minting; public utilities; architectural and engineering related to airfield, communications, and missile facilities; shipbuilding and repair and related engineering; all services, with reference to those goods purchased by the Department of National Defense, the Royal Canadian Mounted Police, and the Coast Guard; services procured in support of military forces located overseas; printing and publishing; transportation services; dredging; contracts tendered on behalf of the Department of Transport	Shipbuilding and repair; urban rail and transportation equipment, project-related materials of iron or steel; communications; detection and coherent radiation equipment; agricultural support programs; oil purchases related to strategic reserve requirements; support of safeguarding nuclear materials or technology
Hong Kong		
Annex 1: purchases of office or residential accommodation	Insurance and pension consulting; money broking; asset management; settlement and clearing services for financial assets; advisory and other auxiliary financial services; trading of financial instruments	Air mail; statutory insurance for vehicles and vessels and employer's liability insurance for employees

(continued)

Table 6-3. *(continued)*

Country/entities	Services and construction	General notes
Israel		
Annex 1: insulin and infusion pumps; audiometers; medical dressings; intravenous solution; Annex 3: cables; electromechanical meters; transformers; disconnectors and switchers; electric motors; telecommunications		Purchase of water and the supply of energy and fuels for the production of energy; acquisition of land and immovable property
Japan		
Annex 2: operational safety of transportation; electricity; Annex 3: operational safety of transportation and telecommunications; geological surveys; advertising, construction, and real estate services; vessels jointly owned with private companies; telecommunication equipment	Maintenance and repair for motor vehicles; courier services; four subcategories of architectural, engineering, and other technical services; printing services for confidential information	
Korea		
Annex 1: airports; Annex 2: urban transport; all entities: satellites		
United States		
For certain states: construction-grade steel; motor vehicles; coal; restrictions		

Table 6-3. *(continued)*

Country/entities	*Services and construction*	*General notes*
attached to federal funds for mass transit and highway projects		
EU-15		
Annexes 1 and 2: drinking water; energy; transport; telecommunications; Annex 3: purchase of water and fuel for the production of energy	Voice telephony, telex, radiotelephony paging, satellite services; financial services in connection with exchange of financial instruments, and central bank services; arbitration and conciliation services	Contracts awarded to an entity that is itself a contracting authority; agricultural support programs; acquisition of land and immovable property; acquisition, development, or production of program material for broadcasting; employment

service being supplied. This provision was introduced during the Uruguay Round renegotiation of the GPA to ensure that nondiscrimination applies to both trade and sales through establishment. This was particularly important for services providers, and many services are bought only from "local" suppliers.

Transparency

The GPA contains a large number of transparency provisions. For example, tendering procedures often involve a preselection of potential suppliers based on a prequalification process. This is permitted, but entities that use this procedure are required to maintain lists of qualified suppliers and publish these at least once a year in an agreed publication, specifying their validity and the conditions for the inclusion of suppliers, as well as the methods used to verify that requirements are met. All qualified suppliers must have the opportunity to bid. There are also publication requirements: procuring entities must publish calls for tender stating the mode of procurement, its nature and quantity, dates of delivery, economic and technical requirements, amounts and terms of payment, and so forth. Such requirements are intended to ensure that all potential bidders have access to the same information and that procuring entities have limited discretion in awarding contracts to favored suppliers.

Government Procurement of Services

Services are often the largest category of purchases made by governments, increasingly so in countries that rely on outsourcing and contracting strategies. In the United States, for example, most federal nondefense procurement comprises services.[2] In 1993 purchases by federal, state, and local authorities in the United States exceeded US$1.4 trillion, which is equivalent to some 20 percent of GDP. Of this amount, federal procurement was $445 billion, 68 percent of which was spent on defense (goods, services, and employee compensation). Of the remaining $141 billion, worker compensation accounted for 48 percent, leaving $73 billion. Most of this was used to procure services. Goods purchases accounted for only $14.4 billion, compared with $47 billion for non-wage-related services (table 6-4). At the state and local level the dominant category of expenditure (excluding wages) is structures (construction and maintenance activities). In contrast to central government purchases, those at lower levels consist more of goods than of services.

An increasing number of governments have been pursuing far-reaching efforts to improve the efficiency of public services by directly subjecting production units to competitive market forces. Some have privatized state-owned enterprises, encouraged entry into sectors traditionally reserved for public entities (such as utilities), and contracted out activities to the private sector. The efficiency gains associated with such policies can be significant.[3] Their influence on the size of procurement markets varies. On the one hand, privatization reduces the size of procurement, as by definition the purchases of inputs by privatized firms are no longer public. On the other hand, outsourcing increases the size of the services procurement market, as the activities of former public employees become "contestable." Virtually

---

2. Francois, Nelson, and Palmeter (1997).

3. Domberger, Hall, and Li (1995) survey the empirical literature on the price and quality effects of competitive tendering and conclude that savings on the order of 20 percent are common; and that these savings do not come at the expense of quality.

Table 6-4. *U.S. Government purchases, 1993*
Billions of U.S. dollars

Purchase	1993
Federal (nondefense)	140.9
Goods	14.4
Services	114.8
Compensation of employees	67.9
Other services	47.0
Structures	11.7
State and local government	704.7
Goods	99.5
Services	505.6
Compensation of employees	483.0
Other services	22.6
Structures	99.6

Source: Francois, Nelson, and Palmeter (1997).

all of the increase in procurement in such cases will lie in services, as the items "bought" are the services of private firms contracted to undertake activities that were previously done "in-house" by government employees.

At present comparable and disaggregated data on procurement of services are not available across countries. In particular, little is known about expenditures by subcentral offices of government or how much of what is procured could be subject to international competition, which depends on various factors: the type of services; the threshold applied to determine if competitive bidding will be required; the policy toward buying from non-nationals; whether small enterprises, minority-owned businesses, or other groups are favored; and so on. Many countries have legislation on the books allowing or calling for price or other preferences to be granted to national suppliers. In most cases, however, no data are available on the extent to which such provisions are enforced and are binding constraints, especially for local affiliates of foreign firms. Often, such firms are treated as "nationals," so that the effect of discrimination may be minimal as long as FDI is the preferred mode of supply. However, some governments may differentiate between locally established firms on the basis of ownership. That is why some GPA members endeavored to widen the reach of the national treatment principle during the Uruguay Round to cover establishment as a mode of supply.

Even less is known about developing country markets for services, except that they are likely to be smaller than those of high-income countries, not only in absolute size, but also in relation to purchases of goods. The thresholds embodied in the GPA are likely to be more binding in developing countries as the average contract will likely be smaller than in a high-income country. The provision of many services might require a local presence, which may be prohibited or restricted. Furthermore, most developing countries have much less in the way of national suppliers than industrialized nations, so the scope for discrimination in favor of domestic industries is more restricted.[4] It is also important to recognize that many expenditures by developing country governments are financed by official development assistance funds, both bilateral and multilateral. Official bilateral development aid is usually tied to procurement from the donor country and hence anything purchased with such funds cannot be subject to international competition.

Information on the importance of aid flows as a share of government expenditure suggests that aid finances a significant share of total purchases of goods and services by the governments of developing countries. The ratio of multilateral flows to expenditure is about 18 percent for low-income countries, while total aid (including bilateral aid) is equivalent to 35 percent of total expenditures on goods and services. For lower-middle-income nations, total aid accounts for 16 percent of expenditures; for upper-middle-income economies, the figure drops to 6 percent.[5] This suggests that for poor countries in particular, much procurement cannot be subjected to preferential policies, even if governments wanted to do so. This significantly reduces the potential benefits for foreign suppliers interested in selling services in these markets.

The Economic Consequences of Discrimination

The effects of discrimination cannot be adequately assessed without distinguishing between two aspects of procurement regimes: policy (whether it discriminates against foreign suppliers) and the implementation of policy. Even if a country has no formal mandate allowing discrimi-

---

4. In the 1980s, developing countries channeled one-quarter of total public investment into the power sector. In most cases, the associated capital equipment could not be procured domestically even if governments pursued discriminatory purchasing policies.

5. Hoekman (1998).

nation, its purchasing practices may be nontransparent, discretionary, and arbitrary. Such behavior can give rise to significant costs for the government insofar as it encourages corruption and rent-seeking. In the following discussion of the economics of discrimination, we assume that purchasing practices are "clean," so even if a nation "cleans up" those practices, explicit procurement discrimination will have the effects described here. The issue of transparency and corruption is discussed later.

Discrimination against foreign bidders may improve welfare if domestic firms are at a competitive disadvantage in producing the goods and services being procured (that is, domestic firms have higher production costs) and if only a limited number of firms bid for a contract. In such situations, foreign firms may exploit their cost advantage by bidding just below what they expect domestic firms to bid.[6] Even though the foreign firm will be the lowest bidder, the bid may be substantially above the firm's actual cost. A policy that gives preferences to domestic firms may then induce foreign firms to lower their bids by a fraction of the preference margin and increase national welfare. Discrimination may also be rational simply because foreign profits do not enter into domestic welfare, or because shifting demand to domestic firms contracts price-cost margins as output expands and so reduces the distortions created by the market power of the domestic firms.[7]

Although in certain situations discriminatory procurement policies can theoretically lower procurement costs, simulation studies suggest that the net welfare benefits are modest at best. Procurement favoritism will generate greater profits for domestic firms, but the cost savings for public entities tend to be meager, if nonexistent.[8] The net effect depends on how the government evaluates national welfare, specifically, the relative weight it puts on the domestic industry's profits as opposed to expected procurement costs. Furthermore, in most instances, the government will not have enough information (about all of the bidders' cost structures, among other things) to set the optimal preference policy, and miscalculations in this regard can result in substantial welfare losses. In sum, favoritism is likely to be more costly than a policy of nondiscrimination.

Procuring entities that have difficulty in enforcing or monitoring contract compliance may increase the likelihood of better performance

6. McAfee and McMillan (1989).
7. Branco (1994); Chen (1995).
8. Deltas and Evenett (1997).

through discrimination, as the excess profits to contractors may be necessary to get them to deliver.[9] In such cases, the required premium may increase as the number of potential bidders rises (because each supplier will take into account the higher probability of not getting repeat business) and thereby strengthen the rationale for discrimination.[10] If asymmetric information and monitoring costs also imply that governments will prefer to source from local firms, foreign firms will then have greater incentive to contest procurement markets through FDI.

The intangible nature of many services implies that asymmetries of information are likely to influence the nature of contracting by increasing the likelihood of de facto discrimination, as purchasers often use the implicit promise of a long-term relationship to induce suppliers to deliver high-quality services in a timely fashion. From a trade policy perspective, the issues are clear-cut: whether there are barriers to entry through FDI; and how entities decide whether suppliers are local "enough," through the rules of origin for legal persons. More generally, the effect of a government's procurement policies depends on competition policy.

The economic effects of procurement discrimination depend in large part on whether the products purchased are tradable. If a service is tradable (if it can be shipped across frontiers by telecommunications technologies), then in the short run the effect of discrimination depends on whether government demand initially exceeds domestic production of the service.[11] Because the service is tradable, it sells at the prevailing world price. And when markets are competitive, all firms selling the same service will have to charge that world price. Should the government suddenly decide not to buy from foreign service suppliers, this discriminatory policy will have no effect on prices, quantities imported, and national welfare. This is because every foreign producer who previously supplied the government will find a domestic consumer to sell to at world prices; while every domestic consumer (who was abandoned by the domestic firms that now supply the government) finds their needs met by foreign suppliers. And no domestic supplier can raise its selling price to the government because other domestic suppliers are willing to step in at the existing world price.

9. See Laffont and Tirole (1991); Rotemberg (1993).

10. See Breton and Salon (1995).

11. For a more detailed analysis of the effects of procurement discrimination, see Baldwin and Richardson (1972); Miyagiwa (1991); and Branco (1994). Evenett and Hoekman (1999) emphasize the importance of allowing for entry in response to procurement policies.

If government demand initially exceeds domestic supply, procurement discrimination will temporarily force the government to pay a higher price, cause a decline in its overall purchases, and give domestic service suppliers an incentive to increase their output. Domestic private sector consumers will be unaffected, as they can always source from abroad at the world price. When discrimination creates excess profits in the domestic industry, new firms will enter the domestic industry (and existing firms will expand their production facilities), expanding total domestic supply and forcing prices down until the excess profits are eliminated and the price charged to the government returns to the world price. Thus in the short run the welfare consequences of procurement discrimination depend on the relative size of government demand and domestic industry output. In the longer run they depend on the strength of a nation's competition policy, as reflected in the ease of entry. The message to policymakers is clear: if markets are contestable, then procurement discrimination in tradable services has no adverse permanent effects.

Since most services products are not tradable, one must examine the applicability of the above analysis. When trade is not feasible, a government's FDI policy stance, and more generally its competition and regulatory policies, become an important determinant of the effect of its discriminatory procurement policies, because establishment is a precondition for contesting the market. In evaluating policies that affect nontradable services, it is essential to recognize that there is no world price to pin down the analysis. National markets will be segmented, and prices will depend to a large extent on local factor costs and production technologies. In the long run, however, prices will be set at minimum average total costs since firms in competitive markets must make zero profits. Long-run prices will therefore be determined not by the "world" price, but by the cost functions of enterprises.

Many forms of procurement discrimination are possible in the procurement of services.[12] One of great interest is a ban on government purchases from subsidiaries of foreign firms that have established a local presence. Assume that both home and foreign-owned firms have access to the same local technology and confront the same factor prices. As in the case of tradable products, if government demand is initially less than the total supply of home firms, the imposition of a ban on purchasing from foreign firms merely reallocates customers, with each foreign affiliate able to find demand from the host country private sector to offset exactly the

12. Hoekman and Primo Braga (1997).

loss of sales to the government. The removal of the ban has no effect on equilibrium prices, the output of home firms, and national welfare.

Suppose, instead, that at the long-run equilibrium price (determined by the minimum cost of production) government demand exceeds the total supply of national firms, so that some foreign affiliates initially sell services to the government. A discriminatory procurement policy that bans sourcing from foreign affiliates then acts to segment the market: national firms supply the government at a price P^I, the price at which the government demand schedule intersects the supply schedule of home firms. This price is higher than C^*, the minimum cost of production, so the home firms are making positive profits (figure 6-1). The foreign subsidiaries can no longer supply the government market and are left supplying only the private sector. The price they receive drops significantly (to P^{II}), reflecting the fact that home private consumers are unwilling to buy all of the foreign subsidiaries' prediscrimination level of output at the initial price C^*. In the short run, a procurement ban would therefore introduce two consumption and two production distortions. In contrast to trade in goods, here the ban raises home consumers' welfare, as they benefit from the lower price that results from cutting foreign affiliates out of the government market.

This short-run equilibrium will not persist, as foreign firms are incurring losses (that is, P^{II} is below the minimum of their average total costs, C^*). As a result, some foreign-owned firms will exit. This pattern will continue until the price paid by home consumers rises again to C^*, the point at which foreign subsidiaries break even. As depicted in figure 6-1, this implies that the demand of home consumers returns to point D from point B. Home

Figure 6-1. *Short- and Long-Run Impact of Procurement Discrimination*

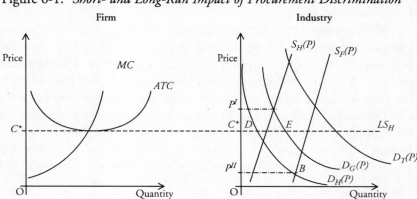

Table 6-5. *The Effect of a Procurement Ban on Foreign Subsidiaries*

		At initial prices (minimum cost of production, C^*)		
		$D_G > S_H$		
Variable	$D_G < S_H$	Short run and long run without entry or exit	Long run with exit only	Long run with entry and exit
Private sector price	0	−	0	0
Price for government	0	+	+	0
Home firm's output	0	+	+	+
Foreign firm's output	0	−	−	−
Domestic welfare	0	−	−	0

firms make positive profits at the short-run equilibrium price P^1, creating incentives for new domestic firms to enter the market. If entry is permitted, this will force down the price paid by the government until firms make zero profits (with price at C^* and government demand at point E). Thus in the long run the ban will tend to attract additional private sector resources into the industry and increase the number of domestic firms, while reducing the number of foreign firms. Free entry and exit eliminate the consumption and production distortions in the long run. Moreover, elimination of the discriminatory procurement ban has no effect on the equilibrium price and so cannot reverse the reduction in the number of foreign-owned affiliates. Table 6-5 summarizes the effects of procurement discrimination in services. It reinforces the importance of the relative size of government demand and the central role that the strength of a nation's competition regime plays in determining how discriminatory procurement policies that operate within rather than at the border will affect welfare in the long run. As table 6-3 makes clear, the long-run effect of a procurement ban on foreign subsidiaries depends greatly on the interaction of a nation's competition policy and its procurement policy, and not solely on the latter.

Policy Implications

Discriminatory procurement regimes for tradable services are unlikely to have permanent adverse effects on the economy. In many, if not most, situations, government demand will be too small to affect outcomes—in which case procurement discrimination need not be a concern, from either a national welfare or a market access perspective.

If the demand of government entities is larger than domestic supply—a situation that is likely to be more common in developing countries—the incentives for entry are particularly important. In the long run, entry is the mechanism by which the price distortions (created by the procurement policy) are eliminated. If entry is unimpeded, the costs of procurement favoritism to the economy are short-lived. Thus governments that pursue active competition policies to ensure markets are contestable will not experience the permanent damage that discriminatory procurement policies can cause. This will not necessarily benefit foreign firms excluded from procurement markets, since procurement favoritism can result in outcomes that are irreversible: the elimination of the policies may have no effect on equilibrium prices, welfare, or foreign sales.

Many of the services purchased by government entities are nontradable, because of technological factors or because economic forces favor procuring from local suppliers, as mentioned earlier. In such cases, procurement preferences will be binding only if foreign firms can contest the market through FDI and government entities are able to differentiate across firms on the basis of their "nationality." If these conditions are not satisfied, procurement regimes based on discrimination will be either redundant or unenforceable.[13]

If a liberal FDI policy stance is pursued, serious consideration must then be given to the rationale for procurement policies. If FDI is allowed, government discrimination against foreign affiliates will have the same effects as it does when products are tradable. The main difference is that if, in the short run government demand is "large," discrimination in procurement will increase the welfare of private sector consumers because they can then source at a lower price. This suggests that powerful political economy forces may favor procurement discrimination, since both domestic firms and consumers gain in the short run. As plants close, domestic labor employed in the foreign affiliates loses, but if the affiliates are taken over by domestic firms, the net employment loss should be zero (if production technologies are similar).[14] The procurement policy is akin to a nationalization or expropriation policy: foreign

---

13. Low, Mattoo, and Subramanian (1997).

14. This is not the case if the product is tradable. Again assuming government demand is large, a procurement ban can expand domestic industry and net employment in the long run.

firms have an incentive to sell out to local firms if sales to the government account for an important share of their revenues. One can thus expect significant opposition to the removal of the procurement policy in the short run, as domestic firms try to snap up foreign firms at fire sale prices.

Any government that actively discriminates against foreign affiliates in its procurement is unlikely to attract much FDI in the first place, unless government demand is small and the government market is therefore not an important target for the investor. If government demand is "large," a procurement ban will act as a de facto FDI barrier even where the FDI regime is open. This may come at a high cost if domestic service providers are less efficient than domestic incumbents, a situation ruled out in our analysis by the assumption that all firms have access to the same technologies.

Multilateral Disciplines and Transparency

Corruption and rent-seeking in public purchasing can be a major source of loss for the government budget and a major irritant in international trade relations. The amounts involved can be significant, and foreign interests may be directly affected. Case studies have demonstrated the cost of corruption to be high, with excess costs per project in the range of 25 to 50 percent.[15] This analysis of discrimination in procurement has focused on the market responses and abstracted from the issues of corruption and nontransparent procurement practices. In practice, of course, the transparency of the procurement process affects the efficiency of purchasing practices. The 1997 WTO ministerial meeting in Singapore established a working group on transparency in government procurement to study the issue and to explore the possible content of an agreement in this area. Such an agreement could have substantial benefits for all WTO members, whether or not a government pursues discriminatory procurement policies.

Putting aside national differences in cultural norms, effective anticorruption strategies must reduce the benefits that can be granted by officials, increase the costs of bribery for the private sector, and limit the market

15. Wade (1982); Rose-Ackerman (1995a).

power of officials.[16] To reduce the prevalence of nontransparent and arbitrary procurement, policymakers could create effective deterrents through ex post punishments that exceed the gains realized (for example, they could ban firms caught in attempts to engage in bribery from bidding for contracts for a number of years); establish external monitoring mechanisms and institutions (this could include encouraging and protecting "whistle-blowers"); introduce new methods to improve public transparency (such as published audits by independent auditors); privatize and impose hard budget constraints on state entities; require the use of standardized products or goods that have well-established market positions; use general retail or wholesale market prices for goods similar to those to be procured as comparators; and create incentives for losers from corruption to complain and seek recourse through the courts or specialized administrative tribunals and ombudsmen. Particularly important in the procurement context are "challenge procedures" of the type required by the GPA. These provide firms with an opportunity to protest before the final procurement decision is completed, as well as thereafter. Most of these are domestic mechanisms. However, multilateral monitoring and the threat of initiating the WTO's dispute settlement procedures can ensure that entities abide by whatever procedural transparency disciplines are agreed at the multilateral level.

Concluding Remarks

Procurement regimes for services, even if explicitly discriminating against foreign suppliers, are unlikely to have permanent repercussions for domestic or foreign welfare as long as the markets are contestable. The main objective for national policy should not be to seek separate multilateral disciplines on service procurement by WTO members through GATS, but to remove market access barriers. Especially important in this regard is the right of establishment (the ability to engage in FDI), as proximity is frequently required to supply services not only for technological reasons—the services being nontradable—but for good commercial reasons as buyers of services source from local firms to ensure, for example, contract compliance. As market access and national treatment commitments expand under GATS, there will be less need for multilateral rules on procurement. Market access is a precondition for foreign firms to contest

16. Rose-Ackerman (1995a, 1995b); Bardhan (1997).

procurement markets. If they are not permitted to gain access to the market—which in practice typically means establishing a commercial presence through FDI—procurement regimes and possible multilateral disciplines are irrelevant.

This is not to say there is no value in any multilateral disciplines on procurement. Disciplines that ensure that procurement mechanisms are more transparent will reduce the scope for corruption and rent-seeking. Even if procurement discrimination has little impact on the efficiency of resource allocation in the long run, corruption and rent-seeking that aim to influence the allocation of procurement contracts is costly. This dimension of procurement was only touched on here, principally because it is not sector-specific. Any procurement disciplines that relate to process and transparency should be applied across the board, for there is no compelling reason to treat procurement of services differently from procurement of goods. This provides another argument against efforts to include procurement disciplines under GATS. Instead, the focus should be on agreeing to a new set of stand-alone rules regarding transparency in procurement, as is being done in the WTO Working Group on Transparency in Government Procurement. In this area WTO members have got the economics right, by emphasizing not procurement policy (discrimination), but procurement practice.

References

Baldwin, Robert, and J. David Richardson. 1972. "Government Purchasing Policies, Other NTBs, and the International Monetary Crisis." In *Obstacles to Trade in the Pacific Area*, edited by H. English and K. Hay. Ottawa: Carleton School of International Affairs.

Bardhan, Pranab. 1997. "Corruption and Development: A Review of Issues." *Journal of Economic Literature* 35: 1320–46.

Branco, Fernando. 1994. "Favoring Domestic Firms in Procurement Contracts." *Journal of International Economics* 37: 65–80.

Breton, Albert, and Pierre Salmon. 1995. "Are Discriminatory Procurement Policies Motivated by Protectionism?" *Kyklos* 49: 47–68.

Chen, Xiangqun. 1995. "Directing Government Procurement as an Incentive of Production." *Journal of Economic Integration* 10: 130–40.

Deltas, George, and Simon J. Evenett. 1997. "Quantitative Estimates of the Effects of Preference Policies." In *Law and Policy in Public Purchasing: The WTO Agreement on Government Procurement*, edited by Bernard M. Hoekman and Petros C. Mavroidis. University of Michigan Press.

Domberger, Simon, Christine Hall, and Eric Ah Lik Lee. 1995. "The Determinants of Price and Quality in Competitively Tendered Contracts." *Economic Journal* 105: 1454–70.

Evenett, Simon J., and Bernard M. Hoekman. 1999. "Government Procurement: How Does Discrimination Matter?" Washington, D.C.: World Bank. Photocopy.

Francois, Joseph, Douglas Nelson, and David Palmeter. 1997. "Government Procurement in the U.S.: A Post-Uruguay Round Analysis." In *Law and Policy in Public Purchasing: The WTO Agreement on Government Procurement,* edited by Bernard M. Hoekman and Petros C. Mavroidis. University of Michigan Press.

Hoekman, Bernard M. 1998. "Using International Institutions to Improve Public Procurement." *World Bank Research Observer* 13: 249–69.

Hoekman, Bernard M., and Carlos Primo Braga. 1997. "Protection and Trade in Services: A Survey." *Open Economies Review* 8: 285–308.

Hoekman, Bernard M., and Petros C. Mavroidis, eds. 1997. *Law and Policy in Public Purchasing: The WTO Agreement on Government Procurement.* University of Michigan Press.

Laffont, J. J., and Jean Tirole. 1991. "Auction Design and Favoritism." *International Journal of Industrial Organization* 9: 9–42.

Low, Patrick, Aaditya Mattoo, and Arvind Subramanian. 1997. "Government Procurement in Services." In *Law and Policy in Public Purchasing: The WTO Agreement on Government Procurement,* edited by Bernard M. Hoekman and Petros C. Mavroidis. University of Michigan Press.

McAfee, R. Preston, and John McMillan. 1989. "Government Procurement and International Trade." *Journal of International Economics* 26: 291–308.

Miyagiwa, Kaz. 1991. "Oligopoly and Discriminatory Government Procurement Policy." *American Economic Review* 81: 1320–28.

Rose-Ackerman, Susan. 1995a. "The Political Economy of Corruption." *Viewpoint,* no. 74. Washington, D.C.: World Bank (April).

————. 1995b. "Redesigning the State to Fight Corruption." *Viewpoint,* no. 75. Washington, D.C.: World Bank.

Rotemberg, Julio. 1993. "Comment." In *Incentives in Procurement Contracting,* edited by Jim Leitzel and Jean Tirole. Boulder, Colo.: Westview Press.

Wade, Robert. 1982. "The System of Administrative and Political Corruption: Canal Irrigation in South India." *Journal of Development Studies* 18: 287–327.

7 Déjà Vu, or New Beginning for Safeguards and Subsidies Rules in Services Trade?

GILLES GAUTHIER, *with*
ERIN O'BRIEN *and* SUSAN SPENCER

SAFEGUARDS AND SUBSIDY DISCIPLINES have a long history in trade in goods.[1] Present since the inception of the General Agreement on Tariffs and Trade (GATT) in 1947, they have now developed into full-blown mechanisms governed by distinct sets of rights and obligations, set out in Annex 1A of GATT 1994. In services trade, the question of whether to include in the General Agreement on Trade in Services (GATS) a safeguard mechanism and subsidy disciplines was on the agenda of the Uruguay Round services negotiations. However, negotiators reached no consensus on whether to develop such rules. But they did agree to explicitly provide for future work, that is, to negotiate on the question of emergency safeguard measures, the results of which would enter into force no later than three years after the World Trade Organization (WTO) agreement itself was to enter into force (GATS Article X); and to develop multilateral disciplines on subsidies to avoid

The views expressed in this essay are those of the authors and should not be attributed to the government of Canada. Many thanks to Malcolm Bosworth for his helpful comments, as well as to participants to the Preparatory Conference Services 2000: New Directions in Services Trade Liberalization, held on June 1–2, 1999.

1. The third element of what is called trade remedies, the antidumping measure, is not addressed here since questions about it have not arisen in the services debate.

their distortive effects on trade in services (Article XV). To date, neither mandate has been fulfilled.

This chapter examines the desirability, feasibility, and prospects for developing multilateral rules on an emergency safeguard mechanism and trade-distorting subsidies, in the context of the upcoming Services 2000 negotiations. Using the existing framework of trade in goods as a model, we evaluate whether, and how, relevant GATT principles might be applicable in these two areas in the context of services trade. The discussion is directed primarily at trade policy practitioners. As such, it focuses not only on the desirability, feasibility, and negotiability of such rules but also on whether new rules would help to deepen and broaden the liberalization objectives of GATS.

Safeguards

Since trade agreements are legally enforceable instruments, terminology is important. Authorities, and ultimately traders, must know what the rules are, how they can be invoked, and what purposes they will serve.

Defining Safeguard Measures

The term "safeguard" can be used to describe various "escape clauses" that can be invoked for different circumstances. In its broadest sense, it can refer to provisions that permit measures to be "safeguarded" from the application of the obligations of the agreement. General exceptions, such as those found in GATT Article XX, GATS Article XIV, and the national security provisions, are examples. The term "safeguard" can also refer to the ability to change or modify a commitment. Article XXI of GATS and Article XXVIII of GATT contain such a mechanism: it provides a safety valve for a government that decides, for one reason or another, to withdraw a concession, subject to the requirement that it make compensatory adjustments in return. Both GATS and GATT also provide for the temporary imposition of restrictions on trade to "safeguard" against a serious deterioration of the country's balance of payments situation.

For the purposes of this discussion, and in the language most commonly used, "safeguards" refer to a mechanism that can be invoked by governments, under specified conditions, to impose or increase protection in order to relieve temporarily difficulties or pressures that have arisen as a result of commitments and obligations undertaken in trade agreements. The main features of a temporary safeguard are that it targets a specific product or industry, it is applied on a most favored nation (MFN) basis, it is of limited duration, it is sometimes progressively liberalized over the period of its application and, in some cases, it is subject to demands for compensation from other members affected by the measure. In most cases, this type of measure is invoked when increased imports resulting from the liberalization are causing or threatening to cause "injury" to domestic producers of the like or directly competitive product. Examples of this type of safeguard can be found in GATT Article XIX (Agreement on Safeguards), Article 5 of the Agreement on Agriculture, and Article 6 of the Agreement on Textiles and Clothing, as well as in numerous regional trade agreements, including the North American Free Trade Agreement and most European Union Association agreements.

In the context of future GATS negotiations regarding an emergency safeguard measure (ESM), it would, as a starting point, appear appropriate to use a definition that resembles most closely this latter category, that is, an emergency mechanism offering temporary protection to a domestic industry adversely affected by liberalization. The other types of measures that can be associated with the notion of a safeguard—general exceptions, renegotiations of commitments, balance of payments, to which one can probably add prudential measures—while relevant from an overall policy standpoint, are not suited to dealing with the same sort of circumstances.[2] Although they are clearly not substitutable for an ESM, their role and function still provide useful guideposts to circumscribe the scope of an eventual ESM. In other words, policymakers must remember that these other instruments do exist and that any such ESM should not apply to circumstances already contemplated by existing provisions.

The Economic Case for Safeguards

The emergency safeguard measure originated in response to the perceived need for some form of safety valve in the event that liberalization created unforeseen problems in trade agreements. Protection of the domestic industry has been an explicit objective. One purpose of the ESM was to help persuade domestic constituencies (as well as trading partners) to

2. Messerlin (1997).

accept greater liberalization. Another was to give domestic industries breathing room to adjust to new competitive realities.

However, the usefulness of such measures in securing greater liberalization and facilitating adjustment is difficult to verify empirically. Few examples come to mind of instances in which successful liberalization has been directly associated with a safeguard provision. In agreeing to the level of liberalization, negotiators tend to attach far greater importance to the perceived degree of sensitivity of the industry or sector than to the availability of a safeguard clause. Moreover, the safeguard is directed at "unforeseen" consequences, whereas negotiators assess risk on the basis of how particular sectors would cope in the face of increased foreign competition.

While the availability of a safeguard measure might not in itself secure greater liberalization, it might help temper opposition to liberalization and thus serve a political economy purpose. As in any negotiated package, the key test is whether the result is balanced and takes into account both the export and import interests at play. One might argue that the availability of the safeguard ensures that "defensive" interests will be taken into account. That is why safeguard measures are common features of trade agreements; that is, they bring a certain political value to the liberalization process as a whole, even though the presence of safeguards may not have a decisive impact on the magnitude of a commitment on a sector-by-sector basis.

The argument regarding adjustment is not very compelling. Research suggests that protection devices such as safeguards carry economic costs. Safeguard actions tend to increase prices and impose additional costs on consumers that outweigh the benefits to the recipient industry, and this produces a net welfare loss.[3] At the microeconomic level, there is little empirical evidence to show that domestic industry actually does take the appropriate steps to "adjust" to conditions of competition when given the opportunity during the application of a safeguard measure. In short, the safeguard can be useful to temporarily appease domestic concerns, but it is no panacea for substantial adjustment.

In the case of services, WTO members have not yet been able to identify the precise circumstances in which an ESM might be used. Indeed, the discussions have by and large been in the abstract. This may be symptomatic of the overall context in which they are taking place. First, no one wants to act as a "demandeur" in the early days of a discussion that

3. See Baldwin (1992).

may lead to negotiations since the price for achieving one's goal might well become inflated. Second, GATS is still in its early days of existence. Actual liberalization has been modest, with the vast majority of bindings reflecting current status (if not less), and minimizing the scope for the "unforeseen" scenario. Moreover, in view of the positive listing of commitments, negotiators always have the option of not making a commitment. Third, it may be that the international trade dimension of many service sectors is only beginning to gain attention. Long considered nontradable or subject to a rigorous domestic regulatory framework, many services industries are just now being exposed to the dynamism of international competition. Hence a paradigm to assess the impact of this openness is not yet fully developed.

An ESM in services trade would not be without its economic consequences. In goods trade, such a safeguard would limit the access to services from foreign suppliers and would generally maintain higher prices than would be dictated by open competition. Since many services play an important role in the structure of the economy, restricting their supply might have adverse effects on the performance of the economy as a whole. In fact, the effects could be dramatic, considering that a proportion of the productivity gains of recent years can be attributed in part to the declining costs of telecommunication and transport, greater sophistication of financial products, improvements in distribution systems. The lessons from trade in goods cannot be ignored: a safeguard action can protect the relevant domestic industry but can also impose additional costs on others and on the economy as a whole.

Applying GATT Safeguards to Trade in Services

Looking at GATT Article XIX as a possible template for services, one must recognize that the concept of "unforeseen" developments, though incorporated there, is not replicated in the Uruguay Round Agreement on Safeguards. Rather, the negotiators of the Agreement on Safeguards wanted more precise tests to govern the application of a safeguard action. The Agreement on Safeguards imposes a two-part test: the imports must have increased in absolute quantities or in relation to domestic production (implicit here is the notion of a surge in imports or import shares); and the imports must cause serious injury to a domestic industry producing like or directly competitive goods.

However, the concept of "imports" is not entirely clear in the services context. The picture is complicated by the fact that a service may be delivered in one of four modes.[4] Thus one of the first steps in attempting to apply an Article XIX mechanism to services would be to decide whether such a mechanism could be designed to apply to "typical" import situations (that is, cross-border trade) and whether it could (or should) apply to situations in which services are supplied through one of the other modes of delivery.

Mode 1, cross-border trade, does not pose particular conceptual difficulties because there is an "import" in the traditional sense, and the limitation on trade can take the form of constraining the sale of foreign service suppliers in the importing country. For mode 2, the "import" transaction takes place in the exporter's market. Instead of the supplier, it is the customer who crosses the border to consume the service abroad. Any limitation on services trade would mean limiting the ability of the customer—as opposed to the supplier—to go abroad to consume a service. In mode 3, the situation is even more complex since the transaction involves the establishment of the service supplier in the importing country. Thus the "importation" issue has two dimensions: it concerns the right to establish, as well as the sales of the established foreign supplier. The former may be dealt with via a limitation on foreign investment, but the latter could not, conceptually, be considered "imports." In the case of mode 4, which entails the movement of persons, the concept of imports appears rather incongruous.[5] Nonetheless certain issues—such as those relating to the repatriation of salaries—could be considered "import" transactions.

Since the traditional purpose of an ESM is to provide short-term protection to the domestic industry, the right to bring a complaint should fall to the "domestic industry." In the services context, the domestic industry could be composed of domestic service suppliers or foreign service suppliers that have established a commercial presence. In this case, the question is whether the term "domestic industry" should include all service suppliers located within the territorial limits of a country, or whether the locally established service suppliers of foreign companies should be excluded. If locally established foreign service suppliers are excluded, then one must consider the ramifications of classifying their services as "imports" and thereby possibly making them subject to whatever safeguard measure is imposed. In addi-

---

4. GATS, Article I. The four modes are cross-border trade, consumption abroad, commercial presence, and movement of persons.

5. One could argue, however, that the use of an economic need test represents a form of safeguard measure since it directly relates to the capacity of the host country to absorb the additional entry of foreign personnel.

tion, the exclusion of foreign suppliers established in the domestic market raises the obvious problem of national treatment.

The next problem to sort out is what constitutes "like or directly competitive services." The very nature of services trade makes this determination somewhat more tenuous since so much of what is delivered as a service is custom-tailored to meet the needs of the consumer of the service. In addition, the intangible nature of service provision creates difficulties in trying to compare a foreign service with a domestic service. Moreover, the concept of "like or directly competitive" would be made considerably more complicated if one had to determine whether a service supplied across borders was similar to one supplied through one of the other modes of supply.

It is clearly essential to establish what constitutes the "domestic industry" and the "like service," for only then can one determine if imports may be causally linked to whatever injury is suffered by that domestic industry. The determination of injury in itself poses a challenge: how to establish causality. Another question that must be answered is whether there has been a "surge" in imports of the like or directly competitive product. The well-known statistical deficiencies in the services sectors could make it difficult to gather sufficient information in a timely manner to resolve the question of surges in imports, and of the injury that has been suffered.

Any measure is useful only to the extent that it is administratively sound and enforceable. There may be serious challenges here. For instance, how would a safeguard measure apply to a large part of the trade in services that takes place electronically across borders under modes 1 and 2? How does one deal with the growing importance of electronic commerce in services trade? How would a measure deal with established firms under mode 3, where "border"-related transactions do not occur?

These are a few of the questions that are bound to arise in applying a safeguard such as Article XIX to the services context. They suggest that an ESM modeled on trade in goods would pose significant conceptual and practical problems for trade in services. If an ESM is to be negotiated, a new approach would be needed to better reflect the intricacies of GATS (particularly the modes of supply), more appropriately relate to the conditions of competition in services trade, and better balance the various interests at play.

An Alternative ESM for Services Trade

Although the case for a safeguard remains ambiguous, the question of an ESM is expected to be on the agenda for the next round of negotiations.

During their deliberations, negotiators should aim at establishing some general criteria for determining when an EMS would be applicable to services trade.

First, they should clearly articulate the types of circumstances for which a safety valve is not already provided. To date, the only such circumstances that appear relevant are those characterized as "unforeseen problems caused by liberalization commitments." It will be incumbent upon countries wanting an ESM to argue the case, and in particular to propose objective tests that can be used to identify such circumstances, especially in light of the difficulties that are associated with concepts such as "imports," "like services," and "like service providers." It can be safely predicted, however, that those countries that do not believe an ESM is warranted, feasible, or desirable will seek a negotiating quid pro quo. In short, the discussion over the question of an ESM will be linked to the discussion of increased liberalization commitments. This does not necessarily mean that an eventual ESM could apply only to new liberalization commitments. Rather, this should be viewed in the aggregate and as a negotiated outcome, whereby the introduction of an ESM is considered in conjunction with further liberalization, which remains the paramount objective for the so-called GATS 2000 negotiations, as mandated in GATS Article XIX.

Second, it will be important to find the appropriate balance between an ESM that purports to address the genuine concerns of countries that have yet to schedule a significant amount of liberalization commitments across their services sectors and an ESM that could be open to abuses and become the instrument of protection of choice.

Third, attention must be given to the potential negative economic effects of an ESM on both domestic and foreign service suppliers. Accordingly, the creation and subsequent use of an ESM should be based on the condition that it is used only for the purpose of permitting the domestic service supplier the time to adjust to new competitive conditions. That is to say, the application of an ESM should be time-bound and perhaps (if feasible) should be liberalized progressively over the period of its application.

The issue of when to apply the MFN criterion will need to be addressed as well. However, this may not be as simple as it sounds given that it might be necessary to take into account the differences in the mode of supply. The issue of regional integration may also come up in this context.

In the matter of implementation, the main concern is whether the ESM should apply indiscriminately to the four modes of delivery. If

GATS were to move away from a universal application of the ESM (that is, coverage of all four modes at once), a question could arise as to the effectiveness and equity of applying the measure. At this point, it is not clear how equitable such a measure would be in view of the lack of uniformity among sectors covered in member countries and the potential for an uneven impact on differing methods of delivery. Moreover, one could argue that applying the ESM to one mode only is inequitable because it would unreasonably penalize service providers that conduct their business in one mode versus those who are diversified and conduct (or have the capacity to conduct) their business through a variety of modes of supply. This may well penalize certain trading partners more than others and raise de facto discriminatory concerns. In addition, an ESM applied to one mode could lose some of its effectiveness, as it might lead businesses to divert supply to another mode, to avoid the ESM restrictions.

The most problematic aspect of applying an ESM relates to mode 3, commercial presence. Several considerations arise here. First, the rule would have to specify whether the safeguard could permit a clawback on existing investment; in other words, it would have to provide for the divestiture of existing investment made by the foreign service supplier. From an economic and policy standpoint, there is little justification for getting into this scenario. Not only does the foreign establishment generate genuine domestic economic activity, but it is hard to imagine that its divestiture will help domestic suppliers eventually adjust to a new, more open, competitive environment. Second, such a move would have serious consequences for the attractiveness of a country's foreign investment regime. In a world of stiff competition for attracting investment, it is not clear that a country would find divestiture to be in its economic interest. Third, a very large number of WTO members are parties to foreign investment agreements providing for rules against forced divestiture and exposing governments to compensation claims. Would it not be simpler (and more efficient) to use government funds to assist in the adjustment of "domestic" firms in the market instead of buying off a foreign competitor? Fourth, in today's increasingly global environment, it is often difficult to deal with the "who is us" phenomenon, that is, to differentiate domestic from foreign entities.

Assuming that forced divestiture is ruled out, the issue then becomes whether mode 3 should be covered in any event, even when the primary concern is cross-border trade. The problem here becomes the interplay between modes 1 and 3. It is not hard to imagine a situation in which an ESM applied across borders would simply entice the foreign supplier to jump the barrier by establishing itself in the importing market. Does it make sense from a trade policy perspective for a protection device such as an ESM to be used to spur foreign investment? Examples of such concerns have sometimes been raised in trade remedy for goods, notably with respect to anticircumvention rules in the European Community. The fact that commercial presence—and thus investment—is itself a commitment under GATS would make this scenario even more questionable from an overall trade policy standpoint. At first glance, there would thus appear to be a strong case for ensuring that an ESM covers mode 3, at least to avoid introducing an investment distortion. Perhaps a "freeze" on new commercial presence by foreign suppliers in the relevant services industry would be an adequate mechanism in this context.

It may well be that if an ESM were created, provision would probably have to be made for both cross- and single-modal types. The single-modal type would have the advantage of being capable of tailoring to a specific problem and could provide a means by which the application of the ESM would be limited to the least restrictive form. This two-level notion of how an ESM might operate would certainly have to rely on the creation of a procedure whereby designated authorities within a member country would review the facts of the allegations of problems made by domestic services suppliers and determine whether a cross-modal or single-modal ESM would be appropriate. In short, transparency (notification and reporting) obligations would have to be well defined.

A Possible Model

The foregoing discussion suggests the rudimentary elements that should be considered in contemplating an ESM for the services context. First it should not duplicate other "safeguard" features of GATS, particularly the positive approach to scheduling commitments in Article XXI (modification of schedule of commitments), the provisions related to prudential measures, or the balance of payments and general exceptions. Second, a temporary safeguard modeled on GATT Article XIX would be difficult to transpose to a services context. Third, negotiators should keep in mind the economics of trade remedy protection, to avoid defeating the purpose of liberalization. Fourth, some basic criteria should be applied in considering an eventual ESM, notably its link to adjustment and liberalization, and to the MFN principle. Finally, it is essential to account for the diverse nature of the services industry and its four modes of delivery.

These considerations suggest that a generic safeguard clause is not worth pursuing. There are too many technical and policy hurdles to justify following that path. How, then, can there still be useful discussion on this question? Perhaps the most logical alternative is to shift the focus to the manner in which commitments are scheduled. Indeed, should an ESM be contemplated for services, the schedules of commitments may provide the only workable structure in which it could operate. This could be done line by line or at the sectoral level, depending on knowledge of the structure, and the conduct and competitive features of that market. If a country wished to invoke a safeguard, it would need to inscribe it in its schedule of commitments pertaining to a particular sector or category.

In addition, it would need to take certain steps to ensure that the ESM is adequately circumscribed: liberalization could be delayed only temporarily (that is, no permanent backtracking would be possible); EMS would be a one-time measure only, of limited (defined, short-period) duration, and would perhaps include progressive liberalization; it would be triggered only by nondiscretionary, objective events, based on statistical results (transparent domestic procedures); appropriate notification and reporting obligations (modeled on Article 12 of the Agreement on Safeguards) would be required; it would be applied on an MFN basis; it would apply to specific sectors and modes of supply; for mode 3, there would be no right to seek divestiture.

The issue of compensation would also need to be addressed. The right to seek compensation is an important principle to observe to ensure that the negotiated outcome remains balanced. It can also be a useful tool in resisting requests for protection that would not be fully substantiated. However, this issue may be linked to the extent of use and duration of the application of an ESM. One would also have to deal with possible measurement difficulties.

Would this type of proposal be attractive in today's negotiating context? The answer to this question remains unclear. It is generally believed that the "demandeurs" will push for a more general approach not directly tied to specific commitments, so as to gain broader discretion and flexibility. In particular, they may press for something that could provide for the complete removal of commitments from a schedule. Such a tactic might be considered unacceptable, however, since this is not a situation warranting an ESM, but rather a policy decision about withdrawing a concession and would be more appropriately dealt with through Article XXI.

The broader context of GATS 2000 may provide a different negotiating dynamic. At present, GATS has no safeguard provision. A new provision that would allow a country to "temporarily" suspend its commitments owing to unforeseen circumstances in accordance with the modalities described earlier would be a major development. No doubt, it will likely continue to be strongly resisted by many WTO members. For these countries, an ESM is not likely to be negotiable unless there is sufficient progress on liberalization.

As in any negotiation, one needs to look at the "reservation price," that which each party to the negotiation is prepared to pay for getting a deal. This will only be revealed through the negotiation itself. There may well be halfway points, for instance, for looking at phase-in commitments, with a possible interruption in establishing new commitments in case of unforeseen circumstances.

Subsidies

To date, the issue of subsidies has attracted far less attention than safeguards in the discussions of the GATS Working Party. Hence it is not clear that there would be any interest in pursuing the issue in the context of GATS 2000.

Article XV of GATS states that "subsidies may have distorting effects on trade in services," which implies that subsidies exist and that some, although not all, forms of subsidies may have trade-distorting effects. No comprehensive information is available on the existence or impact of subsidies in services trade. However, anecdotal evidence indicates that in certain countries sectors such as transportation, audiovisual, tourism, and financial services have benefited from some form of subsidization. The challenge, then, is to show not only whether trade-distorting subsidies do exist but how they could be identified, measured, and, if necessary, disciplined under GATS. This is a tall order given the lack of information, the inherent difficulty in measuring trade in services, and the special characteristics of services trade, notably the modes of delivery. The following discussion is largely conceptual, raising questions that will need to be considered before a conclusion can be reached on further disciplines.

To begin, one needs to define a subsidy, since this is not done in GATS. For present purposes, one can borrow the GATT definition, which states that a subsidy is a financial contribution by a government that confers a benefit to the recipient. Trade-distorting subsidies might include export subsidies, import-displacement subsidies, and production subsidies that materially affect the price and quantity available for export. In addition, subsidies to goods producers may have indirect or downstream effect on services trade.

Existing GATS Disciplines on Subsidies

The existing GATS is not bereft of provisions applying to subsidies. Specifically, subsidies are considered "measures" within GATS, and thus the obligations of MFN and national treatment are applicable. The MFN clause in Article II forbids discrimination between foreign services and service suppliers originating in different GATS member countries. It is a horizontal obligation, applicable to all measures affecting trade in services, in all sectors and modes of delivery. MFN obligations are particularly relevant to the subsidy issue when there is no domestic service supplier. In such a case, a member is not allowed to discriminate between the service suppliers of other members.

National treatment applies to subsidies to the extent that the sector has been listed in the schedule of commitments. National treatment can be a strong discipline on the use of subsidies as it requires governments providing subsidies to domestic services suppliers to make equivalent subsidies available to foreign service providers operating in the country. However, the majority of members have included limitations to national treatment that apply to all subsidy practices. Others have done so with respect to specific modes and specific sectors. A point still being debated is whether the national treatment obligation extends across all modes of supply, or whether members retain the freedom to discriminate between identical services delivered via different modes on the grounds that the suppliers are not "like suppliers." Another point at issue is how the national treatment obligation would apply to "one-off" subsidies and how the concept of "like service supplier" would be interpreted.

GATS articles also cover domestic regulations (Article VI) and monopoly behavior (Article VIII). Services industries tend to be characterized by a higher degree of government ownership, regulation, and intervention compared with goods-producing sectors. Government regulation and monopoly concessions tend to create large, highly competitive service providers who can extend into foreign markets from a highly protected home base. In such circumstances, particular government regulations may have a similar effect as a trade-distorting subsidy: they may drive prices downward in the foreign market. GATS contains a provision on monopolies and business practices that may be relevant to these circumstances.

As trade in services continues to increase, the pressure may build for a more comprehensive set of disciplines to deal with trade-distorting subsidies. Current GATS provisions, including MFN and national treatment obligations, may not be sufficient and may prompt negotiators to consider developing disciplines that would be appropriate to services trade. In this regard, it may be instructive to look at the disciplines in the WTO Agreement on Subsidies and Countervailing Measures (SCM).

Agreement on Subsidies and Countervailing Measures as a Model

The Uruguay Round achieved notable improvements in the area of subsidy disciplines. For instance, the SCM agreement provides a definition of the term "subsidy," expands the list of prohibited practices, strengthens disciplines regarding domestic subsidies, and improves and clarifies the rules concerning the application of countervailing duties.

The SCM agreement (Part 1, Article 1) defines a subsidy as "a financial contribution by a government or any public body within the territory of a Member" that also confers a benefit to the recipient. This definition includes financial contributions provided by any government body or agency, subfederal governments, or even a private firm acting on behalf of a government. The definition also contains an exhaustive list of practices that constitute financial contributions (see SCM, Annex 1).

In the services context, one might ask whether a broader definition is needed, one that would also take into account the subsidy-like effects of regulatory interventions, for instance. An all-encompassing definition might turn into an unwieldy instrument that could be subject to abuse. The trade effects of a direct subsidy would be difficult enough to determine as it is, without trying to calculate the financial costs and benefits bestowed by regulations. Also, the adverse effects of regulatory barriers could presumably be dealt with more appropriately under the auspices of Articles VI and VIII. As a result, the current SCM definition may provide a workable basis for services.

Another main feature of the SCM agreement is its "traffic light" approach to classifying subsidies. Green light subsidies are nonactionable, red light subsidies are prohibited, and amber light subsidies are actionable only if it can be proven that adverse trade effects have resulted from the government assistance.

Green light subsidies encompass four types of activities: generally available subsidies (that is, subsidies not specific within the meaning of the SCM agreement), research and precompetitive development activities (R&D), regional development aid, and certain environmental subsidies (that is, assistance to enable existing plants meet new environmental requirements). Interestingly, these activities can constitute services in their own right. If governments felt it necessary to protect them in the goods context, would the same reasoning be valid for services?

In addition, it might be necessary to examine the possible ramifications for social services (education, health, and pension systems). In principle, subsidies to these types of activities should not be an issue because the services are delivered to "individuals" and not to "producers." However, this may not necessarily be the case in services trade as the person receiving these subsidies may be the producer of a service. Moreover, some of these social sectors represent tradable services, already listed in the schedules of some countries. This would no doubt be a sensitive issue in many jurisdictions and greatly complicate the task of developing acceptable subsidy disciplines.

The SCM agreement prohibits export subsidies and import substitution subsidies. Before this can be transposed to the services trade, however, it is essential to examine what it would mean to each mode of supply. For mode 1, or cross-border delivery of services, the situation is roughly comparable to trade in goods, and theoretically the same prohibition would probably be applicable.

For mode 2, the scenario is reversed, because the consumer travels to the supplier's territory to consume the service. How might an export subsidy be applicable? A domestic producer (of a like service) would have to claim that a foreign service provider received government assistance conditional on attracting a purchaser from the domestic country to consume the service abroad. Is this realistic? For instance, would a subsidy granted by a government to a local tourism authority to build large resort hotels to attract foreign tourists constitute a prohibited subsidy? How is this situation different from the subsidization of an aircraft repair facility that services foreign aircraft companies?

The concept of an export subsidy also becomes quite confusing in terms of mode 3 service delivery, commercial presence. A domestic government is unlikely to provide a subsidy to a firm that is considering relocating or establishing a commercial presence in another jurisdiction. No export subsidy as such exists in this scenario. On the other hand, investment incentives offered by host countries to attract investment from abroad may be a problem. Should the country with the most attractive package be brought before the WTO on charges of providing "unfair" subsidies? Countries often justify investment incentives as a form of economic development assistance even though the trade implications of their actions can be apparent. When are investment incentives trade distorting and when are they legitimate for public policy reasons as recognized by GATS Article XV?

For mode 4, one is hard pressed to think of credible examples of export subsidies that affect the movement of natural persons. Is it realistic for governments to provide a subsidy for persons leaving the country? The importing country would be more likely to provide a subsidy to attract skilled workers to their territory. Owing to the shortage of skilled computer engineers, for example, a government may offer financial incentives (that is, subsidized travel rates) for foreign skilled workers to locate within its territory. The situation is thus similar to the one under mode 3 and the phenomenon of investment or location incentives.

These examples illustrate the complexity of developing guidelines to discipline what is, at first glance, the most obvious form of trade-distorting subsidies. The same is to be expected regarding the treatment of actionable subsidies under the SCM agreement, which does not contain an explicit definition of an "actionable" subsidy. These forms of specific subsidies are subject to remedial action if it is proven that the interests of other members have been adversely affected. Adverse effects include injury to the domestic industry of an importing country; nullification or impairment of GATT benefits; and "serious prejudice" to the interests of another member.

The determination of injury caused by the subsidization is an essential step in the application of countervailing duties. Several problems would arise in attempting to replicate this procedure in the GATS context. To begin with, countervail clearly does not work for modes 2 through 4 because the traditional notion of imports does not apply. For mode 1, implementation would be problematic because of the difficulties associated with measuring and observing trade data, defining "like services" and "like domestic services providers," and enforcing the ruling, especially in the realm of electronic delivery. These problems, which are essentially the same as those raised in the context of safeguard measures, would also be compounded by the difficulty of measuring the degree of subsidization to be countervailed. Given the intangible nature of a service, how would one be able to calculate a "per unit subsidization rate"?[6]

Many of the same difficulties would probably be present in attempting to apply a serious prejudice test to services trade. However, the serious prejudice provision also contains specific tests of total ad valorem subsidization that might be relevant in a service context. Under the SCM agreement, serious prejudice is deemed to exist when the overall rate of subsidization exceeds 15 percent of the total funds invested in a new start-up operation. In a sense, this resembles closely a plausible scenario under mode 3, whereby the subsidization is given to entice the establishment of a commercial presence by a service provider.

In short, some elements of the SCM agreement would appear relevant to a consideration of subsidy disciplines in services trade. The definition of subsidies would offer a starting point, and the traffic light approach would offer a possible structure to work from, although adjustments would be needed to reflect the particular nature of services trade, especially its modes of delivery. However, a countervailing duty mechanism would be very difficult, if not undesirable.

A Possible Way Forward

Before embarking upon the creation of disciplines, it is essential to reflect further on the basic question of whether trade-distorting subsidies are sufficiently pervasive and troublesome in services trade to warrant making special rules. A general transparency provision might represent a useful starting point. In addition, it is important to note that the SCM agreement already provides scope for remedial action against unfair subsidization of services incorporated in trade in goods. It may be that some of the potential concerns about trade-distorting subsidization in services are already taken care of by existing rules on goods.

Perhaps the two issues that require the most attention, although it is yet unclear in a negotiating context, are prohibitions on export subsidies

---

6. Another debatable issue is whether it would be advisable to even contemplate a countervailing duty mechanism for services trade. Countervail implies the use of a unilateral remedy to try to resolve what is inherently a bilateral or multilateral issue: at least two governments are involved, the one providing the subsidy and the complaining party.

and investment incentives in the context of the establishment of a commercial presence. Export subsidies are intrinsically antithetical to fair trade. For reasons already mentioned, this might only be workable for mode 1, in which case one must ask whether it could create distortions between modes of supply, and possibly allow businesses to circumvent the disciplines by delivering the service via a different mode. Nonetheless, from an overall trade policy standpoint, one cannot avoid considering whether the efforts being made to discipline export subsidies in trade in goods should also find their way into services trade.

As for the question of investment incentives, the existing obligations pertaining to commercial presence, on the one hand, and the serious prejudice provision, on the other hand, suggest that it can be addressed incrementally, and that such a move would also represent a useful complement to existing disciplines. The sensitive issues that both of these questions raise must not be discounted, however.

Conclusion

It is generally believed that the art of creating trade policy consists of striking a balance between what "policy makers practice and what economists preach."[7] This is certainly true when considering the appropriateness of an ESM and subsidy disciplines in services trade. Several factors must be carefully weighed: economic rationale and underpinnings, commercial interests, practicability, enforceability, and certainly negotiability.

The question of an emergency safeguard measure in services trade has been on the agenda for several years now. Although the debate has moved forward, it still appears to be quite a distance away from conclusion. The desirability of an ESM is still an open question, given the state of knowledge of services trade. The test of "unforeseen circumstances" that is instrumental to the consideration of an ESM remains fragile, simply because it is difficult to see how it can be put into practice via objective criteria. Even if its desirability is accepted, one must consider its feasibility when several hurdles would need to be overcome, especially with respect to the modes of delivery, the impact of technology, the embryonic nature of statistical information, not to mention the economics and diversity of trade interests. In this context, it may be somewhat premature to venture

7. Tharakan (1995, p. 1550).

into assessing prospects or propose a precise course of action. At this point, as this discussion as shown, a few important points need to be considered in this regard. They suggest that the negotiating dynamic will likely be an important factor in determining whether an ESM is contemplated. The scheduling of commitments, coupled with generic modalities, might represent the most pragmatic way of considering the issue.

The question of subsidy disciplines has not been as hotly debated as the question of safeguards. Whether disciplines are desirable in this area cannot be established without a thorough investigation of the extent to which subsidies exist in services industries and adversely affect trade. As is the case for safeguards, the feasibility of subsidy disciplines will depend on the specificities of services trade. While some guidance could come from the SCM agreement, it is not a panacea. For instance, a countervailing mechanism would appear undesirable, both from a policy and conceptual standpoint. However, export subsidies and investment incentives, particularly in relation to the existing GATS obligation on commercial presence, deserve further consideration.

References

Baldwin, Robert E. 1992. "Assessing the Fair Trade and Safeguards Laws in Terms of Modern Trade and Political Economy Analysis." *World Economy* 15 (March): 186–87.

Messerlin, Patrick. 1997. "The Emergency Safeguard Measures in GATS." Note prepared for a seminar hosted by the Permanent Mission of Thailand to the World Trade Organization, Geneva (September).

Tharakan, P. K. M. 1995. "The Political Economy of Contingent Protection." *Economic Journal* 105 (433): 1550.

8 | *Where Next for Labor Mobility under GATS?*

ALLISON M. YOUNG

T HE MOVEMENT OF NATURAL PERSONS to provide services, as laid out in mode 4 of the General Agreement on Trade in Services (GATS), represents an entirely new area of concern for the multilateral trading system. Negotiated during the Uruguay Round at the instigation of both less-developed countries and multinational corporations (MNCs), mode 4 is the first attempt by multilateral trade negotiators to liberalize the movement of natural persons to provide services. An examination of the schedules of GATS commitments reveals that a significant degree of liberalization of mode 4 was not achieved during the Uruguay Round or in the follow-up negotiations concerning the movement of natural persons.[1] This has led less-developed countries and MNCs to call for greater liberalization of this mode of supply in the next round of services negotiations, to begin in 2000 under the auspices of the World Trade Organization (WTO).

The views expressed in this chapter are solely those of the author and are part of ongoing doctoral dissertation research at Dalhousie University, Halifax, Canada. These views in no way represent the position of the government of Canada.

1. At the end of the Uruguay Round, less-developed countries complained that significant commitments to liberalize mode 4 had not been made during the negotiations. Consequently, a Decision on Negotiations on Movement of Natural Persons was inserted into GATS to create a Negotiating Group on Movement of Natural Persons. This group was to hold its first negotiating session no later than May 16, 1994, and was to conclude negotiations and produce a report no later than six months after the Agreement Establishing the World Trade Organization went into force. Negotiations were concluded in July 1995.

The multilateral trading system no longer deals solely with "at-the-border issues," such as tariff reduction, but is now grappling with behind-the-border domestic regulatory concerns. In effect, the multilateral trading system is bringing the international economy into direct contact with domestic economies, thereby undermining the deliberate separation of these two spheres organized by the post–World War II planners in the late 1940s. Attempting to liberalize the movement of natural persons as service suppliers raises complex domestic regulatory issues concerning immigration and labor market development. Faced with demands from less-developed countries and MNCs for liberalization of this movement, immigration and labor market development officials are being forced to undertake the difficult task, both technically and politically, of figuring out how to respond to these demands as trade negotiators begin to give them serious consideration in preparation for the next round of multilateral services negotiations.

The main concern of this discussion is how mode 4 is deployed within GATS and how this deployment might be improved in the next round of multilateral services negotiations. The suggestions offered take into account industry needs for increased liberalization and strategies designed to draw out more mode 4 commitments from members of the Organization for Economic Cooperation and Development (OECD). Consideration is also given to some of the concerns articulated by regulatory agencies about mode 4 liberalization and to ways in which these concerns can be approached.

What Is Mode 4?

Little attention has been given to mode 4 in the trade literature.[2] This is probably because of the opaqueness of the scheduled commitments, the regulatory sensitivities involved, and the shortage of ways in which to conceptualize this movement, given the instruments used to maintain border integrity, particularly where the movement of working people is concerned.

Much confusion exists concerning how to refer to people who move across borders to deliver services. Are they basically service providers or service sector workers? This confusion reflects the different approaches

2. See Butkeviciene (1998); Ghosh (1997); Mukherjee (1996); WTO (1998b).

taken by trade, immigration, and labor market development officials to analyze this issue, as well as to define the conditions under which the movement of people takes place.

Trade negotiators and trade policy analysts maintain that people providing services under mode 4 are not entering the local labor market because their stay is temporary and because they are not seeking residency or citizenship status. There is therefore no need to refer to them as labor since they are not part of the labor market. Rather, they are service providers.

Immigration and labor market development officials, on the other hand, argue that "temporary" often means stays of more than three years, so even if the service providers do not seek local residency or citizenship status, they are still participating in the local labor market by providing a service a local person could probably do. From this point of view, service providers have entered the local labor market and are implicated in local labor and employment market conditions, including those arising from personal taxation, union representation, and employer tax burdens in relation to employees. The service provider is therefore a "laborer" with all the accompanying economic and social linkages that word implies in terms of the laborer's relationship to the service or work being provided.

One may imagine that the provision of a service by a person moving across a border may be delivered by someone who is self-employed, by the employee of a supplier located in the home country, or by someone being employed by a foreign affiliate (who may or may not come from the country of ownership of the "parent" company), such as a branch, a representative office, or a joint venture. GATS defines mode 4 as "the supply of a service . . . by a service supplier of one Member, through presence of natural persons of a Member in the territory of any other Member" (Article I 2(d)). This definition focuses on the ability of a service provider to cross a border in order to provide a service. It does not define the conditions under which that movement may take place. This is left to the schedules of specific commitments in which member countries are able to schedule broadly within the context of the GATS Annex on Movement of Natural Persons Supplying Services under the Agreement. This annex says that GATS does not:

> apply to measures affecting natural persons seeking access to the employment market of a Member, nor shall it apply to measures regarding citizenship, residence or employment on a permanent basis and does not:

. . . prevent a Member from applying measures to regulate the entry of natural persons into, or their temporary stay in, its territory, including those measures necessary to protect the integrity of, and to ensure the orderly movement of natural persons across, its borders, provided that such measures are not applied in such a manner as to nullify or impair the benefits accruing to any Member under the terms of a specific commitment.

The schedules of specific commitments, then, allow member countries wide latitude in defining mode 4 and determining the extent of liberalization under it. Although GATS recognizes that services can be provided by the movement of service providers, the tension between trade officials and immigration and labor market development officials over the liberalization of movement of service providers is played out in the schedules.

Deployment

The schedules of specific commitments require members to indicate horizontally and sectorally what commitments they are making for mode 4 with regard to market access (Article XVI), national treatment (Article XVII), and any additional commitments (Article XVIII). Although this sounds reasonably straightforward, the scheduling of commitments is complicated by a poor understanding of what constitutes mode 4, and by the general opaqueness of GATS with regard to its rules and its scheduling guidelines.

Schedules of Commitments under Mode 4

Generally speaking, commitments under mode 4, whether horizontal or sectoral, are significantly less extensive than those found in the other three modes. More than two-thirds of the entries concern executives, managers, and specialists, and about one-third of these focus explicitly on intracorporate transferees. This biases the entries in the direction of skilled personnel. Many of these entries do not include specific durations. The commitments are limited mainly by preemployment criteria, economic needs tests, and numerical quotas. The latter two are not well defined in the schedules, though the scheduling guidelines encourage this definition.[3]

3. Though the scheduling guidelines have been circulated as formal documents (MTN.GNS/W/164 and MTN.GNS/W/164.Add.1), paragraph 1 of MTN.GNS/W/164 states that "the answers should not be considered as an authoritative legal interpretation of the GATS."

Without agreed definitions regarding employment category or function, however, interpretations of the schedules are inconsistent and vague. For example, 'specialists' are commonly listed under intracorporate transferees. Presumably, they could refer to any individuals who consider themselves to be specialists.[4] Lacking a clear definition of specialist, regulatory authorities have discretionary powers in deciding what constitutes a specialist. These problems hamper transparency and reduce commitment certainty.

Mode 4 horizontal entries are generally based on three approaches:

—Half of the entries describe measures that are inconsistent with Article XVI concerning market access, in particular with paragraph 2(d), which refers to "limitations on the total number of natural persons that may be employed in a particular service sector or that a service supplier may employ and who are necessary for, and directly related to, the supply of a specific service in the form of numerical quotas or the requirement of an economic needs test."

—Nearly a third indicate a limited commitment by describing what they are offering rather than by stipulating the market access limitation.

—The remaining schedules generally give national authorities broad discretionary power in granting permission for temporary entry and stay of foreign personnel supplying services.[5]

Because of these approaches to scheduling, information on the nature of the limitations for mode 4, either horizontally or sectorally, is sparse. For example, market access limitations on numerical quotas and economic needs tests (Article XVI 2(d)), as well as specific durations for mode 4 entry, are not clearly defined. In addition, schedules fail to offer a precise statement of what is being limited, with the result that other members cannot be sure that no other limitations exist under mode 4. Discretionary power, such as that associated with the specialist category, is often very broad because explicit criteria for defining temporary entry are limited. These transparency problems need to be rectified in order to lend more certainty to the scheduling process and to open up more negotiating possibilities in future rounds.

A more global approach to remedying the opaqueness of the commitments under mode 4 would be for members to agree to submit their

4. In the American Schedule of Specific Commitments, specialists "may include but are not limited to, members of licensed professions." GATS/SC/90 (April 1994, p. 3).

5. See WTO (1994).

schedules to comprehensive reviews where mode 4 is concerned. Such reviews could be organized sectorally, voluntarily, or on demand and attached to a timetable. This approach is more radical than some of the incremental suggestions outlined earlier, which would still allow some room for discretionary scheduling. Members who submitted to such a review might be rewarded in other negotiating areas for temporary periods of time by receiving special or differential treatment, or credit for trade-offs in other places in the negotiating process. At the very least, such reviews could be used as a tactical measure to create negotiating opportunities with respect to other members.

Relationship to Other Modes

Part of the opaqueness of GATS stems from the fact that in reality the agreement does not divide service provision into the modes of delivery defined for negotiating purposes. In the case of mode 4, it is important to remember that its use in providing a service often (though not always) depends on the use of mode 3.[6] This is the case, for example, with regard to distribution services and is reflected in the schedules by the significant number of commitments scheduled for intracorporate transferees that lack value unless complemented by supportive mode 3 commitments.[7]

Because establishing commercial presence through mode 3 requires capital, service sectors in which mode 4 is dependent on the use of mode 3 are carried out mainly by OECD countries. Sectors that can be delivered exclusively through mode 4, such as computer and related services and health services, are often carried out by non-OECD countries, which are then able to realize a comparative advantage in cheaper labor costs. In addition, many sectoral services may be carried out solely by mode 4 and in conjunction with mode 3. None of these definitions or relationships as they exist for service industry realities are particularly evident in the schedules of commitments.[8]

6. It is not clear if mode 4 is also dependent on the use of mode 1 to provide a service. For example, is the increased use of electronic commerce lessening or increasing the need for the use of mode 4 in this area? The answer seems to depend on the sector in question, particularly its need for customized services. Certainly, modes 1 and 4 can be used in conjunction with each other, particularly where certain professional services are concerned.

7. See WTO (1998a).

8. Some schedules do indicate when commercial presence is also required for a service to be supplied by a natural person. The Japanese schedule, for example, identifies this link with regard to professional services. See "Japan, Schedule of Specific Commitments," GATS/SC/45 (April 15, 1994), pp. 6–16.

One strategy for deploying mode 4 across the sectors might be to define when mode 4 delivery tends to depend on mode 3 and when it does not. This might be done sectorally or horizontally, and in either case it would separate mode 4 from some of the problems related to liberalizing mode 3, making it easier to assess the chances for liberalizing mode 4 on its own across the different sectors. Moreover, commitment substance might be better understood, given the close relationship between modes 3 and 4 for particular services, such as business services. Defining mode 4 more clearly in its own right would also make trade-offs in the negotiation process more transparent and the interests of states easier to define across the sectors.

Classification

During the Uruguay Round, negotiators created a services sectoral classification list based loosely on the United Nations Central Product Classification. This list, which is used to organize the schedules, is grouped by sector and further divided by subsector.[9] It is not organized according to skill level or type of job. This means that mode 4 liberalization, either horizontally or sectorally, is clearly not connected to the job being performed but to the service being provided. It is true that GATS rules are based not on what a service is, but on how it is delivered. This makes sense since it is in the delivery that international trade in services occurs.

From a regulatory perspective, it is difficult to develop labor market policy, for example, that accurately protects a designated employment category from the international supply of a service through mode 4 since this supply could encompass any number of undefined employment categories in a particular sector. Hence the broad category "specialist" is used in many schedules. The domestic regulatory response to this problem is often to "play it safe" and implement an overly restrictive policy with regard to mode 4 liberalization. This reduces the effectiveness of the domestic regulatory policy while at the same time hampering liberalization. Moreover, from an international perspective, it raises transparency questions regarding exactly what is being protected by domestic regulation.

One possible answer to this problem is to develop a parallel list that identifies those service occupations relevant to (temporary) service delivery via mode 4. This list could be developed from the International Labor

9. GATT (1991).

Organization's International Standard Classification of Occupations. It could help deal with industry complaints that the Sectoral Classification List does not respond to "the entire network of activities" that are necessary to support sectors such as retail and other distribution services.[10] A parallel service occupation list could provide a flexible 'mix-and-match' way to express the delivery of a service across different service classifications, while making that expression clearly understandable in terms of mode 4. It could also be used by members during the negotiation process to determine the scope of mode 4 service delivery in particular sectors. An important consideration for the development of such an occupation list would be for all members to sign on to the same list in order to avoid confusion and to promote transparency.

Interestingly, a similar idea has been developed in chapter 16 of the North American Free Trade Agreement, which addresses the temporary entry for business persons. This chapter contains a list of professional occupations that is to be used in determining who can enter another member country's market in order to deliver a service. Similarly, many GATS schedules of commitments contain rudimentary occupation lists and categories to help determine who may be allowed to enter a country as a service provider. India, for example, mentions professionals in the physical sciences, engineering, or other natural sciences, and Canada mentions engineers, agrologists, architects, forestry professionals, geomantic professionals, land surveyors, foreign legal consultants, urban planners, and senior computer specialists.[11]

Mode 4 and Article VI.4

Liberalizing the movement of natural persons is complicated not only by the scheduling, definition, and classification problems just mentioned, but also by domestic regulatory practices that severely constrict (often on a nondiscriminatory basis) the ability of natural persons to move across borders to deliver services. Article VI.4 of GATS makes some effort to remedy this problem.

This article is designed to allow members to simultaneously maintain domestic regulatory policies regarding qualification requirements and pro-

10. Coalition of Service Industries (1998, p. 7).
11. "India, Schedule of Specific Commitments," GATS/SC/42 (April 15, 1994), p. 3; "Canada, Schedule of Specific Commitments," GATS/SC/16 (April 15, 1994), p. 14; "Canada, Schedule of Specific Commitments Supplement 2," GATS/SC/16/Suppl. 2 (July 28, 1995), p. 2.

cedures, technical standards, and licensing requirements and to ensure that any trade-distorting effects of those policies are kept to a minimum. Domestic regulatory policies are not scheduled in GATS unless members make additional commitments with respect to qualifications, standards, or licensing matters. These commitments would be scheduled under Article XVIII, Additional Commitments. Most schedules contain no commitments under Article XVIII, presumably because countries would rather first negotiate such commitments under the disciplines set out by Article VI(4) than give anything away unilaterally.

The disciplines set out under GATS Article VI(4) aim to ensure that domestic regulations are based on objective and transparent criteria, such as competence and the ability to supply the service; are not more burdensome than necessary to ensure the quality of the service; and in the case of licensing procedures, are not in themselves a restriction on the supply of the service. Presumably, this article will subject relevant aspects of immigration and labor market development policies to the disciplines listed above. Further transparency could also be improved by "requiring members to explicitly state the public policy objectives served by a regulation."[12] These objectives could then be thought of in terms of their impact on modal delivery. From the perspective of mode 4, such an exercise would be interesting and informative because it could help clarify exactly how public policy objectives relate to the movement of service providers, if at all. It could also be included in the suggestion for conducting voluntary comprehensive schedule reviews of mode 4.

Although GATS does not provide a definition of technical standards, the efforts of the Working Party on Professional Services to develop disciplines in the accountancy sector would suggest that such standards apply both to the rules by which the service must be performed and to the technical characteristics of the service itself. To cite an example, the way architects provide their services on a construction project must meet professional and regulatory standards, while the work done by the construction workers must meet product standards set by government regulators. From the perspective of mode 4, this means technical standards are relevant for professional services and for nonprofessional services alike. The WTO's Working Party on Domestic Regulation is expected to develop disciplines for technical standards for all services in the classification list, whether or not they are delivered by "professionals." This reality would

---

12. Feketekuty (1998, p. 94).

seem to support the position of less-developed countries that movement of natural persons should not be limited to the "skilled professionals" (as is currently the case in most if not all of the schedules of commitments and often indicated through a minimum educational requirements such as a baccalaureate) but should be opened up across the skill spectrum. If disciplines for technical standards are developed for all service sectors, entry restrictions for the "unskilled" based on quality of work and consumer protection criteria would be much more difficult to maintain.

Such an argument brings into sharper focus the relationship between GATT and GATS. Because it is becoming increasingly difficult to distinguish trade in goods from trade in services with regard to the movement of natural persons, the applicability of the concepts underlying the Agreement on Technical Barriers to Trade to services, particularly regarding Article VI.4, seems relevant.[13]

The Problem of Defining Mode 4

All of the scheduling complexities concerning mode 4 are further complicated by the overarching question of what actually constitutes mode 4. This problem has several dimensions. First, the multilateral trading system developed over the past fifty years positions trade as an international transaction. In the case of mode 4, this means that money from country X flows to country Y in exchange for a service being provided by person Y in country X. Clearly, GATS is implicated in such transactions.

From a statistical perspective, this interpretation is supported in part by the balance of payments statistics collected by the International Monetary Fund and published in its *Statistical Yearbook*. When service providers (and any other workers) move across a border for less than one year to provide a service, their wages and other compensation are recorded as income for the sending state. However, remuneration for stays of longer than one year are not subject to such measurement since such workers are considered to be part of the host economy. Many mode 4 commitments accommodate workers wanting to stay for longer than one year. In this case, remuneration statistics may be collected as remittances of workers assumed to have changed their residence (even though they may have not formally done so). Remuneration statistics may also be collected as migrant transfers. It is clear that such reporting techniques do not capture all trade

13. GATT (1994).

in services provided by mode 4, nor do they disaggregate those that are captured in terms of service provision. As has been previously suggested, improving the measurement of mode 4 usage might "be feasible where such movements form part of the employment data from statistics collected on services via commercial presence."[14]

A close reading of GATS reveals that an international transaction as defined above does not have to occur in order for service provision under mode 4 to take place. That is, a provider from country A and a service consumer from country A may both travel to country B, where the provider from country A provides consumer from country A with a service.[15] An example of this would be a tour bus guide who takes tourists to another country and gives them a tour. In this case, there is no import or export of a service and therefore no international transaction to be recorded in the balance of payments statistics; yet the trade of a service as defined under mode 4 has occurred. The question, then, is do GATS provisions come into play in the absence of an international transaction? Can barriers to mode 4 be said to exist if they do?

If the answer to these last two questions is yes, this form of service supply under mode 4 becomes important because any rules that exist in country B will have an impact on the ability of supplier A to provide a service to consumer A in country B. These requirements may be domestic regulations as defined under Article VI or performance requirements not permitted under Article XVI concerning market access. If they are the former, would they be subject to a necessity test as outlined in Article VI(4)(b)? If the latter, can performance requirements be imposed on consumers in cases where they cannot be on producers? Do the requirements constitute some form of indirect barriers to trade? How would any of these issues be taken into account in the schedules or in a dispute settlement case? What happens if the service is delivered in conjunction with a good? There are, as yet, no clear answers to these questions. Perhaps the best place to start would be to create an inventory of problems raised by this form of delivery, group them according to their relationship to Articles XVI and VI(4), and begin to identify what new commitments

---

14. Henderson (1997). See also IMF (1993).

15. Article I of GATS defines trade in services as the supply of a service "by a service supplier of one Member, through presence of natural persons of a Member in the territory of any other Member." Article XXVIII(b) defines supply of a service as including the production, distribution, marketing, sale, and delivery of a service.

might be scheduled or subject to negotiation under Article VI(4) in order to bring them formally into the GATS realm.

Second, the definition of mode 4 does not describe the employer of a service provided under mode 4 or the terms of the employment contract. Is the employer in the sending country or in the receiving country? Is the employment based on a contractor-contractee relationship or on an employer-employee relationship? The schedules of commitments vary in the extent to which they accommodate these possibilities. This question is important at the domestic level because, depending on who the employer is, different regulatory issues will arise concerning taxation, wages, labor market regulation and development, collective bargaining agreements, the collection of statistics, and so on. It is also politically important since the argument by trade policymakers that the use of mode 4 does not displace local labor rests, as has already been discussed, on the (debatable) notion that service providers operating in a foreign market do not enter the labor market. Where foreign service suppliers are hired by a host country employer, they are usually supposed to be filling local labor market gaps. From a trade perspective, these issues have bearing on the ability of service providers and service consumers/employers to be competitive. The extent to which these issues might be examined under GATS—inasmuch as they concern wages, benefits, and other labor standards issues—is probably limited given political sensitivities, but they do serve to underscore the complexity of comprehending and comparing schedules of commitments.

These definitional problems lend some support to the idea that a separate regime needs to be established for labor services or even the movement of labor more generally.[16] Here, the whole range of related issues could be addressed in terms of the challenges this movement poses both for the multilateral trading regime and for other state-related concerns.

Although perhaps attractive intellectually and even as a long-term goal, the extraction of mode 4 in this manner would require structural changes in GATS and, at minimum, majority approval from the WTO membership. In addition, this idea does not account for the political compromise that allowed mode 4 to be established during the Uruguay Round and that continues to exert influence on the preparations for new services negotiations. Moreover, the GATS structure necessitates a comprehensive understanding of mode 4, not only in its own right but also in terms of other modes, particularly mode 3. At this relatively early stage in

16. See Mukherjee (1996, p. 40).

liberalizing trade in services within the multilateral trading regime, it is still essential to retain mechanisms solely for the purpose of understanding exactly what the supply of a service means in terms of movement of personnel.

Liberalization

The discussion now turns to the mode 4 expectations of developing countries in the next round of services negotiations. It also examines how Quad schedules are positioned to respond to the demands of such countries and summarizes the service industry wish list for mode 4 liberalization.

Mode 4 and Less-Developed Countries

During the Uruguay Round, less-developed countries argued that services supplied by the movement of people across borders was as legitimate a concept of service supply as commercial presence and therefore needed to be taken into account by GATS. Liberalization of the movement of people as a factor of production, they contended, needed to be balanced against liberalization of the mobility of capital since the imbalance was not only unfair but it limited the efficient utilization of productive resources. Furthermore, they hoped that liberalization of service delivery via natural persons could be used as a negotiating counterweight to concessions made with regard to mode 3. They also believed that they could probably realize a comparative advantage in this form of service delivery in relation to developed countries because of lower labor costs.[17] As already noted, the results of these efforts were modest and biased in favor of the highly skilled workers being deployed in conjunction with mode 3. Many less-developed countries viewed the resulting GATS commitments as unbalanced in the treatment of labor and capital. This view has become more entrenched since the end of the negotiations on financial and telecommunications services.

In the upcoming round of services negotiations, less-developed countries are likely to try to increase their participation in services trade by

17. Currently, most movement of service providers occurs between OECD countries. For more information on the geographic breakdown of the movement of service providers, see "Presence of Natural Persons (Mode 4)," S/C/W/75 (December 8, 1998).

seeking more mode 4 commitments in relation to developing countries. They will be supported in this strategy by and large by Article IV of GATS (Increasing Participation of Developing Countries). In preparation for the 1999 Ministerial Conference, certain developing countries have suggested that an occupation services list could be used to negotiate occupations and service sectors that might be excluded from the application of economic needs tests. This amounts to an internationally coordinated positive list for certain services occupations, which might include occupations from all skill levels. (Interestingly, such a list is in the early stages of being developed on an ad hoc national basis through the binding of professional occupations, many of which are similar across schedules, particularly for business services occupations). Remaining sectors in which an economic needs test still applied could be subject to agreed-upon principles for the use of an economic needs test such as definition, criteria for their introduction, procedures for application, duration of application, and so on.

These suggestions will no doubt be greeted with caution, since they would narrow the discretionary power of governments to regulate the movement of natural persons to supply services. From an immigration and labor market development perspective, this discretionary power preserves the flexibility required to prevent policy from being locked in to a static set of commitments. However, some sectors might be excluded from an economic needs test, most notably those for which skill shortages are predicted or are already occurring, as is the case in the information technology sector. Still, even this might be problematic in occupations subject to little regulation. In 1995, when India attempted to obtain a special entry category for software service providers entering the United States, the U.S. Immigration and Naturalization Service was reluctant to do so since assessing qualifications in this industry proved too difficult given the unregulated nature of the occupations in the software industry.

By contrast, Canada recently ran a pilot program that brought software development workers to the country temporarily in order to fill labor shortages in this area.[18] Here, the objective was to bring software development workers to Canada by approaching the validation process (or labor market test) differently. Instead of having a national employment officer making one-off decisions about labor market needs, Human Resources Development Canada pre-identified a larger need within the labor market

18. "Pilot Project to Help Canadian Employers Attract Highly Skilled Workers," Citizenship and Immigration Canada News Release, 1998.

for software development workers. It was assisted by sectoral councils and key employers, who also provided ongoing input to ensure the program was meeting labor market, labor standard, and business needs, and who also helped define occupations and qualifications for participation.

Although the Canadian program also faced the challenge of assessing qualifications, applicants who had a job offer from a Canadian employer, the proper qualification, and security clearance, as well as any necessary visa (depending on their country of origin), were automatically validated, issued an employment authorization, and allowed to work in Canada.[19] This program took important steps toward the objectives of mode 4 by assigning higher priority to industry needs over government and labor market needs while at the same time retaining regulatory controls in areas such as working conditions.

The likely resistance of developed countries to be more forthcoming on liberalization of mode 4, beyond the current commitments on intracorporate transferees, executives, managers, and specialists, could find its counterpart in South-South negotiations over mode 4. For this reason, it is perhaps more realistic to first increase the transparency of visa and work permit systems through legislation, provide all interested parties with a say in the proposed changes to relevant legislation, bind current immigration legislation to areas connected with the commitments, and provide a mechanism (either domestically or internationally) for encouraging feedback from the business community and other nongovernmental organizations regarding mode 4 implementation.[20]

Admittedly, some states will find it more difficult to implement these suggestions than others. Members of the European Union, for instance, have no unified migration policy and therefore no comprehensive and effective way to track mode 4 implementation or impact at the European level. Similarly, when GATS members tried to develop international disciplines for accountancy, they were unable to reach an agreement that would have allowed all interested parties to provide input in the development or alteration of relevant legislation. These examples from the realm of mode 4 liberalization reflect both structural and institutional problems at the regional and national levels, as well as broader political issues outside the purview of multilateral trade negotiations.

19. Employment extensions were possible, depending on the employment offer. It is unclear if any foreign workers who used this program applied to become residents of Canada. Many of the workers who applied and came to Canada were from India.

20. This approach is being pursued by the Asia-Pacific Economic Cooperation. See APEC (1996).

Mode 4 and the Development of Emergency Safeguards under GATS

Since the end of the Uruguay Round, the Working Party on GATS Rules has been occupied with developing emergency safeguard measures. This has proven to be a complex endeavor since it is difficult to identify why an emergency safeguard would be needed, and what or who would be targeted by them. Moreover, because many services are supplied by using more than one mode, as is often the case for modes 3 and 4, imposing safeguards for one mode could have an impact on another mode of supply. The question then is how efficient are safeguard measures?

In the case of mode 4, the purpose of such a measure would be to protect domestic employment in a particular sector or to protect a domestic supplier. It would be targeted at natural persons from another country who had already entered the market or those planning to do so. Although it is difficult to imagine how a safeguard mechanism could be effectively designed for the former, the latter group might be captured through a temporary tightening of market access limitations, as outlined in the horizontal or sectoral commitments. Still, such safeguards would be difficult to implement without an effective tracking device for mode 4.

The politically sensitive nature of further liberalization of services trade, particularly for mode 4, lends some credence to the idea that further liberalization will depend on the development of emergency safeguard measures. If that were the case, it would provide the incentive to identify and bind economic needs test criteria and relevant legislation, which in turn would provide other negotiating opportunities for other modes. A safeguard measure targeted at a particular sector might even be made to require a commitment to liberalize in a given sector.

Such ideas, their opponents argue, would make agreements all the more complex and even more difficult to implement, and they would undermine efforts to liberalize, both in practice and in theory. Supporters counter that in any case the implementation of further commitments to liberalize services for mode 4 will automatically be slowed down in many service sectors by the existence of domestic regulatory mechanisms. In effect, domestic regulation is seen as a built-in adjustment mechanism that will reduce the need to use the safeguard measures; the time and effort required to address domestic regulation under Article VI(4) will provide time and knowledge to prepare for the liberalization to come. The existence of safeguard measures, however, might lend additional security to the largely uncharted territory of services liberalization in the multilateral trading environment. They would represent the political price for further services liberalization. The question remaining, then, would not be on what but when safeguard measures could be used.[21]

Mode 4 and the Quad Countries

Scheduled commitments under mode 4 for the United States allow horizontally bound temporary entry and stay of nationals for services salespersons, intracorporate transferees (managers, executives, and specialists), personnel engaged in establishment, and fashion models and specialty occupations.[22] At the sectoral level, some additional limitations exist for both market access and national treatment, and they are usually listed by state. Often, these limitations relate to in-state residency or citizenship requirements. It is important to note that American commitments for mode 4 in GATS bound the status quo. This means that although the commitments in the schedules for intracorporate transferees, for example, appear to provide for unfettered entry, it is still necessary to petition the U.S. Immigration and Naturalization Service to obtain the relevant L-1 visa. One of the main requirements of this petition process is that persons seeking L-1 status must have been continually employed by the petitioning MNC for at least one of the preceding three years.

The category of fashion models and specialty occupations is bound at 65,000 persons annually, in accordance with immigration legislation. This quota is filled largely by foreign skilled workers employed in industries experiencing labor shortages such as the software industry. It is considered to be very low compared with the demand for entry; the quota for 1999 was filled by June. Interestingly, the legislation governing the H-1B visa was revised upward in October 1998, putting the number at 115,000 for 1999 and 2000, and 107,500 in 2001. It will revert back to 65,000 after this period. Obtaining or renewing an H-1B visa now requires new attestation requirements and other provisions (hotly contested by employers) designed to protect American workers.

Whether or not this new legislation will become bound at the higher level and how any new attestation requirements might affect GATS com-

21. One might argue that in any case concern over mode 4 usage might be covered under Article XIV (General Exceptions), which states that "nothing in this Agreement shall be construed to prevent the adoption or enforcement by any member measures (a) necessary to protect morals or to maintain public order."

22. "The United States of America, Schedule of Specific Commitments," GATS/SC/90 (April 1994).

mitments are two questions likely to arise during the new services negotiations. On the American side, the binding of such a quota helps offset the requirements for an economic needs test (such as the requirement that American employers take steps to recruit and retrain American workers before bringing in foreign workers) by providing a well-used visa category for any profession requiring a bachelor's degree.[23] No other Quad schedules bind the number of foreigners eligible to enter and work in the host country. Presumably, entry numbers in the other Quad countries are limitless as long as other criteria are met. Where unofficial targets are maintained for temporary entry, they should be listed in the schedules of commitments as market access limitations.

Canada, for example, has no quota but does limit the professions in which foreigners may work.[24] Japan and the European Community take similar approaches.[25] However, Canada and Japan do not employ economic needs tests in their schedules, though these are still commonly found in the European sector schedules (especially those for the United Kingdom and Italy), but without defining criteria. The Europeans provide only a limited temporary period of three months for contracted work and do not otherwise specify duration of stay since this is regulated nationally. The other Quad countries normally provide between three and five years for most temporary entry categories, except business visitors, where temporary entry usually covers a maximum period of ninety days. Only Japan has not listed additional market access and national treatment limitations in sectors (except for the occasional commercial presence requirement) such as citizenship or residency requirements. Its horizontal limitations instead refer to specialized qualifications in given professions without defining those requirements. Presumably they include residency and citizenship requirements, as well as other educational, licensing, and experience requirements.

The more general problem is that WTO members have not yet reached a consensus on what needs to be scheduled under Articles XVI and

---

23. Because attempts by the U.S. Department of Labor to implement attestation requirements (economic needs tests) are usually hampered by vociferous business charges of bureaucratic micromanagement, the quota serves to limit the number of entries in the absence of a well-received economic needs test policy.

24. "Canada, Schedule of Specific Commitments," GATS/SC/16 (April 1994) and GATS/SC16/Suppl.2 (July 28, 1995).

25. "Japan, Schedule of Specific Commitments," GATS/SC/46 (April 15, 1994); "European Communities and Their Member States," GATS/SC/31 (April 1994) and GATS/SC/31/Suppl.2 (July 28, 1995).

XVII and what falls under Article VI as domestic regulatory issues. This question plagued the negotiations over disciplines for the accountancy sector under Article VI(4) and will presumably continue to be an important agenda item for the WTO's Working Party on Domestic Regulation.

Japan lists the least number of professions (six) under which foreigners might enter and does so only with a preemployment requirement. Canada lists nine without a preemployment requirement, while the European Union lists seventeen areas in which contracts might be undertaken.[26] This makes the fact that Japan may want to seek increased liberalization for mode 4 from other members in the next round of services negotiations an interesting prospect.

Generally speaking, then, the United States will likely be faced with negotiating demands to increase the specialty occupations quota to 115,000 and to eliminate entry requirements such as petitioning in the intracorporate transferee category. Canada and Japan will need to look closely at the number of professions they are willing to bind. In Japan's case, preemployment criteria and nonremuneration by Japanese employers will probably be targeted areas for liberalization. Certain countries in the European Union will face questions directed at pinning down economic needs test criteria, lengthening the time during which foreigners can enter under mode 4, and easing the requirements on third-country nationals. All member countries will need to give more attention to the challenges posed by Articles VI(4) and VII in order to make more transparent and meaningful their commitments under mode 4 regarding professional services and presumably nonprofessional services as well.

Mode 4 and Service Industry Needs

During the Uruguay Round, MNCs that provide business services pressed for the liberalization of the movement of natural persons. In particular, they sought mobility for managers, executives, specialists, and professionals providing legal services, accountancy services, and so on. MNCs were fairly successful in getting these service suppliers into the schedules of commitments under mode 4. However, the commitments scheduled largely bound the status quo and did not achieve new levels of

26. Note that commitments to omit professionals often depend on agreements between or among countries to recognize foreign qualifications and licensing procedures. Such agreements must often be undertaken by self-regulating professional associations. GATS Article VII concerning recognition provides a mechanism for incorporating mutual recognition agreements into GATS commitments.

liberalization. One of the goals for the business service industry in the next round of negotiations is to deepen liberalization with respect to mode 4.

Suggestions for deepening liberalization generally revolve around delivery issues specific to a sector and ease of entry. Those concerned with delivery need to devote more attention to the close relationship between modes 3 and 4 in certain sectors that makes the liberalization of one mode dependent on the other. Suggestions of this nature can be seen in measures deemed necessary to protect consumers, such as requirements for partnership with local service suppliers and requirements that top management be locally licensed professionals. The extent to which consumer protection could be assured via alternative and less discriminatory measures needs further examination, particularly with respect to the concept of "necessity" being developed under Article VI(4). Here again, mode 4 liberalization is closely tied to work being undertaken under Article VI(4). Furthermore, commitment schedules need to take a more flexible approach to how people are effectively employed in business service industries. For example, services may be best delivered by individuals, teams, or on a short-term rotating basis.[27] Schedules also need to accommodate the human resource development needs of business service industries, which often depend on international training opportunities.

With regard to ease of entry, various proposals exist for establishing a GATS visa regime. In the view of MNCs, such proposals should provide for the entry of key personnel who are already employed and who would enter the country for less than one year with no intention of establishing permanent residency. Special tax exemptions would apply, depending on length of stay. Those entering for less than three months, but on a multiple basis within one year, would bypass the visa requirement altogether.[28]

The requirement of previous employment generally links this movement of personnel to mode 3 entry and is therefore mainly for those with the resources to engage in commercial presence. From the point of view of developing countries, this movement should not be limited to so-called key personnel or be limited by pre-employment requirements but rather should be opened up to all service providers, whether or not mode 3 is involved. Time limits would be retained and the movement would remain temporary to avoid permanent migration and brain drain.[29]

27. European Commission (1999, p. 3).
28. U.S. Department of Commerce (1998, p. 37).
29. Ghosh (1997, p. 144).

A growing number of MNC demands for liberalization of mode 4 are being directed at less-developed countries in which important markets for professional services are emerging. By way of example, one might look at three schedules of commitments with regard to mode 4: the schedules of India, the Philippines, and Mexico.[30]

Indian commitments for mode 4 are organized along the lines of the Quad schedules, that is, in terms of business visitors, intracorporate transferees (including managers, executives, and specialists), and professionals. The first two categories appear to be fairly open, with entry allowed for a maximum of five years. Presumably, any economic needs tests and quotas would be listed in the schedules. The professionals category is less liberal, with entry limited to those in the fields of physical sciences, engineering, and other natural sciences and for a time period of only one year, which can be extended for up to three months.[31]

The Philippine schedules of specific commitments for mode 4 are very limited and depend on economic needs tests. Special conditions apply for entry into certain sectors. In the insurance sector, for example, only aliens qualified to hold technical positions may be employed within the first five years of operation of an enterprise, and each employed alien should have at least two Filipino understudies. In the tourism sector, tourism establishments must employ only citizens as a rule. The Tripartite Agreement among the Department of Tourism, the Department of Labor and Employment, and the Bureau of Immigration permits some exceptions, however: these include four aliens at the managerial level in a hotel or resort, three-month contracts for aliens working in special tourism events, and four alien chefs for a maximum of two years in a restaurant with a minimum of seventy-five seats. In the transport sector, aliens may be employed only within the first five years of operation of an enterprise, and each employed alien should have at least two Filipino understudies.

The Mexican commitments allow business visitors to enter for ninety days. Intracorporate transferees (managers, executives, and specialists) are also mentioned, but the schedule does not make clear how long intracorporate transferees are allowed to work in Mexico. Professionals wishing to enter and be employed in Mexico are not included in the schedule.

30. "India, Schedule of Specific Commitments," GATS/SC/42 (April 15, 1994); "Philippines, Schedule of Specific Commitments," GATS/SC/70 (April 15, 1994); "Mexico, Schedule of Specific Commitments," GATS/SC/56 (April 1994).

31. "India, Schedule of Specific Commitments Supplement 2," GATS/SC/42/Suppl. 2 (July 28, 1995), p. 4.

Clearly, the scheduling of mode 4 commitments in these three countries indicates that the movement of service providers is considered important for development-related objectives. The extent to which these limitations advance the development objectives while also encouraging (or discouraging) investment prospects is not known. Greater liberalization by less-developed countries in mode 4 will no doubt have to be rationalized in terms of development objectives.

Mode 4 and the Regulatory Response

The assumption thus far has been that deeper liberalization of the movement of natural persons is desirable economically because it will allow human resources to move freely to areas where they are most productive. Productivity is measured not only in terms of efficiency, but also in terms of knowledge development, the latter being a crucial component of the global service economy.

Although it is necessary to undertake this discussion in order to assess what the movement of natural persons to provide services really means in terms of GATS, such a discussion is essentially focused inward. That is, it has not engaged effectively with other related discussions external to it, such as those carried on by immigration and labor market development authorities. The very limited commitments under mode 4 proves this point. To be fair, negotiations during the Uruguay Round to create mode 4 were necessarily focused on whether and how to include movement of natural persons within the agreement's structure, not on intensive dialogues with national regulatory agencies to move liberalization forward. However, the manner in which mode 4 has been included in the schedules of commitments has raised many new questions for GATS. The answers to these questions will be found by engaging in a comprehensive dialogue with the relevant national regulatory agencies, particularly those responsible for immigration and labor market development. How can this dialogue be approached?

Before thinking about ways to answer this question, it is important to remember that the mission of most immigration authorities is to administer legislative acts that are largely defensive in orientation. It is not to reach out to the international business community to facilitate entry so that services can be provided through the temporary movement of natural persons. Who holds that responsibility at the national level is unclear in many countries. Meeting labor market development needs through temporary labor is within the purview of labor market development officials, yet they do not control entry and have traditionally been concerned with employer-employee relationships at the national level rather than international service providers who claim not to be entering the local labor market. Clearly, national policy has in many cases failed to determine who is best positioned to respond to demands in order to accommodate service provision through the temporary movement of natural persons.

To the extent that immigration and labor market development regulators are being asked to respond to the various ideas for achieving further liberalization of mode 4, they have been (understandably) cautious. A GATS visa regime, for example, poses huge challenges because it requires regulators to reassess or phase out current entry programs, given the existing legislation, the need to coordinate data collection internationally to track implementation, the need for new resources to train border personnel and invest in new automated technology, and so on.[32] Furthermore, they are aware that implementing a GATS visa regime would require a higher threshold of regulation to track implementation and would trigger many other complex regulatory responses concerning labor market development.[33] This means that ease of entry via a GATS visa regime, at least in the short term, may be more difficult than in the absence of such a regime, because it would reveal concerns that might not otherwise have been perceived to exist. This not only politicizes an already sensitive issue but also undermines the raison d'être of transparency as a mechanism for increasing certainty and therefore efficiency.

32. Six members of APEC (Australia; Chile; Hong Kong, China; New Zealand; South Korea; and the Philippines) now have business cards (manually processed) and dedicated immigration lanes to promote ease of entry. However, neither the United States nor Canada is planning to join this program because of separate visa requirements and because they run the INSPass and CANPass programs, respectively, which attempt to promote ease of entry at the border for certain groups using a biometric or automated system. The manual system is not considered a step forward. Not surprisingly, few countries are able to deploy a biometric entry system because of its cost and organizational requirements. Establishing a GATS visa regime, then, would have to somehow account for the differing capacities of WTO members to implement efficient entry systems. International dialogue on immigration issues occurs sporadically between Australia, the United Kingdom, Canada, and the United States in a forum called the Fourth Country Conference. The last such meeting was held in San Francisco in April 1999. Note, too, that the North American Free Trade Association has established a Working Group on Chapter 16 Temporary Entry for Business Persons, which meets every year.

33. The ability of the United States to implement a quota for its H(i)(b) visa depends on a petition process for the verification of prevailing wages. This process allows the Immigration and Naturalization Service to count visas issued when a job is approved and not when employment authorization is issued. Countries that waive such verification processes find it much more difficult to manage quotas.

The idea of special tax exemptions depending on length of stay would require significant cooperation with national revenue authorities, which would be quite separate, for privacy reasons, from the administration of a GATS visa regime. Discussion of such an idea is outside the scope of this essay.

The regulatory response to suggestions for more clearly defining and binding economic needs tests, quotas, time durations, and relevant legislation is generally negative, since labor market needs are viewed as dynamic and therefore not subject to static agreements. Such ideas position the regulatory bodies concerned as redundant and call into question the purpose of maintaining border integrity.

Caution has also greeted suggestions for removing preemployment criteria and for bringing nonprofessionals into the purview of Article VI(4) by focusing on the technical characteristic of services (in addition to looking at the rules by which a service is performed as in the case of professionals). Preemployment criteria usually link mode 4 to mode 3 and therefore guarantee investment rather than entry into the local labor market. While bilateral agreements to admit the so-called unskilled in categories such as fruit pickers do exist, these are usually administered on an ad hoc basis as the need arises. Again, binding such entry would not account for the dynamic needs of the labor market. Although emergency safeguard measures would theoretically address such dynamic needs, they do not receive a great deal of support from regulatory officials because they would be very difficult to implement either at the border or after entry has been granted.

Before immigration and labor market development authorities can engage in a productive dialogue on the further liberalization of mode 4, they will need to shift from their usual inward-looking defensive stance to one geared more toward the needs of agreements such as GATS and the global economy in general. This is already beginning to happen. Australian immigration authorities recently set up service centers for employers who want to petition for foreign workers. This constitutes a proactive outreach program in which a direct link is being made between temporary entry and labor market development issues. The same might be said of the recent Canadian pilot project to recruit foreign computer software workers.

Second, trade officials need to take an incremental approach to mode 4 liberalization. One step in this direction would be to conduct more comparative research on how different kinds of temporary movement in relation to trade agreements affect national economies (in both developed and developing countries), and also on how regulatory authorities have responded to this impact. From here it might be possible to develop best practices for regulating temporary entry based on accepted international trade principles such as necessity, nondiscrimination, transparency, equivalence, and so on.[34] This makes the suggestion for comprehensive reviews of the commitments under mode 4 important.

To the extent that these reviews are not practicable, another way to develop a best practice approach would be to consider negotiating standard minimum commitments for mode 4 liberalization to be applied horizontally and sectorally. These commitments could consist of minimum durations, application to a minimum number of sectors (and occupations), fewer preemployment criteria, and less scope for economic needs tests and quotas. Minimum standards would provide for more liberalization while also retaining scope for regulation. It would then be possible to begin a thorough and comparative assessment of the regulatory responses triggered by such an agreement without overwhelming negative domestic responses from both political and bureaucratic entities. Again, this assessment could begin to identify best practices for regulating temporary entry by applying preestablished efficient regulation principles geared toward trade needs such as transparency, necessity, and equivalence.

Finally, it would be important to develop a formal international process for exchanging and disseminating information on regulatory initiatives designed to liberalize the movement of natural persons providing services. This would facilitate the development of best practices while also establishing a central location from which individuals and businesses could access information on entry procedures and could provide feedback regarding how user-friendly these procedures actually are.

Conclusion

In crafting a way to connect international and domestic perspectives on the provision of services via the temporary movement of natural persons, it is important to remember that the domestic and international authorities involved are operating from diametrically opposed agendas and

34. Such a project would require the joint cooperation of trade officials and those involved in labor market development and migration-related issues. This kind of cooperation is only slowly getting under way as both groups begin to realize how closely their policy concerns have become interwoven because of trade agreement commitments.

mandates. This is no accident, given the deliberate separation of domestic and international economies that took place after World War II. Dismantling this separation with regard to the last frontier of border integrity—the immobility of people—and making the agendas of trade and regulatory officials more complementary will require careful and sustained thought.

From a trade policy perspective, commitments made under mode 4 must be both meaningful and practicable. Examining current commitments and imagining how they may be further liberalized raises many difficult questions, and the attempt to answer some of these questions here really only begins to scratch the surface of what is an enormous project. Without meaningful dialogue between trade officials and those who oversee immigration and labor market development, these questions will not be rigorously answered, and further mode 4 liberalization will be stalled.

References

Asia-Pacific Economic Cooperation (APEC). 1996. "APEC Business Travel Handbook: A Guide to Visa and Entry Requirements for Business Travel to APEC Member Economies." APEC Committee on Trade and Investment (November).

Butkeviciene, Jalita. 1998. "Market Access for the Movement of Natural Persons as Service Suppliers." Geneva: United Nations Conference on Trade and Development.

Coalition of Service Industries. 1999. "Coalition of Service Industry Response to Federal Register Notice of August 19, 1998." Solicitation of Public Comment Regarding U.S. Preparations for the World Trade Organization's Ministerial Meeting, Fourth Quarter 1999. FR Doc. 98-22279. Washington, D.C.

European Commission, Directorate General I. 1999. "GATS 2000: Issues Paper, Domestic Regulation and Mobility of Personnel." Brussels. (March 25).

Feketekuty, Geza. 1998. "Setting the Agenda for the Next Round of Negotiations on Trade in Services." In *Launching New Global Trade Talks: An Action Agenda,* edited by Jeffrey J. Schott. Washington, D.C.: Institute for International Economics.

General Agreement on Tariffs and Trade (GATT). 1991. "Services Sectoral Classification List." Secretariat Note MTN.GNS/W/120. Geneva (July 10).

———. 1994. "Agreement on Technical Barriers to Trade." In *The Results of the Uruguay Round of Multilateral Trade Negotiations.* Geneva (June).

Ghosh, Bimal. 1997. *Gains from Global Linkages: Trade in Services and Movement of Persons.* New York: St. Martin's Press.

Henderson, Hugh. 1997. "On Building Bridges: A Canadian Perspective on Linking Services Categories of the World Trade Organization and of Balance of Payments Compilers." Discussion paper, Tenth Meeting of the IMF Committee on Balance of Payments Statistics, Washington D.C. (October 22–24).

International Monetary Fund (IMF). 1993. *Balance of Payments Manual.* 5th ed. Washington, D.C.

Mukherjee, Neela. 1996. "Exporting Labour Services and Market Access Commitments under GATS in the World Trade Organization." *Journal of World Trade* 30 (October).

U.S. Department of Commerce. 1998. "Results of the Services 2000: A Conference and Dialogue on Global Policy Developments and U.S. Business." Washington, D.C. (October 16).

World Trade Organization (WTO), Council for Trade in Services. 1998a. "Distribution Services." Background Note by the Secretariat S/C/W/37. Geneva (June 10).

———. 1998b. "Presence of Natural Persons (Mode 4)." Background Note by the Secretariat S/C/W/75. Geneva (December 8).

World Trade Organization (WTO), Negotiating Group on Movement of Natural Persons. 1994. "Horizontal Commitments on Movement of Natural Persons." Informal Note by the Secretariat (September 15).

COMMENT BY
Malcolm Bosworth

The insightful analysis by Simon Evenett and Bernard Hoekman in chapter 6 concludes persuasively that government procurement disciplines may not be necessary in the realm of services. They show that the domestic and foreign welfare effects of discriminatory procurement regimes will be negligible and transitory where domestic markets are contestable by new suppliers. Procurement favoritism for local suppliers will not raise domestic prices or reduce welfare significantly in competitive and contestable markets. Even where government demand constitutes a large share of domestic output, such adverse economic effects will be short-lived and relatively benign provided market entry is open.

Many procured services, however, will either be nontradable "cross-border" services, or their preferred mode of supply will be commercial presence because of natural advantages in being located in the home market. For these services, procurement favoritism will only matter if such policies can differentiate between national entities and foreign affiliates. As the authors rightly point out, what really matters to economic efficiency and domestic welfare in these cases is the restrictions on foreign direct investment (FDI). Where government demand is relatively large, they contend, discriminatory procurement practices would be akin to nationalization or expropriation policies. Foreign firms would be encouraged to sell out to local firms. Evenett and Hoekman see a procurement ban on foreign affiliates acting as a de facto FDI barrier. Since restrictive FDI policies are likely to reduce economic efficiency and domestic welfare, governments should resist powerful political economy forces at work on behalf of procurement favoritism.

Some clear and practical policy implications emerge from their discussion of discipline issues. Since the economic damage done by discriminatory procurement policies depends upon the contestability of markets, the policy response should be to encourage open and competitive markets. Therefore Evenett and Hoekman call for the removal of market access barriers, especially on commercial presence, hoping the forthcoming services negotiations will concentrate on improving market access and national treatment commitments under GATS, rather than on developing government procurement disciplines.

In their opinion, general procurement disciplines would be best achieved though a general procurement agreement. Although trade and investment liberalization may well obviate the need for such multilateral rules, they may still have value in promoting transparency of procurement, thereby reducing the scope for corruption and rent-seeking. One multilateral way forward, they suggest, would be to "multilateralize" the plurilateral government procurement agreement, which still clearly has a long way to go.

Evenett and Hoekman give us a timely reminder of just how important open and contestable markets are, a point all too easily lost by negotiators as they grapple with the complexity and political demands of intense multilateral trade negotiations. Anything that reduces the demands on negotiators should therefore be welcomed. In this context, however, it is reasonable to ask whether procurement disciplines may yet be needed until the goal of truly contestable markets is achieved. This is still a long way off, be it for services, goods, or investment. Nevertheless, the best response would seem to be to establish general multilateral disciplines across all trade, and not just on services, a point that also reinforces the need to obtain general disciplines on FDI.

One topic that Evenett and Hoekman do not discuss at any length is the role of competition policy in maintaining open markets. Presumably such policies can play a major role in maintaining open entry. However, enforcement of competition policies can go both ways. A good case in point is merger policy, since new entrants frequently merge with incumbents to enter markets. If competition regulators apply an unduly restrictive merger policy, this could end up reducing market contestability. Also, government policies restricting mergers in sensitive sectors, though often maintained in the interests of competition, risk preventing market forces from working. In addition, one wonders whether the conclusions Evenett and Hoekman reach would apply equally in countries that have weak or no competition policy.

The authors assume that governments behave honestly in procurement matters. This may well be a heroic assumption. In this regard, multilateral disciplines may be one of the few means of combating corrupt practices. Here again, however, general and truly multilateral procurement disciplines would appear more effective than rules for services alone.

In chapter 7, Gilles Gauthier and his colleagues address two important issues that are proving difficult to resolve in GATS. Are disciplines on emergency safeguards and subsidies needed for services? WTO negotiations on these issues have progressed slowly, and for safeguards have gone well over the three-year time limit originally envisaged in GATS.

The authors consider the feasibility, and indeed desirability, of extending these disciplines to services by seeing whether the GATT model on goods would work for services. Like them, I restrict my comments mainly to safeguards, about which Gauthier and his colleagues offer two key conclusions: first, the economic case for them is ambiguous; and second, for a number of practical and conceptual reasons, a GATT-generic safeguard clause would be unworkable for services, and not worth pursuing in GATS. The ambiguous case for safeguards rests on the following propositions:

—Using safeguards to temporarily protect domestic industries is irrational from an economic standpoint. Such measures usually frustrate rather than facilitate the industry's structural adjustment. Import restrictions are seen as an inefficient instrument for remedying serious injury and promoting industry restructuring. They effectively transfer the adjustment burden to someone else.

—Safeguards are costly to consumers, other producers, and to economic efficiency. Price rises for the injured products further penalize lowly assisted producers using them as inputs. This distorts resource allocation and defeats the purpose of trade liberalization. With many services, such as communications, transportation, and financial services, widely used in both consumption and production, these costs could be substantial.

—They have little value in securing more liberal commitments from members.

The first two arguments are, in my view, clear-cut. There are no "straight" economic reasons for having emergency safeguards. Governments should therefore not invoke them lightly; hence the need for tight disciplines on their use. However, I am unsure on the third point. I wonder whether access to emergency safeguards can have a "political economy" value in inducing more liberal commitments. Although it goes against my natural instincts to suggest so, there may be valid "political economy" reasons for having safeguards as a "safety valve" to encourage more liberal service commitments.

The generally poor architecture of GATS has a clear bearing on this debate. Because national treatment and market access are negotiated sectorally in GATS, there may be a greater need for a "safety valve" here than in GATT. Their absence may make members more inclined to enter binding commitments on services below the status quo. Safeguards may therefore provide a beneficial means of "unblocking" the negotiations and encouraging more liberal commitments. This would assist the negotiations by allaying the concerns some governments have against opening services markets, which by being new areas of liberalization have a high degree of uncertainty.

However, I also wonder whether we might not have already missed the boat. To be fully effective in this role, safeguards should have been finalized well in advance of the 2000 negotiations. This failure could have therefore been a lost opportunity to "prime" the upcoming negotiations. The safeguard negotiations have now become embroiled in sectoral negotiations. I am far from certain that this is a desirable outcome.

Gauthier and his colleagues suggest that one factor reducing the case for safeguards on services is that GATS already contains many safeguard-like measures. By way of example, they point to the positive list approach to scheduling commitments, Article XXI modification provisions, the prudential carve-out in financial services, general exemptions, and balance of payments provisions. They correctly state that a new safeguard instrument in services should only deal with those issues that cannot be handled by existing mechanisms. Nevertheless, it would be fruitful to discuss whether these really fulfill the perceived role of emergency safeguards. Members can indeed withdraw concessions in GATS, subject to compensation (Article XXI). But should some "halfway" measure be available to try first? GATT also has these and emergency safeguards.

Another argument for having emergency measures is that "the devil you know is better than the one you don't." According to the authors, some governments already expect such measures to be needed, and if this demand is not met, there is a real danger that other measures may be contemplated. Calls for extending antidumping action to services trade, so far thankfully not part of the services mandate, may not be far off. Given a choice between the two measures, I would strongly favor safeguards. Unfortunately, having emergency safeguards does not necessarily rule out having antidumping provisions, as GATT demonstrates.

The authors propose a new approach, should safeguards be applied to services. Members could inscribe them in their schedules of commitments, either on a line or broader sectoral basis. This approach is preferred because it better handles the intricacies of GATS, especially the multiple modes of supply, the different nature of service markets, and the balance of various interest groups affected by such measures.

GATT-generic emergency safeguards are considered unworkable in part because they are difficult to transpose to services: terms such as "imports," "like services," and "like service providers" can be difficult to interpret for services, as can proving causality between injury and imports. Equally important, they cannot take account of the diverse nature of services and their multiple modes of supply.

There is little doubt that differences between services and goods and the two agreements do raise a number of difficult conceptual and practical problems. Those discussed in chapter 7 relate mainly to the commercial presence mode of supply. However, do these by themselves constitute such insurmountable obstacles to justify walking away from applying GATT-generic safeguards to services? This important issue warrants further discussion, especially as there could be some benefits in adopting common safeguard measures within the WTO across all trade. Indeed, it begs asking whether having different emergency safeguard disciplines in GATT and GATS is desirable, even sustainable. At the very least, if there are to be differences, we need to be clear on the reasons why.

The proposal that members inscribe emergency safeguards in their schedules for individual sectors or categories is seen as a means of fine-tuning them to meet the diverse requirements encountered in services. Thus substantive tests and measures would be negotiated in country schedules, while a set of general disciplines or criteria would still control their use. Gauthier and his colleagues rightly state that such measures should be time-bound to delay trade liberalization only temporarily. Furthermore, the authors note, they should be triggered by transparent domestic procedures, be applied on a most favored nation basis, and be subject to appropriate notification, reporting, and surveillance requirements. However, members would presumably want these modalities agreed before commencing negotiations on what safeguards to schedule. Thus an essential task for this approach is to determine what general disciplines would be appropriate and whether those that currently apply to trade in goods could be used. Are these sufficient, and how would they be implemented?

Just as unclear are the practical consequences of having safeguard measures negotiated individually and inscribed in country schedules. For example, what format would such inscriptions take? Would the precise type of safeguard measures be negotiated and inscribed, and if so, from which set of available measures? Could other measures be invoked?

The proposed approach would also mean that safeguards would be negotiated on some services for certain modes and not others. Would this be a desirable outcome? The authors themselves mention a number of equity and efficiency problems that can arise from not having safeguard measures applied universally across all modes of supply of a particular service. Linking access to safeguards in the negotiations with more liberal sectoral commitments would add another major dimension to what are already complicated negotiations. Would it work in practice, or would it overload the process and make more liberal service commitments even harder to achieve?

One view consistent with that of Gauthier and his colleagues would be that members could use access to safeguards as a lever to obtain improved commitments from less liberal governments. However, this approach could entail high risks that might make it even harder to achieve liberal outcomes. How desirable is it to have important architectural features, such as on emergency safeguards, embroiled as "negotiating fodder" in crucial sectoral negotiations? Although well argued in chapter 7, such a novel approach runs the risk of creating more problems than it solves.

An alternative approach might be to apply generic emergency safeguards to services, while tightening the general disciplines governing their use, perhaps by introducing an effective public interest test and adopting a shorter and nonrenewable sunset clause. Members could then flexibly apply these measures in individual circumstances, subject to more effective controls. The tighter these general disciplines, the less need there would be to negotiate detailed rules on many of the specific issues covered in this chapter.

On the issue of subsidies, Gauthier and his colleagues remind us that some important provisions in GATS already govern domestic subsidies, such as most favored nation and national treatment. National treatment in particular can be a strong discipline on domestic subsidies. The authors therefore ask whether comprehensive disciplines on subsidies are necessary for services. Unfortunately, national treatment applies only to scheduled services, and then is subject to inscribed limitations, which, Gauthier and his colleagues inform us, most members made substantive use of in regard to subsidy measures.

The existing subsidy provisions on goods, they contend, are of only limited use in devising comprehensive subsidy disciplines for services, primarily because of the latter's multiple modes of delivery. Any comprehensive disciplines for services should, they suggest, initially prohibit export subsidies and control the use of investment incentives to encourage commercial presence. As their examples from across the four modes of supply illustrate, however, disciplines similar to those used in goods will not be easy to develop in order to prevent export subsidies in services.

Although these problems do complicate matters for services, one could again ask whether they are insurmountable. At the same time, as the authors point out, one must keep in mind that it would be very difficult, if not undesirable, to apply a countervailing duty mechanism to services.

Controlling fiscal incentives to entice foreign investment is undoubtedly a problem that lies outside the scope of GATS commitments. Such disciplines are badly needed, as Gauthier and his colleagues suggest, but they would seem to be more of a general problem affecting foreign investment in both goods and services. Therefore the question is whether establishing disciplines on their use in GATS under commercial presence is the best place for them. Rather, circumstances argue for a separate investment agreement covering both goods and services.

COMMENT BY
Ken A. Richeson

Nothing is more central to the promotion of trade and investment than the ability of business people to move freely around the world. Allison Young tackles this important subject by describing the current state of play on the issue of labor mobility. She begins her discussion with a definition of "mode 4," one of four ways in which the delivery of professional and business-related services is contemplated under GATS. Mode 4 is defined as "the supply of a service . . . by a service supplier of one Member, through presence of natural persons of a Member in the territory of any other Member" (Article I 2 (d)). Because mode 4 represents the first attempt by multilateral trade negotiators to liberalize the movement of natural persons who provide services, this definition can shed light on the present and future role of labor mobility in the World Trade Organization (WTO).

As Young points out, by addressing "behind-the-border" concerns, mode 4 raises complex regulatory issues regarding immigration and labor market development. During the Uruguay Round, she notes, developing countries took the position that "services supplied by the movement of people across borders is as legitimate a concept of service supply as commercial presence." It is for this reason that developing countries have suggested that an occupation services list could be used to negotiate occupations and service sectors in which "economic needs" or "skill level" tests would not apply as a means of limiting entry.

As is well known, little progress was made during the Uruguay Round or in the follow-up negotiations concerning the movement of natural persons. Commitments under mode 4, whether horizontal or sectoral, are significantly less extensive than in the other three modes. In most cases, where commitments have been made, they only bind the "status quo" and break no new ground.

To remedy this situation and provide the basis for moving forward, Young suggests that mode 4 be defined more clearly, in order to make the trade-offs in the negotiation process more transparent. In addition, WTO members need to agree to comprehensive peer reviews whenever mode 4 commitments are undertaken. Members are urged to increase transparency by explicitly stating the public policy objective of any restrictions. Young also calls on members to develop a parallel list that identifies those service occupations relevant to the delivery of services via mode 4, create technical standards for all service sectors that define "skilled professionals," prepare an inventory of problems raised by mode 4 delivery of services and use them to identify what commitments need to be made, define a separate regime for labor services or even labor movement, and seek agreement on "emergency safeguard measures" to provide incentives to identify and bind "economic needs test criteria" and relevant legislation. It will be impossible to address these issues adequately, Young adds, unless members engage in a comprehensive dialogue with the relevant national regulatory agencies, particularly those responsible for immigration and labor market development.

She urges trade officials to proceed with this task "incrementally." By that, she means they should undertake comparative research on the impact of different kinds of temporary movement in relation to trade agreements on national economies; they should try to develop "best practices" with respect to regulating temporary entry based on accepted international trade principles such as necessity, nondiscrimination, transparency, and equivalence; they should negotiate standard minimum liberalization commitments for mode 4 liberalization, which would be applied horizontally and sectorally; they should establish a formal process for the international exchange and dissemination of information on regulatory initiatives to liberalize movement of natural persons providing services.

The question is, does this approach get us to where we need to go in the necessary time frame? In my view, it does not. It does not address real-world business problems. It focuses on "form over substance" and opens the door to interminable discussions and negotiations. Furthermore, it ensures that the "national regulatory agencies responsible for immigration and labor market development" will succeed in putting protectionism ahead of liberalization.

In the world of business, companies that operate internationally come up against many problems caused by restrictive regulation of the temporary entry of key personnel. Operations may be delayed, for example, and service companies left without the means to meet their clients' needs on a timely basis.

One possible solution to this problem would be an international agreement on the temporary movement of key personnel with specialized knowledge. The agreement could apply to certain types of personnel, who would stay in a country less than one year with no intention of establishing residence. And it could apply only to workers already employed. Such an agreement would thus not create immigration or labor displacement problems.

Among its specific provisions, the proposed agreement would require that a valid passport be used for initial entry. In addition, business visas would be waived for stays of less than ninety days, or they could be applied for after entry; if approved, they would be valid for one year. Work permits would not be required if the stay was less than three months and, if granted, would be valid for one year. Taxes would not be required if the stay was less than 183 days in any twelve-month period. When taxes did apply, they would be applicable only to income earned in that country and would not be subject to withholding. Instead, the employer would be responsible for filing tax payments, and key personnel would be permitted to leave the country before the payment of taxes.

Efficient delivery obviously depends on people, especially in the case of services related to information technology, which are highly dependent on skilled personnel. An essential asset today is the ability to move skills around the globe. Indeed, the mobility of business people is a critical factor in meeting the needs of international customers and ensuring the growth of the information technology services sector.

But a host of problems—business visas, work permits, personal taxes, and others already mentioned—can get in the way of a growing business, as can be attested by IBM New Zealand's Integrated Customer Management Systems for telephone companies, a world-class service that allows a telephone company to gain competitive advantage in rapidly deregulated markets. Efforts to deploy this service in the Philippines ran into delays in getting necessary work permits. There were also tax problems, which could have made it necessary for IBM New Zealand to establish a tax presence in the Philippines. As a result, there were significant delays in establishing the system, which adversely affected the Philippine telephone companies that were going to use it. More important, the transfer of skills was delayed to the Philippines, which IBM hopes to make one of its four international centers for excellence in the installation of telecommunications services.

In another important case, IBM Taiwan won a contract to install five semiconductor fabricator projects for Taiwanese semiconductor manufacturers, which required the services of fifty Japanese engineers from IBM Japan. At that time, however, Taiwan had a quota system limiting a company's ability to bring in foreign workers. As a result, only ten of the engineers were granted work permits, which were good for six months and were readily renewable. Although palliative solutions were eventually developed, the completion of the projects was delayed, much to the annoyance of the firm's customers and the Taiwanese semiconductor industry.

Is an international agreement on the temporary movement of key personnel with specialized knowledge really possible? Several reasons suggest why it might be: it is consistent with the WTO's interest in expanding trade in services; it would address real business issues, which arise in a large number of sectors and are far from unique to the information technology industry; such a proposal focuses on temporary entry as opposed to immigration; the categories of personnel involved are already employed and not seeking employment in domestic labor markets; it would be limited to key personnel with specialized knowledge; precedents already exist in other international agreements, such as the North American Free Trade Agreement; and such an agreement is not impossible from a U.S. policy perspective.

What steps should be taken, then, to promote such an agreement? For one thing, international business—not just U.S. business—needs to make it a high priority. Thankfully, this is already happening. The issue has featured prominently in the recent submissions of the U.S. Coalition of Services Industries to the U.S. Trade Representative. In addition, the Business Advisory Council of the Asia-Pacific Economic Cooperation (APEC) has addressed it in their annual report to the APEC leaders. And the Transatlantic Business Dialogue has launched an effort that is concerned with international personnel mobility. But more needs to be done. Above all, a strong multisector, multinational case will have to be built before the kind of international regime described above can see the light of day.

PART THREE

Domestic Regulation and GATS: Regulatory Reform to Effective Market Access

9 | Regulatory Reform and Trade Liberalization in Services

GEZA FEKETEKUTY

SERVICES ARE AT THE HEART of the new economic revolution. They drive economic activities based on the new production paradigm, enabling countries to adapt new technologies to their own needs, and to link themselves to the broader global economy. No country can expect that paradigm to work, however, without first creating the conditions for a thriving, productive, and innovative services industry.

Regulatory reform and liberalization of trade in services are crucial tools for achieving this objective. They rid the environment of overregulation and restrictions on entry by foreign service providers, which inevitably result in low-quality, high-cost, and outdated services. The economic benefits of regulatory reform can be seen in the United States, following the reduction of government regulation in key sectors, and in the European Community, in the wake of efforts to remove regulatory barriers to trade under the single market program. The new round of negotiations on trade in services has to be seen as a key event in facilitating domestic reform of regulatory systems that up to now have prevented individual countries from seizing the new opportunities for economic growth.

The challenge for governments at present is to devise more effective policies for accomplishing important social goals, not to dismantle the means for pursuing a social agenda. Not all of these issues have a global dimension or can usefully be tackled at the global level at this time, but they help set a theme and a context for informing the broader purposes and vision of the next round of multilateral trade negotiations, which some have labeled the Millennium Round. One appropriate theme would surely be the reform of internal and external measures that hamper domestic economic efficiency and growth.

The Challenge of Regulatory Reform

The need for regulatory reform stems from four recent developments:
—Technological innovations that have expanded the potential for competition in infrastructure services.
—New products and services that do not fit current regulatory provisions.
—New insights into the economics of regulation, which may make it possible to design more economically efficient regulations.
—The globalization of production and markets, which has increased the cost of maintaining large national differences in regulatory standards.

Technological advances have led to an explosion of new goods and services. But these goods and services have difficulty entering markets where regulations mandate the use of goods and services based on current technologies, in order to satisfy various environmental, health, or safety concerns. Such regulations distort trade and competition by preventing enterprises or consumers from accomplishing desired social goals by more efficient means. This can be accomplished by establishing performance-based regulatory criteria. In any case, regulations that are product and technology specific become increasingly ineffective as markets substitute unregulated products and services for regulated ones.

Many infrastructure services have traditionally been thought of as natural monopolies because the major cost in providing the service was in the construction and maintenance of infrastructure facilities, rather than in the marginal inputs required to serve individual customers. Modern technology has fundamentally changed the economics underlying the provision of such services. It has reduced the capital cost of the infrastructure facilities in relation to variable costs, increased the opportunities for interconnecting independently provided services through computer intermediated systems, and made it possible to track, monitor, and price network services supplied over a single network by different enterprises. The net result is that competition has not only become more viable but is now an essential condition for the introduction of more efficient and innovative infrastructure services. Regulations that stifle and limit competition increase the costs of businesses dependent on these networks.

In this fast-changing environment, much has been learned about the incentive structures created by various techniques of regulation and their relative effectiveness in achieving desired social objectives. Much has also been learned about the advantages of and techniques for focusing regulations more closely on the desired regulatory objective. Too often regulatory systems seek to achieve social objectives by controlling entry into the industry by new suppliers or by controlling the provision of new services by existing suppliers, when attention really needs to be on the behavior of suppliers with respect to particular regulatory objectives. Moreover, there is a tendency to regulate more of the activities of an enterprise than is really necessary to achieve a clear social objective. For example, in order to ensure that the owners of telecommunication or power lines do not charge exorbitant prices or abuse their control over the basic distribution network, it is sufficient to regulate access to the network and the price charged for the use of the network. The market can be allowed to determine the types of services that might be offered over the network by competitive suppliers, and the prices charged for such services.

The regulatory scene has also been greatly affected by globalization. The globalization of production has created pressures for harmonizing standards related to the provision of internationally integrated infrastructure networks. The globalization of production makes economic sense only where national regulations allow the adoption of the technologies, information systems, and standards across national frontiers. Large differences in national regulations that have a direct bearing on the operation of globally integrated networks or production systems add to the cost of doing business internationally.

The Internet is pushing regulatory reform one step further by opening up the possibility for the efficient global distribution of many services. Governments will need to rethink the regulation of many services in light of the ability of consumers to buy services directly from foreign service providers. Some thought will also have to be given to the locus of responsibility for services produced abroad but purchased locally though the Internet, and to the desired scope for international cooperation in creating a stable commercial environment for Internet transactions. Already, many information services are provided competitively over the Internet, as are many financial services such as banking.

Principles for Regulatory Reform

A number of principles could help governments formulate sound laws and regulations. Such principles can induce governments to develop regulations that focus on desired social objectives, that do not burden economic activity more than is necessary to achieve those objectives, and that keep the opportunity cost of achieving the objectives at a minimum. At their core, most of these are principles of good governance, and of a sound legal structure.

Each country must decide how best to incorporate these principles into its own laws and regulations. At the same time, these principles can serve a useful purpose in international trade agreements, by helping to reduce the frictions associated with the pursuit of national social agendas in a globalizing world economy. Many of them have found their way into previously negotiated international trade rules and agreements. One of the challenges for a new round of negotiations in the World Trade Organization will be to find more effective ways of applying these principles through an extension of crosscutting rules such as those incorporated in Article VI of the General Agreement on Trade in Services (GATS) and the Code on Technical Barriers to Trade in the General Agreement on Tariffs and Trade (GATT), the negotiation of sectoral disciplines such as those incorporated in the Basic Telecommunications Agreement and the Agreement on Accounting Services, and the specific commitments embodied in national schedules.

Some of these principles are already widely accepted and only need to be incorporated more rigorously in the disciplines of the World Trade Organization (WTO), or extended to new areas of regulation. Other principles can be applied in novel ways to help governments achieve their desired social ends.

Transparency of Laws and Regulations

The first and most important principle is transparency. It holds that governments should publish all the laws, regulations, and administrative proceedings that affect market participants and all changes in such laws, regulations, and administrative procedures. Furthermore, everyone affected should know what the laws and regulations are before they engage in economic activity that may be covered by such laws and regulations.

This ensures fairness in governance and economic efficiency. Market participants cannot make informed decisions about production, marketing, and investment decisions if they do not know how laws and regulations will affect them. A firm cannot plan and organize its activities efficiently if it does not know in advance what rules it will have to follow. Moreover, it will not be able to make sound decisions about what to produce or trade unless it knows all the costs it will incur, including the costs of meeting regulatory requirements.

Second, all potential market participants must have equal knowledge about the relevant laws and regulations; otherwise, market outcomes will be distorted. Success in the marketplace will depend on privileged access to knowledge, rather than on superior economic performance. Every time a firm that exhibits superior economic performance finds itself at a disadvantage, overall economic growth suffers a blow.

Transparent laws and regulations are one of the essential ingredients of good governance. Transparency is equally important to the efficient functioning of a market economy, in that all market participants need to have access to all the available information about laws and regulations before they can make the correct management decisions. If everyone has the same access to such information, their success in the marketplace will be a function of their performance rather than privileged access to information. The principle of transparency is at the core of virtually all trade agreements.

Due Process in the Administration of Laws and Regulations

A second key principle is due process. This principle holds that firms affected by government laws and regulations should be given the opportunity to consult the government on the interpretation and application of the regulations that affect them, to appeal regulatory decisions to appropriate administrative or judicial bodies, and to obtain a timely response to requests for regulatory decisions.

Due process ensures that both market participants and officials have the information they need about the impact of laws and regulations on economic decisions, and that laws and regulations are administered in an impartial and objective manner. The process of consultation is a two-way street. On the one hand, it helps ensure that officials making regulatory decisions have the best possible knowledge about the impact of laws and regulations on economic activity. On the other hand, it helps ensure that market participants fully understand how to interpret and adapt the legal language to real-world situations.

Due process also helps minimize unforeseen but avoidable burdens on economic activity. Changes in the interpretation or application of regulations can help boost economic growth when such changes reduce costs or expand commercial opportunities without compromising the desired social objective.

Due process contributes to economic efficiency in three ways. It ensures that all market participants have the information they need to make sound decisions, that the economic cost of laws and regulations is kept to the minimum level necessary to achieve clearly identified social objectives, and that the most economically efficient firms succeed in the marketplace.

Predictability

Predictability is another important principle. It suggests that governments should not arbitrarily change laws and regulations. According to this principle, such changes should be made only when necessary to achieve stated social objectives and after proper notification and consultation. It implies that laws and regulations should be promulgated only after careful thought has been given to their implementation and effects in the future.

The principle of predictability extends the principles of transparency and due process over time and enables market participants to make sound long-term decisions. The establishment of a predictable legal and regulatory environment helps lower the risk for market participants and thus lowers the risk premium entrepreneurs have to build into their investment decisions. This in turn enables market participants to increase their level of investment and thereby contributes to economic growth.

Predictability enters into trade agreements through negotiated national commitments on policy measures that could affect particular sectors or products. Of course, the negotiation of such commitments does not remove all risk that the rules might change in the future. The rules give governments the flexibility to alter their commitments in the face of unforeseen events, or to adopt policies that affect the commitments under certain well-defined circumstances. However, the commitments assure businesses that the government involved will not change the rules arbitrarily and for less than compelling reasons.

Nondiscrimination

According to the principle of nondiscrimination, governments should not discriminate in the application of laws and regulations to market participants, except insofar as there is an objective and explicit criterion for such discrimination. Discrimination might be appropriate if circumstances differ, or if discrimination serves an objective policy purpose. This principle contributes to economic growth and economic efficiency by ensuring that the most effective firms are not put at a disadvantage through arbitrary discrimination in the design or application of regulations.

In trade parlance, nondiscrimination between firms or products originating from different foreign countries is referred to as the most favored nation principle. Nondiscrimination between domestic and foreign firms and products is referred to as national treatment. The application of the national treatment principle in GATS does not obligate governments to treat all domestic and foreign firms equally in all circumstances. However, any discrimination must be clearly stated, must be based on clearly established criteria, and must serve desirable policy objectives.

Objective, Performance-Based Criteria

In order to be effective, regulations must establish objective, measurable, performance-based criteria for the supply of services. This goal is difficult to achieve fully in all cases. Nevertheless, a regulatory system is more likely to achieve its desired social objective and is less likely to impose a burden on economic performance if its provisions and enforcement are based on objective, measurable, and performance-based criteria. Objective and measurable criteria ensure that the regulation will not be enforced on the basis of arbitrary criteria or on the whim of the regulator, but rather on a standard that is predictable and transparent and can be applied on a nondiscriminatory basis to all market participants. By closely linking the objective and measurable criteria to performance with respect to achieving the desired social objective, the government can help ensure that the regulation does what it is designed to do, namely, achieve the desired objective. It also helps ensure that the achievement of the desired social objective does not impose unnecessary costs or burdens on economic actors and by extension on economic performance overall.

By contrast, regulatory systems that leave a great deal of discretion to regulators are prone to corruption, to underachievement with respect to the desired social objectives, and to economic inefficiency. Similarly, regulatory systems that seek to substitute controls on entry, on production, or on prices for performance-based regulatory criteria will not achieve the desired regulatory goals, support the economically efficient delivery of the service, or enhance the growth of the economy overall.

Minimizing the Regulatory Burden

Another principle of good regulation is that rules should be designed so as to minimize the burden that the achievement of the desired social objective imposes on economic activity. This is obviously closely related to the principle just described, namely that regulations should be based on objective, measurable, performance-based criteria. It is only common sense to want to minimize the cost of achieving any particular goal.

Transparency of Regulatory Objectives

The burden associated with achieving a regulatory objective can be further minimized through the corollary principle that the social objective served by a particular law or regulation should be transparent; that is, it should be clearly stated at the time the regulation is adopted. A clear statement of the desired social objective helps to remove possible confusion over the purpose of the regulation. Such a statement also makes it a great deal easier to judge whether a regulation is the least burdensome necessary to accomplish the desired social objective.

Use of Market Mechanisms

Governments should use a market mechanism to promote desired social objectives, whenever that is feasible. The use of across-the-board economic incentives and disincentives is an economically efficient method of achieving desired social goals because it allows market forces to determine the most economically efficient manner of attaining them. A corollary of this principle is that scarce resources should be auctioned whenever possible rather allocated to incumbent firms on the basis of historic shares.

An auction process is more likely to enable the most efficient firms to gain access to such resources and is more likely to ensure that the opportunity cost of using the scarce resource is properly reflected in the cost of supplying the service and the prices charged to consumers.

Where regulations give existing producers or sellers preferential treatment in the allocation of scarce resources, they not only create domestic economic inefficiencies by discriminating against potentially more economically efficient new suppliers, but they also distort international trade and competition. Moreover, there is a significant risk that the economic inefficiencies and trade distortions will be magnified by political/interest group pressures and corruption.

Minimizing the Scope of Regulations

Closely related to the notion that governments should seek to minimize the regulatory burden is the principle that governments should minimize the scope of any regulation to what is necessary to accomplish the desired social objective. This principle holds that governments should only regulate activities directly related to the achievement of the regulatory objective. Reducing the scope of regulations to the minimum necessary to achieve the desired social objective helps to minimize the economic cost of such regulations.

This principle is particularly relevant to the regulation of infrastructure services such as water, gas, electricity, telecommunications, and rail transportation. In the past governments have shown a tendency to regulate all aspects of economic activity in these sectors because the network for distributing these services often constituted a natural monopoly. In more recent years many governments have recognized that they can more efficiently accomplish their objective of protecting consumers by separating the construction and operation of the distribution network from the provision of services over that network. By separating the production of these infrastructure services from their distribution through the monopoly network, the government can regulate access to and use of the network monopoly, while leaving the supply of the services involved open to market competition. Efforts to minimize the scope of regulations to the minimum necessary to achieve the desired social objective help to minimize the economic cost of such regulations and the potential distortion of international trade and competition.

Application of these principles in a more consistent and vigorous fashion to government measures that affect market competition will help achieve social objectives, improve the economic efficiency of markets, reduce trade distortions, and thus ultimately foster economic growth.

Strengthening the GATS Legal Framework on Regulation

Negotiators working on agreements dealing with regulatory issues should follow a three-prong approach: they should endeavor to strengthen Article VI of GATS (which deals with regulatory issues), negotiate sectoral agreements in heavily regulated sectors along the lines of the telecom agreement, and improve commitments incorporated in national schedules. This kind of approach would serve a number of purposes. It would keep the degree of intrusion by international rule-making in each sector to the minimum necessary to provide a viable framework for market entry and would open cross-border competition; it would provide a pragmatic basis for developing the most effective route to liberalizing trade in regulated sectors while preserving national preferences to the extent possible; and it would provide alternative means for making progress. Negotiating strengthened disciplines in Article VI is likely to prove an adequate basis for minimizing regulatory barriers to trade in many services sectors, particularly the newer professional services and services related to the information economy.

The negotiation of sectoral agreements in heavily regulated sectors makes it possible to address the specific areas of regulatory concern in a sector to the extent that is necessary to permit open competition among firms operating under different national regulatory regimes. It is neither necessary nor desirable to harmonize regulations among all countries. At the same time, open trade and competition cannot be achieved if countries are free to use the regulatory rationale to curb entry and competition at will. The negotiation of the specific commitments embodied in the national schedules allows countries to address specific issues having to do with differences in national legal systems, cultural practices, or institutions.

Exploring the Application of the Subsidiarity Principle

Preparatory discussions on regulatory reform might also explore the application of the subsidiarity principle to WTO negotiations on regulatory issues. In general, the principle of subsidiarity holds that any particular form of regulation should be carried out at the lowest level of governance consistent with the achievement of various social goals. In effect, this principle establishes a downward bias in favor of keeping regulation at the lowest level of governance consistent with the achievement of various social goals, including regulatory effectiveness, economic efficiency, and political legitimacy.

Regulatory decisions at a high level of governance make it possible to prevent the loss of economic efficiency and growth associated with differences in regulations. The economic advantage is a reduction in the compliance costs associated with meeting different regulations in different jurisdictions and an expansion of the potential economies of scale and scope. Decisions made at high levels of governance also have the political benefit of ensuring an equal distribution of the cost of achieving common goals, establishing common ground rules or a level playing field for firms competing across jurisdictional boundaries, and reducing the likelihood that competition will force regulators to adopt lower social goals. On the other hand, decisions at a high level of governance introduce added economic costs by leading governments to adopt regulations that do not suit different local conditions, and by making it more difficult to change regulations in response to changed circumstances. Decisions at higher levels of governance are also more difficult to keep up to date because a larger number of people have to agree to the change. Accommodating the views and interests of a larger number of people is not only more difficult, but also takes more time.

Decisions made a high level of governance also face the political cost of creating a greater distance between decisionmakers and those affected by the decisions, thus reducing the influence and involvement of individual citizens in decisions that affect them. Moreover, regulatory decisions made at a level above the nation-state create fundamental concerns about democratic control of such decisions. Given the central role of the nation-state in political life and the reluctance of nation-states to cede that sovereignty to supranational groupings, decisionmaking in supranational institutions is usually the exclusive province of national governments. Individual citizens usually find it difficult to acquire full information on how a decision was made, much less directly influence a decision. Most supranational institutions lack the political mechanisms that would allow individual citizens to influence such decisions directly.

The negotiation of international agreements on regulatory issues is thus an exercise in balancing the benefits and costs of economies of scale and scope in regulation. Liberalizing trade inevitably creates the need for rules that limit national flexibility. It is all the more necessary to remind oneself regularly that minimizing the intrusion into national decisionmaking is just as desirable as minimizing regulatory intrusion into individual choice by consumers and enterprises. The subsidiarity principle accomplishes this objective.

Generally, the WTO has a solid history of focusing agreements on key substantive and procedural principles, while leaving substantive details to national governments or other private or governmental international bodies with expertise in the area. GATT/WTO disciplines in trade-related areas of domestic policy generally do not establish detailed regulations but rather put forth a set of principles and procedures for the design and application of national measures. The objective is to make sure that policy measures are designed and applied without discrimination and to avoid unnecessary barriers to trade or unnecessary injury to enterprises engaged in trade.

The WTO Code on Technical Barriers to Trade provides a useful model in this regard. Effective international cooperation in many services calls for a judicious blend of legally binding obligations, voluntary guidelines, and references to standards and work carried out in other public and private entities.

GATS and Domestic Political Processes

In parallel with the application of the subsidiarity principle, negotiations should seek to make decisionmaking processes more transparent and more open to domestic democratic processes in member countries. Since future negotiations in trade in services will inevitably be more intrusive in the internal affairs of countries, the work in the WTO will have to become increasingly more transparent in order to meet public concerns about a democratic deficit in the WTO. Much useful progress has been made in reaching out to the public through the greater dissemination of information about WTO activities, through expanded contacts with private interest groups, and through the activities of issue coalitions among WTO members. More will have to be done in the future to assure skeptics that the WTO is not a secret conspiracy to rob them of their democratic rights.

Strengthening Article VI of GATS on Regulations

Article VI of GATS provides a basic framework for minimizing the distortions of trade created by domestic regulation. A strengthening of this article could go a long way toward liberalizing real market access by committing countries to the reform of regulations that impede market-oriented competition. Under the present provisions of Article VI, new regulations that affect services bound by national commitments are to be administered in a reasonable, objective, and impartial manner; must provide procedures for the review of the regulation at the request of service suppliers; and must be based on objective and transparent criteria, must not be more burdensome than necessary to ensure the quality of the service, and in the case of licensing procedures, must not in themselves restrict the supply of the service. These provisions could be strengthened in a number of ways.

First, the scope of the provision could be expanded to cover all regulations that have an impact on tradable services. Moreover, Article VI could expand the scope of GATS Article I on transparency by requiring members to explicitly state the public policy objectives served by a regulation. This would facilitate any examination of whether the regulation is "more burdensome than necessary to ensure the quality of the service," as provided in Article VI (4) (b).

A revision of Article VI could also make clear that the words "quality of service" in VI (4) (b) refer not only to the reliability of the service from the perspective of an individual consumer, but also to regulations aimed at the achievement of the full range of social objectives, including safety, integrity of networks, the provision of services to underserved regions or population segments, and so on. This broader interpretation of the term "quality of service" is consistent with the overall thrust of Article VI but is not necessarily clear if the sentence is taken by itself, outside the broader context of Article VI as a whole.

Article VI could also contain a new provision encouraging members to limit the scope of a regulation to what is necessary to achieve the objective served by the regulation. This would be fully consistent with the spirit of the requirement that regulations not be more burdensome than necessary to ensure the quality of service and would amplify that rule. Countries would be encouraged to regulate only those activities that have a direct bearing on the regulatory objective and not seek to regulate ancillary activities carried out by the same firm. Such a provision would, for example, encourage countries to limit their regulation of infrastructure services to the terms of access to physical infrastructures such as pipelines and electric transmission lines, leaving it to competitive suppliers of services to decide what services to provide over the network at what prices.

Article VI could also include a general restatement of the competitive safeguards built into the Telecommunications Annex and the Agreement on Basic Telecommunications (GBT). Such a provision would help assure that monopoly providers of essential services would not abuse their monopoly position by either charging unreasonable fees or by giving themselves preferential access to essential services in the competitive provision of downstream products. This provision could apply not only to "transport services" provided over electric conduits or pipelines but also to a variety of other monopoly inputs such as water.

Another addition to Article VI could encourage countries to adopt performance-oriented regulations rather than regulations that directly seek to establish bureaucratic control over the specific activities carried out by enterprises. Such a provision would parallel a provision embedded in the GATT Code on Technical Barriers to Trade and would also be fully consistent with and amplify GATS Article VI (4) (a), which requires regulations to be based on objective and transparent criteria.

Yet another possible addition could encourage member countries to use market-based incentives and disincentives to achieve regulatory objectives where that is feasible and appropriate. Market-based regulations tend to achieve desired social objectives with greater economic efficiency than directive regulations that seek to control the behavior of market participants. For example, it would be far more efficient from an economic standpoint to allocate scarce resources such as landing slots through an auction than through a system of licensing that benefits incumbents.

Finally, Article VI could encourage self-regulation by industry where that satisfies the achievement of the desired social objective. At the same time, it should require member governments in such cases to ensure that compulsory private regulatory or standards-making activities are open to all service providers, including foreign service providers.

Sectoral Negotiations

In some heavily regulated sectors, some degree of international rule-making on a sectoral basis is inevitable, particularly where the regulations specifically limit competition or competitive entry, or where the regulations set high performance standards for service providers. Countries with regulations that permit open entry and competition are concerned about market access conditions in countries that limit competition. Countries with strict performance standards are reluctant to grant open entry to foreign firms that are not required to maintain adequate performance standards by their own governments. International trade and competition in these sectors therefore may require some degree of international understanding on the allowable forms and extent of competition, and of the minimum performance standards that should be met.

It would be a mistake, however, for the WTO to establish highly detailed regulations. It needs to take to heart the principle of subsidiarity and avoid excessive rule-making. As was the case with respect to the GATT treatment of standards, the WTO should focus on establishing legally binding obligations centered on some key principles and procedures, while leaving much of the substantive detail to other international organizations, national governments, and voluntary private bodies. This calls for a judicious blend of legally binding obligations on key principles, voluntary guidelines that could serve as reference points for international regulatory norms, and references to standards and work carried out in other public and private organizations.

Concluding Thoughts

The liberalization of barriers to international trade and investment in services can contribute to growth in two ways. First, negotiations on international trade in services can spur the removal of barriers to internal competition within individual countries and thereby eliminate internal constraints to the achievement of greater economic efficiency in the production of services and relieve infrastructure bottlenecks. Second, such negotiations can bring down the barriers to external competition in services, making available the gains from increased trade such as expanded markets for competitively produced services, domestic gains in productivity as domestic producers respond to the foreign competition, and lower prices for consumers. The gainers will be business users of services, as well as household consumers.

Regulatory reform and a search for increased international cooperation on regulatory issues are likely to be central concerns of government policymakers in the years ahead. The recent crisis in the financial markets of many countries was a powerful reminder of the need for reform. In considering how progress can be made, it will be extremely important for any international discussion or negotiation on regulatory reform to focus on the domestic economic benefits of such a move.

Domestic political support for regulatory reform can be bolstered by focusing on the needs and interests of the users of services and on the contribution that the right kind of reforms can make to good governance. That contribution would be to improve the quality, objectivity, and professionalism of the regulatory bodies of government and to reduce the opportunities for bribery and corruption.

10 | From Policed Regulation to Managed Recognition in GATS

KALYPSO NICOLAÏDIS *and*
JOEL P. TRACHTMAN

To DATE, the General Agreement on Trade in Services (GATS) has focused mainly on discriminatory barriers to trade in services, rather than on nondiscriminatory (in EU parlance, indistinctly applicable) measures. However, nondiscriminatory regulatory diversity poses a substantial barrier to international trade in services because of the costs of complying with multiple regulation. What is required, or permitted and normal, in one jurisdiction may be forbidden in another. The benefits of free trade—economies of scale, consumer choice, and competitive discipline—are lost. The types and level of the barriers will vary in different circumstances, as will the trade costs. Even the regulatory benefits from diversity, assuming that they exist, will vary.[1] These complexities make it difficult to balance the trade costs occasioned by regulatory autonomy and the regulatory benefits assumed to arise from autonomy. A theoretical response would be to address this problem on a case-by-case basis, using cost-benefit analysis. However, this approach may be inefficient or otherwise unsatisfactory.[2] Even when the benefits of liberalization are deemed to outweigh its costs, the question remains as to what method should be used to achieve these benefits: general principles

1. See Nicolaïdis (1966); Trachtman (1993).
2. Sykes (1999); Trachtman (1998).

241

applied by panels or specific rules spelled out in political agreements. This essay examines the structure currently in place under GATS to address nondiscriminatory issues and suggests some policy alternatives.

Regulation of Services in Trade and Allocation of Regulatory Jurisdiction

For the purposes of this discussion, the constraints on trade, or what might be called the "trade and . . ." problem, need to be addressed in the specific factual and legal context of services. The "trade and . . ." problem has achieved notoriety in the context of environmental regulation, but it also exists in connection with labor rights, competition, intellectual property, investment, and virtually every other area of economic regulation. In this chapter, the "trade and . . ." problem involves regulation having at least a purported prudential goal but also collateral trade restrictive effects.[3] The "trade and . . ." problem is understandable as a problem of allocation of regulatory jurisdiction. To evaluate the options for addressing the "trade and services regulation" problem, one must first look at the techniques currently available under GATS for allocating regulatory jurisdiction, ex ante or ex post, over services.

Under the GATS model, rules of national treatment alone permit host state regulation to be applied to foreign nationals operating in the host state. Similarly, rules of mutual recognition (or simply rules of recognition) can be understood as rules allocating regulatory jurisdiction to the home state despite the offering of services in, or to residents of, a host state.[4] Rules of harmonization establish a kind of limited transnational regulatory jurisdiction, insofar as they set a transnational substantive rule for application by national authorities, or in some cases by transnational authorities. In addition, there are multiple types and phases of regulation. Thus even under rules of harmonization, regulatory barriers still exist because of the continuing fact that varying enforcers of the law are engaged in licensing and supervision activities.[5] The key distinction here is between the prescriptive

---

3. See Sykes (1996); Trachtman (1998).

4. See Nicolaïdis (1993); Trachtman (1995).

5. When we navigate between goods and services or among services, semantics matter. In the realm of goods, mutual recognition is used to refer to both mutual recognition of standards, and mutual recognition of testing and certification procedures. In the realm of professional qualifications, mutual recognition is also used to refer to both the recognition of equivalence of the content of training and

and enforcement aspects of jurisdiction. "Enforcement" jurisdiction refers to *regulatory control,* which encompasses the accreditation, supervision, and enforcement responsibilities of regulatory authorities. "Prescriptive" jurisdiction refers to the underlying substantive *rules,* that is, the *content* of the regulations that are enforced. Thus regulation is a complex process, with varying "moments," each of which should be evaluated separately.

Prevailing allocations of regulatory jurisdiction are increasingly being challenged by more dispersed methods of providing services (often by means of electronic technology) and by more transnationally dispersed service providers in financial, telecommunications, professional, and other sectors. These providers are engaging in cross-border acquisitions or finding other means to become established in multiple states. In view of these various circumstances, regulation of service providers must be distinguished from regulation of service transactions, and appropriate measures designed for each.

Efforts to Date in the WTO, European Union, and Functional Organizations

Together, the trends just described may put pressure on policymakers to move away from the traditional national treatment paradigm toward home country and transnational jurisdiction, or combinations thereof.

THE WORLD TRADE ORGANIZATION. The World Trade Organization (WTO) and GATS have only recently begun to address the issue of regulatory barriers to trade in services. The original Uruguay Round GATS negotiations led to an open-ended framework agreement centered around denials of national treatment and market access issues (Article XVI and XVII). Although it addressed blatantly protectionist regulation, GATS by and large declined to take on regulation with substantial regulatory justification.[6] Concessions made on these fronts are generalized through most

---

the recognition of the home country's authority to certify such training through the granting of diplomas or other evidence of qualification. When we come to financial services, or more generally services provided by firms and requiring supervision of these firms, mutual recognition along the second dimension is usually referred to as home country control.

6. The preamble to GATS recognizes "the right of Members to regulate, and introduce new regulations, on the supply of services within their territories in order to meet national policy objectives and, given asymmetries existing with respect to the degree of development of services regulations in different countries, the particular need of developing countries to exercise this right."

favored nation (MFN) treatment (Article II), but only separately for each of four modes of delivery.[7]

As will be shown later in the chapter, GATS imposes few specific constraints on national regulatory autonomy. In fact, in the leading sector of financial services, the Annex on Financial Services specifically provides that nothing in GATS shall prevent a state from taking measures for prudential reasons.[8] In addition, Article XIV spells out some general conditions under which domestic regulations that may impose a burden on outsiders ought to be considered legitimate. At the same time, GATS provides several facilities for the development of further restrictions, in Articles VI and VII.

Article VI(4) of GATS calls on the Council for Trade in Services (CTS) to develop any disciplines necessary to ensure "that measures relating to qualification requirements and procedures, technical standards and licensing requirements do not constitute unnecessary barriers to trade in services." Where a state has undertaken specific commitments, Article VI(5) applies, pending the entry into force of disciplines developed under Article VI(4). It prohibits the application of licensing and qualification requirements and technical standards that nullify or impair such specific commitments in a way that could not have been reasonably expected when the commitments were made and in a manner that is not based on objective and transparent criteria, is more burdensome than necessary to ensure the quality of the service, or, in the case of licensing procedures, is itself a restriction on the supply of the service. As shown later in the chapter, there are severe limitations on the possible application of this prohibition. Finally, Article VII encourages signatories to enter mutual recognition agreements: "For the purpose of the fulfillment, in whole or in part, of its standards or criteria for the authorization, licensing or certification of

7. The MFN issue that held up the Uruguay Round financial services agreement was purely an issue of reciprocal trade benefits and, at least initially, had little bearing on national regulatory autonomy. A different MFN issue is quite important in the field of regulation: the authority of states to enter into mutual recognition agreements that do not include all WTO member states. Such action is a departure from MFN, but one that is authorized, subject to specified conditions, under article VII of GATS (as discussed under guidelines for negotiations later in the chapter).

8. Similarly, the Annex on Telecommunications allows for limitations of access to include "measures necessary to ensure the security and confidentiality of messages," restrictions on resale or shared use, requirements to use specified technical interfaces for interconnection, requirements for the interoperability of telecommunication services, approval by type of terminals attached to the network, restrictions on interconnection of private leased or owned circuits, and, last but not least, notification, registration, and licensing of foreign service providers.

service suppliers . . . a member may recognize the education or experience obtained, requirements met, or licenses or certification obtained in a particular country." Presumably, domestic measures that escape the scrutiny of national treatment and Article VI(5) provisions will need to be dealt with (if at all) through Article VI(4) or Article VII.2.

THE EUROPEAN UNION. The European Union has achieved much more in terms of establishing disciplines on local regulatory autonomy, by virtue of the "negative integration" jurisprudence of the European Court of Justice (ECJ), positive integration through harmonizing measures, and positive integration through rules of mutual recognition. In fact, the subtle and dynamic combination of these types of measures in the European Union provides a useful reference, if not a model, for those seeking to address similar kinds of regulatory barriers to trade in services in the WTO or elsewhere.

The negative integration jurisprudence of the ECJ, beginning with *Dassonville*[9] and *Cassis de Dijon*[10] as applied to goods and extending to services in cases such as *German Insurance*[11] has disciplined national regulation of services in the European Union. The disciplines formulated by the ECJ include the principle of *proportionality*, stricto sensu, to the effect that trade burdens should not be excessive in relation to regulatory benefits, and the principle of *equivalence,* to the effect that where the host country's regulatory goal is addressed by home country regulation, the host country should defer. In applying these principles, the court has struck a subtle balance, usually shying away from all-out prohibition of domestic regulations applied to foreign providers, especially with regard to professional and financial services. More recently, it has even seemed to partly reverse its earlier jurisprudence in the field of goods, starting with the *Keck and Mitouard* ruling.[12]

In the European Union, this negative integration jurisprudence has served as a platform, a pathfinder, and a spur to positive integration. It is a platform of positive integration insofar as equivalence is a precursor to

9. *Procureur du Roi* v. *Dassonville,* Case 8/74, [1964] ECR 837.

10. *Rewe-Zentral AG* v. *Bundesmonopolverwaltung für Branntwein,* Case 120/78, [1969] ECR 649.

11. *Commission* v. *Germany,* Case 205/84, [1986] ECR 3755, 2 CMLR 519.

12. The case resulted in a partial shift away from the *Cassis* jurisprudence by limiting the scope of application of Article 30 (free movement of goods) to domestic regulations related to the characteristics of the product itself, rather than those linked with its marketing and distribution. Case C-267 and 268/91, November 24, 1993.

legislative requirements of mutual recognition. It also serves as a pathfinder for legislation, developing approaches to allocation of jurisdiction that may later be legislatively adopted. It is a spur insofar as equivalence, along with proportionality, provides incentives for states to negotiate legislative packages for essential harmonization combined with mutual recognition.

Since the adoption of the Single European Act in 1987, the European Union has engaged in a substantial program of legislation to create essential harmonization and mutual recognition in a wide array of service sectors. These positive integration efforts are supported by, and interact with, the negative integration jurisprudence of the ECJ.

The single-market program included ninety-two directives, regulations, or Commission recommendations aimed at liberalizing the services market.[13] For professional services, member states passed the *General Systems Directive* in 1989 and its supplement two years later, distinguishing between more than and less than three years of study for the purpose of mutual recognition of professional diplomas.[14] The directives introduced a horizontal approach for the 150 or so professions in the European Union, eschewing the sectoral harmonization pursued in the previous decades (mainly in the medical field). Given the lack of harmonization, however, the directive granted only a partly automatic right of entry, spelling out the residual requirements permitted in the host state.

In the financial sector, the *Second Banking Directive,* along with flanking harmonization directives, introduced the Community single-banking license, otherwise referred to as the European passport.[15] But jurisdictional transfer to the home country was not complete: the host country retains responsibility for the supervision of liquidity and enforcing measures related to monetary policy, and exceptions are available to protect the "general good." As discussed below, the European Union has implemented a

13. Covering banking (14), insurance (12), securities (9), transport (18), new technologies and services (21), capital movement (3), and free movement of labor and the professions (16).

14. Council Directive 89/48/EEC on a general system for the recognition of higher education diplomas, COM (1985) 355 final, *Official Journal of the European Communities,* C 217/3, 8.85; Council Directive 92/51/EEC (June 18, 1992) on a second general system for the recognition of professional education and training to supplement Directive 89/48/EEC. *Official Journal of the European Communities,* L 209/25, 24.7.92.

15. Council Directive 89/646/EEC (December 15, 1989) on the Coordination of Laws, Regulations and Administrative Provisions relating to the Taking up and Pursuit of the Business of Credit Institutions, *Official Journal of the European Communities,* L 386, 1989. The directive was made famous outside the European Community because it embodied a reciprocity clause that could exclude non-EC newcomers from its benefits.

complex system—combining home and host jurisdiction, recognition and harmonization, and sovereignty transfers based on mutual monitoring as well as trust—that can be characterized as one of "managed mutual recognition."[16]

THE TRANSATLANTIC MARKETPLACE. Following on the EU experience and on the successful negotiations of six bilateral sectoral mutual recognition agreements (MRAs) for products, the United States and the European Union have launched a new initiative, the Transatlantic Marketplace, which seeks to extend mutual recognition and harmonization to a number of services sectors, including the professions. These MRAs would cover not only the enforcement dimension of jurisdiction, as did the MRAs on products signed in 1996, but also prescriptive jurisdiction—the applicability of substantive rules—as the two are much harder to disentangle in the case of services.

FUNCTIONAL ORGANIZATIONS AND COOPERATION WITH THE WTO. The WTO has expressed a willingness to defer to action by functional specialized organizations, such as the International Telecommunications Union and the International Organization for Standardization in telecommunications, the International Federation of Accountants, the International Accounting Standards Committee and the International Organization of Securities Commissions in accounting, the Bank for International Settlements for banking, the International Civil Aviation Organization for aviation, Codex Alimentarius in food standards, and the International Labor Organization in labor standards, in connection with issues involving the overlap between trade competencies and other functional competencies.[17] Indeed, given the limitations on the applicability of non-WTO law in the context of WTO dispute resolution, it seems odd that the WTO defers to these other organizations.[18] It will most likely be necessary to amend WTO law to incorporate the results of the legislative efforts of these functional organizations, or to address these issues in WTO law initially. Furthermore, the WTO may prove an attractive forum for these types of negotiations, insofar as the WTO facilitates cross-sectoral exchanges of concessions.

16. See Nicolaïdis (1993, 1996). Also chapter 11 in this volume.
17. Renato Ruggiero, the outgoing director-general of the WTO, has proposed the creation of a "World Environmental Organization" to serve as an environmental counterpart to the WTO.
18. See Trachtman (1999).

What Is Left to Be Done?

It is difficult to determine how much more action needs to be taken to reduce regulatory barriers to trade in services. The determination cannot be made in the abstract but must be made by reference to particular sectors in particular states. The determination must be made on the basis of the benefits to those particular states of reducing regulatory barriers, including compensation provided by other states in other sectors. Thus it will be important to evaluate the costs and benefits of such barriers, and to place them on the table for negotiations alongside other types of concessions in services, goods, investment, intellectual property, and the like, in the next round of trade negotiations. States will no doubt make sector-specific proposals and may find that there is enough congruence, or institutional spillover, among these proposals to adopt a more horizontal arrangement. In light of sectoral diversity, however, horizontal arrangements will generally be framed broadly, as standards for general application.

WHY DO MORE? COMPARING THE COST OF TRADE BARRIERS AND THE VALUE OF REGULATORY AUTONOMY.   Regulatory autonomy is valuable for a number of reasons. States may simply have different regulatory goals or methods, consumers different needs and habits. Regulatory competition may provide benefits, first through regulatory autonomy, perhaps enhanced by rules of recognition without harmonization. However, regulatory competition may bring an unwelcome race to the bottom. Moreover, the value of regulatory autonomy must also be weighed against three additional considerations. First, regulators are increasingly subject to the same pressures as commercial service providers: they need to regulate efficiently, at the least cost to the tax payer; waiving their regulatory prerogatives over foreign service providers helps in this regard. Second, regulatory cooperation can be good, spreading best practices, in addition to facilitating trade. Third, given transnational enterprise, regulators will need to cooperate in order to address the full jurisdictional scope of regulatory issues. Thus no single answer will apply across all sectors and for all countries. Rather, it is necessary to devise an institutional structure that will provide context-sensitive responses to particular regulatory circumstances.

DETERMINING APPROPRIATE INSTITUTIONAL OR REGULATORY STRUCTURES TO DO MORE.   Several options are open to GATS negotiators, assuming they have a desire to impose greater disciplines on nondiscriminatory domestic regulation.

Laissez-Régler. The first option is to do nothing legislatively (by "legislatively," we mean via treaty-making or other international law making). This approach might be suggested by considerations of subsidiarity: let the national government regulate as it sees fit (laissez-régler). This can be understood as the classical version of the national treatment principle. Interestingly, laissez-régler (freedom of states from restraints on regulation) is in some sense in opposition to traditional concepts of laissez-faire (freedom of business from regulation). This, of course, leaves open the question of whether some negative integration (or limited positive integration) should be effected adjudicatively. Laissez-régler is often accompanied by rules of national treatment, which may shade into more intrusive standards. Laissez-régler would be the right approach where there is no value to be gained from further integration, from further reduction of trade barriers.

Enhanced Policed Regulation. A second option would be to provide substantially stronger standards for domestic regulation in the resolution of disputes. These standards might approximate those applied by the ECJ in the European Union. They would go farther toward disciplining non-discriminatory national regulation on the basis of disproportionality, necessity, or equivalence, or a more wide-ranging balancing test. Interestingly, the national treatment principle is so difficult to limit that it can be applied in a way that may constitute enhanced policed regulation.

Harmonization and Recognition. The WTO can continue to expand its legislative program, with negotiations at the CTS under Article VI(4) toward increased rule-based discipline, leaving less discretion to the dispute resolution process than under the first and second options. Such a program might include rules of harmonization or rules of recognition negotiated and enforced multilaterally but is more likely in the short term to develop through the use of Article VII and restricted negotiations on recognition that might later be expanded. Within this program, case-by-case choices of the combination of harmonization and recognition would be appropriate.

FOUR SCENARIOS TO RECONCILE TRADE AND REGULATORY GOALS. As negotiators seek to "map boundaries" between these different modes and levels of constraints, they will need to decide where various regulatory measures and policies ought to fall along two separate dimensions: general standards versus specific rules, and a multilateral regime versus plurilateral arrangements.

Regulatory Approach: General Standards versus Specific Rules. Following a distinction used in the legal lexicon, negotiators need to decide on the role of general standards usually applied through dispute resolution, on one hand, and more specific rules usually established through treaty-making, on the other hand. In other words, to what extent should domestic regulation be policed through legal principles or political agreement?[19] Laissez-régler can fall in either of these categories, whereas enhanced policed regulation generally belongs to the former and recognition/harmonization generally belongs to the latter. This choice ought to be based on criteria of feasibility and legitimacy, as will be discussed later. Clearly, these options can easily be combined on a case-by-case basis, for example, for a given service sector and mode of delivery.

Institutional Framework: Multilateral Regime versus Delegation to Plurilateral Arrangements. In addition, the WTO could rely on preexisting and new plurilateral arrangements that pertain to domestic regulations outside the full-blown multilateral framework (table 10-1). Alternatively, or in combination, these can develop either more restrictive general standards among a subset of contracting parties or establish specific rules made through political deals, such as MRAs. Such plurilateral arrangements could be bilateral, regional, or functional. That regulatory measures might be handled under this category would not mean that they would fall outside the scope of the WTO, however, but simply that liberalization would be pursued under a bilateral or regional waiver or under a code-like approach. In this case, the authority to manage domestic regulatory measures is delegated, or at least relinquished, by the WTO. Four broad categories of approaches are thus available under the WTO trade regime. Obviously, these approaches are not mutually exclusive and can be combined across as well as within sectors.

The boundaries between these alternative approaches can be better understood by examining the characteristics, limits, and potentials of the key GATS provisions relevant to option 1—namely, national treatment under Article XVII, legitimate exceptions under Article XIV, and nullification and impairment under Article VI(5)—and then seeing how these

---

19. We believe that the actual distinction used in the literature between "standards" and "rules" might be misleading in our context, in that here "standards" is also used to refer to some of the domestic regulations per se, as in banking standards or professional standards. In this latter sense, it conveys a notion of specificity rather than generality. To avoid confusion, we will use the terms "general standards" or "legal principles" interchangeably.

Table 10-1. *Mapping Boundaries in GATS*

	Institutional framework	
Regulatory approach	Multilateral (directly under WTO)	Plurilateral (authority delegated by WTO)
General standards (legal principles)	Article XVII national treatment	EU/ECJ equivalence/ proportionality
	Article VI(5) proportionality vs. Article XIV exceptions	Possible further plurilateral arrangements
Specific rules (political agreements)	Article VI(4) agreements	Bilateral or plurilateral MRAs under Article VII
	Possible further agreements	Possible further regulatory cooperation mechanisms

relate to the other three options. At that point, it will be possible to propose a general framework for dealing with alternative regulations under GATS.

National Treatment under Article XVII

National treatment—which requires that foreigners be treated at least as well as locals—is a fundamental component of any structure for economic (and indeed political) integration. In GATT, national treatment obligations under Article III were initially intended to protect from defection the tariff concessions under Article II of GATT. However, Article III has grown in its use, in part because of the inherent difficulties in applying the standard of national treatment itself. The central problem—never solved in GATT—is how to determine when two products are similar enough (are "like products") to implicate the obligation to treat them alike. In order to find two products alike when they are regulated differently, it is often necessary to disregard—to implicitly invalidate—the regulatory distinction applied under national regulation. Article XVII(1) of GATS provides that

> in the sectors inscribed in its schedule, and subject to any conditions and qualifications set out therein, each Member shall accord to services and service suppliers of any other Member, in respect of all measures affecting the supply of services, treatment no less favorable than that it accords to its own like services and service suppliers.

Thus national treatment under GATS is not universal but is subject to the positive listing of the relevant service sector in the relevant state's schedule. In addition, it is subject within each listed sector to the negative listing of any exception to the national treatment obligation in that schedule. The decision that national treatment should not be a general principle as in GATT, but a concession to be bargained over, is one of the distinctive features of GATS, reflecting the fact that the starting point with services is a "zero tariff situation."[20] The core of a nondiscrimination obligation such as national treatment is the comparison between the favored good, service, or service supplier and the disfavored one. Article XVII sets up the comparison as being one between "like" services or service suppliers, referring on its face to the "like products" concept articulated pursuant to Article III of GATT.

Like Services and Service Suppliers

What makes two services "like?" For example, is the underwriting of a bond issue "like" a bank lending transaction? If so, why are different reserve requirements and capital requirements applicable? Does it matter for regulatory purposes that one transaction is effected by a bank that accepts insured deposits? Similarly, is Internet telephony "like" standard telephone service? More fundamentally, is it permissible to make distinctions between services on the basis of the identity and structure of the service supplier as well as the way the service appears to the consumer?

PRODUCT/PROCESS DISTINCTIONS AND INSTITUTIONAL REGULATION VERSUS TRANSACTIONAL REGULATION.   Under some GATT Article III jurisprudence, referring to ad Article III, the regulation of production processes is not "subject to" Article III, and is therefore an illegal quantitative restriction under Article XI, unless an exception applies under Article XX.[21] The product/process distinction serves as a kind of territorially based allocation of jurisdiction, in which the product, which travels to the importing state, may be regulated by the importing state. On the other hand, the production process, which is assumed to take place in the exporting state, is not "subject to" Article III, and therefore is unprotected from the strict scrutiny of Article XI (and regulation by the host state is permitted only if justified under

20. Drake and Nicolaïdis (1992).
21. Trachtman (1998c). Ad Article III is the designation for treaty language that is appended to Article III.

Article XX). The situation is quite different in GATS, where the regulation of service providers is expressly validated and subjected to the national treatment criterion.[22] Because the service provider—person or firm—may itself be a part of the continuing nature of the service, a different arrangement seems appropriate. That is, it seems less obvious (if it is at all obvious in the goods sector) that the service-importing state should not have equal rights to regulate the service provider itself, even though on the territory of the home country. In other words, the process by which a service is "produced" (a loan issued, a professional trained) as it were, may determine the actual characteristics of the ultimate service "product" (the loan, the advice, the treatment). This would validate traditional institutional regulation of most types of financial institutions, as well as regulation of the structure of law firms or other types of service providers.

Furthermore, we must distinguish between the two main vehicles for trade in services: cross-border provision (including consumption abroad) and commercial presence.[23] In cases of commercial presence, the foreign service provider would, at least to some extent, be present in the territory of the service "importing" state and thus would be more naturally subject to the full territorial jurisdiction of that state.[24] The need for commercial presence indeed reflects the fact that a service is often "produced" and "consumed" simultaneously and in the same place. We have a much less "natural"—and more difficult—regulatory jurisdiction problem in connection with the cross-border provision of services, whereby production and consumption need not happen in the same place.[25] However, as seems to be recognized in Article XVII, the "importing" state should not, prima facie, be prevented from regulating the service provider in these cases.

On its face, the structure of Article XVII seems to indicate that a na-

22. Mattoo (1997).

23. GATS distinguishes among four modes of delivery, allowing states to list different exceptions to liberalization under each mode. With the advent of e-commerce, the distinction between modes 1 and 2 is becoming more and more blurred, and mode 4 can be seen as a variant on 3 for our purposes. The four modes are from the territory of one nation into the territory of another; in the territory of one nation to a consumer in another nation; by a service supplier of one nation through commercial presence in the territory of another nation; and by a service supplier of one nation through presence of natural persons of a nation in the territory of another nation. This categorization is one of the keys to the evolutionary nature of GATS: it achieves two seemingly contradictory purposes by casting the widest net possible for liberalization while allowing nations to carve out areas to exempt from liberalization, even within subsectoral categories listed in their schedules.

24. Of course, with a multinational corporation such as a bank, especially one that operates through branches, it may be difficult to regulate the corporation without regulating extraterritorially.

25. Nicolaïdis (1995); Trachtman (1998a).

tional service regulation imposed on a foreign service provider must meet two tests: it must provide treatment no less favorable than that accorded domestic like services, and the treatment must be no less favorable than that accorded domestic like service providers. Therefore, even if the service providers are not "like," and there is thus no possible basis for finding illegal discrimination between them, it is still possible that the services they provide may be "like," giving rise to a claim of violation of the requirement of national treatment. This might on its face seem an absurd result, and might invalidate, for example, a regulation that requires a bank to maintain reserves different from those maintained by an insurance company before making a loan, for while the service providers might not be "like," the services are.

Thus it would be better to read the two requirements above in the disjunctive, that is, to separate the evaluation of treatment of services from the evaluation of treatment of service providers. One would simply evaluate regulation of services, as services, by determining whether the regulation treats "like" services alike, full stop. If this were the case, regulation of service providers would be evaluated to determine only whether like service providers, as service providers, are treated alike. Using this interpretation, there would be no violation of national treatment if like services were treated differently where the reason for the difference in treatment is the regulation of the service provider, as service provider. This is likely to be the interpretation that a WTO panel or the Appellate Body would apply. *In effect, such an approach would replicate a kind of product/process distinction as a service/service provider distinction.* But contrary to the general understanding of the case of products, host state regulation of the "process" or the service provider—often geographically located in the host state— would be validated (subject only to a strict national treatment constraint). Laws regulating the service, as such, would only be evaluated to determine whether like services are treated alike, while those regulating the service provider, as such, would only be evaluated to determine whether like service providers are treated alike. The WTO Dispute Settlement Body would be required to distinguish between regulation of services and regulation of service providers. In addition, the analogy to products might be taken one step further, suggesting stronger constraints on host state regulation of the service provider than of the service.

WHO SHOULD DETERMINE THE VALIDITY OF REGULATORY DISTINCTIONS?
As noted at the beginning of this section, GATT/WTO dispute resolution has been unable to provide a predictable, consistent approach to determin-

ing when products are "like." We cannot expect GATS dispute resolution to do better. Thus, for example, we might ask whether two accountants, each with advanced university degrees from universities in different states, are "like service providers." Are two banks, each from different states where they are required to establish different levels of reserves, "like service providers"? Similarly, are the loans provided by these two banks "like services"? Under GATT jurisprudence, these questions cannot be answered predictably, or in the abstract, but must be determined on a case-by-case basis. While this jurisprudence results in a degree of unpredictability, the Appellate Body has now addressed several cases, providing experience in how these multiple factors are likely to be viewed and applied. The question for us, answered later in the chapter, is whether this situation of case-by-case analysis by the dispute settlement mechanism is superior to a more discrete, ex ante, specification that could be provided by a treaty-making or other quasi-legislative process?

PRUDENTIAL EXCEPTIONS.   Under Article 2.1 of the GATS Annex on Financial Services, nothing in GATS prevents members from taking any measures for "prudential reasons," including for "the protection of investors, depositors, policy holders or persons to whom a fiduciary duty is owed by a financial service supplier, or to ensure the integrity and stability of the financial system." The scope of this "prudential carveout" is unclear, especially as Article 2.1 continues to state that "where such measures do not conform with the provisions of [GATS], they shall not be used as a means of avoiding the Member's commitments or obligations under the Agreement." This language seems to deny the exception where there is an intent to evade other GATS commitments. The exceptions included in the Telecommunications Annex do not contain such a caveat. In addition, one might expect that a measure might be attacked on the basis that it is not properly considered "for prudential reasons." It is difficult to predict how a WTO panel or the Appellate Body would approach this requirement. One possibility might be that it would be treated analogously to the treatment of Article XX(g) of GATT, which provides an exception from other GATT disciplines for measures "relating to the conservation of exhaustible natural resources." WTO dispute resolution jurisprudence has required that measures sought to be justified under this provision be "primarily aimed" at such conservation. By analogy, in order for a measure to benefit from the "prudential carveout" of Article 2.1 of the GATS Annex, it would need to be "primarily aimed" at prudential regulation.

This is just one of several possible ways that a WTO panel might approach the prudential carveout.

Relationship with General Exceptions, Article XIV

Importantly, even if a state is otherwise found to violate the national treatment obligation of Article XVII (or other provisions of GATS), its regulation might still be permitted under the exceptional provisions of Article XIV. Of course, Article XIV would only apply where there was an original violation of another provision of GATS. Article XIV parallels Article XX of GATT, providing certain domestic policy exceptions from the otherwise applicable GATT obligations. The most relevant bases for exceptions under Article XIV are for measures

> (b) necessary to protect human, animal or plant life or health;
> (c) necessary to secure compliance with laws or regulations which are not inconsistent with the provisions of this Agreement including those relating to:
> (i) the prevention of deceptive and fraudulent practices or to deal with the effects of a default on services contracts; (ii) safety.

Both of these clauses incorporate a "necessity" test, which has been interpreted in the GATT context to require that the national measure be the least trade-restrictive alternative reasonably available to achieve the regulatory goal. Least trade-restrictive alternative analysis in the European Union has often turned to labeling requirements, which might be less applicable in some service areas than they are in goods. The necessity test is discussed in more detail in the next section.

Furthermore, the exceptions under Article XIV would be available only if the national measures met the requirements also of the chapeau of Article XIV, which requires that such measures "are not applied in a manner which would constitute a means of arbitrary or unjustifiable discrimination between countries where like conditions prevail, or a disguised restriction on trade in services." The recent *Gasoline* and *Shrimp/Turtle* decisions of the WTO Appellate Body have interpreted the same language in the context of Article XX of GATT in a fairly restrictive manner. In the *Shrimp/Turtle* case, the Appellate Body applied a balancing test (referred to as a search for a "line of equilibrium"), evaluating whether the application of the national measure is appropriate to achieve the regulatory goal, whether it is the least trade-restrictive alternative reasonably available to achieve the regulatory goal, and whether it is applied equally to all member states. Given that the chapeau of Article XIV is identical to that of Article XX, one would expect the same type of scrutiny to be applied in services cases.

Nullification or Impairment and the Necessity Test under Article VI(5)

Article VI (Domestic Regulation) spells out general obligations for service sectors that have been included by contracting parties in their national schedules, except for measures that are the object of reservations in these schedules under Article XVII (National Treatment) and XVI (Market Access). In very vague terms, it provides that domestic regulations applied in a sector that a member has agreed to include under specific liberalization commitments must be administered in a "reasonable, objective, and impartial manner." Article VI also includes procedural guidelines requiring that decisions in cases where the supply of a service requires authorization in the host country must be issued "within a reasonable period of time," and that signatories must establish tribunals and procedures to process potential complaints by foreign service suppliers.

Article VI(4) of GATS calls on the Council for Trade in Services to develop any necessary disciplines to ensure that measures relating to qualification requirements and procedures, technical standards, and licensing requirements do not constitute unnecessary barriers to trade in services.[26] Prior to the agreement and entry into force of more specific rules under Article VI(4), disciplines on national measures are available under Article VI(5) in sectors in which the importing member has undertaken specific commitments. In order for these disciplines to apply, two sets of criteria must be satisfied:

—The licensing or qualification requirements or technical standards must nullify or impair specific commitments in a manner that could not reasonably have been expected at the time the specific commitments were made.

—The measure must fail to be based on objective and transparent criteria, or be more burdensome than necessary to ensure the quality of the

---

26. It is worth asking what is left out of this list of types of measures. Was this provision intended to exclude any particular type or method of regulation?

service, or in the case of licensing procedures, be in itself a restriction on the supply of the service.

Nullification or Impairment

Nullification or impairment (N/I) has served as a central feature of GATT and WTO dispute resolution. Under Article XXIII of GATT, redress pursuant to the dispute resolution system of GATT is only available in the event of N/I. In fact, it is possible, although infrequent, for N/I to serve as the basis for a successful complaint in the absence of an actual violation of GATT: in a so-called nonviolation nullification or impairment. Article VI(5) of GATS incorporates this concept of nonviolation nullification or impairment.

In a recent nonviolation nullification or impairment case, *Film,* the panel reviewed in detail the basis for certain U.S. expectations, in order to decide whether the United States had "legitimate expectations" of benefits after successive tariff negotiation rounds.[27] As the complaining party, the United States was allocated the burden of proof as to its legitimate expectations. In order for the United States to meet this burden, it was required to show that the Japanese measures at issue were not reasonably anticipated at the time the concessions were granted.[28] Where the measure at issue was adopted after the relevant tariff concession, the panel established a presumption, rebuttable by Japan, that the United States could not have reasonably anticipated the measure.

The import of this approach in the services context is clear. The complaining party must show that the measures attacked were not reasonably anticipated. Thus long-standing regulatory practices or circumstances are protected. This means that the domestic circumstances as they are form a background for all concessions; as a matter of negotiation strategy, members of GATS must recognize this and bear the burden of negotiating an end to existing measures that reduce the benefits for which they negotiate.

It is useful to compare this structure with that applicable to goods under GATT and under the two WTO agreements pertaining to regulatory standards: the Agreement on Technical Barriers to Trade and the

---

27. "Japan—Measures Affecting Consumer Photographic Film and Paper," Panel Report WT/DS44/R (98-0886), adopted by Dispute Settlement Body (April 22, 1998) [hereafter, Film Report].

28. Film Report, para. 10.7.

Agreement on the Application of Sanitary and Phytosanitary Measures. Neither GATT nor these agreements include the N/I requirement in the prohibition itself. Therefore, in connection with trade in goods, determination of a violation of a provision of a covered agreement results in prima facie N/I under Article 3(8) of the Dispute Settlement Understanding, placing the burden of rebutting the existence of N/I on the respondent. In the context of Article VI(5) of GATS, without N/I, there is no violation. Without a violation, there is no prima facie N/I. Consequently, it will be the responsibility of the complaining party to show nullification or impairment. This will make it more difficult for national services regulation to be addressed under Article VI(5).

We may speculate as to why GATS relies on the N/I concept so heavily in this context. N/I is an extremely vague standard, but one that by itself has been difficult to meet. Thus, without the means to negotiate more specific disciplines on national regulation, N/I provides a modicum of more general discipline. It might be viewed as a "least common denominator," insofar as the parties could agree not to nullify or impair concessions earnestly made, but could not agree on more pervasive, blanket restrictions on their national regulatory sovereignty. Thus Article VI(5) is first and foremost merely a standstill obligation.

The Necessity Test

Under this additional component of the Article VI(5) test, we focus on the requirement (incorporated from Article VI(4)(b)) that the national measure not be more burdensome than necessary to ensure the quality of the service. Even if it is possible to show that a national measure nullifies or impairs service commitments, a complainant would still be required to show that the national measure does not comply with the criteria listed in Article VI(4), the most likely of which is the necessity test examined here.

GATT dispute resolution panels have taken a narrow view of what is "necessary" under Article XX of GATT, which contains language on which Article VI(5) is modeled.[29] In order to be deemed necessary, the measure must be the least trade-restrictive measure reasonably available to achieve the regulatory goal. In the context of Article VI(4)(b), the reference is to measures "not more burdensome than necessary to ensure the quality of

29. "Thailand—Restrictions on Importation of and Internal Taxes on Cigarettes," DS10/R, GATT Basic Instruments and Selected Documents 200 (37th Supp. 1990).

the service." The last clause could be very interventionist. It could restrict not just the means to attain a given regulatory goal but even the types of regulatory goals that might be achieved, as when the regulatory goal is not to maintain the quality of the service but to avoid some other externalization or regulatory harm by the service provider. For example, if a bank is required to maintain a particular reserve in relation to a loan, is that necessary to ensure the quality of the service? Many types of service regulation might be subject to similar, inappropriate, attack. This provision should be corrected in the next round of negotiations.

Furthermore, in a placement comparable to the inclusion of the N/I criterion in the substantive prohibition, the necessity criterion here is included as a parameter of the substantive prohibition, in addition to being included in the exceptional provisions of Article XIV(c). Therefore, in order to make out a violation of Article VI(5) under this clause, one must show the national measure to be unnecessary in the sense described above. Then, in order for the respondent to claim an exception under XIV(c), one must show that it is necessary in the broader sense defined there. One interesting question here involves the burden of proof. Under the products jurisprudence of the Appellate Body, it appears that the complainant will be required to show the lack of necessity under Article VI(5), while the responding state would ordinarily be required to prove the affirmative defense of necessity under Article XIV(c). This is at least an odd legal circumstance, where both sides are allocated the burden of proof on the same issue at different phases. The complaining state, say, the European Union in an attack on U.S. separation of commercial from investment banking, would be required to show that the U.S. regulatory approach is "unnecessary" under Article VI(5), while the United States would be required to demonstrate that it is necessary under Article XIV(c).

Recognition and Necessity

Necessity has a complex relationship with recognition. That is, a necessity test, interpreted as a requirement that the national measure be the least trade-restrictive alternative reasonably available to address the regulatory concern, can be either an absolute requirement or a relative requirement. Thus a less restrictive option might make sense irrespective of the home regime, or conversely it might be justified only in reference to the home country regulatory regime, as a *complementary* measure. Judgments based on the former assessment reflect a high degree of judicial activism and are unlikely to be found legitimate. In the latter case, where the home country regulatory regime satisfies the host country concerns, necessity may require recognition. This would be an extreme interpretation of necessity, stating in effect that no regulatory intervention on the part of the importing country is necessary at all. The least restrictive alternative is to do nothing. We have seen this in the ECJ's jurisprudence,[30] and also in treaty provisions in Article 4 of the WTO Agreement on Sanitary and Phytosanitary Measures[31] and Article 2.9 of the WTO Agreement on Technical Barriers to Trade (TBT).[32] Under this interpretation, recognition is mandated by judicial fiat. Note that Article VII of GATS and paragraph 3 of the Annex on Financial Services, in contrast, do not require recognition but merely authorize it. Although a strong GATS standard of necessity might eventually lead to such judicially required recognition, this is unlikely to be the case under current treaty language for reasons we will come to later. But the necessity test might nevertheless mandate partial recognition of some regulations and not others, whereby partial recognition becomes the operational consequence of the principle of proportionality.

New Disciplines under Article VI(4)

It is useful to begin an inventory of possible disciplines under Article VI(4), and to compare the operation of these potential disciplines with those already in place. These fall into two broad categories. On one hand, more stringent legal standards are most likely in the short run. On the other hand, Article VI can serve as the legal basis for the inclusion of specific rules of recognition and harmonization in the longer run.

30. See, for example, *Sager* v. *Dennemeyer*, Case C-76/90, [1991] ECR I-4221. In this case it was found that a national regulatory measure is enforceable against a service provider only if the public interest at stake "is not protected by the rules to which the person providing the services is subject in the Member State in which he is established." This indicates a possibility of judicially required recognition based on a necessity test, although it is noteworthy that the definition of "public interest" is notoriously open-ended. See also European Commission, interpretative communication concerning the free movement of services across frontiers, O.J. C334, 9.12.1993, p. 3.

31. "Members shall accept the sanitary or phytosanitary measures of other Members as equivalent, even if these measures differ from their own or from those used by other Members trading in the same product, if the exporting Member demonstrates to the importing Member that its measures achieve the importing Member's appropriate level of sanitary or phytosanitary protection."

32. "Members shall give positive consideration to accepting as equivalent technical regulations of other Members, even if these regulations differ from their own, provided they are satisfied that these regulations adequately fulfill the objectives of their own regulations."

Enhanced Policed Regulation

On December 24, 1998, the CTS adopted the *Disciplines on Domestic Regulation in the Accountancy Sector*, developed by the WTO Working Party on Professional Services.[33] These disciplines apply to all member states that have made specific commitments in accountancy (positive list), but they do not apply to national measures listed as exceptions under Articles XVI and XVII (negative list). For the most part, they articulate further and tighten the principle of necessity, according to which the least trade-restrictive method should be used to effect a legitimate objective. In fact, these provisions replicate requirements that have been imposed in the European Union pursuant to the ECJ's single-market jurisprudence.[34] They also replicate the approach of the EU's General Systems Directive on Professions, codifying principles of proportionality or necessity.[35] They concentrate not only on necessity, but also on transparency, licensing requirement, qualification requirements, and technical standards.

Necessity. Member states are required to ensure that measures relating to licensing requirements and procedures, technical standards, and qualification requirements and procedures are not prepared, adopted, or applied with a view to or with the effect of creating unnecessary barriers to trade in accountancy services. Such measures may not be more trade restrictive than necessary to fulfill a legitimate objective, including protection of consumers, the quality of the service, professional competence, and the integrity of the profession. As will be clear from the discussion above, this necessity requirement is substantially stronger than that contained in Article VI(5) of GATS.

Transparency. Member states are required to make information regarding relevant regulation public, and upon request, to provide the rationale behind domestic regulatory measures in the accountancy sector. When introducing measures that significantly affect trade in accountancy services, member states must endeavor to provide an opportunity to comment and give consideration to such comments before adoption. This type of discipline is drawn from the TBT agreement.

---

33. WTO *Focus,* December 1998, pp. 10–11.

34. This suggests that the EU jurisprudence can serve as a source of principles for articulation through nonjudicial means in other contexts.

35. Proportionality, stricto sensu, examines whether the means are proportionate to the ends: whether the costs are excessive in relation to the benefits. A wider definition of proportionality developed in the EU context includes three tests: proportionality, stricto sensu; a least trade-restrictive alternative test; and a simple means-ends rationality test.

Licensing Requirements. With respect to residency requirements that are not subject to scheduling under Article XVII of GATS, member states must consider whether less trade-restrictive means could be employed to achieve the relevant purposes, taking into account costs and local conditions. Where membership in a professional organization is required, member states must ensure that the terms of membership do not include conditions unrelated to the fulfillment of a legitimate objective. If professional indemnity insurance is required, members must take into account any existing coverage, insofar as it concerns relevant activities and is consistent with the requirements of the host country legislation. Note that relaxing licensing requirements is especially important in the context of e-commerce and cross-border provision of professional services.

Qualification Requirements. Member states must take account of qualifications acquired in the territory of another member state, on the basis of equivalency of education, experience, or examination requirements. Examinations or other qualification requirements must be limited to subjects relevant to the activities for which authorization is sought. This last clause—expanding on the expression "take account"—is obviously the most prone to different interpretations and will need to be spelled out through more specific rules.

Technical Standards. Technical standards must be prepared, adopted, and applied only to fulfill legitimate objectives. In determining conformity, member states must take account of internationally recognized standards of international organizations to which they are party.

From Policed Regulation to (Partial) Recognition and Harmonization under Article VI(4)

All the above options constitute alternative or complementary legal standards that can be enforced by dispute resolution bodies. Article VI(4), however, could also be used as a basis for more specific rules of harmonization or recognition that would apply to all GATS contracting parties. This is what is suggested by the development of a framework MRA agreement for accountants, even if in a first stage this agreement is to be adopted by members on a bilateral or plurilateral basis under Article VII.

Specific rules with regard to licensing and qualification could be developed in two ways. GATS contracting parties could progressively establish a database—from the bottom up—clarifying what the relevant host country residual requirements might be for different professions in different countries. This database could also be based on lists of professional training institutions. Alternatively, the parties could develop and adopt more specific rules on the process by which remaining "complementary requirements" could be administered by the host country, including procedures for designing entry exams and for determining the length and characteristics of "adaptation" or "training" periods in the host country. Finally, harmonization, or at least the development of common "essential requirements" as in the EU context, could be envisaged under Article VI(4). Up to now, members have been reluctant to use the WTO to develop substantive international standards or regulations, preferring to delegate the task to regional or functional bodies. But if the disciplines outlined above were to create a certain amount of regulatory convergence among parties, perhaps the WTO could afford to become more pro-active. For one thing, WTO disciplines could do more than simply urge contracting parties to "take into account" international standards (as stated in the technical standards clause) and could officially endorse specified international standards as the mandatory basis for the recognition of foreign enforcement of these standards. Furthermore, WTO committees could themselves work on the wording of "multilateral essential requirements" even if such requirements were to be spelled out by more specialized bodies.

Additional Options: Delegation, Recognition, and Harmonization

While Article VI(5) and the Article VI(4) work program contemplate policed regulation, and perhaps legislation of multilateral rules of harmonization and recognition, Article VII of GATS provides for unilateral, bilateral, and plurilateral recognition regimes.[36] In the longer run, it could even be the basis for a multilateral mutual recognition regime.

Delegated Authority under Article VII

As already mentioned, Article VII does not mandate recognition, but authorizes it. Through this provision, the WTO gives its stamp of approval to nonmultilateral deals, as in the case of regional agreements. As such,

---

36. See also chapter 11 in this volume.

Article VII provides an exception to the MFN obligations of Article II of GATS, but makes up for it on the procedural front by outlining disciplines on recognition arrangements designed to prevent them being used to dilute entirely the MFN obligation.[37]

Whatever the emphasis in the recognition arrangements—whether supervision and enforcement of regulations, or the underlying substantive regulations—GATS envisages them as requiring "horizontal" recognition of the regulatory regimes of other members. But this recognition can be conditional on "vertical" recognition of underlying regulatory criteria pertaining to non-national, perhaps multilateral, regulatory regimes. Although attention is usually on horizontal recognition, it is important to recognize, especially in the context of necessity, that vertical recognition may also be required. Article VII(5) of GATS provides that "wherever appropriate, recognition should be based on multilaterally agreed criteria." This is useful, but not as strong as, for example, Article 2.5 of the TBT agreement, which states that a national technical regulation that is in accordance with relevant international standards shall be rebuttably presumed not to create an unnecessary obstacle to trade.

Harmonization and the Limits of Recognition

A degree of harmonization is often a prerequisite for recognition. This is so because recognition requires acceptance of foreign regulation. Earnestly maintained national regulation cannot simply be replaced by foreign regulation through a rule of recognition without a determination that the foreign regulation satisfies enough of the host state's regulatory goals to serve as a satisfactory replacement. This can occur through regulatory convergence over time, facilitated by informal regulatory cooperation, exchange of data, and regulatory analysis. But if liberalization becomes a short-term political imperative, it is more likely to occur through formal harmonization. In the European Union, as well as in certain North American contexts, mutual recognition has often been predicated on "essential" harmonization. This experience indicates the need for a stronger link between Articles VI(4) and VII of GATS.

Of course, laissez-faire adherents would argue for recognition without harmonization, thereby promoting regulatory competition. This is indeed an option and has been used to varying extents in particular EU contexts.

37. Mattoo (1999); Nicolaïdis (1999).

The issue here is, first, whether regulatory competition will result in a race to the bottom or a race to the top; second, whether the goal is to reach the bottom, the top, or somewhere in between; and, third, how one defines the top and the bottom. In practice, this choice is made in the European Union whenever a harmonizing directive is legislated. The directive will contain a particular degree of recognition and of harmonization, anticipating and establishing the conditions for a particular level of regulatory competition.

This being said, it is important to note that although harmonization is an alternative for eliminating barriers to access in the case of underlying standards and criteria, on the enforcement side, mutual recognition is the *only* mechanism for liberalization, short of supranational control. Barring the creation of supranational agencies for controlling services firms, training professionals, and the like, mutual recognition of home country jurisdiction is the only alternative to host country control and traditional national treatment. Even in cases where countries adopt the same rules or rely on international rules, mutual recognition of enforcement prerogatives is generally not extended as a matter of course.[38] In other words, "harmonization" as an alternative to either home or host country jurisdiction is not available along this second dimension. As a result, when one says that harmonization of the standards themselves provides a single rule from the economic actors' viewpoint, it does not necessarily follow that harmonization provides a single point of control. In this light, mutual recognition of regulatory authority is the only path to complete market access.

Managed Recognition

But what is recognition in practice? Recognition agreements between countries—whether in the European Union or under currently negotiated bilateral MRAs—do not generally apply mutual recognition in its "pure" form: meaning full unhindered rights of access reflecting full reallocation of authority from the host to the home country jurisdiction. Instead, mutual recognition agreements require a great degree of ex post and ex ante regulatory cooperation beyond harmonization, as discussed above. At a

---

38. This point is often overlooked by those who present harmonization as a complete alternative to mutual recognition. See, for instance, Sykes (1996). On the other hand, agreements such as the "positive comity" agreement between the European Union and the United States regarding competition law enforcement might be interpreted as providing a degree of mutual recognition of enforcement jurisdiction.

minimum, recognition requires an ex ante analysis of the foreign regulatory regime. Most often, it requires mutual regulatory adaptation. In the end, mutual recognition agreements themselves vary in their regulatory scope and usually leave residual powers to the host state; they are not based on blind trust but involve mutual monitoring between regulatory authorities; they require preconditions to ensure some degree of mutual convergence before the implementation of mutual recognition, and they involve reversibility clauses whereby the host country can take back regulatory power if it is not satisfied with the regulations of the home country. Both in the European Union and in bilateral MRAs, safeguard clauses have been inserted allowing the host state to reverse home state jurisdiction if it conflicts with legal provisions protecting the "general good."

This set of characteristics can be referred to as "managed mutual recognition."[39] It differs from "pure" mutual recognition in the same sense as managed trade differs from total free trade. Pure mutual recognition implies granting fully unconditional and open-ended rights of access. In contrast, mutual recognition in operational terms actually involves complex sets of rules and procedures that may serve to reduce, if not eliminate, the open-endedness of mutual recognition. As a process, managed mutual recognition sets up a dynamic whereby transfers of sovereignty are partial and reversible, conflicts are managed in a manner acceptable to the majority of the population, and the adoption of the norm is only the beginning of a progressive regulatory, sectoral, and geographic expansion. In short, managed mutual recognition is an exercise in designing limits to and safeguards against regulatory competition through a much more diversified set of instruments than simple harmonization.

Complementarity and Boundary between Articles VI and VII

Is such an approach transferable from the European Union to another context? In the WTO context, what is missing, of course, is an entity like the European Commission, with real authority to initiate a legislative process toward "managed" recognition, including minimal harmonization, and with the ability to bring cases before a dispute resolution tribunal to discipline national regulation. Also missing is broad agreement on the utility of the project. With an integrated program of rules, standards, and prospective rule-making involving both dispute resolution institutions and

39. Nicolaïdis (1993, 1996).

legislative institutions, sector-based solutions could be found to the problem of regulatory barriers to trade in services. What is lacking, in short, is an institutional setting conducive to establishing a productive complementarity between general legal standards and specific treaty-based rules.

Nevertheless, the GATS framework provides an embryo for such conditions in the twin pillars of Articles VI and VII. We discussed earlier the relationship between the necessity test and recognition. In effect, in certain cases a strict reading of Article VI could eventually preempt the need for treaty-based recognition. But this is highly theoretical. Our diagnosis of widespread "managed mutual recognition" in practice would support the view that even politicians do not dare embark on a pure form of recognition amounting to total regulatory disarmament. This is, however, the only form of recognition judges would have at their disposal on the basis of an expanded interpretation of the necessity test. Judges cannot readily create systems, networks, and procedures for "managed" recognition.

Yet Article VII does not exist in isolation from Article VI. These provisions work together to provide a complex system for managed mutual recognition. That is, the weak disciplines of Article VI(5), combined with the strengthened disciplines developed under Article VI(4), can provide incentives for recognition under Article VII, or under other circumstances can accomplish the same goals as those sought under Article VII. We now turn to a more general analysis of the rationale, potential, and limits for choosing between or linking these two paths to liberalization.

Designing a Coherent Approach to Regulatory Jurisdiction

At the outset of this chapter, we argued that negotiators for services will be facing two fundamental choices both in determining a regulatory approach and in designing an institutional framework. In terms of regulatory approach, the choice will be between specific rules and general standards. In the case of the institutional framework, it will be between multilateral and plurilateral arrangements. We now suggest some possible guidelines on how negotiators may go about these choices.

Regulatory Approach

The main considerations in determining the regulatory approach are degree of specificity and locus of decision.

GENERAL STANDARDS VERSUS SPECIFIC RULES.   The first core question facing GATS negotiators in the next trade round will be one of specificity. How specific should any new amendments be in policing domestic regulations? Even if regulatory options lie on a spectrum between two extremes, we have framed this at the outset of this chapter as a choice between general standards of policed regulation (including national treatment, nullification or impairment, proportionality, and necessity) and specific rules of recognition or harmonization. In doing so, we draw on a literature dealing mainly with the U.S. domestic context, which we seek to transfer to the international trade context.[40] We will speak of an "agreement" in the latter case, when analysts speak of a "law" in the domestic context.

In general terms, a law is a "rule" to the extent that it is specified in advance of the conduct to which it is applied. Thus a law against littering is a rule to the extent that "littering" is well-defined therein.[41] A law is a "standard" when it establishes general guidance both to the person governed and to the person charged with applying the law but does not specify in detail in advance the conduct required or proscribed.[42] Clearly, even with laws-as-rules there are always questions to ask, so that every law is incompletely specified in advance, and therefore incompletely a rule. But with standards, the lack of specificity is more apparent and intentional.[43]

40. The literature in question is mainly concerned with the relationship between the U.S. Congress and regulatory agencies and the extent of autonomy that should be left to the latter. It distinguishes between standards (often, but not necessarily, involving ex post specification by panels or courts) and rules (often, but not necessarily, involving ex ante specification through treaties or political agreements). Notwithstanding our semantic reservation expressed at the beginning of this chapter regarding the use of the term "standard" in this way in the context of services liberalization and regulation, we revert to this term here, reflecting the prevailing use in the literature.

41. Even with the simple example of littering, there are issues that a law may not address. Must there be an intent not to pick up the discarded item? Are organic or readily biodegradable substances covered? Is littering on private property covered? Is the distribution of leaflets by air protected by rights of free speech?

42. Familiar constitutional standards in the U.S. legal system include requirements such as "due process," prohibitions on uncompensated "takings," or prohibitions on barriers to interstate commerce. A well-known statutory standard is "restraint of trade" under the Sherman Antitrust Act.

43. The distinction between a rule and a standard is not necessarily grammatical or determined by the number of words used to express the norm or by who expresses the norm; rather, the critical distinction relates to how much work remains to be done to determine the applicability of the norm to a particular circumstance. Furthermore, this distinction assumes, with H. L. A. Hart, and contrary to certain tenets of critical legal theory, that language may be formulated to have core meanings, penumbral influence, and limits of application (Hart 1991, chap. 7; Schauer 1994). If all language were equally indeterminate, there would be no distinction between a rule and a standard.

GATS itself provides examples of both approaches. Its General Obligations and Disciplines (GODs) are obviously standards. Even the more specific *Disciplines on Domestic Regulation in the Accountancy Sector* still fall under this category. The model MRA in accountancy, on the other hand, constitutes a specific set of rules that are most likely to be adopted on a bilateral or a regional basis. Similarly in the European Union, the Treaty of Rome provides general standards—for example, a ban on "measures with equivalent effect" to tariffs and quotas—while EU directives and regulations are specific rules. In general, standards will need to be interpreted by courts and panels to become truly operational, while rules are self-enforcing to a greater extent.

Rules and standards should also be distinguished on the basis of the locus of decision they each privilege. Clearly, who makes the law affects its form and impact.[44] With rules, the legislature often "makes" the decision, while with standards, the adjudicator determines the application of the standard, thereby "making" the decision (the tribunal does not, as in naive belief, simply "find" the law). Of course, courts can make rules pursuant to statutory or constitutional authority: the hallmark of a rule is that it is specified ex ante, not that it is specified by a legislature. However, at least in the international trade system, rules are largely made by treaty, and standards are largely applied by tribunals. Legislators in this case are national representatives negotiating on behalf of their member states, and adjudication takes place through ad hoc panels (except for the WTO Appellate Body). This has profound implications for the costs and benefits of the two approaches, as discussed below.

THE COSTS AND BENEFITS OF RULES AND STANDARDS.   The choice of negotiating over rules or standards, and concurrently of determining whether national representatives or panels ought to make particular decisions, should be made using cost-benefit analysis, taking into account normative and strategic criteria. Standards, it should be mentioned, have more visible and immediate benefits than rules, and that is why they are more prevalent in treaties, including trade agreements.

As for costs, first and most obviously, standards avoid *specification costs* associated with rule-making, including drafting costs, negotiation costs, and the use of general administrative resources. These savings can be

---

44. See Komesar (1994).

significant in a multilateral context where more than 130 countries are negotiating together.

Second, standards can be chosen on *efficiency grounds*. In a public interest analysis, legislatures or trade negotiators may not have enough information or predictive capacity to specify ex ante all of the details of treatment of particular cases. In the same vein, the rate of change of circumstances over time may favor the ability of courts to adjust over relatively inflexible rules. This is especially true in the context of services, where technological change, particularly in relation to the Internet, risks overtaking an attempt at laying out too specific rules.

Efficiency may also result from differences in the strategic calculations of the actors involved that make agreement possible.[45] "When the parties bargain over the entitlement when there is private information about value and harm, bargaining may be more efficient under a blurry balancing test than under a certain rule."[46] This is because under a more specific rule, the holder of the entitlement will have incentives to "hold out" and decline to provide information about the value of the entitlement to that holder. The cost of insecure contracts will generally not be equally shared. Under a standard, where presumably it cannot be known with certainty ex ante who owns the entitlement, the person not possessing the entitlement may credibly threaten to take it, providing incentives for the other person to bargain.[47] Over time, rules may provide such benefits if tribunals develop exceptions to rules in a way that introduces uncertainty to their application.

Third, there are *strategic benefits* in avoiding ex ante specification. The choice of standards may be a more explicitly political decision to either agree to disagree for the moment, to avoid the political price that may arise from immediate hard decisions, or to cloak the hard decisions in the false inevitability of judicial interpretation.[48] Standards may even help to mask or mystify a decision made.[49] In the trade area, the strategic benefit is both

45. A number of analysts have argued that the allocation of a legal entitlement may be more efficient if specified ex post by a judge rather than ex ante. For instance, Johnston (1995) analyzes rules and standards from a strategic perspective, finding that, under a standard, bargaining may yield immediate efficient agreement, whereas under a rule, this condition may not obtain. See also Rose (1988); Trachtman (1998b).

46. Johnston (1995, 257).

47. Johnston (1995, p. 272) points out that this result obtains only when the ex post balancing test is imperfect, because if the balancing were perfect, the threat would not be credible. This provides a counterintuitive argument for inaccuracy of application of standards.

48. See Hadfield (1994), citing Cohen and Noll (1991).

49. See Abbott and Snidal (1998).

external and internal. Externally, as with any ambiguous agreement, all sides may claim victory, at least initially. Internally, incompleteness is often a means to suppress mobilization by protectionist elements and, more generally, the intense domestic scrutiny associated with treaty-making. In the *Disciplines on Domestic Regulation in the Accountancy Sector,* the negotiators avoided the political costs that would come with either recognition or harmonization. It may be that costs are borne later by the WTO dispute resolution process, if it holds domestic regulation to violate the standards set, but these costs are less general: they are felt in only one state at a time. (Interestingly, there is no formal rule of *stare decisis* or of general invalidation by virtue of the establishment of a legal principle.) They are incurred later and are thus reduced in terms of present value.

Fourth, general standards help avoid *policy linkages* in deciding, for example, how the policy expressed relates to other policies. This is critical in the trade area, where often the incompleteness of a trade agreement relates to its declining to address, or incorporate, non–trade policies. Thus the *Disciplines on Domestic Regulation in the Accountancy Sector* allow some integration, without the need to constrain, in advance, the domestic regulation of accountants.

What are the arguments, then, for turning to more specific rules? First and foremost, rules are likely to provide a greater degree of *trade liberalization,* at least at first, than general standards. They are mechanisms that deepen and accelerate economic integration through political deals and reciprocal concessions. But this need not always be the case; in fact, agents can sometimes capture rule-making processes to carve out exceptions and safeguards that would not be specified under a standards-based approach.

Second, rules are generally thought to provide greater *predictability,* both ex ante, as actors are able to plan and conform their conduct to the rule in question, and ex post, after the relevant conduct has taken place and the parties can predict the outcome of dispute resolution. The so-called primary and secondary predictability provided by rules can reduce costs for economic agents. Rules provide compliance benefits: they are cheaper to obey, because the cost of determining the required behavior is lower. Rules are also cheaper to apply by a court: the court must determine only the facts and compare them with the rule. To be sure, tribunals or even panels may construct exceptions in order to do what is, by their lights, substantial justice, thus reducing predictability. Moreover, predictability may not be a terribly important value, if, as with the *Disciplines on Domestic Regulation in the Accountancy Sector,* the constraints imposed are not very intrusive, and thus unlikely to affect many states or economic actors. In many cases, predictability is obtained at the cost of efficiency.

Third, the final outcome is likely to gain in *legitimacy*. At the core of the legitimacy issue is the degree of representativeness of constituents. Which institution will most accurately reflect citizens' desires? There is no denying that in most liberal democracies the judicial branch has gained in legitimacy in relation to the legislative branch. At the international level, on the other hand, binding adjudication is still in its infancy and is not part of citizens' expectations of representative institutions. Even if nongovernmental organizations succeed in making dispute resolution more transparent, the process will continue to be perceived as remote and unaccountable. Conversely, even if contested, more specific rules are the result of a process whereby elected governments trade away concessions in exchange for some calculated benefits. They are, in effect, the extension at the international level of the social contract that underlies the regulatory state at the domestic level.[50] It is also true, however, that just like legislatures at the domestic level, national representatives can become captive to a small group of actors on the international scene. Panels might then more "objectively" represent the public interest. But they may still not be perceived as such.

RECOMMENDATIONS.   Given the pros and cons of alternative approaches, we recommend the adoption of three guiding principles: choosing a standard that maximizes the level of liberalization permitted in the WTO, combining rules and standards where possible, and adopting an evolutionary approach to rule-making.

Choosing a Standard That Maximizes the Level of Liberalization within the Limits of Legitimacy in the WTO. Of course, the choice between rules and standards depends, in part, on what standard is to be applied and who is to apply it. A number of standards are available for different circumstances. Naming them briefly does not do justice to their diversity and subtlety in actual practice, or to the fact that they overlap in actual practice. They have to do with national treatment, simple means-ends rationality, necessity/least trade-restrictive alternative tests, proportionality, balancing tests, and cost-benefit analysis.

In the recent Appellate Body report in the *Shrimp/Turtle* case, all of these standards were arguably applied together. As noted earlier, all are

50. See Howse (1999).

included to different extents either in current GATS provisions or in possible extensions of these provisions under the general principle of "enhanced policed regulation." In economic theory, the "standard" that would be most efficient would be cost-benefit analysis, maximizing the combination of trade benefits and regulatory benefits, net of trade costs and regulatory costs. However, there are good reasons—in terms of administrability and predictability, distributive concerns, commensurability, and interpersonal comparison of utility—that cost-benefit analysis is generally not used.[51]

In order to use standards properly, GATS negotiators will have to consider these issues as they try to determine which standard or combination of standards should be applied to particular services issues or services sectors. Of course, an issue-by-issue or sector-by sector analysis might not mean that each issue or sector is treated differently. Rather, there may be economies of scale or economies of scope that provide incentives for homogeneity of treatment.

Combining Rules and Standards When Possible. When it is necessary to negotiate specific rules as a signal of political commitment to deeper liberalization but the complete fine-tuning of the rules is too costly and inefficient, negotiators can seek to combine rules and standards in a single agreement. In particular, standards can be nested within rule-like agreements as safeguard mechanisms. Thus most mutual recognition clauses inside or outside the European Union, for instance, include vaguely worded standards to the effect that host states are allowed to reassert regulatory jurisdiction in order to "protect the general good." It will be up to the courts to interpret such a vague standard, hopefully with restraint, so as to respect prevailing notions of the "general good" in the countries concerned.

Adopting an Evolutionary Approach to Rule-Making. Negotiators may more consciously and explicitly adopt a staged approach to liberalization. Clearly, the strategic relationship between legislators and courts in this back-and-forth game cannot be mapped out in advance.[52] Nevertheless, standards may be used earlier in the development of a field of law, before sufficient experience is acquired to form a basis for more detailed specification. In many areas of law, courts develop a jurisprudence that serves as a road map and forms the basis for codification—or even rejection—by legis-

51. See Trachtman (1998c).

52. Such strategic analysis is based on the tools of public choice or positive political theory. See, for example, Ferejohn and Weingast (1992); Cooter and Drexl (1994); Sunstein (1995, p. 9613).

latures. With this in mind, legislatures (or adjudicators) may set standards at an early point in time, and determine to establish rules at a later point in time.[53] Thus over time the *Disciplines on Domestic Regulation in the Accountancy Sector* may form the basis for elaboration of a more detailed jurisprudence in the accountancy sector. As instances of the relevant behavior are more frequent, economies of scale will indicate that rules may be worth developing. Even if the European Court of Justice had come to apply recognition very liberally (which it did not), and even if the court had the authority to establish complex relations of recognition and harmonization (which it does not), it would have taken decades to complete the single European market by judicial fiat. For circumstances that arise only infrequently, it is more difficult to justify promulgation of specific rules.

The Institutional Framework

Choices centered on the balance between general standards and specific rules will certainly depend on the institutional setting. The question is, what level of aggregation among states should negotiators focus on in addressing particular issues or sectors? Different groupings of states will have different preferences and affinities. They may work together in regional groups, in bilateral pairs, or in other plurilateral groups, and these groups may overlap with one another and with the multilateral system in varying ways.

States will choose whether to engage in regional or multilateral integration on the basis of their own preferences and their own views as to how to maximize their preferences. We do not address this substantive problem here but note that the choice of level of integration will depend, in part, on the degree of shared preferences in particular sectors, as well as on the institutional mechanisms available at each level. Furthermore, economies of scope will arise from treating multiple issues together.[54]

THE MFN PROBLEM AND MULTILATERALISM, PLURILATERALISM, AND TRANSITIVITY. MFN may or may not be an appropriate rule in circumstances where liberalization is more unidimensional, as in negotiations over tariff

---

53. Kaplow (1992, 1998). See also Sunstein (1995). It is clear that a rule of *stare decisis* is not necessary to the development of a body of jurisprudence by a court or dispute resolution tribunal. See Palmeter and Mavroidis (1998). Note, too, that in a common law setting, or any setting where tribunals refer to precedents, the tribunal may announce a standard in a particular case and then elaborate that standard in subsequent cases until it has built a rule for its own application.

54. Trachtman (1996).

barriers or discriminatory barriers to foreign service providers. MFN becomes more complicated under the more subtle circumstances of regulatory barrier reduction. Conditional MFN, or equality of opportunity, is an easier approach to apply. Article VII(2) of GATS recognizes this, by allowing disciplined departures from MFN for recognition arrangements, on the condition that members afford adequate opportunity for other interested members to negotiate accession to such arrangements. This can be described as "procedural" MFN as opposed to "substantive" MFN. Procedural MFN consists of spelling out what adequate opportunity might mean, who bears the costs of demonstrating equivalence of regulations, and what are the concrete procedures by which third parties may be brought into this process. Substantive MFN would imply that once an MRA has been negotiated at a bilateral or plurilateral level, a panel would be able to decide that third parties ought to be allowed to participate simply by assessing the equivalence of its standards to any of the partners in the MRA. Given the cooperation-intensive nature of managed recognition, the latter avenue does not seem likely. In this context, the MFN requirement of Article VII constitutes a general standard applied to develop specific rules over time.

Plurilateralism in arrangements to reduce regulatory barriers raises the question of stumbling blocks versus building blocks. Is plurilateral integration a barrier or a contributor to multilateral integration? A dynamic time-path model might suggest that plurilateralism can be more productive in addressing regulatory barriers than in addressing traditional trade barriers, insofar as there are even stronger reasons relating to regulatory heterogeneity for earlier plurilateral action.[55] On the other hand, regulatory heterogeneity will indicate varying paths for harmonization. As these varying paths are followed, they may make subsequent wider harmonization more difficult. That is, if different groups of states harmonize around different standards, it will be more costly to engage in multilateral harmonization at a later time. Ideally, this path-dependence problem would be considered from a multilateral standpoint before a decision was made to follow a plurilateral track.

Perhaps an appropriate midpoint between MFN and simple plurilateralism would be a requirement of transitivity.[56] A requirement of transitivity would effectively link plurilateral arrangements in particular sectors,

55. See Bhagwati (1991).
56. See Nicolaïdis (1996).

by calling on states that are hubs of several plurilateral arrangements to effectively merge such arrangements. That is, if the United States has a plurilateral arrangement with Mexico and Canada, on the one hand, and a bilateral arrangement with the European Union, on the other hand, a rule of transitivity would require the European Union, Mexico, and Canada to establish (or simply to accept) a similar arrangement. This approach is not completely satisfactory from a regulatory standpoint, as, in this example, the European Union might not be satisfied with Mexico or Canada's regulatory regime. However, the argument would proceed as follows. If the U.S. regulation addresses the EU's regulatory concerns sufficiently for the European Union to enter into bilateral relations with the United States, and if for its part the United States is satisfied with the regulatory regimes of Mexico and Canada, the European Union should also be so satisfied. This argument would substitute the judgment of the United States for that of the European Union, and, even less defensibly, would assume that the concerns of the United States are the same as those of the European Union. Perhaps this is true in enough cases to argue for a presumption of transitivity, but even this might appear threatening to national regulatory autonomy.

FROM BILATERAL MRAS TO A MULTILATERAL FRAMEWORK FOR MANAGED MUTUAL RECOGNITION.   More broadly, a requirement of transitivity will need to be considered under the question of how to bring back under the multilateral framework plurilateral arrangements pursued on a separate track. Services negotiators should aim to develop a multilateral framework for managed mutual recognition. This would include guidelines for rule-making (for example, guidelines for a model framework MRA and for expansion), enforceable standards of nondiscrimination and transitivity, and the provision of institutional infrastructure for both accreditation and minimal harmonization.[57]

Designing a Model Framework Agreement. One of the most important obstacles to the negotiation of MRAs is their apparent complexity.[58] In a few rare cases, bilateral MRAs have been negotiated ex nihilo. But generally, MRAs will likely follow from two prior steps: adoption of framework agreements calling for MRAs; the crafting of detailed work programs, road maps, and guidelines for designing MRAs that can provide a precious basis

57. See Nicolaïdis (1999).
58. See Nicolaïdis (1997).

for learning from precedents and developing trust between regulators. The development in the WTO of a framework for an accountancy MRA constitutes a first step that now can be generalized. This would involve a pledge by WTO members that the same formats and procedures would be adhered to in all MRA negotiations. Such a pledge would lead to an open and transparent negotiating system for such agreements.

Designing a Strategy for Progressive Expansion. In addition, such guidelines should encourage parties to view MRAs as a dynamic process and should include provisions to that effect. These can be related to the stated purpose (to set in place a process for the progressive enhancement of the understanding with the ultimate goal of full mutual recognition); the combination of different mechanisms for recognition within a single MRA; indications as to how the degree of automaticity of access granted by the MRA may progressively increase; the need to maximize the range of choice regarding compensatory requirements imposed by the host state; progressive expansion in scope of access (activities, title, time frame, mode of delivery); and reversibility.

Enforcing Requirements of Procedural Nondiscrimination. Although the above framework would constitute optional guidelines, all parties would need to respect nondiscrimination requirements, at least in a first stage. Existing requirements not only need to be fine-tuned, but WTO should provide support for access to MRA agreements, especially for nongovernmental bodies with public authority but few resources.

Developing and Enforcing Requirements of Transitivity. As outlined in the previous section, requirements of transitivity might also help expand the multilateral character of managed mutual recognition.

Developing a Multilateral System of Accreditation or Supervision. Enforcing these norms might not be sufficient, however, to provide a genuinely multilateral dynamic. One of the main obstacles to generalized recognition is incompatibility resulting in difficulty and high cost of assessment of other countries' accreditors. The WTO could come to manage a system of "accreditation of accreditors" that would be shared globally. This would involve setting up networks of such meta-accreditors. In effect, generalized mutual recognition would not need to be based on trust but on constant shared monitoring of those at the national levels accrediting certifying institutions.

Developing a Multilateral Consensus on Minimal Harmonization. The WTO could become involved in the development of minimal harmonization, even if only as an initial step, by officially enforcing regulations developed within functional international organizations.

MULTIFUNCTIONALISM VERSUS PLURIFUNCTIONALISM.   Another important question to consider is what organizational structure is best to address particular sectoral or functional issues? Should financial regulation issues be addressed by the Basle Committee or the International Organization of Securities Commissions, but not by GATS? This is not unlike the question of whether the WTO should address environmental and labor issues or leave these to specialized organizations or negotiating processes, such as the Rio process or the International Labor Organization.

There are two main reasons for aggregating functions in a single organization. First, if there are enough, it may be attractive to integrate similar and linked responsibilities in the interest of institutional economies of scale and scope. Second it is important to be able to provide cross-sectoral "basket deals" in negotiations, as has been done successfully in the EU context. These cross-sectoral deals, whether in treaty-making or other legislative activities, are matched, and extended temporally, by the possibility of cross-retaliation in dispute resolution, as has been established in the WTO context.

Conclusions

The choice between specific rules and general standards must be based on the particular service contexts in which it arises, and the choice may change over time. The choice of forum for these measures will depend on the degree of shared interests among states. GATS is wisely flexible in these respects, providing a facility for the development of rules and standards in multilateral, plurilateral, and regional contexts. But the default option in GATS today is a relatively weak set of general standards for application to domestic regulation, weaker than that applicable to technical standards relating to goods. We have sought to provide a road map to some of the boundaries that will need to be drawn in the upcoming round of negotiations that will be revisiting GATS.

Clearly, these boundaries will have to be flexible and fluid and will need to adapt to prevailing economic, technological, and political circumstances. It is impossible to predict how these circumstances will change the constraint on regulatory jurisdictional allocation. But we can indicate possible alternative "worlds."

On the technological front, advances in e-commerce technology might force states to contemplate transfers in regulatory jurisdiction that they never envisaged before, simply because no recoverable assets would be located in the host territory.[59] Alternatively, electronic identification technologies might develop to allow for the control of the territory of origin of potential clients or consumers and thus for the continued subjection of these consumers to their country's regulatory regime.

On the political and economic fronts, globalization combined with heightened emphasis on consumer needs, health, and protection might induce a citizen's revolt against further encroachment of regulatory sovereignty; a couple of highly publicized cases of flawed services subject to foreign regulations in key countries might suffice in turning the tide against deeper regulatory integration, especially if led by anonymous courts rather than elected politicians. Conversely, public opinion and politicians might become convinced that global governance is a necessary corollary to globalization and accelerate the pace toward trade-friendly global regulatory management. The regulatory reform process under way in most countries of the Organization for Economic Cooperation and Development will surely support such an evolution.

References

Abbott, Kenneth W., and Duncan Snidal. 1998. "Why States Act through Formal International Organizations." *Journal of Conflict Resolution* 42 (Fall): 3–32.

Bhagwati, Jagdish. 1991. "Jumpstarting GATT." *Foreign Policy* 3 (Summer): 105–18.

Cohen, Linda R., and Roger G. Noll. 1991. "How to Vote, Whether to Vote: Strategies for Voting and Abstaining on Congressional Roll Calls." *Political Behavior* 13: 97.

Cooter, Robert, and Josef Drexl. 1994. "The Logic of Power in the Emerging European Constitution: Game Theory and the Division of Powers." *International Review of Law and Economics* 14 ( ): 307.

Drake, William, and Kalypso Nicolaïdis. 1992. "Ideas, Interests and Institutionalization: 'Trade in Services' and the Uruguay Round." *International Organization* 46 (Winter): 37–100.

Ferejohn, John, and Barry Weingast. 1992. "A Positive Theory of Statutory Interpretation." *International Review of Law and Economics* 12: 263.

Hadfield, Gillian K. 1994. "Weighing the Value of Vagueness: An Economic Perspective on Precision in the Law." *California Law Review* 82: 541–53.

Hart, H. L. A. 1994. *The Concept of Law.* 2d ed. Clarendon Law Series.

Howse, Robert. 1999. "Managing the Interface between International Trade Law and the Regulatory State: What Lessons Should (and Should Not) Be Drawn from the Jurisprudence of the United States Dormant Commerce Clause." In *Regulatory Barriers*

59. See Trachtman (1998a); also chapter 14 in this volume.

and the Principle of Non-Discrimination of World Trade Law: Past, Present and Future, edited by Thomas Cottier, Petros Mavroidis, and Patrick Blatter. University of Michigan Press.

Johnston, Jason Scott. 1995. "Bargaining under Rules versus Standards." *Journal of Law, Economics and Organization* 11: 256.

Kaplow, Louis. 1992. "Rules Versus Standards: An Economic Analysis." *Duke Law Journal* 42 (December): 557–629.

———. 1998. "General Characteristics of Rules." In *Encyclopedia of Law and Economics,* edited by B. Bouckaert and G. De Geest. Edward Elgar Publishers.

Komesar, Neil. 1994. *Imperfect Alternatives.* University of Chicago Press.

Mattoo, Aaditya. 1997. "National Treatment in the GATS: Corner-Stone or Pandora's Box?" *Journal of World Trade* 31 (February): 107.

———. 1999. "GATS and MFN." In *Regulatory Barriers and the Principle of Non-Discrimination of World Trade Law: Past, Present and Future,* edited by Thomas Cottier, Petros Mavroidis, and Patrick Blatter. University of Michigan Press.

Nicolaïdis, Kalypso. 1993. "Mutual Recognition among Nations: The European Community and Trade in Services." Ph.D. diss., Harvard University.

———. 1996. *Mutual Recognition of Regulatory Regimes: Some Lessons and Prospects, Regulatory Reform and International Market Openness.* Paris: Organization for Economic Cooperation and Development.

———. 1997. *Promising Approaches and Principal Obstacles to Mutual Recognition, International Trade in Professional Services: Advancing Liberalization through Regulatory Reform.* Paris: Organization for Economic Cooperation and Development.

———. 1999. "Non-Discriminatory Mutual Recognition: An Oxymoron in the WTO Lexicon?" In *Regulatory Barriers and the Principle of Non-Discrimination of World Trade Law: Past, Present and Future,* edited by Thomas Cottier, Petros Mavroidis, and Patrick Blatter. University of Michigan Press.

Palmeter, David, and Petros C. Mavroidis. 1998. "The WTO Legal System: Sources of Law." *American Journal of International Law* 91 (3): 398.

Rose, Carol. 1988. "Crystals and Mud in Property Law." *Stanford Law Review* 40.

Schauer, Frederick. 1991. *Playing by the Rules.* Clarendon Law Series.

Sunstein, Cass R. 1995. "Problems with Rules." *California Law Review* 83 (July): 953–1023.

Sykes, Alan O. 1996. *Products Standards and International Integrated Goods Market.* Brookings.

———. 1999. "Regulatory Protectionism and the Law of International Trade." *University of Chicago Law Review* 66: 1.

Trachtman, Joel P. 1995. "Trade in Financial Services under GATS, NAFTA and the EC: A Regulatory Jurisdiction Analysis." *Columbia Journal of Transnational Law* 34: 37.

———. 1996. "The Theory of the Firm and the Theory of the International Economic Organization: Toward Comparative Institutional Analysis." *Northwestern Journal of International Law and Business* 17 (2/3): 470–555.

———. 1998a. "Cyberspace, Sovereignty, Jurisdiction and Modernism." *Indiana Journal of Global Legal Studies* 5 (2): 561–81.

———. 1998b. "Externalities and Extraterritoriality." In *Economic Dimensions of Interna-*

tional Law, edited by Jagdeep Bhandari and Alan O. Sykes, 642–83. Cambridge University Press.

———. 1998c. "Trade and . . . Problems, Cost-Benefit Analysis and Subsidiarity." *European Journal of International Law* 9 (1): 32–85.

———. 1999. "The Domain of WTO Dispute Resolution." *Harvard International Law Journal* 40 (2): 333–77.

11 | *Market Access through Mutual Recognition: The Promise and Limits of GATS Article VII*

AMERICO BEVIGLIA ZAMPETTI

FURTHER LIBERALIZATION OF TRADE in services is one the most important challenges facing World Trade Organization members at the turn of the twenty-first century, and a framework for negotiations has been provided for in the General Agreement on Trade in Services. National regulations may have a particularly restrictive effect on trade. In many service sectors, in the absence of any significant restrictions on national treatment or establishment, domestic regulation constitutes the main barrier to the provision of services by foreign businesses or individuals. Although many service sectors will always be subject to regulation to protect the interest of the public, the extensive differentiation of such domestic regulations, often developed with no consideration for the impact on third parties, may and often does seriously hamper trade. Thus this is an important area where renewed negotiating efforts need to be concentrated. A promising avenue to be considered relates to the ample, but certainly not fully used, opportunities provided for by GATS to conclude agreements or arrangements for the mutual recognition of education, qualifications, or ability to provide services.

In the industrial sector the instrument of mutual recognition has been one of the main contributing factors to the success in the European Community (EC) of the 1992 Internal Market program.[1] The recognition

I am grateful to Julian Arkell, Maria Deli, Robert Howse, and James Mathis for useful discussions and comments.

1. See Commission of the European Communities (1985).

that the fragmentation of markets resulting from different and inconsistent regulatory requirements was a powerful barrier to trade between the member states of the Community came early. The policy aimed at eliminating technical barriers to trade goes back to the beginning of the 1960s.[2] However, it took more than two decades to fine-tune the mutual recognition instrument that has been one of cornerstones of the establishment of a single internal market. Such a principle provides that, once a product meets the technical requirements in one EC member state, it cannot be denied access to another EC market. National regulations have to comply with the essential requirements or minimum conditions set at the EC level, but otherwise compliance with national regulations is sufficient to allow free movement inside the internal market of the Community.

The same philosophy has been applied to services.[3] Indeed, the phrase "mutual recognition" appears in the original Treaty of Rome of 1957 with regard to the recognition of diplomas, certificates, and qualifications for suppliers of professional services.[4] At that time various forms of mutual recognition in services were already widely used, albeit in a very diversified fashion. More recent developments have not brought more coherence to the international practice. Thus to see how WTO rules could be improved and expanded to foster greater recourse to mutual recognition, it is important first to review existing international practice and highlight the problems that have emerged. This will be followed by an analysis of current GATS rules to show that the problems have not been fully addressed and resolved. The chapter concludes with some suggestions on how they could be tackled in the context of the WTO to make more extensive use of mutual recognition agreements and enjoy more fully the trade facilitation and liberalization benefits they can bring about.

International Mutual Recognition in Services

The international practice of mutual recognition in services is long established and fairly diversified.[5] A very large number of bilateral and

---

2. For a detailed analysis, see Mattera (1990).

3. Mattera (1991).

4. Article 57(1) reads in part, "In order to make it easier for persons to take up and pursue activities as self-employed persons, the Council shall . . . issue directives for the mutual recognition of diplomas, certificates and other evidence of formal qualifications."

5. The Convenio de Montevideo, signed by Argentina, Bolivia, Colombia, and Ecuador, dates to 1889.

sometimes multilateral (often regional) agreements for scientific and cultural cooperation have mutual recognition provisions.[6] These agreements are more common between countries sharing the same language or strong cultural links. They are very common between Latin American countries.[7] Generally, through these agreements, diplomas granted by signatory countries are mutually recognized on the basis of reciprocal trust with regard to the equivalence of educational institutions and study programs. Sometimes the recognition is specifically intended for academic purposes to allow enrollment in training, specialization, or further study. In other cases general mutual recognition provisions of professional qualifications are included.[8] Sometimes the objective of allowing the exercise of professional activities is specifically mentioned.[9]

At the bilateral level there are also examples of mutual recognition agreements in financial services. The 1989 agreement between the European Community and Switzerland on direct insurance other than life insurance aimed to create through mutual recognition identical conditions for access to, and carrying out of, direct insurance activities.[10] For the purpose of granting authorization, the two signatories recognize each other's proof of solvency of insurance companies with head offices situated in the territory of any of the parties. As a result, no lodging of a deposit or provision of other security is required for authorization. Switzerland and Liechtenstein have also recently concluded a far-reaching agreement in direct insurance.[11]

6. An important example of a regional agreement is the 1974 Convenio regional de convalidación de estudios, títulos y diplomas de educación superior en America y el Caribe. Mutual recognition provisions are also included in treaties of friendship, commerce, and navigation, such as the 1891 treaty between Ecuador and El Salvador.

7. This is the picture that appears by perusing the WTO notifications under Article VII:4 of GATS.

8. See, for instance, the 1976 Convenio de Cooperación Cultural y Cientifica between Chile and Brasil that states in Article V: "Los diplomas y títulos para el ejercicio de profesiones liberales y técnicas, expedidos por instituciones de enseñanza superior de una de las Partes Contratantes, tendrán plena validez en el territorio de la otra Parte, una vez satisfechas las formalidades legales de cada Parte Contratante."

9. See, for instance, the 1992 Convenio de Reconocimiento Mutuo de Certificados, Titulos y Grados Academicos de Educacion Primaria, Media y Superior between Argentina and Colombia, which states in Article III: "Las Partes promoverán, por medio de los organismos pertinentes de cada país, la obtención del derecho al ejercicio profesional a quienes acrediten un título reconocido, sin perjuidicio de la aplicación de las reglamentaciones que cada país impone a sus nacionales, de acuerdo con las normas legales vigentes para cada profesión."

10. See the agreement between the European Economic Community and the Swiss Confederation on direct insurance other than life insurance, in *OJEC (Official Journal of the European Communities)* L 205, July 27, 1991. The agreement entered into force on January 1, 1993.

11. See World Trade Organization, "Notification pursuant to Article VII.4 of the General Agreement on Trade in Service," S/C/N/75, August 14, 1998.

Germany has concluded bilateral agreements with the United States and Japan exempting branches of credit institutions established within its territory but having their registered office in the United States and Japan from the provisions of the German Banking Act concerning limits on credit volume, price risk, certain investments, and availability of additional capital.[12]

The European Union and the United States are also actively involved in mutual recognition talks. After recently concluding a mutual recognition agreement on conformity assessment for goods, the two partners are endeavoring to broaden the use of this instrument to cover services as well.[13] In the context of their Transatlantic Economic Partnership initiative, the European Union and the United States are negotiating a framework agreement for mutual recognition in services to which sectoral annexes should be appended on a rolling basis.[14] Insurance and engineering services are already discussed as potential candidates.[15]

It is not surprising that the European Union is particularly active in this area. Mutual recognition has been instrumental to the realization of market integration in the European Union. Although openly protectionist regulations designed to exclude foreign persons and enterprises existed in some member states, most barriers resulted from nondiscriminatory regulation meant to achieve legitimate public policy objectives. Actions to eliminate overt discrimination but also to coordinate and harmonize the

12. See the Decree of 21 April 1994 in Bundesgesetzblatt 1994, Teil I S. 887, and Decree of 13 December 1995 in Bundesgesetzblatt 1995, Teil I S.1703, implementing exchanges of letters between the German and, respectively, U.S. and Japanese authorities.

13. The text of the agreement is reproduced in *OJEC* L 31/3, February 4, 1999.

14. The Transatlantic Economic Partnership was launched at the EU-U.S. London summit, May 18, 1998. It is set out in a joint statement of political intent, which does not introduce any legally binding obligations on the parties. The statement is reproduced in UK Presidency of the European Union, Press Release, May 19, 1998, and in U.S. *Federal Register,* vol. 63, no. 110, June 18, 1998, pp. 31546–48. Both the Council of Ministers on May 28, 1998, and the European Council on June 15–16, 1998, took note of the statement. Subsequently, the European Commission and the U.S. administration drafted an action plan to carry out the statement. The European Council at its November 9, 1998, meeting endorsed the plan. The council also decided that the commission is authorized to enter into negotiations in four areas, including technical barriers to trade and services. The annexed negotiating directives make clear that in both cases the focus is on the removal of regulatory barriers through mutual recognition. See EU Press Release, IP/98/974, November 9, 1998, and U.S. Trade Representative Press Release, November 11, 1998. The text of the plan is reproduced in *International Trade Reporter,* vol. 15 (November 11, 1998), pp. 1897–1904.

The text of the framework agreement is reproduced in *OJEC* L 31/3, February 4, 1999.

15. It is unclear whether this negotiation will be successful. However, if it fails, it will do so because of disagreement on the binding of subfederal states and other entities.

national rules that fragmented markets and hindered the provision of services and establishment were started in the early 1960s. However, notwithstanding a broad legislative effort and the development of case law, by the mid-1980s progress was still limited. The 1985 white paper, *Completing the Internal Market*, urged a new approach based on mutual recognition.[16]

For instance, in professional services this led to the adoption of a general system of recognition of higher education diplomas that largely replaced the previous approach aimed at harmonizing the conditions for access.[17] In this way member states accept the comparability of their higher education diplomas, particularly for granting the authorization to exercise a regulated profession. The necessary mutual trust premise is also present in financial services, where except for the limited harmonization of basic prudential rules, all controls are now left up to the home country and must be accepted by the other member states.[18] This means that a credit institution can conduct its activities in all member states provided that it is approved by the authorities of its country of origin. Where a service supplier is proven to be subject to adequate supervision in its home state, no further unnecessary controls can be required by the state in which it provides its services.[19]

Another example of extensive use of mutual recognition in a regional context is the Trans-Tasman Mutual Recognition Arrangement (TTMRA) between Australia and New Zealand, which covers both goods and services.[20] It is based on the experience acquired within the Australian federal system, where a domestic mutual recognition scheme was established in 1992. Under the TTMRA terms, goods that can be legally sold in one country can, in principle, be sold in the other. Similarly, people registered to practice an occupation in one country are able to practice the same occupation in the other (apart from medical practitioners) without the need for complete harmonization of standards and professional qualifications.

If the Trans-Tasman approach is very far-reaching, at the other end of the spectrum are the Canada-U.S. Free Trade Agreement and North American Free Trade Agreement experiences. The former provided for the

16. See Commission of the European Communities (1985). For a recent assessment see Commission of the European Communities (1999).

17. Directive 89/48 of December 21, 1988, in *OJEC* L 19, January 24, 1989.

18. Directive 89/646 of December 15, 1989, in *OJEC* L 386, December 30, 1989.

19. See, for instance, case 279/80 in *Common Market Law Review* (1982), p. 406.

20. The TTMRA entered into force on May 1, 1998. See Hay, Taylor, and Webb (1997).

possibility of negotiating mutual recognition of licensing and certification requirements.[21] Specific provisions were set out for the architectural profession.[22] However, the use of mutual recognition is not in any way mandated, and in professional services it is left to the professional organizations to decide whether to make use of it. In this context the U.S. National Council of Architectural Registration Boards (NCARB) and the Committee of Canadian Architectural Councils (CCAC) signed an agreement in 1994 that provides for the reciprocal registration of architects who are practicing in a subfederal jurisdiction that has signed a letter of undertaking.[23] These letters provide for the acceptance of the conditions of the agreement and also permit the individual state or province to stipulate any special requirements, such as demonstration of knowledge of local laws or seismic forces, personal interview, or other unique requirements that all applicants for registration must meet.[24] Discussions to extend the arrangement to Mexico are under way.

In accountancy the American Institute of Certified Public Accountants (AICPA), the U.S. National Association of State Boards of Accountancy (NASBA), and the Canadian Institute of Chartered Accountants (CICA) agreed in 1991 to Principles of Reciprocity and recommended them to state boards of accountancy in the United States and provincial authorities in Canada.[25] After reviewing the respective examination, education, and experience requirements for licensure, the participating organizations agreed that the respective qualifications were comparable. As a consequence, only an abbreviated examination designed to demonstrate satisfactory knowledge of national and local legislation, standards, and practices of the jurisdic-

21. See Article 1403 (Licensing and Certification) of the Canada-U.S. Free Trade Agreement, which states: "The Parties shall encourage the mutual recognition of licensing and certification requirements for the provision of covered services by nationals of the other Party."

22. See Annex 1404 A.

23. The NCARB is a nongovernmental national federation of fifty-five state and territory architectural registration boards in the United States. The CCAC is a committee comprising all of the Canadian provincial architectural associations.

24. Thirty-four states and seven provinces have submitted letters of undertaking. See World Trade Organization, "Notification pursuant to Article VII.4 of the General Agreement on Trade in Services—Architecture," S/C/N/52, February 10, 1997.

25. The AICPA is a national association responsible for the profession's self-regulatory activities in coordination with the state societies of certified public accountants. NASBA is a national association of subfederal regulatory authorities representing the fifty-four U.S. licensing jurisdictions. CICA is a national professional association that represents the chartered accountancy profession and facilitates coordination among the provincial institutes of chartered accountants responsible for the regulation of the profession in the twelve Canadian subfederal jurisdictions.

tion in which licensure is sought should be required. The arrangement is implemented only by those states and provinces that accept it.[26]

Again in the North American context, the same approach has been carried over into NAFTA.[27] Despite the significant liberalization in services, professionals from a NAFTA party are not able to practice a licensed profession within the territory of another NAFTA party, even on a temporary basis, without meeting all licensing criteria and receiving a license from the host jurisdiction.[28] Mirroring the Canada-U.S. Free Trade Agreement, NAFTA tries to remedy this by providing a framework under which interested professions can work toward mutual recognition based on objective and mutually acceptable standards for licensing and certification.[29] The relevant professional bodies are encouraged to submit recommendations to that effect to the NAFTA Commission. Adoption of the recommendations is reserved for the respective competent authorities of the parties, individual states in the case of the United States, and provinces in Canada. So far only the representatives of the engineering and legal professions have developed and recommended arrangements in mutual recognition.[30] The engineering document specifies the education, experience, and examination requirements that are to be recognized in the other NAFTA jurisdictions to obtain a temporary or permanent license to practice engineering. The legal document recommendation is meant to permit lawyers from any one of the three NAFTA countries to act as foreign legal consultants in either of the other

26. Thirty-six states and nine provinces have accepted the recommendations set out in the agreement. See World Trade Organization, "Notification pursuant to Article VII.4 of the General Agreement on Trade in Services—Accounting," S/C/N/51, February 10, 1997.

27. On the NAFTA experience see Sauvé (1995).

28. NAFTA Article 1210 (Licensing and Certification) in paragraph 3 eliminates any citizenship or permanent residency requirement for the licensing or certification of professional service providers.

29. See NAFTA Annex 1210:5 (Professional Services).

30. For engineering see "Mutual Recognition of Registered/Licensed Engineers by Jurisdictions of Canada, the United States of America and the United Mexican States to Facilitate Mobility in Accordance with the North American Free Trade Agreement," signed on June 5, 1995, in Washington by representatives of the Canadian Council of Professional Engineers (CCPE), the U.S. Council for International Engineering Practice (USCIEP), and the Comité Mexicano para la Práctica Internacional de la Ingeniería (COMPII).

For the legal profession see "Joint Recommendations of the Relevant Canadian, Mexican and American Professional Bodies under Annex 1210.5, Section B, of NAFTA," June 19, 1998. The government of Canada designated the Federation of Law Societies of Canada as the relevant professional body for Canada. The Mexican Committee on the International Practice of Law, representing several lawyers' voluntary organizations, and the Mexican Ministries of Education and Commerce were designated by Mexico. The American Bar Association and the National Conference of Bar Examiners were designated by the United States.

two countries. Although it is too early to judge the success of the recommendations established by the legal profession, the mutual recognition document established by the representative of the engineering profession has found approval in Mexico and Canada. In the United States, only Texas has decided to implement the provisions of the document.[31]

At the multilateral level both UNESCO and the Council of Europe have done extensive work in recognition of educational qualifications, which has led to several conventions. As in the case of the bilateral cultural treaties, the emphasis is on fostering educational and cultural links and academic mobility more than the provision of services. For instance, the recent Convention on the Recognition of Qualifications Concerning Higher Education in the European Region aims to facilitate the recognition of qualifications granted by one party in another party. [32] It stipulates that requests should be assessed in a fair manner and within a reasonable period of time. The recognition can only be refused if the qualification is substantially different from that of the host country, and the onus is on its educational institution to prove that it is.

In the WTO some work on mutual recognition has been carried out by the Working Party on Professional Services, which recently issued its "Guidelines on Mutual Recognition Agreements or Arrangements in the Accountancy Sector."[33] It "provides practical guidance for governments,

31. For engineering see "Letter of Intent to Implement the Document of Mutual Recognition of Registered/Licensed Engineers to Facilitate Mobility in Accordance with the North American Free Trade Agreement," signed on November 18, 1996, by the Texas State Board of Registration for Professional Engineers. See Lewis (1998).

32. The Convention, done in Lisbon on April 11, 1997, is opened for signature by the member states of the Council of Europe, the member states of the UNESCO Europe Region, any other signatory, contracting state, or party to the European Cultural Convention of the Council of Europe or to the UNESCO Convention on the Recognition of Studies, Diplomas, and Degrees concerning Higher Education in the states belonging to the Europe Region. The convention entered into force in February 1999. Australia, Canada, and the United States, among others, have signed but not yet ratified the convention. Two bodies, the Committee of the Convention on the Recognition of Qualifications concerning Higher Education in the European Region and the European Network of National Information Centres on Academic Mobility and Recognition (the ENIC Network), are to oversee, promote, and facilitate the implementation of the convention. The committee is responsible for promoting the application of the convention and overseeing its implementation. To this end it can adopt, by a majority of the parties, recommendations, declarations, protocols, and models of good practice to guide the competent authorities of the parties. Before making its decisions the committee seeks the opinion of the ENIC Network. As for the ENIC Network, it upholds and assists the practical implementation of the convention by the competent national authorities.

33. World Trade Organization, "Guidelines on Mutual Recognition Agreements or Arrangements in the Accountancy Sector," S/L/38, May 28, 1997.

negotiating entities or other entities entering into mutual recognition negotiations on accountancy services." These guidelines are intended for use on a voluntary basis and are nonbinding. There are sections on how to conduct mutual recognition negotiations, how to fulfill WTO notification requirements, and how to construct the form and content of agreements. The form and content section deals with the possible scope of agreements and the way of designing mutual recognition of qualifications, registration, and licensing systems and their eligibility criteria.

To conclude this nonexhaustive review of the international practice, it is essential to mention the significant number of arrangements concluded by professional bodies. An arrangement titled "Principles of Reciprocity" was reached in 1996 between the US AICPA and NASBA and the Institute of Chartered Accountants in Australia (ICAA).[34] It sets out reduced examination requirements and experience requirements for the licensed accountants of the two jurisdictions. The arrangement is carried out in Australia on a national basis, but individual state boards of accountancy have to accept it in the United States.[35]

In architecture the Commonwealth Associations of Architects (CAA) has established many recognition arrangements between institutes in the Commonwealth countries, based on the inspection and accreditation of the architectural training provided in specific educational establishments.[36] Qualifications are mutually accepted subject to local interview. The validation of courses and examinations for exemption is carried out on behalf of member institutes by the Royal Institute of British Architects, using a procedure modeled on its own long-standing practices.

The International Union of Architects (UIA) has developed voluntary guidelines, the so-called Barcelona Accord, meant to provide practical guidance for governments and negotiating entities seeking mutual recognition for architectural services.[37] Therefore they cover not only the recog-

34. The ICAA is a national professional association that represents the chartered accountancy profession across all states.

35. Nineteen boards have done so. See World Trade Organization, "Notification pursuant to Article VII.4 of the General Agreement on Trade in Services—Accounting," S/C/N/68, March 13, 1998.

36. There were twenty-two founder member institutes, and new institutes have since been admitted, bringing membership to thirty-nine. It is estimated that through its member institutes the association represents more than 45,000 architects throughout the Commonwealth.

37. The Union Internationale des Architectes (UIA) was founded in 1948 in Lausanne, Switzerland, as a federation of professional societies of architects from twenty-two countries. It now has a membership of the professional societies of more than one hundred countries representing around 1 million architects.

The official name of the accord is "Accord on Recommended International Standards of Profession-

nition of an academic diploma but also the waiving of examinations, adaptation periods, or tests; the issue and registration of a practicing certificate for cross-border and establishment practice; and membership of the local order and use of their title. In particular, the "Guidelines on Registration/Licensing/Certification of the Practice of Architecture" require that an applicant for recognition hold an accredited professional degree in architecture, have appropriate practical training, pass examinations, possibly undergo a personal interview, and be of good moral character. Anyone thus accepted and licensed should have his or her current and valid registration recognized by other jurisdictions.

The Engineering Accreditation Commission (EAC) of the Accreditation Board for Engineering and Technology (ABET) of the United States and the Canadian Engineering Accreditation Board (CEAB) of the Canadian Council of Professional Engineers (CCPE) reached a mutual recognition agreement in 1997 that superseded a 1980 agreement. The two parties agree that the accreditation criteria, policies, and procedures used by the EAC and the CEAB in their processes are comparable and that the accreditation decisions rendered by one party are acceptable to the other party.

A wider arrangement is represented by the so-called Washington Accord. It was signed in 1989 by professional bodies from six countries (Australia, Canada, Ireland, New Zealand, the United Kingdom, and the United States). Since then, two more bodies have become signatories (Hong Kong and South Africa), but only the Hong Kong Institution of Engineers has been accepted by the other parties. Signatories to the agreement recognize the substantial equivalency or comparability of the respective accreditation process of engineering education courses and programs leading to the first professional degree or basic education in engineering (the "accredited engineering degree").[38] The signatories agree that decisions rendered by one signatory are acceptable to the other signatories and they will make every reasonable effort to ensure that the bodies responsible for registering or licensing professional engineers to practice in their respective

---

alism in Architectural Practice," adopted in 1996 in Barcelona and subsequently revised. It was adopted by UIA members at a general assembly in Beijing in June 1999.

38. The rules and procedures of the Washington Accord provide that the accreditation systems in each signatory country be subject to a comprehensive review and report by the other signatories every six years, or earlier if a substantial change in its accreditation criteria, policies, or procedures is reported. The outcome of such a review can be acceptance of the accreditation system for a further six years, or three years if there are specific issues identified to be addressed, or a downgrading to provisional status. Termination of signatory status needs the support of two-thirds of all signatories.

countries accept the substantial equivalence of engineering academic programs accredited by the other signatories. The agreement does not address the mutual recognition of professional credentials, such as the professional engineer or chartered engineer, but only of educational credentials that are the basis for seeking practice credentials.

Legal Issues and the Negotiation of MRAs

Regulatory activities in services involve many different parties within countries and at the international level.[39] In the United States, for instance, most service sectors are the subject of federal, state, local, and industry regulation, or some combination of these. Even in unitary states, self-regulating bodies and regulatory agencies are widespread. This has led to a diversified and patchy international practice of mutual recognition. The various domestic regulatory systems and approaches, while often similar in their public policy objectives and effects, frequently remain very different. This often engenders problems that hamper progress in mutual recognition at the international level.

Multilayer regulatory regimes pose a particular challenge. The presence of regulatory competence at subcentral level is a well-known problem in the conduct of international relations between unitary and nonunitary states, which has also directly affected the negotiations of trade agreements such as the WTO Government Procurement Agreement.[40] However, the situation becomes even more complicated when regulation is achieved, as it is in many countries, both through legislation and self-regulation. In many cases self-regulatory bodies are created by law, and their regulatory and disciplinary authority is statutorily recognized together with their autonomy from the government.[41]

Although the awareness of the usefulness of mutual recognition as a trade-facilitating and liberalizing tool seems to be growing, three preliminary issues need to be clarified to foster the use of this instrument. What

39. World Trade Organization, "International Regulatory Initiatives in Services," S/C/W/97, March 1, 1999.

40. For an interesting analysis of the issue from a U.S. constitutional perspective, see Schaefer (1999).

41. As pointed out by Robert Howse in commenting on this chapter, in these cases drawing appropriate lines of accountability for the negotiation and implementation of MRA commitments between different levels of government or regulatory authority and nongovernmental voluntary bodies would be highly desirable, not only for effectiveness, but also from a perspective of democratic legitimacy.

does "recognition" mean and imply? Who is competent to negotiate and enter into legally enforceable mutual recognition commitments? And who is responsible for ensuring their implementation? These matters are certainly at the heart of the current difficult discussions between the United States and the European Union on mutual recognition in services in the context of the Transatlantic Economic Partnership.[42]

Current international practice does not seem to provide straight answers. What is meant by mutual recognition in services and what legal obligations such recognition gives rise to are obviously crucial to allowing greater use of the recognition instrument. The uncertainty surrounding this idea is partly due to significant differences between service sectors.[43] Recognition of an engineering diploma is different from the recognition of prudential measures in banking. It is also partly due to the different aims of the agreements, particularly in the recognition of qualifications. In some cases the mutual recognition is aimed at facilitating movements of students and scholars, and any trade impact occurs only as a side effect. In other cases, facilitating provision of a professional service is the main goal. Recognition thus has different meanings and entails different consequences in each agreement.

Similarly, in current international practice, diverse entities are involved in some kind of mutual recognition activity. Although there are a number of classic international agreements, both bilateral, such as the various cultural conventions, and multilateral, including the UNESCO conventions, there are also other combinations that directly involve competent authorities at the subcentral level. In particular, there are arrangements between professional bodies, to be implemented by subcentral regulatory authorities, that are provided for in turn by regional integration agreements, such as the Canada-U.S. Free Trade Agreement and NAFTA. There are also bilateral and multilateral arrangements developed by professional bodies with no connection with any government-to-government agreement.

The characterization of these arrangements poses a number of legal problems.[44] Arrangements such as those between architects under the Canada-U.S. FTA or between lawyers under NAFTA should be regarded as recommendations offered by the professions to the subcentral authori-

---

42. See note 14 and accompanying text.

43. For an analysis of mutual recognition in professional services, see Nicolaïdis (1997).

44. For a general discussion of the issues posed by the agreements' so-called *infra-étatiques*, which is also relevant in this context, see Burdeau (1981).

ties of the parties involved on how to implement some form of mutual recognition. Despite the treatylike style with which these recommendations are drafted and despite a formal link with a proper intergovernmental agreement, the signatories are not capable of entering into agreements that are binding under international law. Professional or other self-regulatory organizations do not possess the status of international legal persons and, even if created by domestic law, they are not generally part of the governmental structure. They do not appear to be capable of binding the state to which they belong unless they have received a clear delegation of authority to this effect.[45] Even a general delegation of public authority would probably not be sufficient to establish a clear capacity to enter into an international agreement; a specific confirmation would be required to ensure legal clarity.

However, if it could be ascertained that the drafters of these kinds of documents, in their private capacity, were willing to enter into legal obligations, these arrangements could be regarded as contracts. But the arrangements, first under the Canada-U.S. FTA and now NAFTA, are meant to be put into practice by state and provincial authorities when they are competent. These voluntary implementation activities appear to be unilateral acts that could be reversed without engendering any kind of legal responsibility. At most, a contractual engagement of a private nature could be identified.[46]

Similar considerations apply to the arrangements reached by professional or other self-regulatory bodies. These documents can be considered

---

45. NAFTA Article 1213 (Definitions) in paragraph 1 provides that references to a federal, state, or provincial government are deemed to include "any non-governmental body in the exercise of any regulatory, administrative or other governmental authority delegated to it by that government." The mutual recognition document drafted by the engineering professions of Canada, Mexico, and the United States (see note 30), in its Article II defines the signatories as "Representative Engineering Organizations" from the three countries. For instance, the U.S. government limited itself to support and encourage the efforts of the U.S. Council for International Engineering Practice. There is no mention of any delegation of power.

For delegation of authority it is interesting that GATS Article I (Scope and Definition) states in paragraph 3 that "'measures by Members' means measures taken by . . . (ii) non-governmental bodies in the exercise of powers delegated by central, regional or local governments or authorities." The Vienna Convention on the Law of Treaties, in Article 7, recognizes heads of state, heads of government, and ministers for foreign affairs as having the capacity to enter into treaties on behalf of their nations. In certain cases diplomats or official representatives to an international conference are also recognized as having such capacity. Otherwise a document authorizing the person to enter into the treaty must be provided by the "competent authority" of the nation.

46. See Lissitzyn (1968, p. 83).

either nothing more than an expression of goodwill or a private contract. Even if parties to an arrangement are on one side a self-regulatory body, which through a specific delegation of power can be considered part of the governmental structure (and thus competent to enter into an international agreement), and on the other side a private, nongovernmental body, the arrangement would remain a contract at best.[47] In those cases where the existence of a contract could be ascertained, significant additional legal issues would have to be tackled, including the choice of the governing law, which is generally not designated by the parties to this type of arrangement.

It appears that international practice in this area has not changed the general tenet whereby nation-states remain the most appropriate parties to negotiate and conclude internationally binding agreements. This does not mean that the current varied practice should be discounted as irrelevant. Subcentral bodies that are competent at the domestic level need to be involved in the negotiations, if for no other reason than that they have the necessary expertise in a given field. However, to ensure legal security, predictability, and transparency, their participation needs to be integrated into a broader legal framework. In this way the various and patchy mutual recognition efforts could be brought into a more coherent whole.

Because nations are the best suited to negotiate and conclude mutual recognition agreements, they also remain ultimately responsible for ensuring implementation of any commitment undertaken. Arrangements such as those reached in the Canada-U.S. FTA and NAFTA, which are meant to be carried out by state and provincial bodies, basically rely on their voluntary decisions to do so.[48] These documents, even when they include detailed provisions, do not introduce any obligation to carry out the arrangements. In general, arrangements between professional or other self-regulatory bodies with no specifically delegated powers can only be carried out and enforced as contracts. But arrangements between such

---

47. So-called state contracts, such as a contract between a state granting concessions to a private company, for example, are not international agreements or treaties. See "Anglo-Iranian Oil Case," *ICJ Reports* (1952) 111.

48. For instance, in its "Letter of Intent to Implement the Document of Mutual Recognition of Registered/Licensed Engineers to Facilitate Mobility in Accordance with the North American Free Trade Agreement," signed on November 18, 1996, the Texas State Board of Registration for Professional Engineers says, "The Board intends to deliberately identify and pursue courses of action, consistent with the Document and with licensing standards of the Texas engineering profession, that can serve to improve the mobility of professional engineers across the borders of Texas and throughout North America." This does not seem to go beyond a unilateral promise.

bodies enjoying specific powers could be construed as engaging the respective states, thus creating an obligation for implementation.

International practice shows that even for mutual recognition of education, qualifications or ability to provide services that involves many layers of central, subcentral, and even private authority, international commitments need to be entered into and put into practice by governments or at least through government involvement. Specific provisions may be included in an agreement to address the issue of competence of subcentral authorities.[49] Any attempt to bypass central governments results in voluntary engagements or in private contractual obligations that are generally not suited for the conduct of international trade relations between states. This does not in any way suggest that implementation should be achieved in a centralized way. Each country will carry out its international commitments according to its internal constitutional structure. Flexibility and engagement of the responsible authorities at all levels will be crucial in many cases.[50] However, as it is generally recognized under international

49. An interesting example of such a provision is Article II:1 of the UNESCO/Council of Europe Convention on the Recognition of Qualifications concerning Higher Education in the European Region, referred to earlier (see note 37 and accompanying text), that states:

1. Where central authorities of a Party are competent to make decisions in recognition cases, that Party shall be immediately bound by the provisions of this Convention and shall take the necessary measures to ensure the implementation of its provisions on its territory.

Where the competence to make decisions in recognition matters lies with components of the Party, the Party shall furnish one of the depositories with a brief statement of its constitutional situation or structure at the time of signature or when depositing its instrument of ratification, acceptance, approval or accession, or any time thereafter. In such cases, the competent authorities of the components of the Parties so designated shall take the necessary measures to ensure implementation of the provisions of this Convention on their territory.

2. Where the competence to make decisions in recognition matters lies with individual higher education institutions or other entities, each Party according to its constitutional situation or structure shall transmit the text of this convention to these institutions or entities and shall take all possible steps to encourage the favourable consideration and application of its provisions.

3. The provisions of paragraphs 1 and 2 of this Article shall apply, *mutatis mutandis*, to the obligations of the Parties under subsequent articles of this Convention.

50. For an important example of agreement reached between governmental agencies, see the so-called Basle Capital Accord ("Report on International Convergence of Capital Measurement and Capital Standards") established in 1988 by the Basle Committee on Banking Supervision, which comprises representatives of the central banks and supervisory authorities of the so-called Group of Ten countries (Belgium, Canada, France, Germany, Italy, Japan, the Netherlands, Sweden, Switzerland, the United Kingdom, the United States) and Luxembourg. With regard to implementation it states in paragraph 51: "The arrangements described in this document will be implemented at national level at the earliest possible opportunity. Each country will decide the way in which the supervisory authorities will introduce and apply these recommendations in the light of their different legal structures and existing supervisory arrangements. In some countries, changes in the capital regime may be introduced, after consultation, rela-

law, "a party may not invoke the provisions of its internal law as justification for its failure to perform a treaty."[51]

Mutual Recognition in the GATS Context: Article VII

Article VII of GATS does not provide direct responses to the legal questions I have outlined. It nonetheless establishes an important enabling principle for mutual recognition: it allows WTO members to enter into mutual recognition agreements with regard to "education or experience obtained, requirements met, or licenses or certification granted," thus deviating from the MFN principle enshrined in Article II.[52] This wording appears to be broad enough to cover virtually all domestic regulatory instruments with a direct impact on the ability to provide services. Members are thus allowed to enter into bilateral agreements reciprocally granting a more favorable treatment—recognition—without being obliged to extend that treatment to other members. But neither Article VII nor Article 3 of the GATS Annex on Financial Services elaborates on what that treatment may entail in terms of legal obligations. The question of what recognition means remains open. The two GATS provisions only state that recognition "may be achieved through harmonization."[53] Article VII:5 adds that "wherever appropriate, recognition should be based on multilaterally agreed criteria."

Article VII and Article 3 of the Financial Services Annex establish a clear requirement for WTO members party to a bilateral mutual recognition agreement to "afford adequate opportunity" for accession of other members or for negotiation of comparable agreements.[54] Furthermore,

---

tively speedily without the need for legislation. Other countries may employ more lengthy procedures, and in some cases these may require legislation. In due course the member states of the European Community will also need to ensure that their own domestic regulations are compatible with the Community's own legislative proposals in this field. None of these factors needs result in any inconsistency in the timing of implementation among member countries. For example, some countries may apply the framework in this report, formally or informally, in parallel with their existing system, certainly during the initial period of transition. In this way banks can be assisted to start the necessary process of adjustment in good time before substantive changes in national systems are formally introduced."

51. See Article 27 of the Vienna Convention on the Law of Treaties.

52. Articles 2.7 and 6.3 of the TBT Agreement and Article 4.2 of the SPS Agreement also provide for entering into mutual recognition agreements.

53. Art VII:1 of GATS and Article 3(a) of the Annex on Financial Services.

54. Similar albeit weaker standards are included in the TBT Agreement with regard to mutual recognition of technical regulation (Article 2.7) and of conformity assessments (Article 6.3).

members wishing to enter into negotiations for a mutual recognition agreement are required to inform the Council for Trade in Services about their intent so as to "provide adequate opportunity to any other Member to indicate their interest in participating in the negotiations before they enter a substantive phase."[55] These provisions clearly indicate a preference for a plurilateral approach to mutual recognition. Bilateral agreements are allowed, but even before conclusion the two parties are to be receptive to the possibility of letting other parties join in the negotiation. In any case, bilateral agreements need to remain open. Although it is unclear what an "adequate opportunity" to negotiate accession would entail, the inclusion of a clear accession clause would be the preferable solution. Finally, even if accession proves impractical, parties to a bilateral agreement are required to pursue negotiations for similar agreements with all other interested parties.

Members also have the option of granting recognition autonomously. In so doing they shall not discriminate between like services and service suppliers or introduce disguised restrictions on trade in services.[56] Recognition, both in services and goods, requires lengthy technical work and comparison between domestic and foreign requirements. This is a resource-intensive process that, in light of the reciprocal offensive interests of domestic service suppliers in third markets, is unlikely to happen frequently on a unilateral basis.

With regard to who is competent to negotiate mutual recognition commitments, Article VII and Article 3 of the Financial Services Annex clearly refer to agreements or arrangements between WTO members. No other possibility is contemplated. Although arrangements for which members are not responsible may still be permissible, their legal status remains open to question and the applicability of the requirements of Article VII unresolved. It could be argued that there is no accession requirement in arrangements between professional associations that may well remain closed and discriminatory. As mentioned, if an agreement is concluded by members, the signatories are also responsible for implementation. Although Article VII does not address implementation of mutual recognition agreements by subcentral regulatory authorities, the general GATS standard is that members shall take all "reasonable measures" to ensure imple-

---

55. Article VII:4(b).
56. Article VII:1 and 3.

mentation "by regional and local governments and authorities and non-governmental bodies" within their territories.[57]

A Plurilateral Agreement on Mutual Recognition

GATS rules allowing for the negotiation of mutual recognition agreements clearly point toward plurilateral agreements. Negotiating a plurilateral agreement would provide the opportunity to clarify some of the legal issues that the current unwieldy international practice leaves open, thus ensuring the necessary legal security and predictability. In particular, an agreement that is included in Annex 4 of the WTO Agreement would also firmly ground mutual recognition in the multilateral trading system, thus limiting any possible discriminatory temptation.[58]

Because of the considerable variations among regulatory regimes of service sectors, there are limits to the possibility of setting general rules. However, a plurilateral agreement could clarify the idea of recognition, the issue of competence to negotiate and implement, and the role of subcentral regulatory authorities. It could also include more precise rules on accession, the scheduling of the mutual recognition commitments, and the various other necessary provisions relating to definitions, entry into force, institutions and management, amendment, emergency safeguards, and termination. This effort would certainly clear away some often thorny issues, leaving the competent regulatory authorities to concentrate on the negotiation of the actual recognition commitments.

With regard to the meaning of recognition, it is useful to consider the approach followed in trade in goods.[59] Article 2.7 of the Agreement on Technical Barriers to Trade (TBT Agreement)—as well as Article 4 of the Sanitary and Phytosanitary Agreement—refers to the idea of equivalence. Members are encouraged to accept "as equivalent technical regulations of other Members . . . provided they are satisfied that these regulations adequately fulfil the objective of their own regulations." When two parties accept the equivalence of any regulatory requirement, they are in effect waiving the application of otherwise mandatory requirements that would

---

57. Article I:3(a) (Scope and Definitions).

58. The inclusion of any trade agreement in Annex 4 of the WTO Agreement needs to be approved by WTO members by consensus. See Article X:9 of the Marrakesh Agreement Establishing the World Trade Organization.

59. Article 2.1, TBT. See Mathis (1998); and Beviglia Zampetti (forthcoming).

need to be fulfilled to market a specific product or group of products. Although regulatory requirements for domestic products remain unaltered (the treatment applied to nationals and national products), the mutual recognition partner receives a more favorable treatment. Because third countries' products would still have to fulfill the same requirements as domestic products, the national treatment obligation is respected. However, on MFN grounds, more favorable treatment of this type, granted to the mutual recognition partner, would have to be extended. But in light of the very information-intensive and technical work that needs to underpin the decision to accept the equivalence of any regulatory requirement, the unconditional application of the MFN treatment would render mutual recognition virtually impossible. Recognizing this reality, the TBT Agreement provides a legal basis for proceeding with bilateral (or plurilateral) mutual recognition.

In services the same "bilateral equivalency" could apply, and indeed Artcle VII of GATS allows a bilateral solution. As in the case of goods, the mutual acceptance of equivalence would not exclude the possibility of pursuing the harmonization of domestic rules and regulations bilaterally or adopting the recommendations of international standardization bodies.[60] However, full harmonization remains a difficult and long-term process in most cases. If, obviously, complete harmonization would eliminate the need for mutual recognition, partial harmonization could indeed be complementary and facilitate the mutual recognition of specific rules and regulations that stem from common principles.[61]

However, as far as services are concerned, it is indeed the mutual acceptance of equivalence that is the core commitment that the two parties will have to make reciprocally. In general, equivalence would entail that the parties agree that the respective licensing, qualification, and other technical requirements are interchangeable because they are satisfied that the objectives sought by domestic regulation are also fulfilled, in a different but equivalent way, by the other party's regulation. This means that the latter can be applied in lieu of the domestic regulation that is effectively waived with respect to services and service suppliers originating in the partner's jurisdiction. Because foreign regulation would become applicable with a bearing on procedures before domestic courts, it may be useful to include

60. Article VII:5.
61. This is basically the EU approach of only harmonizing essential requirements and then proceeding with extensive mutual recognition.

in the plurilateral agreement appropriate rules on conflict of law.[62] Furthermore, members can accept the equivalence of licensing and other regulatory requirements such as prudential measures or ethical, disciplinary, and other behavioral rules that entail a continued supervisory function of the regulatory authority. Particularly with a view to ensuring consumer protection, in these cases the mutual recognition commitments may have to be accompanied by provisions for consultation and cooperation between regulatory authorities.

In addition, the equivalence of qualifications, licensing, and other technical requirements for services will probably necessitate—more frequently in some service sectors than in others—the introduction of agreed compensatory requirements to ensure the quality of the service or the fulfillment of the public policy objectives pursued in the country where the service is supplied.[63]

Any commitment to adopt an international (or common) standard and to accept specific regulatory requirements or the majority of them as equivalent, would freeze the situation at the time when the commitment is undertaken. Such a constraint on the sovereign regulatory authority would not be—at least entirely—acceptable to WTO members. The mutual recognition partners would want to preserve the possibility of altering their regulatory requirements for various reasons, including the advancement of science and technology as well as possible shifts in environmental and consumer protection objectives.[64] A substantial modification of the applicable regulatory requirements, including a departure from a previously adopted international (or common) standard by one party, would entail the withdrawal of the equivalence recognition.

An important issue would be to consider ways of dealing with this eventuality, which has the potential of affecting the trade facilitation benefits originally negotiated. One possibility would be for the parties to allow themselves a completely free hand, although obviously subject to some form of reciprocity. If a party decides to change its regulatory requirements and as a consequence to withdraw a mutual recognition commitment, or does so in response to the other party's change in its technical regulations (which are no longer deemed equivalent), the other

62. This would be the case, for instance, of professional liability suits.

63. For instance, the WTO Accountancy Guidelines, S/L/38, May 28, 1997, specifically provide for this possibility.

64. This issue is addressed for instance in Article 39 (Evolution of the Domestic Legislation of the Contracting Parties) of the EC-Switzerland agreement on direct insurance (see note 10).

party would be free to withdraw all other commitments pertaining to the specific product or sector.[65] This appears undesirable and could be only partially corrected by a strong procedural commitment to transparency and regulatory cooperation, as much upstream in the regulatory rule-making process as possible, to try to minimize the possibility that diverging requirements would be developed. Preferably, parties could decide to make this change in the original commitments subject to consultation and dispute settlement procedures. The plurilateral agreement would need to include provisions to this effect, including the standard of review. Relevant principles such as those included in Article VI:4 (Domestic Regulation) of GATS would need to be inserted by reference and perhaps elaborated.[66]

As mentioned earlier, Article VII allows members to join in existing bilateral agreements for mutual recognition. A plurilateral agreement could enshrine this in a proper accession clause. This aspect is obviously linked to the overall architecture of the plurilateral agreement. General obligations in this area cannot go beyond the setting out of an overall framework. The actual mutual recognition commitments need to be negotiated country by country because of the marked differences between regulatory regimes. They could be scheduled as additional commitments as provided for by Article XVIII of GATS or could take the form of bilateral sectoral annexes.[67] For this new type of commitment it would probably be useful for the plurilateral agreement to acknowledge the prevailing bilateral nature of mutual recognition and to explicitly confirm the basic but qualified MFN exemption that stems from Article VII. This qualification would consist of stronger procedural requirements in order to afford other members a fuller opportunity to negotiate mutual recognition commitments, thus ensuring a truly open system. The commitments would remain as a

65. By way of simplification, two cases could present themselves. First, one of the mutual recognition partners may decide to make its own technical regulation "more stringent" and thus consider that the regulation of the other party originally deemed equivalent is no longer so. In such a case protectionist motives could also be alleged. Otherwise, one partner may decide to make its own domestic regulation "less stringent," leading the other party to consider that the new version of the regulation is no longer equivalent. A form of competitive deregulation could be alleged in this case. Here the possibility of withdrawing mutual recognition commitment would neutralize any "race to the bottom" pressure, allowing for the preservation of high levels of safety and protection.

66. The primary issue here would be how deferential the standard of review should be vis-à-vis the sovereign autonomy of national legislators and regulators. See Hudec (1998).

67. Article XVIII (Additional Commitments) specifically refers to "commitments with respect to measures . . . including those regarding qualifications, standards or licensing matters."

general rule bilateral, but the process of extending the number of partici-
pant members and the scope of the commitments would be put on a firmer
ground.[68]

At the same time, the plurilateral agreement could clarify the role of
subcentral regulatory bodies in the negotiation and implementation of
the mutual recognition commitments. It would be useful to include a
clause that would enable clear delegations of powers for negotiation and
implementation of the commitments. Transitional and provisional periods
and safeguard provisions could be added to increase the comfort level of
the subcentral regulatory bodies during implementation. However, from
a political economy perspective, a complete delegation to subcentral or
self-regulating bodies or both may not be advisable since parochial, sector-specific or corporatist, and protectionist attitudes would probably prevail. With regard to subfederal coverage, and in light of the differences
in regulatory regimes that may exist at the state and local level, the
plurilateral agreement could make clear that members are allowed to carve
out from their mutual recognition commitments those subcentral entities
that are unable or unwilling to agree to be bound. Obviously, such possibility will affect the willingness of the other party to enter into any
mutual recognition commitment, and a procedure to verify the existence
of a critical mass of participating subcentral entities would need to be
included.

Finally, a plurilateral agreement could include provisions for the settlement of disputes. A WTO plurilateral agreement would also have the
significant advantage that, as provided by Appendix 1 of the Dispute
Settlement Understanding, the WTO dispute settlement system could be
used to enforce such an agreement, also through its deterrent power.
"Special and additional" provisions could then be introduced to supersede
the normal DSU provisions as appropriate to the specific case. Because
disputes in mutual recognition of licenses and regulatory requirements
may often be very individualized, it may be useful to consider the possibility of allowing private parties access to a customised dispute resolution
system. Specific arbitration procedures could be devised to settle differences between individual service providers, both natural and juridical

---

68. Some extension of the benefits of the mutual recognition commitments to like services and
service providers even if "originating" from a third country could be envisioned. For instance, if licensed
engineers from the United States are, through mutual recognition, admitted to practice in the European
Union, the same treatment could be accorded to a Canadian engineer that has acquired a license in the
U.S. jurisdictions.

persons and the host country's regulatory authorities and self-regulating bodies.[69]

Conclusion

Internationally, mutual recognition in services has developed in an unwieldy fashion. A certain lack of transparency also leaves the possibility of discrimination. Although this experimentation is useful and indeed natural, the potential trade facilitation and liberalization benefits that mutual recognition promises have been limited. GATS allows members to use this instrument while providing only very basic principles on how to do it. The main preoccupation of Article VII is to permit the necessary departure from the MFN rule while ensuring the openness of any bilateral mutual recognition agreement. This framework, although necessary, is probably not sufficient because it is too rudimentary to foster the use of an instrument that raises a number of delicate legal issues. The development of a WTO plurilateral agreement may provide the opportunity to clarify them, while definitively anchoring the mutual recognition instrument in the multilateral system of trade rules. At the same time, a plurilateral agreement that provides the necessary rules to which sectoral (bilateral) commitments are attached will allow for the necessary flexibility to cater to all the specificities of the various service-related regulatory regimes. It will also ensure the necessary coherence and transparency that will lead to learning economies and demonstration effects, thus encouraging the use of the mutual recognition instrument by an increasing number of WTO members.

References

Beviglia Zampetti, Americo. Forthcoming. "Mutual Recognition in the Transatlantic Context: Some Reflections on Future Negotiations." In *Regulatory Barriers and the Principle of Non-Discrimination in World Trade Law: Past, Present and Future*, edited by Petros Mavroidis and Thomas Cottier. University of Michigan Press.

Burdeau, Geneviève. 1981. "Les accords conclus entre autorités administratives ou organ-

---

69. The NAFTA mutual recognition document for engineers (see note 28), provides for such an arbitral dispute resolution system. In the WTO context an arbitral mechanism open to aggrieved private parties is already provided for in the Agreement on Preshipment Inspection, Article 4 (Independent Review Procedures).

ismes publics de pays différents." In *Mélanges offerts à Paul Reuter—Le droit international : Unité et diversité*, pp. 103–26. Paris: A. Pedone.

Commission of the European Communities. 1985. *Completing the Internal Market*. COM (90) 283 final. Brussels.

———. 1999. *Mutual Recognition in the Context of the Follow-up to the Action Plan for the Single Market*. COM (1999) 299 final. Brussels.

Hay, Q., M. Taylor, and D. Webb. 1997. "Trans-Tasman Mutual Recognition: A New Dimension in Australia-New Zealand Legal Relations." *International Trade Law and Regulation* 3 (1): 6–13.

Hudec, Robert. 1998. "GATT/WTO Constraints on National Regulation: Requiem for an 'Aim and Effect' Test." *International Lawyer* 32 (Fall): 619–49.

Lewis, L. G. 1998. "Engineering Mobility under the NAFTA." *Licensure Exchange* 2 (April): 6–7.

Lissitzyn, Oliver. 1968. "Territorial Entities Other than States in the Law of Treaties." *Recueil des Courses de l'Academie de Droit International* 125: 1–92.

Mathis, James. 1998. "Mutual Recognition Agreements: Transatlantic Parties and the Limits of Non-Tariff Barrier Regionalism in the WTO." *Journal of World Trade* 32 (December): 5–31.

Mattera, Alfonso. 1990. *Le marché unique européen; ses règles, son fonctionnement*. Paris: Jupiter.

———. 1991. "Les principes de 'proportionalité' et de la 'reconnaissance mutuelle' dans la jurisprudence de la Cour en matière de libre circulation des personnes et des services; de l'arrêt 'Thieffry' aux arrêts 'Vlassopoulou', 'Mediawet' et 'Dennemeyer.'" *Revue du Marché Unique Européen* (4): 191–203.

Nicolaïdis, Kalypso. 1997. "Managed Mutual Recognition: The New Approach to the Liberalization of Professional Services." Working Paper. John F. Kennedy School of Government, Harvard University.

Sauvé, Pierre. 1995. "The Long and Winding Road: NAFTA and the Professions." In *Liberalisation of Trade in Professional Services*, pp. 61-69. Paris: OECD.

Schaefer, Mark. 1999. "Twenty-First Century Trade Negotiations, the US Constitution, and the Elimination of U.S. State-Level Protectionism." *Journal of International Economic Law* 2 (March): 71–112.

COMMENT BY
Robert Howse

Geza Feketekuty's chapter is an eloquent restatement of the neoliberal orthodoxy about regulation and its reform, complemented by a fine appreciation of the important role of services in economic growth and development and a real sensitivity to the legal architecture of the General Agreement on Trade in Services. There is much that I would agree with in Feketekuty's essay, and so I will concentrate in this brief comment on points of divergence.

The first divergence is perhaps as much a matter of emphasis and tone as of substance. Feketekuty is clearly right to emphasize that the key to effective competition in so-called network industries like telecommunications and electricity is the separation of the natural monopoly element—the core "infrastructure"—from the provision of goods and services (basic electricity would actually appear to be a good)[1] by competing firms, some of which will of course have to be delivered over the network. Yet I sense in his chapter perhaps too much optimism that once such a separation has occurred, it is a relatively straightforward matter to define equal terms of access and secure a competitive level playing field for network users. Given that the network remains a monopolist, pricing access to maximize technical efficiency incentives to that monopolist while ensuring an appropriate amount of investment in upgrading and expansion of network capacity is a tricky business with no obvious answer from economic doctrine. How various users interconnect to a network may affect its reliability and impose externalities on other users. At the same time, rules about interconnection, the pricing of such externalities, and so forth can become trade barriers if they are devised in such a way as to intentionally or inadvertently advantage local in-jurisdiction providers, including new companies that may previously have been part of a horizontally integrated monopoly provider.

Another kind of re-regulation that may have an important impact on the openness of newly competitive services markets to out-of-jurisdiction providers is constraints on anticompetitive behavior by dominant players. In the case of electricity, this includes, for instance, gaming behavior by major suppliers of generating capacity to the grid, which can result in

1. Howse and Heckman (1996).

manipulated spot prices for electricity. Feketekuty would seem to prefer non-industry-specific competition rules to deal with such problems—one advantage of that is perhaps less likelihood of the rules and their application being captured by a particular industry. However, this may involve not only a reworking of the general competition law of a jurisdiction but the acquisition of specialized industry expertise by the competition authorities, not always an easy achievement. In the end, Feketekuty acknowledges that some sectoral rule-making is inevitable.

This relates to the issue of the appropriate form and institutional context for global competition rules as they relate to trade in services in network industries. The principles in the reference paper appended to the Basic Telecommunications Agreement in GATS represent a recognition of the need to ensure appropriate competition policy with a view to liberalized trade in basic telecommunications services. But is the WTO the appropriate institutional context in which to determine whether the competition and related policies of individual parties to the agreement uphold these basic principles? Feketekuty makes the interesting suggestion that only general principles should be binding obligations under the WTO framework, with more specialized international agencies, as well as national authorities and voluntary associations, responsible for addressing more specific issues in the regulatory interface between jurisdictions. Would these agencies or organizations also have a role to play in interpreting whether the basic principles were being implemented in specific contexts?

Feketekuty emphasizes transparency and due process in regulation; at the same time he calls for minimalist and market-based regulation. I think there are some interesting tensions in putting all these notions into practice together. For instance, industry self-regulation, delegated regulation, and use of voluntary, private-sector-generated standards may well be indicated by the preference for minimalist and market-based regulation. However, the ideas of due process, specification of detailed rules and criteria, and so on as developed by Feketekuty seem based on an "administrative state" paradigm, more fitted to traditional "command and control" regulation. In rapidly changing industries, where regulators and regulated entities must rapidly adapt to new technologies and grasp the competitive significance of new products and ways of doing business, discretion and flexibility may be necessary if regulation is not to be heavy-handed, thereby straightjacketing innovation. However, as Feketekuty also notes, discretion can be abused, with protectionist, anticompetitive, or even corrupt decisions made "invisibly." In any case, even with explicitly stated rules and criteria, rights of appeal, and so forth, I am skeptical that close surveillance by transnational authorities of the application of domestic rules and regulations by officials and agencies in specific contexts is feasible. Precisely because there is no set of European Union–type institutions—with legitimacy, though limited, to regulate and judge regulation—at the global level, we are likely to be stuck with a large amount of subsidiarity. If it is any consolation, perhaps, from a lawyer's perspective, I could suggest that Feketekuty is somewhat too optimistic about the capacity of transparent legal formalism to constrain corrupt or captured regulatory decisionmaking. One should not underestimate the ability of interested parties to get around the most detailed and public formal rules and regulations in a regulatory context characterized by corruption or capture. I think transnational initiatives to improve the *competence* of regulators who do exercise discretion are, by contrast, more likely to bear fruit—technical assistance in the case of developing or newly liberalizing countries, seminars, exchange of information and perspectives on regulatory problems, evolution of best practices for regulation in specific sectors (Ann Marie Slaughter's recent work on globalization and expert networks is of considerable interest).[2]

Like the Feketekuty chapter, the chapter by Kalypso Nicolaïdis and Joel P. Trachtman displays a range of important virtues. I admire the way that the authors unpack the complexities of the concept of mutual recognition, an apparently simple idea that has within it a range of subtle institutional, legal, and political economy choices (some of these are also explored with finesse in the chapter by Americo Beviglia Zampetti).

Nicolaïdis and Trachtman are right not to assume that there is, in principle, a good case for further disciplines on regulations that purport to have an impact on services trade. Their position that one should pose the question of whether further disciplines are warranted on a sector-by-sector basis is a judicious one. At the same time, at various places in the chapter, the authors seem to assume some kind of generic meaning to the notion of a regulatory trade barrier. Yet this is not an obvious or uncontroversial notion. When thinking about the scope of such legal disciplines, it may be easier to start from common ground—namely, the central concern of trade law with the constraining protectionism, that is, measures that entail either facial or de facto discrimination against foreign goods, services, firms,

2. Slaughter (1997, p. 183).

capital, and workers, and then consider why it is institutionally appropriate or legitimate to expand beyond this concern the ambit of the global trading regime such that it subjects nonprotectionist regulations to discipline through legal rules.[3]

In terms of the basic legal architecture of GATS, where the authors are absolutely right is to emphasize the complexity of the legal rules that discipline *discriminatory* regulations. One issue they discuss in detail is that of determining the meaning of a "like service" for purposes of determining whether a member's regulations have provided as favorable treatment to the services of another member as to domestic "like" services. The authors' analysis could be advanced by keeping in mind the basic premise that an analysis of National Treatment, in aiming to scrutinize regulatory measures for *discrimination*, should not seek to invalidate or question general regulatory distinctions but only those that are cast in a directly or indirectly protectionist manner and do not have a foundation in criteria that are apparently neutral or unrelated to protection of domestic markets against foreign competition.

The authors suggest, in my view wrongly, that there is a solid legal basis in GATT for the process/product distinction—the notion that National Treatment relates only to the physical characteristics of products and not the manner in which they are produced. This was a distinction invented ex nihilo by the two most discredited (and never adopted) panels in GATT history—the Tuna/Dolphin panels—in a misguided attempt to make GATT-illegal even nondiscriminatory environmental measures.[4] Article III:4 applies to all regulations and requirements "*affecting* [the] internal sale, offering for sale, purchase, transportation, distribution or use of products"—what matters, logically enough for a trade agreement, is the commercial issue of whether the measures have discriminatory effects on the conditions of international competition, not the metaphysical question of whether the measures address some matter related to the becoming of the product or its being. Thus, in the adopted GATT panel ruling in the Section 337 case, the panel had no difficulty applying the National Treatment obligation to measures that treated domestic and foreign products differently in regard to intellectual property violations that may have occurred in the process of their production, which of course goes to the

---

3. Sykes (1999).

4. The following draws from a coauthored manuscript in progress on the conceptual and jurisprudential groundlessness of the products/PPMs distinction. Many of my insights on this issue owe much to my coauthor, Don Regan.

juridical characterization of the production process, not any physical, or metaphysical, essence of the "product."[5]

Given the incoherence of the product/PPM distinction, it is not surprising that I have serious concerns about the attempt to carry it over somehow to the application of the National Treatment obligation in GATS, distinguishing between like services on the one hand and like service providers, on the other.[6]

The authors make another legal interpretation that is problematic. In their discussion of the WTO Appellate Body judgment in the Turtles case, they suggest that balancing of trade costs versus regulatory benefits was undertaken by the Appellate Body and that it also used a necessity test. I do not see any attempt to engage in cost-benefit analysis in this ruling, nor any employment of a necessity test. The confusion seems to be surrounding the Appellate Body analysis of the chapeau of Article XX of the GATT as opposed to its analysis of the main operative paragraph in Article XX. Following its decision in *Reformulated Gasoline*, and contrary to the impression left by the authors, the Appellate Body rejected an approach to Article XX that was based on the notion that all Article XX exceptions must be interpreted strictly. Instead, the Appellate Body stated that careful attention must be paid to the exact wording of each provision in Article XX. In this case, the United States relied on Article XX(g), which refers to measures

---

5. The authors refer to the interpretative note to GATT Article III (Ad. Article III). The interpretive note states that any internal tax, charge, or regulation that is applied to an imported product at the border is nevertheless within the scope of Article III. This provision is aimed at distinguishing Article XI, which prohibits nontariff border restrictions, from Article III, clarifying that just because a measure is applied at the border, it does not become for that reason alone a prohibited border restriction within the meaning of Article XI. There is no language in it that even suggests a hint of a distinction between characteristics of products and the characteristics of their production processes. It is true that the interpretive note refers to a kind of measure that "applies" to products, but it does not say that all Article III measures only apply to products—it only deals with a certain subset of measures, applied domestically to domestic products and applied at the border to imported products, for purposes of stating that the latter are nevertheless within the ambit of Article III. And of course, a measure may apply to a product—that is, be implemented through control of the import of the product itself—while the regulatory distinction that determines to which product it applies is based on the process and production method. Thus, a measure that controls imports of dolphin-unfriendly tuna obviously "applies" to the product (it stops the product at the border rather than fining the fisher, for example), while the basis of its application is the manner in which the tuna was fished. However, based on the analysis in the Section 337 case, it is questionable whether to be within the ambit of Article III, measures even have to be applied to a product in this attenuated sense. The procedures to deal with intellectual property violations at issue in the Section 337 case included not only measures that applied to the product (border control of entry of products manufactured in violation of intelel+lectual property laws), but also to the producers themselves, that is, the legal liability to which they were subject as firms.

6. See Howse and Regan (1999), available from the author on request.

"relating to" the conservation of exhaustible natural resources. Here, the Appellate Body correctly suggested that the language in question demanded only a rational connection between the measure in question and the policy objective at issue, conservation of exhaustible natural resources, and it rightly found a connection between the goal of preserving sea turtles as endangered species and the banning of imports of turtle-unfriendly shrimp. When it turned to the chapeau, however, and examined how the U.S. shrimp ban was being applied, it was examining evenhandedness in administration and enforcement of the measures and *not the measures themselves.* The Appellate Body found elements of arbitrary and unjustifiable discrimination in the manner in which the measures were being implemented, owing to an absence of administrative due process in determinations under the scheme, and the fact that some countries were being offered alternatives through negotiated arrangements that others were not. I simply do not see in the language of the Appellate Body any indication that it was applying any kind of "test"—it was interpreting the language of the treaty which refers to the concepts of "arbitrary" and "unjustified" discrimination. And the scheme itself was sustained on a rational connection basis.

In general, with their emphasis on the various "tests," the authors at times seem to assume that the WTO dispute settlement organs are, or should be, doing normative economic and policy analysis, in the face of generically similar kinds of trade-offs to those which other tribunals (the U.S. Supreme Court or the European Court of Justice)[7] face in effecting court-driven economic integration. At least what the WTO Appellate Body says it is doing is interpreting a treaty—a legal text that exists within the context of international law and its distinctive sources and interpretive principles. There may be important reasons of institutional legitimacy for this apparent formalism, and one should not assume that such formalism is simply based on ignorance by the Appellate Body of the more sophisticated sciences in which the authors are learned.

The very interesting discussion of rules versus standards in their chapter suggests that the authors are not unaware of the issues of institutional legitimacy in international adjudication. In some cases, we simply cannot expect legitimate outcomes through adjudicators applying vague or general standards on a case-by-case basis, and that is when it may well be desirable to negotiate specific rules and understandings about particular regulations

---

7. And at other points in the essay they bring out quite nicely differences of institutional context and their importance. See below.

and their application across the border. The authors rightly point out that there can be a dynamic relationship between application of general standards in dispute settlement and negotiation of rules that constitute a kind of *lex specialis*, or detailed code. In particular, the former can be a trigger to the latter: if states are dissatisfied with the adequacy of case-by-case jurisprudence applying general standards, then this simply acts as a spur to negotiation of more specific legal rules. I want to tease out some of the implications of this insight in the WTO context. Under the WTO Dispute Settlement Understanding, unlike with the old GATT, dispute settlement rulings are adopted as binding law unless a consensus is held *against* their adoption—in other words, even the winning party must be opposed to adoption to block it. However, adoption of new rules or even definitive interpretative understandings of old ones requires, generally speaking, a positive consensus. Now if there is a dispute settlement ruling that risks institutional legitimacy by being quite intrusive with respect to a democratic outcome in a particular country on the basis of vague standards or norms, the challenge of solving the problem posed by that decision through creation of new rules will be formidable. At a minimum, the winning party will be asked to give up, to an extent at least, something it has received as an *acquis* in dispute settlement. In such cases, we may be as likely to see bilateral settlements or "deals" as the development of new rules—and the former may be an obstacle to the evolution of the latter (see the very insightful section of the chapter on bilateral versus plurilateral and multilateral options). But, more generally, I think the reason why, as the authors conclude, standards-based disciplines are "weak" has much to do, in the WTO context, with the constraints on political adjustment of judicial activism, where it creates or threatens to create a legitimacy crisis (consider the problems the system would have faced had the Tuna/Dolphin rulings had to be adopted as legally binding). Thus, directly relevant to how "standards" adjudication should be approached in the WTO context, is the use of the *in dubio mitius* principle by the Appellate Body in *Hormones*—a treaty interpreter, when faced with a provision capable of being interpreted as either having a meaning that is very intrusive with respect to domestic sovereignty or a relatively deferential one, should (at least in the WTO context) adopt the relatively deferential reading. Further, as the authors indicate in a key paragraph of their chapter on the relationship between judicial tribunals and representative institutions, the conferral of an expansive mandate for judicial activism on international tribunals poses some particular legitimacy issues. The problem of ex ante democratic control over international agreements is severe enough as it is in most democracies.[8] The employment of general "standards" in such agreements makes intelligent public and legislative deliberation about the implications of ceding more regulatory autonomy even more difficult and elusive. This related point also helps explain why "standards" provide, quite often, "weak" disciplines with respect to trade-impacting domestic regulation—thus, in the original GATT, the "standards" that deal with domestic regulation are ones implicit in the very idea of a comprehensive agreement on reduction of tariffs and abolition of most other discriminatory border measures (Article XI)—these specific commitments shall not be undermined, or cheated on, by equally or more *discriminatory* treatment of imports in internal regulation and taxation. Since the architecture of GATS is different (the market access claims in services relate to different measures, by and large) the concept that what is being disciplined by general "standards" is that which undermines bargained concessions is expressed differently—thus, National Treatment applies only to sectors in which specific commitments have been made. And where disciplines on regulatory autonomy in GATS go beyond the basic idea of nondiscrimination (Article VI), as the authors note, nullification and impairment of benefits must be proved by the complainant to make its case. This requirement ensures that governments are not faced with open-ended depredation of their (democratic) regulatory autonomy but only those constraints implicit in the logic of the actual concessions they have given. Notably, the kind of justification of government policies required by the various provisions in Article VI of GATS is only indicated in GATT once the policies have been found to violate a provision of the General Agreement, which means they usually have been determined to be *discriminatory*.

The Beviglia Zampetti chapter provides a splendidly lucid overview not only of actual experience with Mutual Recognition Agreements (MRAs) but also of the important challenges in designing successful arrangements of this type. There is hardly anything he says that I would not endorse. I would only draw attention to a couple of points in the chapter that I think are worthy of special attention. First of all, Beviglia Zampetti rightly notes that designing MRAs in the context of multilevel regulation (federal states, economic unions, and so on) is a challenge. Certainly from a democratic legitimacy perspective, drawing appropriate lines of accountability between different levels of government or regulatory authority for the negotiation and imple-

8. Benvenisti (forthcoming).

mentation of MRA commitments is highly desirable. Second, Beviglia Zampetti points out the special challenge for accountability where nongovernmental, voluntary bodies have a crucial role in the realization of MRAs. I agree with Beviglia Zampetti that creation of direct legal obligations even of a contractual nature between such bodies directly is undesirable, for it breaks the lines of democratic accountability. At the same time Beviglia Zampetti is right that collaboration and input from such bodies in the negotiation of MRAs and their implementation are crucial, given that these bodies have needed expertise and are close to the marketplace on a daily basis. Here I come back to a point made earlier in discussing the Feketekuty chapter—there is a trade-off between the value on the one hand of transparency and clear democratic accountability and the benefits on the other hand of informal networking between experts, governmental and nongovernmental, of different jurisdictions, emphasized, for example, by scholars such as Ann Marie Slaughter. Perhaps part of the answer lies in making informality itself more inclusive and more transparent—do trust and understanding between regulatory experts necessarily depend on clubbish secrecy and exclusionism?[9] In any case, Beviglia Zampetti displays a fine sensitivity to the values of administrative democracy, not always exemplified by the more dogmatic free trade advocates who work in this area. Finally, Beviglia Zampetti draws attention to a crucial issue (also raised by Nicolaïdis and Trachtman), that of the relationship between MRAs and most favored nation treatment. Noting the partial GATS exception from MFN treatment for MRAs, Beviglia Zampetti wonders whether without the integration of MRAs into some more general multilateral or at least plurilateral legal framework, such bilateral arrangements will run the risk of increasing discrimination in international trade. I think it is indeed worth considering how one could create such a framework, which would specify certain minimum requirements of MRAs that hem in the MFN exception and work to ensure that managed recognition does not become a scheme for covert managed (discriminatory) trade.

References

Benevenisti, E. Forthcoming. "Exit and Voice in the Age of Globalization." *University of Michigan Law Review.*

Howse, R. 1999. "Transatlantic Regulatory Cooperation and the Problem of Democracy."

---

9. I develop this notion in Howse (1999).

Paper prepared for U.S.-EU Symposium on Transatlantic Regulatory Cooperation. Columbia Law School, April.

Howse, R., and G. Heckman. 1996. "The Regulation of Trade in Electricity: A Canadian Perspective." In *Ontario Hydro at the Millenium: Has Monopoly's Moment Passed?* edited by R. Daniels, 104–55. Montreal and Kingston: McGill-Queens.

Howse, R., and D. Regan. 1999. "The Product/Process Distinction: An Illusory Basis for Disciplining Unilateralism." Paper preared for the European Journal of International Law–University of Michigan Symposium on Unilateralism and Its Limits. University of Michigan Law School, September 24.

Slaughter, A. M. 1997. "The Real New World Order." *Foreign Affairs* 76 (September-October): 183–97.

Sykes, Alan, O. 1999. "Regulatory Protectionism and the Law of International Trade." *University of Chicago Law Review* 66 (Winter): 1–46.

COMMENT BY

Aaditya Mattoo

There seems to be agreement that the current disciplines on domestic regulations in the General Agreement on Trade in Services are weak. The question is how best to strengthen them, without unduly curtailing national regulatory freedom. These three chapters on the subject are very good. I cannot do justice to them in the limited time available. So I will make two points, which draw upon the chapters but reflect my own views.

—It is desirable and feasible to develop horizontal disciplines for domestic regulations.

The diversity of services sectors, and the difficulty in making certain policy-relevant generalizations, has tended to favor a sector-specific approach. However, even though services sectors differ greatly, the underlying economic and social reasons for regulatory intervention do not. And focusing on these reasons provides the basis for the creation of meaningful horizontal disciplines.

Such a generic approach is to be preferred to a purely sectoral approach for at least three reasons: it economizes on negotiating effort, leads to the creation of disciplines for all services sectors rather than only the politically important ones, and reduces the likelihood of negotiations being captured by sectoral interest groups. It is now widely recognized that the most dramatic progress in the European Union single-market program came from willingness to take certain broad cross-sectoral initiatives.[1] In the context of the World Trade Organization, the experience of the accountancy negotiations shows the propensity for single sectoral negotiations on domestic regulations to produce a wishy-washy outcome

Even if a horizontal approach is desirable, is it feasible? The economic case for regulation in all services sectors arises essentially from market failure

---

1. Bernard M. Hoekman and Patrick A. Messerlin (in this volume) see multilateral negotiations as secondary to domestic policy reform and GATS merely as a mechanism to tie in unilateral liberalization. This view underrates the powerful stimulus that multilateral disciplines can provide to national policy reform—by making such reform more likely and at the same time ensuring that the impact is widespread. Just as it has proved easier to deal with border measures in a multilateral context, so it should be easier to address the protectionist effect of domestic regulations multilaterally. It might be easier for countries to collectively accept the across-the-board application of basic disciplines of the kind that are suggested here, than for each country to institute such disciplines unilaterally sector by sector. A striking example of the rapid generalization of the benefits of pro-competitive regulatory developments was the institution of independent regulators in the telecommunications sectors of nearly sixty WTO members.

attributable primarily to three kinds of problems, natural monopoly or oligopoly, asymmetric information, and externalities, while the social case for
regulation is based primarily on distributional considerations. Market failure because of natural monopoly or oligopoly may create trade problems because incumbents can impede access to markets in the *absence* of appropriate
regulation. Because of its direct impact on trade, this is the only form of market failure that needs to be addressed directly by multilateral disciplines. The
relevant GATS provision, Article VIII dealing with monopolies, is limited in
scope. As a consequence, in the context of the telecom negotiations, the Reference Paper with its competition principles was developed to ensure that
monopolistic suppliers would not undermine market access commitments.
The first element of our proposal is that these principles should be generalized to a variety of other network services, including transport (terminals
and infrastructure), environmental services (sewage), and energy services
(distribution networks). How precisely is this to be done? By granting access
to all suppliers, national and foreign, to essential facilities, be they roads, rail
tracks, terminals, sewers or pipelines, at cost-based rates.

In all other cases of market failure, multilateral disciplines do not need
to address the problem directly but rather to ensure that domestic measures
to deal with the problem do not serve unduly to restrict trade. (The same
is true for measures designed to achieve social objectives.) Such trade-restrictive effects can arise from a variety of technical standards, prudential
regulations, and qualification requirements in professional, financial, and
numerous other services, as well as from the granting of monopoly rights
to complement universal service obligations in services like transport and
telecommunications. The second element of our proposal is that the trade-
inhibiting effect of this entire class of regulations is best disciplined by
complementing the national treatment obligation with a generalization of
the so-called necessity test. This test essentially leaves governments free to
deal with economic and social problems provided that any measures taken
are not more trade restrictive than necessary to achieve the relevant objective. We suggest that the test can be used to create a presumption in favor
of economically efficient choice of policy in remedying market failure and
in pursuing noneconomic objectives.

I believe that the necessity test is not just an add-on discipline. It is
difficult to see how even the basic disciplines of most favored nation and
national treatment can be enforced without the application of some sort
of necessity test. Consider national treatment, which requires that foreign
services and service suppliers receive no less favorable treatment than the

like national services and suppliers. But if we apply the traditional two-step approach of first establishing likeness and then deciding on whether like foreign suppliers are receiving less favorable treatment, we end up in a legal cul-de-sac. Say a doctor from Greece arrives in the United States and wishes to practice. And say the U.S. authorities ask the doctor to fully requalify. Is this inconsistent with national treatment? The United States says that a doctor trained in Greece is not comparable to a doctor trained in the United States. What would a WTO panel say? If it says that a Greek doctor is "like" a U.S. doctor, then the United States does not have the right to impose even a slightly greater burden on the Greek doctor. This is hardly sustainable and could with justification be seen as a huge threat to regulatory autonomy. If, however, a Greek doctor is not comparable to a U.S. doctor, the national treatment discipline simply does not apply, and the Americans are free to do what they want. We might as well defenestrate GATS and the doctor. Neither is a very satisfactory outcome.

The most reasonable argument would be to ask what the U.S. authorities really need to do to ensure that foreign doctors do not constitute a threat to the health of U.S. citizens. The basic problem is one of asymmetric information: our inability to observe the true skills of the doctor. And the economically efficient way of remedying it is through a test of competence. Hence, full requalification is not necessary, and therefore this measure could be found inconsistent with GATS. In this context, Geza Feketekuty's suggestion that regulators be required to be transparent about their objectives makes a lot of sense. At the multilateral level, it is difficult to pronounce on the legitimacy of objectives, but one can discipline the choice of instruments, and transparency of objectives can help to establish whether this choice is appropriate.

In sum, the telecommunications and accountancy models, suitably developed and generalized, can together ensure that domestic regulations achieve their objectives without sacrificing economic efficiency. This is not to say that there is no need for sector-specific disciplines. For instance, valuable work could be done to establish how best to deal with asymmetric information and differences in standards between countries. But we can make a powerful beginning by taking a cross-sectoral approach.

—At the multilateral level, harmonization and mutual recognition are not meaningful alternatives to the application of a necessity test—though they may play a role at the bilateral or plurilateral level.

First consider harmonization. The pessimism about this option is based on the absence of widely accepted international standards in services. Where such standards exist, as in banking or maritime transport, meeting them is seen as a first step toward acceptability, rather than as a sufficient condition for market access. Moreover, it is unlikely that we will see meaningful international standards for most services developed soon.

Next consider mutual recognition agreements (MRAs). The chapters have generally taken a positive of view of MRAs. They even speak of a possible multilateral agreement on MRAs. I have three related problems with this approach. First, one cannot make MRAs happen; second, they do not seem to be happening—at least not on any major trade-influencing scale; and finally, even if they were to happen, it is not clear that they would always be desirable. Let me elaborate a little.

A multilateral agreement like GATS cannot oblige countries to conclude MRAs—just as any provision such as Article V of GATS or Article XXIV of GATT cannot make regional integration happen. As in the case of regional agreements, multilateral disciplines can be more or less permissive about mutual recognition.

This raises a key question: where and how strong are the incentives to conclude MRAs? First, Americo Beviglia Zampetti's partial survey suggests that the scope of MRAs is quite limited, and they are invariably concluded between very similar countries. Then, Kalypso Nicolaïdis and Joel P. Trachtman suggest that even in strongly integrationist Europe, despite a significant level of prior harmonization, the effect of MRAs may have been limited by the unwillingness of host country regulators to concede complete control. So the bottom line is that MRAs do not seem to have had a significant effect on services trade.

Which brings me to the question of the benefits and costs of MRAs. The analogy with regional integration agreements is useful, for MRAs are like sector-specific preferential arrangements. Now if regulatory barriers are prohibitively high, that is, if you begin with autarky, then recognition can only be trade creating. But if they are not, then selective recognition can have discriminatory effects and lead to trade diversion. The result may well be to create trade according to a pattern of mutual trust rather than the pattern of comparative advantage. For instance, we may well see the United States and the EU make progress toward MRAs in professional services, but can anyone see either partner concluding an MRA with India, Egypt, or the Philippines? In sum, we would probably see some encouragement of gentle intraindustry trade rather than the more challenging and more rewarding interindustry trade.

Article VII of GATS on recognition strikes a delicate balance by allowing such agreements, provided third countries have the opportunity to accede or demonstrate equivalence, and so on. Thus, Article VII has a desirable open-ended aspect that Article V (dealing with integration agreements) does not. This makes it particularly worrying that many MRAs are notified under Article V rather than VII. In any case, the key concern for any multilateral agreement should be not how those who have preferential access are treated but how those who do not have preferential access are treated. And the only defense of the rights of these third countries is precisely the necessity test, which ensures that they will not be subject to unnecessary burdensome regulation even if they are not part of an MRA.

COMMENT BY
Peter Morrison

A key debate during the GATS 2000 round will center on "domestic regulation." During their discussions, negotiators will attempt to develop new disciplines in the General Agreement on Trade in Services that push well beyond traditional ones based largely on the origin of a service or service supplier, or on quota restrictions. The new rules will ensure that government regulations are based even more broadly on principles of economic efficiency and good governance. The hope is that the barriers to trade in services will be further reduced. Should the negotiators succeed, the focus of the WTO will broaden even further from "trade" to "commerce." But how far should the WTO go in tying governments to pure economic principle? And how should its members go about it?

These three excellent chapters attempt to answer such important questions and along the way provide many useful pointers for negotiators during the new trade round. They do not prescribe a single path for all situations but advance a series of proposals. The chapters make important contributions to the debate, and I discuss each one in turn.

The chapter by Geza Feketekuty sets out lucidly the various regulatory principles governments should follow to achieve maximum economic efficiency and good governance and how GATS should be modified to reflect these principles. The principles—transparency, due process, nondiscrimination, and half a dozen others—are familiar, but it is helpful to see them enumerated and discussed together. They are largely based on U.S. and European Union experience of reducing government regulation. The principles are not aimed at imposing social objectives on governments but rather in ensuring that these objectives are achieved in an efficient way.

Although in theory these principles seem desirable and would promote efficiency and economic welfare, in my view making a legal requirement of governments to apply them would in many cases be problematic for two main reasons. First, governments might simply refuse to bind themselves so closely to pure economic doctrine. Second, any binding regulatory disciplines introduced in Article VI would have to be carefully coordinated with similar obligations already existing in GATS. Feketekuty recognizes this problem, and many of his suggested modifications to the text of Article VI, incorporating his principles, would be best-efforts clauses. That is not to say that the principles would serve no purpose; on the contrary, they could be a first step to obligations at a later stage and could help a panel or the Appellate Body in interpreting other provisions of GATS.

In implementing these regulatory principles, Feketekuty advises a sensible three-pronged approach to reform: first, a strengthening of Article VI disciplines on domestic regulation, which would be suited for most sectors; second, the negotiation of sectoral agreements, designed for heavily regulated sectors; third, negotiations on commitments in national schedules that could take account of particular national differences. He rightly emphasizes that negotiators must constantly bear in mind the principle of subsidiarity, which would stipulate rules at the WTO level of governance only when a lower level would not be appropriate.

The chapter touches also on harmonization, recognizing that its systematic application is neither necessary nor desirable for liberalization. But the focus of the chapter is not on this topic, nor on the related issue of mutual recognition under Article VII of GATS, dealt with at length in Beviglia Zampetti's contribution. Overall, Feketekuty has provided a clear framework for the introduction into the world trading system of new disciplines reflecting principles of regulatory reform.

Kalypso Nicolaïdes and Joel P. Trachtman, in contrast to Feketekuty, focus their chapter more closely on exploring the nature of domestic regulation and the factors that influence the negotiation of appropriate regulatory disciplines. The chapter contains many intriguing insights but occasionally risks overwhelming the reader by the variety of analytical tools it deploys.

At the outset, Nicolaïdes and Trachtman make several interesting and important points on who is entitled to regulate. They rightly point to the neat allocation of regulatory jurisdiction in goods trade (although perhaps not on the textual basis they suggest) and show that in services trade the model is far more complex. Based on the notion of jurisdiction, the authors also show how mutual recognition and harmonization can be progressive extensions of national treatment. Using the example of a foreign goods producer resident in a host country, they demonstrate how the producer could be subject first to host state regulation (under simple national treatment), then home state regulation (under mutual recognition), and finally a type of "transnational" regulation (under harmonization). The authors also make the vital distinction between prescriptive jurisdiction (the right to make the substantive rules) and enforcement jurisdiction (the right to interpret and enforce). They show how both play a vital role and, in the case of enforcement jurisdiction, how mutual recognition is the only option (short of supranational control) available to ensure proper liberalization.

Nicolaïdes and Trachtman borrow two key attributes of regulation to organize their thoughts. First, *who* should negotiate the new regulatory disciplines: the WTO or another institution? Second, *how* should the new regulatory disciplines be formulated: as general standards or specific rules? These two important regulatory dimensions allow the authors to draw up a useful four-way classification to pigeonhole categories of regulatory disciplines: WTO general standards, WTO specific rules, non-WTO general standards, and non-WTO specific rules.

In examining the category of WTO general standards (their first of four categories) Nicolaïdes and Trachtman consider the existing disciplines within GATS. Starting with national treatment, they note that in cross-border goods trade, the accepted notion of "like product" implies that the host (importing) country may not make regulatory distinctions based on processes, producer characteristics, and other matters that are not incorporated in the product. In cross-border goods trade, therefore, there is a general rule of home country regulation of the producer, coupled with a host country jurisdiction of the product once imported. As demonstrated in the WTO Appellate Body's Shrimp-Turtle decision, only the Article XX exceptions clause may (potentially) justify host country jurisdiction over the home country goods producer.

In trade in services, however, the situation is different. GATS, reflecting the nature of services trade, covers two situations: where production and consumption occur in the same jurisdiction and where they do not. Where production and consumption occur in the same place, regulation is relatively straightforward, since usually all the elements of the transaction—supplier, consumer, and service—are in the same jurisdiction. However, in the cross-border situation, multiple jurisdictions complicate the issue, since several host countries may attempt to apply their own differing regulations to a single service supplier providing a service from its home country (danger of conflicting requirements on the supplier), or a uniform service of a supplier from its home country (danger of conflicting requirements on the service). Nicolaïdes and Trachtman are right to point out that the Appellate Body will have to deal sensitively with the scope of host country regulation in these cases.

Nicolaïdes and Trachtman also offer an intriguing analysis of the relationship between recognition and necessity. GATS Article XIV requires that a measure, to be covered by an exception, must be "necessary" to accomplish one of the listed policy goals. Necessity has been defined in the analogous GATT provision as requiring that a measure be the "least-trade-restrictive" measure reasonably available. As suggested in the Shrimp-Turtle case, a WTO member seeking to justify a measure under the exceptions clause of Article XX, can be required, when attempting to show that the measure was the least-trade-restrictive one reasonably available, to take into account the situation of other countries to which the measure is being applied. The authors rightly point out that this requirement, if carried to an extreme, could introduce a type of recognition by judicial *fiat*. The basis of such a requirement to take into account other countries' regimes could also be based on a strict reading of Article VI. But such judicial recognition, if pushed too far, could be a form of "regulatory disarmament" unacceptable to most governments.

Nicolaïdes and Trachtman also usefully remind us what mutual recognition entails in operational terms. Far from being a simple, static rule of recognition, they demonstrate that it is a process, requiring elements such as a certain degree of prior harmonization, partial and reversible transfers of recognition powers, and verification procedures.

In weighing the use of general standards and specific rules, Nicolaïdes and Trachtman make useful points on their respective worth in different situations. They analyze the relative costs to develop and apply these norms and the degree of predictability they afford. The authors find that general standards are more often used in the early development of a field of law and where there are not enough actual cases to justify the elaboration of specific rules. They also weigh the relative institutional benefits of standards and rules, noting on public choice and other grounds that legislatures, as opposed to courts, do not always reflect best the desires of their citizens.

In analyzing the value of the general standards available in GATS, Nicolaïdes and Trachtman touch on a very difficult issue that is not often discussed. They note that the least-trade-restrictive test does not maximize trade and regulatory values as well as a pure cost-benefit analysis, because the least-trade-restrictive test is overbroad and underinclusive. But under any cost-benefit analysis the awkward question arises: whose welfare is being calculated, that of the member taking the measure, or the collective welfare of all WTO members? The authors do not develop this important aspect of the issue.

In implementing regulatory disciplines, Nicolaïdes and Trachtman argue, like Beviglia Zampetti, for the negotiation of a Framework Agreement setting out requirements for mutual recognition agreements. The

Framework Agreement could usefully contain provisions encouraging the parties to continue progress, transitivity clauses (requiring recognition between all members of interlocking mutual recognition agreements), the setting up of a multilateral system of "meta-accreditors" on the enforcement side, and at least some minimal harmonization.

On the institutional question of where regulatory disciplines should be negotiated and enforced, Nicolaïdes and Trachtman point out the advantages of grouping disciplines within a single body such as the WTO. This practice affords the possibility of cross-sectoral deals and of cross-retaliation. However, the authors realize sensibly that different solutions may be needed for different sectors and countries.

The authors conclude on a pragmatic note, recognizing that sectoral, country, and regional variations among the elements analyzed in their chapter can lead to different optimal approaches to regulatory disciplines.

The chapter by Americo Beviglia Zampetti focuses squarely on the topic of recognition. It provides an extensive and informative view on actual practice in the area, which the author uses to illustrate the variety of legal problems that arise from recognition agreements. He then analyzes Article VII of GATS (on mutual recognition), proposing that it should be bolstered by the negotiation of a Framework Agreement on mutual recognition.

Among the legal problems identified by Beviglia Zampetti, many arise from the multilayer nature of many regulatory regimes, especially those that contain a mix of legislation and self-regulation by independent bodies. But even more fundamental legal problems exist, such as the basic meaning of "recognition." Surprisingly, no straightforward answer to this question can be gleaned from international practice, perhaps because of fundamental differences among services sectors.

A further legal problem concerns the capacity to negotiate and be bound by recognition agreements. Many such agreements exist between professional bodies, and they may or may not be linked to government agreements. In Beviglia Zampetti's view, if a recognition agreement is made between purely private bodies, then it can be nothing more than an expression of good will or at most a private contract. The author thus arrives at the sensible view that state actors, not private bodies, need to conclude recognition agreements to ensure their legal enforceability. They would draw on advice from all appropriate bodies and could of course delegate implementation to private bodies.

Beviglia Zampetti notes that GATS Article VII does not answer most of the legal puzzles about recognition. It does, however, state clearly *who* may negotiate and bind a mutual recognition agreement: only members may do so. Beviglia Zampetti further notes that GATS does ensure that members take all reasonable measures to ensure implementation by subcentral governments and nongovernmental bodies. The GATS provision also expresses a preference for a plurilateral approach.

The deficiencies in Article VII lead Beviglia Zampetti to argue for a Framework Agreement on mutual recognition. He recognizes at the outset that there are limits to the specificity of such an agreement, since each sector is different. However, certain legal aspects of recognition could usefully be clarified. The meaning of "recognition" could, for example, be defined as a type of "equivalency." This would grant better than national treatment to the partners' goods and would need to allow for the modification of equivalencies over time. The roles of subcentral bodies would also have to be clarified. Dispute settlement provisions could usefully be incorporated and could be brought under the relevant rules of the WTO.

The author shows conclusively that the international development of recognition has until now been unwieldy and lacking in transparency. He is right to conclude that Article VII is not enough to ensure the proper functioning of an international web of mutual recognition agreements. A Framework Agreement containing core principles of mutual recognition is needed to clarify the basic legal issues.

The authors all agree that flexible solutions are needed to reduce regulatory barriers to trade in services. These include strengthening Article VI disciplines on domestic regulation, increased use of Article VII on mutual recognition, and the negotiation of a Framework Agreement on mutual recognition. While these are all sensible solutions, the obligations and commitments already existing in GATS may also be capable of leading us farther along the road of liberalization than the authors indicate.

The national treatment commitment, in particular, has the powerful potential of disciplining many regulations that are normally considered "domestic." This may seem paradoxical, since the focus of domestic regulation is understood to be nondiscriminatory measures. The truth is that national treatment, as it has evolved in GATT and GATS, has become a test that focuses less on actual discrimination based on origin and more on "likeness"—that is, whether a government is entitled to make a regulatory distinction between two categories of services or suppliers. This change in focus results largely from the wording of Article XVII, which accepts de facto discrimination and from past findings in GATT that changes in conditions of competition triggering national treatment violations, as well as actual presence in the market of competing foreign products, can be *de minimis*. In assessing "likeness," panels have tended to find that it exists only when the functional characteristics of the products compared (as reflected in their physical characteristics and market substitutability) are the same or similar. The focus on "likeness" so defined reveals the underlying basis of the national treatment test: a regulation can only be maintained if it is based on functional differences between categories of services or suppliers that it creates. In a very real sense, therefore, the national treatment commitment has become a "rule of objective regulation" that compares with the disciplines on domestic regulation set out in Article VI.

This is not to say that the national treatment commitment has become totally divorced from its roots in origin-based discrimination. And the general exceptions under Article XIV may always be applicable in particular cases. But with the dramatic increase in world trade, and thus of potential if not actual foreign competition in most markets, the conditions of application of the national treatment commitment are easier than ever to satisfy.

Other existing GATS obligations may also discipline domestic regulation. What has been said about the wide applicability of the GATS national treatment commitment can also be repeated for the MFN obligation, which contains a similar "likeness" requirement, and has been interpreted by the Appellate Body in the Banana III decision to include de facto discrimination. Finally, it should not be forgotten that the market access commitment in Article XVI, in addition to discriminatory measures, also covers wholly nondiscriminatory ones.

PART FOUR

New Issues on the Horizon: Investment, Competition Policy, and the E-Commerce Revolution

12 | *Investment Liberalization in GATS*

PIERRE SAUVÉ *and*
CHRISTOPHER WILKIE

A SIDE FROM THE POSSIBLE EXCEPTION of cross-border environ-mental factors affecting international trade rules, invest-ment stands out as the policy domain in which the need for multilateral rules is most readily apparent. The reasons for this are well known and do not bear repeating at length, though governments have been prone to take what one observer has dubbed "a rearview mirror"approach to policymak-ing in this area.[1]

The absence of a credible and coherent framework for international investment is increasingly apparent as investment, more than trade, be-comes the driving force of deepening integration in the world economy.[2] The patchwork of bilateral treaties, regional arrangements, and limited plurilateral or multilateral instruments relating to investment stands in

The authors are grateful to Stephen J. Canner, Edward M. Graham, Mark Koulen, Charles S. Levy, François Nadeau, Daniel M. Price, Jeffrey J. Schott, Stephen Thomsen, Andrew Walter, and Douglas Worth for helpful comments and discussions.

1. Ostry (1997).

2. As with multilateral competition policy disciplines, the absent investment regime has a long history, one that starts with the failure to establish the International Trade Organization at the end of the 1940s. The Havana Charter had proposed including investment as well as trade provisions, although the investment provisions were limited owing to fears of many countries, particularly developing ones, of foreign control over natural resources and strategic industries. See Ostry (1997). See also Hart (1996).

sharp contrast to the comprehensive system of norms and principles governing international trade. The absence of an international framework is all the more surprising in light of the change in attitudes in favor of investment regime liberalization that has taken root in developed, developing, and transition economies alike in recent years. The world has witnessed an unprecedented unilateral liberalization of foreign direct investment regimes.[3]

Although embedding a coherent set of investment disciplines in the World Trade Organization rests on compelling rule-making and economic grounds, this objective is unlikely to be secured very soon. Investment rules in the WTO will more likely evolve incrementally, with most attention devoted to expanding the scope of existing investment-related disciplines while seeking progressively greater investment regime protection and liberalization under them.

Of all existing WTO agreements pertaining to investment, the General Agreement on Trade in Services offers by far the greatest potential for meeting both objectives.[4] Important steps may nonetheless be taken during the next WTO negotiations in laying the basis for the possible future adoption of generic rules for investment, notably by encouraging some forward thinking on the longer-term architectural implications of an integrated approach to trade and investment in the WTO.

A key to securing the longer-term objective will be for WTO members to renew and refine the mandate of the Working Group on the Relationship between Trade and Investment that was established at the WTO's first ministerial meeting in Singapore in December 1996. The group's mandate will be up for review at the organization's ministerial gathering in Seattle. The Seattle meeting offers WTO members a good opportunity to affirm a shared belief in the usefulness of a longer-term, pedagogical journey on trade and investment issues (with no a priori judgments on its ultimate destination) and to take steps to improve the fairness, transparency, and predictability of global conditions of market presence.

As the recent failure to conclude negotiations on an OECD-based Multilateral Agreement on Investment (MAI) suggests, investment rulemaking journeys have a tendency to be bumpy and take many unanticipated turns. Much, as usual, will depend on the political economy of

---

3. See Graham (1998a).

4. For an excellent discussion of some of the economic and political forces supporting such an assertion, see Hoekman and Saggi (1999).

"getting there." A useful starting point is thus to determine the kind of policy landscape against which trade and investment discussions may take place. This landscape, as it happens, has much already to say about the journey ahead, including some of the forks in the road that ministers might wish to consider in Seattle. We turn our attention to these matters before focusing more squarely on what we consider the only workable medium-term agenda: that of improving the "investment-friendliness" of GATS.

The Global Investment Policy Landscape

Economic, legal, and political forces suggest a continuing bumpy road with respect to investment matters in both the short and medium terms in the WTO.

—Inflows and outflows of foreign direct investment (FDI) remain at unprecedented levels around the world. International direct investment is of growing importance in global economic integration as firms expand their presence in foreign markets and as industries consolidate in response to the new competitive environment. The most recent figures from the Organization for Economic Cooperation and Development suggest that the Asian financial crisis and its aftermath have exerted surprisingly little effect on aggregate cross-border investment activity. Far from dampening corporate enthusiasm for overseas expansion, the crisis may have encouraged more FDI in some of the countries most affected by lowering the price of many attractive assets.

—Failure to satisfactorily conclude twice-delayed negotiations on the Multilateral Agreement on Investment, whose swift demise deserves closer scrutiny before a new multilateral roadmap for investment can be devised.

—Internet-based policy advocacy by nongovernmental organizations (NGOs), particularly those concerned with environment, labor, and human rights issues (but also public interest groups concerned with consumer and development issues), has come of age. NGOs cut their teeth during the MAI negotiations, and their presence and voices, dissonant as they sometimes are, will be a factor in all future WTO negotiations.

—The growing shadow of U.S. presidential politics means that policy initiatives in areas deemed controversial or potentially "antigreen" or "antiblue"(antilabor), which is arguably how the multilateral investment agenda has come to be portrayed in public debate (and not only in the United States), are unlikely to enjoy much support by the administration.

Box 12-1. *The Case for a Multilateral Approach to Investment Rules at the WTO*

The changing nature of business behavior in a globalizing environment illustrates the need for new thinking on trade and investment. Multinational corporations increasingly treat trade and investment as complementary means for carrying out global production activities rather than as alternative strategies for penetrating markets. They consider trade and investment sides of the same market access coin.[5]

The emergence of a seamless relationship between trade and investment carries potentially significant policy and rule-making implications, ultimately calling into question the traditional separation of trade and investment in domestic policy formulation and in international negotiations and agreements.

Achieving greater policy coherence between trade and investment is all the more important when one considers that, as the principal means of delivering goods and services to foreign markets and the leading factor in organizing international production, foreign direct investment has become a major determinant of the size, direction, and composition of world trade. Moreover, the marked intensification of worldwide locational competition for high value added investment in recent years has brought a proliferation of distorting incentives in its wake. The global and potentially competition-impairing effects flowing from such links suggest the need to integrate comprehensive investment disciplines into the multilateral trading system.[6]

(continued)

Moreover, a hesitant U.S. government and private sector, both of which had championed the MAI, continue to profess a cautious view of the WTO's potential on investment rule-making.

—The Working Group on Trade and Investment (WGTI) in the WTO has been moving slowly, reflecting both the steepness of the learning

---

5. See Ruggiero (1996).

6. Traditionally limited to OECD countries, investment incentive projects in technology-intensive industries have in the last few years received considerable resources in developing countries, particularly in Southeast Asia. A desire to maintain and further such practices undoubtedly explains the otherwise paradoxical resistance shown by some emerging economies to OECD countries' call for launching comprehensive negotiations on investment at the WTO. The emergence of a global community of investment-incentive "sinners" shows that multilateral cooperation and bargaining probably offer the best, and perhaps the only, way out of a classical prisoner's dilemma. Graham (1998a); and Moran (1998).

Box 12-1. *(continued)*

The case for a global rule-making response to the trade-investment interface can also be inferred from the direction of trends in cross-border investment. Although the bulk of foreign direct investment still originates within OECD countries and is destined for other markets within the OECD area—some 80 percent of outflows and 65 percent of inflows on average in the 1990s—the past decade has witnessed a significant expansion of the relative share of non-OECD countries (especially in Asia) in global investment flows, both as recipient and FDI-originating countries. FDI flows into developing countries exceeded $100 billion for the fourth year in a row in 1998, compared with $10 billion in 1985. Meanwhile, outward investment from developing countries reached $63 billion in 1997, a threefold increase since 1992.[7] The share of non-OECD countries in world FDI inflows can be expected to expand as developing and transition economies accelerate structural reform efforts, move into higher value added and more technology-intensive manufacturing and services, and open up much needed investment in basic infrastructures to greater foreign participation.

The growing presence of developing and transition economies in global investment emphasizes the desirability of and commensurate gains from multilateral rules. Because the multilateral trading system already features several components of a comprehensive investment framework, further work at the WTO can help to ensure overall coherence in rule design and command the political legitimacy required to bring all member countries to the negotiating table. In addition, MFN-based multilateral disciplines at the WTO, particularly in services, where the greatest potential for investment liberalization lies, could contain concerns over free riding in negotiations among smaller, nonregionally based WTO members, an issue that helped halt prospects for liberalization during the MAI negotiations.[8]

curve in this complex policy domain (even for resource-rich OECD countries, as the MAI negotiations so clearly demonstrated) and the fact that the Paris-based negotiations affected the WGTI talks in Geneva. This, in

7. OECD (1998a). Note, too, that the tendency of multinational enterprises' affiliates to finance expansion with funds from host or third countries often serves to underestimate real levels of the enterprises' investment activity contained in figures that measure cross-border financing activity for balance of payments purposes only.

8. On the political conundrum associated with MFN status under a prospective MAI, see Wimmer (1996).

turn, has created the caution exhibited by many important developing country members of the WTO whose exclusion from the MAI has provided them with a ready-made, if all too facile and somewhat tactical, excuse to show continued reluctance on this policy front.

—A still compelling case is to be made on both economic and rule-making grounds to adapt the multilateral trading system to the realities of a globalizing world economy by doing for investment what has been done so successfully for trade since the inception of GATT. In essence this means allowing the benefits of open and contestable markets to be more easily and fairly reaped by developing a body of legally binding disciplines with which to uphold the procompetitive values of transparency and nondiscrimination (box 12-1).

Outstanding Issues in International Investment

The policy landscape described above suggests that a multilateral journey on investment matters is likely to be a slow, difficult affair. Our contention is that it would be wise to scale back ambitions on trade and investment in the Seattle meeting. Various reasons argue the need for—indeed the longer-term usefulness of—more realistic short-term expectations.

To begin with, what market or policy failure would a body of multilateral rules for investment seek to redress? Stated succinctly, how crippling has the absence of multilateral disciplines on investment protection and liberalization proven for cross-border investment? Part of the answer is provided in figure 12-1, which shows the growth in FDI over the past decade and a half. Asking this question helps one understand why it proved so difficult in the Uruguay Round and the MAI to enlist significant and determined private sector support for a strong effort on investment rule-making. Part of the answer also seems to lie in what could be called the positive bias in domestic policymaking on FDI—a natural inclination of countries to do the right thing—that sets it apart from trade policy, whose political economy of cyclical protectionist capture is far likelier to generate deliberalizing policy reversals.

It bears recalling that the increasing noise generated by the investment debate is taking place against a trend of continued unilateral liberalization in virtually all countries, developed, developing, or in transition. This can only increase the liberalization that could be locked in during future

Figure 12-1. *Trends in Global Trade, Output, and Foreign Direct Investment, 1981–98.*

Index, 1981=100

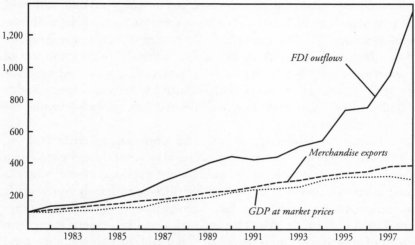

Sources: OECD (1998a); WTO, *Annual Report 1998*; and World Bank *World Development Indicators, 1998.*

multilateral negotiations, should these ever come to fruition. Meanwhile, there are simply no compelling empirical signals that suggest reversing liberalizing trends in the continued absence of comprehensive, integrated multilateral investment rules. As recent surveys by the UN Conference on Trade and Development (UNCTAD) suggest, policy change on FDI has been and remains a one-way street, and a liberalizing one at that.[9] It should come as little surprise then that calls to develop a multilateral regime for investment have been likened to a "bureaucratic solution in search of a [market] problem."[10]

A second reason to scale down rule-making ambitions is that investment policy has already made its way into the WTO system, albeit in an incidental manner that calls for continued attempts to achieve greater overall coherence in rule design. Multilateral discussions of investment are anything but starting from scratch. Although much remains to be done by

9. See the annual *World Investment Reports* published by the UNCTAD Secretariat, which provide yearly updates of trends in policy change in national investment regimes.

10. Smythe (1998).

way of improving existing disciplines, the Uruguay Round probed deeper than any previous negotiating round into investment-related matters. And the Marrakech Agreement that established the WTO contains provisions concerning investment liberalization and investment protection.[11] Most of the provisions can be found in the Agreement on Trade-Related Investment Measures (TRIMs) and GATS. Other components of the Final Act of the Uruguay Round bearing directly or indirectly on the treatment of investment include the Agreement on Subsidies and Countervailing Measures (SCM), the Agreement on Trade-Related Intellectual Property Rights (TRIPs), and the Understanding on Rules and Procedures Governing the Settlement of Disputes.

A basic policy challenge is to make such provisions cohere by building a consensus in favor of revamped multilateral rules for doing business in a global economy. Ultimately this should involve the development of investment disciplines that no longer make artificial and largely bureaucratic distinctions between goods, services, business people, or intellectual property-related matters, or indeed between trade and investment as the twin modes of acceding to world markets.[12] That said, there is still not a great deal of appreciation among WTO members of the extent to which existing rules address investment-related matters, let alone of the case to be made for, and the likely operational consequences of, an integrated approach to rule-making.

A third reason to temper expectations is that the WTO Working Group on Trade and Investment has made little progress toward formal investment negotiations. Letting the working group soldier on with its much needed and excellent pedagogical work would better ensure that attention remains focused on the substantive elements of the trade-investment interface than formal negotiations would allow.

In addition, comprehensive negotiations on investment would also carry significant political visibility, providing a ready-made platform for renewed NGO activism on investment matters. Such activism must be expected in today's negotiating environment and indeed welcomed as a potentially legitimizing force for global rule-making. But there is little denying that a discussion based in the working group, particularly one premised on existing WTO rules (which already command some political and, especially, juridical legitimacy), is more difficult to oppose than a

11. Sauvé (1994, 1997). See also World Trade Organization (1996).
12. See Schott (1996); and Beviglia Zampetti and Sauvé (1996).

full-blown negotiation in a "new" policy area.[13] This is particularly true of investment discussions centered on GATS, given the significantly lower incidence of environmental problems that arise in services (particularly the high-growth, information technology–intensive sectors) as opposed to manufacturing or mining.[14]

Pushing too hard and too early for formal negotiations on investment would also give rise to premature, if inevitable, expressions of mercantilism on the part of WTO members at a time when substantive command of the issues at stake would not yet have taken root. The result would risk diluting the substance of possible new rules and of liberalization commitments.

A prime objective of the Seattle ministerial meeting should thus be to renew the working group's mandate for three more years (which many see as the desirable length of time the WTO negotiations flowing from the Uruguay Round's built-in agenda should take), recognizing that we are on a long and complex journey, substantively and politically. The working group's renewed mandate should, however, focus more narrowly on the elements of a workable framework for foreign direct invention within the trading system and on the implications of linking such a framework to the design and operation of existing agreements. Were the working group to fulfill its mandate, it could be in a good position to recommend—or possibly reject—launching formal negotiations on a generic investment instrument at the WTO by the end of 2003.

As noted earlier, the heightened political sensitivity of international investment rules after the failure of the MAI negotiations has arguably hampered progress in the WTO. There is thus need to separate the two processes: to reap the economies of scale in rule-making that the pursuit of a pedagogical agenda among *all* countries allows and for that agenda to be "owned" by a broader and more diverse WTO constituency. Ultimately, such a process will deliver a verdict on whether, all things considered, a consensus exists in favor of developing a more comprehensive WTO regime for investment. The bias toward unilaterally liberalizing changes in domestic investment policy regimes that was described earlier suggests that

13. The sensitivity of investment issues in the WTO in the wake of the breakdown of MAI negotiations is undeniable. This has implications for investment in GATS as well. The potential overlap of GATS and MAI is evident in the GATS coverage of investment through mode 3 and the definition of investment in the draft MAI text (albeit qualified through footnotes indicating unresolved issues) that implicitly included investment in services industries. Thus a higher profile for investment in GATS will not be immune to controversy.

14. OECD (1998, chap. 6).

such patience could produce significant policy- and rule-making benefits in the longer run. It would also provide WTO members with much needed time to develop the kinds of communication tools required to assuage legitimate public concerns over the effects of market liberalization and respond more effectively to (and, where needed, debunk) the counteroffensive of many NGOs.

There remains, finally, the important task of internalizing the many useful, if ultimately sobering, lessons flowing from the decision to abandon negotiations on an OECD-based MAI. Such a process has already begun, both at the WTO itself, and among commentators.[15] Many of these lessons will be germane to how investment might be addressed in the future in the WTO and to the more immediate issue of whether changes to the architecture of existing rules (for example broadening the remit of prohibited TRIMs or modifying the scheduling of liberalization commitments under GATS) are ultimately feasible. Four of those lessons would appear to warrant the more immediate scrutiny of policymakers:

—Should a multilateral regime address all forms of investment, including portfolio investment, or be confined to flows of foreign direct investment? Much as it may be difficult to draw an operational distinction between portfolio investment and FDI, the Asian financial crisis and its aftermath have shaken confidence in what used to be an important element of the so-called Washington consensus: support for a fully open capital account, including in regard to short-term capital flows.[16] Renewed support for the not so new idea of throwing sand in the wheels of international capital flows can be expected to have—indeed already has had—a bearing on the global investment debate, financial instability being considered by many as offering proof of the inherent dangers of market openness, be it trade- or investment-induced.[17] How that debate might be arbitrated in future WTO discussions of investment is hard to predict, but it seems a fair assumption that some member countries could be attracted to proposals that steer discussions away from non-FDI forms of investment, resulting in a narrower scope of coverage than was envisaged under the draft MAI or than currently exists under the North American Free Trade Agreement.

—Just how robust is the case for developing sweeping multilateral disciplines on investment protection? The MAI negotiations, involving as

15. In the WTO (1998). See also Henderson (1999); and Graham (forthcoming).
16. Sauvé (1998).
17. Rodrik (1999).

they did countries with high levels of regulatory and NGO activism, ultimately revealed a limited political appetite for what came to be seen as an intrusive agenda on expropriation-related matters. This revealed preference of OECD countries sits somewhat uncomfortably with their continued keenness to see developing countries adopt such rules in proposed bilateral investment protection treaties (or BITs). Yet because the developing countries, particularly the smaller, more peripheral ones, derive potentially important signaling benefits from providing high standards of investment protection, there are grounds to believe that bilateral treaties will continue to be the preferred way of securing significant levels of investment protection. Although there would appear to be legal and economic merit (particularly in reducing transaction costs) in codifying best bilateral or regional practices in a multilateral setting, recent developments suggest that investment protection may well be a policy domain where multilateral efforts may yield significantly inferior levels of protection than bilateral agreements.

—Is a negative list approach to scheduling liberalization commitments politically and bureaucratically feasible? There is little doubt that conceptually speaking using this means to liberalization is superior in domains of high regulatory density, such as investment and services. A negative list locks in the regulatory status quo (ensures a standstill by allowing no wedge to be exploited between bound commitments and applied regulatory practices), guarantees the nondiscriminatory nature of all future regulatory undertakings, helps promote procompetitive regulatory reform, and forces governments to document in a highly transparent (and perhaps embarrassing) manner all discriminatory and restrictive practices they maintain.[18] Nonetheless, as discussed by Patrick Low and Aaditya Mattoo in chapter 15, negative listing is also fraught with difficulties and perverse incentives. Indeed the practice of negative listing in NAFTA has been generally disappointing. It has proven to be taxing for bureaucracies (and would thus be problematic for most developing countries), sits uncomfortably with the political economy of federalism, particularly because subnational states tend to be regulatory activists in services and investment, and tends to prompt a knee-jerk resistance to change from regulatory authorities while exacerbating the already formidable mercantilistic instincts of trade negotiators. The sobering result has been the production of a messy telephone book of nonconforming measures (among which there are many trivial

18. On the advantages of negative listing, see Sauvé (1996). See also Snape and Bosworth (1996).

ones on precautionary grounds) maintained at the federal level only, a need for open-ended unbound reservations in sensitive areas, and considerable caution over the legal and political consequences of buying into a permanent regulatory freeze. None of the above bodes well for an overhaul of the GATS scheduling technology any time soon.

—Is there a political market for introducing credible multilateral disciplines on investment incentives? The MAI, like NAFTA before it and the lingering fate of long-standing efforts by the OECD's Industry Committee to monitor and promote greater transparency on government subsidies, attests to the lack of political support, particularly in federal countries, for efforts to curtail the ability of governments to attract foreign investors through incentive schemes (whose distorting effects on trade and investment flows are well known and indeed largely acknowledged). Although the WTO's Agreement on Subsidies and Countervailing Measures may provide some indirect discipline in this area, this is another revealed preference that will complicate attempts to broaden the scope of the WTO's existing investment-related provisions.[19] This is particularly true of the TRIMs Agreement, given the close links between the granting of investment incentives by governments and the undertaking of performance requirements by foreign investors.[20] Still, it bears recalling that a modest start has been made in the WTO Working Group on Trade and Investment with respect to the additional analytical work that may be necessary to help develop the political momentum to address this issue in the context of international investment.[21]

What May Be Feasible on Investment at the WTO

Two routes can be taken in the WTO with respect to investment policy issues over the short to medium term (figure 12-2). Both as it

19. See Sauvé (1997, pp. 59–63).

20. See Moran (1998, pt. 2) for an excellent discussion of the policy links between investment incentives and performance requirements.

21. Notably, in its December 1998 report to General Council, the WTO's Working Group on Trade and Investment included a sizable section on "country experiences regarding national investment policies, including investment incentives and disincentives." WTO Working Group (1998, paras. 69–100). In addition, the OECD's Committee on International Investment and Multinational Enterprises (CIME) has also highlighted "investment incentives and investment promotion" as one of the five substantive issues for discussion in its current work program relating to international investment. See http://www.oecd.org/daf/cmis/cmisindex.htm.

Figure 12-2. *WTO Potential Future Investment Agenda, Two Approaches*

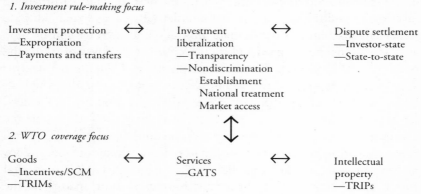

1. Investment rule-making focus

Investment protection   ⟷   Investment   ⟷   Dispute settlement
—Expropriation   liberalization   —Investor-state
—Payments and transfers   —Transparency   —State-to-state
                                         —Nondiscrimination
                                           Establishment
                                           National treatment
                                           Market access

                                              ↕

2. WTO coverage focus

Goods   ⟷   Services   ⟷   Intellectual
—Incentives/SCM   —GATS   property
—TRIMs   —TRIPs

happens lead in the same direction and emphasize yet again the incremental nature of the rule-making journey ahead.

A first way of looking at the WTO's investment agenda is to focus on the three core elements of any rule-making initiative on investment: protection, liberalization, and dispute settlement (both state to state and investor-state) and determine what is feasible at the WTO in a post-MAI setting. As we have mentioned, recent negotiations have revealed a limited appetite for a high-standard, BIT-like investment protection agenda, an issue that seems better suited to bilateral initiatives and the political and economic asymmetries that typically characterize negotiations between developed and developing or transition economies.[22] Given the large and growing network of existing bilateral investment protection treaties and prevailing sensitivities over protecting investors against indirect forms of expropriation (so-called regulatory takings), the question ultimately arises of the extent to which developing multilateral norms in this area represents a priority of the business community. Improving the ability of investors to make payments and transfers in an unimpeded way across borders, as is affirmed under the Articles of Agreement of the International Monetary Fund and provided for in scheduled sectors under GATS (but not GATT), is arguably a more pressing and commercially valuable objective to pursue.

---

22. The rationale for embedding the highest standards of investment protection in the MAI was never clear to start with, given the exclusion of developing countries from the negotiating table. The lack of a rationale is reinforced by the empirical observation that OECD countries have concluded among themselves only a minute fraction of the more than 1,700 bilateral investment protection treaties in existence.

The absence of a political market for an ambitious multilateral agenda on investment protection all but obviates the need to consider providing investors with direct recourse to the multilateral trading system's dispute settlement machinery. Investor-state arbitration, a sine qua non of BITs and, when properly designed and circumscribed, a good way of taking the politics out of investment disputes, is simply not on Geneva radar screens. There are both political and technical reasons to believe that this will remain so. Politically, perhaps the greatest difficulty in justifying the need for investor-state arbitration is that it would implicitly affirm, in the continued absence of a commensurate desire on the part of WTO members to provide equivalent rights to environmental groups or labor unions or other private stakeholders, the superior rights of holders of capital within the trading system. On technical grounds, quite apart from the thorny (and politically charged) aspect of how adverse investor-state rulings might affect the delicate balance of benefits brokered between WTO members under various agreements, one of the main problems would lie in the inability of the WTO's current institutional machinery to accommodate the proliferation of cases that could arise should private-party recourse to dispute settlement be allowed.

So where does that leave us? Basically with one workable agenda item: investment liberalization (promoting transparency and nondiscriminatory conditions of entry and operation through a commercial presence) with potential disputes arbitrated through traditional state-to-state WTO practice.

Determining where the largest potential for investment liberalization happens to lie requires one to take a different route and consider the WTO coverage continuum shown in figure 12-2. The continuum focuses attention on the three subject matters covered by WTO disciplines: goods, services, and intellectual property. The challenge here is to decide what may be feasible by way of improving the "investment friendliness" of existing WTO disciplines.

With respect to goods (chiefly manufacturing), two matters stand out as most difficult from an investment perspective: locational incentives and performance requirements. Their fates are linked in ways that do not generally bode well for using either the Agreement on Subsidies and Countervailing Measures or the Agreement on Trade-Related Investment Measures as the main vehicles for improving the WTO's treatment and coverage of investment-related matters. Although an increasing number of voices are willing to address investment incentives, many of the system's most important stakeholders are reluctant to address this admittedly complex issue.

As for TRIMs, whose compliance record on notifications has been mixed, developing countries have little desire to broaden the scope of the agreement's illustrative list of prohibited measures. This is all the more understandable in the absence of a compensatory bargain on investment incentives (although many developing countries have become sinners themselves in this area) and competition policy, both of which are linked to the TRIMs agreement through Article 9, where many developed countries cannot bring themselves to utter the words "restrictive business practices," let alone agree to rules aimed at curbing private anticompetitive conduct in the WTO.

There is, additionally, the increasing perception that the TRIMs Agreement remains unbalanced, with little to offer developing countries. Although recent empirical work has shed useful light on the generally adverse economic effects performance requirements can have (especially local content, joint-venture, and technology-sharing requirements), the politics of maintaining such practices is compelling for many developing countries. This is truer still in the continued absence of a compensatory quid pro quo and in light of the policies enacted by developed countries that range from the discriminatory rules of origin maintained in many regional free trade agreements to aggressive recourse to antidumping rules. The effect of these policies is to divert or hold back FDI that should otherwise flow to developing countries.[23]

Turning to matters related to intellectual property and the scope for improving the WTO's treatment of investment through the TRIPs Agreement, one is left with similar, if more strongly stated (and substantively compelling) perceptions of political and juridical illegitimacy. The agreement's attributes for improving global welfare have been increasingly questioned and its antidevelopmental effects for the world's poorer nations vociferously decried.[24] These perceptions suggest that future negotiations in this area, which the Uruguay Round's built-in agenda has set for January 1, 2000, are likely to be difficult under the best of circumstances. What is more, and despite the fact that the agreement constitutes an important, if indirect, source of investment protection, it is unclear how such a generic attribute could be made any more specific with regard to investment within the remit of the TRIPs Agreement. The MAI experience proved

23. See Moran (1998, chap. 10); and Hoekman and Saggi (1999).
24. Rodrik (1999, p. 148).

highly sobering in this regard because negotiators were ultimately unable to decide whether or how issues related to intellectual property rights could be addressed in the draft agreement's proposed coverage.[25] Thus even as one can agree that the TRIPs Agreement performs a useful investment protection function, the freedom to alter it significantly to address investment-related issues may be limited.

The simple logic of policy deduction flowing from figure 12-2 suggests that, just as investment liberalization stands out as the only workable agenda to consider from a rule-making perspective, GATS may well offer the only serious vehicle to strengthen the WTO's existing investment-related rules and achieve a greater number of bound liberalization commitments. Both objectives are worthy of pursuit, and genuine forward movement on both fronts seems possible in ways that might well have longer-term consequences for whether and how a generic, more comprehensive approach to investment may be pursued in the WTO.

Investment and GATS: A Pragmatic Way Forward

Of all sectors of economic activity, services offer by far the greatest potential for rolling back discriminatory and burdensome regulations that inhibit globally active firms from contesting and serving national and international markets through an established presence. A number of factors may be adduced as proof of this liberalizing potential. To begin with, as GATS implicitly revealed, and the NAFTA lists and the draft MAI's approach with respect to a negative list of reservations indicate, most presence-impeding measures maintained by governments in investment, including governments of developed countries, concern crucial service industries—telecommunications, broadcasting and related audio-visual services, satellite services, energy services, financial services (especially securities), civil aviation, and maritime transport.[26] Global investment liberalization is very much focused on services, there being few significant barriers to entry via foreign direct investment in manufacturing or primary industries.[27]

The significant liberalization potential of services was also much in

25. See Gervais and Nicholas-Gervais (1999).

26. For a cogent description of the predominance of services in the NAFTA reservation lists, see Rugman and Gestrin (1994). See also Gestrin and Rugman (1993).

27. See Hoekman and Saggi (1999).

evidence in its impact on the draft MAI, the inability of which to satisfy the criteria laid down in GATS Article V on economic integration arrangements revealed the breadth of an otherwise virtuous (in economic terms) but ultimately political (and tactical) free-rider problem vis-à-vis non-MAI-acceding members of the WTO. Indeed, realization that the greater liberalization commitments sought under the MAI would need to be extended on a most favored nation basis to all WTO members arguably lessened interest in rolling back prevailing investment restrictions within OECD countries. In turn, this deprived the draft agreement of much of its value-added from a private sector perspective.

As already noted, there is considerable investment coverage in the GATS agreement. And although investment in service industries represents an important component of the agreement by means of mode 3 (commercial presence), all modes of service supply affect investment behavior. The openness of a service sector to the provision of a service even without commercial presence (through modes 1 and 2) can affect the decision to establish in a particular market. That which former WTO Director General Renato Ruggiero so presciently observed with respect to the agreement as a whole also applies to investment in services industries:

> the GATS provides guarantees over a much wider field of regulation and law than the GATT; the right of establishment and the obligation to treat foreign services suppliers fairly and objectively in all relevant areas of domestic regulation extend the reach of the Agreement into areas never before recognized as trade policy. I suspect that neither governments nor industries have yet appreciated the full scope of these guarantees or the full value of existing commitments.[28]

How then should an incremental yet still useful investment policy agenda be pursued under GATS? We conclude by offering a few thoughts on how best to maintain forward momentum on investment matters through the more narrow confines of GATS, it being understood that much complementary progress on the why and how of a more comprehensive and longer-term journey on investment need also be made in parallel in the Working Group on the Relationship between Trade and Investment.

A GATS-centered push on investment at the WTO can usefully tackle two core matters: making existing rules more investor friendly and achiev-

28. Ruggiero (1998).

ing greater investment regime liberalization than was possible in the first round of services negotiations.

Improving the Investment Friendliness of GATS Rules

Several possibilities, some direct, others more incidental, offer prospects for improving the global investment climate through advances in GATS rules.

Clarifying the Definition of Commercial Presence

GATS negotiators could usefully focus on how the narrow, enterprise-based manner in which GATS defines "commercial presence" differs from the broad, asset-based way in which "investment" is commonly defined in various investment agreements (BITs, NAFTA, the European Charter Treaty, or the draft MAI). Clarifying the meaning of commercial presence as it is defined in Article XXVIII(d) (Definitions) of GATS is of considerable importance given the primacy of investment as a means of delivering services to markets. Indeed, the scope of covered investments is a prime determinant of the extent to which GATS affords extensive investment protection and liberalization.[29]

Although the definition of commercial presence used in GATS covers matters relating to both pre- and postestablishment (a matter of some debate in the MAI talks) and applies to both existing and de novo investments, its enterprise-based remit appears more narrowly confined to foreign direct investments proper than to the spectrum of assets typically covered by mainstream investment agreements (portfolio investments, interests that entitle an owner to share in the income or profits of an enterprise, real estate, and all forms of tangible and intangible property).

Adopting an asset-based definition of commercial presence would most likely broaden the protection and liberalization potential of GATS and result in a better understanding of the agreement's scope with regard to investment matters. Doing so would, however, likely clash with the greater overall caution with which many countries have now come to view the regulation of capital flows. This suggests that not all elements of a broader definition of investment would be considered for adoption under an expanded definition of commercial presence. A possible solution to this

29. For a fuller discussion of definitional matters, see Sauvé (1997, pp. 63–65). See also Price (1996).

problem would be for WTO members to treat definitional matters asymmetrically under GATS, using a broader definition to underpin the agreement's investment protection provisions while relying on a more narrow, FDI-centered definition for scheduling liberalization commitments.

Failing this, further elucidation of the reach of commercial presence would help clarify the protection and liberalization potential of GATS. An attempt to achieve further elucidation was made in 1994 in the Understanding on Commitments in Financial Services.[30] But even this limited step may not be easy. As the debate over electronic commerce has shown, it has become increasingly difficult and perhaps counterproductive to differentiate among modes for service delivery. This blurring can be expected to spread in the coming years and ultimately call into question the usefulness of the current GATS practice of scheduling by mode of supply.

Strengthening the Investment Protection Features of GATS

A recurring criticism of GATS is that the bulk of its provisions apply only to scheduled sectors and modes of supply, subject to the possibility of maintaining discriminatory or access-impairing restrictions in scheduled areas. Given that GATS explicitly aims to promote progressive liberalization, the shortcoming is perhaps best addressed by focusing more narrowly on ways of strengthening the agreement's investment protection features.

Some elements of investment protection already exist. In particular, Article XI (Payments and Transfers) states that restrictions on international transfers and payments may not be applied to current transactions relating to specific commitments. Also relevant is footnote 8 to Article XVI:1 (Market Access), which stipulates that if a market access commitment is undertaken through mode 3, the member is "thereby committed to allow related transfers of capital into its territory." Although there are caveats concerning the jurisdictional reach of the International Monetary Fund (IMF) on these matters as well as related balance of payments safeguards in Article XII, these

---

30. Paragraphs 5 and 6 of this understanding, under the heading "Commercial Presence," state: "5. Each Member shall grant financial service suppliers of any other Member the right to establish or expand within its territory, including through the acquisition of existing enterprises, a commercial presence. 6. A Member may impose terms, conditions and procedures for authorization of the establishment and expansion of a commercial presence in so far as they do not circumvent the Member's obligations under paragraph 5 and they are consistent with the other obligations of the Agreement." Paragraph 7, under the heading "New Financial Services" reads: "A Member shall permit financial service suppliers of any other Member established in its territory to offer in its territory any new financial service."

obligations cannot be circumscribed in member countries' schedules of commitments, as is also significantly the case under GATS Articles VI (Domestic Regulation) and VIII (Monopolies and Exclusive Suppliers).

Although the investment protection provisions of GATS are strong already and focus on an area of priority interest for investors, the level of protection they afford international investors could be strengthened by making them general rather than commitment-specific obligations. Their status could indeed become the equivalent of the core GATS obligations of transparency (Article III) and MFN treatment (Article II). Making them general obligations would also bring WTO practice more in line with those already obtaining under the IMF's Articles of Agreement.

Improving the Clarity of GATS Scheduling Terminology

Inconsistencies, or at the very least widely divergent approaches to the nature and extent of bound commitments, were a hallmark of the scheduling experience of the first GATS round. Because of the agreement's hybrid approach to scheduling, a number of barriers to market access, and most certainly to establishment (though probably more so on cross-border trade), were not scheduled to begin with. Moreover, even where commitments were scheduled, country practices often diverged noticeably.[31]

The inconsistencies noted earlier reflect the strongly didactic nature of the first GATS round as well as the considerable regulatory diversity of GATS members. Still, there clearly remains scope for negotiators to press for much greater legal clarity, precision, and uniformity with respect to how investment-related commitments are lodged and restricted by limitations to market access and national treatment.[32] In particular, efforts

31. For instance, with respect to commercial presence, Australia listed its foreign investment policy guidelines and Foreign Acquisitions and Takeovers Act of 1975, and Brazil its registration and other legal requirements for foreign investors (including caveats with respect to "sole proprietorship" and "partnership" under Article XXVIII (Definitions) of the GATS). Canada listed elements of its investment review mechanism under limitations to market access (but not with respect to national treatment); the European Union listed "public utilities" vis-à-vis public monopolies and exclusive rights of private operators (as well as various French, Spanish, Portuguese, and Italian limitations) and Malaysia its limitations with respect to "Acquisitions, Mergers and Takeovers." See "MAI Draft Text 24 April 1998"; http://www.oecd.org/daf/cmis/ii/reports.htm.

32. Related to this is another issue for negotiators to clarify in the next round: how to deal with dispute settlement procedures and other issues related to investment agreements that were overlooked in the GATS schedules. For example, only two countries (Canada and Poland) took the precaution of listing investor-state dispute settlement procedures in their list of MFN exemptions, although clearly other WTO members intend to continue not to grant such procedures on an MFN basis. What is less clear is whether this will be at all possible given the closed nature of Article II exemptions.

should focus on clarifying, circumscribing, and ultimately limiting horizontal scheduling with respect to mode 3. This could be done, for instance, on the basis of a sunset clause specifying a period over which restrictive measures would need to be eliminated or their restrictive incidence significantly curtailed.

GATS signatories could similarly be encouraged to apply sunset provisions to a given percentage (once again this might vary in timing and importance according to countries' level of development) of nonconforming measures scheduled under Articles XVI and XVII. This would help address the lack of a built-in dynamic for liberalization that characterized the outcome of the GATS 1994 negotiations. Such built-in momentum would lessen if not obviate the need for periodic negotiations, providing internationally active firms with a more predictable roadmap with which to plot longer-term corporate strategies.

Promoting Greater Transparency on Investment Incentives

Despite the sobering analysis of the prospects for agreeing to a credible set of multilateral disciplines on investment incentives, promoting stronger regulatory transparency on investment incentives warrants greater attention. The Working Party on GATS Rules, which is currently focusing attention on subsidies and services, could usefully turn to documenting the extent, nature, and economic incidence of investment incentives extended to businesses supplying services, including incentives at the subnational level. Such an endeavor would provide WTO members with a sounder empirical basis from which to make more informed decisions about the scope for collective action. Although investment incentives are probably more prevalent in manufacturing than in services, tackling this subject in the GATS context might still generate an interest in looking at it in a generic manner or through the prism of the SCM Agreement.

Other Incremental Approaches

Other GATS-centered rule-making avenues may allow WTO members to improve the agreement's investment friendliness. Not incidentally, this will also promote the greater contestability of services markets worldwide and likely prove of benefit to and enjoy the support of the business community. These include matters such as government procurement, the political economy of which almost by definition requires an established presence (see chapter 17). Although efforts to equip GATS with a set of disciplines on government procurement would be better deployed to multilateralize the WTO's generic but plurilateral Government Procurement Agreement (GPA), there is little doubt that the opening of markets in government procurement offers attractive opportunities to foreign investors and developing countries alike. Nowhere is this truer than for infrastructure services.

Similarly, tightening existing GATS disciplines on the conduct of monopolies (including their purchasing conduct) and exclusive or dominant suppliers could help ensure that conditions of entry and operation in markets remain fair and open.[33] This could notably be done by drawing up under GATS Articles VIII (Monopolies and Exclusive Service Suppliers) and IX (Business Practices) a more detailed illustrative list of anticompetitive practices (including investment practices—for example, granting "golden"or blocking shares to governments when privatizing state-owned enterprises) to which a de facto prohibition or rule of reason might subsequently apply.

Replicating the approach that led to the adoption of the procompetitive regulatory principles in the WTO's landmark Agreement on Basic Telecommunications, whether in sectoral annexes or by making recourse in members' schedules to GATS Article XVIII (Additional Commitments), represents another means of ensuring that conditions of entry and presence in markets promote contestability (see chapter 13). Indeed, it has been observed that these principles could serve as a blueprint for sectoral negotiating approaches to GATS as a whole in the next round.[34]

The regulatory intensity of some service industries means that domestic regulatory conduct represents a potentially important source of nullifi-

33. The European Union's citation in its GATS schedule of public utilities vis-à-vis public monopolies and exclusive rights of private operators, and of Malaysia under its heading "Acquisitions, Mergers and Takeovers," suggests the more general point that the treatment of public monopolies under GATS will likely require greater attention in the next negotiating round. Monopolies emerged as an important investment issue in the MAI negotiations, as an examination of several relatively complex provisions related to monopolies in the draft text reveals.

34. As the U.S. Coalition of Service Industries (1998) argued, "The 'Reference Paper' negotiated as part of the WTO Agreement on Basic Telecommunications is a model that should guide the development of a framework for dealing with regulatory reforms in the Services 2000 Negotiations. The regulatory principles embodied in this paper have already had an important influence on reshaping national regulatory systems toward a more market-oriented approach. The key is effective implementation of those principles—in their common, procompetitive, open market interpretation and application. We must learn from experience. The Reference Paper, we are discovering, must be interpreted clearly and forcefully for dispute settlement to be effective in most instances."

cation or impairment of liberalization commitments, including those for investment. More generally, the adoption of procompetitive regulatory principles in opening up such services markets as audio-visual, broadcasting, shipping, air transport, or finance, where market concentration and private anticompetitive conduct may be prominent and where regulatory and other exemptions from the full application of domestic competition laws are often found, means that GATS may well continue to offer the strongest vehicle for furthering the internationalization of competition policy in the WTO.

There remains, finally, the challenge of improving the ways the WTO system addresses labor mobility (see chapter 8). Although many countries (developed and developing) may not be receptive to promoting greater flows of even skilled labor, the economic case for promoting greater labor mobility is just as robust as that applying to capital. Affirming the equivalence of those flows is what NAFTA attempted to do by developing two generic chapters in these areas. Doing so in the WTO would be desirable on grounds of both equity and efficiency if and when a decision was made to include generic investment disciplines in the WTO. That being considerably down the road, it is important to focus attention on how GATS may strike compensatory bargains on labor mobility. Such bargains must satisfy both the business imperative of allowing internationally active firms to deploy key personnel of their choice more easily and speedily across borders and offer labor-rich developing countries a chance to gain a more meaningful temporary foothold in developed country markets, notably in areas where skill shortages are most acute.

Achieving Greater Investment Regime Liberalization

Creating better access and presence in markets has become a prime objective on the GATS agenda for the next round. Former European Trade Commissioner Sir Leon Brittan outlined the "hope that the next round will focus overwhelmingly on market access. No sector will be excluded, and the aim must be, in no more than 3 years, to conclude an ambitious package of additional liberalization by developing as well as developed countries, in politically difficult as well as in other sectors."[35]

Yet just how should such an objective be pursued? Reflecting the political sensitivity of negotiations on investment, few concrete suggestions

35. Brittan (1998, p. 3).

on how best to tackle investment liberalization in GATS (or the WTO) have emerged. However, two suggestions are worthy of note in recalling the links between GATS and investment. One of these emanates from the private sector in the United States and the second from the European Commission.[36]

Of the six objectives for services in the next round outlined by the U.S. Coalition of Service Industries, two in particular concern mode 3 (investment): ensuring rights of establishment and ownership for U.S. investors abroad through wholly owned or other forms of business ownership and ensuring national treatment for U.S. companies operating abroad so that foreign investors enjoy the same access to local and foreign markets as domestic companies have.[37]

Similarly, in late 1998 the European Commission published an issues paper on GATS 2000 titled "Investment/Establishment" that outlined an approach to both horizontal issues and sector-specific priorities.[38] Horizontal issues were broken down into questions on "regulatory issues," "horizontal 'formula' approaches," and "interaction of different sectors." The European Union submission paid generally less attention to sector-specific priorities, although some ranking of sectoral obstacles was pro-

---

36. By May 1998 negotiating priorities had begun to be articulated at the political level. U.S. Trade Representative Charlene Barshefsky pointed to the following "minimum" for the United States on services. "Services, in which we hope to see specific commitments for broad liberalization and market access in a range of sectors, including but not limited to audiovisual services, construction, express delivery, financial services, professional services, telecommunications, travel and tourism, and others." Barshefsky (1999, p. 4). The EU position stated by Trade Commissioner Brittan (1998) was that "GATS negotiations should take place on all services sectors with no prior exclusions. As a starting point, improvements should be made in the existing offers: market access restrictions should be further removed; and full national treatment ensured. We also need to consider the so-called new services or those which received less attention during the Uruguay Round, for example business and courier services, environment services, and education and health services" (p. 5). Despite these markers from the two most important service powers, the structure and format of the next negotiating round remained unclear at the time of writing,with many trading partners not willing to reveal their proposals until the late summer ("WTO Ministerial Preparations Slowed by Major Trading Partners," *Inside US Trade*, April 23, 1999, p. 1). Nonetheless, positions were beginning to emerge. Witness the Canadian trade minister calling for a review of international rules on unfair pricing in the new round, "including how trade remedies could be applied to services" ("Marchi Calls for Review of Trade Remedies, Unveils Canada Priorities," *Inside US Trade*, April 9, 1999, p. 1), and a Canadian consultations process and background paper on investment in the WTO; available at http://strategis.ic.gc.ca/SSG/ii00003e.html.

37. O'Hare (1999).

38. European Commission (1998). Canada, too, has posed a number of questions on investment in the WTO in its background paper on the issue, in which the investment focus in the WTO is not limited to GATS; available at http://strategis.ic.gc.ca/SSG/ii18319e.html.

vided, suggesting an initial EU agenda of sorts.[39] In investment, important topics included restrictions of the form of establishment, ownership limitations, economic needs tests, discretionary authorizations, and "other" restrictions.

Having identified the objectives and types of investment-related restrictions whose removal should command priority attention, both in the horizontal and sector-specific components of GATS signatories' schedules, the question remains how best to pursue these objectives in a negotiating setting.[40]

Securing the Regulatory Status Quo

Recalling the analogy between applied and bound tariffs in relation to trade in goods, there is a large difference between the level and quality of bound services and investment commitments that countries have lodged in various agreements, most notably under GATS, and the actual openness that domestic regulations permit. Taking advantage of the GATS 2000 Round to narrow that gap by chipping away—indeed eliminating—the perverse mercantilistic incentive to maintain a wedge will do much to affirm the tarnished liberalizing credibility of the agreement in the business community. Somewhat remarkably, GATS is silent on this critical issue, the agreement's scheduling guidelines having been somewhat hurriedly improvised toward the end of the first round of negotiations. A primary objective of the GATS 2000 Round should thus be to develop language aimed at securing the regulatory status quo in those sectors where GATS members voluntarily agree to schedule commitments.[41]

An unfortunate GATT import, allowing WTO members to bind their services and investment regimes at less than the regulatory status quo,

---

39. As part of an "exchange of information exercise" the WTO has recently derestricted twenty-one sectoral papers. The information contained in them offers interesting clues as to possible sectoral negotiating priorities to pursue during the next round. The studies address the following sectors: distribution services, construction and related engineering services, postal and courier services, audiovisual services, legal services, architectural and engineering services, computer and related services, environmental services, advertising services, education services, health and social services, tourism services, energy services, air transport services, land transport services (in two parts), maritime transport services, financial services, accountancy services, and telecommunications and presence of natural persons (mode 4). See http://www.wto.org/wto/services/w65.htm.

40. See also the suggestions with respect to promoting horizontal improvements in mode 3 commitments in the schedules in chapter 16.

41. Sauvé (1999a).

makes little sense from the perspective of foreign investors and service suppliers, who may be reluctant to commit resources under conditions of regulatory uncertainty. The practice makes even less sense from the perspective of host countries, particularly those that have shown the greatest proclivity to maintain a large wedge. In so doing they waste much of the signaling benefits that should otherwise flow from undertaking bound commitments in GATS. Sadly, many developing countries are likely to resist locking in the regulatory status quo in their bound GATS commitments. For this reason, thought should be given to the best means of implementing such a provision in a flexible manner, allowing developing countries greater time in honoring this new commitment-specific obligation (allowing them to close the gap between applied and bound regulations over agreed transition periods).

Reflecting Unilateral Liberalization Measures in Country Schedules

Aside from binding the regulatory status quo, another important means of imparting a greater liberalization dynamic to GATS would be to consider adopting a ratcheting provision whereby unilateral liberalization measures passed between periodic negotiating rounds in sectors subject to scheduled commitments are reflected in GATS schedules and extended on an MFN basis. Such a provision can be found in numerous regional integration agreements covering trade and investment in services, particularly those concluded recently within the Western Hemisphere.[42] Such a proposal would not extend to liberalization measures taken pursuant to IMF or World Bank adjustment programs because this would run counter to the voluntary and consensus-based nature of WTO bindings.

For developed countries in GATS this ratcheting should be automatic, while developing countries could extend such benefits progressively, with transition periods once again determined according to the countries' level of development. Two essential complements would likely be required to make such an approach operational and politically attractive to GATS members. First, the agreement's notification machinery would need to be strengthened to allow for speedier and more transparent dissemination of information on changes to countries' regulatory regimes affecting services trade and investment. Second, and perhaps more important, a credible system for tabulating "liberalization credits" for autonomous liberalization

---

42. Prieto and Stephenson (1999).

undertakings between negotiating rounds would need to be devised and administered, most likely by the WTO Secretariat (possibly in collaboration with UNCTAD and the World Bank).

Formula-based Approaches to Liberalization

The first GATS round saw most efforts on liberalization devoted to servicing time-consuming and resource-intensive "request-offer" negotiations, most of which focused on demands for the removal of barriers maintained in sectors of special export interest to those countries making requests. Given the regulatory intensity of barriers to services trade and investment, there is little doubt that request-offer procedures will continue to figure prominently in attempts at increasing the breadth and quality of liberalization commitments under GATS.

Yet because of the inherent difficulty of measuring the quality of liberalization commitments that flow from bilateral request-offer procedures (a problem that is endemic in all areas subject to regulatory barriers), attention has recently begun to focus on devising formulaic approaches to liberalization with a view to achieving some economies of scale while reducing negotiating transaction costs (see chapter 16). As one proponent of such an approach has noted, formula-based liberalization could be either horizontal, focusing on barriers whose restrictive effects cut across several sectors and are common to many countries (for example, quantitative thresholds on foreign ownership), or more narrowly sectoral in design and scope.

> Negotiators should consider the adoption of a "formula" approach to market access negotiations, whereby countries would agree to a percentage reduction or elimination of particular types of market access restrictions such as quotas, citizenship requirements, and limitations on locally established foreign firms' volume of activity. For certain types of barriers it might be possible to apply a formula to all sectors, while for other barriers it may be necessary to develop formulas adapted to the unique characteristics of that sector. Both horizontal and sectoral formulas could establish separate targets for developed countries, developing countries, and least developed countries.[43]

The European Commission has hinted that horizontal formulas would be preferable, noting that "such approaches should ideally be applied to sev-

43. Feketekuty (1998).

eral sectors, by all or many WTO Members. This would be useful in the
GATS, where the lack of generally applied approaches to the listing of commitments makes it very complex to negotiate and to assess the value of what
is offered by each WTO Member."[44] In devising formula-based approaches
the European Commission sought suggestions on the following proposals:

—making national treatment a basic right for service suppliers (which
is seemingly incompatible with the GATS hybrid approach to scheduling
commitments);

—allowing service suppliers to have the right to majority share ownership in sectors where mode 3 commitments are scheduled;

—in light of the rising prominence of electronic commerce, removing
unduly burdensome and overt restrictions on cross-border access;

—freedom of choice with regard to the form of establishment in
scheduled sectors under mode 3; and

—securing greater commitments to be applied by all WTO members
in the movement of persons in order to facilitate the flow of service
suppliers, in particular intracompany transfers.

A quick perusal of both NAFTA reservation lists of nonconforming
measures and GATS commitments suggests that countries maintain many
similar types of restrictions to trade and investment in services to which a
formulaic approach might usefully be applied. To take one example, it is
common for countries to constrain the ability of foreign investors to own
or control a national airline. This suggests the scope, perhaps yet again on
the basis of some variable geometry across countries and over time, to set
a liberalization target through which to increase progressively the contestability of foreign markets for investors and service providers. Some horizontal, or nonsector-specific, liberalization formulas for investment in
services are shown in box 12-2 (drawn from chapter 16).

Practicing What All Preach: Operation Transparency

There is little doubt that greater recourse to formula-based approaches
to liberalization would require greater regulatory transparency on the most
egregious and commercially damaging obstacles to access and presence
than that which the current approach to scheduling provides under GATS.
In this regard, and with proper technical assistance from the WTO, UNC-

44. European Commission (1998).

Box 12-2. *Horizontal Formulas for Liberalizing Investment in Services*

> Removal of economic needs test for approval, removal of quotas on number of firms permitted, and removal of limitations on majority foreign ownership as general principles for establishment of new services businesses.
>
> Consequent on establishment, guarantee of national treatment for foreign firms in
>
> —scope and geographic location of permitted business activities;
>
> —types of permitted legal entity;
>
> —application of domestic business and professional laws and regulatory licensing;
>
> —removal of limitations on ability of foreign firms to lease or buy land and buildings for their direct commercial use;
>
> —removal of limitations concerning possibility of forced divestiture of existing foreign shareholdings in services businesses; and
>
> —removal of nationality requirements for board members, directors, and senior executives.

TAD, and World Bank Secretariats (which are already involved in efforts in this direction), GATS members should be encouraged to launch what could be called an Operation Transparency. Its purpose would be to shed much needed light on the nature, sectoral incidence, and economywide effects of barriers to trade and investment in services. This should ultimately involve the production of nonlegally binding lists of key nonconforming measures maintained by GATS members. Such lists would become powerful instruments to promote procompetitive domestic regulatory reform and underpin efforts at achieving still greater liberalization in future negotiating rounds.[45]

Such an effort would also generate valuable information to foreign investors and service providers contemplating entry or expansion in new markets. One of the keys to securing long-term foreign direct investment is to ensure that the treatment of established or would-be investors is predictable. Indeed, difficulties in establishing knowledge of the laws and regulations of the host country have consistently been identified by international investors as an important brake to their propensity to invest abroad. The most basic of all WTO obligations, transparency is easily preached, less seriously practiced. The time has come for GATS members to be more transparent and to

45. Sauvé (1996, pp. 45–46); see also Sauvé (1999b).

focus more serious efforts and energy on documenting commercially meaningful obstacles to trade and investment in services.

Concluding Remarks

Our depiction of the post-MAI policymaking and rule-making context leads to the conclusion that a pragmatic, incremental, and GATS-centered approach to the next round of WTO negotiations can meaningfully broaden the coverage of investment-related matters within the multilateral trading system. Although the recent past has seen increasingly frequent calls for integrating a comprehensive set of investment disciplines into the WTO, it is most unlikely that wholesale architectural reform will be up for consideration during the next round.

That said, there are useful things to be done within the multilateral trading system to improve and sustain investment as a force of integration among nations. We have suggested three ways of doing so under GATS:

—clarifying the status, scope, and economic incidence of investment restrictions;

—making GATS rules more investor friendly; and

—showing continued imagination in trying to secure greater liberalization commitments, notably through efforts at locking in the regulatory status quo in sectors where countries voluntarily undertake specific commitments, ratcheting up autonomous liberalization measures taken between negotiating rounds, and adopting formula-based approaches to liberalization where these prove feasible.

We end on a cautionary note, however. Investment coverage in GATS should not obscure the point that the international trade and investment system may ultimately be best served by simplifying the structure of GATS and that investment rules in their own right may warrant full and comprehensive integration into the multilateral trading system. Patience, humility, foresight, and diplomacy should eventually win out, bearing in mind the all-important tendency toward unilateral virtue in domestic investment policymaking.

References

Barshefsky, Charlene. 1999. Testimony before U.S. House of Representatives Appropriations Subcommittee. March 17. http://www.ustr.gov/testimony/index.htm.

Beviglia Zampetti, Americo, and Pierre Sauvé. 1996. "Onwards to Singapore: The International Contestability of Markets and the New Trade Agenda." *World Economy* 19 (3).

Brittan, Leon. 1998. "European Objectives for Services Worldwide: How the WTO Can Help." Address to the Conference on Trade and Services, "Towards GATS 2000—A European Strategy." Brussels, June 2; http://gats-info.eu.int/gats-info/g2000.pl.

———. 1998. "Europe's Prescriptions for the Global Trade Agenda." Address at the CSI Annual Meeting. Washington, September 24; http://www.globalservicesnetwork.com.

European Commission. 1998. "GATS 2000 Issues Paper: Investment/Establishment." October; http://gats-info.eu.int/gats-info/gatslib.pl.

Feketekuty, Geza. 1998. "Setting the Agenda for Services 2000—The Next Round of Negotiations on Trade in Services." Under "Editorial Contributions" in http://www.globalservicesnetwork.com/.

Gervais, Daniel, and Vera Nicholas-Gervais. 1999. "Intellectual Property in the Multilateral Agreement on Investment: Lessons to Be Learned." *Journal of World Intellectual Property* vol. 2 (March): 257–74.

Gestrin, Michael, and Alan M. Rugman. 1993. "The NAFTA's Impact on the North American Investment Regime." C. D. Howe Commentary 42. Toronto: C. D. Howe Institute, March.

Graham, Edward M. 1998a. "Contestability, Competition and Investment in the New World Trade Order." In Geza Feketekuty and Bruce Stokes, eds., *Trade Strategies for a New Era: Ensuring U.S. Leadership in a Global Economy*, pp. 204–22. New York: Council on Foreign Relations with the Monterey Institute of International Studies.

———. 1998b. "The Economic Effects of Investment Incentives on Host Economies." In Dennis J. Encarnation and Boris Velic, eds., *Competing for Foreign Direct Investment: Government Policy and Corporate Strategy in Asia*. Oxford University Press.

———. Forthcoming. *Anti-Globalism and the Demise of the Multilateral Agreement on Investment.* Washington: Institute for International Economics.

Hart, M. 1996. "A Multilateral Agreement on Foreign Direct Investment: Why Now?" In Pierre Sauvé and D. Schwanen, eds., *Investment Rules for the Global Economy: Enhancing Access to Markets,* pp. 36–99. Policy Study 28. Toronto: C. D. Howe Institute.

Henderson, David. 1999. *The MAI Affair: A Story and Its Lessons.* Pelham Papers. University of Melbourne Business School. Also published in French, *L'accord multilatéral sur l'investissement: Leçons d'un échec.* Paris: Groupe d'économie mondiale, "Sciences Po."

Hoekman, Bernard, and Kamal Saggi. 1999. "Multilateral Disciplines for Investment-Related Policies?" Paper prepared for the conference "Global Regionalism." Internazionali, Rome: Instituto Affari, February.

Low, Patrick. 1995. "Market Access through Market Presence: A Look at the Issues." In *New Dimensions of Market Access in a Globalising World Economy,* pp. 49–60. Paris: OECD.

Moran, Theodore H. 1998. *Foreign Direct Investment and Development: The New Agenda for Developing Countries and Economies in Transition.* Washington: Institute for International Economics.

O'Hare, Dean. 1999. Statement before the Subcommittee on Trade of the House Committee on Ways and Means. March; http://www.uscsi.org.

Organization for Economic Cooperation and Development. 1998a. "Recent Trends in Foreign Direct Investment." *Financial Market Trends,* 70.

————. 1998b. *Open Markets Matter: The Benefits of Trade and Investment Liberalization.* Paris.

Ostry, S. 1997. "A New Regime for Foreign Direct Investment." Occasional Paper 53. New York: Group of Thirty.

Price, Daniel M. 1996. "Investment Rules and High Technology: Toward a Multilateral Agreement on Investment." In OECD, *Market Access after the Uruguay Round: Investment, Competition and Technology Perspectives,* pp. 171–86. Paris.

Prieto, F. J., and Sherry Stephenson. 1999. "Multilateral and Regional Liberalization of Trade in Services." In M. Rodriguez Mendoza, P. Low, and B. Kotschwar, eds., *Trade Rules in the Making: Challenges in Regional and Multilateral Negotiations,* pp. 235–60.Washington: Organization of American States and Brookings Institution Press.

Rodrik, Dani. 1999. "The New Global Economy and Developing Countries: Making Openness Work." Economic Development Policy Essay 24. Washington: Overseas Development Council.

Ruggiero, Renato. 1996. "Foreign Direct Investment and the Multilateral Trading System." *Transnational Corporations* 5 (April): 1–8.

————. 1998. "Towards GATS 2000—A European Strategy." Address to the Conference on Trade and Services. Brussels, June 2; http://gats-info.eu.int/gats-info/g2000.pl.

Rugman, Alan M., and Michael Gestrin. 1994. "NAFTA's Treatment of Foreign Investment." In Alan M. Rugman, ed., *Foreign Investment and NAFTA,* pp. 47–79. University of South Carolina Press,.

Sauvé, Pierre. 1994. "A First Look at Investment in the Final Act of the Uruguay Round." *Journal of World Trade* 28 (October): 5–16.

————. 1996. "Services and the International Contestability of Markets." *Transnational Corporations* 5 (April): 37–56.

————. 1997. "Qs and As on Trade, Investment and the WTO." *Journal of World Trade* 31 (August): 55–79.

————. 1998. "The Benefits of Trade and Investment Liberalization: Financial Services." In Douglas H. Brooks and Monika Quiesser, eds., *Financial Liberalization in Asia: Analysis and Prospects,* pp. 173–88. Paris: Asian Development Bank and OECD Development Center.

————. 1999a. "Creating the Climate for Investment in Services in the Western Hemisphere." Paper prepared for the conference "Global Trade in Services and the Americas." San Jose, Costa Rica, July; available from the author at pierre_sauve@harvard.edu.

————. 1999b. "Preparing for GATS 2000: An Overview." Paper prepared for Industry Canada, Ottawa, February.

Schott, Jeffrey J. 1996. *WTO 2000; Setting the Course for World Trade.* Policy Analyses in International Economics 45. Washington: Institute for International Economics.

Smythe, Elizabeth. 1998. "Agenda Formation and the Negotiation of Investment Rules at the WTO: The History of a Campaign." Paper prepared for the annual meeting of the International Studies Association. Washington.

Snape, Richard, and Malcolm Bosworth. 1996. "Advancing Services Negotiations." In Jeffrey J. Schott, ed., *The World Trading System: Challenges Ahead,* pp. 185–204. Washington: Institute for International Economics.

U.S. Coalition of Service Industries. 1998. "Services 2000 USTR Federal Register Submission: Coalition of Service Industries Response to Solicitation of Public Comment Regarding U.S. Preparations for the World Trade Organization's Ministerial Meeting." Fourth quarter.

Wimmer, A. M. 1996. "The Impact of the General Agreement on Trade in Services on the OECD Multilateral Agreement on Investment." *World Competition* 19 (June): 109–20.

World Trade Organization. 1996. *Annual Report 1996.* Volume I: *Special Topic: Trade and Foreign Direct Investment.* Geneva.

————. 1998. *Report (1998) of the Working Group on the Relationship Between Trade and Investment to the General Council.* WT/WGTI/2–8 December; http://www.wto.org/ddf/ep/C4/C4920e.doc.

13 | Competition Policy and GATS

MARK A. A. WARNER

A GREAT DEAL HAS BEEN WRITTEN and spoken about the "new" trade issue of the relationship between competition and trade policy since the beginning of the Uruguay Round of trade negotiations. With the passage of time, it is tempting to see this as no longer a new issue at all. But because of the limited progress made in translating this cacophony into actual rule-making, the trade and competition interface arguably still qualifies as a new issue. Two elements of this relationship genuinely qualify for consideration as new issues. These are the relationship of competition policy to investment policy and the liberalization of services. This chapter addresses the relationship of investment, competition, and services.

It is becoming increasingly apparent that grand approaches to multilateral investment rule-making are fraught with many difficulties.[1] Accordingly, the difficulties that resulted in the narrow WTO Agreement on Trade Related Investment Measures in the last round of trade negotiations will probably present themselves again. Therefore, once again greater scope for investment liberalization may be achieved in negotiations on the liberalization of trade in services. In that respect the built-in agenda of GATS 2000 represents an important opportunity for pursuing both investment and services rule-making of an incremental but yet still significant nature.

1. See chapter 12 in this volume.

That being said, experience with GATS negotiations demonstrates that competition and competition policy will in many sectors be critical to the willingness of WTO members to liberalize their trade in services. The question then arises as to how issues of competition and competition policy should enter into these negotiations. One approach might be to pursue negotiations relating to an agreement on trade-related aspects of anticompetitive measures (TRAMs). Another approach, however, would be to build on the existing competition provisions of GATS in future sectoral negotiations or in even more horizontal understandings of principles of domestic regulation with respect to services.

This chapter examines the prospects for achieving both approaches and the relative strengths and weaknesses. The first section examines the state of rule-making for multilateral competition policy. The second discusses existing competition policy provisions in GATS. The third examines the ways in which concern for competition policy might arise in particular services sector negotiations.

Rule-Making in Multilateral Competition Policy

It is worth distinguishing between two ways of thinking about competition policy rule-making. One focuses on the international aspects of competition law enforcement. That could include consideration of cooperation and coordination among competition law authorities. The cooperation and coordination could involve investigations of private anticompetitive measures or the enforcement of remedies for such conduct. The cooperation and coordination could occur across the full panoply of competition policy concerns or could be focused on particular concerns such as prohibiting cartels and reviewing mergers. This rule-making could take the form of binding obligations or the expression of nonbinding principles the relevance of which members consider case by case.

Another way of thinking about rule-making for multilateral competition policy is to focus on traditional concerns with trade distortions and market access. This approach would emphasize establishing significant anticompetitive measures that have a substantial impact on international trade and negotiating appropriate rules to discipline violators. The approach would not necessarily focus solely on competition law authorities but would instead be aimed at principles by which members would agree to be bound to make their other trade liberalization commitments stronger.

Most progress on rule-making has been achieved by focusing on traditional concerns. At the multilateral level the Organization for Economic Cooperation and Development, not the World Trade Organization, has been the institutional forum for that work. Specifically, the OECD Competition Law and Policy Committee (CLP) has generated a number of recommendations of the OECD Council of Ministers. Notable examples of these are the 1998 Recommendation Concerning Effective Action against Hard Core Cartels (HCC Recommendation) and the 1995 Revised Recommendation Concerning Cooperation Between Member Countries on Anticompetitive Practices Affecting International Trade (Cooperation Recommendation).[2] Like all recommendations, these are nonbinding. There is no particular form of dispute settlement provided in either. At most, under the HCC Recommendations, the CLP can upon the request of the member countries involved serve as a forum for consultations on the application of the recommendation.[3] Under the Cooperation Recommendation, the CLP can serve as a forum for exchanges of views on matters related to the recommendation "on the understanding that it will not reach conclusions on the conduct of individual enterprises or governments."[4] Further, the CLP can consider requests for conciliation submitted by member countries and can assist "by offering advice or by any other means in the settlement of the matter between the Member countries involved."[5]

Not surprisingly, the dispute settlement provisions, such as they are, of these nonbinding recommendations have never been used. Without a substantial change of heart among OECD member countries, they will probably never be used. Countries so far have seemed hesitant to multilateralize their bilateral competition policy disputes.

Part of the reason for this reluctance may be the imprecise nature of these consensus recommendations. For instance, the HCC Recommendation defines a hard core cartel as "an anticompetitive agreement, anticompetitive concerted practice, or anticompetitive arrangement by competitors to fix prices, make rigged bids (collusive tenders), establish output restrictions or quotas, or share or divide markets by allocating customers, suppliers, territories or lines of commerce." In the United States, however, the adjective phrase "hard core" used in relation to cartels is restricted to a

---

2. The HCC Recommendation can be found at http://www.oecd.org/daf/clp/rec9com.htm. The Cooperation Recommendation can be found at http://www.oecd.org/daf/clp/rec8com.htm.

3. HCC Recommendation, C/M(98)7/FINAL, Article II:2.

4. Cooperation Recommendation, C(95)130/FINAL, Article III:1.

5. Cooperation Recommendation, Article III: 3.

limited class of per se offenses for which no proof of anticompetitive effects would be required. Accordingly, vague consensus recommendations that neither reflect member countries' laws nor require change in such laws to reflect the recommendation are not conducive to binding or even non-binding dispute settlement.

A second reason for the limited use of these dispute settlement provisions is that the CLP has not adopted guidelines for conducting such proceedings, especially to deal with confidential information that might have to be disclosed for the matter to be adjudicated or to provide for working parties consisting of less than all CLP members to serve as the forum.

In fairness it should be noted that the CLP has functioned more successfully as a forum for promoting convergence of competition policies among member countries and also for providing technical assistance to certain observers and nonmember countries. There may well be an inherent tension between the committee's role as a forum for promoting convergence and as a forum for settling disputes, which may also account for its reluctance to embrace the dispute settlement function.

Similar competition provisions exist in certain bilateral agreements for competition policy enforcement. But none of these appear to be fully binding or subject to dispute settlement.

It is useful to ask what can be learned from applying this experience with rule-making to the specific context of investment and services liberalization. One possible conclusion is that this approach to rule-making will probably not encourage countries concerned about securing competitive safeguards to fully liberalize. They will probably want firmer assurance that their concerns about anticompetitive measures can be addressed. Further, in the services context many of the anticompetitive measures might relate to governmental or regulatory conduct. It is not clear that this approach to rule-making would be suited to address those kinds of concerns.

That being said, to a limited extent the HCC Recommendation, with all of its attendant weaknesses, may demonstrate that countries can agree to certain principles or common approaches (if not common standards) to dealing with particular anticompetitive measures. That in itself might be a useful element in any architecture for services competition policy rule-making.

With the second approach to competition policy rule-making—commitments relating to trade distortions and market access—there has been precious little progress. In terms of the WTO agreements, putting the GATS aside because it will be discussed more fully later, it is possible to identify a number of competition provisions.[6] For instance, in GATT 1947, Article II:4 deals to some extent with import monopolies; Articles III:2 and III:4 deal with maintaining the competitive conditions between domestic goods and imported like products; Article XI prohibits certain quantitative restrictions on imports and exports; and Article XVII deals with certain conditions for state trading enterprises. Article 11:1(b) of the Agreement on Safeguards provides that "a Member shall not seek, take or maintain any voluntary export restraints, orderly marketing arrangements or any other similar measures on the export or the import side." The "similar measures" are specified to include "export moderation, export-price or import-price monitoring systems, export or import surveillance, compulsory import cartels and discretionary export or import licensing schemes, any of which afford protection" to the importing country's industry. Furthermore, Article 11:3 provides that "members shall not encourage or support the adoption or maintenance by public and private enterprises of nongovernmental measures equivalent to those referred to in paragraph 1." The Agreement on Trade-Related Aspects of Intellectual Property Rights (TRIPs) also contains provisions on licensing that can be considered related to competition law and policy.

As a formal matter, competition policy per se arises only indirectly in Article 9 of the Agreement on Trade Related Investment Measures (TRIMs). Article 9 provides that by the end of 1999 the Council for Trade in Goods shall review the operation of TRIMs and, as appropriate, propose to the ministerial conference amendments to its text. Furthermore, the Council for Trade in Goods shall consider whether this review should be complemented with provisions on investment policy and competition policy.

At the WTO Ministerial Conference held in Singapore in December 1996 the Working Group on the Interaction between Trade and Competition Policy (WGTCP) was established as was the Working Group on Trade and Investment.[7] These groups were instructed to draw on each

6. Organization for Economic Cooperation and Development (1999a).
7. Paragraph 20 of the Ministerial Declaration provides that
   Having regard to the existing WTO provisions on matters related to investment and competition policy and the built-in agenda in these areas, including under the TRIMs Agreement, and on the understanding that the work undertaken shall not prejudge whether negotiations will be initiated in the future, we also agree to:
   —establish a working group to examine the relationship between trade and investment; and
   —establish a working group to study issues raised by Members relating to the interaction between trade and competition policy, including anti-competitive practices, in order to identify any areas that may merit further consideration in the WTO framework.

other's work if necessary and also draw on and be without prejudice to the work in the United Nations Conference on Trade and Development (UNCTAD) and other appropriate intergovernmental forums such as the OECD. The Ministerial Declaration further clarified that "it is clearly understood that future negotiations, if any, regarding multilateral disciplines in these areas, will take place only after an explicit consensus decision is taken among WTO Members regarding such negotiations."[8] The General Council was instructed to keep the work of each body under review and to determine after two years how the work of each should proceed. In December 1998 the mandate of the WGTCP was extended and refined to "continue the educative work that it has been undertaken pursuant to paragraph 20 of the Singapore Ministerial Declaration."[9] To this point the working group has served primarily as a useful educational forum for developed and developing countries to discuss competition policy and only secondarily as a prenegotiation forum. Among the items considered by the group in the first two years of its mandate were:

—The relationship between the objectives, principles, concepts, scope, and instruments of trade and competition policy. Their relationship to development and economic growth.

—Stocktaking and analysis of existing instruments, standards, and activities regarding trade and competition policy, including experience with their application; national competition policies, laws, and instruments as they relate to trade; existing WTO provisions; and bilateral, regional, plurilateral, and multilateral agreements and initiatives.

—The interaction between trade and competition policy: the impact of anticompetitive practices of enterprises and associations on international trade; the impact of state monopolies, exclusive rights, and regula-

8. Ministerial Declaration, para. 20.

9. In light of the limited number of meetings that it will be able to hold in 1999, the working group, while continuing at each meeting to base its work on the study of issues raised by members relating to the interaction between trade and competition policy, including anticompetitive practices, would benefit from a focused discussion on the relevance of fundamental WTO principles of national treatment, transparency, and most favored nation treatment to competition policy and vice versa; approaches to promoting cooperation and communication among members, including in the field of technical cooperation; and the contribution of competition policy to achieving the objectives of the WTO, including the promotion of international trade. The working group will continue to ensure that the development dimension and the relationship with investment are fully taken into account. It is understood that this decision is without prejudice to any future decision that might be taken by the general council, including in the context of its existing work programme." *Report (1998) of the Working Group on the Interaction between Trade and Competition Policy to the General Council* (WT/WGTCP/2), para. 154 (December 1998).

tory policies on competition and international trade; the relationship between the trade-related aspects of intellectual property rights and competition policy; the relationship between investment and competition policy; and the impact of trade policy on competition.

The WGTCP's work before December 1998 included identifying any areas that may merit further consideration in the WTO framework, but it never reached that point in its deliberations. It remains to be seen whether in this second phase of the work the group will move to more of a prenegotiation or negotiation mode. At this stage it seems unlikely that it will move to a negotiation mode because the positions of various parties still seem far apart. Nonetheless, it may be useful to canvass the positions of major players to assess the implications for horizontal competition policy rule-making with respect to the liberalization of trade in services.

The European Union has perhaps the most expansive proposal for horizontal rule-making about competition policy. The "Communication from the Commission to the Council and to the European Parliament on the EU Approach to the Millennium Round" enumerates four elements on the negotiation of a binding framework of multilateral rules on competition as part of a comprehensive round.

—Core principles and common rules relating to the adoption of competition law and its enforcement (a commitment to adopt a comprehensive competition law, limits on sectoral exclusions, application of principles of transparency and nondiscrimination, rights of firms, and private actions in national courts).

—Common approaches on anticompetitive practices with a significant impact on international trade and investment (hard core cartels, criteria for assessment of vertical restrictions or abuses of dominance with a foreclosure effect, and principles for cooperation on export cartels and international mergers).

—Provisions on international cooperation, which could include provisions on notification, consultation, and surveillance in relation to anticompetitive practices with an international dimension; exchanges of nonconfidential information; and positive and negative comity (although without a binding obligation to investigate on behalf of another country).[10]

10. The 1991 Agreement between the United States and the European Commission Regarding the Application of Their Competition Laws adopted the idea of "positive comity," that is, one country's authorities may ask another country to take measures against anticompetitive activities in that country that violate its competition laws and that harm the requesting country's interests; http://www.us-doj.gov/atr/public/international/docs/ec.txt. In April 1998 the United States and the European Com-

—Dispute settlement to ensure that the domestic enforcement structures for competition law are in accordance with the multilaterally agreed principles, but in no event should there be a review of individual decisions.[11]

Finally, with respect to dispute settlement the position of the European Commission appears to be that WTO panels should consider whether a member is in breach of the principles or whether competition law appropriately covers the common approaches. This dispute settlement would not apply in individual cases and not in respect of positive comity. Although there appears to be a consensus that dispute settlement should not apply to individual cases because of the complex and fact-intensive nature of competition law and policy, it is worth noting that the WTO already deals with complex and fact-intensive cases under the Agreement on the Application of Sanitary and Phytosanitary Measures (SPS Agreement) or involving environmental measures.[12] It should also be noted that Article 2:2 of the WTO Understanding on Rules and Procedures Governing the Settlement of Disputes provides that panels may seek the counsel of experts with respect to "a factual issue concerning a scientific or other technical matter raised by a party to a dispute."[13]

As proposed, the dispute settlement would apply to alleged patterns of failure to enforce competition law in cases affecting international trade and investment.[14] It is not clear how this proposal could in practice avoid

---

munities refined the 1991 agreement with a further Agreement on the Application of Positive Comity Principles in the Enforcement of Their Competition Laws; http://www.usdoj.gov/atr/public/international/docs/1781.htm.

11. Released July 8, 1999; http://europa.eu.int/comm/dg01/dglnewround.htm. See also Brittan (1999a, 1999b); and Van Miert (1998).

12. "United States: Measures Concerning Import Prohibition of Certain Shrimp and Shrimp Products, Report of the Appellate Body" (AB/DS58/AB/R 12 October 1998); "EC: Measures Concerning Meat and Meat Products (Hormones), Report of the Appellate Body," AB1997-4 (WT/DS26/AB/R, WT/DS48/AB/R), January 16, 1998, adopted; "Australia: Measures Affecting Importation of Salmon, Report of the Appellate Body," AB1998-5 (WT/DS18/AB/R), June 20, 1998, adopted; and "Japan: Measures Affecting Agricultural Products, Report of the Appellate Body," AB1998-8 (WT/DS76/AB/R), February 22, 1999, adopted. See generally Horlick (1999); and Cottier (1999).

13. Professor Frederic Jenny, vice chair of the French Competition Council, chair of the WTO Working Group on the Interaction between Trade and Competition Policy, and chair of the OECD Competition Law and Policy Committee, has recently made this point and also noted that similar provisions can be found in the SPS Agreement and the Agreement on Technical Barriers to Trade (TBT Agreement). See Jenny (1999).

14. See Brittan (1998a). "Furthermore, we have been reflecting within the Community on whether dispute settlement should also apply to a pattern of non-enforcement of domestic competition law. My personal view is that once such a pattern has been established, it should also be subject to some appropriate form of dispute settlement." See also Mehta (1999).

judging individual cases, especially when what is alleged is a pattern of nonenforcement. Presumably, this will be clarified in subsequent interventions from the EU. In this regard it is worth considering the observations of Joel Klein, U.S. assistant attorney general for antitrust, who "does not know what it means to say . . . that individual cases will not be reviewed but that a 'pattern' may be; a pattern is a series of individual cases, and even if the whole were greater than the sum of its parts, any meaningful dispute resolution powers in this field could not ignore the parts."[15]

The U.S. position is much less comprehensive. The U.S. antitrust agencies—the Department of Justice and the Federal Trade Commission—emphasize bilateral cooperation and coordination in investigation and enforcement. This has sometimes been described as an attempt to multilateralize Canada-U.S. practices of enforcement cooperation and coordination.[16] They emphasize the use of treaties on mutual legal assistance in criminal matters and interagency cooperation agreements, which include positive comity provisions, but not the automatic deferral mechanism as in the U.S.-EU context.

This Canada-U.S. approach is based largely on the development of U.S. antitrust law over time under a common law, judge-driven, case-by-case model.[17] Accordingly, the United States seeks to replicate the model through a network of cooperation agreements with countries that already have competition laws, technical assistance to encourage the adoption of competition laws in those countries without them, and convergence though dialogue in forums such as the CLP and WGTCP.[18] The United States (like Canada and the European Union) also supports peer review of competition law and policy matters using the Trade Policy Review Mechanism (TPRM) modeled on the OECD experience with country reviews in regulatory reform.[19]

The Canadian approach is more enigmatic. Like the European Union, Canada supports multilateral rules, but there are indications that Ottowa is more skeptical about dispute settlement. Canada has called for negotiations that build on the OECD work such as the HCC Recommendation, the 1998 CLP Framework for Premerger Notification, and ongoing work

15. Klein (1999).
16. Klein (1997a, 1997b).
17. See A. Douglas Melamed, principal deputy assistant attorney general, Antitrust Division, U.S. Department of Justice (1999).
18. Ambassador Charlene Barshefsky (1998).
19. Klein (1997a, 1997b).

on rights to remedy and positive comity. Canada has emphasized the need to establish a common approach to abuse of dominance, complying with core principles, and the elements of a minimum competition law institutional framework (an independent investigative agency, independent judicial review and appeal, and fair adjudication). Canada has proposed a plurilateral agreement with a dispute settlement mechanism designed to ensure that members carry out their minimum commitments in accordance with their jurisprudence and legal traditions. However, like the EU Canada suggests rather unconvincingly that this could be done in a way that does not question how countries apply their laws in particular cases.[20]

A recent consultation discussion paper described the Canadian position as favoring

> a multilateral agreement on competition policy [that] could include a commitment to fundamental principles such as transparency and nondiscrimination; common substantive approaches to address private anticompetitive practices (including hard core cartels, abuse of dominance, merger review); mechanisms to enhance cooperation among countries; as well as dispute settlement provisions. Provisions to encourage effective domestic enforcement of competition laws could also be considered. In addition to facilitating cooperation between parties in addressing anticompetitive behaviour, such an agreement could assist in providing firms with needed assurance as

20. Konrad Von Finkenstein, commissioner of competition (1998). Compare with a more recent speech by Patricia Smith, deputy commissioner of competition, Economics and International Affairs Branch, Competition Bureau (1999):

> Some may argue that the workings of the WTO dispute settlement mechanism under these circumstances would not significantly differ from work currently being done in regard to other WTO obligations. But this needs to be scrutinized much more closely. Our concern is that it might be difficult if not impossible to confine the dispute settlement procedures to *only* these issues and that, inevitably, dispute settlement would lead to the review of decisions of competition authorities in individual cases.

> The competition bureau has concerns about the applicability of the existing WTO dispute settlement procedures to competition policy cases. The WTO has no mechanism to deal with the intense fact finding investigation that is fundamental to the economic analysis of competition cases, let alone a proven track record on confidentiality matters.

> As you can no doubt gather from this and reading between the lines in the paper, we strongly question whether it's full speed ahead on this one! Nevertheless, we believe a lot can be accomplished short of a dispute settlement mechanism. Before we start down the slippery slope of dispute settlement, WTO members may wish to examine other means of reviewing members' records in implementing their competition policy obligations.

Smith further advocated the creation of a Competition Policy Review Mechanism and Trade-Related Aspects of Anticompetitive Measures Council to conduct such reviews in lieu of a dispute settlement forum within the WTO.

to the rules of business conduct in foreign markets and in ensuring they are treated in a nondiscriminatory way.[21]

Japan has tended to align itself with certain developing countries, mostly from the Asia-Pacific region, in stressing the need to look at the anticompetitive effects of trade remedies. Japan is more open in support of the EU initiative for multilateral investment rule-making in the context of the WTO, and there may be a certain implied linkage to the EU competition as well. The proposed Japanese framework would include the following elements:

—Certain basic principles that all rules of the framework should meet, including most favored nation treatment, national treatment, transparency, and competition-oriented principles.

—Anticompetitive practices to be banned (hard core cartels, horizontal concerted boycotts, import cartels, and abuse of dominance).

—Common procedures for review and analysis of mergers.

—Minimization of exemptions and exceptions from national competition laws.

—Effective national enforcement structures.

—Cooperation, notification, and exchange of information and conflict avoidance.

—Dispute settlement procedures applied to failure to adopt domestic legislation in conformity with obligations stipulated in the framework, measures that directly violate the framework (for example, expansion of exemption systems), and inappropriate actions or tolerances against specific cases.[22]

As for developing countries, there does not appear to a groundswell of interest in either the EU proposals for investment or horizontal competition rule-making. In fact the compromise between developed and developing countries implicit in the narrow TRIMs Agreement and the explicit linkage between trade and competition in the Singapore Declaration re-

---

21. Canada, "Discussion Paper, Competition Policy and the International Trade Agenda," March 1999.

22. "WTO Working Group on the Interaction of Trade and Competition Policies Communication from Japan," WT/WGTCP/W/134, July 14, 1999; and "WTO Working Group on the Interaction of Trade and Competition Policies Communication from Japan," WT/WGTCP/W/119, May 27, 1999. See also Hisamitsu Arai, vice minister for international affairs, MITI (1999). In particular Arai remarked with respect to the application of dispute settlement to individual cases that "even under existing WTO rules, a similar problem could arise in the case of a dispute relating to . . . under the TRIPS Agreement."

main relatively unchanged. Developing countries have not made clear exactly what they are looking for in terms of the competition link to investment, although this may become clearer as UNCTAD's work (begun in June 1999) on the latest revision to the Set of Mutually Agreed Equitable Principles and Rules for the Control of Restrictive Business Practices progresses.[23] One thing that is clear is that developing country views are unlikely to be homogeneous. But there will likely be sufficient opposition, combined with divisions within the quad to mean that as a practical matter successfully achieving horizontal competition policy rule-making will be very difficult.

Aside from the practical difficulties of achieving an agreement for the liberalization of trade in services, there is the further question of its desirability. A Canadian public consultation discussion paper identified certain market access barriers to trade in services:

> limitations on the numbers of service suppliers (i.e., in the form of quotas, monopolies, rights for exclusive supply); limitations on the total number of services transactions or assets or operations (i.e., usually expressed in terms of a quota); limitations on the total number of persons that may be employed in a particular service sector; measures which restrict the legal entity through which a foreign service supplier may deliver the service (e.g., subsidiaries, branches, joint ventures); and limitations on the level of shareholding or investment that a foreign service supplier may make.[24]

This is a useful point of departure because it identifies monopolies, quotas, and rights of exclusive supply as crucial problems. Competition law, particularly if applied to public sector entities, other state-owned enterprises, and firms operating with exclusive and special rights, could be helpful in addressing these problems. Further examples of anticompetitive practices that could create market problems for service suppliers can be found in the U.S. Trade Representative's 1999 report on foreign trade barriers. For example, the report lists some computer airline reservation practices of dominant EU firms that may adversely affect the ability of U.S. airline firms to compete in certain markets.[25] This case was the subject of the first and so far only formal positive comity request under the U.S.-EC

23. UNCTAD, "Agreed Conclusions of the Intergovernmental Group of Experts on Competition Law and Policy at Its Second Session," TD/B/COM.2/CLP/L.5, June 10, 1999.

24. Canada, "Services Issues Paper," March 1999.

25. U.S. Trade Representative (1999, p. 131). *1999 Report to the President on Foreign Trade Barriers (1999)*.

Cooperation Agreement. After almost one year the case against one of the owners of the reservation system was settled, and the EC filed a statement of objections against the practices of the other owner of the system.[26] That part of the case continues, but the example illustrates the link between anticompetitive practices and trade in services. Other potential examples include airport ground handling services reserved to national carriers. In this instance the European Commission has issued a directive phasing out the practice.[27] The point to be made is that in energy, postal services, telecommunications, and other sectors where exclusive rights remain, some multilateral agreement on competition policy could be beneficial in securing market access.

At this point it is worthwhile listing a few other potential anticompetitive measures and the sectors in which they might arise: abuse of dominance (financial and postal services, transportation, energy); price fixing (shipping, airlines, professional services); bid rigging (infrastructure, construction), state aids (airlines), and exceptions that inhibit market access. I will discuss these later.

The GATS Framework

GATS Article 8 requires a member country to ensure that a monopoly supplier does not "abuse its monopoly position" when it competes in the supply of services outside its monopoly rights. Article 9:1 says "members recognize that certain business practices of service providers, other than those falling under Article 8, may restrain competition and thereby restrict trade in services." Article 9:2 obliges members to accede to any request for consultation with any other member concerning such practices "with a view to eliminating" them. It also imposes a duty to cooperate in providing nonconfidential information of relevance to the matter in question.

To date there has been only one request for consultations concerning GATS Article VIII: a U.S. complaint that Belgian law and regulations on the reform of public enterprises impose conditions for obtaining a license to publish commercial directories in Belgium, and measures governing the acts, policies, and practices of Belgacomm N.V. with respect to telephone

26. Prepared statement of Joel I. Klein, assistant attorney general, Antitrust Division, U.S. Department of Justice, before the Senate Subcommittee on Antitrust, Business Rights, and Competition of the Committee on the Judiciary, May 4, 1999.

27. Klein (1997b, pp. 131–32).

directory services contravene GATS Article VIII.[28] Belgacomm, the former telephone monopoly in Belgium, is 51 percent owned by the Belgian government (the other 49 percent is held by Ameritech, Tele Danmark, and Singapore Telacomm) and is responsible to the Ministry of Telecommunications, which supervises the Institute for Postal Services and Telecommunications.[29]

The United States did not request consultations with the European Commission at the same time it made the request to Belgium. There appears to be some suggestion that Belgacomm's actions may also be under investigation by the commission for violating an EC directive.[30] This is a very nice example of the potential for competition policy to be used for further liberalization in trade in services and to address market access barriers. That the United States has complained raises the interesting possibility that although some U.S. potential entrant is being hurt by the alleged infringement, a U.S. firm, Ameritech, is also benefiting from the alleged practice. What is clear is that consumers in Belgium are probably being hurt by higher prices than would otherwise prevail and reduced choice. Competition policy, therefore, may be a useful complement to services liberalization because its tradition of nondiscriminatory application of certain principles can benefit both domestic consumers and potential foreign entrants with market access concerns.

We are still in the very early day of GATS Articles VIII and IX, but this case shows the underutilized potential in GATS to apply competition policy to address anticompetitive practices. Thus, apart from the much more talked about sectoral context, GATS is already equipped with competition provisions. This discussion, and the earlier discussion of sectors potentially posing anticompetitive problems, suggests that in thinking about making GATS an even more promising tool for achieving liberalization, perhaps some thought should be given to making Articles VIII and IX even more powerful, directly or through some reconsideration of GATS Article VI on domestic regulation. I will return to this idea later.

Telecommunications

The negotiations on basic telecommunications were not completed by the time the Uruguay Round drew to a close in December 1993. It had

28. Belgium, "Measures Affecting Commercial Directory Services," WT/DS80/1, May 12, 1997.
29. Ameritech, a U.S. company, also owns 42 percent of Tele Danmark.
30. Horlick (1998, note 25); and generally, European Commission (1998).

become apparent as the negotiations on services proceeded that governments saw telecommunications as special. Without access to telecommunications, many other services cannot be delivered, making specific
commitments to supply them of dubious value. Thus paragraph 5(a) of the
Telecommunications Annex states that each member "shall ensure that any
service supplier of any other Member is accorded access to and use of
public telecommunications transport networks and services on reasonable
and non-discriminatory terms and conditions for the supply of a service
included in its Schedule."[31]

Suppliers of such services are entitled to access to and use of any public
telecommunications transport network or service offered within or across
the border, including private leased circuits. Suppliers also have the right
to purchase or lease and attach terminal or other equipment to the network
and to interconnect private leased or owned circuits with public telecommunications transport networks and services or with circuits leased or
owned by another service supplier. These rights are qualified by the right
of the entity owning or controlling the network to impose conditions on
access and use to safeguard public service responsibilities, protect the
technical integrity of the networks or services, and restrict network use
where this is not required pursuant to a scheduled commitment. The
obligations of the annex extend not only to service suppliers in other
sectors, but also to those in the telecommunications sector who would
compete with incumbent network operators.[32]

Thus to some extent, issues related to competition policy concerning
interconnection, market conduct safeguards, and transparency had already
been touched upon in GATS and its associated Annex on Telecommunications. However, some negotiators felt that the annex commitments were
too general to guarantee new entrants adequate opportunity to compete.

The obligations of GATS and the annex apply only to those telecommunications sectors that the WTO members incorporated in their schedules. Mostly, the schedules contained what is commonly referred to as
"enhanced telecommunications services." Enhanced services are those in
which the voice or nonvoice information being transferred from one point
to another undergoes an end-to-end restructuring or format change before

---

31. Nondiscrimination in this context comprises both MFN and national treatment.

32. It should be noted that annex commitments only apply in those sectors where governments have
accepted specific market access and national treatment commitments. Under GATS, governments have
negotiated these commitments sector by sector, and in sectors that are not covered in this manner, the
only obligations that apply relate to MFN treatment and transparency.

it reaches the customer. In 1994 the members' schedules generally included enhanced services such as electronic mail, voice mail, on-line information, electronic data interchange, value-added facsimile services, code and protocol conversion, and data processing.

The members were not ready in 1994 to make commitments on basic telecommunications services because, unlike enhanced services, the basic services have been provided by state-owned operators or state-sanctioned monopolies. Thus it became increasingly apparent that if negotiations were limited to the traditional trade approach of scheduling commitments on market access and national treatment, there would not be a guarantee that liberalization commitments would translate into effective access to markets.[33] The removal of regulatory entry barriers is clearly a necessary condition of access, but such action would have little impact in the face of nongovernmental barriers based on the ability of regulated incumbent firms to frustrate market entry.

Thus a significant component of the extended negotiations focused on a quest for acceptable regulatory principles that would be enforceable through WTO dispute settlement procedures. Accordingly, proposals were made to define interconnection rights more specifically. Market conduct safeguards were also sought to ensure that suppliers with market power would refrain from various anticompetitive practices. Finally, transparency requirements were sought to reassure the countries that adopted the Reference Paper.

The Reference Paper

The Reference Paper to the GATS Agreement on Basic Telecommunications (ABT) is a prominent example of a framework in a WTO agreement that already involves competition principles. Specifically, the Reference Paper contains a general commitment of members to maintain appropriate measures to prevent suppliers unilaterally or collectively from engaging in or continuing anticompetitive practices. A major supplier is defined as one with the power "to materially affect the terms of participation (having regard to price and supply), either due to control over essential, network facilities or its market position."

In addition, the Reference Paper gives specific examples of anticompetitive practices:

—anticompetitive cross-subsidization;

33. Low (1995).

—use of information obtained from competitors (with "anticompetitive results"); and

—withholding technical and commercially relevant information.

The Reference Paper also applies to "interconnection" issues: linking with suppliers providing public telecommunications transport networks or services to allow the users of one supplier to communicate with users of another supplier and to access services provided by another supplier. However, the extent of this obligation is limited to the specific commitments undertaken by a member in the various schedules of GATS and the Agreement on Basic Telecommunications commitments. Interconnection must be provided

—under nondiscriminatory terms, conditions (including technical standards and specifications), and rates and of a quality no less favorable than that provided for its own like services or for like services of nonaffiliated service suppliers or for its subsidiaries or other affiliates;

—in a timely fashion on terms, conditions (including technical standards and specifications), and cost-oriented rates that are transparent and reasonable, have regard to economic feasibility, and are sufficiently unbundled so that the supplier need not pay for network components or facilities that it does not require for the service to be provided; and

—upon request, at points in addition to the network termination points offered to the majority of users, subject to charges that reflect the cost of construction of necessary additional facilities.

The Reference Paper also builds on transparency to ensure that the agreement can be put into practice. The procedures applicable for interconnection to a major supplier will be made publicly available, and a major supplier must make publicly available either its interconnection agreements or a reference interconnection offer.

With respect to settlement of disputes under the agreement, the Reference Paper appears to distinguish between disputes about anticompetitive practices and disputes about interconnection. There is no particular form of settlement provided for disputes over anticompetitive practices of major suppliers, but presumably a Reference Paper signatory's failure to maintain appropriate measures would be subject to dispute settlement. With respect to interconnection the Reference Paper indicates that for dispute settlement, recourse is to be made to an independent domestic body. A service supplier requesting interconnection with a major supplier will have recourse either "at any time" or "after a reasonable period of time which has been made publicly known" to an independent domestic body, which may be a regulatory body.[34] That body must be given the authority to resolve disputes regarding appropriate terms, conditions, and rates for interconnection within a reasonable period of time to the extent that these have not been established previously. It is conceivable (and not precluded by the terms of the Reference Paper itself) that the body might not be a sector-specific regulator but, for example, a competition authority.

The Reference Paper also reflects a balance between the objectives of both trade liberalization and competition policy and other social or policy objectives of interest to governments and civil society. Article 3 provides that any member has the right to define the kind of universal service obligation it wishes to maintain, and such obligations will not be regarded as anticompetitive per se. However, those requirements must be administered in a transparent, nondiscriminatory, and competitively neutral manner and cannot be more burdensome than necessary for the kind of universal service defined by the member. Similarly, any procedures for the allocation and use of scarce resources, including frequencies, numbers, and rights of way, must be carried out in an objective, timely, transparent, and nondiscriminatory manner.

When the Agreement on Basic Telecommunications entered into force in February 1998, some 69 of the 130 WTO members committed to some liberalization of their telecommunication markets. Of these, 44 (representing 99 percent of basic telecommunications revenue among WTO members) permitted entry by foreign carriers. Fifty-five countries agreed to adhere to the rules of the Reference Paper.[35]

Implications of the ABT

This section discusses the implications of the Agreement on Basic Telecommunications for future multilateral rule-making for trade and competition policy. First, I identify factors that, in part, made possible this

34. When this is a regulatory body, it must be separate from and not accountable to any supplier of basic telecommunications services, and the decisions of and procedures used by regulators must be impartial with respect to all market participants.

35. Takigawa (1998, pp. 39–40). Compare Spiwak (1998, p. 176), who notes that certain of the signatory countries "agreed to uphold certain 'pro-competitive regulatory principles' yet, at the same time, these signatory countries also condone those signatory countries which refuse to allow any new competitors to enter their market."

sectoral agreement. Second, I discuss ways the architecture of the agreement might be applied in other sectoral contexts or to other multilateral rule-making. Finally, I conclude with a discussion of several normative caveats that suggest this model should be invoked with some caution when it comes to other contexts.

Factors Facilitating the ABT

During the past two decades and more the explosion in technological developments in the telecommunications industry has been matched with tremendous growth in demand for traditional and new forms of telecommunications services.[36]

This growth in demand is linked in part to the fact that telecommunications services are an important component of or input into traded or tradable services. The demand and supply of improved services and the growth of foreign suppliers in these services have also tended to highlight the further gains that could be achieved by liberalizing basic telecommunications services as well. As barriers between nations decrease and economic interdependence grows, so too does the demand for more links between national telecommunications networks. This interdependence has highlighted the need for a multilateral approach to negotiations as opposed to a network of bilateral approaches. And given the prominence of this sector in the global economy, certain growth-oriented developing countries may have chosen to signal their commitment to open trade and investment policies by agreeing to liberalization in this sector.[37]

During these decades also many of the leading markets for the demand and supply of telecommunications services have unilaterally liberalized their regulations of enhanced telecommunications services and then basic telecommunications services. This liberalization has sometimes also involved significant privatization of domestic monopolies. This trend has been accompanied by increasing application of competition principles by telecommunications regulators or in some cases the application of competition policy.[38] There is wide agreement that the transition of telecommunications from a highly regulated industry with public monopolies to a less regulated one with more entrants and service providers was a crucial and

36. See generally Organization for Economic Cooperation and Development (1997c, p. 31; 1997a).
37. Low and Mattoo (1998, p. 26).
38. See generally Organization for Economic Cooperation and Development (1996, 1997b).

unique feature the recognition of which helps to explain the competition provisions of the Reference Paper. Once governments had decided to emphasize entry and to open this network to international competition, there was a feeling that traditional trade approaches to market access through national treatment and MFN commitments alone would not be sufficient to ensure successful entry by foreign service suppliers without additional competitive safeguards. Thus the Reference Paper builds on both traditional market access concepts as well as competition principles, although some might argue that in this respect it could be seen as going beyond the existing approaches to access to "essential facilities" under the competition laws of many countries.

The successful negotiation of the ABT may have something to do with the character of trade in services as compared to trade in goods. It may be that trade in services is seen as inherently implicating domestic regulation beyond the border to a much greater extent than the traditional at the border tariff or nontariff barriers' emphasis of the liberalization of trade in goods. Even where the national treatment commitment applies within the border to imported "like" products, it is less likely to call into question the existing domestic regulatory scheme and choices, as appears to be the case in trade in many services. Accordingly, nations have been more hesitant to adopt the traditional approach to applying most favored nation and national treatment principles than they have been with trade in goods.

Therefore, from a pragmatic viewpoint a negotiating approach based on some up-front liberalization and disciplines on domestic regulation could have been important. It may be that for this reason trade liberalization and competition law and policy can work in a particularly focused and complementary fashion to promote procompetitive reform of domestic regulation. Although competition authorities will be concerned with promoting competition within the domestic market, trade officials will also be concerned with the relationship between domestic market regulation and export and foreign investment opportunities of domestic firms.

These four factors may not be necessary but rather sufficient conditions for trade and competition policy to work in a complementary fashion in respect of multilateral rule-making. Accordingly, one might suggest that other highly regulated tradable service sectors characterized by network effects (electricity, for example) may be candidates for the ABT approach to multilateral rule-making. I will return to this point later.

Architecture of the ABT

Although the Agreement on Basic Telecommunications is a sectoral agreement with respect to trade in services, its architecture might have implications for both trade in goods and more general multilateral competition rule-making. As discussed above, the ABT builds on the GATS commitment of MFN and national treatment linked to schedules of commitments, transparency, disciplines on the abuse of a monopoly position by a monopoly supplier, and multilateral dispute settlement. In addition the ABT incorporates the Telecommunications Annex to GATS, which addresses issues of access and use of public telecommunications transport networks and services. Similarly, the ABT incorporates the Reference Paper, at least insofar as concerns the fifty-five countries that have agreed to adhere to it. The Reference Paper also addresses issues of anticompetitive practices and interconnection.

It may be worth giving further consideration to this aspect of the Reference Paper. The Reference Paper defines a major supplier as one that has a material effect on price or quantity by virtue of controlling an essential facility or using its market position. No further definition is given of the term "essential facility," suggesting that each jurisdiction has at least some regulatory flexibility. With respect to the major supplier's abuse of its market position, more guidance is given by a nonexhaustive list of anticompetitive practices: cross-subsidization, the misuse of competitors' confidential information (presumably obtained from interconnection or through horizontal collusion), and withholding important information relating to an essential facility. In the context of the application of competition policy in most OECD members, at least as regards telecommunications, this list is probably uncontroversial. However, what is important is that members have agreed to a framework for thinking about anticompetitive practices in telecommunications while retaining considerable freedom to implement their regulatory policy choices. This point holds true even with respect to interconnection issues discussed in the Reference Paper. Again, if there were a failure to meet this obligation permanently, this would likely be a matter for multilateral dispute settlement.

Thus the Reference Paper provides a flexible way of dealing with certain trade and competition concerns. This flexible architecture is also manifested in the dispute settlement provisions. Countries have an obligation to maintain "appropriate measures" to prevent major suppliers from engaging or continuing to engage in anticompetitive practices. There is no obligation with respect to the detailed application of those laws. However, the WTO dispute settlement provisions could address whether a particular measure is "appropriate" without making a judgment about the application of the measure in any particular case. With respect to interconnection issues, countries are required to provide access to an independent regulator, and such regulator is subject to certain other procedural requirements.

Caveats

Three important caveats about the ABT model of dealing with trade and competition concerns can be identified at this stage. First, if governments agree to create mutual obligations to enforce a given set of regulatory principles, they could be viewed as having tied themselves into an established pattern of regulation. This may be appealing from the point of view of opening up market access on a broadly reciprocal basis. However, it also has the potential of locking in a uniform approach in circumstances that might be quite different from country to country. In the context of the ABT and the Reference Paper and of possible future multilateral initiatives that might build on the flexible architecture, this will not necessarily be the case. That is so because the Reference Paper does not set forth a detailed or mechanical common standard for regulation of the telecommunications sector. Rather, it provides an approach to applying principles of competition to the sector while leaving significant freedom and flexibility for members to implement their regulatory policy choices.

This problem, to the extent that it exists, can also be addressed through the design of the regulatory principles that do not apply when a given threshold of diversification in relation to the sources of supply available in a market has been attained. Even so, multilateral uniformity may in some circumstances lead to a suboptimal degree of regulatory intervention. In other words, the regulatory authorities or the governments to which they are ultimately responsible could find that multilateral commitments make regulatory forbearance harder in circumstances where it might otherwise seem desirable. Again, for the reasons already described, in the context of the ABT and the Reference Paper and the more general context of possible future multilateral initiatives that might build on its flexible architecture, there is no a priori reason to expect this to occur.

The third caveat is the risk that regulatory interventions putatively designed to promote competition instead become primarily used to protect competitors. But given the flexible architecture of the ABT and the Reference Paper, there does not appear to be any a priori reason to expect the problem of rent seeking to be worsened by the multilateral agreement. On the contrary, the emerging consensus among trade and competition officials about telecommunications regulation would seem to strengthen rather than weaken the hands of those authorities wrestling with these forms of rent seeking. It must also be recognized that antitrust laws and their enforcement may, in certain jurisdictions (inside and outside the OECD) reflect multiple objectives, including industrial policy considerations. It is also true that antitrust authorities may be subject to some of the problems of capture and political influence faced by other types of regulators.

I have attempted to set forth some of the implications of the ABT for multilateral rule-making with respect to trade and competition policy issues while recognizing that there are discrete factors that have led to the creation of what one commentator has called "a unique and slightly divergent method for the establishment of international competition."[39] Where similar conditions are present, the ABT might provide a useful model for dealing with these issues in other sectors such as electricity.

The Understanding on Financial Services

The Understanding on Financial Services is similar to the Basic Telecommunications Agreement. It has no independent status as a WTO or GATS agreement except to the extent that it has been reproduced into members' schedules of specific commitments as provided for in the GATS Annex on Financial Services.

The understanding sets forth market access provisions with respect to monopoly rights. It provides that in addition to Article VIII of GATS each member "shall list in its schedule pertaining to financial services existing monopoly rights and shall endeavour to eliminate or reduce them."[40] Furthermore, this additional commitment applies to other activities conducted by a public entity for the account or with the guarantee or using the financial resources of the government.

---

39. Rill and others (1998, p. 23).

40. Article B(1) of the Understanding on Domestic Regulation in the Accountancy Sector. Legitimate objectives are defined in Article II:2 as, among other things, the protection of consumers (which includes all users of accounting services and the public generally), the quality of the service, professional competence, and the integrity of the profession.

Disciplines on Domestic Regulation in the Accountancy Sector

The WTO Disciplines on Domestic Regulation in the Accountancy Sector were adopted by the Council on Trade in Services in December 1998. Unlike the Reference Paper or the Financial Services Understanding, the Accounting Disciplines have not yet been incorporated into any country's schedule of commitments. The Working Party on Professional Services continues to develop general disciplines for professional services while retaining the possibility of developing or revising sectoral disciplines, including accountancy. No later than the conclusion of the forthcoming round of services negotiations, the disciplines developed by the WPPS are intended to be integrated into GATS. Until then, members are enjoined, to the fullest extent consistent with their existing legislation, not to take actions that would be inconsistent with these disciplines. As such, their status at present represents that of hortatory guidelines.[41] They do not appear to be subject to the dispute settlement provisions of the WTO. This architecture may serve as a useful precedent in the event that the OECD nonbinding recommendations approach to rule-making for international competition policy were adopted within the WTO.

In addition to that architectural point, the Accounting Disciplines contain provisions on licensing that are similar to concerns of those who enforce competition policy. For instance, they provide that where membership of a professional organization is required to fulfill a legitimate objective specified in the text, members shall ensure that the terms for membership are reasonable and do not include conditions or preconditions unrelated to the fulfillment of such an objective. Furthermore, where membership of a professional organization is required as a prior condition for application for a license (an authorization to practice), the period of membership imposed before the application may be submitted shall be kept to a minimum. Both conditions focus on reducing barriers to entry that could pose both market access and competition problems.[42]

In addition, the market access provisions prohibit, in sectors where market access commitments are undertaken, a member from maintaining or adopting either on the basis of a regional subdivision or on the basis of its entire territory, unless otherwise specified in its schedule, limitations on the number of service suppliers, whether in the form of numerical quotas,

41. World Trade Organization (1998).
42. Disciplines on Domestic Regulation in the Accountancy Sector, S/L/64, December 14, 1998, Article IV:10.

monopolies, exclusive service suppliers, or the requirements of an economic needs test.[43]

This section of the paper has reviewed the competition provisions in GATS and its associated agreements. A main conclusion is that GATS itself may be a strong tool with which to apply competition policy to the liberalization in trade in services. However, certain sectors require additional tailored competitive safeguards to make parties willing to make reciprocal market access concessions. Furthermore, GATS shows some interesting architectural ways of introducing new and complicated subjects into the WTO. This is demonstrated in the sectoral plurilateral commitments in the Reference Paper with respect to basic telecommunications and in the Understanding on Financial Services. On a more basic level the Accounting Disciplines integrate a transitional concept of nonbinding guidance into the framework of WTO agreements. In addition, each of these examples warrants further consideration to determine what competition principles might be applied horizontally within the GATS framework through the Article VI provisions on domestic regulation.

An Expanded GATS Article VI

Article VI of GATS deals with domestic regulation. At its most basic level it provides that in sectors where specific commitments are undertaken, each member shall ensure that all measures of general application affecting trade in services are administered in a reasonable, objective, and impartial manner.[44] Further provisions require each member to maintain or institute as soon as practicable judicial, arbitral, or administrative tribunals or procedures that provide, at the request of an affected service supplier, for the prompt review of, and where justified, appropriate remedies for administrative decisions affecting trade in services. However, these provisions are not be construed to require a member to institute such tribunals or procedures where this would be inconsistent with its constitutional structure or legal system.[45]

Article VI:4 sets out rules to apply to measures relating to qualification requirements and procedures, technical standards, and licensing require-

43. Disciplines on Domestic Regulation in the Accountancy Sector, S/L/64, December 14, 1998, Article XVI:2.

44. Article VI:1.

45. Article VI:2.

ments to ensure that they do not constitute unnecessary barriers to trade in services. The Council for Trade in Services is given the authority to develop any necessary disciplines aimed at ensuring that such requirements are, among other things,

—based on objective and transparent criteria, such as competence and the ability to supply the service;

—not more burdensome than necessary to ensure the quality of the service; and

—in the case of licensing procedures, not in themselves a restriction on the supply of the service.

Pending the agreement on those disciplines, Article V provides that in sectors in which a member has undertaken specific commitments, it shall not apply licensing and qualification requirements and technical standards that nullify or impair such specific commitments.

As currently structured, Article VI applies to measures relating to qualification requirements and procedures, technical standards, and licensing requirements. Competition law and policy may be relevant to all such measures. The further requirement in Article VI is that such measures in domestic regulations not constitute unnecessary barriers to trade in services. Again, competition law and policy can be an important instrumemt in ensuring that these measures are administered in a way that pays particular attention to strategic or other regulatory barriers to trade in services.

The question that emerges is whether in the GATS 2000 negotiations a way can be found to integrate more directly into Article VI certain competition law and policy concerns and other competitive safeguards.[46] Relevant experience may be found in the history of Article VI of GATT 1947, which sets forth the discipline on antidumping measures and the successive interpretations, codes, and understandings that culminated in the Uruguay Round with the Agreement on the Interpretation of Article VI of GATT. One could consider a gradual expansion of the GATS Article VI commitment through a similar iterative process. To the extent that a horizontal agreement on competition policy is not feasible at this time or that an endless series of sectoral agreements with competition policy is not desirable, gradual expansion might be a useful option to consider.

One immediate way of conceptualizing this would be to back the commitments in GATS Article VIII with respect to monopoly leveraging

---

46. See Feketekuty (1999) and chapter 9 of this volume.

and Article IX with respect to anticompetitive practices into an expanded understanding of domestic regulatory requirements. Further insights might be gained from looking at the experience in those sectors where agreements embodying competition policy have already been achieved. However, it should be plainly stated that not all such features as "essential facilities" concepts might properly form part of a generic GATS Article VI competition provision.[47] This half-way provision in a sense would build on the recognition of the ties between competition law and policy and domestic regulation.

Other Sectoral Issues for Competition Policy in GATS

In this section, I briefly review some potential competition policy issues to be addressed in further sectoral GATS negotiations. The analysis is of a summary nature, drawing on GATS sectoral working background notes and recent OECD studies.[48] My purpose is to flag some of the possible competition concerns that might arise as the sectoral negotiations progress. My intention is not to be definitive but rather to suggest some lines of consideration for negotiators.

Distribution Services

A lot can be said about distribution services and the application of competition policy. However, since my goal is not to settle that issue here, I simply pose some questions for further analysis in the event that negotiations on liberalization in this sector are pursued. Do private practices create welfare-reducing barriers to trade in distribution services? If so, is there a case for developing procompetitive regulatory guidelines to address those distortions? Alternatively, would excessively stringent competition policy norms themselves inhibit the development of efficient distribution arrangements? Is it sufficient for national competition law and policy to be administered on a nondiscriminatory basis in examining distribution issues, or does entry into retailing by foreign service providers require some special analysis to account for qualitative differences between foreign and domestic firms?

47. Recent OECD work on competition policy and regulation might also provide some useful insights. See Organization for Economic Cooperation and Development (1999c).

48. The twenty WTO Sectoral Papers on Trade in Services can be found at http://www.wto.org/wto/services/w65.htm.

Postal and Courier Services, Energy Services, and Rail Transport

The postal, energy, and rail transport services sectors are network industries similar to telecommunications.[49] They raise competition concerns ranging from abuse of dominance to precluding access to essential facilities. They may thus be particularly well suited for a consideration of the extension of competitive safeguards similar in type to those set forth in the Reference Paper with respect to Basic Telecommunications.

Air Transport Services

The air transport sector seems to be particularly ripe for competition policy safeguards for the liberalization of trade in services. Among the issues that could be considered are abuse of dominance (by private or state-owned carriers), price fixing, market (slot) allocation, precluding access to and use of essential (ground-handling) facilities, and perhaps even predatory pricing.[50] Some of these concerns might be more suited to the approach taken in the Reference Paper.

Maritime Transport Services

In June 1996 the post–Uruguay Round negotiations on liberalization in maritime transport were suspended pending the resumption of comprehensive negotiations in the context of GATS 2000.[51] Among the issues that could be considered in future negotiations are the application of competition policy safeguards to liner shipping alliances (whether consortiums or conferences), the continued need for exemptions from competition laws, and the enforcement of laws against price fixing and other cartel behavior with respect to harbor services.

Land Transport Services: Road Transport

The road transport services sector is unlike the other transportation services in that it is not inherently a network industry. For that reason,

49. See generally Organization for Economic Cooperation and Development (1999b).
50. See generally Organization for Economic Cooperation and Development (1999d). Competition Policy and International Airport Services, DAFFE/CLP(98)3 (14 May 1999b).
51. WTO, Decision on Maritime Transport Services, adopted by the Council for Trade in Services June 26, 1996, S/L/4, July 3, 1996.

concerns relating to monopolization and abuse of dominance using vertical restraints seem less important than horizontal concerns relating to bid rigging, price fixing, and market allocation. In other words a general competition law should address the market access concerns in this sector. Other possible concerns relate to regulatory standard-setting measures and licensing agreements administered in a discriminatory or unnecessarily restrictive manner to the detriment of foreign entrants. This sector also would seem to illustrate the limitations of a purely sectoral approach to addressing competition concerns. It might be that multimodal regulations have anticompetitive effects.

Environmental Services

Several questions arise from the highly concentrated nature of environmental services in most countries because of the sector's "public monopoly" characteristics. How far do the disciplines of GATS Article VIII ensure that the behavior of monopolies supplying environmental services is not discriminatory? Is there a case for developing certain procompetitive regulatory principles? Are broad exemptions from the application of competition policy necessary to achieve the objectives of the regulations that give rise to this industry in many cases?

Construction and Related Engineering Services

The construction sector raises a number of potential problems for which competition policy safeguards might be considered in future negotiations. These concerns range from bid rigging and other cartel behavior to licensing and standard setting.

Audiovisual Services

With the increased number and variety of network-based services, competition policy also needs to do more to regulate the conduct of audiovisual service providers. However, the evolutionary nature of convergence also means that competition policy may need to be applied with a more constant and detailed attention to market, sectoral, product, and technological evolution. Given the political sensitivity of this sector in some countries, perhaps some benefit could be gained by studying the

balance between the competitive safeguards and universal service requirements in the Reference Paper with respect to Basic Telecommunications.

Advertising, Legal, Architectural and Engineering, Education, and Health and Human Services

The basic approach to issues of licensing in the Accounting Disciplines
might be applicable in such sectors as legal and education services. However, the matters of concern are potentially deeper than just licensing in the
professions. They also include restrictions on advertising and who gets to
participate in the decisionmaking on market regulation. Consideration
might also be given to the transitional architecture of nonbinding guidance
in the Accounting Disciplines to begin to apply competition principles to
cross-border trade in professional services.

Tourism Services

Tourism does not appear at first glance to present the need for any
particular competition policy safeguards. However, in some cases licensing
agreements might be granted in anticompetitive ways, and local or national
service providers might be given preferential treatment that would raise
concerns about monopolization or abuses of dominant provision. The
tourism sector is a good example of how downstream service sectors can
be affected by anticompetitive upstream behavior. Tourism might very well
be affected by anticompetitive distortions caused in transportation or in
advertising. Thus the sector is a good illustration of how a purely sectoral
approach to dealing with competition concerns might not yield the full
benefits of trade in services.

Computer and Related Services

The computer services sector may be characterized by some aspects of
network industries. To that extent it may share some of the same competition concerns about access to essential facilities that were identified in
relation to other service sectors. It is also a sector that may demonstrate the
limitations of a sectoral approach to dealing with competition concerns.
For instance, it may be that restrictions and distortions in another service
sector such as telecommunications also are the source of competitive
distortions in this sector.

I have tried to sketch some preliminary ideas of where competition concerns might arise in various service sectors and where those restrictions might have adverse effects on trade. As negotiations proceed, much more detailed work will have to be done to put flesh on these bones. Table 13-1 represents an attempt to draw some subjective judgments about the relative importance of rudimentary competition concerns in each sector. Each sector is analyzed to give an idea where horizontal concerns (agreements among competitors), vertical concerns (agreements between firms at different levels of production and distribution), abuse of dominance, and exceptions or exemptions from national competition laws might pose problems. The problems are rated from low concern to high concern. At some later stage, one could think of grouping the identified concerns in a way that might be useful for an expanded GATS Article VI. On first impression, however, it appears that simply bringing GATS Articles VIII and IX more closely into the ambit of Article VI would provide a first stab at a more robust approach to achieving procompetitive domestic regulation in a manner that promotes trade in services.

Conclusions

I have examined the implications for GATS of integrating competition policy disciplines in the World Trade Organization. Horizontal rule-making would potentially contribute greatly to the liberalization of trade in services. However, it seems unlikely that comprehensive binding rule-making for horizontal competition will be successful. By contrast, the existing GATS and its associated sectoral agreements are fairly strong instruments for integrating competition policy safeguards into sectoral liberalization initiatives and perhaps into domestic regulation by some gradual expansion of Article VI. In this context, I suggested that in thinking about Article VI, we should scrutinize the experience under Articles VIII and IX and the provisions in the Basic Telecommunications Reference Paper, Financial Services Undertaking, and Accounting Disciplines. If an incremental sectoral approach to integrating competition policy into the WTO is pursued, I showed possible issues for consideration in each of the service sectors identified by the Council for Trade in Services.

Finally, this discussion also showed that the provisions in the Basic Telecommunications Reference Paper, Financial Services Undertaking, and Accounting Disciplines offer useful architectural approaches to thinking

Table 13-1. *Potential Service Sector Competition Concerns*

Service sector	Concerns			
	Horizontal	*Vertical*	*Abuse of dominance*	*Exceptions/exemptions*
Distribution	Medium	High	Medium	Low
Postal and courier	Low	Medium	High	High
Energy	Low	High	High	High
Transport				
Land				
Road	High	Medium	Low	Medium
Rail	Medium	Medium	High	High
Air	High	High	High	High
Maritime	High	High	High	High
Environmental	Medium	Medium	High	Medium
Construction and related engineering	High	Low	Medium	Low
Audiovisual	Low	Low	High	High
Advertising	Medium	Low	Low	Medium
Legal	High	Low	Low	Medium
Architectural and engineering	High	Low	Low	Medium
Education	Low	Low	Low	High
Health and human	High	Medium	Medium	High
Tourism	Medium	Medium	Medium	Medium
Computer and related services	Low	Medium	Medium	Low

395

about horizontal rule-making in competition policy within the WTO. These approaches apply both to binding and nonbinding rules.

Whatever the approach taken to integrating competition policy disciplines into the WTO, it will be difficult to achieve the full gains from the liberalization of trade in services without some serious consideration of issues of competition. It may well be that without the integration of competition policy disciplines in some manner, it will also be very difficult politically for countries to make the necessary reciprocal market access concessions that are essential to move beyond the status quo.

References

Arai, Hisamitsu. 1999. "Global Competition Policy as a Basis for a Borderless Market Economy." Address to the Columbia University Conference "The Next Trade Negotiating Round: Examining the Agenda for Seattle." New York, July.

Barshefsky, Charlene. 1998. Address to the "Global Trading System: A GATT 50th Anniversary Forum." Brookings Institution, March.

Brittan, Leon. 1999a. "The Contribution of the WTO Millennium Round to Globalization: An EU View." Speech to the First Herbert Batliner Symposium, "Europe in the Era of Globalization: Economic Order and Economic Law." Vienna, April.

————. 1999b. "The Need for a Multilateral Framework of Competition Rules." Address to the OECD Conference on Trade and Competition. Paris, June.

Cottier, Thomas. 1999. "SPS Risk Assessment and Risk Management in WTO Dispute Settlement: Experience and Lessons." Paper prepared for the Conference on Risk Analysis and International Agreements. Melbourne, February.

European Commission. 1998. "Fourth Report on the Implementation of the Telecommunications Regulatory Package." December.

Feketekuty, Geza. 1999. "Competition Policy and the WTO: Implications of Recent Developments in the Services Sector." Paper prepared for the Third WTO Symposium on Competition Policy and the Multilateral Trading System. Geneva, April.

Horlick, Gary N. 1998. "The Consultation Phase of WTO Dispute Resolution: A Private Practitioner's View." *International Law* 32 (Fall 1998): 685.

————. 1999. "The World Trading System at the Crossroad of Science and Politics." Paper prepared for the Columbia University Conference "The Next Trade Negotiating Round: Examining the Agenda for Seattle." New York, July.

Jenny, Frederic. 1999. "Globalization, Competition and Trade Policy: Issues and Challenges." Paper prepared for the Columbia University Conference "The Next Trade Negotiating Round: Examining the Agenda for Seattle." New York, July.

Klein, Joel I. 1997a. "Criminal Enforcement in a Globalized Economy." February. http://www.usdoj.gov/atr/public/speeches/jik97220.htm.

————. 1997b. "Anticipating the Millennium: International Antitrust Enforcement at the End of the Twentieth Century." October. http://www.usdoj.gov/atr/public/speeches/1233.htm.

———. 1999. "A Reality Check on Antitrust Rules in the World Trade Organization, and a Practical Way Forward on International Antitrust." Address to the OECD Conference on Trade and Competition. Paris, June.

Low, Patrick. 1995. "Multilateral Rules on Competition: What Can We Learn from the Telecommunications Sector?" Paper prepared for an OECD workshop, "Trade Policy for a Globalizing Economy." Santiago, Chile, November.

Low, Patrick, and Aaditya Mattoo. 1998. "Reform in Basic Telecommunications and the WTO Negotiations: The Asian Experience." WTO Staff Working Paper ERAD9801. February.

Mehta, K. 1999."The Role of Competition in a Globalized Trade Environment." Speech at the Third WTO Symposium on Competition Policy and the Multilateral System. Geneva, April.

Melamed, A. Douglas. 1999. "International Cooperation in Competition Law and Policy: What Can Be Achieved at the Bilateral, Regional and Multilateral Levels?" Speech to the Third WTO Symposium on Competition Policy and the Multilateral System." Geneva, April.

Organization for Economic Cooperation and Development. 1996. *Competition in Telecommunications.* OCDE/GD(96)114. Paris.

———. 1997a. *Communications Outlook 1997.* Paris.

———. 1997b. *Developments in Telecommunications: An Update Aide Memoire.* Paris.

———. 1997c. *Information Technology Outlook 1997.* Paris.

———. 1999a. *OECD Competition Elements in International Trade Agreements: A Post-Uruguay Round Overview of WTO Agreements.* OECD/COM/TD/DAFFE/CLP(98)26/FINAL. Paris.

———. 1999b. "Promoting Competition in Postal Services Background Note." DAFFE/CLP/WP2(99)1. Paris, January.

———. 1999c. *Promoting Competition in Sectors with a Non-Competitive Component: Report by the Secretariat.* DAFFE/CLP/WP2(99)4. Paris, April.

———. 1999d. *Competition Policy and International Airport Services.* DAFFE/CLP(98)3. Paris, May.

Pitofsky, Robert. 1998. "Competition Policy in a Global Economy: Today and Tomorrow." Remarks to the European Institute's Eighth Annual Transatlantic Seminar on Trade and Investment. Washington, November.

Rill, James F., and others. 1998. "Institutional Responsibilities Affecting Competition in the Telecommunications Industry: A Practicing Lawyer's Perspective." Draft Paper prepared for the European University Institute 1998 EU Competition Workshop.

Smith, Patricia. 1999. Remarks to a Symposium at the University of Toronto. May.

Spiwak, Lawrence J. 1998. "From International Competitive Carrier to the WTO: A Survey of the FCC's International Telecommunications Policy Initiatives 1985–1998." 51 *Federal Communications Law Journal* 111.

Takigawa, Toshiaki. 1998. "The Impact of the WTO Telecommunications Agreement on U.S. and Japanese Telecommunications Regulations." Journal of World Trade 33 (December).

U.S. Trade Representative. 1999. *1999 Report to the President on Foreign Trade Barriers.* Washington.

Van Miert, Karel. 1998. "The WTO and Competition Policy: The Need to Consider Negotiations." Address to ambassadors to the WTO. Geneva, April.

Von Finkenstein, Konrad. 1998. Speaking notes to the International Competition Policy
    Advisory Committee to the Attorney General. Washington, November.
World Trade Organization. 1998. *Report to the Council for Trade in Services on the De-
    velopment of Disciplines on Domestic Regulation in the Accountancy Sector.* S/WPPS/4.
    December.

14 | Global Electronic Commerce and GATS: The Millennium Round and Beyond

WILLIAM J. DRAKE *and*
KALYPSO NICOLAIDÏS

O F ALL THE TRENDS SWEEPING the international trade environment, none has engendered more discussion (and hype) than the rapid expansion of global electronic commerce (GEC). The Secretariat of the World Trade Organization (WTO) and the U.S. Department of Commerce predict that GEC—the production, advertising, sale and distribution of products via electronic networks—will soon will reach $300 billion.[1] Some analysts would argue that this is a conservative estimate, but either way a significant amount of money is involved, and the effects of GEC activity on companies, markets, and economies around the world is substantial.

GEC is not a new phenomenon. Businesses have long employed telecommunications networks to produce and market goods and services and have traded them internationally by telephone, fax, and so on. Moreover, the explosion since the 1970s of business data communications via leased cir-

We would like to thank Virginia Haufler, Michiko Hayashi, Pierre Sauvé, Rachel Thompson, Lee Tuthill, and Dimitri Ypsilanti for their helpful comments on an earlier version of this essay.

1. The WTO suggests that the "value of electronic commerce has catapulted from virtually zero to a predicted US$300 billion in the ten years up to the turn of the century." See WTO (1998a, p. 2). It is not entirely clear how the figure for ten years ago could have been zero, unless one is referring solely to commerce over the Internet. For its part, the U.S. Department of Commerce more straightforwardly predicts a value of $300 billion by 2002. See WTO (1998a, p. 7).

399

cuits and later, private networks, significantly increased the commercial activity conducted over networks in a wide variety of sectors. What is new, though, and is driving the explosion of GEC is the Internet. The rapid globalization, commercialization, and mass popularization of the Internet since 1991 has transformed completely the information and communications technology (ICT) environment, which in turn is having a profound effect on all realms of global economic activity that rely on ICT goods and services. Indeed, the Internet is so central to GEC that it has become common—albeit misleadingly—to use the term "global electronic commerce" as a synonym for Internet commerce (pity the forgotten telephone).

The purpose of this chapter is to examine some of the issues that GEC, and especially Internet commerce, raise for the General Agreement on Trade in Services (GATS) in the upcoming Millennium Round and beyond. To be sure, GEC is not a sector and it is not confined to services; agricultural, manufactured, and intangible goods are also traded electronically, so there are implications for GATT as well. Further, the growth of GEC raises interesting questions with respect to the Agreement on Trade-Related Aspects of Intellectual Property Rights (TRIPs) as well as for other WTO instruments and issues. But the focus of this book is on GATS, so an assessment of these other aspects will have to wait for another occasion.

We argue that GATS may need to be reformed in important respects to more clearly apply to trade in GEC services. This trade includes electronic transmission services (telecommunications and Internet access), content services (banking, entertainment, and so on, where the substantive service is directly delivered over a network), and distribution services (in which goods and services are ordered electronically but delivered in nonelectronic form).

In arguing for GATS reform, we are mindful of two constraints. First, from a technical standpoint, it may be that not all gaps or ambiguities in GATS coverage need to or can be resolved in the next trade round. Its explosive growth notwithstanding, Internet-based GEC is still a new phenomenon. The technology is changing rapidly, and transactional dynamics, business models, and national policies are still in flux. Under these circumstances it may be difficult for WTO negotiators to devise rules that promote trade and remain appropriate in the years ahead. Moreover, WTO members will confront many other difficult issues during the next round, including moving beyond the standstill commitments of the Uruguay Round to roll back trade restrictions in line with the existing GATS framework.

Second, from a political standpoint, some of the ideas we offer run counter to the prevailing political winds. Indeed, while members' negotiating strategies are still taking shape, both the United States and the European Union (EU) could find points to disagree with in our assessment. This is inevitable because we have attempted to evaluate the issues in terms of strengthening the multilateral system, not in terms of promoting players' interests or identifying opportunities to cut a deal. In consequence, some of our suggestions will probably be ignored, at least in the coming round. We nevertheless hope that by outlining various challenges we can contribute to the debate, which is only in its early stages, about how the trade system will have to adapt to GEC in the years ahead. Thus the "beyond" in this chapter's title is a recognition that some problems we identify may have to wait until the round after next, if then.

The chapter is organized as follows. The first section briefly discusses the WTO's Global Electronic Commerce Work Program and then outlines four nonmutually exclusive options for dealing with the various services issues associated with GEC. The sections that follow take up the items explored in the work program with respect to GATS. The second section addresses the definitional and classification problems raised by the electronic network environment. The third examines the applicability to GEC of the core GATS disciplines concerning market access, regulation, and the like. Finally, the fourth section assesses two additional questions of particular interest to developing countries: whether to apply customs duties to electronic transmissions and how to increase their participation in GEC.

The Institutionalization of Global Electronic Commerce in the WTO

This section briefly discusses the WTO's Global Electronic Commerce work program and then outlines four options (not mutually exclusive) for dealing with the various services issues associated with GEC.

The Global Electronic Commerce Work Program

In May 1998 the WTO's second ministerial conference at Geneva adopted a declaration on GEC. The declaration had two major components. The first pertained to the application of customs duties to electronic transmissions across borders. To date, governments have not attempted to treat such transmissions—via telephone, fax, or data communications services—as imports subject to border duties. With the rapid growth of the Internet the United States has argued that breaking with that tradition would send the wrong signal and risk stifling GEC early in its development. As such, it proposed a standstill on the application of new duties until the next ministerial meeting, an initiative that other industrialized countries supported. Many developing countries were unsure as to whether this was in their interests, but because GEC over the Internet is for them a nascent and still negligible phenomenon, they were willing to go along with a temporary ban.

The 1998 ministerial meeting approved a Declaration on Global Electronic Commerce stating that "we also declare that Members will continue their current practice of not imposing customs duties on electronic transmissions."[2] Governments remained free to levy duties on goods ordered over the Internet and shipped through conventional means, but they were to defer doing this with products shipped electronically over networks. The moratorium is to be reviewed at the Seattle ministerial meeting, where a decision will be made on its extension or codification as a permanent ban.

Second, the declaration called on the WTO's General Council to adopt at its September 1998 session "a comprehensive work programme to examine all trade-related issues relating to global electronic commerce." The council was to produce a report on the progress of work done under this program, including any recommendations for action, for consideration at the Seattle meeting.

Adopted on September 25, the work program laid out items to be examined by WTO organs. The agenda was not designed to be a far-reaching exploration of every trade-related issue associated with GEC, but instead gave priority to assessing the adequacy of WTO instruments. The Council for Trade in Goods was to consider seven issues with respect to GATT's coverage of GEC: market access, valuation issues, import licensing procedures, customs duties, standards, rules of origin, and classificaiton issues. The Council for TRIPs was to address the protection and enforcement of copyright and related rights, trademarks, and new technologies and access to technologies. The Committee on Trade and Development was to examine the effects of GEC on the trade and economic prospects of developing countries, especially their small and medium-sized enter-

---

2. World Trade Organization (1998b).

prises; the challenge of increasing the participation of developing countries as exporters in GEC; the use of information technology in the integration of developing countries in the multilateral trading system; the development implications of GEC's potential impact on traditional means of distributing physical goods; and the financial implications for developing countries.

The Council for Trade in Services was given twelve items to consider with respect to GATS's current and future application to GEC services: scope, including mode of supply (Article I); most favored nation, or MFN (Article II); transparency (Article III); increasing the participation of developing countries (Article IV); domestic regulation, standards, and recognition (Articles VI and VII); competition (Articles VIII and IX); the protection of privacy and public morals and the prevention of fraud (Article XIV); market access commitments on the electronic supply of services, including commitments on basic and value-added telecommunications services and distribution services (Article XVI); national treatment (Article XVII); access to and use of public telecommunications transport networks and services (the Annex on Telecommunications); customs duties; and classification issues.[3] The sections following address each of these subjects.

Dealing with Global Electronic Commerce in GATS

The various bodies' interim reports to the General Council in the spring of 1999 suggest that there has been considerable progress in thinking through the often complex issues raised by GEC. Governments are collectively learning about conceptual issues and their own interests, a process that has similarities to the debates about trade in services that occurred before and during the Uruguay Round.[4] Some of the questions that have been explored clearly do not require any particular sort of action in the coming round. But what about those matters on which the merits of action are at least debatable? How should WTO negotiators proceed?

We outline four institutional approaches to dealing with GATS's application to GEC services. To reiterate, these are not mutually exclusive options: no one approach would provide a satisfactory response to all

---

3. World Trade Organization, General Council (1998).

4. On the nature of those debates and their significance for the eventual GATS agreement see Drake and Nicolaïdis (1992).

the outstanding issues. Rather it is a matter of mix and match, with some options being well suited to some issues and others to others. In our view the optimal outcome in this round would comprise a blending of all four.

RELY ON THE EXISTING GATS FRAMEWORK.   A first option is simply to rely on the disciplines set out in the current GATS. Any clarification of their application to GEC's trade in services aspects would be pursued in two contexts. First, the issues might be sorted out in the scheduling exercise, with solutions being built into the national commitments. Second, the dispute settlement mechanism would be important. Decisions interpreting how the principles apply to GEC would be made case by case, and their accumulation would help to provide order and stability in the near term and to clarify any gaps in the disciplines that could be filled in, with the benefit of experience, in an ensuing round of negotiations.

For Millennium Round negotiators this is the easiest solution. Sticking with the status quo would allow governments to focus their energies on broadening, deepening, and implementing existing national commitments under GATS. This approach is also appealing for governments and other stakeholders who worry that the pace of technological development will render obsolete or counterproductive any new trade rules negotiators devise, especially if they are unduly restrictive. In this view it would be better to let the Internet mature, business practices stabilize, and any trade problems become manifest before attempting to establish tailored disciplines in GATS or other WTO instruments.

Others, however, might argue that the easiest solution is not necessarily the best and that the current GATS framework does not provide enough clarity and precision to deal with the unique properties of Internet-based commerce between now and the trade round after next. If this is true, when conflicts arise the dispute settlements mechanism might be placed in the position of having to legislate, potentially on very sensitive issues, rather than interpret existing agreements. Of course, the panels could always exercise restraint and return a "can't rule" verdict when GATS does not provide adequate guidance, but that would hardly be an optimal solution in cases where WTO rules really are needed to promote trade or legitimate regulatory objectives. In this view it would be better for WTO members to express their collective intent through a negotiated agreement on how GEC should be governed, ideally one that is flexible enough to accommodate a rapidly changing environment.

REVISE THE GATS PRINCIPLES. A second option is to revise the GATS principles to address the most pressing unanswered questions raised by GEC. If there are situations where the general obligations and disciplines (GODs) and other provisions are too broadly stated to be clear about Internet-based transactions or are manifestly out of synchronization with them, negotiators could do some tinkering with the wording or even add to the Articles of Agreement.

If done correctly, selective revisions of GATS might solve any problems created by a mismatch between the rules and the game being played. These revisions might help mitigate any concerns about dispute settlement panels not having enough guidance to render well-grounded decisions. After all, the realignment of multilateral frameworks and changing operational environments is not uncommon in other domains of international cooperation, and in principle it could also be pursued in the WTO.

However, this road could also lead to problems. Technically, it could be difficult to balance the needs to address ambiguities regarding GEC and to avoid overly detailed language that is ill suited to other contexts. The GODs are broadly framed to apply across sectors and modes of delivery. Loading them up with provisions geared toward particular kinds of transactions might be a mistake. And politically, launching a new debate about the fundamentals of the agreement could open a Pandora's box of competing objectives and demands. Thus given that GATS is only five years old, is replete with shallow stand-still commitments, and remains largely untested, one could argue that it would be better to let the principles be for the time being.

ADD A NEW GEC INSTRUMENT TO GATS. A third option is to add a new instrument to GATS that would deal with the unique properties of the network environment. It could take one of two forms. First, negotiators could establish an annex on GEC alongside the other GATS annexes. A minimalist version might entail broad principles that are specific to Internet-based and other forms of GEC, such as a permanent ban on the applications of customs duties to electronic transmissions, strengthened transparency requirements, guidelines for determining applicable national jurisdiction in the event of regulatory disputes, and so on. A more ambitious version might involve detailed rules on how GATS principles apply in potentially ambiguous circumstances.

An annex could provide a more targeted, coherent, and readily understood set of rights and obligations than would be achieved by selectively revising current GATS principles. However, some might argue that attempting to develop an annex would invite governments to add unnecessary provisions or that the result would be to ghettoize GEC issues as being somehow apart from the rest of the framework.

Alternatively, negotiators could create a GEC reference paper akin to the one agreed upon in 1997 for basic telecommunications. Such a paper could contain the same substantive principles and rules that an annex would have; the difference would simply be that governments would choose whether to be bound by the new disciplines in the additional commitments sections of their national schedules.

Clearly, an annex is the stronger and more demanding of these two forms. All WTO members could be required to apply its provisions to all their scheduled commitments. A reference paper would allow governments at different stages of development or with varying degrees of interest in openness to choose their level of commitment at the outset in the hope that they would choose full participation later on. Such differences in obligations might be a blessing in terms of facilitating negotiations and bringing governments on board at a comfortable pace, but they might also be a curse in the near term because they would not promote an open and global system subject to consistent norms.

PURSUE HORIZONTAL REFORMS OF WTO INSTRUMENTS.   A fourth option would be to look beyond GATS and focus on horizontal reforms that cut across the major WTO instruments. There is growing concern that GATS, GATT, and TRIPS are unduly fragmented because they involve varying levels of liberalization, sometimes inconsistent commitments on related transactions, conceptual gaps, and other disparities.[5] Such problems may take on particular urgency with respect to certain aspects of GEC, especially the issues of classifying digital products and promoting technological neutrality (ensuring that products are treated the same regardless of the technological means used to deliver them). Thus negotiators could attempt to devise harmonized solutions across instruments in certain cases or, much more ambitiously, address any relevant GEC issues in the context of a horizontal revamping of WTO instruments.

From a technical standpoint, a horizontal approach to selected GEC problems, or even to the WTO architecture, may well make sense. Developing coherent disciplines that cut across goods, services, investment, and

5. For an argument along these lines, see Pierre Sauvé and Robert Stern's overview to this volume.

intellectual property issues has a particular appeal in the ICT environment where technological change has frequently rendered obsolete artificial delineations between systems and services that were devised by governments for regulatory purposes. In the future, one can expect instances in which the lack of technological neutrality and the presence of differing obligations across goods and services generate conflict—the Canada-U.S. magazines case may be a harbinger in this regard.[6]

But politically it could prove difficult to develop horizontal disciplines in the next round. Making the existing GATS work is challenging enough, and filling in its potential gaps with respect to issues such as GEC would be even more demanding. To pursue cross-instrument reforms would be harder still in some respects, and it is unclear whether negotiators would be able to invest the energy needed to pursue a macroeconomic restructuring of WTO instruments this time around. Nevertheless, even if broad revamping is impossible, it may turn out that in a few instances a horizontal approach is the only logical solution to GEC issues.

Definitions and Classifications

We now turn to those aspects of the WTO's GEC work program relevant to GATS. We start with two questions related to definition and classification. How should we distinguish between goods and services and thus GATT and GATS jurisdiction in an era where both goods and services increasingly cross borders in digital form? How should GEC be classified within GATS itself?

Classifying between GATS and GATT

As was recognized during the Uruguay Round, it is sometimes difficult to distinguish clearly between goods and services.[7] The boundary gets

6. The Canadian government's reliance on GATS to curtail imports of so-called split-run was rebuked by the WTO Appellate Body on the basis of GATT. Canadian policy was to prevent Canadian advertisers from buying advertising space at dumped prices in magazines with little Canadian editorial content, thereby confining the advertisers to the Canadian magazine market. Canada maintained that the measure was covered under GATS because it related to advertising and that Canada had not scheduled any liberalization commitments. But the Appellate Body argued that the measure nullified benefits under GATT because the inability to sell magazines, a good, was what was at stake.

7. This is especially obvious when goods and services are bundled together and jointly marketed or otherwise commingled in a given commercial transaction. For a broad discussion of the problem see Grubel (1987).

especially fuzzy when the products take the form of digital information. The rapid growth of GEC raises this problem anew and with increased urgency. International trade in such products could expand significantly in the years ahead, especially as the next generation of Internet infrastructure is created, but market access commitments will be needed to establish a facilitating environment. Under what instrument should commitments be made? Are digital information products services subject to GATS or goods subject to GATT?

Certainly, a great deal of global economic commerce unambiguously consists of services. But how do we classify products normally recognized as goods—books, magazines, and software—when they are delivered or downloaded in digital form and then embodied in a tangible medium or are simply stored on a computer? What about television programs, movies, and music? Should they all be treated as services? Alternatively, should they be considered as goods if they are embodied in a physical medium such as videotapes or compact discs but as services when they are supplied and consumed simultaneously rather than being stored?

This problem has become a political issue on which governments and international businesses are at times divided. The European Commission argues that all transmissions of digital products constitute services and fall under the scope of GATS. In addition to presumably being convinced of this on the technical merits, the commission has some other factors to consider. For example, the "all services" approach is embodied in the EU's single market agenda, and the EU is, of course, keen to ensure consistency between its internal reforms and its WTO commitments.

Moreover, the European Union excluded audio-visual services from its liberalization commitments in the Uruguay Round at the urging of various national ministries of culture. A classification that could result in television programs, movies, and music being treated as goods would allow foreign suppliers to operate under GATT rules and bypass this carve-out under GATS. Particularly with future services negotiations falling under mixed rather than exclusive EU competence, France's dogged insistence on the point is certainly a constraint. Further, a services classification would ensure that EU policies on privacy protection and so on apply to the supply of digital products. And given that GATT is stricter on quantitative limitations and that its market access and national treatment principles are GODs rather than negotiated specific commitments as in GATS, acknowledging that digital products can be goods may be perceived as a recipe for a flood of imports from the dominant supplier of such items—the United States.

Predictably, the U.S. government has raised an eyebrow about the European position and has suggested that "given the broader reach of WTO disciplines accorded by the GATT . . . there may be an advantage to a GATT versus GATS approach to such products which could provide for a more trade-liberalizing outcome for electronic commerce."[8] The business community appears divided: for example, while some in the U.S. software industry argue that their offerings must be treated as goods, others in the private sector maintain that all electronically transmitted products should be classified as services. The Alliance for Global Business and the International Chamber of Commerce have remained neutral thus far and have called for further study of the matter.

The WTO Secretariat is of course neutral but has prepared a background note that leans toward an all-services classification. One may speculate as to whether there are organizational reasons for this interpretation, but what really matters is the reasoning. The secretariat argues that the only issue is the character and treatment of electronic transmission itself. "What is done with the information after downloading is another matter. If hard copies are produced, whether legally or not, this is a manufacturing process resulting in the production of goods, into which the electronic transmission could be seen as a services input."[9] Presumably, when a program is downloaded, what is sold is (at least in part) the electronic transmission itself. But what consumers are buying from Disney is Mickey Mouse, not an electronic transmission, which is incidental to the transaction.

Certainly, it is not obvious that there is an intrinsic difference between downloaded music or movies and CDs or videotapes bought at a store. Moreover, newspapers, CDs, and so on have long been manufactured through a process involving the international transmission of data over private networks to production facilities. If transmission to a printing company is part of a trade in goods transaction, why would transmission to an individual consumer be trade in services? It would seem that a good has been sold irrespective of whether it was intangible on delivery or of who made it tangible afterwards.

There are some ways to proceed. First, negotiators could leave it to dispute settlement panels to decide which products are goods and which are services. In our view it would be better for the panels to be used to

8. World Trade Organization, General Council (1999a, p. 5).
9. World Trade Organization, Council for Trade in Services (1998, pp. 10–11).

interpret WTO members' collective intent as expressed in WTO instruments than to force governments to legislate on such fundamental issues because governments cannot reach agreement, especially insofar as goods and services are not defined in the instruments. Second, negotiators could establish a new category of "hybrids" for products that have the properties of both goods and services. This might seem to be the most sound approach conceptually, and it could contribute to promoting the horizontal consistency of WTO instruments. But it might also add unneeded complexity, risk undermining the individual coherence of both GATS and GATT, and make bargaining more difficult. Third, one could argue, as Indonesia and Singapore have suggested, that such products "be simply considered as trade in intellectual property rights and not be classified as a good or a service."[10] But this may be fudging the issue, and given the nature of the TRIPs agreement, it would not seem to contribute heavily to the cause of trade liberalization.

By default, then, the fourth and most difficult option seems unavoidable: negotiators should define and agree on clear criteria differentiating goods from services. They may need to tackle issues of consistency between GATS and GATT in the next round anyway, so sorting out this issue seems an obvious starting point. In effect, this is a question of technological neutrality between goods and services and not only within services.

In our view an operational definition must include both physical and contractual considerations. Two criteria that may be relevant are that digital products can be categorized as goods if they become locally stored and transferable between buyers. "Locally stored" means that the product is downloaded onto a physical medium. It need not take on a tangible form: a magazine, CD, or movie can be downloaded onto a computer and controlled by the consumer without any involvement by the producer and without making a separately packaged hard copy. But even this simple distinction raises problems. For example, companies are developing the means to transmit on-line movies that can remain on a consumer's hard drive either for a few days as a rental or permanently as a purchase.

"Transferable" means that the value of the product can be preserved independently of the initial consumer and transferred to another consumer without the intervention of the producer. An airline ticket is a part of a service that is bound to a specific person unless and until the seller transfers it to another. An architect's drawing or a teacher's comments on a paper in

10. World Trade Organization, General Council (1999b, p. 2).

a long distance course are services that are intrinsically bound to the input of the buyer. But downloaded instructions for do-it-yourself learning or textbooks would not be services under the definition. This criterion does not reserve the feature of customization for services: a CD can be downloaded in a customized form and still be of value to another customer. It is still off the shelf in that the initial customization is not absolutely specific to a given customer and that the producer need not intervene again in the customization process.

In short, the definition that we suggest is that a product delivered electronically must be considered as a good if it is locally stored and transferable between buyers, that is if its function and contractual value become independent from the intervention of the supplier at the time of transaction.

The political problem is that classifying such arrays of digital bits as goods would fail to address European concerns that audiovisual products are part of national culture and ought not to be treated in the same way as classic goods. Other governments would agree to a solution involving a cultural exception for both goods and services, but this seems unlikely. The EU may, however, be less concerned about music, games, software, news, and the like, so there could be room for at least some progress. In any event, clarification of the boundary could be effected through several of the institutional options we have listed.

Classifying within GATS

Related issues concern the classification of GEC services and their supply within GATS. Article I (Scope and Definition) specifies that GATS covers any service in any sector except those supplied in the exercise of government authority, and that its disciplines apply to measures affecting trade in services that are taken by central, regional, or local governments and authorities as well as by nongovernmental bodies exercising authority delegated by such governments. Moreover, trade in services is defined as the supply of services (a) from the territory of one member into the territory of another member (cross-border); (b) in the territory of one member to the service consumer of any other member (consumption abroad); (c) by a service supplier of one member through commercial presence in the territory of another member; and (d) by a service supplier or one member through the presence of a natural person in the territory of another member. This formulation can cover all services relevant to GEC.

And indeed, as the WTO's GEC report points out, a wide range of e-commerce services are already covered by existing commitments.[11]

At least three interesting categories of questions arise. First, there are a number of services associated with GEC that have been developed since the Uruguay Round. It is not entirely clear whether existing commitments in more generically defined sectors automatically extend to them. For example, as the United States has asked, "do Web-hosting services, electronic authentication services, or data 'push' services fall under any traditional categories such as value-added services or data processing, or would more explicit commitments provide valuable certainty for the provision of these services?"[12] Some WTO members also wonder whether the activities of firms that administer and assign Internet domain names and IP addresses are covered as "measures" subject to such GATS disciplines as MFN and transparency, or whether they should be explicitly covered to the extent that they can be said to occur under authority delegated by governments.

Moreover, the Internet allows for a great deal of bundling between sectors. In these circumstances it is not entirely clear what services ought to be bound: only the "primary" services or any associated content services as well? In the same vein, should back-office services such as payment and encryption services be classified separately or as an integral part of each sector?[13] When services are intrinsically bundled, should concessions and access rights also be bundled? WTO negotiators may need to sort these and related issues out while scheduling commitments.

Second, discussions in the course of the work program have emphasized that GEC can be involved in all four modes of delivery. Some observers are wondering whether this raises any questions about existing commitments on mode 3 and mode 4. If a member has agreed to allow market entry via commercial presence or the movement of natural persons, do the suppliers automatically have a right to provide electronic services within the member's territory? Some clarification during the scheduling process may be required here as well.

Third, as experience in the financial sector has already demonstrated, GEC raises a dilemma about the boundary between modes 1 and 2. With

11. World Trade Organization (1998, p. 51).

12. World Trade Organization, General Council (1999b, p. 2).

13. Rachel Thompson suggests that other examples of bundled services might include Internet access services, the operation of server farms, rich e-mail, electronic data interchange bulletin boards, on-line auctions, community groups on the Web, museum and cultural services, and electronic books. See Organization for Economic Cooperation and Development (1999).

the mass popularization of the Internet, millions of customers can now "virtually visit" a foreign country and import services, so the question of whether the service is being delivered within or outside the territory of the consumer gets blurry. Although the question is interesting, the practical consequences are more pressing. As the WTO Secretariat notes,

> There is no operational need, in the administration of GATS, to classify transactions according to the modes of supply, though it may be interesting to do so for statistical purposes. The real function of the modes is to categorize commitments in national schedules. The question of the mode under which a transaction takes place only becomes important if there is disagreement about the legitimacy of a measure taken by a Member affecting the transaction, in which case the measure would be judged against the Member's commitments.[14]

Not surprisingly, there is a political dimension to this issue. In the Uruguay Round the commitments undertaken under mode 1 were often limited, in part because many governments preferred that suppliers enter their markets through commercial presence. Mode 2 commitments tended to be stronger, although most governments were probably not assuming they applied to electronic transactions when they were made. The United States, which is the leading exporter of GEC services, has expressed interest in the idea that mode 2 commitments are applicable, but some governments appear reluctant to embrace this interpretation.

Aside from its implications for the scheduling of commitments, the boundary problem also raises the problem of determining which nation's legal and regulatory jurisdiction applies to a given transaction. In general, and pending exceptions, if a transaction is classified under mode 1, the jurisdiction of the buyer applies; if a transaction is classified under mode 2, the jurisdiction of the seller applies. In the latter case, by "moving" to the seller's territory the buyer has willingly put himself under the seller's home jurisdiction. Determining the applicable jurisdiction for remote transactions is a key problem to sort out, especially because the solution chosen will bear on consumer protection and other important matters.

There are at least three choices. First, some observers have suggested the negotiators might be able to sidestep the problem by simply listing identical commitments on both modes 1 and 2. But this would be an ugly solution and would not resolve the jurisdictional dimension with any

14. World Trade Organization, Council for Trade in Services (1998, p. 2).

clarity. Second, in one of his chapters in this book, Geza Feketekuty has suggested that consideration be given to adding a new, fifth mode of supply for the Internet. The reasoning is clear, but this approach arguably risks ghettoizing GEC somewhat, and there might be problems in defining the boundaries between mode 1 and the new mode.

The third option is for negotiators to define an unambiguous criterion for distinguishing between modes 1 and 2. A simple solution would be to amend Article I by specifying that mode 2 involves the physical presence of the person being serviced in another member's territory. Some may argue that this is actually too simple; for example, what if a person's blood or tissue is sent abroad for testing? Is this not the movement of a person? It seems to us that what is moving here is simply data, and that if the person remains at home for diagnosis and treatment, it is a definite mode 1 scenario. A more practical problem with this option might be what to do if a WTO member argues that its original commitments were based on a different understanding of the mode 1–mode 2 boundary, but this may not be too controversial because the effect is to narrow down the more liberal mode 2 commitments.

To ensure that this solution does not reduce the overall openness in the trading system, it would be imperative to make a major push to enrich the commitments on mode 1. Whether the risk of such an effort's failing would make our solution unacceptable to parties arguing for a mode 2 approach to on-line transactions is another question.

Competition and Regulation in Networked Markets

A second set of issues addressed by the GEC work program deals with the applicability of core GATS principles to electronic commerce. These include market and network access, competition, likeness, the necessity test with regard to regulation, recognition and harmonization, and legitimate domestic regulation.

Access to and Use of Telecommunications Transport Networks and Services

Conditions in the electronic network environment obviously have a major impact on the ability of individuals and organizations to engage in GEC. The dominant incumbent public telecommunications operators

(PTOs) in particular have the ability to employ restrictions that effectively limit the value of market access commitments across the board, that is in network access and transport services, electronic content services, and distribution services. As such, assessing the adequacy of GATS in relation to telecommunications services has been a critical part of the GEC work program. In addition to the application of the general obligations and disciplines, two targeted instruments are crucial: the Telecommunications Annex, and the Reference Paper that was adopted by fifty-seven countries (as additional commitments) during the Group on Basic Telecommunications negotiations that concluded in February 1997.

Arguably, the Telecommunication Annex is the most user-oriented component of GATS. It deals with access to and use of public telecommunications transport networks and services as a mode of supply for services on which countries have made commitments. The annex requires that access to and use of public networks and services be provided on a reasonable and nondiscriminatory basis. Thus governments are required to grant foreign suppliers access to and use of privately leased circuits. Moreover, governments must ensure that foreign service providers purchase or lease and attach terminal or other equipment interfacing with public networks; interconnect privately leased or owned circuits with public networks or with circuits leased or owned by another service supplier; and use operating protocols of the service supplier's choice, provided that they do not disrupt telecommunications transport networks and services to the public generally. Governments must also make sure that foreign service suppliers can use these networks and circuits to transfer information without undue impediments within and across national borders and that they can access information contained in databases held in any member country.

In addition, governments must not establish conditions on access and use other than those necessary to safeguard an incumbent carrier's public service responsibilities, protect the technical integrity of public networks, or ensure that foreign service suppliers provide only services that have been designated open to competition in market access commitments. If the measures are necessary to meet these criteria, however, governments may adopt policies that restrict resale and shared use of public services; require the use of specific technical interfaces and protocols for interconnection; require the interoperability of services; require type approval of terminal or other equipment interfacing with public networks; restrict the interconnection of privately leased or owned circuits with either public networks or the circuits of other service suppliers; and require the registration or licensing of foreign suppliers.[15]

Although it is not a part of the GATS framework agreement, the fact that the Reference Paper on basic telecommunications has been incorporated into the schedules of countries representing perhaps 90 percent of the global telecommunications market makes it an important tool for promoting GEC as well. The Reference Paper comprises six principles for the redesign of national regulatory rules and institutions to ensure compatibility with trade disciplines.

—Competitive safeguards. Governments are required to ensure that major suppliers, especially the national public telecommunications operators, do not engage in anticompetitive cross-subsidization, use information gathered from competitors with trade-restricting results, or fail to make available on a timely basis the technical information about their facilities and operations needed by competitors to enter the market.

—Interconnection. PTOs are to provide market entrants with interconnection at any technically feasible point in the network. Interconnection is to be provided at nondiscriminatory terms, conditions, and rates, and should be of a quality no less favorable than the provider gives its own services. Moreover, interconnection rates are to be cost-oriented, transparent, and where economically feasible, unbundled. A dispute mechanism administered by an independent body is called for to handle disputes over interconnection terms and other issues.

—Universal service. Such obligations are to be administered in a transparent, nondiscriminatory, and competitively neutral manner that is not more burdensome than required to meet the policy objectives.

—Public availability of licensing criteria. Where licenses are needed, information and decisionmaking procedures are to be transparent.

—Independent regulators. Regulatory bodies are to be separated from service providers and not accountable to them.

—Allocation and use of scarce resources. Procedures for allocating and using frequencies, numbers, and rights-of-way are to be carried out in an objective, timely, transparent, and nondiscriminatory manner.[16]

At least three issues arise regarding these disciplines. First, the Telecommunications Annex applies only to sectors where specific commitments

---

15. On the workings of the Telecommunications Annex see Tuthill (1996).

16. For discussions of the Group on Basic Telecommunications deal and the Reference Paper see Drake and Noam (1998); and Drake (1999).

have been made, and in sectors crucial to GEC many governments have not made significant commitments. We discuss later the question of commitments, but in this context the point is that the benefits of the annex's application are thus somewhat limited.

Second, the language of both instruments is broadly framed. For example, the annex does not contain strong disciplines on points of interconnection, pricing, numbering, unbundling, and promptness of access, all of which are crucial for GEC. The Reference Paper is more explicit on some of the relevant issues but even so is broadly cast. In consequence, governments might argue that a variety of PTO practices are legal under GATS although to others they appear to restrict market access. For example, there have already been battles on interconnection, with incumbent PTOs and their governments defending prices and operating requirements that potential entrants have argued prohibit market entry.

One could argue that GATS is perfectly capable of tackling such matters through the dispute settlements mechanism, and that it would be difficult to negotiate more precise language, especially when governments' domestic regimes vary and are in flux. Government regimes do vary, but the annex may not provide sufficient guidance for optimal panel rulings, and anyway it would be better to provide all stakeholders with a clearer set of rights and obligations in one place. Similarly, while more explicit national commitments elaborating on the Reference Paper principles would help, relying on this alone still might leave too much regulatory variability across markets. Unlike some of the other GEC issues, the problems in telecommunications are well understood; as such, strengthening these disciplines should be a priority in the coming round.

Third, there is a looming problem concerning the networks and services to which these instruments apply. Governments designed the annex and the Reference Paper to deal with basic telecommunications and public switched telephone networks (PSTN), especially (and explicitly, in the latter case) where these are supplied by the incumbent PTOs. Now with the emergence of major Internet access providers that are not providers of basic telecommunications and PSTNs, some WTO members are asking whether the obligations contained in the two instruments should not be extended to these firms as well. In effect, Internet access providers would be deemed basic telecommunications providers and subject to the full range of WTO obligations pertaining to such providers. Of course, the decision on this issue also would bear on whether Internet access is deemed to be covered by existing commitments.

At present, the European Commission appears to be leaning in this direction. But such a change would pose difficulties for the United States, where the Federal Communications Commission has repeatedly refused to designate Internet access a basic telecommunications service subject to common carrier legislative and regulatory obligations. Moreover, U.S.-based Internet access providers would be vehemently opposed to such a classification, which they would undoubtedly decry as an effort by foreign governments to impede entry into the foreign markets and to boost their own firms' prospects via administrative power rather than consumer choice.

There is no question that a major reason for the Internet's extraordinary growth, especially in the United States, is that it has been treated as an unregulated enhanced (or value added) service. Except where the incumbent PTOs have prevented this, the global Internet access market generally is competitive. In that context, imposing extensive new regulations on independent Internet access providers—even if only on the larger ones—would be a premature solution in search of a problem, and one that carries a substantial risk of limiting competition and slowing the deployment of new infrastructure and services. It would be better for the WTO to focus on clearing the way for competition with the PTOs and perhaps to take up other issues raised by media convergence, including competition in cable television infrastructure.

Competition

GATS Article VIII (Monopolies and Exclusive Service Providers) requires members to ensure that monopoly suppliers do not act in a manner inconsistent with their obligations in a relevant market. In particular, the members must take care that such providers not abuse their positions when competing in markets outside the scope of their monopoly rights. Similarly, Article IX (Business Practices) notes that certain suppliers' actions may restrict trade in services and requires members to enter into consultations at the request of any other member to eliminate such practices.

These articles clearly have direct bearing on telecommunications services, and intentionally so. What requires further consideration is how they may apply to other GEC services. It may well be that global electronic commerce reduces the scope for trade-restrictive business practices by improving access to and the transparency of markets, which are especially important for small suppliers. But a problem could arise involving monopolies and restrictive practices in certain software services as well as certification and authentication or Internet address assignment services. In these and other cases it would seem important to reach a clear understanding of whether the rules apply only to monopolies that are formally established or authorized by governments or also to suppliers who have attained such positions without government intervention. The latter may also have the effect of limiting market access and the expansion of the GEC generally.

Because the dispute settlement mechanism has not been brought to bear on such problems yet, it is difficult to make a strong judgment about whether the existing GATS disciplines are sufficient. But the kinds of services we have mentioned are fundamental to the operation of the Internet and GEC, and governments were not thinking of them when they devised GATS and their national commitments. It may be unwise to leave such matters to dispute settlement panels, which would essentially have to legislate on new and critically important terrain. Whether the specificities of GEC competition issues would best be addressed in an annex or in another manner merits further consideration.

Market Access Commitments on the Electronic Supply of Services

Maybe the most distinctive feature of GATS is that the withdrawal of actually restrictive domestic measures is governed only through negotiated commitments included in national schedules. Under Article XVI (Market Access) members that want to retain such measures may either exclude sectors in their schedule or include them with reservations for the measures in question. Thus the procedure for registering commitments in national schedules combines positive and negative undertakings: there are no liberalization obligations unless a sector or subsector is positively included in the schedule, but once it is, a member cannot maintain measures in that sector that are inconsistent with Article XVI. The article specifies that members are to accord services and service suppliers of any other member treatment no less favorable than that provided for in their schedule. Where commitments are made, members are to avoid numerical restrictions unless otherwise specified in their schedules. These restrictions are listed as follows: limitations on the number of service suppliers, on the total value of service transactions and the number of people that may be employed in a sector, and limitation on the participation of foreign capital, either in terms of a percentage limit on foreign shareholding or on the total value of foreign investment, either in the aggregate or by a single entity.

Article XVI provides adequate guidance for global electronic commerce, but relevant national commitments need to be broadened and deepened. This is especially obvious in telecommunications, where—despite progress in the Group on Basic Telecommunications—many members have only partial and phased-in commitments on basic telecommunications, while many others still have none at all. As we have mentioned, the coverage of Internet access services under existing commitments may need to be clarified where some members have included specific entries while other have not. In general, commitments on electronic transport should cover telecommunications and Internet access, commitments on distribution services should cover the on-line ordering and delivery of products, and the relevant sectoral commitments should apply to "content" services like financial and professional services.

Nondiscrimination and the Problem of "Likeness"

In GATS, Article II (Most Favored Nation) requires members to extend to the services and service suppliers of members treatment no less favorable than they accord to like services and service suppliers of other countries—unless, of course, they have listed exemptions in their schedules of commitments. Similarly, Article XVII (National Treatment) requires members to accord foreign service suppliers treatment within their territories that is no less favorable than that which they apply to their own suppliers of like services. National treatment is meant to affect qualitative, discriminatory measures, implying that the treatment of foreign and national suppliers must be equivalent in substance, not just in form. Measures that may have restrictive effects on trade but are not deemed discriminatory need not be scheduled, although they could be questioned under Article VI (Domestic Regulation) or other obligations. There is nothing about electronic commerce that requires a fundamental rethinking of these cardinal principles; rather the challenge is to clarify their application, especially since discriminatory measures may be magnified in a network world where a national point of entry can give access to a global service market.

Article II is mandatory whereas Article XVII is optional. But in both the same question arises: does the criterion of "likeness" raise new issues in the GEC environment? One problem is that the ability to customize digital products may make it difficult to judge their likeness when adjudicating disputes. For example, an on-line supplier may offer a customized service that is nominally classified like a standardized service. How are the two services to be compared? They appear to be different to the customer, but should they be treated differently under trade disciplines?

Another problem concerns the ability to supply services remotely. Clearly, a given electronic service should be treated the same whether it is delivered from home or abroad. But should a service that is delivered electronically from abroad be treated in the same manner as one that is delivered domestically through nonelectronic means? The technological neutrality requirement would dictate that there is no reason for differential treatment. But since GATS allows the regulation of foreign service providers by importing states, there may be no violation of national treatment if like services are treated differently in order to apply such regulation. That the supplier is not located, even partially, in the host country might be deemed to change the very nature of the service. The traditional criteria for assessing likeness (for example, product characteristics and consumer attitudes) may not be sufficient here. A consumer may not realize that the provider is less accessible for the purpose of ex post liability claims and would thus consider the two services to be alike even if they are different from a regulator's viewpoint.

In general the issue of likeness has become one of the most contentious in the WTO for both goods and services.[17] In the long term a horizontal solution may be needed, and not only for GEC. In the short run, however, electronic commerce is likely to be where disputes arise, so it may be important to clarify how MFN and national treatment are to be applied in the coming round. For example, one approach to the first problem noted earlier might be to specify that the service being assessed for likeness is actually the service input to a transaction rather than the subsequently customized end product.

From an institutional standpoint the most straightforward approach here could be to improve scheduling methods and practices by specifying in members' commitments the regulatory reasons for any restrictions. Dispute settlement panels then would have a clearer benchmark to assess the legality of domestic measures, and those that do not significantly contribute to accepted regulatory objectives would be struck down.

Domestic Regulation and Standards

Article VI (Domestic Regulation) applies to national measures for which contracting parties have not scheduled exceptions in their national

17. For a general discussion see Cottier, Mavroidis, and Blatter (1999).

schedules, whether or not their delivery is electronic. It indicates that members should ensure that measures of general application affecting trade in services are administered in a reasonable, objective, and impartial manner. It also calls for domestic measures relating to qualification requirements and procedures, technical standards, and licensing requirements not to constitute unnecessary barriers to trade in services. Recognizing that this injunction is very broad, Article VI(4) calls on the Council for Trade in Services to develop further disciplines. In the meanwhile, Article VI(5) applies, prohibiting the application of licensing and qualification requirements that would nullify commitments under articles XVI (Market Access) and XVII (National Treatment).

These provisions apply equally to electronic transport services, distribution services, and content services. Content services are of particular interest here. The electronic supply of these services generally has not been targeted by extensive domestic regulation. However, there is a significant risk that this will change as the volume, value, and variety of transactions expand. Thus there may be a need to begin clarifying some of the issues. For example, how are the necessity or proportionality tests to be applied in as complex and fluid a realm as GEC? What do terms like "reasonable" and "not more burdensome than necessary" mean in this context (or any other, for that matter)? What should be done about the problem of applicable national jurisdiction?

It may be difficult to handle these and related regulatory problems in the upcoming round. Crucial parties are divided: some in the international business community worry that Article VI might give regulatory authorities too much license to "regulate the net" and argue that GEC issues should be left to them to sort out through self-regulatory initiatives whenever possible. In contrast, many WTO members worry about their capacity to enforce their sovereign regulatory rights under the article, and the European Union has been particularly vocal in maintaining that self-regulation cannot be the only basis for GEC regulation. For example, distant sourcing of input services makes it especially difficult for regulatory authorities to make recognition of qualifications a condition of market entry. This is a concern expressed especially by the Europeans.

Given the negotiating difficulties that would be encountered, one might argue that Article VI should be left as it is until all the gaps in schedules have been filled, and that WTO members could then see whether disputes abound before seeking clarification. Further, one can always hope that industry self-regulatory initiatives undertaken in the meantime would provide workable enough solutions to facilitate the growth of electronic commerce, at least in the near term.

But as unpalatable as it may seem to some parties, there probably is a need to establish at least some intergovernmental guidelines on what is permissible regulation of GEC content services. After all, government regulations protecting basic public interests such as public health and safety, consumer rights, and the security of transactions ought to apply equally in both the virtual and physical worlds. There is nothing sacred about the Internet that should or will preclude governments from, for example, attempting to regulate the on-line supply of medical or educational services to their citizens. And if they are going to establish such regulations, there should be some level of multilateral agreement about what kinds of regulations are legal under GATS. Moreover, shared principles could help mitigate the growing threats to the Internet of governments unilaterally regulating cyberspace or subjecting service providers and transactions to multiple and totally incompatible national regulations.[18]

Of course, in addition to industry self-regulatory initiatives on these issues, there are intergovernmental efforts under way in bodies like the Organization for Economic Cooperation and Development. To the extent that these are successful, WTO negotiators might be able to avoid at least some of these murky waters or even make reference to other agreements within GATS. But in the end at least some guidelines will become necessary in the near term if trade in content services is to flourish. Whether developing these can be left entirely to whatever trade round will follow the one beginning in 2000 is a real question.

The European Commission has suggested that "it would be worth discussing whether a list of regulatory objectives—for example, consumers' protection, universal service, and security of the transactions, as well as those covered by Article XIV [General Exceptions] of the GATS, among others—could be established."[19] One can quibble about which objectives should be so listed, and governments undoubtedly would, which is a problem. Nevertheless, a list may be a reasonable first step, regardless of

18. The Bavarian government's December 1995 threat to prosecute CompuServe points to early lessons in this vein. The ISP was attacked for serving as carrier to discussion groups producing material violating German pornography law and, as a result, had to block access to these discussion groups worldwide. The issue was finally resolved through technological devices, but similar conflicts are bound to arise.

19. World Trade Organization, Council for Trade in Services (1999, p. 2).

whether it is done generically for all services transactions in a reworked Article VI or in a more network-specific instrument like a GEC annex.

If they go this route, WTO negotiators may also find it useful to begin considering what kinds of regulations on electronic content services could pass the GATS necessity test. One option to consider might be a registration requirement, under which content suppliers must register in every country in which they wish to do business. This would provide a basis for consumer protection and liability redress and would be all the more justified if there was a quid pro quo relaxation of commercial presence restrictions. Another possibility might be a labeling requirement under which content services provided over the Web must include all relevant information regarding the regulations to which they are subject. Countries could design formats for mandatory services labeling. The impact would range from simple informed access for certain types of consumers to conditional access. A third possibility might be an identification requirement under which suppliers require consumers to use identification devices to provide them with information on their jurisdiction of origin. In any event, harnessing technologies that help create "virtual borders" may be legitimate to the extent that regulatory authorities have exploited the specific opportunities for least restrictive regulations offered by the Internet.

With any such requirements there would clearly be problems of enforcement and the mutual recognition of enforcement. Most governments may not have the necessary domestic institutions, laws, and regulations to handle these matters yet. This is just one of the many challenges that will have to be confronted if networked trade in educational, health, and other consumer-related services in particular is to flourish.

A related matter explored in the GEC work program is technical standardization, which presents a special problem in the electronic environment. Clearly there is a need to ensure that governments and private firms do not establish standards that are unduly trade restrictive. But judging whether standards have that effect using the language in GATS could be difficult. The issues of domestic regulation and nondiscrimination are intrinsically linked in this regard. Under the status quo even admittedly like products might be denied entry by technical choices that are not clearly driven by discriminatory intent. As the Alliance for Global Business suggests, this could arise with "regulations that are neutral on their face but nonetheless affect some countries more than others. So, for example, a WTO member nation might decide to favor a certain digital signature or encryption technology and not others, thereby favoring contracts for services provided from countries that also recognize that technology."[20]

Standards issues can be extremely complicated, and assessing them often requires a high level of technological expertise. Moreover, the GATS language on standards is very broad. It therefore is not obvious that dispute settlement panels would have an easy time rendering well-grounded judgments if, as it seems reasonable to expect, conflicts arise with the expansion of GEC. As it would not make sense to burden the general obligations and disciplines with rules specific to the networked environment, this seems like another area in which additional clarification might best be pursued in a new instrument like an annex.

Transparency

Under Article III (Transparency) members must publish all relevant measures of general application that pertain to or affect the operation of GATS, promptly or at least annually inform the WTO of the introduction of new regulations or guidelines or changes to existing ones, and promptly respond to requests from other governments for specific information on any of its measures. To facilitate prompt response, WTO members are also to establish inquiry points. The Internet and GEC do not pose any particular problems for this loose provision, and in fact should help governments carry out their obligations under its terms, including channeling information to the relevant parties.

In fact, one could argue that WTO members should be required to publish on the Internet—in an accessible, one-stop shopping manner—all regulations or guidelines affecting GEC services exports into their markets. This would be especially helpful to individual entrepreneurs and small and medium-sized businesses. After all, one of the widely celebrated virtues of the Internet is that it can lower some barriers to entry for such businesses. But that promise may be negated if they cannot readily determine what rules apply to providing services to foreign customers who visit their Web pages and so on (assuming a mode 1 solution to the classification issue). As governments begin to adopt domestic regulations on the supply of electronic content services, small businesses should be able to find out what the rules are without having to hire a fleet of consultants. Governments

---

20. International Chamber of Commerce (1999, p. 55).

probably would not be willing to even consider taking on this obligation for administrative and other reasons, so perhaps it is just wishful thinking. Nevertheless, GEC-specific transparency requirements in either an annex or a revised Article III would be a good thing, especially in light of the WTO debates over transparency, relations with civil society and nongovernmental organizations, and so forth.

Mutual Recognition and Regulatory Cooperation

Under GATS, domestic measures that are trade restrictive but nondiscriminatory and are likely to escape the reach of Article VI (Domestic Regulation) provisions at times may need to be dealt with through more far-reaching and restricted agreements.[21] Thus Article VII (Recognition) encourages signatories to enter mutual recognition agreements bilaterally or plurilaterally, or even to engage in unilateral recognition of "the education or experience obtained, requirements met, or licenses or certification obtained" under each other's jurisdiction.

The Internet could make implementing mutual recognition agreements (MRAs) easier, so governments may want to explore how to use this potential to its fullest. In addition to helping enforce procedural MFN status, the Internet could help create the basis for MRAs by fostering cooperation between regulators and collaboration between private bodies with delegated authority (such as university accreditation bodies or professional boards). Recognition may eventually be extended to electronic accreditation bodies whose stamp of approval would constitute a right of entry for Web delivery to specified jurisdictions. The existing GATS may provide an adequate basis for the WTO to assess any charges of discrimination and such involving these operations.

An example relevant to GATS of how the Web can change things involves professional services. The proportionality principle requires that the professional associations or public authorities granting rights to activity in the importing country "take account" of the qualifications obtained in the professional's home country. This idea of taking into account can be greatly fine-tuned and operationalized through bilateral or plurilateral MRAs. The widespread "managed" character of recognition simply means that there is always a residual degree of control by the host country. The questions are

21. For a discussion on the boundary between articles VI and VII, see the chapter by Nicolaïdis and Trachtman in this volume.

over what, how much, and on what grounds. Whether regulators seek to implement the necessity test embodied in Article VI (Domestic Regulation) or whether they seek to implement MRA obligations, regulating access by professionals on the basis of proportionality could be facilitated by cyberspace. Taking into account foreign qualification requirements to determine what residual requirements may be warranted is a customized process that is very information intensive. Regulators need to evaluate the foreign system and the path followed in it by the candidate for access. The availability of Web-based information on curriculum content, training requirements, and foreign accreditation conditions and grades can serve as the basis for more routine assessment. Common comparative databases of certifying institutions could be developed to facilitate this process and build the foundation for a global decentralized accreditation regime.

Societal Protections

Article XIV (General Exceptions) states that members may adopt and enforce measures necessary to protect the privacy of individuals in relation to processing and disseminating personal data and protecting confidentiality of individual records and accounts; protect public morals or maintain public order; and prevent deceptive and fraudulent practices. However, any such measures must not constitute a means of arbitrary or unjustifiable discrimination between countries where like conditions prevail, and they must not serve as disguised restrictions on trade in services. Article XIV kicks in when measures have been ruled illegitimate under Article VI (Domestic Regulation).

As with GATS generally, the article has not been tested. But the mass popularization of the Internet and the direct and unmediated involvement of potentially millions of consumers in global electronic commerce will mean that there will be an infinitely larger number of transactions in which the issues Article XIV covers could come into play, so the question of whether it should be clarified (and used) may become unavoidable. The clause on public morals is unlikely to raise problems: it is unlikely that any government will go to bat for a firm that is being prevented from selling pornography in another country or that the democracies would challenge authoritarian governments' restrictions on political speech in the WTO. But on the other matters there are challenges to be faced.

With regard to privacy protection, the primary problem is the transatlantic division. The United States remains strongly committed to a "self-regulatory" approach to Internet privacy that is favored by its well-organized business community but regarded as completely ineffective and unenforceable by almost all independent privacy advocates and consumer groups. In contrast, the EU's Data Directive provides stronger requirements for business compliance and legal remedies for violations, but it was designed before the Internet boom and may now be overly rigid. Neither approach is satisfactory in its current form, but we are left with a heated debate about their relative merits nonetheless.

Bilateral negotiations to square the circle are still under way, with the United States insisting against all evidence that self-regulation provides the same or better protection than laws and that the two approaches are simply different means to the same ends. The OECD's 1981 Guidelines and 1998 Declaration on data protection—which was issued at its ministerial meeting on GEC in Ottawa—are sometimes held up as evidence that there is at least transatlantic agreement on governing principles, but there are healthy grounds for skepticism because these instruments are vague and toothless by design.[22] Thus although one can hope that the United States would have the good sense not to challenge the EU's obligation to protect its citizens' privacy as a trade barrier, it might be useful to clarify what means to that end are acceptable under GATS.

Similarly, there is a need to go beyond the single focus on fraud by adding to GATS a broader exception for consumer protection. Consumer protection is absolutely essential if people are to have confidence that transactions on-line are as safe as those in the physical world. The biggest division here is between international business and consumer groups. The consumer groups are demanding strong protections and a recognition that the consumer's country is the applicable national jurisdiction in any disputes (a mode 1 approach). International differences on the point were in evidence at the OECD's GEC ministerial meeting, which was able to adopt only a vague declaration calling for continued dialogue. Consumer groups also are becoming increasingly critical of the WTO, and many are planning to band together with environmental and other nongovernmental organizations to protest outside the WTO's Seattle ministerial meeting. Given the importance of the issue for the expansion of electronic commerce and in light of the larger WTO debate on transparency and relations

22. The OECD's work and reports on e-commerce issues are available at http://www.oecd.fr/dsti/sti/it/ec/index.htm. The materials from the Ottawa ministerial conference are available at http://www.oecd.fr/dsti/sti/it/ec/news/ottawa.htm.

with civil society, it would make sense to address the issue in GATS, as the European Union seems inclined to do.

The problem for negotiators is that as with the calls for the WTO to address environmental, labor, and human rights questions, the issues above involve the proper balance between trade and wider social objectives. Given the sharp differences on such matters, addressing them in any detail in the WTO would be opening the proverbial can of worms. But not addressing them could entail risks as well. The result is a "damned if you do, damned if you don't" scenario for the WTO.

In this heated environment, it would be inappropriate to leave to dispute settlement panels to decide what national policies are (un)justifiable. To have panels making judgments on sensitive social issues in closed deliberation could present a threat to the legitimacy of and public support for the WTO. In the context of the Internet, where individuals and organizations can easily make a lot of noise and mobilize networks of like-minded correspondents around the world—as was demonstrated by the OECD's failed effort to establish the Multilateral Agreement on Investment—it is not difficult to imagine campaigns being launched in response to panel determinations deemed adverse by some stakeholders or observers somewhere. This could raise domestic political problems for a member government faced with an adverse ruling on privacy or consumer protection.

Of course, WTO negotiators need not attempt to devise detailed instruments on these issues and indeed are probably not well placed to do so. Ideally, governments and other parties would reach a workable level of consensus in other international forums, although the efforts thus far have yet to yield meaningful results. Absent that, the negotiators could evade a given issue with a "gentlemen's agreement" to avoid resorting to dispute settlements until there is greater consensus, as the Group on Basic Telecommunications did with regard to international telephone accounting and settlements rates. However, it is not clear that this would be a trade-expanding or institution-strengthening outcome.

Thus it would be useful to add an explicit exception for consumer protection to Article XIV and to consider whether it is possible to provide at least some clarification as to what kinds of policies are or are not arbitrary, unjustifiable, or disguised restrictions on trade in services. This would give any dispute settlements panels greater guidance and political cover in interpreting the principles. Whether it would be better to provide that guidance in a revised Article XIV or in a new instrument like an annex would depend on the level of context-specific detail deemed necessary.

Additional Issues of Particular Interest to Developing Countries

Finally, we turn to GEC matters of particular interest to developing countries. We start with the current controversy about customs duties, perhaps the hottest issue on the GATS agenda. We then turn to recommendations on how to ensure increasing participation in the world trading system by these countries in the age of electronic commerce.

Customs Duties

In principle, whether to extend or make permanent the standstill on applying customs duties to electronic transmissions may not seem to be solely an issue in developing countries. After all, customs duties are routinely applied around the world on other kinds of transactions, and ministries of finance everywhere are typically loath to forgo sources of revenue. Moreover, the European Commission has announced that it will not support the U.S. proposal for a permanent moratorium until work on other aspects of the GEC work program is completed to its satisfaction. But insofar as EU governments have previously supported a permanent ban, this is probably just a bargaining tactic being used to advance the commission's agenda regarding other items on which it is at odds with the United States.

In practice then, this issue is primarily relevant to developing countries. One problem is that many developing countries believe they will be net importers of GEC in the years ahead, so forswearing customs collection at the virtual border would be depriving themselves of a new source of foreign revenue. In the same way, when the Internet is used as an alternative to the conventional delivery of products that are subject to customs, this substitution effect is seen as eroding an existing source of revenue. Complicating things further, even though border duties and the internal taxation of transactions are separate issues, many governments seem to think of them as being closely linked. In light of these concerns, some developing countries have expressed interest in keeping open the possibility of applying customs duties in the future.

Nevertheless, the assumptions on which this position rests are problematic. For one thing, opponents of a ban seem to have a rather static analysis of their own prospects. Some developing countries may well develop vital GEC export markets. Furthermore, if appropriate national policies are in place, GEC should contribute enough to overall economic activity to offset the absence of customs revenues on transmissions.

It is also important to emphasize that taxes and customs duties are indeed separate issues. Internet commerce certainly does raise a number of thorny taxation issues for national governments, but many of these go beyond the border measures and nondiscrimination issues dealt with by the WTO. And while some countries such as the United States may choose to limit taxes in order to stimulate the growth of GEC in their territories, it is entirely legitimate for other countries to pursue a different strategy. This is consistent with WTO instruments; for services, GATS Article XIV (General Exceptions) allows domestic measures aimed at ensuring "the equitable or effective imposition or collection of direct taxes." But any such taxes should be imposed internally on the value of the transactions' content and must not be applied only to foreign-originated services if national treatment commitments apply.

There also is a noteworthy practical problem. Technologically, it would be difficult to distinguish from other traffic, measure, and ascribe values to commercial electronic transmissions, and this may be especially true for developing countries. Insisting on the right to do something they probably do not have the means to do anyway arguably results in the worst of both worlds if revenues are not collected and the market is given a signal that GEC is unwelcome. Certainly, attempting to simply apply customs duties to all Internet traffic, rather than just to commercial transactions, would be profoundly self-destructive.

Such considerations aside, the question remains as to whether customs duties on transmissions would be consistent with developing countries' WTO obligations. Customs duties are of course routine for trade in goods and compatible with GATT, including duties for goods ordered over the Internet and delivered in physical form. In contrast, customs duties on trade in services are almost nonexistent. However, as the WTO Secretariat notes, "there is no reason in principle why customs duties should not be applied to services, whether supplied electronically or in any other way." But any such measure "which would increase the bound level of protection of a committed service would be inconsistent with a Member's commitments."[23]

There is nevertheless an ambiguity when one focuses on the transmission per se in the GATS context. None of the countries that have scheduled

23. World Trade Organization, Council for Trade in Services (1998, p. 9).

commitments in the telecommunications sector have thought to schedule duties on transmissions. If the technological neutrality principle is taken seriously, the question arises as to whether they can therefore claim the option for Internet transmissions. Contracting parties need to decide if doing so would be a breach of bindings in such cases.

There is growing opposition to the U.S. proposal for the coming round among Latin American and Asian governments. It is unclear how deep the divide is or whether opposition is just a bargaining tactic. But in the end, if the application of customs duties on transmissions is determined to be consistent with their commitments, developing countries have every right to give it a try. It unclear that the effort would promote any national objectives; more likely it would stifle their participation in GEC. Several years of being left out of the expansion of GEC might bring these countries around to reducing or eliminating the duties.

If developing countries do dig their heels in on electronic customs duties, it would be a mistake for the industrialized countries to insist on banning the duties and risk lending credence to the wrongheaded view that an open GEC environment is yet another example of rich countries imposing their will on poor countries. Persuasion is far preferable to pressure here, especially insofar as a ban may be of greater symbolic than practical value. If an agreement cannot be reached, the industrialized countries could always develop a plurilateral agreement that would cover much of the GEC in the near term. But if an agreement can be reached, codifying a ban in a new instrument like a GEC Annex would be a nice touch.

Increasing Developing Countries' Participation in GEC

Article IV (Increasing Participation of Developing Countries) calls on WTO members to undertake specific commitments to helping developing countries by, among other things, strengthening their domestic services capacity through access to technology, improving their access to distribution channels and information networks, and liberalizing market access in sectors of interest to them. Members are also to establish contact points to facilitate access to trade-related information regarding qualifications and other aspects of doing business in members' markets.

The Internet is perfectly compatible with these minimalist provisions and can readily be used to promote the objectives they present. For developing countries the Internet should be a godsend relative to the days when data networking was largely about proprietary networks operated by transnational firms. Its open architecture and related attributes can facilitate easy access to a wealth of trade-related information from government, nongovernment, and business sources, as well as to a seamless distribution channel; the Trade Point program of the UN Conference on Trade and Development (UNCTAD) is a model that could be built on in this respect. Indeed, the Internet may well be the biggest transfer of technology and information the world has ever seen.

Although Article IV does not require any clarification, WTO members could undertake some useful steps to implement it more fully in the context of GEC. For example, the developed countries should strengthen their commitments in GEC-related sectors where developing countries might have a comparative advantage. Identifying those sectors, and any barriers that may obtain in them, should be a priority in both the WTO technical cooperation efforts and in UNCTAD.

One area that deserves particular attention involves labor-intensive exports from developing countries. Part of the political bargain of the Uruguay Round was supposed to be that the developed countries would make commitments with respect to mode 4 exports in exchange for developing countries making commitments on commercial establishment under mode 3. But in the end the industrialized countries' mode 4 commitments generally had to do with the movement of corporate executives and the like; both low-skill and high-skill workers or professionals from developing countries were treated more under the category of "movement of labor"—subject to immigration laws—than under the GATS category of movement of a natural person service supplier.

In this round the industrialized countries could take a more liberal approach to the movement of professionals from developing countries who deliver services such as software or architectural design, including where the periodic movement of such persons is ancillary to Internet-based services supply. They might also enter into mutual recognition agreements that acknowledge the credentials and ease the temporary entry of professionals and technicians from developing countries. Given the industrialized countries' shortage of skilled personnel in some high-technology industries, which in the United States has led Silicon Valley to advocate immigration reform, there should be a way to make this politically palatable.

For their part the developing countries urgently need to undertake domestic reforms. For example, many of these countries maintain market-restricting practices in the telecommunications sector—prohibiting infrastructure competition, curtailing the entry of independent Internet access providers, imposing high prices on the leased circuits needed by these providers, requiring end users to pay per-minute dial-up fees, and so on—that constrain the expansion of Internet usage and GEC.[24] Often the incumbent national telecommunications operators still dominate policy-making and insist that they must limit competition to recover past invest-ments and build out the bandwidth necessary for Internet and other service offerings. It is not impossible that some governments may even believe that an underdeveloped information infrastructure is beneficial insofar as it limits foreign entry in network-dependent markets and thus provides time for local infant industries to develop. Reforming self-defeating national policies would go a long way toward helping the developing countries benefit more fully from the international trading system.

Finally, there is an urgent need to expand technical cooperation pro-grams with regard to the Internet and GEC. Although some still insist on seeing the Internet as a tool of cultural imperialism and economic domi-nation, many developing country governments have come a long way in the past few years in their thinking about it. Even so, making commit-ments to an open GEC environment will be a difficult pill for some to swallow. Much more technical support will be needed if developing coun-tries are going to establish appropriate national policies on a range of GEC issues so that they can participate effectively in both the world market and in WTO negotiations. Governments, the international business commu-nity, the WTO, and other international organizations like the World Bank, UNCTAD, and the International Telecommunication Union all have roles to fill here.[25]

Conclusion

Although this chapter has covered a good deal of ground, in a real sense it has only begun to scratch the surface. The trade issues associated with GEC services are complex and wide ranging, and they will undoubt-edly become more so as the technologies, business practices, and national policies continue to develop in the years ahead. Nevertheless, as a snapshot

---

24. For a thorough discussion of such issues see International Telecommunication Union (1999).

25. These concerns were first raised in World Trade Organization, Committee on Trade and Development (1998).

of the current terrain, we hope our discussion provides useful contribution to the evolving policy debate.

While recognizing the political difficulties entailed in the alternative, we are not convinced that a quick fix consisting of only the most minimal additions to or clarifications of GATS would be the best outcome of the coming round. Even if the round actually concludes in 2003, GEC will by then have already expanded dramatically, which will probably lead governments to adopt a variety of national policies to deal with emerging problems. Who knows what the situation will look like by the time the round after next gets under way, much less concludes? Without a multilateral consensus on at least core principles during the Millennium Round, there may be a risk that such policies will stifle GEC somewhat or lead to conflicts that the dispute settlement system is not well equipped to handle yet.

Thus while the adoption of detailed rules on certain points may have to wait, it would be advisable to establish flexible guiding principles that take into account the specifics of the GEC environment. Among the most pressing items are the classification problems; strengthening the Telecommunications Annex; establishing at least a list of permissible domestic regulatory objectives, including consumer protection (although specifying some criteria of permissibility would be even better); and banning customs duties on transmissions if the developing countries can be convinced that it is in their interest. As to the other issues we have discussed, it might be worth trying to develop language clarifying the workings of the transparency, national treatment, and competition principles in the GEC environment or at least to reach an informal agreement on their interpretation. In addition, national commitments need to be strengthened across the board, including those on electronic transmission services (telecommunications and Internet access) and on sectors and modes of supply that are of particular interest to the developing countries. Even if formal agreement cannot be reached on all these issues, working through them could yield greater consensus in some respects. And if the alternatives are unilateral rule or no rules at all, the only thing worse than negotiating is not negotiating.

References

Cottier, Thomas, Petros Mavroidis, and Patrick Blatter, eds. 1999. *Regulatory Barriers and the Principle of Non-Discrimination in World Trade Law: Past, Present and Future.* University of Michigan Press.

Drake, William J. 1999. *Toward Sustainable Competition in Global Telecommunications:*

From Principle to Practice—Summary Report of the Third Aspen Institute Roundtable on International Telecommunications. Washington: Aspen Institute.

Drake, William J., and Kalypso Nicolaïdis. 1992. "Ideas, Interests and Institutionalization: Trade in Services and the Uruguay Round." *International Organization* 45 (Winter): 37–100.

Drake, William J., and Eli M. Noam. 1998. "Assessing the WTO Agreement on Basic Telecommunications." In Gary Clyde Hufbauer and Erika Wada, eds., *Unfinished Business: Telecommunications after the Uruguay Round,* pp. 27–61. Washington: Institute for International Economics.

Grubel, Herbert G. 1987. "All Traded Services Are Embodied in Materials or People." *World Economy* 10 (September): 319–30.

Hill, Peter. 1997. "Tangibles, Intangibles, and Services: A New Taxonomy for the Classification of Output." Paper prepared for the CSLS Conference on Service Sector Productivity and the Productivity Paradox, Ottawa, April 11–12.

International Chamber of Commerce. 1999. "Draft Alliance for Global Business Discussion Paper on Trade-Related Aspects of Global Electronic Commerce." March.

International Telecommunication Union. 1999. *Challenges to the Network: Internet for Development.* Geneva.

Nicolaïdis, Kalypso. 1995. "International Trade in Information-Based Services: The Uruguay Round and Beyond." In William J. Drake, ed., *The New Information Infrastructure: Strategies for U.S. Policy,* pp. 269–302. New York: Twentieth Century Fund.

——. 1999. "Non-Discriminatory Mutual Recognition: An Oxymoron in the New WTO Lexicon?" In Petros Mavroidis and Patrick Blatter, eds., *Non-Discrimination in WTO: Past and Present.* World Trade Forum series. University of Michigan Press.

Organization for Economic Cooperation and Development. 1999. "Electronic Commerce: On-Line Supply of Services–Market Access Issues." Draft Working Paper, Trade Committee, February.

——. 1998. "Documents of the Ministerial Conference on Global Electronic Commerce, Ottawa"; http://www.oecd.fr/dsti/sti/it/ec/news/ottawa.htm.

Tuthill, Lee. 1996. "Users' Rights? The Multilateral Rules on Access to Telecommunications." *Telecommunications Policy* 20 (March): 89–99.

U.S. Department of Commerce. 1998. *The Emerging Digital Economy.* April; http://www.ecommerce.gov/emerging.htm.

World Trade Organization. 1998a. *Global Electronic Commerce and the Role of the WTO—Special Studies 2.* Geneva.

——. 1998b. "Declaration on Global GEC." WT/MIN(98)/DEC/2 (May 20). http://www.wto.org/wto/anniv/ecom.htm.

World Trade Organization, Committee on Trade and Development. 1998. "Global Electronic Commerce in Goods and Services—Communication from the Delegation of Egypt." WT/COMTD/W/38 (March 3).

World Trade Organization, Council for Trade in Services. 1998. "The Work Programme on Electronic Commerce: Note by the Secretariat." S/C/W/68 (November 16).

——. 1999. "Work Programme on Electronic Commerce—Communication from the European Communities and Their Member States." S/C/W/98 (February 23).

World Trade Organization, General Council. 1998. "Work Programme on Electronic Commerce." WT/L/274 (September 30).

————. 1999a. "Preparations for the 1999 Ministerial Conference: Work Program on Electronic Commerce—Communication from Indonesia and Singapore." WT/GC/W/247 (July 9).

————. 1999b. "Work Programme on Electronic Commerce—Communication from the United States." WT/GC/16 (February 12).

COMMENT BY
Merit E. Janow

These are exceptional and interesting, albeit somber, essays. Their authors suggest that horizontal rules in the WTO covering investment (Sauvé and Wilkie) or competition policy (Warner) may be desirable, but such rules are not achievable. Thus each essay offers suggestions in a more narrowly confined area of trade law and policy, GATS. Indeed, both essays are mindful (perhaps somewhat excessively) of the cheerless climate of the upcoming Seattle trade summit. And each offers insightful yet incremental suggestions and modest architecture rather than the bold vision and architecture that one might wish for when envisioning a more fully integrated international trading system.

Indeed, the investment essay heeds a number of economic, political, and other forces that have adversely shaped international sentiment toward negotiation of investment rules, including the lessons of the failed Multilateral Agreement on Investment negotiations at the OECD. I concur with those observations and cannot help but wonder if the MAI had been structured as a nonbinding instead of a binding instrument, whether it would have avoided the contagion effect on the negotiation of international investment rules. Recent years have shown that many countries are prepared, indeed have chosen on their own, to liberalize their investment regimes yet are loath to bind those more open systems at the international level. This has been, for example, the paradox of the Asia-Pacific Economic Cooperation (APEC) experience. The risk of reintroducing more restrictive investment regimes remains, but it may be less of a worry for international capital flows than the backlash that could occur in developing countries against the presumed ambitions of developed economies. I found the investment essay by Sauvé and Wilkie particularly insightful in identifying specific areas for improvement over the short and medium term in the GATS framework. Government officials and business executives should pay serious attention to these proposals for they are practical and constructive.

The competition discussion is also intriguing, yet let me advance a slightly different conceptualization of the competition law policy discussion now occurring in many capitals around the world. Much of the international debate surrounding competition policy has centered on what forms international cooperation should take in light of the perceived market problems. The debate is taking the form of three related but distinct expressions of appropriate future policy directions.

First, how can nations best increase the effectiveness of antitrust regimes, both with respect to national or domestic competition problems and those problems that have international spillover effects? In a world where more than eighty countries have introduced competition laws or policies and more than half have done so in the 1990s, this question is not academic. Happily, it appears that in many countries, competition laws and policies have been introduced because they are considered useful companions to economic deregulation, privatization, and in general the introduction of market forces. This proliferation of competition policy regimes has not resolved the international challenges to the sufficiency of national competition laws. International spillover effects can arise—for example, by virtue of transnational cartels—that may require cooperation between authorities for effective prosecution. Also, mergers involving corporations with multinational operations or international effects have become commonplace. Such is the impact of globalization.

A second focus has, of course, been on the future role of the World Trade Organization. Is the WTO currently, or can it become, well suited to serve as the forum for the negotiation of rules on competition (horizontal commitments) that would then be subject to WTO dispute settlement rules? Or are there other steps that could usefully be taken in the WTO to ensure that it is a constructive force for resolving competition problems that also raise trade or market access problems?

The European Union is on the record as strongly advocating the negotiation of competition rules at the WTO, suggesting that early efforts at negotiation oblige countries to have competition laws, enforce them in a transparent and nondiscriminatory fashion, provide for international cooperation, and gradually consider broader coverage. The EU proposal also suggests that these rules should be subject to dispute settlement, but instead of examining individual cases, "patterns" of cases would be examined.

I do not think that there is now sufficient consensus around the world to support the negotiation of horizontal competition rules, nor am I convinced that nations should create at the WTO an obligation that countries have competition laws and policies. More important is that countries take steps to promote competition in their markets. If they choose to do so through the introduction of competition laws and policies, then certain features of those policies such as transparency and due process can be reinforced at the WTO and other places. This is the opportune time for governments and their publics to consider incremental next steps at the WTO that will increase understanding of the interface of trade and competition problems and find specific areas for action that are mutually reinforcing. The essay by Warner makes the important observation that GATS, the Basic Telecommunications Reference Paper, and the Accounting Disciplines, among others, offer interesting architectural ways of introducing competition policy safeguards into sectoral liberalization initiatives. I concur. As other sectors with comparable features (state enterprises, strong government regulation, network features) become the subject of negotiations, competition safeguards should also be considered.

One can think of still other modest but useful steps: developing an on-going work program on trade and competition problems; including a competition policy review within the context of country reviews undertaken as part of a Trade Policy Review Mechanism examination; expanding discussion, seminars, and other initiatives between the WTO and other international bodies such as the OECD, the United Nations Conference on Trade and Development (UNCTAD), and the World Bank in consideration of competition policy matters. These incremental measures may be small steps toward developing consensus. Next steps should not chill prospects for constructive and continuing consultations. And, considering the credibility of the WTO, it is also important that any rules negotiated at the forum prove judicable. It is not clear whether the EU proposal, including the idea of a dispute panel reviewing patterns but not specific cases, would truly address competition problems, except for those that stem from obviously discriminatory and distortive practices. Although those problems may exist, the disputes now sustaining the international friction on trade and competition tend to center on more subtle questions of failure to enforce laws and violations of rule of reason.

Finally, because more competition problems are international but not all competition problems are trade problems, it may be time to consider whether a new forum is needed to bring together competition officials from around the world to address a full range of issues confronting competition policy in the global economy. The OECD has served as an important forum for deliberation among its members on competition matters and has recently achieved an important recommendation with respect to cooperation in fighting hard core cartels. Yet the OECD does not routinely include all jurisdictions that have competition laws. The WTO, for its part, is mostly focused on trade and competition interface issues. Perhaps both organizations in collaboration with other international entities could more affirmatively collaborate to provide an inclusive forum for discussion of procedural and substantive elements of best practices in competition policy. This is not to suggest attempting formal harmonization of substantive law but rather developing greater policy coherence around the world, informed where possible by shared views on ways that private, hybrid, and governmental anticompetitive or exclusionary practices can adversely affect national economic well-being and international trade. And for those nations that have chosen to introduce competition policy regimes, an expanded international dialogue could be useful to support institution building, the development of systems based on rule of law, and possibly even the arbitration of disputes. This international discourse, if useful, should not come in lieu of continued work at the WTO but rather in support of it.

COMMENT BY
Jeffrey J. Schott

The General Agreement on Trade in Services was the first truly multilateral investment and competition policy accord. Its skeletal provisions have established a useful basis for future negotiations to promote liberalization of existing barriers to global commerce. To date, however, little liberalization has been achieved despite the more recent conclusion of agreements on financial and basic telecommunications services.

Linking the essays by Mark Warner on competition policy and Pierre Sauvé and Christopher Wilkie on investment issues in GATS has a clear logic. More open investment regimes encourage participation by foreign companies and thus promote competition in the domestic market. World Trade Organization rights and obligations in these areas are mutually reinforcing.

Both chapters describe the provisions of GATT and GATS relating to investment and competition and put forward modest proposals for WTO reforms in the next trade round. Warner discusses the numerous GATT provisions that deal with competition policy issues (Articles III, XI, XVII, XX:d, and the Safeguards Code); the mandate to review the relationship between investment and competition policy in Article 9 of the Agreement on Trade-Related Investment Measures (TRIMs); GATS Articles VIII and IX; and the Reference Paper on Regulatory Principles of the Agreement on Basic Telecommunications (which has been accepted in whole or part by about one-third of the WTO membership). He notes that competition rules can be useful in promoting market access in services, particularly where there are public sector firms, state-owned enterprises, and entities with exclusive and special rights to operate (energy, postal, and telecommunications services providers).

Warner argues for a continuation of incremental rule-making, following the precedent of the negotiation of the Agreement on Basic Telecommunications. Taking his cue from the pronouncements of U.S. Trade Representative Charlene Barshefsky, he proposes that WTO members pursue competition policy objectives through regulatory guidelines in specific service sectors, and only then try to derive common lessons from that experience to develop horizontal rule-making.

Such an incremental approach to competition policy in services makes sense given the dense regulatory environment that entangles commerce in many countries. But the new GATS 2000 Round should not limit its efforts in competition policy issues to narrow sectoral talks. As Edward Graham and David Richardson have proposed, WTO members could usefully begin to develop better working relationships among competition policy authorities, perhaps starting first by agreeing that their officials would consult with counterparts in other WTO countries about practices that impede the rights of foreign investors or exporters.[1] In time such closer contacts could help the development of common standards (starting with some for cartels and mergers) that could be codified in a new horizontal pact on trade-related antitrust measures, or TRAMs.

The chapter by Pierre Sauvé and Christopher Wilkie on investment issues contends that the services sector is where the action is on investment issues in the WTO, and that work on investment in the new WTO Round should focus predominantly in GATS (at least for the near future). They note that global investment liberalization is very services-centered, there being relatively few significant barriers to entry via foreign direct investment in manufacturing or in primary industries. Like Warner, they propose incremental rule-making and caution that the political backlash from the acrimonious experience of the OECD negotiations on the Multilateral Agreement on Investment (MAI) precludes more ambitious initiatives.

In addition, Sauvé and Wilkie put forward three reasons why a comprehensive investment accord may not be feasible in the prospective WTO Round:

—bilateral investment treaties already adequately cover a lot of concerns regarding investment protection;

—OECD members seem unwilling to address distortions arising from their own investment policies, especially investment incentives; and

—less developed countries (LDCs) seem unwilling to expand Agreement on Trade-Related Investment Measures (TRIMs) or Agreement on Trade-Related Intellectual Property Rights (TRIPs) obligations given the unwillingness of OECD countries to deal with their own investment restrictions, including preferential rules of origin and antidumping practices "whose overall effect is to divert or hold back foreign direct investment that should otherwise flow in the direction of LDCs." Instead, they suggest what they call a "pragmatic way forward." Their narrowly focused GATS reform proposals call for

---

1. Graham and Richardson (1997).

—clarifying the definition of commercial presence to conform more closely to the "asset-based" definition found in the North American Free Trade Agreement (NAFTA), the draft MAI, and many bilateral investment protection treaties (BITs);

—transforming investor protection provisions into general rather than commitment-specific obligations equivalent to the core GATS obligations of transparency (Article III) and most favored nation treatment (Article II);

—securing the regulatory status quo in sectors where GATS members voluntarily agree to schedule liberalization commitments (no bindings should be allowed at less than the status quo);

—ensuring that unilateral liberalization measures agreed to between negotiating rounds are reflected in country schedules through a ratchet mechanism;

—developing a sunset clause for restrictions in national schedules and nonconforming measures scheduled under Articles XVI (Market Access) and XVII (National Treatment);

—promoting greater transparency on investment incentives; and

—developing a formula-based approach to liberalization in sectors in which countries maintain similar types of trade and investment restrictions (for example, civil aviation). Because such an arrangement would require increased transparency of barriers, they advocate that countries circulate "nonlegally binding lists of key nonconforming measures."

Limiting investment issues in the new WTO Round to pragmatic reforms in GATS could yield some important results. In particular, it would focus attention on the importance of investment in finance, telecommunications, and other infrastructure services that are critical for the use of information technologies and are thus essential for the production of a broad range of goods and services.

Sauvé and Wilkie cite the substantial investment reforms by LDCs over the past decade and the continuing strong foreign direct investment inflows to them despite the global financial crisis as evidence that FDI restrictions are not a big problem that requires the development of a comprehensive investment pact. Moreover, they argue that investment issues already are on the WTO agenda as part of the review of TRIMs and the deliberations of the WTO working group on investment. Indeed, they suggest that given the poisoned political climate since the MAI debacle, it is better to continue the de facto negotiating process of the working group, which allows negotiators to become educated on the subject, instead of commissioning formal de jure negotiations.

But Sauvé and Wilkie are too dismissive of investment problems that continue to plague global commerce and that would not be addressed by their limited proposal. I see several problems with their approach.

The first problem is fundamental. Although the data clearly show that FDI continues to flow to developing countries (mostly to a few countries such as China and Brazil that offer attractive inducements), I wonder whether the policies of many of those countries are not distorting investment decisions and promoting overinvestment (via incentives, performance requirements, and trade protection) in certain sectors, creating the seeds of new trade problems and directing resources away from other economic activities.

I agree with Sauvé and Wilkie that investment reforms in these countries have been impressive and are unlikely to be reversed. Indeed, there is a self-enforcing market mechanism against policy reversal—investors vote with their feet. But what if the investment distortion is due to subsidy and thus attracts rather than deters foreign investors?

I am also less sanguine about the current modest initiatives in the WTO that address investment issues. To date, both the TRIMs review and the working group deliberations have primarily focused on developing country issues and have blunted efforts to address investment distortions caused by developed country practices. Although these deliberations have produced useful background information on investment regimes, the authors somewhat overstate the educational value of this work for prospective negotiations. To be sure, negotiators learn by doing, but national economic officials generally are informed about the importance of investment for economic development and trade even if their trade bureaucrats in Geneva are not. Moreover, one cannot argue, as the authors implicitly do, that the working group's deliberations can be looked at as de facto negotiations. The participants do not bring a strong political commitment to the process, and some countries have used the working group as a means to defer rather than advance new negotiations.

In sum, Warner and Sauvé and Wilkie have put forward useful proposals for advancing WTO rules on competition and investment policy through incremental changes in GATS. Their analysis reflects a cautious pragmatism befitting the current political temperament in the United States. But what about the interests of other WTO participants?

Given the importance of FDI for the growth of crucial service sectors in developing countries, one may wonder why these countries do not champion comprehensive investment rules in the WTO.[2] They can ill afford to pay the subsidies often required to compete against other countries for FDI in new production plants. Most LDCs already recognize the value of FDI in transferring technology and management skills to their economies and have instituted investment reforms that have substantially opened their markets to foreign investors (with a few notable sectoral exceptions). LDCs clearly should give investment issues higher priority on the WTO agenda.

References

Graham, Edward M., and J. David Richardson, eds. 1997. *Global Competition Policy.* Washington: Institute for International Economics.

Moran, Theodore H. 1998. *Foreign Direct Investment and Development.* Washington: Institute for International Economics.

2. See Moran (1998).

PART FIVE

GATS 2000:
Challenges Ahead

15 | Is There a Better Way? Alternative Approaches to Liberalization under GATS

PATRICK LOW *and*
AADITYA MATTOO

T HE GENERAL AGREEMENT on Trade in Services (GATS) was a bold and long overdue innovation in international rule-making. While many writers and observers of trade policy readily acknowledge this achievement, they are also inclined to note that GATS needs improvement in several important areas. This includes both the rules and continuing betterment of the somewhat modest liberalization achieved or committed to so far under the agreement.[1] The purpose of this paper is to identify some aspects of the GATS structure and approach to liberalization that seem particularly deserving of attention. If the rules do not impose unambiguous disciplines upon the design and conduct of policy at the national level, they will not be enforceable internationally. Nor will they foster a strong commitment to continuing trade liberalization.

Improving the Clarity of GATS

Many practitioners and observers have pointed to aspects of the design of schedules and scheduling techniques that introduce an unwelcome element of opacity and interpretative ambiguity into GATS, making the

1. See, for example, Hoekman (1996); Feketekuty (1998); Sauvé (1995); Snape (1998).

agreement less effective as a system of rules and vehicle for further liberalization. In this section, we specify some of the more important areas where modifications—sometimes of a relatively straightforward nature—could make a significant contribution to the effectiveness of GATS.

Market Access and National Treatment

GATS schedules of specific commitments consist of market access undertakings potentially subject to six limitations (Article XVI) and national treatment undertakings that may be conditioned by any kind of specified discriminatory measure (Article XVII).[2] This bifurcation between market access limitations and discriminatory measures potentially raises some confusion about the true nature of members' scheduled commitments.[3] The problem is confounded by a scheduling convention set out in Article XX:1. This provision is intended to deal with situations where discriminatory market access limitations are scheduled, or in other words where restrictive measures fall within the scope of both Articles XVI and XVII. In such cases, Article XX:2 states that the relevant measures should be inscribed in the market access (Article XVI) column of the schedule and would be understood to provide a condition or qualification to Article XVII as well. Thus the market access column contains measures that are inconsistent with Article XVI only (nondiscriminatory market access limitations) and with both Article XVI and XVII, but there is frequently no indication whether the measures concerned are nondiscriminatory or discriminatory.

Since the precise overlap between Article XVI and Article XVII is not identified, the scope of the national treatment obligation remains ill-defined. This is already a problem. But in addition, suppose a member only undertakes to provide national treatment and not full market access. In this case, there is no way of knowing (in the absence of a proper definition of national treatment in relation to market access) whether any unscheduled improvements in market access would have to respect full national treatment. The problem of identifying the scope of national treatment is most acute in mode 3, bearing in mind that securing market access under this

---

2. The six permitted restrictions encompass limitations of the number of service suppliers, the value of transactions or assets, the number of operations or total quantity of output, the number of natural persons that may be employed, the nature of legal entities permitted to supply services, and the extent of participation of foreign equity in an enterprise.

3. For a full analysis of these issues, see Mattoo (1997).

mode is in practice a two-stage process—one set of measures will define the terms of entry for a foreign investor, and another will establish the conditions for postentry activity.

At least three possibilities suggest themselves in relation to the scope of national treatment in these circumstances.[4] The first possibility is full national treatment, which would cover both the right to establish, as well as postestablishment treatment. This interpretation is in line with the text of Article XVII, which states that this provision applies to "all measures affecting the supply of services." The second possibility is postentry national treatment, which would exclude the right to establish from the scope of the national treatment obligation. It is possible that scheduling practice (of at least some members) was based on the view that the national treatment obligation is only effective once a foreign company has been established in the territory of a member. A third possibility is limited national treatment, which would exclude all measures falling within the scope of Article XVI, including discriminatory quantitative restrictions, from the scope of the national treatment obligation. This interpretation would eliminate the overlap between the two provisions.

The differences among these three options are stark in terms of the value of a national treatment commitment, and the fact is that there are many entries in members' schedules where it would be impossible to determine which of these definitions of national treatment is to apply. What would be the value, for example, of a schedule entry in mode 3 recording no commitment under market access ("unbound"), or specifying the requirement of an economic needs test, and a full commitment under national treatment ("none," meaning no limitations)? Under one interpretation, national treatment would apply to all measures covered by Article XVII. An alternative interpretation is that national treatment would only provide a guarantee of nondiscrimination in relation to measures covered by Article XVII other than those covered by Article XVI. Clearly, this is an issue in need of attention.

Defining Specific Commitments in Terms of Modes of Supply

GATS defines trade in services in terms of the four modes of supply—cross-border supply (mode 1), consumption abroad (mode 2), commercial presence (mode 3), and the movement of natural persons (mode

4. Mattoo (1997)

4). These modes are also used for scheduling purposes. Two issues have arisen about the use of modes for scheduling purposes. The first is about overlap between modes, specifically modes 1 and 2. Second, the definition of "likeness" of foreign and national services and service suppliers across modes of delivery raises interpretative difficulties about the rights acquired through specific commitments at the modal level.

The problem of modal overlap attracted particular attention in the context of the negotiations on trade in financial services. In essence, the question is whether a crossborder financial service transaction should be classified as a mode 1 or a mode 2 transaction. At the margin, the answer can be virtually impossible to determine under existing definitions. If the transaction is deemed to have originated with a supplier in one jurisdiction selling a service to a consumer in another, then from the point of view of the jurisdiction in which the consumer is located, this would be classified as crossborder delivery, or a mode 1 transaction. If, however, the consumer initiates the transaction or solicits the service, it could be classified as consumption abroad. This potential confusion between mode 1 and mode 2 transactions obviously becomes important if the commitments scheduled by a member are not identical in both modes.

Several solutions to this problem have been mooted. One is to work toward ensuring that mode 1 and mode 2 commitments are indeed identical. The choice of modal definition could then turn on other matters—in particular, the question of whose regulatory system, or which territory, would have legal jurisdiction in respect of a transaction. Jurisdiction has not been addressed in the GATS context, and it is going to become increasingly important with the growth of electronic commerce. Part of the solution will presumably be to clarify the relationship between mode 1 and mode 2. Other suggestions for dealing with the modal definition issue include the amalgamation of both modes into a single one, the redefinition of mode 2 to require the physical movement of a consumer, and the requirement that every sectoral activity involving an interjurisdictional transaction is predefined in terms of the mode to which it belongs. Space limitations preclude a more systematic analysis of this issue, but in the absence of clarification, doubt will remain about the value of certain commitments.

The second problem concerns the possibility that a commitment on a particular service in one mode can be undermined by the absence of a commitment in another mode, or by an interpretation of the relationship among modes that treats a given service as an "unlike" product because it is delivered via one mode rather than another.[5] If, for example, a member has accorded unrestricted access to the foreign supply of a service under mode 1 in respect of both market access and national treatment, and then offers a subsidy to national producers of the same product in the domestic market —a measure seemingly consistent with GATS in the absence of a national treatment obligation under mode 3—then clearly the subsidy will alter the conditions of competition and undermine the value of the mode 1 commitment. Similarly, even if the subsidy were granted to both foreign and national producers operating in the national economy, or in other words, even if the member concerned had a national treatment commitment under mode 3 as well as mode 1, the grant of a subsidy to domestically based producers would undermine the value of the mode 1 commitment. Conversely, a tax on mode 3 production would undermine the rights of suppliers under this mode in relation to suppliers under mode 1.

There is nothing in the national treatment provisions of GATS (Article XVII) which suggests that the mode of supply is a determining factor in defining the "likeness" of a service—alternative modes of delivery may be used to supply "like" services. If this interpretation were adopted, then something would need to be done about the effects of an intervention under one mode on the value of a commitment under another. At present, probably the only recourse would be a nonviolation complaint under the World Trade Organization's (WTO's) Dispute Settlement Understanding.[6] However, the manner in which trade in services is defined through the modes, and the schedules designed, suggest that commitments are indeed mode specific. This issue needs attention.

Agreeing on Technological Neutrality in Scheduling

The description of a service under GATS may not be sufficiently developed or explicit for it to be clear whether a commitment is intended to be technology neutral. Technological neutrality refers to the idea that a commitment covers all means by which the service in question might be delivered within a mode of supply. It became apparent that WTO members were aware of these kinds of difficulties in the negotiations on basic telecommunications. A chairman's understanding was developed during

5. Mattoo (1997).

6. For a nonviolation complaint to prosper, it would need to be shown that the source of the difficulty could not have reasonably been anticipated at the time the commitment was entered into. This may prove a high standard to meet in the situations described above.

those negotiations to clarify the coverage of scheduled commitments. The understanding established a presumption that unless indicated to the contrary, the description of a basic telecommunication service in a member's schedule encompassed the full spectrum of ways in which a service could be supplied. A commitment on voice telephony, for example, would cover radio-based as well as wire-based technologies unless otherwise indicated. Similarly, in discussions in the WTO on electronic commerce and in the Committee on Specific Commitments, members seem to have agreed that a commitment on a service should be invariant with respect to the means by which the service is delivered.

In considering whether the means of conveying a service should be regarded as a distinguishing feature from a legal perspective, the concept of like product is crucial. It can be argued that products should be deemed alike regardless of the means by which they are conveyed from the supplier to the consumer. Suppose, for example, that a member claimed that legal services could be supplied crossborder through mail delivery but not through electronic delivery. To sustain the argument that such a regime is nondiscriminatory, it would be necessary to assert that identical products delivered by different means of conveyance were not like products in a legal sense. In the sphere of goods, a comparable case would be one in which garments transported by road would be subject to one regime and those transported by air would be subject to another. To justify this differentiated regime against a charge of national-treatment-inconsistency, garments entering by road and identical garments entering by air would have to be deemed unlike products. It is highly unlikely that a WTO panel would see matters in this light.

A further consideration is whether the market access restrictions permitted under Article XVI:2 of GATS, which are all expressed in quantitative terms, could encompass restrictions on the means of delivery of a service. It would appear that such restrictions are not covered. Since the only restrictions that may be scheduled under Article XVI:2 are those that are listed, this implies that limitations on the means by which a service is delivered can neither be scheduled nor directly disallowed. In the absence of an explicit understanding by governments in favor of neutrality toward alternative means of delivering a service, along the lines of the chairman's understanding developed in the basic telecommunications negotiations, such limitations could presumably be challenged through the two provisions in GATS dealing with nondiscrimination—the Article II MFN requirement and the Article XVII provisions on national treatment. These provisions would apply, for example, where some suppliers were permitted to use electronic means and others were not, and in the case of national treatment, if a service had been scheduled without national treatment limitations. Clarity and legal certainty would be improved if these different aspects of technological neutrality were clearly addressed.

The Relationship between Scheduled Commitments and Domestic Regulation

The structure of GATS requires that a tenable distinction be made between measures intended as limitations on access to the domestic market by foreign-produced services and service suppliers and measures adopted in pursuit of public policy objectives. This is the distinction between measures falling under Articles XVI and XVII on the one hand, and Article VI on the other. The approach has been to maintain that if a regulatory intervention embodies a market access restriction, the measure should be inscribed under Article XVI. If there is a discriminatory element, then the measure should be scheduled under Article XVII. In all other cases, the disciplines of Article VI apply. Regulatory interventions cannot of course be characterized as either restricting trade or not restricting trade, which is why the requirement exists that regulatory interventions must be the least-trade restrictive possible.

In practice, how clear will the distinction be between Article XVI and Article VI? Whether a public policy measure falls under one or other of these provisions may not always be clear at the margin and will require legal interpretation. Similarly, a discriminatory measure that is "excessive" in the sense of going beyond what is necessary to achieve a public policy objective would not be dealt with as an unnecessary barrier to trade under Article VI but as a measure in need of liberalization under Article XVII. In the work on accountancy of the Working Party on Professional Services, it became apparent that some members felt that embracing certain regulatory disciplines could imply de facto acceptance of market access commitments. A range of measures considered to fall within the ambit of Article XVI or Article XVII were consequently excluded from consideration. Furthermore, the Disciplines on Domestic Regulation in the Accountancy Sector drawn up by the WPPS apply only when members have entered into specific commitments. While it might be argued that the application of regulatory disciplines independently of the existence of specific commitments would be desirable because it would enhance the conditions of competition in the market, as a practical matter the value of regulatory disciplines in the absence of trade liberalization commitments would be very limited. The legal device of maintaining Articles XVI and XVII entirely separate from Article VI facilitates interpretation but does not alter the fact that in the absence of specific commitments, limitations on market access and national treatment can render Article VI disciplines ineffective. This conclusion suggests the need for a parallel approach to regulation and liberalization.

Why Schedules Must Not Double as Vehicles for Transparency nor Lack Legal Specificity

In many schedules, members have provided information that does not, on the face of it, concern the substance of the legal commitment being undertaken. The schedules are intended to specify in precise terms the nature of commitments on market access (Article XVI), national treatment (Article XVII), and additional commitments (Article XVIII). If descriptive material with no bearing on the legal commitments is included in the schedules, this may lead to legal uncertainty. Members may have chosen to include explanations and additional information because they felt it would clarify the nature of the policy regime to which they were making a commitment. To the extent that this is the case, it indicates a need for better mechanisms to provide such transparency. The schedules are not the place to do it.

At the same time, there are many examples in members' schedules where the precise nature of legal obligations is not spelled out. Perhaps the most egregious of these are the references to economic needs tests, permitted under Article XVI:2. When the nature of these needs tests is unspecified, uncertainty and scope for arbitrariness follow. Even if such measures were spelled out fully, they would raise problems about the security of market-access commitments if they were in any way made contingent on unforeseeable circumstances. And if this is not their intent, then it is unclear why the concept is necessary in the first instance.[7] No member inscribed an economic needs test in its schedule of commitments in the post–Uruguay Round negotiations on basic telecommunications and fi-

---

7. The question whether market access should be made contingent on unpredictable circumstances is under consideration in the ongoing negotiations on a possible emergency safeguard mechanism under GATS. If such a mechanism were to be agreed, it would surely contain provisions against its careless or excessive use.

nancial services, perhaps indicating a willingness by members to dispense with this instrument of trade restriction.

A more general point about clarity in schedules is that the product nomenclature used in GATS has severe shortcomings. First, many members have used their own definitions of certain sectors, subsectors, or particular services activities, sometimes with no reference to any established nomenclature. Second, the nomenclature developed by the Group of Negotiations on Services during the Uruguay Round (document MTN.GNS/W/120), which was relied on by many members to a significant degree, is too aggregated to provide adequate standardized definitions in many sectors. Work is under way under UN auspices to improve the nomenclature. The development of an adequate system of nomenclature is an essential part of improving the clarity of scheduled commitments.

Promoting Further Liberalization

Three questions help to determine the quality of liberalization commitments. The first concerns the relationship between foreign equity participation and the conditions of competition in the market. The second relates to the use of GATS schedules as a mechanism for precommitments to future liberalization, and the third relates to the gap between commitments and actual policies (ceiling bindings).

Increased Competition versus Foreign Equity Participation

One aspect of the existing commitments that evokes concern is the emphasis on change of ownership rather than on the introduction of entry. For instance, for the commitments on financial services, the pattern differs across regions: in Latin America, many members have retained discretion on whether to allow entry, but few have imposed limits on foreign equity participation.[8] In Asia, the two types of limitations are frequently encountered together. Apart from economic considerations, these differences in policy reflect differences in political attitudes to foreign direct investment and varying degrees of concern about the prospect of foreign ownership and control in financial services.

8. It is possible that the discretionary licensing in some Latin American countries could pertain to both entry and equity participation.

A multilateral commitment by a government to allow entry influences the degree to which markets are contestable. Regardless of the existing market structure, established suppliers in the market are likely to behave more competitively if there are no legal barriers to entry. Increased competition brings benefits through promoting allocative efficiency, that is, pricing close to costs, and internal efficiency, producing at least cost. Conversely, privately efficient profit seeking behind protective barriers cannot be expected to lead to socially efficient results. Restrictions on entry benefit producers at the expense of consumers. The earnings of producers are then greater than the social productivity of the inputs because there is a component that is a transfer from consumers. It is therefore desirable for the scope of competitive forces to be enhanced by the effective removal of barriers to entry.

In light of the emphasis in the GATS negotiations on increasing permitted (or maintaining existing) levels of foreign equity participation, it is interesting to consider the implications of a situation in which foreign participation has been permitted, without an increase in the degree of competition allowed to occur in the market. In other words, what are the welfare consequences of foreign ownership without adequate competition? Foreign investment clearly brings benefits even when it does not lead to enhanced competition. First, allowing foreign equity participation may relax a capital constraint that could otherwise result in socially suboptimal levels of investment in the sector. Furthermore, the benefits of increased investment in helping to recapitalize troubled financial institutions in many developing countries cannot be underestimated. In fact, one reason why countries may have chosen this particular combination of policies, that is, to restrict new entry while allowing foreign equity participation, is probably because they would like new foreign capital to help strengthen weak domestic financial institutions rather than to come in the form of highly competitive new banks and insurance companies that might drive their domestic rivals out of business. Second, foreign equity participation may serve as a vehicle for transferring technology and know-how. The benefits come not only in the form of technological innovations, such as new methods of electronic banking, but also in terms of improved management and credit assessment techniques, as well as higher standards of transparency and self-regulation.

Against these benefits, there may well be costs associated with foreign direct investment when competition is restricted. If foreign investment comes simply because the returns to investment are artificially raised by restrictions on competition, then the cost to the host country may exceed the benefits, because the returns to the investor will be greater than the true social productivity of the investment. The argument may be presented in an alternative form. Aggregate national welfare in a particular sector can be seen as the sum of consumers' surplus and national producers' profits (plus government revenue). In competitive markets, welfare is greatest because marginal social benefit is equated to marginal social cost. In imperfectly competitive markets, welfare is reduced because output is restricted to a level at which marginal social benefit exceeds marginal social cost. Producers gain at the expense of consumers. Now if foreign participation enhances competition, welfare may increase, but if foreign participation takes place with limited change in competition, then there is a further reduction in national welfare because of the transfer of rents from national producers to foreign producers.[9]

In this context, it is important to consider a scheduling innovation that helped solve one of the central problems in the financial services negotiations. The conflict arose because certain countries were unwilling to make commitments that reflected the status quo with respect to commercial presence. Thus, they were either inclined to bind foreign ownership levels below those that currently prevailed or insist on legal forms (local incorporation) other than those currently in the market (branches), or both. In some cases, the problem arose because domestic law had changed since the foreign firms first established commercial presence, for example, in Malaysia, where the indigenization policy was being implemented after the establishment of many foreign firms. In other cases domestic law became less restrictive than the binding, for example, in the Philippines, where the law enacted in 1994 stipulates maximum foreign equity of 60 percent in banking, but new entry is bound at 51 percent.

The three types of grandfathering provisions, foreign equity-related, legal form-related, and general, are to be found in the financial services schedules. It is evident that grandfathering was primarily an Asian phenomenon, prompted presumably by the introduction of more restrictive

---

9. To some extent rent appropriation can, of course, be prevented by profit taxation or by holding competitive auctions of licenses or equity. The rents would then accrue to the government or to existing national shareholders. But the static and dynamic inefficiencies consequent upon lack of competition would still exist. Creating discriminatory profit tax regimes would have negative incentive effects on new foreign investment, but such regimes are ruled out of course where commitments are undertaken to provide national treatment. Furthermore, while equity auctions may prevent net profit transfers abroad through new acquisitions, and license auctions achieve the same vis-à-vis new entrants, neither addresses appropriation by existing foreign share owners. In this context, the grandfathering commitments assume particular significance.

regimes pertaining to foreign equity and legal form than had prevailed when the foreign firms first entered. The grandfathering provisions reflect the relative emphasis in these negotiations on guaranteeing the rights of incumbents. They provide the benefits of security to investors who are already present in the market rather than to new investors. Furthermore, they may even place new entrants at a competitive disadvantage where differences in ownership and legal form affect firm performance.

It would seem desirable in future negotiations to put a greater emphasis on the introduction of competition rather than maintaining or creating foreign ownership. One way in which this could be done is by creating a stronger presumption against restrictions on the number of suppliers even when they are accompanied by a relaxation of restrictions on the number of foreign suppliers. But it is not clear whether any rule could prevent countries from negotiating patterns of liberalization that are mutually acceptable but not economically optimal.

Precommitting to Future Liberalization

What is the potential role of the WTO as a vehicle for promoting future liberalization? One of the reasons why governments are unwilling to liberalize immediately can be seen as a variant of the traditional "infant industry" or "infant regulation" arguments. The first is based on considerations of potential comparative advantage, whereby currently disadvantaged national suppliers, if provided with protected markets, are expected to learn by doing and eventually become internationally competitive. The failure of these policies in the past, and the innumerable examples of perpetual infancy, may well be attributed to the inability of a government to threaten credibly to liberalize at some future date—either because it has a stake in the national firm's continued operation, or because it is vulnerable to pressure from interest groups that benefit from protection.[10]

GATS offers a valuable mechanism to overcome the difficulty of making credible commitments to liberalize. Commitments to provide

---

10. National firms often behave as if they prefer to operate as high-cost, poor-quality producers in protected markets than as low-cost, high-quality producers facing international competition. This may be because of the profitability of protection, or the greater utility that managers and workers derive from operating in sheltered environments. In any case, when the government cannot credibly threaten to liberalize, then national firms may have an incentive to precommit to high costs or poor quality, in an environment of slow learning and underinvestment in research and development. Such behavior by the firm, either for strategic reasons or on account of inertia, forces governments to prolong socially costly protection. See Staiger and Tabellini (1987) for a variant of this argument.

market access and national treatment at a future date are binding under WTO law. Failure to honor these commitments would create an obligation to compensate those who are deprived of benefits. This need to compensate does in fact make the commitment more credible than a mere announcement of liberalizing intent in the national context.

Several governments have already taken advantage of this mechanism to strike a balance between, on the one hand, their reluctance immediately to unleash competition on protected national suppliers, and, on the other hand, their desire not to be held hostage to these suppliers in perpetuity. For instance, in basic telecommunications, several governments made commitments to future liberalization, including a number of Asian and Latin American countries.[11] In financial services there was less evidence of such commitments. This could be seen as a consequence of the uncertain economic climate in which the negotiations were concluded, but it could also be argued that precommitment to future liberalization would have contributed to creating stability. In future negotiations, it would seem desirable to encourage such precommitments where there are difficulties in immediate liberalization. In fact, it may be required of countries to demonstrate why it is not possible to make such commitments, at least on the basis of a pessimistic, delayed liberalization scenario—unless it is the intention to provide protection in perpetuity.

Ceiling Bindings

Many members, especially developing countries, have undertaken specific commitments that define minimum access guarantees that are less than the status quo in terms of access permitted to foreign services or foreign service suppliers. Commitments of this kind are to be contrasted with those that define actual levels of access and those that promise improved access in the future. In both financial services and basic telecommunications, there are examples of each of these levels of commitment.[12] In the sphere of trade in goods, Joe Francois and Will Martin have used a model constructed on a probability distribution of policy outcomes to argue that ceiling bindings are likely to give rise to more liberalization than situations in which there are no bindings at all.[13]

11. Low and Mattoo (1997).
12. Kono and others (1997); Low and Mattoo (1997); Mattoo (1997).
13. Francois and Martin (1996).

While ceiling bindings may have positive value, however, they clearly offer less guaranteed access or legal security than bindings that reflect actual or future additional levels of binding. There is an argument, therefore, for seeking ways of bringing bindings closer to the policy status quo. In practical terms of course the gap can widen again as markets become more open unless an undertaking exists automatically to ratchet up scheduled commitments in the face of liberalizing policy changes. In discussions on the possible development of a safeguard mechanism in GATS, it has been suggested that the possibility of taking safeguard action might be linked to commitment levels that reflect the status quo or entail a precommitment to future liberalization.

Deepening Disciplines

This section looks very briefly at what is arguably the single most important area in which GATS disciplines are in need of deepening—that of domestic regulation. However, we only seek to lay out an analytical framework that seems useful in addressing the issues involved. Considerable further analysis of these issues is needed, especially in light of the importance of adequate disciplines on domestic regulation as an accompaniment of liberalization.

Strengthening Domestic Regulation

Trade in services, far more than trade in goods, is affected by a variety of domestic regulations. A central task in the coming GATS negotiations will be to develop disciplines which ensure that such regulations support rather than impede trade liberalization. One basic discipline, the national treatment obligation, requires that regulations do not discriminate in any way against foreigners. However, trade can be inhibited even by regulations that do not discriminate, like certain standards and licensing requirements, and by the absence of pro-competitive regulations. While important initiatives have recently been taken to remedy these problems in accountancy and telecommunications, the general disciplines on domestic regulations in the General Agreement on Trade in Services remain weak. As we approach the next round of services negotiations, the question arises as to whether it is best to rely on further sectoral initiatives or whether it is possible to adopt a more general approach.

The diversity of services sectors, and the difficulty in making certain policy-relevant generalizations, has tended to favor a sector-specific approach. However, it can be argued that even though services sectors differ greatly, the underlying economic and social reasons for regulatory intervention do not. And focusing on these reasons provides the basis for the creation of meaningful horizontal disciplines. Before elaborating on the suggested way forward, note that such a generic approach is to be preferred to a sectoral approach for at least three reasons: it economizes on negotiating effort, leads to the creation of disciplines for all services sectors rather than only the politically important ones, and reduces the likelihood of negotiations being captured by sectoral interest groups.

The basic argument can be summarized as follows.[14] The economic case for regulation in all services sectors arises essentially from market failure attributable to three kinds of problem—natural monopoly or oligopoly, externalities, and asymmetric information. The social case for regulation, however, is based primarily on considerations of equity. Market failure owing to natural monopoly or oligopoly may create trade problems because incumbents can impede access to markets in the absence of appropriate regulation. Because of its direct impact on trade, this is the only form of market failure that needs to be addressed directly by multilateral disciplines. The relevant GATS provision, Article VIII dealing with monopolies, is limited in scope. As a consequence, in the context of the telecom negotiations, the Reference Paper with its competition principles was developed to ensure that monopolistic suppliers would not undermine market access commitments. These principles should be generalized to a variety of other network services, including transport (terminals and infrastructure), environmental services (sewage), and energy services (distribution networks).

In all other cases of market failure, multilateral disciplines do not need to address the problem per se but rather to ensure that domestic measures to deal with the problem do not serve unduly to restrict trade. The same is generally true for measures designed to achieve social objectives. Such trade-restrictive effects can arise from a variety of technical standards, prudential regulations, and qualification requirements in professional, financial, and numerous other services, as well as from the granting of monopoly rights to complement universal service obligations in services like transport and telecommunications.

14. Gamberale and Mattoo (1999).

The trade-inhibiting effect of this entire class of regulations is best disciplined by complementing the national treatment obligation with a generalization of the so-called "necessity" test. This test essentially leaves governments free to deal with economic and social problems provided that any measures taken are not more trade restrictive than necessary to achieve the relevant objective. Such a test already appears in GATS, weakly in Article VI on domestic regulations, and more effectively in Article XIV on general exceptions, and has been further developed in the accountancy negotiations. One of the shortcomings of the necessity test is that it has often been less than clear what criteria are to be used in determining whether a measure can be judged "necessary" in relation to alternative interventions. Criteria built explicitly on the notion of economic efficiency could reduce uncertainty on this point, offering a sound and consistent methodology for choosing interventions to remedy market failure or to pursue noneconomic objectives.

Improving the Negotiating Methodology

Part IV of GATS carries the title "Progressive Liberalization" and the associated text talks of achieving "a progressively higher level of liberalization" through successive rounds of negotiation. As noted at the outset, many commentators have observed that the level of liberalization achieved or committed to is quite modest so far. GATS is certainly designed to accommodate gradualism. Is there, nevertheless, potential for concerted or more coordinated approaches to liberalization, such that members end up making more far-reaching commitments, generally and at the sectoral level?

In the sphere of trade in goods, governments have sometimes agreed to a formula on the basis of which they cut tariffs across the board by a uniform amount. In the Tokyo Round (1973–79), a weighted formula was devised so that higher tariffs would be cut more deeply than lower ones. This approach had the effect of moving the liberalization process ahead on multiple fronts, although exceptions to the formula applied in certain sectors. Such an approach is easier to conceive where there is a single policy instrument—the tariff—to consider. In the sphere of services, the situation can be more complex. Many different instruments determine the prevailing degree of liberalization, and the lack of adequate nomenclature may complicate efforts to ensure uniformity of commitments among members.

But already in services, there are examples of concerted liberalization packages through which a number of members have agreed to a uniform set of commitments. These are approaches that could be built upon.

Alternative Formulas for Negotiation

Three different "models" of a concerted approach to liberalization suggest themselves from the experience accumulated so far in the GATS context. First, model schedules were developed in the maritime and basic telecommunications negotiations. The basic purpose of the model schedules was to identify a set of subsectors and commitments that would be assumed by all parties to the negotiations. The premise was that agreement on standardized commitments would secure a higher level of commitment overall than if members devised their liberalization offers independently. A package would not only guarantee an acceptable degree of reciprocity but also define areas for exclusion and areas where differing degrees of liberalization were feasible. In maritime services, for example, there was agreement to exclude cabotage altogether from the picture. And the separation of bulk and liner shipping services permitted members to offer more in the former area than they would have been willing to do without this separation. Similarly, it was essential in basic telecommunications to separate out international, domestic long-distance, and local loop telephony services. In any event, the maritime negotiations did not come to closure, nor did the draft model schedule in basic telecommunications prosper greatly among members, but the approach clearly holds significant promise in future negotiations.

Second, in financial services, a formula approach was developed, although only a restricted number of (mostly developed) countries adopted the formula. The Understanding on Commitments in Financial Services specified the content of market access commitments and in addition contained provisions dealing with procurement, the treatment of new financial services, and a standstill commitment.[15] Two points are significant about this initiative. First, by addressing such questions as a standstill, procurement rules, and the treatment of financial services, the understanding took members further than they would otherwise have been able to go in terms of the GATS framework of rules and the normal approach to liberalizations commitments. Second, the members that accepted this

15. Kono and Low (1997).

approach were willing to do so on a most favored nation basis, thereby ensuring a higher level of openness without compromising the basic non-discriminatory structure of a multilateral agreement.

Third, the Reference Paper in basic telecommunications was a set of regulatory commitments entered in the additional commitments column (Article XVIII) of the schedules of those members that accepted the disciplines. This instrument attracted many more signatories (more than fifty) than the Understanding on Financial Services and was regarded by many as a sine qua non for rendering meaningful the market access and national treatment commitments contained in members' schedules. Without effective regulation, it was feared that monopolistic market power in the telecommunications sector could be used to neutralize the competitive and market-opening effects of market access and national treatment commitments. The Reference Paper was about more than market access, in the sense that it entailed regulation, but it is a good example of a cooperative effort around a common set of commitments that led to more effective market opening than would have otherwise been possible. A similar effort was in the making in the maritime negotiations, where additional commitments were drawn up to safeguard access to and use of port services.

These experiences demonstrate different ways in which formula approaches might be crafted. We would suggest an appropriate generalization of the above three models along the following lines. The model schedule approach is most suitable to situations where there may be ambiguity about sectoral definition and a degree of consensus between members on the areas where liberalization is feasible. One area in which such an approach may be fruitful is with respect to the presence of natural persons: clear definitions could be agreed for the categories of skilled workers (currently listed as managers, executives, and specialists), and a strong presumption could be created in favor of a certain threshold level of liberalization built into the model schedule. Then the burden would be on a member to justify its refusal to concede the threshold level rather than for other members to extract the minimum concessions through painful negotiations. The approach may also be useful in other sectors where segmentation facilitates the establishment of clear focal points on the acceptable level of liberalization. It would seem appropriate for members with special interests in particular sectors to prepare such model schedules and to secure their general acceptability by striking the necessary balance between their own ambitions and the feasibility of widespread liberalization.

The Financial Services Understanding approach is most suitable for areas where only a subset of members are willing to develop deeper disciplines, but are, nevertheless, willing to extend the benefits on a most favored nation basis to all other members. Whereas the model schedule reflects a situation in which all members simultaneously accept certain commitments, the understanding is more on the lines of a leader-follower model—though, given the nature of the negotiating process, the leaders would understandably be reluctant to reveal their identity too early. This approach (or outcome) would obviously be feasible where participating members are satisfied by the acceptance of disciplines by a critical mass of members rather than all of them. The approach has the advantages of the Tokyo Round Codes without their disadvantages: it would facilitate effective and quick negotiations among like-minded members and create a positive demonstration effect on initially nonparticipating members, without creating a discriminatory arrangement. Thus the acceptance of disciplines in more sectors on government procurement, the treatment of new services, and a standstill on new restrictive measures are among the possible candidates for such an approach.

Finally, as has been argued earlier, it would make sense to generalize the basic telecommunication Reference Paper model to other network-based industries, where procompetitive regulations are called for at the sectoral level in order to underwrite effective market access.

"Negative" Lists versus "Positive" Lists of Liberalization Commitments

Much discussion has taken place about the difference between a positive and negative list approach to identifying specific commitments. A positive list approach is one where parties to an agreement specify which sectors are covered. A negative list approach, by contrast, requires that parties specify the sectors that are not covered by commitments. GATS uses a positive list approach to identify sectoral coverage and then a negative list approach to indicate limitations to market access and national treatment commitments in respect of sectors listed in schedules. NAFTA, by contrast, relies on a negative list approach. Pierre Sauvé has argued strongly in favor of a negative list approach, which has also been advocated by R. Snape.[16]

The issue can be considered at two levels. One is somewhat trivial, in that it concerns little more than the choice between saying what is to be done and what is not to be done. In these terms, the case for a negative list turns on

16. Sauvé (1999); Snape (1998).

three arguments.[17] First, a negative list approach will foster greater transparency, as it will be immediately obvious which sectors or activities are excluded from coverage. However, exclusions can be identified by deduction under a positive list approach, and arguments about the need for transparency might be better addressed more directly through appropriate transparency provisions. Second, a negative list approach may generate a greater pro-liberalization dynamic, as governments might be embarrassed by long lists of exceptions. It is not obvious, however, why governments would be more embarrassed by long negative lists than by short positive ones. Finally, a negative list approach would imply that any new services developed as a result of innovation or technological advancement, or for any other reason, would automatically be subject to established disciplines. This is potentially a strong liberalizing argument for a negative list approach but may also be the one that makes governments cautious about adopting this approach.

A more fundamental interpretation of a negative list approach is that, unlike a positive list, it would entail an across-the-board binding with respect to all services activities. The negative listing would then apply only with respect to specifically identifiable nonconforming measures in particular sectors. The liberalizing consequences of such an approach would obviously be more far-reaching than what exists today under GATS. But as soon as a negative listing permits the exclusion of sectors, the difference between the two approaches becomes less interesting (as suggested above). We would argue that members are simply not ready to make commitments in all services sectors, and that even if they did, they would be tempted to specify heavy-handed restricting measures in their negative lists that would take the substance out of commitments in sectors that they regarded as sensitive. Instead of arguing for what would amount to a significant structural change in GATS, therefore, we conclude that the preferable approach for the time being would be to emphasize reductions in limitations currently inscribed in schedules—especially with respect to the "unbound" entries—and at the same time to press for widening the scope of sectoral coverage in existing schedules.

Conclusion

A basic conclusion of this chapter is that it is possible to make significant improvements in GATS and to make it a much more effective

17. Low (1997).

instrument of liberalization, without fundamental structural changes, which are, in any case, of doubtful political feasibility. This chapter has identified four broad themes: improving the clarity of the agreement, using the existing structure to generate more effective liberalization, deepening the disciplines on domestic regulations, and improving the negotiating dynamic. To an extent, our proposals build on the existing commitment to successive rounds of negotiations aimed at "achieving a progressively higher level of liberalization" (Article XIX:1 of GATS), and on the existing negotiating mandates to develop new rules. However, we believe that there is also need for an explicit mandate for work on improving the clarity of the agreement. Some of the ambiguities in GATS are quite fundamental, turning on questions of interpretation that make a significant difference to the nature of members' obligations and the extent of market access and rule-based certainty delivered by the agreement. The main suggestions made in the chapter are summarized below.

Areas for Clarification

—Clarifying the relationship between market access and national treatment in order to specify precisely the scope of existing and future national treatment commitments. At present, credible alternative interpretations carry starkly different implications.

—Clarifying the relationship among modes of supply with respect to commitments on a given services activity. Is a service delivered under different modes considered a "like" service regardless of the modal distinctions made in schedules? If not, as the structure of the schedules suggests, then the rights of members should be clarified with respect to policy interventions in one mode that may undermine the value of a commitment in another.

—Confirming that the principle of technological neutrality applies within modes. In other words, within a mode of supply, a service is to be regarded as "like" independently of the means by which it is delivered. It should also be confirmed that no scope exists under Article XVI for scheduling restrictions based on the manner of conveyance of a service within the same mode. This would confirm, for instance, that existing commitments cover electronic delivery of services.

In view of the clear separation that GATS seeks to establish between market access and national treatment on the one hand, and domestic regulation on the other, it is clear that meaningful progress in strengthening the domestic regulation provisions of GATS Article VI only makes sense where specific market-access commitments have been undertaken. Otherwise, the value of good regulation can simply be nullified by restrictions on access to the market. For this reason, work on domestic regulation and improving the quality of liberalization commitments should proceed in tandem.

—Eliminating extraneous descriptive material from the schedules of commitments to prevent interpretative confusion regarding the true scope of bound market access and national treatment commitments. Only commitments should be inscribed in schedules, and members should consider whether it would be useful to supplement existing transparency provisions with an additional mechanism of a nonbinding nature for information that will contribute to a better understanding of commitments.

—According priority to the development of a detailed nomenclature that should be generally applicable. The absence of an adequate nomenclature works against transparency and the enforceability of commitments.

Promoting Further Liberalization

Attention should be focused on the manner in which market access liberalization is defined. In particular, emphasis should be focused upon ensuring foreign market entry to enhance contestability and improve the conditions of competition in the market. Merely increasing foreign equity participation in existing enterprises is less likely to achieve these beneficial effects and could lead to losses in national welfare in imperfectly competitive markets.

Members should use services negotiations more to make phased-in commitments to liberalization, as a number of countries did in the basic telecommunications negotiations. Precommitment is a valuable instrument for planning future market opening in a credible manner and guaranteeing adequate time to ensure that the necessary conditions are in place when additional competition is introduced into the market.

Deepening Disciplines

Meaningful liberalization requires that the provisions on domestic regulations are strengthened. The basic approach should be horizontal in nature, to take advantage of economies of scale in rule-making and lessen the risk of regulatory capture. Sector-specific regulatory provisions may sometimes be necessary to supplement the horizontal approach. Horizontally based regulation implies generalization of existing initiatives, depending on the source of market failure that the regulatory intervention is designed to address. Where a problem arises from monopolistic or oligopolistic control over essential facilities, the approach should be to develop regulatory principles along the lines of those negotiated in the basic telecommunications sector. Where other market failures are present, the "necessity" test should be applied, on the basis of criteria built explicitly on economic efficiency criteria.

Improving the Negotiating Methodology

Different formulas have been used in sectoral liberalization negotiations so far, and these approaches should be built upon. A model schedule can be helpful where ambiguity over sectoral definitions coexists with potential consensus on the degree of liberalization that is achievable. Providing collective focal points (that function like a negative list approach) is likely to lead to more liberalization. Understandings such as those developed in the financial services sector make sense where some members are willing to undertake deeper commitments or accept stricter rules but need to develop a common understanding as to the content of such liberalization or rules. Such initiatives will unambiguously raise the level of liberalization, provided they are built around the MFN principle. The idea of developing standardized sets of additional commitments, such as the pro-competitive regulations in the basic telecommunications Reference Paper, has significant appeal and may find a place in negotiations in other network-based industries, as discussed above.

References

Feketekuty, G. 1998. "Setting the Agenda for the Next Round of Negotiations of Trade in Services." In *Launching New Global Trade Talks: An Action Agenda*, edited by J. Schott, 91–110. Washington: Institute for International Economics.

Francois, J. F., and W. Martin. 1996. "Multilateral Trade Rules and the Expected Cost of Protection." WTO Working Paper. ERAD 96-010. Geneva: WTO.

Gamberale, C., and A. Mattoo. 1999. "Domestic Regulation and the GATS." Mimeo. Washington: World Bank.

Hoekman, B. 1996. "Assessing the General Agreement on Trade in Services." In *The Uruguay Round and the Developing Countries*, edited by W. Martin and L. A. Winters, 88–124. Cambridge: Cambridge University Press.

Kono, M., and others. 1997. *Opening Markets in Financial Services and the Role of the GATS.* WTO Secretariat Special Study. Geneva: WTO.

Low, Patrick. 1997. "Impact of the Uruguay Round on Asia: Trade in Services and Trade-Related Investment Measures." In *The Global Trading System and Developing Asia,* edited by A. Panagariya, M. G. Quibria, and N. Rao, 481–544. London: Oxford University Press.

Low, Patrick, and Aaditya Mattoo. 1997. "Reform in Basic Telecommunications and the WTO Negotiations: The Asian Experience." WTO Working Paper. Geneva: WTO.

Mattoo, Aaditya. 1997. "National Treatment in the GATS: Corner-Stone or Pandora's Box?" *Journal of World Trade* 31 (1): 107–36. Geneva: Kluwer Academic Publishers.

Sauvé, Pierre. 1995. "Assessing the General Agreement on Trade in Services, Half-Full or Half-Empty?" *Journal of World Trade* 29 (4): 125–45. Geneva: Kluwer Academic Publishers.

———. 1997. "Qs and As on Trade, Investment, and the WTO." *Journal of World Trade* 31: 55–79. Geneva: Kluwer Academic Publishers.

———. 1999. "The Benefits of Trade and Investment Liberalisation: Financial Services." In *Financial Liberalisation in Asia: Analysis and Prospects,* edited by D. Brooks and M. Queisser, 173–88. Paris: Asian Development Bank and OECD Development Center.

Snape, R. 1998. "Reaching Effective Agreements Covering Services." In *The WTO as an International Organization,* edited by A. Krueger, 279–95. University of Chicago Press.

Snape, R., and M. Bosworth. 1996. "Advancing Services Negotiation." In *The World Trading System: Challenges Ahead,* edited by J. Schott, 185–203. Washington: Institute for International Economics.

Staiger, R., and G. Tabellini. 1987. "Discretionary Trade Policy and Excessive Protection." *American Economic Review* 77: 823–37. Menasha, Wis.: American Economic Association.

16 | *Formula Approaches to Improving GATS Commitments*

RACHEL THOMPSON

THIS CHAPTER SETS OUT some practical options for what tend to be described as "cross-cutting" or "quasi-formula" approaches to multilateral services negotiations. In the Geneva preparations for the new GATS round there is an exploratory level of interest and discussion of the formula issue as a potential means of contributing to the efficient conduct of the negotiations and the production of significant results. However, there is uncertainty about whether and how formula approaches are applicable to the services negotiating context, what the practical benefits are likely to be, and how to ensure "balance" and flexibility in the application of such approaches while yielding commercially meaningful results. The aim of this chapter is to provide a practical analysis of these issues.

What's in a Name?

A key issue at the outset is whether the term "formula approaches" is appropriate in the GATS context. This question arises because for many trade negotiators the word "formula" has a scientific or mathematical connotation, signifying the use of quantitative equations for reductions in trade barriers, as in past GATT rounds. However, according to many dictionaries, a formula, as well as being mathematical equations or formal logical expressions, can also be qualitative or normative in nature, comprising for example:

473

—Any immediately recognizable sequence of events defined by rules and composed of a finite number of steps;

—A prescribed normative set, form, or example; established rule; or conventional method by which anything is to be done, arranged, or said; and

—A standard procedure for solving a class of problems.

Why Use Formula Approaches?

In multilateral trade negotiations, formula approaches to the reduction of trade barriers and trade-distorting measures are really a way to ensure that participants make a broadly comparable contribution to the liberalization goals, notwithstanding that their starting points may differ. As such, formulas represent a method or model for securing a core level of liberalization overall and by individual participants. There may be a single formula or a set of them, they may be quantitative or qualitative (or a combination) in nature, and they may be used for a specific sector or across several or all sectors covered by a negotiation. In tariff negotiations, formula approaches (target cuts) have tended to be agreed to at the outset; while in agriculture and services negotiations, the formula approaches (agreed scope of tariff and subsidy cuts, model services scheduling practices) have emerged in the course of the negotiations.

One of the principal rationales for formula approaches to the reduction of trade barriers and trade-distorting measures is to facilitate the negotiating process among a very large WTO membership. This is because the formulas constitute a set of common benchmarks for undertaking a collective effort. This can generate several political, economic, and technical benefits:

—Allowing a hierarchy of targets to be set, both overall and for particular sectors, against which negotiating progress and results can be benchmarked;

—Improving public comprehension of those negotiating goals and results;

—Generating efficiencies of scale and effort in the negotiation of cross-sectoral issues, freeing up time to focus on sector-specific and rules issues; and

—Improving the consistency, clarity, and user-friendliness of resulting schedules.

In the GATS context, where the new round will entail negotiating specific commitments for some 160 subsectors and among more than 130 members, the use of formulas as a starting point for negotiations may be expected to yield significant gains in the efficiency and transparency of the negotiations. Formula approaches can also help to promote awareness that open markets—and the WTO bindings to demonstrate it—are in a country's own economic interest rather than simply "concessions" to be granted in response to a demand from negotiating partners and "exchanged" on a reciprocal basis. This is particularly the case for services, where trade is largely composed of growth-enhancing and employment-generating inward investment, technology, and expertise.

For developing countries, formula approaches provide an opportunity to shape a package approach to market access commitments into which their particular interests are integrated from the outset. In the case of services, where stand-alone negotiations on movement of natural persons and the maritime transport sector have not succeeded in the past, and where developing countries' other commercial interests are likely to be very specific (for example, computer services, health services, access to electronic advertising, reservation and distribution networks, and so on), a formula package that includes specific liberalization for these issues could be an extremely important way for developing countries to secure results on their services priorities.

By contrast, in bilateral request-offer processes, many developing countries either do not receive requests from OECD countries, making it difficult for them to draw attention to their own requests on OECD countries; or else they receive lengthy sectoral and horizontal request lists from OECD countries while themselves submitting much shorter requests, making for a lopsided negotiation. As well, conventional request-offer approaches are very resource-intensive, particularly for smaller delegations. By contrast, formula approaches, supplemented where necessary by focused request-offer negotiations with main trading partners, help to maximize the use of scarce human resources in the negotiations.

The success of formula approaches depends in large part on reconciling somewhat contradictory considerations. On the one hand, it is important to allay concerns that formula approaches—particularly cross-sectoral or generic ones—will produce only token or minimalist results because the formulas will be watered down, provide too much scope for exceptions, or participants will be unwilling to go "further than the formula" in specific sectors. On the other hand, it is important to ensure that the formulas cover the interests of all participants and provide scope for flexibility for particular countries (for example, longer time frames for developing countries) and particular sectors (for example, the prudential carve-out in financial services, the particular sensitivity of broadcasting services for many countries).

Thus formulas need to be sufficiently ambitious, specific, balanced, and flexible if they are to produce commercially meaningful initial offers from most participants while not foreclosing the opportunity to build a bigger package through further request-offer negotiations or sectoral approaches. Moreover, while the formulas themselves will probably need to be negotiated, it will be important that questions of principle pertaining to their use in a new GATS round are resolved early in the negotiations if negotiators are to avoid the protracted theological debate about formulas that characterized the Uruguay Round negotiations on industrial tariffs. This will be particularly important in view of the widespread desire to conclude the new WTO round within three years.

A Complementary Role

The use of formula approaches does not nullify the traditional "request-offer" approach so much as streamline it into a more efficient process in which bilateral negotiations and trade-offs have a more focused role. In effect the formulas are used as the basis for preparing initial offers, after which requests can be made for further improvements through revised offers and bilateral negotiations. For example, some participants may seek an exception from one formula by offering more than is required by another formula. Disagreements may arise over whether an initial offer adequately reflects a formula requirement, and some participants may be willing to go beyond the formulas if a "critical mass" of others do as well. Certainly this is the experience from the use of formula approaches in past rounds of GATT tariff and agriculture negotiations.

The use of formula approaches, supplemented in this way with more focused request-offer approaches, is likely to be a more efficient basis for proceeding for several reasons. First, by requiring all participants to submit initial offers based on the formulas rather than waiting for trading partners to submit requests, a certain amount of time is saved. Second, a higher level of country and sectoral coverage is secured at the outset. By contrast, when only traditional request-offer approaches are used, the negotiations among the largest participants absorb a high proportion of their time and effort and smaller participants often feel marginalized or excluded from the shaping of the negotiating parameters. As well, at least some of the existing gaps in GATS specific commitments arise from the fact that requests were not made of some countries in the Uruguay Round. Third, conducting an initial round of offers based on a formula approach will provide governments and business with a solid "information base" on what remains to be achieved through bilateral requests for improved offers. This permits negotiating time and energy to be focused on outstanding priorities not covered by the formula-based initial offers, and on rules negotiations.

Quantitative Formula Approaches

In past GATT rounds, *quantitative* formula approaches have been used, in tandem with request-offer negotiations, to secure numerical cuts in individual types of price-based measures such as tariffs and agricultural subsidies (that is, percentage cuts in ad valorem tariff levels and in budgetary outlay and quantity levels of subsidies) (box 16-1).

By contrast with those particular goods trade measures, services trade liberalization involves the removal or relaxation of numerous and diverse barriers to trade and investment arising from domestic laws, regulations, and practices that have social as well as economic objectives. Only some of these measures are "fixed" in terms of value/volume and point of application (for example, quotas on foreign investment or foreign specialists), while others involve the exercise of regulatory discretion or have ongoing application inside the market. As well, multiple measures may apply to the provision of a particular service.

These factors make it very difficult to establish discrete and comparable data sets on specific types of measures and to determine their effects on trade flows in price, volume, or other quantifiable terms. Consequently, the types of quantitative formulas for the reduction of primary trade barriers that have been used in GATT negotiations will not translate across to services at this time; although they may become technically feasible over the medium term when measuring and modeling work on services trade barriers is more developed.[1]

For now, only very basic quantitative approaches to services appear possible. For example, in the Uruguay Round the GATT Secretariat sug-

---

1. See chapter 3 in this volume. It is worth noting that quantification difficulties also arise for some nontariff barriers in the goods context. To date the multilateral approach to those measures has focused on rule-making (for example, technical standards), which is undeniably also part of the solution to market access barriers for services.

Box 16-1. *Use of Formulas in GATT Negotiations*

The Kennedy Round: Participants from OECD countries agreed to a goal of 50 percent linear cuts in tariff bindings, with exceptions to be negotiated.

The Tokyo Round: Using applied tariffs as the starting point, a weighted formula was devised to achieve 50 percent cuts in higher tariffs and 30 percent cuts in lower ones; although exceptions to the formula applied in some sectors. Results were achieved through a combination of formula cuts and request-offer negotiation.

The Uruguay Round: Formula approaches were used in negotiations on industrial tariffs and on agricultural tariffs and subsidies.

For industrial tariffs, an overall target of at least one-third cuts was set at Punta del Este. There followed in the next years a lengthy debate over the use of sectoral formulas versus request-offer approaches to achieve the overall target (as well as on coverage issues, as there were initially separate negotiating groups on textiles, tropical products, and natural-resource-based products). After 1990, the focus moved to various U.S.-sponsored formulas that could be counted against the overall target cut; such as tariff elimination ("zero-for-zero") for select sectors (for example, pharmaceutical products, construction equipment, medical equipment, agricultural equipment, steel, furniture, beer, distilled spirits, toys, and paper) and harmonization of tariffs at levels of 5–10 percent (for example, chemicals). In the end, most OECD countries participated in the zero-for-zero sectoral results; and the OECD countries and a few developing countries achieved an overall average tariff cut of more than 40 percent.

For agriculture, formula cuts emerged in the course of the negotiation rather than at the outset. The resulting formulas were as follows:

Tariffs: New tariffs resulting from the "tariffication" process together with existing tariffs were to be reduced by a simple average of 36 percent in six years by developed countries and 24 percent in ten years by developing countries, with minimum reductions per product line of 10 and 15 percent, respectively. No reductions were required by least-developed countries.

(continued)

gested that a potential formula for the evaluation of GATS offers could be to assess the value of offered sectors as a proportion of the total contribution of services to an economy's GDP. That is, setting a target whereby an economy in which services contributed 30 percent of GDP would offer to bind at least 30 percent of all sectors, while an economy in which services

Box 16-1. *(continued)*

Current and minimum access commitments: For products covered by the tariffication process, the negotiating modalities provided for the maintenance of current market access opportunities and the establishment of minimum access tariff quotas (at reduced-tariff rates), where current access was less than 5 percent of domestic consumption. These minimum access tariff quotas (generally at 4-digit HS level) are to be expanded from 3 percent to 5 percent of domestic consumption over the implementation period.

Reductions in export subsidies and subsidized exports: Developed countries were required to reduce the value of direct export subsidies to a level 36 percent below the 1986–90 base period level over the six-year implementation period and the quantity of subsidized exports by 21 percent over the same period. Reductions by developing countries are two-thirds those of developed countries over a longer time period (10 years). No reductions were required of least-developed countries. In certain circumstances, where subsidized exports had increased since the 1986–90 base period, 1991–92 may be used as the beginning point of reductions although the end-point remains that of the 1986–90 base period level.

Reductions in domestic support: The Total Aggregate Measure of Support (Total AMS) reduction commitments, which cover all domestic support provided on either a product-specific or non-product-specific basis that does not qualify for exemption (that is, under the "green box") were 20 percent in six years by developed countries and 13.3 percent in ten years by developing countries. There were no reduction commitments required by least-developed countries.

contributed 70 percent of GDP would offer to bind at least 70 percent of all sectors, and so on.[2] It is also possible to conceive numerical formulas for the preparation of GATS offers, for example, an overall target of 30 percent reductions in "the number of limitations in schedules." Each country could work out how many limitations it currently has and reduce that number accordingly. Overall, a 30 percent reduction in, for example, the more than 3,000 horizontal limitations scheduled against national treatment would mean eliminating some 1,000 of them.

These types of simple "numerical reduction" approaches may represent useful general negotiating goals or benchmarks and probably can be a

2. See Uruguay Round document MTN.GNS/W/118.

useful tool for summarizing and "selling" the results. However, as negotiating tools they lack specificity on the "barriers that matter the most" as there is no link to or focus on the actual trade restrictiveness of limitations in schedules. Thus the foregoing types of simple numerical formulas could be met even though the most restrictive limitations are left in place. As well, the burden of meeting formulas for simple numerical reductions in types of scheduled limitations would fall disproportionately on those countries that already have bindings across a broad range of sectors.

Thus negotiating tools that aim to lift the scope and quality of *all* countries' services bindings would seem a more effective approach at this time. And the regulatory origins of most services trade barriers suggests that any cross-cutting or formula approaches are likely to need to be qualitative and focused on specific types of trade-restrictive measures.

Precedents

The GATS sectoral negotiations that were conducted after the Uruguay Round provide several examples of "standardized" or "model" qualitative approaches to both the scheduling of specific market access and national treatment commitments and additional "regulatory" commitments. These were the model schedules for Basic Telecom Services Commitments and Maritime Transport Services Commitments; the Understanding on Commitments in Financial Services; and the Reference Paper to the GATS Agreement on Basic Telecommunications (box 16-2).

Additionally, several WTO members scheduled "pre-commitments" on intended future liberalization in the basic telecommunications and financial services negotiations, and some commentators have proposed this should also be made a standard practice in the new round.[3] While there was not widespread take-up of the model schedules in the (suspended) maritime negotiations or the (successful) basic telecom negotiations, nor of the Understanding on Commitments in Financial Services, these approaches can be seen to represent sectoral building blocks of a qualitative nature. It may be that model schedules can be developed and utilized for other sectors or that some elements of the Basic Telecom Reference Paper could be applied across all sectors that are scheduled. But whether these approaches can be described as "formula approaches" is open to debate:

3. See chapter 15 in this volume.

Box 16-2. *Standardized or Model Approaches to GATS Sectoral Negotiations*

Model schedules were developed in the course of the post-Uruguay Round negotiations on maritime transport and basic telecommunications. The aim was to secure a package of core commitments that could where desired be supplemented by request-(further) offer approaches. The model schedules sought to contribute to this by identifying a core set of subsectors in which commitments would be undertaken by all participants, defining areas of exclusion (such as cabotage) and areas where differing degrees of liberalization were feasible. While the models did not propose the content of specific commitments, they encouraged greater clarity and standardization in classifying and listing of commitments, so they would be more user friendly. However, the maritime negotiations were suspended until 2000, and the basic telecom model schedule was not widely adopted.

The Reference Paper for Basic Telecommunications represents a set of common regulatory commitments to be inscribed into schedules as additional commitments, which was done in part or in full by a high proportion of participants. Its basic purpose is to buttress the market access and national treatment commitments made in the sector through commitments on domestic regulatory transparency, access to essential facilities in this and related sectors, and competitive safeguards. A similar approach was being considered in the maritime negotiations to develop additional commitments on access to and use of port facilities.

The Understanding on Commitments in Financial Services represents a set of core commitments for the sector on market access, public procurement, the treatment of new financial services, and a standstill commitment. The understanding was incorporated into schedules of most OECD countries on a most favored nation basis.

some commentators do, while many participants prefer not to. It may be that for services, a term such as "model approaches to core commitments" could attract broader support than the term "formulas."

Potential "Measures-Based" Formula Approaches to GATS Commitments

As well as model schedules and precommitment approaches, it is also possible to envisage other sets of qualitative "core commitments" that could be employed in the effort to broaden and deepen commitments on market access and national treatment in individual sectors and across sectors. The focus of such an approach would be on removal or phase-out of specific types of limitations, or their replacement with less trade-restrictive requirements, across the four GATS modes of supply. This approach could be incorporated into sectoral "model schedule" proposals or constitute a discrete set of objectives for the negotiations. Insofar as they would constitute "targets" to be met in the negotiations, and "guidelines" for the submission of initial offers, they could also be termed "formula" or "model" approaches to the negotiation and scheduling of core commitments; and be utilized in conjunction with request-offer approaches.

"Measures-based" formula approaches may also play a useful role in integrating several of the goals for the GATS round (for example, achieving broader and deeper specific commitments while maintaining the existing GATS structure and the flexibility inherent in "bottom-up" scheduling). That is, by constituting agreed guidelines or targets for the preparation of initial offers, formulas could contribute to all three of those goals and thus reduce the need for "top-down" architectural and rules-based approaches to scheduling of market access and national treatment commitments.

In this regard, it is important to emphasize that the context for considering the use of formula approaches in the services negotiations is to help meet the challenge of achieving higher levels of bound market openness under GATS and to do so across members, sectors, and modes of supply. This suggests that the feasibility and ultimate effectiveness of formula approaches for services cannot be considered in isolation from certain other issues related to meeting this challenge in practice. In particular, the need to clarify the relationship between market access and national treatment commitments and between them and Article VI disciplines on nondiscriminatory domestic regulation; and the question of whether to provide some form of safeguard mechanism in exchange for significantly improved levels of bound commitments.[4] However, those issues involve GATS rules, whereas formula approaches usually do not. That is to say, the results achieved by the use of formulas are incorporated in WTO schedules

---

4. Several chapters in this volume address these GATS rule-making issues in detail, so they are not belabored here, other than to emphasize their relevance to the ultimate workability of measures-based formula approaches to the negotiation and scheduling under GATS of specific commitments for services.

as binding commitments, but the formulas themselves represent guidelines or targets rather than rules for incorporation into GATS Articles. In the services context, this distinction is important because of the mostly qualitative nature of potential formula approaches, which can thus appear similar to rule-making proposals.

In principle, measures-based formula approaches could be developed for application across all services sectors covered by GATS, for "clusters" of closely related sectors, and for individual sectors. Indeed, in view of both the sector-specific regulatory features and the political sensitivity of some services sectors, it may be difficult in practice to take an "all-sectors" approach for some formula or model approaches. For example, while some categories of measures tend to be applied to all service sectors, in some cases additional sector-specific measures of the same type also apply (for example, foreign investment restrictions, restrictions on legal form of entity, limitations on foreign personnel). Then there are some types of restrictions that are almost entirely sector specific (for example, to audio-visual services, retail services, health services); sectors with unique regulatory features (for example, financial services); or sectors where market access commitments could need to be buttressed with sector-specific additional "regulatory" commitments. Additionally, participants may be willing to abide by particular "across-the-board" formula approaches so long as they were permitted some scope for exemptions or longer time frames for their adoption.

Moreover, a number of OECD countries are likely to want to pursue sectoral as well as cross-sectoral approaches. And because developing countries' commercial interests in services rely heavily on services supplied under modes 2 and 4, they are unlikely to regard any "formula package" as balanced unless it contains at least as many "deliverables" for modes 2 and 4 as for modes 1 and 3.

These factors suggest that a combination of across-sectors and sector-specific formula approaches may be needed. To illustrate the potential approaches, box 16-3 contains an overview of some indicative sectoral and across-sectors approaches, and box 16-4 contains a matrix of potential approaches by GATS mode of supply that could be employed across sectors or, alternatively, for individual sectors or clusters of sectors.

A key challenge is to minimize the opportunity for "cherry-picking" from an open-ended list of formulas. Thus it is probably advisable for negotiators to establish a core package of formula approaches that would form the starting point for offers and could be supplemented by further

Box 16-3. *Indicative Overview of Potential Model and Formula Approaches*

Sector-specific

Model schedules for individual sectors (standardized classification lists and scheduling guidelines);

Sectoral Understandings on content and interpretation of specific commitments;

Sectoral Reference Papers on additional "regulatory" commitments;

Sectoral "zero-for-zero" commitments (for example, no market access and national treatment limitations of the type described in Articles XVI and XVII) among a critical mass of participants;

"Harmonization" of commitments within a sector (for example, where one or more subsectors is already bound as no limitations, this would be extended to other subsectors currently less than fully bound. Where there are no sectoral commitments at present, at least partial commitments would be made in all subsectors).

Cross-sectoral (all scheduled sectors unless exceptions agreed by negotiation)

All participants to make offers in substantially all subsectors where they do not currently have any commitments. The guiding principle for such an approach could be to create commercially meaningful market access on nondiscriminatory terms;

Precommitment to further liberalization in the future;

Elimination or phase-out of measures described in Articles XVI and XVII for as many sectors as possible;

Removal of specific types of limitations and expanded coverage of commitments under each mode (see box 16-4).

sectoral initiatives and request-offer negotiations. The core package could be constructed with strict limits on exemptions, longer phase-in periods for developing countries, and a best endeavors approach for least-developed countries, for example on the following lines:

—Maximum of two exemptions and implementation within two years for OECD countries (an exemption may be either exemption from a particular formula across-the-board or exemption of a particular sector from all formulas);

—Maximum of four exemptions for developing countries and imple-

Box 16-4. *Matrix of Potential Formulas by GATS Mode of Supply*

All modes

All participants to make initial offers in sectors where they presently have no commitments.

Measures listed in GATS Article XVI (Market Access) to be phased out by all participants by a designated date.

Measures restricting the provision, transfer, and processing of information and data to be eliminated or phased out, apart from "necessary" measures as provided in GATS Article XIV (General Exceptions).

Mode 1

Replace any commercial presence and local certification requirements with local registration and liability insurance requirements.

Eliminate or phase out any requirements that provision may take place only through joint ventures with local providers or by approved "brand-name" providers.

Mode 2

Elimination or phase-out of all limitations on the consumption of services abroad by a service consumer or consuming unit.

Mode 3

Removal or phase-out of economic needs test for approval, quotas on number of firms permitted, and limitations on majority foreign ownership, as general principles for establishment of new services businesses.

Upon and after establishment, guarantee of national treatment for foreign firms in:

—Scope and geographic location of permitted business activities;

—Types of permitted legal entity;

—Application of domestic business and professional laws and regulatory licensing.

Removal or phase-out of limitations on ability of foreign firms to lease or buy land and buildings for their direct commercial use.

Removal or phase-out of limitations concerning possibility of forced divestiture of existing foreign shareholdings in services businesses.

Removal or phase-out of nationality requirements for board members, directors, and senior executives.

(continued)

Box 16-4. *(continued)*

Mode 4

Expand and standardize the classification of service occupations and professions for use in schedules.

Phase-out or relaxation of:

—Economic needs tests and quotas for entry and stay of skilled service providers for defined periods;

—Nationality and permanent residency requirements for intracorporate transferees and contracted service providers.

Removal or phase-out of other limitations on intracorporate transferees, business visitors, and services salespersons.

Creation of a new category for small teams and self-employed foreign specialists and professionals to undertake services activities on a contract basis.

Requirement to specify minimum and maximum time frames for initial period of stay and extension for all categories of personnel.

Develop a reference paper for additional commitments on transparency, due process, and redress on visa and licensing procedures, taxation matters.

---

mentation within four years (an exemption may be either exemption from a particular formula across-the-board or exempting of a particular sector from all formulas); and

    —Least-developed countries encouraged to adopt at least half of the formulas in at least half the sectors.

17 | Liberalizing Trade in Services: Reciprocal Negotiations and Regulatory Reform

BERNARD M. HOEKMAN *and*
PATRICK A. MESSERLIN

A T THE TIME the Uruguay Round was concluded (1994), many observers were critical of the structure of the General Agreement on Trade in Services (GATS). They argued that schedules are hard to interpret and would not generate a powerful momentum for future liberalization of markets. The "positive" list approach toward scheduling commitments was perceived as an opaque instrument (it is difficult to know what is not liberalized). The sectoral focus (illustrated by specific annexes for financial services and telecoms) was seen as a danger because it limited the potential for intersectoral trade-offs and concessions by GATS members.[1]

Developments subsequent to the Uruguay Round have given some cause for optimism but also provide cause for concern. On the positive side, the sectoral approach worked better than expected. Two agreements on key services sectors (financial services and basic telecoms) were successfully negotiated. Although these agreements introduce only a limited dose of liberalization, that they were concluded at all suggests the critics may have been too pessimistic. The pessimists can point to the failure of efforts

We are grateful to Geza Feketekuty, Patrick Low, Juan Marchetti, Aaditya Mattoo, and other participants for helpful comments and discussions.

1. See, for example, Hoekman (1996) and the references cited therein.

to conclude sectoral talks to liberalize maritime transport (under GATS) and to negotiate a Multilateral Agreement on Investment (MAI) (under the Organization for Economic Cooperation and Development). Among the many disturbing aspects of the MAI negotiations was that it revealed that a "negative" list approach to scheduling commitments is not necessarily a much better way of dealing with complex barriers to competition: the lists tabled by MAI negotiators were so long that they tended to make the general MAI disciplines irrelevant. The MAI experience illustrates that although there is value in transparency, this alone is not sufficient to move a liberalization agenda forward. It needs to be supported by domestic political forces that favor the pursuit of liberalization. The existence of such a domestic consensus was a major factor behind the successful conclusion of the GATS basic telecom talks.

In many countries attempts to liberalize services during the Uruguay Round were not accompanied by a wide and lively debate on national interests and objectives. Often negotiating positions were largely driven by specific industry interests. This was one factor underlying the limited liberalization that was achieved—rational "status quo bias" prevailed. After its inception, GATS continued to attract little public attention. Its provisions, let alone its existence, remain relatively unknown or little understood even among those who have an interest in the functioning of the trading system (multinational business). No major disputes about the implementation of the agreement have been brought forward. This suggests the agreement is not perceived as particularly relevant to the various stakeholders (business, consumer groups). At the same time, there is a strong sense of disquiet in many countries about the impact on national welfare of multilateral liberalization commitments.

New negotiations on services are due to be initiated in 2000—as called for in the Uruguay Round Agreement. Members of the World Trade Organization will have to determine how and what to negotiate. The MAI experience must be internalized, but how to do this is not clear, especially given vociferous opposition by some influential nongovernmental organizations to strengthening the trading system. Meanwhile, there is a wide recognition among the business community and officials that the status quo is not an acceptable option, simply because the existing schedules of commitments in the GATS are not particularly useful. The correspondence between what is scheduled and the effective barriers to trade and investment that are in force is rather loose, to say the least. The question of how to proceed on services is particularly acute for developing countries. Al-

most all governments increasingly recognize the vital role that an efficient
and vibrant service industry plays in the process of economic and social
development (certain services are basic inputs or components of the economic infrastructure, whereas other services can be a provisional shelter
useful for social stability).

This chapter discusses how the coming WTO negotiations might best
be used to help achieve national economic objectives.

Rules of Thumb: Think General Equilibrium and Pursue Neutrality

Governments intervene in markets for a number of reasons: to provide
public goods; to redistribute income in the pursuit of equity objectives;
and to protect and support favored industries or activities. Such support is
provided among other ways through trade protection and fiscal incentives
(tax concessions, subsidies). The tariff peaks and the tariff "escalation"
found in most national tariff schedules reflect the desire to favor certain
industries over others. As a result, effective rates of protection can be very
high or very low—*negative* rates of effective protection are not rare—that
is, activities may be taxed rather than supported. Table 17-1 provides
general evidence on the survival of tariff escalation and dispersion after
more than forty years of GATT-based rounds of negotiations to reduce
barriers to merchandise trade.

The economic justification for government intervention to favor certain economic activities over others generally rests on the existence of
market failure, that is, externalities. While the theoretical case for intervention is clear cut, in practice the interventions observed in most countries
to favor some industries over others are not aimed at offsetting market
failures. Instead, they simply reflect the outcome of political processes and
rent-seeking (directly unproductive profit-seeking) activities. From a national welfare perspective such selective intervention is costly, leading
economists to suggest that a good rule of thumb for policy is to establish
a level playing field in the sense that incentives to engage in different types
of economic activities are neutral. While government should intervene to
ensure that firms and households take into account the negative externalities that are created by their activities (through pollution taxes, zoning
restrictions, and so on) and can benefit from positive spillovers (for example, education, infrastructure), these are non-industry-specific types of

Table 17-1. *Nominal Rates of Assistance via Trade Policies, 1992 and Post-Uruguay Round Implementation*
Percent

Item[a]	Advanced industrial economies	Newly industrialized economies[b]	Low- and middle-income economies
1992			
Agriculture and processed food	39	43	7
Other primary and manufacturing industries	3	8	12
Post-Uruguay Round			
Agriculture and processed food	33	33	6
Other primary and manufacturing industries	2	6	11

Source: Hoekman and Anderson (1999). Unpublished compilation from the GTAP (Global Trade Analysis Project) version 3 database prepared by Anna Strutt. See http://www.agecon.purdue.edu/gtap for details of the GTAP database.

a. The nominal rates of assistance to each sector are calculated from the detailed industry estimates by using production for each sector in each region of the database valued at distortion-free prices as weights.

b. Hong Kong, Korea, Singapore, and Taiwan.

actions. At the firm or industry level the incentive structure should be neutral. The rationale for this is largely a political economy one. Although in theory industry-specific intervention might be justified on a variety of "strategic" grounds, as was pointed out by Friedrich Hayek more than fifty years ago, in practice governments will lack the information necessary to realize the potential gains.[2] If parties recognize that in addition to the information problem, political imperatives and rent-seeking will inevitably induce governments to diverge from "optimal" interventions, a strong case can be made for pursuing neutrality as a fundamental rule of policy toward industries.

Many governments around the world are far from achieving this policy prescription. Although in practice it will be impossible to achieve fully, neutrality is a useful lens through which to assess status quo policies and identify reform priorities. One reason is that neutrality requires an economy-wide or general equilibrium framework to be used that considers the

2. Hayek (1945).

impact of one industry-specific policy on the economy at large. The absence of such a framework often results in highly nonuniform patterns of protection for industries that are detrimental to the long-term growth prospects of the economy. An example is the treatment of agriculture in many developing economies. Policies such as manufacturing protectionism and overvalued exchange rates tend to discourage farm production. Within the farm sector, the developing countries discourage exporters more explicitly than farmers who compete with imports.[3] The emerging markets that were embroiled in financial crisis in the late 1990s are another illustration. There is a strong parallel between the steel crisis in Europe in the 1970s and the banking crisis in Asia in the 1990s. In both cases, one sector remained highly protected during a period in which substitute goods or services were being liberalized. In Europe, protection for aluminum and other substitutes for steel were gradually reduced at a time of decreasing transportation costs; similarly in the banking case, short-term capital flows were being liberalized when the electronic "transportation" costs of moving funds was declining rapidly, whereas inward foreign direct investment (FDI) in the financial services industry in many Asian economies remained restricted.

These examples show the need for a comprehensive as opposed to a piecemeal approach toward liberalization and reform in order to reduce the dispersion in the incentives to undertake investments across sectors and activities. This is not to deny the role governments must play in redistribution and the provision of public goods or to deny that in the pursuit of these activities governments will invariably affect economic activity. Central decisionmakers have become increasingly aware of the benefits of a "general equilibrium" approach in terms of improving resource allocation incentives. For example, growing recognition that differences in domestic indirect tax rates can be damaging has led to a reduction in the dispersion in tax rates. A relative shift away from subsidies has also occurred, motivated by the same factor of distrust of selective public actions (of course, driven also by budgetary constraints).

Of particular importance in the context of the prospective WTO negotiations is that a "general equilibrium" assessment should cover both goods and services to consider interaction effects. Actions taken in services markets can affect competition in goods markets and vice versa. Restrictions on competition in European car distribution as a means to support the European Community voluntary export restraint agreement with Ja-

---

3. Schiff and Valdes (1992).

pan on cars are one example.[4] Similar effects may be caused by legislation allowing exclusive distribution or sole agency, or by restrictions on parallel imports of branded goods. These practices can prevent the benefits of trade liberalization being realized by consumers—instead, the effect may be to transfer what was previously captured as tariff revenue by the government to the private interests that control distribution of imports. Such indirect effects are not limited to manufactures: a major trade reform program undertaken by India in the early 1990s, which reduced import-weighted average tariffs from 87 percent in 1991 to 27 percent in 1996, induced a disappointing agricultural supply response because of policies that restricted competition in the provision of key inputs such as credit, transport, storage, and communication services.[5]

Achieving Greater Uniformity: Implications for GATS Negotiations

As is well known, the process of liberalizing trade in goods through reciprocal negotiations under GATT auspices has been successful because the intrinsically mercantilist behavior of trade negotiators (who focus exclusively on obtaining better access to the export market for their national industries, using domestic trade barriers as negotiating coin) was consistent with (and led to) the economically sound policy that focuses on the benefits for the domestic economy from cheaper imports and an improved allocation of resources that better reflects comparative costs. Because negotiating coin had to be expended to obtain better access to export markets, the process led to a gradual move toward the globally efficient outcome—free trade. Each GATT round led to successive reductions in foreign tariffs that were profitable for domestic exporters and decreases in domestic tariffs that were beneficial to domestic consumers. The latter were made feasible because export interests were willing (required) to support liberalization in domestic political markets.

Of course, the GATT focus on reciprocity is not ideal by any means. Abstracting from the nontrivial opportunity costs of maintaining protection, it results in a nonuniform pattern of protection. Uniformity in protection across activities is a key element for getting the most out of trade liberaliza-

---

4. Mattoo and Mavroidis (1995).
5. Gulati (1998).

tion. In this perspective, the frequent focus on the "average" tariff by countries in trade negotiations is virtually meaningless: even if the average is low, the real costs of protection can be high if the dispersion of tariff rates across commodity groups is large. This is because the consumer deadweight losses from protection increase more rapidly than the level of protection and because distortions in terms of resource allocation tend to be more harmful as the dispersion of tariffs increases (such costs are a square function of the tariff level in the case of linear demand and supply curves). Account should also be taken of the administrative costs of nonuniform tariffs, rent-seeking, and corruption. Notwithstanding these caveats, GATT rounds resulted in greater uniformity: as tariffs were brought down, they also became increasingly similar. The mercantilist approach of negotiators also helped to reduce the dispersion of tariffs directly: some of the negotiating formulas that were developed targeted high tariffs more than low tariffs in an attempt to increase access to more protected markets more than proportionately. Reciprocity worked well because two conditions were satisfied: tariffs constituted the dominant barrier on trade in goods, and most of the other major nontariff barriers (quotas, antidumping measures, and so on) are not too difficult to "translate" in tariff terms. As a result, the value of "reciprocal concessions" associated with tariff or nontariff barrier reduction has not been too difficult to estimate: it was simplistically defined as the value of the concerned imports multiplied by tariff changes—a definition that allows across-the-board calculations. The relative transparency and simplicity of the instruments used also allowed the technique of tariff bindings to be used as an effective commitment device: "nullification and impairment" tactics by countries seeking to reimpose protection through the back door are difficult to hide, as they will generally fall foul of the GATT national treatment rule and the prohibition on quotas (Article XI). Without the constraint of tariff bindings many of the GATT disciplines become unenforceable.

These two conditions are not fulfilled in the services context. Tariffs on services are rare. Nontariff barriers in services are difficult to translate into tariff equivalents, if only because governments are not always aware of their existence (regulations inhibiting trade in services often were introduced so long ago that it becomes difficult to recognize their effects as an impediment). This issue is serious because services are much more regulation intensive than goods (and often good reasons exist for such regulations) and because the economic linkages and interdependencies between services and between services and goods sectors (the input-output coefficients in national accounts) are less well understood than those that prevail between goods. Policymakers are more cognizant of the importance of steel for auto production than they are of efficient insurance or marketing services. As commitment mechanisms in the GATS are inherently weaker than in the GATT, the ultimate consequence is that it is much easier for a government to find a way to undo (deliberately or unintentionally) what has been agreed to in a GATS negotiation—in other words, nullification and impairment will be more difficult to prove.[6]

This situation has an important implication: trade and investment liberalization in services will inevitably be less susceptible to the reciprocal, market access dynamics that drive WTO negotiations. Governments must supply a large dose of "unilateralism" if they are to achieve the goal of uniform protection. Paradoxically, this necessity may be a smaller burden for developing countries than for industrial WTO members. In the past twenty years, trade liberalization in goods by developing countries has largely been the result of unilateral measures. What the developing countries did in the Tokyo and Uruguay Rounds was mostly limited to the partial binding of these unilateral reforms—they did not actively engage in the GATT game. As a result, for most of the developing countries, the coming years of negotiations in services will have an "*air de déjà vu.*" The high dose of unilateralism required for liberalizing services will be supported by the recognition of the high costs of granting services high rates of protection against foreign competition (and often domestic as well).

Current levels of services protection are as high if not higher than those applied to goods ten or fifteen years ago. In many instances, the available information on the level of protection suggests average ad valorem tariff equivalents ranging from 50 percent to 100 percent for large sectors—clearly more than rates observable for manufactured goods in OECD countries, but similar to the rates existing in developing countries in the early 1980s. Some analysts estimate that the U.S. Jones Act (which restricts maritime cabotage to U.S. flag vessels) increases prices by 100 to 300 percent over the average world price.[7] The effects of similar restrictions in developing countries are analogous.[8] Fees charged by the (monopoly) public companies providing port services for handling and storage of goods

6. These differences between trade in services and trade in goods may be eroded in the future because of the increasing importance of (environmental, technical, health-related, and other) regulations in the production of many industrial products.

7. Messerlin (1999); chapter 3 in this volume; Francois and others (1996).

8. Chile is analyzed in Bennethan, Escobar, and Panagakos (1989); a number of African countries are analyzed in World Bank (1997).

in Egypt are some 30 percent higher than in neighboring countries.[9] Adopting a more competitive regulatory regime for telecommunications in Egypt has been estimated to generate a net welfare gain of $800 million, or 1.2 percent of GDP.[10]

The need for unilateral action to undertake the reforms required to attain neutrality has implications for the process of formulating negotiating positions in multilateral (or regional) forums and determining who should take the lead in negotiations on services. In sharp contrast with trade in goods, services liberalization efforts must rely much more firmly on central decisionmakers as opposed to the negotiating process if these efforts are to be an effective tool for economic development. In liberalization of trade in goods, mercantilist trade negotiators could play a central role with only limited potential to do significant economic harm to the national economy—the principal harm done derived from the opportunity costs of not pursuing deeper (unilateral) reforms, something that presumably was not a feasible option for many GATT members because of domestic political constraints; and the nonuniformity that inherently emerges from "offer-request" type negotiations. The main reasons for the beneficial outcome were that the mechanics of reciprocity were needed to overcome resistance to liberalization, and that trade barriers (tariffs or nontariff trade barriers) were prevalent enough and of a type that allowed the process to work. Trade negotiators had an obvious focal point (the level of trade barriers) and could go about their business, "doing good" in the process.[11] This dynamic is less likely to prevail in services. Reciprocity can play less of a role because exporters play a smaller role, and nonborder protection is dominant. The former implies that in many developing countries opposition to reform and liberalization cannot be counterbalanced by export interests seeking better access to foreign service markets; the latter implies that trade negotiators do not have equivalent focal points and the necessary information to employ the tools of their trade in a manner that guarantees the outcome is welfare improving. At issue in the services context are generally regulatory regimes that cannot (should not) be altered in incremental ways. In contrast to tariffs that can be changed smoothly and continuously, regulatory regimes are often "lumpy"—any change will generally be discrete and not necessarily in the national inter-

9. Mohieldin (1997).
10. Galal (1998).
11. Hoekman (1997).

est. In short, the onus will be on autonomous, national reform that must be undertaken and led by central decisionmakers.

From this perspective, contrary to what is often said, developing countries may not need to expand greatly the capacities of their trade negotiators to "negotiate." Instead, the focus of attention should be on strengthening and maintaining a robust capacity for identifying, understanding, and designing the *domestic* regulatory reforms that need to be undertaken in services in order to enhance the efficiency of the economy and bolster economic growth prospects. Multilateral negotiations and institutions should be seen and used as a facilitating device to support the process of implementing the reforms, not as the driver of reform.[12]

Implementing the Uniformity Principle

Regulatory reforms in services should aim, directly or indirectly, at the establishment of a more uniform system of intervention. Attaining this objective will involve deregulation—elimination of outdated, hence costly and inefficient, regulations, including restrictions on foreign entry—and re-regulation—the adoption of appropriate, market-(efficiency-) enhancing regulations. Although services liberalization does not raise new conceptual issues, it does raise new technical issues. Being less tradable than goods, services are more directly dependent on factor markets in the country of consumption—the market for labor, land, and specific bundles of factors often described in certain network services under the generic name of "essential facilities." In the case of goods, a specific (nonuniform) treatment of factors of production can be circumvented by firms by moving production to the cheapest available location: specificity in the policy stance toward factors does not hurt foreign competitors, nor domestic consumers, as long as protection is uniform. As the degrees of freedom for choosing the location of production are more limited in services, the costs of specific policies toward essential facilities can be higher. This point is well known in relationship to barriers to access to essential facilities in telecoms. However, it is not limited to network services such as telecoms, energy, railways, or air transport. For instance, essential facilities in retail-

---

12. Of course, unilateral reform has always been the norm for developing countries, not having been players in GATT negotiations past. The reciprocity dynamics have been important primarily in reducing OECD trade barriers.

ing may consist of a piece of well-located real estate and associated transport infrastructures that are well designed to attract shoppers: restrictions on large shops (or even mere zoning regulations on the authorized type of buildings for different areas) could then constitute a serious barrier to potential entrants because they create an artificial scarcity of usable land or infrastructures.

Thus services liberalization requires a strong focus on attaining and maintaining uniform nonborder protection. The domestic reform agenda is frequently complex, with progress being hampered by resistance by vested interests. Entry barriers often create significant rents for incumbents, who have a strong interest in blocking attempts by governments to increase the contestability of "their" markets. The primary need is to ensure that potential entrants are free to enter service markets and that policies do not discriminate against foreign as opposed to domestic entrants. Entry barriers in many service activities tend to be justified by invoking market failure rationales that revolve around information asymmetries, fears of excessive entry, the need for universal service, and so on. While there is often a valid rationale for intervention (regulation), this does not generally require the creation of significant legal entry barriers.

In the case of developing countries, pursuit of a domestic reform agenda may be easier to pursue because some of the aspects of regulatory reforms that are important in industrial countries are less prevalent. For example, the number and political strength of domestic service industries are often smaller than in industrialized countries as there tends to be excess demand for efficient services. Moreover, "sunk" costs (costs generated by components of an infrastructure that have few if any alternative uses) are likely to be small in many least-developed countries because past investments have been small or have not been maintained (as illustrated by the situation of many public telecom companies in least-developed countries). Moreover, sunk cost bottlenecks related to network infrastructures may be slow to emerge in developing countries if central decisionmakers make choices in terms of service-led competition, rather than infrastructure-based competition. For many developing countries, what is needed are well-functioning services consistent with the prevailing scarcity of capital so as to minimize the cost of needed infrastructure.

This reasoning can be applied, *mutatis mutandis*, to nonnetwork services as well. For instance, in many least-developed countries, many of the state-owned ships that were purchased in a wave of implementation of the UNCTAD liner conference codes have little value, except as a source of scrap iron. In some countries state-owned shipping companies often consist of a small management team, which grants operating licenses under the costly (collusive) rules of the UNCTAD codes and eventually (but not always) derives rents from this situation. Here again sunk costs are less of a constraint than in OECD countries.

Another possible difference between regulatory reforms in developing and industrial countries concerns the trade-off between equity and efficiency. In industrial countries, regulatory reforms can be detrimental to certain groups of consumers or citizens. This possibility seems more remote in developing countries (particularly in the least-developed countries) because most of the existing service monopolies are currently far from providing universal service of uniform good quality (telecoms, airlines, roads, and so on). In other words, the concerns about "universal service" in certain industrial countries (with their strong protectionist potential) may be less important in many developing countries, simply because this objective has not (yet) been attained.

Because there is less scope for international outsourcing (geographic "splintering" of production), the political economy of services liberalization should be easier than it is for goods. Labor is less likely to be put into a situation where whole industries are confronted with a high probability of total demise because the country is unable to produce the goods concerned efficiently. Instead, new entrants will need to employ local labor and produce services locally. Users of services—which include manufacturing firms—are more likely to be sensitive to the argument that inefficient service industries cannot be tolerated because many services are vital determinants of their ability to compete on world markets.

Determining Priorities and Designing Domestic Reforms

Regulatory reform is a complex process, especially if the objective of uniformity is taken seriously. Nonetheless, both economic theory and cross-country experience suggest a number of steps that can be taken by governments in determining the need for—and the design of—policy reforms.

First, regulatory reforms require a proper definition of the "relevant markets" that are affected or involved. Although in principle a general-equilibrium approach is required in the assessment of policies—all activities have to be put "on a par"—in practice this is impossible to put into operation. Instead, efforts should be made to identify the appropriate nexus of related, interdependent activities. For instance, liberalizing air transport without liberalizing airport slots does not lead very far: the price of air tickets will mirror *both* competitive pressures in terms of routes (if there are several airlines in presence, which is not necessarily the case) *and* monopoly rents related to airport slot monopolies.[13] Another example is maritime transport—Joe Francois and Ian Wooton estimate that the welfare gains from trade liberalization (better access to markets) may be doubled if complementary actions are taken to increase competition in the shipping sector.[14] Yet another example is cross-subsidization between network services, such as between telecom and electricity (a electricity monopolist could cross-subsidize its telecom activities, in particular if the technology is developed to use electricity cables to send telecom signals). A "general" general-equilibrium framework is too complicated to be conceived and managed by decisionmakers. Thus "partial" general-equilibrium frameworks should be developed, each of which constitutes a cluster of interrelated services activities. This pragmatic approach could be based on the well-known "effective rate of assistance" (ERA) concept.[15]

Such an approach could build on two tracks. First, a government could estimate ERAs based on all taxes and subsidies that apply to a broadly defined service activity (such as audiovisuals, tourism, telecoms, and so on), the major inputs into this activity (goods and services), and the factors of production used. Input-output tables and social accounting matrices are a vital tool in determining the various clusters of activities and their major inputs. This "public budget-based" component of the ERA can be complemented by a "private" sector component where businesses producing the services involved would be invited to identify the border and nonborder policies that they perceive to be crucial impediments to their ability to contest markets (at home and abroad), and to provide qualitative (quantitative, if they exist) information on these elements. For example, the ERA for tourism in a Sub-Saharan African country could take into account the explicit taxes and subsidies on hotels, wildlife parks, telecoms, airport slots and airlines, as well as the impediments, more difficult to measure, that limit the country's capacity to attract, ship, and host foreign visitors to and between its major tourism sites. It is important to underline that the goal

13. A vertically integrated firm maximizes its profits precisely when it behaves as a monopoly at only one stage of its activities.

14. Francois and Wooton (1999).

15. GATT (1989).

of such an exercise is not to favor any particular activity but rather to ensure that all the services under examination are roughly treated the same way in terms of explicit support (or taxation).

Clearly such an exercise will be information- and resource-intensive and require substantial analytical input. The institution that is given the task of undertaking the required analysis should have the ability to collect, compile, and process a wide range of quantitative and qualitative information. The type of institution that is required is one that has been termed a transparency or competition-advocacy body in the literature. The Australian Productivity Commission is a good example. In a number of economies in transition this role has been played to some extent by the Competition Office. Many governments may find it difficult to establish and staff such an institution, and many may not be able to devote adequate resources for its operation. However, almost all countries have access to competent officials, legal experts, and academics. What is required is a policy decision to establish the required institution, provide it with the necessary mandate to undertake the work required, and, most importantly, to consider seriously the results of its work.

Given information on the ERAs across clusters, a number of simple rules of thumb for regulatory reforms can be identified. First, such efforts in services should aim at reducing the highest ERAs first. Besides directly targeting policies that give rise to high ERAs, efforts should center on increasing the level of competition in markets. Competition is the engine for providing the benefits expected from regulatory reform. This requires the abolition of legislated and administrative barriers to entry in sectors where there is no compelling economic rationale for maintaining such barriers. To maximize the benefits of such initiatives, no distinction should be made between domestic (national) and foreign firms as benefits from increasing access to markets are generally maximized if foreign firms are able to contest markets. A lesson from the experience of OECD countries in this connection is not to rely too much on the ability of competition law and rulings to deliver a high level of competitive pressure in services. For instance, there is an emerging recognition that competition cases in the telecoms area have led to stalemate situations, rather than enhancing competition. When initiating domestic regulatory reforms, developing countries should consider adopting direct mechanisms to deliver a prompt increase in competitive pressures. For instance, Guatemala has introduced a dispute settlement mechanism based on "final offer arbitration" (administered by a specific industry regulator), and this method seems to have delivered more rapid gains from service liberalization than competition law court-based disputes.[16] A growing literature provides rules of thumb or criteria to identify whether an "acceptable" level of competition exists in a given service industry at a given period. For instance, air routes with fewer than three operating airlines are unlikely to be under intensive competition, and large gains from regulatory reforms can be expected.[17] In the case of multimodal competition (such as between trains and airlines), price comparisons between similar air routes with and without multimodal competition can be a good proxy for assessing the capacity of regulatory reforms to deliver the benefits of increased competition.

Both the OECD and emerging market experience illustrate the need to consider strengthening regulatory supervision for some sectors where asymmetric information and related problems prevail—regulatory reform can entail re-regulation as well as de-regulation. The OECD experience also underlines the need to enhance the ability of governments to generate and have access to a wide body of accurate information to allow an assessment of the impact of policy changes and to identify priorities for reform. Where regulation is called for, this is best done by ad hoc specialized agencies. However, such institutions will give rise to high risks of nonuniform protection and are also open to capture by vested interests. Another rule of thumb is therefore that regulatory agencies, and more generally the government broadly defined, be subjected to the scrutiny of the "apex" transparency institution mentioned earlier that has the mandate to assess the economic impact of their activities and is responsible for providing recommendations to assist government in the pursuit of neutrality of policy.

The importance of strengthening capacity to collect and analyze information cannot be overemphasized. A common mistake made by governments involved in regulatory reform is to reduce the ability of agencies to compile the information needed to monitor the impact of reforms. Relatively good information on prices prevailing in liberalized services can be obtained rapidly and cheaply, as illustrated by telecoms or energy.[18] These encouraging developments suggest that the absence of information in services may be more a consequence of old regulations and market closure

16. Spiller and Cardilli (1997).

17. Morrison and Winston (1997).

18. For instance, see Productivity Commission (1999). In services sectors not dominated by public monopolies, the information could also be limited, though not too difficult to get (such as land prices for large retail stores).

than an intrinsic feature of service industries. It also suggests that the ERA approach could be more useful than might be expected today for estimating ad valorem tariff equivalents of regulatory barriers.

Harnessing GATS Negotiations to the Domestic Reform Agenda

The reliance on unilateral, autonomous initiative that is required to pursue a growth-enhancing domestic regulatory reform agenda and increase competition on service markets does not eliminate the benefits from multilateral cooperation. A multilateral liberalization effort can be beneficial in moving the world closer to the ideal of free trade by helping to remove regulatory barriers to entry in service industries and increasing the global information base on the level and impact of these barriers.

In some countries, vested interests are powerful enough to block welfare-improving reforms. In such cases, multilateral negotiations offer an opportunity to break the political deadlock. This of course is a basic rationale for reciprocity in WTO negotiations—as long as the agenda includes enough items that can help change the domestic political equilibrium, it can support beneficial reforms. However, as discussed, the relevance of this argument is likely to be limited for many developing countries. In the case of services, in the early stages of liberalization, little support for reform can be expected to emerge from (potential) exporters of services. In general, in most countries there are unlikely to be many (potentially) competitive exporters of services, if any. When there is a political economy rationale for pursuing reforms through a multilateral mechanism, issue linkages will be required to areas outside services, as that is where developing countries have the greatest export interests—examples include disciplining the use of contingent protection and reducing barriers to trade in agricultural products.

At the same time, the opposition of domestic firms to the prospect of increased pressure from imports may not be as strong in services as in goods, especially if there are scale or scope economies. Indeed, those that liberalize first may have a strategic advantage—a point underlined by economic analysis and present in the minds of many service providers who are more eager to liberalize, even in the absence of narrow reciprocity, that is, "equivalent" concessions being offered by trading partners. This suggests care should be taken not to fall into a "negotiation trap"—seeking to apply standard GATT techniques of regarding liberalization commitments as "concessions" for which compensation must be obtained. What is required is the pursuit of the national reform agenda. The approach should be akin to a more or less explicit joint or concerted exercise in unilateral liberalization. Any "concessions" to be negotiated should center on the time frame for reaching a common threshold of liberalization or the implementation of an agreement that is required to develop and strengthen the institutions needed to implement a particular reform that is deemed welfare enhancing. Conversely, all proposals that are not welfare enhancing should be rejected.

Although this approach may sound idealistic and unrealistic, it is a good description of the European Community's (EC's) Single Market exercise in services. Perhaps the best illustration is the recent electricity case, where some member states did not hesitate to liberalize much more quickly and deeply than others, underlining the nonreciprocal approach. Similar dynamics arose in the WTO negotiations on financial services and telecoms. The success of these sectoral talks largely reflected the fact that most of the governments involved were convinced of the need to pursue regulatory reforms in these sectors, including liberalization and elimination of entry barriers. This was a precondition for the agreements to materialize—it was clear that the associated regulatory reforms did not go beyond what had already been accomplished or decided in the national (unilateral) context.

To be able to participate effectively and maximize the benefits of GATS negotiations it is vital that governments come prepared, that is, develop a well-defined domestic reform agenda they desire to pursue. Only countries that have already identified their domestic regulatory reform agenda can arrive at the negotiating table with an adequate sense of what proposals are in their interest and the ability to reap the benefits from the exchange of information that occurs during negotiations. A country having no or little information on its own services-sector-related policies and without a clear domestic strategy will be flying blind in GATS discussions. As mentioned, this is less of a problem in merchandise trade talks because a country always has information on its own tariffs and related trade policies, and in any event, the policies that are on the table are generally policies that it would be desirable to eliminate. This is not the case with services, which points again to the need to come prepared with a clear *domestic* reform agenda that aims to attain a more uniform pattern of protection (that is, neutrality). Economically meaningful choices regarding the design and sequencing of regulatory reforms aimed at increasing competition in domestic service markets require a profound knowledge about effective resource allocation and ERAs in the economy that trade negotiators do not have. Central decisionmakers must therefore not only design and pursue a national reform strategy but provide clear instructions and briefs to their officials who represent them in negotiations.

A major beneficial role that can be played by GATS/WTO is to assist member governments attain and maintain a neutral economy-wide sectoral policy stance. This can be done through design of the disciplines (rules) that are negotiated and enforced and through the creation of mechanisms that foster transparency and generate information. A first and minimum requirement is that GATS covers *all* services. There is no rationale for excluding certain sectors or modes of supply from the national treatment and market access disciplines of GATS. Given that GATS allows for derogations to both principles, at the very least comprehensive scheduling will ensure that a government is forced to consider the justification and economic rationale for the policies it maintains that are not in conformity with these principles. One way of moving toward this is to apply a formula approach to expanded coverage in the next round of negotiations, setting minimum coverage targets for GATS members, to be attained by a specified date (which may vary depending on per capita income level to allow for a transition period).[19] A more ambitious approach would be to seek agreement on a deadline for full coverage to be reached. It seems unlikely that WTO members will be willing to consider moving from a positive to a negative list approach to scheduling commitments—but there is nothing to prevent individual countries from doing so. Whatever formula or focal point is established for the negotiations, individual countries should consider going beyond this. In the process valuable information can be obtained on how different policies affect clusters of activities that are interrelated and interdependent.

Second, the focus of attention should be on identifying what horizontal, cross-sectoral disciplines can contribute to the realization of the principle of uniform protection. In the GATS context this implies that scheduling of liberalization commitments should shift from the sectoral (specific) to the horizontal (general). Ideally, given universal scheduling of services sectors by a country, restrictions should be of a horizontal (across-the-board) nature, and negotiating efforts should center on developing

19. Hoekman (1997).

disciplines that make sense from the perspective of long-term growth and economic development. In general, these are likely to focus on safeguarding the contestability of markets while maintaining national sovereignty to regulate activities to attain health, safety, prudential, and related objectives. In this perspective, it would be useful to consider "generalizing" the appropriate parts of the so-called Reference Paper in telecoms in order to make it a "horizontal" set of disciplines to be included into GATS as such. The Reference Paper includes concepts such as "affecting the terms of participation" and "essential facilities" that could usefully be extended to all services, even those without any background of monopoly or public ownership or control.

Third, a strict policy of most favored nation treatment is desirable. The appropriate geographical scope of regulatory reforms depends on the extent to which decisions by national authorities do not internalize external effects across jurisdictions. In this context, regional liberalization of transactions in services can provide a positive economic outcome, in contrast to the case of trade in merchandise where there is more cause for concern about trade diversion. However, to the extent that regulatory reforms pursued in the regional context can be applied on a nondiscriminatory basis—which the available evidence suggests is generally the case—there is less need to worry about the discriminatory effects of regional cooperation.[20] On all these dimensions—identifying prevailing policies and their effects on clusters of activities, assessing modalities of disciplines that seek to increase the contestability of service markets, and determining whether (how) regulatory reforms are (can be) applied on a nondiscriminatory basis—a multilateral institution such as the WTO can play a very constructive role in assisting governments to implement and maintain a coherent development strategy. Designing a regulatory reform program to achieve greater uniformity in incentives is difficult. Multilateral surveillance of domestic policies can help in monitoring the prevailing policy stance and identifying areas where action may be required. Moreover, multilateral cooperation is required to reduce the competition-reducing effect of domestic regulations, especially in mandatory standards—for product safety, professional certification, prudential regulation, and so on. This is perhaps the major area where future efforts should focus, not least because it is one where unilateral action is inherently limited.

20. World Bank (1999).

Concluding Remarks

This chapter has sought to identify a number of rules of thumb for decisionmakers in developing countries in the run-up toward the next round of multilateral negotiations to be launched in 2000. The characteristics of services markets have several implications for the process of multilateral negotiations.

First and foremost, decisionmakers should seek to adopt a policy stance that reduces the existing dispersion in the level of support or assistance that is given to activities. Uniformity of protection should be the primary rule of thumb. This in turn requires that information be collected and compiled to allow decisionmakers to identify priorities and the indirect effects of existing regulatory interventions across sectors and activities.

Second, governments cannot rely on the familiar process of reciprocal exchange of "concessions." Instead, a pro-active policy stance is required that is firmly centered on a domestic reform agenda. Much of what is required to ensure that the WTO process is a facilitator of the adoption of policies that will support economic development will have to be undertaken unilaterally. Developing countries can expect very little from playing the traditional reciprocity game that has been pursued by OECD countries to good effect in liberalizing their merchandise trade. In many cases, developing countries' informational deficit will be bigger, their service export interests less powerful, and their import-related interests more friendly to liberalization—a modern development strategy requires cheap and abundant differentiated intermediate services, and the sunk-cost-motivated resistance to liberalization that is observed in OECD countries is less likely to prevail.

Many observers have noted that GATS is an imperfect instrument.[21] Notwithstanding the deficiencies, it can be used as a commitment and signaling device by governments that have decided that regulatory reforms are in the national interest. Specific commitments can be made for all modes of supply, including FDI, and governments that have decided to open access to services markets to foreign providers should pursue the option of locking in policy reforms as much as possible through the existing GATS mechanisms. Future efforts to expand GATS disciplines should center on expanding the sectoral coverage of the agreement and

21. See, for example, chapter 15 in this volume; Snape (1998).

strengthening the transparency and information collection and dissemination functions of the WTO Secretariat.

References

Bennethan, Esra, Luis Escobar, and George Panagakos. 1989. "Deregulation of Shipping: What Is to Be Learned from Chile?" World Bank Discussion Paper 67. Washington.

Francois, Joseph, and Ian Wooton. 1999. "Trade in International Transport Services: The Role of Competition." Tinbergen Institute, Erasmus University. Rotterdam (mimeo).

Francois, Joseph, and others. 1996. "Commercial Policy and the Domestic Carrying Trade; A General Equilibrium Assessment of the Jones Act." *Canadian Journal of Economics* 29 (February): 181–98.

Galal, Ahmed. 1998. "Towards More Efficient Telecommunications Services in Egypt." Policy Viewpoint 2. Cairo: Egyptian Center for Economic Studies (January).

General Agreement on Tariffs and Trade (GATT). 1989. "Effective Rate of Assistance and Related Methods." MTN.GNG/NG2/W/47. Geneva (November 20).

Gulati, A. 1998. "Indian Agriculture in an Open Economy: Will It Prosper?" In I. J. Ahluwalia and I. Little, eds. *India's Economic Reforms and Development: Essays for Manmohan Singh*. London: Oxford University Press.

Hayek, Friedrich. 1945. "The Use of Knowledge in Society." *American Economic Review* 35: 519–30.

Hoekman, Bernard. 1996. "Assessing the General Agreement on Trade in Services." In *The Uruguay Round and the Developing Countries*, edited by W. Martin and L. A. Winter. Cambridge: Cambridge University Press.

———. 1997. "Focal Points and Multilateral Negotiations on the Contestability of Markets." In *Quiet Pioneering: Robert M. Stern and His International Economic Legacy*, edited by Keith Maskus and others. University of Michigan Press.

Hoekman, Bernard, and Kym Anderson. Forthcoming. "Agriculture and the New Trade Agenda." *Economic Development and Cultural Change*.

Mattoo, Aaditya, and Petros Mavroidis. 1995. "The EC-Japan Consensus on Cars: Interactions between Trade and Competition Policy." *World Economy* 18: 345–65.

Messerlin, Patrick. Forthcoming. *Measuring the Costs of Protection in Europe*. Washington: Institute for International Economics.

Mohieldin, Mahmoud. 1997. "The Egypt-EU Partnership Agreement and Liberalization of Services." In *Regional Partners in Global Markets: Limits and Possibilities of the Euro-Med Agreements*, edited by Ahmed Galal and Bernard Hoekman. London: CEPR.

Morrison, Peter, and Clifford Winston. 1997. "The Fare Skies: Air Transportation and Middle America." *Brookings Review* (Fall): 42–45.

Productivity Commission. 1999. *International Benchmarking of Australian Telecommunications Services*. Research Report. Melbourne: AusInfo (March).

Schiff, Maurice, and Alberto Valdes. 1992. *The Political Economy of Agricultural Pricing Policy: Vol. 4, A Synthesis of the Economics in Developing Countries*. Johns Hopkins University Press.

Snape, Richard. 1998. "Reaching Effective Agreements Covering Services." In *The WTO as an International Organization,* edited by A. Krueger. University of Chicago Press.

Spiller, Pablo T., and Carlo G. Cardilli. 1997. "The Frontier of Telecommunications Deregulation: Small Countries Leading the Pack." *Journal of Economic Perspectives* 11:127–38.

World Bank. 1997. *Trade and Transport in West and Central African States.* Sub-Saharan Africa Transport Policy Program Working Paper 30. Washington.

———. 1999. "Trade Blocs and Beyond: Cooperating to Create Competition." Development Research Group. Washington (mimeo).

18 | GATS and Regional Integration

SHERRY M. STEPHENSON

ARTICLE V (ECONOMIC INTEGRATION) of the General Agreement on Trade in Services provides for World Trade Organization (WTO) members to participate in regional trade arrangements that discriminate against the services or services providers of other countries. Thus Article V grants coverage for preferential treatment extended to services trade in derogation of the most favored nation obligation of GATS Article II. The underlying rationale behind this derogation is that the preferential arrangement should contribute to the further liberalization of the multilateral trading system. The exemption from the MFN obligation, however, must be based on certain requirements set out in GATS Article V, some of which are similar to those of Article XXIV of the General Agreement on Tariffs and Trade (GATT), while others are different.

Considerable confusion and lack of clarity surround the interpretation of GATS Article V conditions. Just as a lack of agreed-on interpretation over the conditions set out in GATT Article XXIV for goods proved to be one of the major weaknesses of GATT, a similar impasse is developing under the WTO about the application of GATS Article V for services. Those few regional agreements notified by their members to the WTO and whose service provisions are being examined under the latter's Committee on Regional Trading Arrangements have not yet been the object of any pronouncement on their compatibility with multilateral disciplines. This lack persists even though this process has been ongoing for several years in certain cases. And most regional agreements containing provisions on services have not been notified by their members to the WTO and are therefore without multilateral oversight.

The need for strong and viable Article V disciplines is more pressing than ever, given the many regional trading agreements that have been signed or extended since 1990 containing provisions to liberalize trade in services. Some countries are members to more than one integration agreement; for them, the consistency of these agreements is also an important question. A further complication arises because several sectoral stand-alone agreements on services have been concluded that contain liberalizing provisions and that may have no legal cover for their status under GATS.

For all of the above, it is imperative that agreed guidelines be developed for the interpretation and application of the conditions set out in GATS Article V. This article alone is the nexus between multilateral disciplines and market access commitments on services that countries agreed to in the Uruguay Round and the already numerous and growing set of integration agreements that contain services provisions. Without a clarification of Article V for services (and Article XXIV for goods), the contribution of regional trading arrangements (or integration agreements) to multilateral trade liberalization will remain controversial and the link between the two imprecise and undefined.

This chapter considers the background to the drafting of GATS Article V and examines the main areas of ambiguity surrounding the interpretation of the article that are problematic now. The chapter also reflects on the questions raised by the application of GATS Article V to a future agreement on services within the Western Hemisphere in the context of the Free Trade Area of the Americas (FTAA) process.

Background to the Drafting of GATS Article V

During the Uruguay Round negotiations, a draft provision on preferential trade for services was introduced by the European Union and supported by Switzerland, Australia, and New Zealand. Economic integration agreements only became an issue in the negotiations as of the end of 1988, and ministers agreed at the Montreal midterm review to include this discussion in the services negotiations. In December 1989 a text was circulated by the chairman that included language providing for a derogation to the nondiscrimination principle, under conditions to be negotiated (for example, regional integration arrangements, free-trade areas, preferential trading arrangements among developing countries.) "Such arrangements shall, among other things, not create any new, or raise existing, barriers to trade in services in relation to other signatories and shall in this respect be subject to multilateral discipline and surveillance."[1] During the discussions of the negotiations on how to draft Article V, some participants felt it important to use Article XXIV of GATT as a basis and only examine regional agreements on services falling under Article XXIV of GATT. Other participants felt that each economic integration agreement should be examined on its own merit with respect to services, independently of its content covering trade in goods. In the end a rather opaque compromise was reached. An economic integration agreement on services is to be examined under specific criteria enumerated for services trade only. However, the agreement may also be considered in its entire economic context. As will be seen later in this chapter, the meaning of the latter was not clarified.

GATT Article XXIV provided the background for the inclusion of the concept "substantially all trade" in GATS Article V. It was generally felt that certain criteria were needed to apply to the services area in order to allow agreements to deviate from the nondiscrimination principle. The Dunkel text of December 1991 contained a proposed draft of Article V. At the end of 1991 the footnote to Article V:1(a), setting out these criteria for substantially all trade in the area of services, was added to the draft text. The final version of Article V found in the WTO GATS is almost identical to that set out in the Dunkel draft.

Article V of GATS is distinctive from its GATT counterpart in two important ways. Article V is labeled Economic Integration Arrangements rather than Customs Unions and Free Trade Areas. It contains no reference to formal integration structures, and its provisions do not distinguish between the two. Similarly, there is no need for economic integration to be regional, as is explicitly required for goods under GATT. This fact corresponds to economic logic, since the nature of services

---

1. WTO Committee on Regional Trade Agreements, "Systemic Issues Related to Substantially All Trade." Background Note by the Secretariat, WT/REG/W/21/Rev.1, February 5, 1998, derestricted. Geneva.

trade under the four modes of supply is not linked to a regional dimension, nor does it necessarily gravitate toward regional markets.

GATS Article V Disciplines and Multilateral Examinations

The main provisions of GATS Article V pertinent to the discussion in this chapter are set out as follows for easy reference.

WTO General Agreement on Trade in Services
Article V
Economic Integration:
This Agreement shall not prevent any of its Members from being a party to or entering into an agreement liberalizing trade in services between or among the parties to such an agreement, provided that such an agreement:
has substantial sectoral coverage,[2] and
(b) provides for the absence or elimination of substantially all discrimination, in the sense of Article XVII, between or among the parties, through:
    (i) elimination of existing discriminatory measures, and/or
    (ii) prohibition of new or more discriminatory measures,
either at the entry into force of that agreement or on the basis of a reasonable time-frame except for measures permitted under Articles XI, XII, XIV and XIV bis.
In evaluating whether the conditions under paragraph 1(b) are met, consideration may be given to the relationship of the agreement to a wider process of economic integration or trade liberalization among the countries concerned.
4. Any agreement referred to in paragraph 1 shall be designed to facilitate trade between the parties to the agreement and shall not in respect of any Member outside the agreement raise the overall level of barriers to trade in services within the respective sectors or subsectors compared to the level applicable prior to such an agreement.

The three requirements set out in Article V that must be met by all economic integration agreements that provide for preferential, discriminatory treatment on trade in services are that such agreements must: cover substantially all trade (in number of sectors, volume of trade, and modes

---

2. This condition is understood in terms of number of sectors, volume of trade affected, and modes of supply. To meet this condition, agreements should not provide for the a priori exclusion of any mode of supply.

of supply); result in the removal of substantially all discrimination between the parties to an agreement; and not raise the overall level of barriers to trade in services to service suppliers from countries outside the agreement. From a reading of the text, it is clear that the above requirements were loosely drafted and consequently gave rise to a great deal of imprecision. Many of the concepts have been borrowed from GATT Article XXIV but do not seem to be readily applicable to trade in services with the very aggregate data that are available. Interpretation of the above requirements has therefore proved very difficult.[3]

The WTO Committee on Regional Trading Agreements (CRTA) was created in 1997 with the mandate to examine regional trade and economic integration agreements and to develop a consensus on the interpretation of both GATT Article XXIV and GATS Article V. Although much discussion has taken place over a number of years in the earlier GATT Committee on Trade and Development and in the present CRTA on how to interpret the systemic issues arising under preferential agreements in the area of goods, little discussion has taken place about services. In fact, to date only two papers have been submitted to the committee on this topic. A detailed consideration of the systemic issues arising under GATS Article V only began in late 1998.

At the end of 1998, WTO members reported that their progress in the adoption of reports on the compatibility of integration agreements with WTO requirements had been impeded by a lack of consensus on the interpretation of the rules relating to RTAs, such as those discussed in the following section.

The lack of clarity in the rules governing services also exists in a more fundamental sense, with respect to the kind of barriers that an economic integration agreement should be expected to eliminate. Barriers to trade in services are by their nature very different from barriers to trade in goods, as they consist of measures set out in laws, decrees, and regulatory practices. Liberalization of trade in services as defined under GATS consists of the removal of discriminatory practices by sovereign governments in the treatment granted to foreign, compared with domestic, service providers. This would be applicable to any manner in which a service might be supplied (that is, either through cross-border trade or through commercial

---

3. Geza Feketekuty has written that it is difficult to see how the conditions set out in Article V can effectively be monitored with the kind of data that are currrently available on trade in services. See Feketekuty (1999).

presence in the domestic market, or through movement of personnel). Removal of discrimination can be effected through a change in domestic legislation, the conclusion of mutual recognition agreements that provide for the equivalency of foreign service providers with domestic service providers, or the harmonization of national laws and regulatory practices. Doing so completely would provide for almost a total merging or integration of a country's domestic market with a foreign market. Doing so less than completely means that a certain amount of discrimination remains present in the various services sectors in favor of domestic suppliers. Exactly what degree of integration the WTO members should expect in areas such as foreign direct investment, labor mobility, and the recognition of professional qualifications is extremely unclear.

Areas Needing Clarification in the Interpretation of GATS Article V

The issues raised by the interpretation of GATS Article V are complex, and discussion of such systemic issues to assist in the determination of the compatibility of regional agreements with multilateral obligations has barely begun. While a few agreements on services have been notified to the WTO with examinations ongoing since 1995, only in 1998 did the committee begin to consider systemic issues. Thus the interpretation of the issues raised in this section is still an open question. No WTO understanding has been reached, nor has any precedent been established.

Meaning and Measurement of Substantial Sectoral Coverage

One of the fundamental requirements that all economic integration agreements on services must meet is that of carrying out liberalization for substantially all sectors. However, the meaning of GATS Article V is not clear in this regard nor is the concept of how substantial sectoral coverage should or can be measured. Should this be determined on a sector-by-sector basis, on a subsector-by-subsector basis, or on a completely disaggregated basis? Would a liberal interpretation of this requirement allow for the exclusion of one or more subsectors? Would it allow for the exclusion of an entire sector (such as that of air transport services in various agreements in the Western Hemisphere)? Should members to an economic integration agreement be expected to meet a higher standard than that set in GATS (under which much of the transport sector, including air transport and maritime transport services, is effectively excluded at present)?

When a sector might be excluded from the coverage of liberalization, the question arises as to how much weight to allot this sector. This consideration brings up the difficulty of measurement of trade in services. It is almost impossible now to assess the volume of trade covered by an integration agreement on services because of the severe limitations on the availability of accurate data on services trade and the aggregate nature of the categories reported in statistical publications.[4] The only internationally comparable source setting out categories of services trade is that of the *IMF Balance of Payments Yearbook*. However, even after the fifth revision, the number of categories of services trade that are to be reported and published are very few (only around twenty). The difficulty is compounded because what is needed for the relevant calculation is not the value of trade in services for the world market but the value of intraregional trade in services (among the members of a given integration agreement). When they exist, these data must be extracted from national accounts and national trade statistics and may not be comparable from country to country or agreement to agreement.

Therefore a key question is how to calculate the affected volume of trade when an entire sector may be excluded from an agreement or when a given services sector may be less than fully liberalized. If a services sector is fully or partially excluded from the coverage of an integration agreement, it would be almost impossible to determine its economic importance in the present circumstances owing to the difficulty of obtaining the required data necessary to calculate the percentage represented by that sector in the total intraregional trade in services for members of a given agreement. In the absence of such data, a more feasible alternative would be to calculate the importance of the excluded sector or subsector in the combined GDP of the members making up a given agreement. A suggestion has been made to adopt a minimum percentage target for the volume of services trade to be covered by an integration agreement, as measured by the combined volume of domestic services activity of the included services sectors.[5]

---

4. See Stephenson (1999).

5. This suggestion was made in an informal paper presented by Hong Kong, China, to the members of the WTO Council for Trade in Services in May 1999.

However, no discussion has taken place about what this minimum percentage might be.

In terms of coverage, it is unclear whether or not the GATS requirements in Article V would allow for the exclusion of a mode of supply for one services sector only (such as the cross-border supply of financial services in the case of the agreements signed by Chile). It is equally unclear whether the admonition to not exclude from the outset any mode of supply extends to certain categories within one of the modes (such as the exclusion of the movement of labor categories other than those of professional service providers in the case of the majority of the agreements in the hemisphere). Should all labor mobility as it relates to trade in services be included?[6]

Equally important, does an integration agreement have to cover investment as it relates to trade in services? As investment is the most important mode of supply for services trade, as defined by GATS, it would seem that no agreement excluding investment would be consistent with multilateral rules. However, in some services sectors, governments require foreign suppliers to establish themselves locally before they are allowed to sell their services to local consumers, a requirement amounting to an automatic exclusion of cross-border trade in these services. Can this be considered a violation of Article V?

In the Western Hemisphere all of the integration agreements on services either include a separate chapter containing comprehensive investment disciplines (those agreements modeled on the approach of the North American Free Trade Agreement) or define investment as a mode of supply within the agreement (Mercosur; Andean Community). In the NAFTA approach, investment protocols have been developed separately or are being completed. It will be important to see how the link between the investment and services components of these two integration agreements is articulated and whether the approaches to liberalization are compatible.[7]

---

6. This is a requirement under all of those agreements with the stated aim of being customs unions. This is not the case for free trade agreements. GATS Article V requirements do not distinguish, however, between the two forms of integration agreements, which in the case of labor mobility does have strong implications.

7. For example, it would be problematic for service suppliers to be faced with an agreement providing for a positive list of services commitments on the one hand including those on foreign direct investment, with a comprehensive agreement on investment that adopted a negative list approach to investment decisions overall (for both goods and services), that is, an investment agreement adopting a pre-establishment discipline for liberalization, on the other hand.

If not, service suppliers will be subjected to a confusing situation that would also be unclear from the legal standpoint.

Meaning of Substantially All Discrimination

Another of the main requirements set out in GATS Article V is the necessity for integration agreements to provide for the absence or elimination of substantially all discrimination as understood in terms of Article XVII of the GATS on national treatment. That article provides for treatment granted to service suppliers from other parties to an integration agreement to be no less favorable than that accorded to domestic service suppliers. Granting unqualified national treatment among members to an integration agreement would be the equivalent of free trade for services as no discriminatory barriers (except possibly those of a quantitative nondiscriminatory nature) would exist to the establishment of member firms or to cross-border sales of services by member firms. The main question is whether such a requirement can be measured on some quantitative basis. Further, to which sectors should it apply? Clearly all of those sectors included within an integration agreement should be covered; for these sectors, the question is how to measure the extent of liberalization achieved. What types of discriminatory measures, besides those that fall under the enumerated GATS articles, should be considered legitimate exceptions from this requirement?

Article V lists certain other GATS Articles under which measures are to be excepted from the requirement of eliminating substantially all discrimination. These are GATS Articles XI (IMF Provisions on Payments and Transfers), XII (Balance of Payments), XIV (General Exceptions related to health, safety, taxation and public order), and XIV bis (National Security). Notably, this list does not include Article VII (Recognition), Article X (Emergency Safeguard Measures), Article XIII (Government Procurement), or Article XV (Subsidies). Nor does it make reference to the two annexes on Air Transport Services and Financial Services. This raises a number of questions, namely, whether or not such omissions make it impossible for members of an integration agreement to discriminate against one another in important areas such as the licensing of professional service suppliers, the granting of domestic subsidies, and government procurement of services. Equally, does it mean that members of an integration agreement are not allowed to apply Emergency Safeguard Measures to their services trade with one another?

The agreements on services in the Western Hemisphere clearly do not yet eliminate or harmonize licensing requirements for professional service suppliers, although a few mutual recognition agreements in the services area have been elaborated under NAFTA (for accountancy, engineering, legal advisory services, and architectural services). Many of the agreements contain chapters on professional services, with an aim of attempting to recognize the equivalency of these requirements, or in the case of the Andean Community, foresee the future elaboration of a decision on professional services. However, clearly the stringent application of such a requirement would make it difficult for all agreements covering services to be compatible with multilateral disciplines.

With respect to safeguards, while many of the services agreements in the hemisphere do not include articles foreseeing recourse to such action (NAFTA, the Group of Three, and the bilateral agreements between Chile and Mexico and between Chile and Canada, as well as the Andean Community agreement), other agreements do include such a provision. For four agreements details on safeguard action are to be worked out in the future. It is difficult, however, to imagine how safeguard action among members to an integration agreement would be compatible with the requirement to both liberalize trade among members and not raise the level of barriers to outside members.

Most agreements in the hemisphere do not include an explicit provision to eliminate subsidies or trade between members to the agreement. Therefore this area remains unclear, as does the interpretation of the disciplines expected on subsidies by GATS.

When discrimination in a given service sector is not eliminated among members to an integration agreement, how this situation should be evaluated in terms of its economic impact is still open to debate. Does the existence of discrimination between suppliers of professional services by members to a regional agreement hold more weight than the maintenance of discrimination in the provision of educational or health services? How to evaluate the economic significance of remaining discrimination is a question that has not yet been explored.

Lastly, GATS Article V does not require the immediate elimination of substantially all discrimination by members to economic integration agreements but requires it within a reasonable time frame. The question is, what is a reasonable time frame? In the Understanding on the Interpretation of Article XXIV of the GATT 1994 that resulted from the Uruguay Round, this is taken to mean no longer than ten years in the case of goods. A recent proposal to the Council for Trade in Services has suggested that this time frame be no longer than five years.[8] However, the time frame has not been discussed yet for services.

Meaning of Not Raising Overall Level of Barriers to Services Trade

Once again Article V is unclear about what is meant by the injunction not to raise the overall level of barriers to trade in services vis-à-vis parties outside the integration agreement in individual services sectors or subsectors. In practice, how can such a requirement be tested or evaluated? Several questions arise.

First, the impossibility of calculating the overall level of barriers to services trade in effect prior to the formation of an integration agreement makes this requirement difficult to translate into practice. As the barriers to trade in services are present in the form of laws, decrees, and regulatory practices, the qualitative nature of such barriers makes it virtually impossible to attach to them a quantitative value. Calculating tariff or price equivalents for the trade restrictive effect of most national laws and regulatory practices has proved impossible at present and most likely will continue to run into insurmountable data and methodological difficulties. An alternative test has been proposed on the basis of the requirement that an agreement on services not reduce the level of trade in any services sector or subsector following its entry into force, or that it not reduce the growth of trade in any sector or subsector below a historical trend.[9]

A related question on this requirement has to do again with the nature of changes to barriers to trade in services. In the case of a customs union arrangement, regulatory barriers to services trade are to be gradually harmonized among members. Is this a significantly different means to lower or remove such barriers than under free trade agreements? Regulatory barriers are addressed on the basis of equivalency or mutual recognition agreements. Are these two approaches significantly different? Does the choice of an approach to eliminating discrimination among members affect the treatment of third parties? Would it be easier for service suppliers

8. This proposal was tabled in a paper by Japan at an April 1999 meeting of the WTO Council for Trade in Services. The proposal suggests that the WTO requirement to eliminate discrimination in the sectors covered by an economic integration agreement be met within five years after the agreement is in place. A similar proposal was made by Japan in 1997.

9. This suggestion for an alternative means of evaluating this Article V requirement has been proposed by Hong Kong, China, in its paper to the WTO Council for Trade in Services of March 1999.

from third parties to gain access to a mutual recognition agreement than to comply with harmonized regulatory standards? Does this also relate to the concept of the wider process of economic integration set out in GATS Article V:2?

Other Problems Surrounding GATS Article V

Besides the problems of a systemic nature mentioned above that surround the interpretation and application of GATS Article V, other problems have appeared in connection with this article that render it somewhat unsatisfactory. These include the lack of notifications of regional and economic integration agreements to the WTO for examination in the Committee on Regional Trading Arrangements and the hesitation of developing countries to participate in this process, the existing sectoral standalone agreements on services and their relationship to GATS Article V obligations, and the status of Article V in relation to the regional and economic integration agreements included in the list of MFN exemptions.

Reluctance to Notify Economic Integration Agreements

A general reluctance to notify both regional trading arrangements and economic integration agreements to the WTO for examination within the WTO Committee on Regional Trade Agreements prevails. A study done by the WTO Secretariat for the purpose of drawing a global picture of RTAs identified more than 130 such agreements (not a comprehensive count), of which only 60 had been notified to the GATT/WTO. This leaves 74 nonnotified RTAs.[10] Several of these RTAs have now incorporated provisions on trade in services, meaning that the members of the majority of integration agreements on services are presently not in compliance with WTO disciplines and seem unwilling to participate in this important review process.

The situation in the Western Hemisphere follows this pattern. To date, ten bilateral or subregional integration agreements covering services have been signed or have entered into force.[11] These agreements, and the date of their signature or entry into force, are the following:

10. Not all of these seventy-four agreements would need to be notified to the WTO, however; only those containing binding provisions for preferential treatment fall under multilateral obligations. This would still leave a considerable number of non-notified agreements.

North American Free Trade Agreement	January 1994
Group of Three Free Trade Agreement	January 1995
Mexico/Bolivia Free Trade Agreement	January 1995
Mexico/Costa Rica Free Trade Agreement	January 1995
Chile/Mexico Free Trade Agreement	January 1997
Chile/Canada Free Trade Agreement	June 1997
Mercosur Protocol on Services	December 1997
Andean Community Decision 439 on Services	June 1998
Mexico/Nicaragua Free Trade Agreement	July 1998
Central America/Dominican Republic Free Trade Agreement	January 1999

Only two of the above ten agreements encompassing trade in services have been notified to the WTO for examination under GATS Article V. These agreements are NAFTA (notified in March 1995) and the free trade agreement between Canada and Chile (notified in November 1997). The absence of compliance with one of the basic requirements of the GATS by the members of the other eight integration agreements in the Western Hemisphere is clearly a matter of concern. This is particularly so when all of these agreements would appear to be so-called GATS plus agreements, in terms of their present content or their objectives with respect to the long-term goal of liberalization.

Two of the agreements on services foresee the complete removal of barriers to services trade among the members to the arrangements within a stated period, namely, within ten years for the members of Mercosur and within five years for the members of the Andean Community. The stated objective of the former agreement is to carry out "successive rounds of negotiations in order to complete the Mercosur liberalization program for services within a ten-year period, counted from the date of entry into effect of the Services Protocol." And for the latter "the progressive liberalization of subregional trade in services, in order to reach a Common Market in Services, through the elimination of restrictive measures within the Andean Community."[12] This degree of liberalizing ambition is not present in any of the other regional agreements on services (except for the European

11. Organization of American States (forthcoming).

12. This objective would clearly meet as well the requirement of Article V that integration agreements achieve the absence or elimination of substantially all discrimination within a reasonable time frame. For most WTO members this is understood as not more than ten years.

Union.[13] However, all of the agreements initiated and signed by Mexico (namely, the Group of Three, and the bilateral free trade agreements with Bolivia, Costa Rica, Chile, and Nicaragua) do contain a built-in dynamic for future liberalization in the form of an obligation to continue to open services markets through future negotiations *"aiming to eliminate the remaining restrictions set out in the list of nonconforming measures."*[14]

The lack of willingness to notify agreements that cover all services sectors and modes of supply (Mercosur; Andean Community) or the large majority of sectors and modes of supply (with the Mexico free trade agreements excluding only air transport and labor mobility for nonprofessional categories of workers) while providing for the future removal of substantially all discrimination in services trade among members through their extremely ambitious stated liberalization objectives seems puzzling. However, this reluctance may be linked to the fact that the liberalizing process for services has not yet really begun in earnest: Mercosur members have not made publicly available the lists of commitments they have begun to exchange among themselves, and the Andean Community has not yet developed the inventories of national legal and regulatory measures from which they are to begin negotiating removal of discrimination. In the case of the free trade agreements, only the members of the Group of Three Agreement have so far published the lists of reservations or nonconforming measures to the scope of services liberalization that are to accompany the treaties. So have the members to the NAFTA and Chile/Canada agreements, where such lists are set out as an integral part of the text, making these agreements highly transparent (for measures at the federal level only). Thus a critical element of transparency is missing from the process of services liberalization for all other agreements within the hemisphere, which certainly would be a stumbling block in a multilateral examination.

However, in their reluctance to notify recent economic integration agreements on services, countries in the Western Hemisphere may be overlooking one of the provisions of Article V, which allows for more

13. Notably, all of the integration agreements that postulate the complete removal of restrictions to internal services trade are agreements that by their stated objective are customs unions in nature and not free trade agreements.

14. Emphasis added. This obligation for future liberalization appears in Article 10.09 of the Group of Three Treaty, Article 10.09 of the Mexico/ Chile Free Trade Agreement, Article 9-08 of the Mexico/Bolivia and Mexico/ Costa Rica Free Trade Agreements, and Article 10.9 of the Mexico/Nicaragua Free Trade Agreement. Mexico is currently on the verge of concluding a new free trade agreement with the three countries of the northern triangle in Central America, namely, El Salvador, Guatemala, and Honduras.

lenient examination to be extended to such agreements when the agreement is composed solely of developing countries:

> 3. (a) Where developing countries are parties to an agreement of the type referred to in paragraph 1, flexibility shall be provided for regarding the conditions set out in paragraph 1, particularly with reference to subpara (b) thereof, in accordance with the level of development of the countries concerned, both overall and in individual sectors and subsectors.

This paragraph clearly speaks to flexibility in the interpretation of Article V provisions for developing WTO members about the elimination of substantially all discrimination in services trade, although the notion of more favorable treatment is not precisely defined in the article. Eight of the ten integration agreements in the Western Hemisphere that cover services have developing country membership only, yet not one of these has been notified by the members to the WTO. In the absence of third-party notification, the lack of compliance with the Article V notification requirement can only weaken the one link that should be functioning effectively to ensure the compatibility and congruence of the parallel multilateral and regional liberalization processes.[15]

Overlapping Membership of Regional Trade Agreements

Another phenomenon of relevance is the increasingly common tendency for WTO members to join more than one economic integration agreement simultaneously. According to the study prepared by the WTO Secretariat, twelve countries in the Western Hemisphere signed more than four RTAs.[16] In the case of those agreements covering services, Mexico is a party to no less than six different agreements, while several countries are parties to two different agreements (Bolivia, Canada, Chile, Colombia, Costa Rica, Nicaragua, and Venezuela). Certain anomalies have arisen in this context. For example, in Central America, the members of the Central American Common Market have signed a free trade agreement with the Dominican Republic covering services, even while they do not yet have such provisions among themselves. Colombia and Venezuela have agreed

15. Outside of the Western Hemisphere where several agreements on services have been signed with developing-country membership, this appears to be the case elsewhere only for the members of the Association of Southeast Asian Nations, who signed a Protocol on Services in 1995.

16. The WTO Secretariat also noted that fourteen European countries were party to thirty-five different RTAs.

to the elimination of barriers to services trade between themselves in the context of the Andean Community but have not agreed to the same objective in the context of the Group of Three Treaty they signed with Mexico. The members of the Central American Common Market are now negotiating with Chile at the same time that they are finalizing a services agreement among themselves. And members of Mercosur and of the Andean Community are carrying on discussions about the possible negotiation of a subregional agreement. What would happen to services in the case of such an agreement will be interesting, as the former agreement has adopted a bottom-up approach to services liberalization, while the latter has adopted a top-down approach, creating a possible conflict in attempting to carry out simultaneous liberalization among members of both groupings.

This overlapping membership of RTAs and economic integration agreements in the case of services has resulted in a complex web of rules for the purpose of administering and enforcing the provisions of such agreements. Such multiple rules may run counter to the primary objective of RTAs, which is not to raise barriers to the trade of third countries but to facilitate trade among members, resulting in net trade creation.

Stand-Alone Sectoral Agreements

It is a little known fact that within the Western Hemisphere a great number of stand-alone agreements have been reached in services. In a study carried out in 1997 for the FTAA Working Group on Services on the basis of information received from the participating countries, the Organization of American States Secretariat classified no fewer than 167 sectoral agreements on services of various types (41 at the subregional level and 126 at the bilateral level).[17] Most of these agreements are in professional services and transport services (with 67 agreements relating to air routing alone). Strikingly, more than half of the sectoral agreements have been signed since 1990.

The legal status of these agreements is unclear. For those agreements of a cooperative and technical assistance nature that do not contain liberalizing provisions, there would seem to be no basis for conflict with GATS Article V requirements. However, those agreements that provide for statutory preferential treatment better than that provided to other trading partners should have been notified to the WTO as part of the Annex II of

---

17. Organization of American States (1998).

MFN Exemptions to GATS or otherwise should have been the object of a waiver request, as discussed in the following paragraphs. Since there have been no requests to the WTO for waivers on services measures, certain of these sectoral agreements now presumably exist in a legal gray area, inconsistent with multilateral disciplines.

In telecommunications, a Draft Convention on the provision of value-added telecommunications services was negotiated in 1997 by members of the OAS under the aegis of the Inter-American Telecommunication Commission (CITEL). The convention covers such matters as the standard of treatment, interconnection with the public network, terminal equipment, rights of end-users, and others. It is not clear whether the convention is meant to be applied on a nondiscriminatory basis or a preferential basis among countries in the Western Hemisphere only. If the intention is to give preferential treatment, then the Draft Convention would conflict with the basic MFN principle and would need to comply with GATS Article V provisions. It would appear extremely problematic to accept that a single services sector could qualify under these provisions. Although it was possible for WTO members to list measures and agreements such as a sector-specific telecom agreement as exemptions from the MFN principle, this possibility expired when GATS entered into force in 1995. The only other channel open for making such a sector specific agreement consistent with GATS would be to seek a waiver from the MFN obligation under Article IX:3. Such waivers, when sought, must be justified by exceptional circumstances, should in principle be temporary, and are subject to annual review.

In light of the above, members of CITEL decided to transmit the Draft Convention to the FTAA Negotiating Group on Services in August 1998 for consideration and use in the FTAA process.

Notification of Integration Agreements as MFN Exemptions

Another possibly worrisome development is that many WTO members have claimed wide-ranging exemptions for preferential trade agreements through notifying these under Annex II, or their list of MFN exemptions to GATS, rather than having such agreements examined under the WTO Committee on Regional Trade Agreements. Presumably the reason for such a course of action would be to avoid the examination process under GATS Article V because of uncertainty over whether or not such agreements would be deemed compatible with multilateral obligations.

This brings into question the purpose of the existing Annex II on MFN Exemptions and the MFN article itself. Article II:1 of GATS states that the MFN obligation must be immediate and unconditional for services supplied by any other WTO member, and that it is to apply to any measure covered by this agreement. Although the scope of application of such measures is wide, they would not include the provisions of preferential economic integration agreements, which are to be subject to the provisions of Article V. Measures falling under preferential agreements that contain comprehensive disciplines on services are part and parcel of a larger package and should not be considered on an individual sectoral basis, nor listed in the GATS MFN Annex.

In the GATS MFN Exemptions Lists, several sector-specific discriminatory measures are included that originate in preferential integration agreements: most of these are in the audiovisual sector (thirty-seven), in road transport services (twenty-four), maritime transport services (fourteen), telecommunications services (eighteen), and financial services (ten).[18] Additional analysis would be necessary to determine which of these measures are stand-alone in nature and which fall under services agreements with comprehensive disciplines and sectoral coverage.

Application of GATS Article V to a Future Free Trade Area of the Americas (FTAA) Agreement on Services

What will the relationship of GATS Article V be to a future FTAA agreement on services? The first level of response to this question is very simple: a future hemispheric agreement on services must fulfill Article V requirements to be deemed compatible with the rules and disciplines of the multilateral trading system, and therefore must cover substantially all sectors and remove substantially all discrimination among participants in the Western Hemisphere. From the preceding sections, however, it is apparent that no common interpretation of these multilateral obligations has yet been agreed to by WTO members. Much will depend on the outcome of the present deliberations in the WTO Committee on Regional Trade Agreements.

Political and economic reality will dictate, however, that a regional agreement encompassing countries in the Western Hemisphere that account for one-quarter of the world's GDP and one-fifth of the world's trade

18. This information is contained in Mattoo (1998, table 2) on MFN and GATS. This paper contains a thorough and interesting discussion on the role of the MFN provision in services.

will come under close scrutiny in the WTO. Such an FTAA agreement would rival that of the European Union in economic and trade terms. Thus the conditions of GATS Article V would most likely be closely reviewed and strictly applied in this context, as the FTAA agreement would have such a large weight in international trade.

At another level, the question is, what type of subregional preferential treatment could be envisaged, if any, among the parties to a future FTAA agreement? While the MFN principle in its unconditional form has been the backbone of all of the subregional integration agreements and of the vast majority of trading agreements in the world economy, the question of whether the MFN principle could be interpreted in a conditional manner in a future hemispheric agreement on services has arisen.[19]

This concern prevails because the FTAA process is taking place in a region where several integration agreements already exist and where members of some agreements may wish to achieve deeper levels of integration than that which will be sought at the broader regional level. This reality is reflected in the San Jose Ministerial Declaration which states, "The FTAA can co-exist with bilateral and sub-regional agreements, to the extent that the rights and obligations under these agreements are not covered by or go beyond the rights and obligations of the FTAA."[20]

The declaration could be interpreted as allowing special preferences between smaller groups of countries in the hemisphere (which go beyond the obligations or liberalization of a future FTAA agreement) to be maintained alongside a regional trade agreement. But if the declaration is read in this manner, then several questions arise:

—How would it be possible for a broader FTAA agreement on services containing a conditional MFN clause to be compatible with GATS Article V, which requires an economic integration agreement to achieve the absence or elimination of substantially all discrimination in the sense of Article XVII (National Treatment) between or among the parties?

—How would such an agreement fulfill the mandate given by ministers and endorsed by heads of state to create a free trade agreement for the hemisphere?

19. As is well known, the MFN principle requires not only that a trading partner (of the WTO or of a regional agreement) be treated no less favorably than any other member but also that any advantage that is withdrawn from any member has to be withdrawn from all. The MFN principle thus requires that the best treatment be made available to all members of the agreement in question.

20. Paragraph f of the section on General Principles. San Jose Ministerial Declaration adopted by trade ministers of the Western Hemisphere on April 19, 1998, in San Jose, Costa Rica.

—If varying degrees of MFN treatment were envisaged within the FTAA, how could free trade and investment be achieved?

—Can the MFN principle be thought of as open to gradual implementation in the region so that at some point all countries would reach the same level of liberalization and MFN treatment?

—Should exceptions to the MFN principle be thought of as permanent exemptions or temporary, time-bound reservations subject to future negotiation?

Liberalization could be thought of as moving in concentric circles, with the WTO GATS obligations at the heart of the circle, a future FTAA in the next layer, and the subregional agreements in the farthest layer. Clearly, all subregional agreements and the FTAA itself would have to comply with GATS Article V disciplines; however, would it be possible within the region for the subregional agreements to have a relationship to the FTAA similar to that to the WTO, which is subject to a similar Article V–type discipline allowing for differential preferential treatment under the broader hemispheric agreement?

Besides the questions posed by the application of the MFN principle in a future FTAA on services by countries in the Western Hemisphere, the question also arises of whether differential or conditional MFN treatment be given to countries *outside* the Western Hemisphere? This might be the case for members of different subregional agreements who are involved in simultaneous integration processes, within and outside the FTAA, and who might wish to enter into a mutual economic integration agreement.

Conclusion

At this point it is difficult to draw any definitive conclusions about the interpretation or application of GATS Article V. This is the case whether one is analyzing the nexus between the multilateral and regional disciplines or the possibility of an Article V–type clause in a future FTAA agreement. The lack of definition and respect surrounding multilateral requirements for preferential trade agreements can be contrasted with the number of RTAs and economic integration agreements that continue to multiply. It is clear that this absence of clarity is one of the weak links in the chain of multilateral and regional trade disciplines.

References

Feketekuty, Geza. 1998. "Setting the Agenda for Services 2000: The Next Round of Negotiations on Trade in Services." Paper presented at the Conference on the Future of Services Trade Liberalization Services 2000, sponsored by the Coalition of Services Industries. England (April).

———. 1999. "Assessing the WTO General Agreement on Trade and Improving the GATS." Paper presented to the Conference on Services 2000: New Directions in Services Trade Liberalization, Washington (June)

Mattoo, Aaditya. 1998. "Most-Favoured Nation Treatment and the GATS." Draft paper presented at the World Trade Forum Conference on Most-Favoured Nation: Past and Present. Switzerland (August).

Organization of American States. 1997. *Provisions on Trade in Services in the Trade and Integration Agreements of the Western Hemisphere.* Washington.

———. 1998. *Sectoral Agreements on Services in the Western Hemisphere.* Washington.

———. Forthcoming. *Provisions on Trade in Services in the Trade and Integration Agreements of the Western Hemisphere.* Washington.

Sauvé, Pierre. 1997. "Preparing for Services 2000." CSI Occasional Paper 4. Washington: Coalition of Services Industries.

Stephenson, Sherry. 1999. "Regional Agreements on Services within APEC and Disciplines of the Multilateral Trading System." Paper presented to the meeting of the APEC Group on Services. New Zealand (February).

COMMENT BY
Juan A. Marchetti

The background papers prepared for this session are all interesting, thought provoking, and provide challenging insights into the main issues involved in the forthcoming services negotiations. I find myself in the situation of trying to convey a developing country's perspective as I come from a developing country that has undertaken an ambitious economic reform agenda in the past decade. Before I touch upon some of the issues raised in these chapters, I would like to state one proviso about the context of these negotiations.

The scope of what is sometimes called the Millenium Round is not yet clear. What we do know, however, is that a round of negotiations on trade in services will take place as foreseen in GATS. As an economist, I must acknowledge that convincing arguments in favor of trade and investment liberalization abound. They should suffice to support the basic idea of further services liberalization and a meaningful round of services negotiations (in terms of binding such liberalization). But, although services negotiations are important, they should not be looked at as if they were isolated from the rest of the package. This view would clearly be unrealistic. In fact, for most developing countries, the willingness to liberalize their services sectors and, more important, to translate that liberalization into meaningful commitments in the WTO, will largely depend on the benefits accruing to them as a result of other negotiations, such as those in textiles or agriculture. Cross-sectoral trade-offs will be part of the next round of negotiations, and building momentum for the services negotiations will depend on building momentum in other sectors of interest to developing countries.

Having said that, let me turn to the substantive issues raised in the first three background papers prepared for this session. The following comments are essentially based on what might be called "basic economic instincts." First and foremost, I fully agree with the basic conclusion of the chapter by Patrick Low and Aaditya Mattoo that "it is possible to make significant improvements in GATS, and to make it a much more effective instrument of liberalization, without fundamental structural changes, which are, in any case, of doubtful political feasibility."

As you already know, one of the key principles of GATS, at least for most developing countries, is that of progressive liberalization. Article XIX of GATS provides for appropriate flexibility for opening fewer sectors or liberalizing fewer types of transactions. And GATS certainly accommodates gradualism, in its approach to scheduling commitments and in its four modes of supply. I would argue that it does not seem politically feasible at this stage to introduce major changes to the GATS structure—changes that could be perceived as undermining that flexibility.

The question then becomes, from a political economy perspective, that of turning GATS into a more effective instrument of trade liberalization for developed and developing countries alike. Priority should be given to clarifying provisions that have a direct bearing on the scope and clarity of existing and future commitments. Low and Mattoo have identified the main areas for clarification. Some of them could be addressed by way of understandings and, in my view, do not necessarily call for a modification of the existing provisions. These are the applicability of the so-called principle of technological neutrality; the development of a detailed nomenclature of general application; and the improvement of scheduling guidelines. An understanding could also be envisaged for the clarification of the relationship between mode 1 (cross-border trade) and mode 2 (consumer abroad) in the context of the work on scheduling guidelines, but it should be acknowledged that a definitive solution to this question could require the amendment of the agreement. The clarification of the relationship between market access and national treatment, however, would certainly require an amendment to the agreement. Close attention should also be given to the improvement of the general level of specific commitments. Some commentators have rightly argued that the liberalization effects ensuing from current commitments have proved rather modest, a result that applies to developed and developing countries alike. While developing countries should make an effort to widen the sectoral coverage of their schedules, developed countries should start focusing on eliminating restrictions affecting sectors or modes of supply of interest to developing countries. Full commitments on consumption abroad of tourist services are simply not enough. What about health, construction, computer-related services, maritime transport services, and the like?

A second area that I would like to touch on refers to the relationship between disciplines on domestic regulation and the scheduled commitments. The chapters by Low and Mattoo and by Bernard M. Hoekman and Patrick A. Messerlin address the question of liberalization and regulatory reform. Both chapters agree on the need for a parallel approach to regulation and liberalization. However, it seems to me that they look at the issue from different perspectives.

Low and Mattoo consider the issue from a trade policy perspective. They put greater emphasis on the liberalization commitments for market access and national treatment than on domestic regulatory reform, and they therefore stress the importance of adequate disciplines on domestic regulation as an accompaniment of liberalization. They look at the issue from what I would call a typical GATS perspective, that is, considering domestic regulations as a way to making the scheduled commitments operational in terms of meaningful market conditions. Domestic regulation is understood of course as those nondiscriminatory measures that may have nevertheless a restrictive effect on trade. That is to say, what we call Article VI.4 measures.

I certainly agree with this approach. Clearly a need exists to strengthen the disciplines on domestic regulation. Since the conclusion of the disciplines on accountancy services, the debate in the WTO has focused on whether we should develop horizontal or sectoral disciplines. I agree with Low and Mattoo that the generic approach is better because it economizes on negotiating effort, leads to the creation of disciplines for all services sectors rather than only the politically important ones, and reduces the likelihood of negotiations being captured by sectoral interest groups. However, I think there is still room for some sectoral disciplines besides the general ones. I do not believe that both approaches are mutually exclusive. It seems to me that a two-layered approach could be applied. The first layer would be constituted by generic principles, applicable to all services sectors. Principles such as a necessity test and transparency could be core elements. On top of that, as a second layer, we could develop additional disciplines, especially meant for heavily regulated sectors.

Hoekman and Messerlin consider the issue from an economic policy perspective. In fact, their stated objetive is to develop some useful rules of thumb for policymakers to harness the negotiations on services to the domestic regulatory reform agenda. A basic corollary is that governments should seek to lock in regulatory reform policies undertaken at a national level, and that is why these authors make a plea for an increased dose of unilateralism in the way countries commit themselves in the WTO. Therefore, they look at the scheduled commitments as a way to ensure and complement domestic regulatory reforms.

I found their argument for a greater uniformity in protection very interesting. It could certainly do a lot in favor of trade liberalization.

However, although unilateralism is a necessary condition, it is not a sufficient one. And I also fail to see why this may be a smaller burden for developing than for developed WTO members. One of the features that distinguishes the former from the latter, as far as WTO services negotiations are concerned, is the scope of their schedules of committments. Coverage in terms of sectors and subsectors tends to be much wider in industrialized countries, although there are exceptions. However, this does not mean that developed country schedules are free from market access and national treatment restrictions. But it is not uncommon to find clean commitments from developing countries, even in strategic sectors such as telecommunications and financial services. Therefore, if we are to seek a more uniform pattern of protection, then there is clearly a case for a concerted multilateral effort, both from developing and developed countries.

And that is where the words Trade Policy (in capital letters) come into play. In spite of Hoekman and Messerlin, the WTO is about trade policy, and the forthcoming negotiations are about trade policies affecting services, among other things. And what allows for successful agreements is the possibility of reaching a politically acceptable balance in the commitments we are assuming. Trade-offs are inevitable. And trade officials and negotiators may need to use the services lever to obtain concessions in other sectors, whose developmental implications are at least as important as those arising in services.

Finally, let me turn to negotiating modalities, in particular, formula approaches, negative versus positive lists, and precommitments to future liberalization. On the question of formula approaches, it must be noted at the outset that developing countries tend to favor, in principle, a traditional request-and-offer approach. And the negotiations on basic telecommunications and financial services have proved that this approach is useful to achieve further liberalization.

However, complementary approaches should not be discarded. Some analysts refer to such approaches as negotiating formulas or concerted efforts. It is important to know exactly what we are aiming at. It seems to me that two broad objectives can be identified: expanding the sectoral coverage and improving the quality of commitments. The chapters by Low and Mattoo and by Rachel Thompson explore different options for the design of formulas. And both of them make a good case for greater doses of complementarity between formula approaches and bottom-up scheduling. Formulas may also contribute to achieving a more uniform pattern of protection across countries and sectors, as advocated by Hoekman and Messerlin, as a consequence of the elimination of the same trade restrictions across the board. The question arises, however, of whether one should put priority on downstream user industries or on infrastructural services. These considerations seem to suggest that, although useful a priori, formula approaches should be carefully conceived. Account must also be taken of the fact that, for many developing countries, balance and flexibility play an important role. In other words, formulas should also cover sectors and modes of supply of interest to developing countries, and appropriate flexibility should be provided for them to apply certain formulas.

I would like to refer to the question of the negative versus positive list approach to scheduling specific commitments. The case for a negative list approach turns on two broad arguments: greater transparency in terms of the identification of sectors excluded from coverage; and greater pro-liberalization dynamic. The case against a negative list approach rests similarly on two main arguments: it is not so transparent as to the regime of the services sectors covered by the commitments, especially in relation to nondiscriminatory forms of regulatory intervention; and it is not necessarily more liberalizing since negative lists of exceptions may well be quite long, making the general disciplines irrelevant. In fact, as Hoekman and Messerlin clearly state, this is exactly what happened in the Multilateral Agreement on Investment (MAI) negotiations. Besides, would all countries be prepared to automatically liberalize any new services sector and technology that may be introduced in the future?

I would argue, together with Low and Mattoo and several other contributors to this volume, that revisiting the debate over top-down versus bottom-up approaches is not time well spent. It does not seem politically feasible at this juncture to introduce such a major structural change to the agreement, and the debate misses the more important issue about the precision and clarity with which a country spells out the limitations in its schedule of specific commitments. I would also argue that there is a need for improving the clarity and legal specificity of schedules through the drafting of better scheduling guidelines and the improvement of the nomenclature used for the purposes of negotiations.

Finally, I would like to refer to the issue of committing to future liberalization, so-called precommitting. Low and Mattoo raise this issue, which in my view is closely related to the adjustment process required to overcome the costs of opening markets. In fact, trade and investment liberalization can bring clear benefits if countries' commitment to reform is sustained. However, liberalization is not painless. I would argue indeed that precommitments or phased-in commitments are useful not only as a mechanism to make credible commitments to liberalize but, by the same token, as a clear signal to incumbents that the time to adjust is coming.

COMMENT BY
Michel Servoz

A few months ago when I took my current position in the European Commission, I met an old colleague who is now retired and was involved in the Uruguay Round's services negotiations. He told me, "I built a nice house in the Uruguay Round, with all the modern equipment, large windows, and a strong foundation. Your task now is to decorate the house and find the right furniture. I can see that it takes time." He was referring to the failure of the subsequent maritime transport negotiations and to the time it took to complete talks in the financial services and basic telecommunications sectors. With a bit of hindsight and putting the joke aside, I can now see how his remark serves as a useful reminder of the challenges ahead as preparations for the GATS 2000 round of negotiations intensify.

A primary goal for GATS 2000 should be to preserve the house that was built. Before negotiations commence, WTO members should collectively acknowledge the need to refrain from all that would risk undermining or unraveling the existing agreement. In other words, to use European legislative language, the Uruguay Round "acquis" must be protected. This will be all the more important if the next round brings new and important WTO members around the table.

Efforts must additionally be directed toward strengthening the foundation of the house. This task may not necessarily require fully fledged negotiations leading to new or amended GATS provisions. In most cases, negotiations leading to understandings on interpretation and implementation may suffice. Their potential can be seen in the case of Article V, the economic integration agreement that has been crucial to the development of the European Union (EU) and our partners in central and eastern Europe, and in the related case of Article XXI, which deals with the modification of schedules of commitments.

I see from the chapter by Low and Mattoo that considerable potential exists to clarify the scope of existing disciplines, for example, the overlap between market access and national treatment commitments, the overlap between modes of supply, and the question of likeness of services across various modes or of technological neutrality of commitments. Again, this clarification does not necessarily require amendments to existing provisions but rather gaining a shared understanding on interpretation—fixing problems to make the house more solid.

On the choice of furniture, GATS members have a mandate that flows from Article XIX. I see two possible ways of fulfilling this mandate:

—A first route would consist of identifying sectors in which WTO members want to achieve a "progressively higher level of liberalization" to quote Article XIX language. I call this route restrictive, simply because it would limit the scope of discussions to a number of sectors and by definition would have a strong sectoral bias.

—A preferred route would involve taking up comprehensive negotiations, addressing sectoral and horizontal issues simultaneously.

Before I outline what the EU sees as the substantive elements of such an agenda, let me note an important principle affecting the negotiating process. Ambassador Charlene Barshefsky recently recalled how three years had been lost in Uruguay Round discussions of what should and should not be on the negotiating table. We certainly agree that this delay should be avoided by all means. We also concur that the negotiating mandate flowing from the WTO's next ministerial declaration should be specific enough to avoid any such ambiguity. We would also suggest the principle that services negotiations be approached with an open mind: any country that may want to raise any issue should do so, without however expecting a response from other members. That might help avoid needless discussions about what we should or should not talk about.

The first objective on the comprehensive agenda the EU countries have in mind should be to secure broader and deeper liberalization commitments in several sectors. Given the current imbalance of commitments across countries, sectors, and modes of supply, the possibilities are great. It should not come as a surprise, however, that we have some preferences. For starters, we want to do better in traditional areas such as finance and telecommunications. But we also want to make progress in maritime transport and consider what may be possible in air transport, where the exclusion foreseen by the Annex will have to be reviewed.

In addition, some sectors appear increasingly important to us, and we would like to see a higher level of commitments in them. They include environmental, construction, distribution, health, and education services. Our shopping list is very similar to that of our Quadrilateral partners.

There is also the question of most favored nation exemptions, where no model or precedent for purposes of review currently exists. Two approaches could be taken. A first option could be to sit back and relax, and indeed for members with MFN exemptions to wait until evidence is brought by another showing why and how the exemption should be removed. A second option would see all GATS members with MFN exemptions submit information to the Council on Trade in Services justifying the need for maintaining the exemption in the future.

The second item on our agenda is horizontal and relates to the complex issue of domestic regulation, whose importance is widely acknowledged. We see this issue at the core of the GATS 2000 negotiations. For us, market access and national treatment commitments are of little value if they are not coupled with proper pro-competitive regulatory disciplines. As far as we can see, a lot of good work has been done in the WTO Working Party on Professional Services, whose mandate has been enlarged to encompass the broad challenge of market access–friendly domestic regulation issues. This working group could well become one of the subcommittees for the GATS 2000 negotiations. It is indeed worth considering early on whether the disciplines adopted for the accounting profession could be extended to other sectors, in particular those on transparency.

The most difficult issue to address is obviously the necessity test. Even if we were to agree quickly on what constitutes least-trade-restrictive forms of regulation, nonperforming regulation, or the highest level of regulation required, the challenge of translating such a shared understanding into a general principle applicable to all sectors will represent a formidable challenge.

The Reference Paper for Telecommunications addresses several elements we could usefully apply to other services sectors. They include access to essential facilities, the provision of universal services, the independence of regulatory authorities, and competition safeguards. In our view, it is worth considering whether the reference paper could be extended in one form or another to other services sectors.

The third item on our agenda would be to complete work on the trinity of issues left over from the Uruguay Round: safeguards, subsidies, and government procurement. EU member states remain to this date undecided on the need to have services-specific disciplines on safeguards and subsidies. What is clearer, however, is the considerable difficulties encountered in extending to services the kinds of GATT disciplines that currently apply to goods trade.

Our member states continue to question the logic of defining a like product subject to investigation, establishing clear injury tests to a domestic industry, or calculating in the case of subsidies the benefit to the recipient per unit of product. None of these matters applies in a straightforward way to services, What's more, such rules would in practice only apply to the cross-border mode of supply (mode 1). That said, our members appreciate the importance of developing a safety valve, particularly for developing countries given their stated preference for an opt-out clause should liberalization generate serious and unanticipated adjustment problems for domestic providers. Our members accept that certain types of subsidies, for instance, export subsidies, could have highly detrimental effects and may undermine what we aim to achieve on improved regulatory disciplines.

The fourth item on our agenda relates to so-called horizontal formulas, which we think will be a crucial tool to optimize the efficiency of liberalization discussions, an issue that features prominently in the chapter by Patrick Low and Aaditya Mattoo and in the one by Rachel Thompson. We think that horizontal formulas are crucial for two reasons. First, because some issues are inherently horizontal in nature. We have learned, for example from recent negotiations on China's accession to the WTO, that ownership restrictions are typically best addressed in an across-the-board fashion, not least because such a way of proceeding heightens negotiating leverage vis-à-vis the country that maintains such restrictions. A second reason is highlighted in the chapter by Bernard M. Hoekman and Patrick A. Messerlin and concerns the need to move away from traditional "give and take" reciprocity if we want to make a success of the GATS 2000 talks on the liberalization front.

We have drawn up a list of possible horizontal formulas on which we are currently consulting our member states. Examples include creating clusters of sectors: for a foreign company to operate in a given sector, whether goods or services, it frequently requires access to certain related services sectors that are key inputs. For instance, we have just received a proposal by Finland to consider a specific initiative on advanced technology services that represents a package of liberal market access and national treatment commitments that countries would undertake to facilitate trade flows on all services related to information technologies. Thompson's chapter contains several examples of other possible formulas, such as those on environmental or business services, which we see as worthy of more active pursuit. Yet another formula would target the removal of majority ownership restrictions and would also include a general grandfathering clause aimed at preventing the types of forced divestiture problems that arose in the financial services negotiations. Similarly, WTO members could be encouraged not to increase restrictions affecting consumption abroad. It bears recalling that several horizontal formulas have already been put to good use. Examples include the drafting of model schedules, the understanding on commitments in financial services, and the Reference Paper on Telecommunications. We should continue working with these formulas in the coming round.

COMMENT BY
Toru Aizawa

To Japan, it is important to cast the looming GATS negotiations in the context of the country's current economic situation. The Japanese economy is now facing a severe situation. High unemployment and significant corporate restructuring prevail. The need for drastic economic reform to revitalize the economy is well understood among Japanese people, as is the need to expand employment opportunities.

Under the prime minister's leadership, various government ministries are currently discussing how best to stimulate the economy and reformulate the country's economic system, with the Ministry of International Trade and Industry playing a key role. Focusing first on deregulation, Japan is now deliberating the new steps to take in the priority sectors of telecommunications and information technology as well as in a host of other sectors. In so doing, it is widely acknowledged that promoting the domestic service industry, through deregulation and other measures, holds the key to business expansion and greater employment. It is also recognized that an efficient and dynamic service industry will be a basis for sound and efficient overall economic activity in Japan. Accordingly, I believe that the next set of negotiations offers a unique possibility to bring greater vitality to the Japanese services sector and indeed to the entire Japanese economy.

Recent data reveal the excellent performance of foreign-affiliated service industries in the Japanese market, and we can see, in our daily life, the success stories of these industries all over the country. The latest figures issued on foreign direct investment inflows to Japan revealed a tremendous increase in services sector investment into Japan: fully two and a half times bigger in 1998 than that registered the previous year. In the crucial financial services sector, a 182 percent increase took place; in telecommunications, an even more remarkable 400 percent increase was noted.

In February 1999 the Committee of Industrial Structure Council chaired by Professor Iwata from Tokyo University submitted an interim report on the GATS 2000 negotiations. The report advocated a comprehensive negotiation, with no sectors excluded on an a priori basis. It also recommended a horizontal approach and the development of multilateral disciplines on domestic regulation. The report drew further attention to the need to introduce more transparency and predictability in government procedures for the supply of services in all markets. Another novel feature of the report is its championing of the service user's perspective in the analysis. For instance, the report stressed how Japan's manufacturing industry relies on an efficient service supply inside and outside the country.

As far as preparatory work for the GATS 2000 round is concerned, the government of Japan is focusing on a comprehensive negotiation excluding no specific sector a priori; a minimum of most-favored-nation exemptions; and a combination of horizontal and request-and-offer approaches for liberalization purposes. Japan fully subscribes to the view of the Quadrilateral group of countries that the next round be a short one, lasting no more than three years. Japan also concurs with the Quadrilateral view that a horizontal approach be pursued in developing multilateral disciplines on domestic regulation affecting services.

Japan's position toward investment rule-making remains one that favors general rules in the WTO, affecting both goods and services. Based on the recent experience of the Multilateral Agreement on Investment (MAI), as well as on domestic consultations with Japanese industry, the Japanese government's proposed focus is on foreign direct investment, to the exclusion of portfolio investment. The government is strongly supportive of attempts at promoting greater transparency, including of government procedures. We also wish to exclude investor to state arbitration as a means to settle disputes, relying instead on traditional WTO approaches and instruments.

Finally, let me state my belief that activities such as this conference contribute significantly to the successful outcome of services negotiations. I would like to encourage the Japanese business community to establish a forum in which the same thing can be done.

Contributors

Rudolf Adlung
World Trade Organization

Toru Aizawa
Ministry of International Trade and Industry, Japan

Americo Beviglia Zampetti
European Commission and Harvard University

Malcolm Bosworth
Productivity Commission, Australia

Willliam J. Drake
Carnegie Endowment for International Peace

Simon J. Evenett
Rutgers University

Geza Feketekuty
Monterey Institute of International Studies

Christopher Findlay
University of Adelaide, Australia

Gilles Gauthier
Department of Finance, Canada

Bernard M. Hoekman
World Bank

Robert Howse
University of Michigan

Merit E. Janow
Columbia University

Guy Karsenty
World Trade Organization

Patrick Low
World Trade Organization

Juan A. Marchetti
Argentine Mission to the World Trade Organization

Aaditya Mattoo
World Bank

Patrick A. Messerlin
Institut d'Etudes Politiques, Paris

Peter Morrison
Clifford Chance, London

Kalypso Nicolaïdis
St. Anthony's College, Oxford

Erin O'Brien
Department of Finance, Canada

Ken A. Richeson
Consultant

Pierre Sauvé
*Harvard University and
Organization for Economic
Cooperation and Development*

Jeffrey J. Schott
*Institute for International
Economics*

Michel Servoz
European Commission

Susan Spencer
Department of Finance, Canada

Sherry M. Stephenson
Organization of American States

Robert M. Stern
University of Michigan

Rachel Thompson
*Organization for Economic
Cooperation and Development*

Joel P. Trachtman
Tufts University

Tony Warren
Australian National University

Mark A. A. Warner
*Organization for Economic
Cooperation and Development*

Christopher Wilkie
*Organization for Economic
Cooperation and Development*

Allison M. Young
*Department of Foreign Affairs and
International Trade, Canada*